THE ANSWER

ickonic
publishing

First published in August 2020.

ickonic
publishing

1a Babbington Lane,
Derby,
DE1 1SU
UK

email: info@davidickebooks.co.uk

Cover Design: Gareth Icke
Illustrations: Neil Hague.com

British Library Cataloguing-in
Publication Data
A catalogue record for this book is
available from the British Library

ISBN 978-1916025820

Printed and bound by
CPI Group (UK) Ltd, Croydon, CR0 4YY

THE ANSWER

DAVID ICKE

Dedication:

To *All That Is, Has Been, And Ever Can Be*

What is the point of life?

There does not have to be a point.

It just is.

Enjoy.

David Icke

Quotes by 13th century Persian mystic Jalāl ad-Dīn Muhammad Rūmī widely known simply as Rumi. His words are confirmation that nothing is new. It has only been forgotten:

The universe is not outside of you. Look inside yourself; everything that you want, you already are.

You are not a drop in the ocean.
You are the entire ocean in a drop.

Stop acting so small. You are the universe in ecstatic motion.

Why do you stay in prison when the door is so wide open?

Raise your words, not voice. It is rain that grows flowers, not thunder.

Take someone who doesn't keep score, who's not looking to be richer, or afraid of losing, who has not the slightest interest even in his own personality: He's free.

And one that I can seriously relate to …

Run from what's comfortable. Forget safety. Live where you fear to live. Destroy your reputation. Be notorious. I have tried prudent planning long enough. From now on I'll be mad.

I've been 'mad' for 30 years. Try it – it's wonderful.

I'm Not Crazy.
My Reality is Just Different Than Yours.
People might think you're crazy for what
you believe or wear or say, but it doesn't matter.

Cheshire Cat in *Alice in Wonderland*

Alice: 'Have I gone mad?'

Mad Hatter: 'I'm afraid so, but let me tell you something,
the best people usually are.'

Alice in Wonderland

Though I may not know the answers,
I can finally say I'm free.
And if the questions led me here, then,
I am who I was born to be.

From *Who I Was Born to Be*, written by Audra Mae
and recorded by Susan Boyle.

Contents

The Prologue

When I discover who I am, I'll be free – Ralph Ellison

I am going to expose from 30 years of research and experience in a long list of countries what I say is *really* happening in the world and why. These are my perspectives and they don't have to be yours, but in the wake of the 'Covid-19' police state impositions worldwide they surely become near impossible to deny any longer.

It is ever more blatantly obvious that what I have been saying for decades was planned to happen *is* happening as global society transforms so quickly in the image I have predicted. Events have never moved so fast in that direction than during the manufactured 'Covid-19' hysteria and fascistic national lockdowns in which billions were put under actual and virtual house arrest across the world. Eighty-five percent of this book was written before these draconian impositions were rolled out – based on a lie –and I have decided to hold back on the 'Covid-19' story and its catastrophic human impact through economic Armageddon until the late-added chapters near the end which expose in detail both the nature of the 'virus' scam and why it was perpetrated. I will of course refer to the 'virus' briefly here and there before then, but I want you to read the rest of the book and the information that I laid out *before* the 'virus' blitzkrieg because then the who and why of the 'virus' hoax will be devastating in their clarity and context. Nothing in my lifetime has so proved my point about global control than the staged illusion of 'Covid-19'. To emphasise – *Please note when you see my comments relating to the 'virus' that the text around them was written before the 'virus' hysteria and lockdowns began.*

Is it really random coincidence that what I have written for three decades was planned for humanity is now so clearly happening? Or is it the most glaring evidence and confirmation of a calculated agenda for total human enslavement? I vociferously say the latter and I am confident that by the end of this book with the dots and strands connected you will agree that coincidence theory is simply not credible in the face of the evidence. I'll make it very clear what I say is going on, but I want the *evidence* to speak for itself and for you to decide what it means. With that said we shall begin. I have been exposing for 30 years a conspiracy to enslave humanity in an Orwellian global tyranny of total control – ultimately (and very soon if we don't wake up fast) by connecting artificial intelligence to the human brain so that AI *replaces* the human mind. That's crazy? It's happening step-by-step before our eyes right now. 'Human' thinking and emotions would be history and our perceptions dictated directly by AI and those that control AI. It's no good people screaming

Figure 1: All these decades later the mainstream media is still using the same CIA propaganda term for those who are aware that governments lie to us.

'conspiracy theory' – a term brought into widespread use by the CIA in the 1960s as it sought to discredit those questioning the ludicrous official story of the Kennedy assassination (Fig 1).

These are definitions of the term 'conspiracy': An evil, unlawful, treacherous, or surreptitious plan formulated in secret by two or more persons; a combination of persons for a secret, unlawful, or evil purpose; an agreement by two or more persons to commit a crime, fraud, or other wrongful act; any concurrence in action or combination in bringing about a given result. On that basis the world is drowning in conspiracies at every level of society, but to the mainstream media, indeed the Mainstream Everything, conspiracies don't exist and anyone who says so is a kook peddling a 'conspiracy theory'. Yes, even in the light of the draconian, fascistic impositions of the 'Covid-19' hoax. What I have been exposing since 1990 is not multiple unconnected conspiracies (though they do exist by those definitions alone). I have uncovered *one* conspiracy with multiple faces driving human society to the same despicable end and what I have revealed is not a 'theory'. It is an obvious reality unfolding by the day as AI takes over human life and freedom is deleted. The crazies in the Devil's Playground of Silicon Valley are now telling you that what I have been warning about for so long is indeed what is planned to happen. They are doing so because they have no choice as AI takes over and cannot be hidden any longer. The sales-pitch is the emergence of a new era in which humans will be 'gods' thanks to a connection to AI when, in truth, the 'new human' will be post-human and no longer 'human' at all. Insiders like Google executive Ray Kurzweil even point to the year of 2030 for when this will be seriously underway and human brains will be connected to the AI 'cloud'. He said:

Our thinking … will be a hybrid of biological and non-biological thinking … humans will be able to extend their limitations and 'think in the cloud' … We're going to put gateways to the cloud in our brains ... We're going to gradually merge and enhance ourselves ... In my view, that's the nature of being human – we transcend our limitations.

As the technology becomes vastly superior to what we are then the small proportion that is still human gets smaller and smaller and smaller until it's just utterly negligible.

This is what I have called 'the assimilation' as human awareness is absorbed into AI and that which is truly behind AI. I don't mean the middlemen and women of Silicon Valley. Even the tech billionaires are not the engineers of all this. They are merely the oil rags, albeit very rich ones. What is happening today is the endgame in a story that has spanned thousands of years as we perceive the illusion of 'time'. Our human sense of reality was infiltrated long ago by a force that is not human which has created a global hierarchy of control with its representatives and agents manipulating human perception century after century on the road to *total* enslavement (Fig 2). By controlling perception you control experience individually and collectively in a cause-and-effect that I will be explaining in detail. The plan has demanded the constant centralisation of power as a bottom-line imperative. With every step in that direction fewer and fewer people seize more control over the population. Tribes became nations and nations are becoming superstates like the European Union and trading blocs controlled from the centre. Decisions are being made increasingly through global corporations and institutions like the United Nations and the World Health and Trade Organizations. People have long called this conspiracy (while not realising it's a conspiracy) 'globalisation'. What is this? The global centralisation of power over every aspect of human life – the very plan I have been exposing for decades. We now have the centralisation of control in Silicon Valley over the flow of information from which people form their perceptions of events

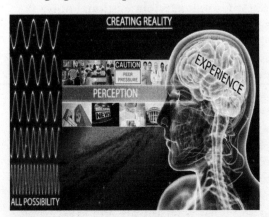

Figure 2: How human perception is manipulated into a myopia of possibility. Control information and you control perception. (Image Gareth Icke.)

and reality. Hysterical Silicon Valley censorship by Google, Facebook, Twitter, Amazon and all the rest (controlled from the shadows by the same force) is aimed at dictating everything you see and hear and, through that, manipulating your *perception* of everything. Even that won't be necessary with an AI connection to your brain. Your perceptions would then be delivered directly.

This has always been the goal of the non-human infiltration of human society via its agents and operatives in apparently human form. The technological cutting edge that we see in the public arena is as nothing compared with technological knowledge in other realities where what is today called 'smart' was known about while history records humans knocking rocks together and living in caves. The constant flow of 'new inventions' that daily deepen human control have been waiting for humanity to reach a point of intellectual development where it could build and operate its own technological prison. This is where we are today. Gadgetry and communication systems required by the global prison are playing out into public awareness from underground bases and secret projects with cover stories and cover people hiding the truth of where it all comes from. The flow of technology is seamless for this reason. There are no 'seams' or big delays as the manipulators wait for the next stage to be 'invented'. There are no gaps as technological limitations are pondered for decades and overcome. Almost by the week the next stages of technological AI are revealed and the pace is ever quickening. Humanity has been perceptually-manipulated to develop the intellectual capacity ('cleverness') to build and operate its own technological Alcatraz while not developing the wisdom to see that this is what we are doing. I have been saying for decades: Cleverness without wisdom is the most destructive force on earth. So it is proving and not by accident, but design. Cleverness is so often confused with wisdom. Cleverness knows about information while wisdom knows what it means and sees its consequences. It is clever to build an atomic weapon, but not wise to do so. I have exposed the conspiracy, ancient and modern, in enormous detail and the non-human force orchestrating from the shadows and realities unseen by the human eye. You can find this information in ... *And The Truth Shall Set You Free, The Biggest Secret, Children of the Matrix, Tales From The Time Loop, The David Icke Guide to the Global Conspiracy, The Perception Deception, Human Race Get Off Your Knees, Phantom Self, Everything You Need To Know But Have Never Been Told, The Trigger*, and other books. My focus here is on how human perception has been manipulated to follow the path the control system has decreed and from this knowledge point to *The Answer* that will set us free. That answer relates to who and what we really are and to escaping the fake self-identity that we are told and pressured to believe in. To know who we are, where we are and how the two interact is the whole foundation of human freedom which is why every effort is made to keep us in ignorance of that information and awareness.

How it's done

Some brief but essential background is required for those new to my work about the overwhelmingly hidden hierarchical structure driving the direction of human society on behalf of the non-human force that it represents. Without awareness of this structure and how it works the context of world events simply cannot be understood. I have long used the concept of the spider and the web. The Spider is the non-human force operating beyond the *extraordinarily* narrow frequency band of five-sense human perception.

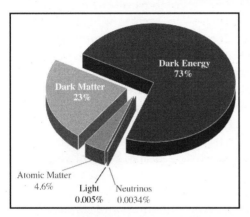

Figure 3: The almost infinitesimal band of frequency that we call 'light' or the electromagnetic spectrum. Scientists call that which we can't see 'dark' which I contend is erroneous in their version of reality. 'Dark' should be simply considered beyond human sight.

People think they can see all there is to see in the 'space' they are observing; but they can't. They are seeing only a tiny fraction of what exists around us and within us. The electromagnetic spectrum (including radio waves, microwaves, infrared, ultraviolent, X-rays and gamma rays) is only 0.005 percent of what exists in the universe in various forms of energy and reality. Some scientists say it's a bit more, but not much. The point is that the electromagnetic spectrum is a fraction of what exists beyond its band of frequency and humans can't see the almost totality even of that spectrum. Human sight – everything we perceive as a visual reality or 'the world' – is confined to a micro-segment of the 0.005 percent known as visible light (Figs 3 and 4). We are limited in our visual

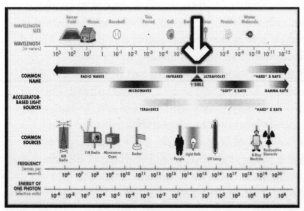

Figure 4: Visible light, which is the only reality we can 'see', is a fraction of the 0.005 percent. The human five senses are aware of only one 'TV channel' within Infinite Existence.

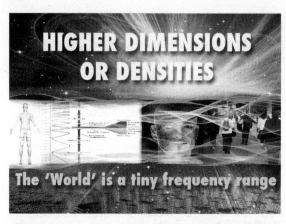

HIGHER DIMENSIONS OR DENSITIES

The 'World' is a tiny frequency range

Figure 5: Our 'world' is a band of frequency within Infinite Reality.

perception to a minuscule band of frequency and that is only by the terms that mainstream science can currently measure or thinks it can (Fig 5). In truth what we 'see' is even more myopic in comparison to Infinite Reality that exists beyond the firewalls of visible light and the illusory limits of the speed of light. Watch television or listen to radio and you perceive only what is being broadcast by the channels and stations you have chosen. All the other channels and stations exist in the same room but you are not aware of them unless you change the channel or move the dial. When people ask why if this non-human force is real we can't we see it – this is why. It operates from realms of frequency outside the human band of visual reality and is invisible to us in the same way that when you are tuned to TV station 'A' you can't see TV stations 'B', 'C' or 'D' even though they exist. Change channel and you switch from station 'A' and connect with one of the others. Station 'A' doesn't disappear when you switch; it's only that you are no longer connected to its wavelength or output and so you can't see it. I have just described what happens when we 'die' (or rather don't – only the body does). Our consciousness changes 'channels' or moves its point of attention. This is that all death is – a transfer of *attention* from one reality to another. The source of human control is hidden from us although non-human entities representing this force can move in and out of our reality by entering our band of visual frequency and then withdrawing. Accounts are legion of people claiming to have seen entities or craft 'appearing out of nowhere' and then 'disappearing' in a flash. They don't appear or disappear. They enter the human band of visual frequency and then leave. To the observer they have appeared from nowhere and disappeared into nowhere when it is just a case of now you see it, now you don't, as it comes and goes from visible light. What does a TV channel do when you switch to it? What does it do when you switch away from it? The channels, or realities, appear 'out of nowhere' and then 'disappear into nowhere' when in fact they don't go *anywhere*. We only connect and disconnect with them.

The Web

What I call 'The Web' is the interconnecting secret society structure that allows the Spider in the hidden to dictate events in the seen (Fig 6). Strands in The Web close to the Spider are the most exclusive secret

societies and their initiates will know the detailed Spider agenda and where it is planned to go. Communication with the Spider directly and through satanic ritual allows these inner-strand initiates to know about technological possibility way before it appears in the world of the seen and to

Figure 6: The compartmentalised web of secret societies, semi-secret and public organisations that allow the 'Spider' hidden at the centre to impose its agenda on human society. (Image Neil Hague.)

secure the transfer of technological knowledge long before its official time of release. If you have access to this inner sanctum of The Web, or penetrate it through decades of work, you can predict what we perceive as the 'future' – including the technology involved – because the 'future' in this sense is only the Spider agenda being spun. If there is a plan for the world and nothing intervenes to stop that plan then it will happen and revealing the plan becomes predicting the future. My books over the decades have proved extraordinarily accurate in predicting events for this reason – including a plan for 'pandemics'. The whole point of what I do is to alert enough people so that humanity *does* intervene and stop the planned outcome of total human control. Famous 'see-the-future' writers such as Aldous Huxley (*Brave New World*, published in 1932) and George Orwell (*Nineteen Eighty-Four*, published in 1948) have proved to be so accurate because by whatever means they were able to penetrate the Spider agenda and could predict technology and other possibilities that didn't exist at the time of their writing. As we move out in The Web from the Spider and the inner-sanctum initiates we meet the secret societies that we do know about in terms of name if not actions. These include the Knights Templar, Knights of Malta, Opus Dei, the Jesuit Order, Freemasons and many others which have an interlocking

The Masonic Structure

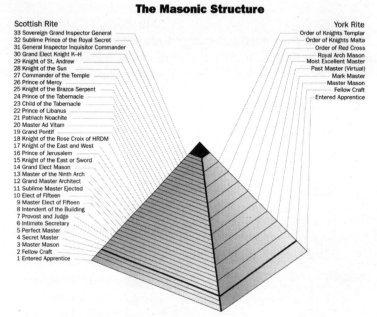

Scottish Rite
33 Sovereign Grand Inspector General
32 Sublime Prince of the Royal Secret
31 General Inspector Inquisitor Commander
30 Grand Elect Knight K–H
29 Knight of St. Andrew
28 Knight of the Sun
27 Commander of the Temple
26 Prince of Mercy
25 Knight of the Brazca Serpent
24 Prince of the Tabernacle
23 Child of the Tabernacle
22 Prince of Libanus
21 Patriach Noachite
20 Master Ad Vitam
19 Grand Pontif
18 Knight of the Rose Croix of HRDM
17 Knight of the East and West
16 Prince of Jerusalem
15 Knight of the East or Sword
14 Grand Elect Mason
13 Master of the Ninth Arch
12 Grand Master Architect
11 Sublime Master Ejected
10 Elect of Fifteen
9 Master Elect of Fifteen
8 Intendent of the Building
7 Provost and Judge
6 Intimate Secretary
5 Perfect Master
4 Secret Master
3 Master Mason
2 Fellow Craft
1 Entered Apprentice

York Rite
Order of Knights Templar
Order of Knights Malta
Order of Red Cross
Royal Arch Mason
Most Excellent Master
Past Master (Virtual)
Mark Master
Master Mason
Fellow Craft
Entered Apprentice

Figure 7: The compartmentalised 'degrees' that keep each level of Freemasonry in ignorance of what the others know is the structural basis for all organisations within The Web.

command structure if you go deep enough. Most of their members will not be aware of their interlocking nature and the agenda their controlling core is pursuing. Different levels or 'degrees' are compartmentalised from what those above them know (Fig 7). Human society is arranged in the same way with the great majority in any organisation kept in ignorance of what the few at the top know and are seeking to impose. They are pawns and foot-soldiers for an agenda they don't even know exists. Intelligence agencies (themselves structured as secret societies) are classics of this compartmentalisation or 'need to know' technique.

There is a point in The Web where the hidden meets the seen and here we have what I call the 'cusp' organisations that include the Royal Institute of International Affairs (established in London in 1920); Council on Foreign Relations (US, 1921); Bilderberg Group (US, Europe, worldwide, 1954); Club of Rome (Europe, US, worldwide, 1968); and the Trilateral Commission (US, Europe, worldwide, 1972). These groupings and others answer to the Round Table secret society founded in London in the latter years of the 19th century by the House of Rothschild and its frontman lackey, Cecil Rhodes (Fig 8). The definition of 'cusp' describes perfectly the role of these organisations – 'a point of transition between two different states'. In this case those two states are the hidden and the seen between which they act as a conduit. Cusp groups gather together

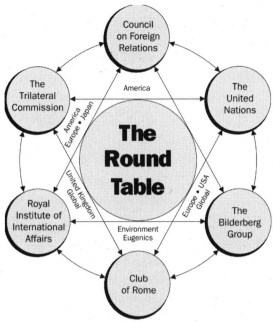

Figure 8: Major 'cusp' organisations that take the hidden agenda of the Spider and play it out across human society.

Figure 9: What happens in the world of the 'seen' is hatched in the unseen.

politicians, government administrators, financiers, corporations, intelligence operatives and media to advance a common direction for the world although many of the gofers and stooges involved will have no idea because of compartmentalisation. Cusp organisations include a fantastic list of 'think tanks' and non-governmental organisations (NGOs). Their role is to take the Spider agenda hatched in the hidden part of The Web and impose that in the world of the seen through governments, government agencies, banks, corporations, intelligence and military groupings, media conglomerates and all the pillars and institutions that dictate the direction of human society. We see apparently random and unconnected decisions made by governments, groups and organisations, but the society-transforming ones are not random and certainly not unconnected. They are the Spider agenda being introduced through its countless proxies which in the end all answer to the same master (Fig 9). At the inner-core of The Web governments and politics *are* the banking system *are* the global corporations *are* the Silicon Valley giants *are* the mainstream media *are* the education system *are* mainstream science *are* the pharmaceutical cartel, or 'Big Pharma', and so on. Key decisions that change the direction of human life are not taken randomly or independently. They are part of the Spider's plan for total control. The vast majority of people working in these groups and organisations who daily take Spider-instigated actions are clueless about the origin of those decisions, changes and policies, and what they are designed to collectively achieve. This is the structure that allows the very few to control and manipulate the very many while the many remain in ignorance of what is really happening and why. Who is going to tell them – the *mainstream media*? That is owned by The Web and most mainstream 'journalists' are as ignorant and often more so about the agenda than the rest of the population.

The Death Cult

The inner core of the secret society global network locks into human-sacrificing Satanism – literally making sacrifices to their hidden 'gods' and masters beyond human sight which are obsessed with death. They feed off the energy and terror associated with death and especially sacrificial death. Most people think that human sacrifice to the 'gods' came to an end in the ancient world. If they read some of my other books they will see otherwise and how many of the global rich and famous are practitioners of this horror to this day. They will also realise that Satanism involves vampiring the energy of children which is where the whole theme originates of 'sacrificing young virgins to the gods'. This is code for children. Satanic and paedophile rings often work in unison in the targeting of children in their service to The Web and the 'gods'. These ancient practices have passed through what we experience as history under the cover of this network and that's why I refer to the inner elite of The Web as a Death Cult. You can read the detailed background to the Cult going back thousands of years in other books like *The Trigger* and *Everything You Need To Know But Have Never Been Told* (*Everything You Need To Know* from hereon). One central network within the Cult is known as Sabbatian (or Sabbatean)-Frankism which emerged in the 17th century and was the driving force behind the creation of Israel and Zionism, Saudi Arabia and the head-chopping (Death Cult) 'ISIS' version of extreme 'Islam' known as Wahhabism. Sabbatian-Frankism is named after two dark occultists, Sabbatai Zevi (1626-1676) and Jacob Frank (1726-1791) and is a form of Satanism. Jacob Frank teamed up with Sabbatian-Frankist Mayer Amschel Rothschild, founder of the Rothschild banking dynasty, to establish the infamous Illuminati in 1776 as another important strand in The Web. I expose Sabbatian-Frankism in *The Trigger* in relation to the *real* perpetrators of 9/11 (a mass death ritual) and all that has followed in regime-change wars (death of millions) and deletion of freedom. I will refer to the inner-core controlling The Web within human society throughout the book as 'the Cult' and it is important to keep in mind the central part played by its Sabbatian-Frankism wing in relation to Israel, the United States, United Kingdom, Europe and worldwide in the manipulation of global events. Tiny Israel has so much power and influence because it is the fiefdom of Sabbatian-Frankism (the global Cult) and no one needs to know this more urgently than the Jewish community which it has infiltrated while posing as Jewish.

The great majority of my research on Sabbatian-Frankism has come from Jewish sources that were and are well aware of how their community has been hijacked. Sabbatian-Frankism and the rest of the Cult specialise in infiltrating societies, cultures and religions by posing as members of those communities while pursuing a very different goal. This infiltration allows the Cult to create and control groups of all kinds while most of those involved have no idea there even is a Cult let alone that it is directing their organisation, religion, culture or society. How many of those who blindly repeat the official nonsense about human-caused climate change and demand the dystopian transformation of society to 'solve the problem' know about the Cult's cusp-cult the Club of Rome? This was specifically created to exploit environmental

Figure 10: The ever-growing obsession with death.

Figure 11: Occult symbol and Extinction Rebellion ('ER') symbol.

concerns (real and imagined) to transform society into a global centralised Marxist-like tyranny in precisely the image demanded by 'climate change' protestors such as Extinction Rebellion and promotors of the 'Green New Deal' in America. Who string-pulls from the shadows such protests and demands? The *Death Cult* does. You can even see the obsession that groups like *Extinction* Rebellion (ER) have with death and blood (Fig 10). We are told that the group's symbol represents an hourglass in a circle to mean time is running out (Fig 11). It is, however, a symbol long used in occultism and 'sex magic' and referred to as 'The Mark of the Beast'. The O is female and X is male. 'Ceremonial magician' Kenneth Grant was secretary

and personal assistant to the elite British occultist Aleister Crowley. He
explains in his 1973 book, *Kenneth Grant, Aleister Crowley & The Hidden
God*, that the symbol also related to a Celtic god called Nodens:

> The Heart of the Sigil of Nodens is identical with the Mark of the Beast: Ⓧ the
> fusion of O and X which produces the lightning flash. Nodens is the God of
> the Great Deep or Abyss, microcosmically identical with subconsciousness.
> He reigns over the Abyss and controls and harnesses its lightnings … The Seat
> of Stone is [Egyptian goddess] Isis, and upon this foundation the Goddess is
> established and rules the heavens, the earth and the deeps beneath the earth.
> In other words, the Goddess who grants all desires is invoked by the union of
> the X and the O …

Extinction Rebellion protests are incredibly ritualistic with groups of
people with white faces and blood-red robes walking through the
streets. I am not saying that all followers of Extinction Rebellion and
supporters of the Green New Deal know they are assets of the global
Cult. They are still more pawns in a game they don't understand. If they
read this book to the end they might see how monumentally they are
being had. Human-caused climate change is being hoaxed to justify the
centralisation of global power over the fine detail of our lives and as I
write so is – *big time* – the 'pandemic' which ticks every box for those
seeking to impose the global Orwellian state.

Permanent government is the real government

Every country and the world as a whole has a permanent government
controlled by the Cult through compartmentalisation and these are
always in power no matter what the nature of the here-today-gone-
tomorrow political parties that only *appear* to be the origin of societal
change. Permanent government is widely referred to as the 'Deep State'
today although that is only part of the permanent control. The Deep
State consists of Cult-directed intelligence, military and law enforcement
personnel along with government administrators and insider politicians
that seek to advance the Cult agenda for the world. They direct,
manipulate and undermine elected government and non-Cult personnel
(the overwhelming majority) to ensure that what the Cult wants it gets.
Other sections of permanent governments include the banking and
financial networks, Big Tech, Big Biotech, Big Pharma, Big Media (and
some of the 'alternative'), Big Oil, other major corporations, the legal
system and courts. Politicians come and go, but the hidden government
is always there and no matter what the colour of the briefly-elected
political rosettes the same direction of the world incessantly continues
(Fig 12). America is a perfect example of how this works although it's
the same in every country. The United States is governed (at least

Figure 12: Permanent governments operate nationally and globally and dictate the direction of countries and the world while 'elected' politicians of all parties come and go.

officially) by either the Democratic or Republican parties and the Permanent Government controls both of them. Whichever you vote for the Cult is in power. The Republican Party is controlled by a group known as the Neocons or neoconservatives (major funder casino billionaire Sheldon Adelson) and the Democrats have a similar group that I call the Democons (major funder financier billionaire George Soros). Adelson and Soros both answer to those that control Israel which in the shadows is the Sabbatian-Frankist wing of the Cult. Soros would deny that Israel connection to maintain his cover of being different from Adelson. He's not. Do these people and others always like each other? No, they don't and there is rivalry between them. Levels above them, however, make sure that any mutual contempt doesn't get out of hand or in the way. Woe betide them if it does. We see the US presidency passing between 'Democrat' Bill Clinton, 'Republican' Boy George Bush, 'Democrat' Barack Obama or 'Republican' Donald Trump who are described in office as the most powerful people in the world. They are in reality only temporary puppets of the Permanent Government because the Neocons and Democons both take their orders from the same Cult (Fig 13).

Political squabbles, attacks and counter-attacks are sideshows as the Cult agenda for total human control moves incessantly forward. Public squabbles played out in the media also help to convince the population that they really do have different political choices within what is called 'democracy'.

Figure 13: Politicians are here today and gone tomorrow, but the Hidden Hand that I call the Cult is always there and ultimately controls all of them. (Image Gareth Icke.)

This term is used as interchangeable with 'freedom' when democracy is really only the ability to mind-manipulate enough people to vote for you by lying to them. You lie in election campaigns about your planned policies and then largely do the opposite once you win office. You are then free to officially run the country until the next lie-fest when you may be replaced by another party controlled from the shadows by the same force that controls you. It happens all the time across the world. People vote for Party 'A' and they get into power. The public don't like what they do and next time the majority vote for Party 'B'. People don't like what they do because it's pretty much the same in outcome and the only way they can remove them is to return to Party 'A' that they threw out the election before. Round and round the garden generation after generation. Heads you lose, tails you lose. In some countries there may be a Party 'C', but the principle is the same. The government that you see is subordinate to the Permanent Government that you don't see and national Permanent Governments fuse into a global Permanent Government that dictates to the world through The Web. Against this background the massive divisions in the population between the political 'Right' and 'Left' take on a whole new light and state of ridiculousness. They are manipulated divide and rule to set the target population at war with itself while believing they have 'choice'(Fig 14).

Figure 14: Get the public to support different masks on the same face and divide and rule will always follow. (Image Gareth Icke.)

Cult wars

War after war in the Middle East is testament to the existence of the Permanent Government behind all political faces and facades. A Neocon 'think tank' called the Project for the New American Century (PNAC), founded and dominated by ultra-Zionists with fanatical allegiance to Israel and Sabbatian-Frankism, published a document in September, 2000, calling for American troops to 'fight and decisively win multiple theatre wars' in the Middle East and elsewhere to regime change governments in a list of countries including Iraq, Libya, Syria and Iran as well as bringing about regime-change in North Korea and eventually China. The Cult seeks to control the whole landmass of Eurasia from Europe to China and from Russia down to the Middle East and this further explains the constant demonisation of Russia. The PNAC document said that to justify this policy to the American public and secure the enormous required increases in military spending the United States had to experience another attack on the homeland like the one by the Japanese at Pearl Harbor, Hawaii, in 1941. To quote the document:

> ... [The] process of transformation ... [war and regime change] ... is likely to be a long one, absent some catastrophic and catalysing event – like a new Pearl Harbor.

A year to the month later America had what President Bush called 'the Pearl Harbor of the 21st century' – 9/11. Members of the Project for the New American Century behind the document came to office with Bush in January, 2001. They included Dick Cheney (Vice-President and de-facto President); Donald Rumsfeld (Defense Secretary); Paul Wolfowitz (Deputy Defense Secretary); Dov Zakheim (Comptroller of the entire Pentagon budget); and many others allied to Israel and committed to the PNAC list of regime-change targets. I show beyond doubt in *The Trigger* that the satanic Sabbatian-Frankist network of the Cult operating out of Israel and in league with its agents in the US Deep State were the real perpetrators of 9/11 which they then used as the excuse to launch the 'war on terror' (war *of* terror) to pick off their list of target countries. They invaded Afghanistan to 'get' the fake 9/11 villain Osama bin Laden and followed this by targeting the countries on the original PNAC list – Iraq, Libya, Syria and Iran with much finger-pointing also at North Korea and increasingly China. The nature of the Permanent Government comes into focus when you observe how those countries have been targeted by different presidents from apparently 'opposing' parties: George Bush ('Republican', Iraq); Barack Obama ('Democrat', Libya and Syria); and Donald Trump ('Republican', Iran). We also had UK Prime Minister and war criminal Tony Blair (Labour Party) working with Bush to invade Afghanistan and Iraq while David Cameron (Conservative Party) was Prime Minister when Britain supported Obama in laying siege to Libya and Syria. They may appear to be 'different' presidents, prime ministers and parties, but they follow the same script written by the Permanent Government.

Unhooking the mind

All this brings me to the focus of this book which is escaping the human mind-prison by taking back control of our own perceptions and self-identity. I mean by that our perceptions of *everything* from world events to the nature of the True 'I' and reality itself. The number of Cult operatives working in full knowledge of what they are doing is microscopic compared with a global population heading towards eight billion. The only way so few can control and direct so many is by hijacking their perception of everything. You can use 'physical' control only over relatively small groups through military and civilian law enforcement (unless the population acquiesce en masse through perception control as with the 'pandemic'). For global control you require perception control. Behaviour comes from perception and if you control perception you control behaviour and what people will do or won't do, challenge or support. Hijack perception and you hijack behaviour; hijack behaviour and you hijack the world. The sequence of control is perception = behaviour = collective human society. The next question is where do perceptions come from? They come from *information* received. We develop our perceptions through information that we absorb from personal experience, a bloke down the bar, the ten o'clock news, a posting on Facebook, and countless other sources. We can therefore extend the sequence to information = perception = behaviour = collective human society. Control information and you control that whole sequence. The Cult already overwhelmingly controls information and it seeks total control. Perceptions are *assumptions* based on the brain's best guess in the light of information received. Humanity would increase by a ginormous leap its potential for knowledge and creativity if we realised that perception and truth do not have to be the same thing and in fact rarely are. What is perceived 'truth' anyway except assumptions that become perceptions that become 'this is how it is'? Donald Hoffman, a professor in the Department of Cognitive Sciences at the University of California, Irvine, said that perception is a controlled illusion and reality is when we agree about our hallucinations. Yes, but who controls the illusion and elicits agreement on hallucinations by controlling information and the assumptions that come from that? The Cult is seeking to enforce total control by imposing perception directly through a brain-connection to AI, but for now they must control information to control perception to hijack collective reality. Here you have the reason the Cult is obsessed with controlling sources of information through ownership of the mainstream media and Silicon Valley while suppressing other information through the ever-increasing censorship documented at length in my other books and experienced by more people every day. The Cult seeks to delete or suppress any source of information and opinion that questions and challenges the official narrative of almost any subject, including government (Cult) policy, 'Covid-19', vaccines, regime-change wars, human-caused climate change, the nature of human biology and political correctness which is manipulating the population to censor itself. All these subjects and so many more are aspects of the Spider agenda and they are imposed by the Cult via The Web. The coordination of censorship by this network is obvious and it's cheered on by the Cult-created fake-'progressive'

'Woke' culture. 'Woke', ironically, is another word for 'fast asleep'. The climate change hoax, the imposition of extreme transgender doctrines, beliefs and language, and the obsession with seeing racism absolutely everywhere are all facets of 'Woke' and, not coincidentally, facets of the Cult agenda for the world as I will be explaining.

Fake self-identity

The foundation and bottom-line of mass perception programming is to maintain humanity in ongoing ignorance of who we are and where we are. The idea is to program the belief from cradle to grave that we are cosmic accidents of random 'evolution' and to define self-identity only by the labels we are given and give ourselves. Life has a beginning and an end and when you're dead you're dead. For those who won't buy the latter you tell them they are subject to the demands of an angry, judgemental external 'God' with rules and regulations (Cult rules and regulations) which must be followed to avoid the fires of hell or secure a date with multiple virgins waiting only for believers. Whether religious or atheist the labels of limitation still apply. These are the labels of 'I-am-a' as in: I-am-a man, woman, gay, transgender, black, white, rich, poor, Christian, Muslim, Hindu, Jew and all the rest. These labels are not who we are. They are merely what we are briefly *experiencing*. We – the eternal 'I' – are an expression of an Infinite State of Awareness *having* those experiences. Think how impossible it would be to pressure, frighten, intimidate and manipulate people to do what the Cult demands if we knew that we are a point of attention within a state of Infinite Awareness having a brief experience called human in whatever form, colour, race or sexuality. How even harder would it be to divide and control people aware that we are all aspects of the *same* consciousness and who understand that our temporary labels are illusory divisions and not real in the way that they seem to be? How would the Cult instigate the essential divide and rule and conflict between labels of race, culture, sexuality, politics and income bracket if we all knew they were temporary illusions and that our reality is just another type of 'dream'? Or that human life is like donning a headset and playing virtual reality? Such games may seem so real, but take off the headset (symbolic of 'death') and you see that it was all a technologically-generated illusion, a dream or nightmare that we believed in the moment to be real. Such is the nature of human life. As Rumi, a 13th century Persian mystic, said:

> This place is a dream. Only a sleeper considers it real. Then death comes like dawn and you wake up laughing at what you thought was your grief.

These truths must be kept from us for the Death Cult conspiracy to

Figure 15: The human illusion.

prevail. This book is about how that is being done and how we can return to the true and eternal 'I' that we are and always will be beyond the illusory diversions of the five senses. The inner circle of the Cult knows what reality is and how it works and their power comes from keeping that knowledge from the population. They do this by dismissing or demonising such information in the public arena while passing it on to generations of chosen initiates in the secret society networks of The Web. Secret societies and other assets of The Web answer in the end to the Cult which itself answers to its non-human masters or Spider. We have in this way been manipulated to forget our real nature and live in an isolated 'Bubble' of self-identity and limitation that I call Phantom Self – *label* self (Fig 15). This is the whole foundation of human control, but it doesn't have to be. Open your mind and it's wakey, wakey time.

CHAPTER ONE

What is 'reality'?

**If you don't know who you truly are,
you'll never know what you really want – Roy T. Bennett**

Dictionary definitions of 'conscious' include: 'The state of being aware of, and responsive to, one's surroundings'; and 'the state of understanding and realising something'. My definition for the purposes of this book is going to be very different.

I am making a clear distinction between what I will call 'mind' and 'consciousness'. I will use the term 'mind' and 'Body-Mind' to describe the perception of five-sense reality and 'consciousness' for expanded awareness beyond the walls – firewalls as we shall see – of the five senses. From this perspective those two official definitions can be seen in another way. Take the first one: 'The state of being aware of, and responsive to, one's surroundings.' Okay, but aware of *what* surroundings? Perceived 'surroundings' (quite the wrong term as I shall explore) are actually illusory when compared with how we appear to experience them. The world is not 'solid', for example. It only seems that way to *senses* that are not consciousness in its prime form. Our five senses, or information decoding systems, 'sense' our 'surroundings' while not in the widest meaning of the word being 'conscious' or 'aware' of what those surroundings are. If that was the case we would see through the illusions and mind-trickery to perceive the world as it really is. Then there is that other definition of conscious: 'The state of understanding and realising something.' Can anyone truly understand *any*thing, never mind *some*thing, when we appear to be experiencing a 'physical' world of 'solidity' which is, in fact, neither? How can we understand anything *in* the world if we don't understand the nature *of* the world? We can't and yet all the institutions of human society are making decisions and forming perceptions based on an illusory reality which is nothing like the one they think they are living 'in'. How can such decisions and perceptions be anything except skewed and misguided? These are the same institutions of education, science, medicine, politics and media etc. from which all but a few glean their perceptions and make their decisions. Put all that together and it captures in its totality the meaning of the phrase 'the blind leading the blind' or, as I would put it, the unconscious leading the unconscious. Five-sense mind is not *conscious* in my definition so much as *sensory* – 'relating to the physical senses'. It doesn't perceive and instead *decodes*. I will explain the hows and whys as we go along. This entrapment in five-sense perception is why so many (especially in academia, science and medicine) only believe in what they can see, touch, taste, smell or hear – *sense, decode*. They are not *conscious* beyond sensory self. By my definition, therefore, such people are *un*conscious and slaves of five-sense mind. Our senses are not conscious any more than a computer is conscious when it *decodes* data and presents it on the screen in a form that we recognise.

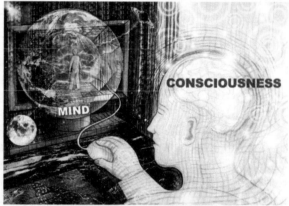

What I am calling 'conscious' is that which operates beyond the merely sensory. You could think of this as the person sitting at the computer with the keyboard and mouse while sensory mind is the computer which should be responding to that input (Fig 16).

Figure 16: The symbolic – but very accurate – depiction of the human plight. The computer operator (consciousness) becomes disconnected from the computer (Body-Mind) which is then programmed with false perceptions of everything to secure mass human control. (Image Neil Hague.)

When a computer virus infiltrates a system and takes it over – takes 'possession' – the operator is tapping the mouse and banging the keys without response. The computer takes on a life of its own with something else seizing control. I say this is what has happened to humanity. A 'virus' – the Death Cult and it's non-human masters – have infiltrated human

Figure 17: Who are we? We are awareness, a state of being aware. The body is only a temporary vehicle for a brief experience by that awareness as a 'human'.

Figure 18: We may experience ourselves as 'individual', but we are all expressions, too, of the same infinite flow of awareness that at one level I will call 'The Field'. (Image Neil Hague.)

Figure 19: When our point of attention enters the human frequency band we should be guided from our expanded levels of consciousness. Instead most are manipulated to operate only in the realm of the five senses where the Cult controls what they see and hear. The result is 'physical' enslavement through perceptual enslavement. (Image Neil Hague.)

perception and essentially disconnected sensory mind (Body-Mind) from expanded awareness. We are not our body or sensory perception. They are only experiences for the True Self which is simply awareness – a state of being aware (Fig 17). Everything in all existence is consciousness, the *same* consciousness in different states of awareness, and we, like *everything*, are an expression of that state of Infinite and Eternal Awareness (Fig 18). Our expression or *point of attention* is currently having a brief experience called human and our Body-Mind (the symbolic computer) is the vehicle for that experience. Humanity has been manipulated by the Cult to forget our true nature and identify with the 'me' of the five senses and all its illusory labels and sense of apartness and division (Fig 19). We are meant to retain a connection to the True 'I' (the hands on the mouse and keyboard) and we can open our minds potentially to Infinity itself. When our minds are closed that influence is lost to our *experiencing* awareness, or Body-Mind, and we becomes isolated in the 'Bubble' within which our sense of reality is dominated by five-sense perception (Fig 20 overleaf). Instead of being influenced by our expanded levels of awareness we become mesmerised by information constantly fed to the

BUBBLE PEOPLE

Figure 20: The whole foundation of human control – isolation in the Bubble of perception. See Neil Hague colour section.

brain and five senses by Cult-controlled media, politics, science, medicine and academia while all except a few in those professions have no idea they are serving a Cult-directed agenda. They are as perceptually mesmerised by their Bubbles as everyone else.

Perceptions within the isolated 'Bubble' are programmed to *sense* reality while not being *conscious* of reality and this allows the Cult to impose its will via manipulated ignorance on human experience. From this has come the collective madness of war, division and conflict of every kind and this possession of Body-Mind is planned to be completed through the mass-connection of AI to the human brain. That would take us beyond mere perception programming to full-blown assimilation into artificial intelligence and the force behind it. I don't mean assimilation of the True 'I', but of the five-sense Body-Mind Bubble isolated from True 'I'. It's like a virus taking control of an entire computer network by bypassing and disconnecting the operators (True 'I') and connecting the system to another source (the Cult and its masters in the unseen). Everything is conscious because everything *is* consciousness manifesting in infinite states and forms. Not everything, however, is *equally* conscious and hence my distinction in this book between what I am calling Body-Mind and consciousness. Observe humanity for five minutes to see multiple states of awareness. Sensory mind is a form of awareness which is incredibly limited in its perception of reality compared with consciousness beyond the Body-Mind Bubble.

What is this 'God'?

We are a point of attention within an Infinite state of awareness/consciousness that some refer to as 'God'. I don't use that term with all its religious connotations and diversions. For those who do, we are not *apart* from 'God'; we are a part *of* 'God'. We are a unique point of attention through which Infinite Awareness, or 'God', can infinitely experience itself (Fig 21). Infinite Awareness means Infinite Possibility and Infinite Potential for Infinite Experience. We are all

Figure 21: Our 'individual' awareness is Infinite Awareness experiencing itself. We are the 'individual' and the whole.

expressions of the same consciousness and separation is a five-sense illusion that the Cult works so hard to maintain. American cosmologist Carl Sagan said:

We are a way for the universe [I prefer The Infinite] to know itself. Some part of our being knows this is where we came from. We long to return. And we can, because the cosmos is also within us. We're made of star stuff.

What is 'human' except a state of awareness experiencing itself in multiple ways? The level of awareness of the 'part' is decided by the strength of connection that it has to the whole. The more we lose a perception of self-identity with the whole (I am Infinite Awareness having a human experience) and perceive ourselves to be isolated random 'labels' (I am Ethel on the checkout or Charlie at the drive-through) the more the connection and influence of Infinite Awareness is lost and we become trapped in illusion and forget who we really are. This can be accurately symbolised as living in a Bubble of isolated Body-Mind in which the perception of everything is formed only from the information available within the Bubble (Fig 22). Beyond its walls lies infinite possibility, potential and awareness that would give you a completely different understanding of who you are and where you are. The Cult works incessantly to keep humanity

Figure 22: Humanity is entrapped in perceptual Bubbles and programmed by Cult-controlled mainstream information sources operating in the Bubble. Isolate and program. See Neil Hague colour section.

entrapped in the Bubble because only then can its will prevail. Isolate Body-Mind from expanded states of consciousness and program Body-Mind with the perceptions and self-identity that allow the imposition of mass servitude. Crucial to this is to use the inner-core of the secret society network to communicate the nature of reality through the generations of the Cult while keeping that knowledge from the target population.

Descriptions of Infinite Reality that I have outlined here can be found throughout history long before the Cult instigated mainstream 'science' to tell us that we are all random cosmic accidents, that consciousness only comes from the brain, and death is the end. The perceptual outcome of promoting this nonsense has been to embed the belief that we are not an eternal expression of an infinite whole and only a meaningless assembly of randomly-evolved cells. We are told by 'experts' that the brain is the origin of consciousness and life depends on the brain being active. When it's not then consciousness ceases to be. Selling this Bubble illusion is an essential precursor to mass control. Cult-created 'education' and academia download this baloney to each generation of young people who largely pass it on to the next generation. Academia and this-world-is-all-there-is 'scientists' have themselves downloaded the same script (otherwise they would never get the job) and their funding and authorities demand that this is what they teach to others in a perpetual-perceptual motion machine in which ignorance speaks lies unto ignorance and calls it 'education'. For those who won't buy this perceptual program there is the associated entrapment of religion in which some have eternal life if they do what 'God' (the Cult) demands while others are condemned to the Fires of Hell for having a mind – or consciousness – of their own. Religion in a sentence: 'Do what 'God' (we) say or you'll be in deep shit.' Ancient cultures across the world knew that consciousness is eternal and their societies were founded on that understanding in the thousands of years before Cult 'science' and religion dropped in to tell and sell another story which was imposed by Cult-orchestrated colonisation from Britain and Europe. The Cult headquartered itself in Britain (hence the British Empire) after its journey of the centuries out of Sumer and Babylon (today's Iraq), Egypt, Asia, and elsewhere. Italy and Germany are other major Cult centres (so is China) and it expanded into North America with colonisation while establishing itself in the pivotal land of Palestine through Sabbatian-Frankism with the creation of Israel (see *The Trigger*).

Unravelling the illusion

Before I explore reality more deeply I should summarise the illusory 'normal' that we are told to believe in. This requires us to accept that what we appear to be experiencing is *really* what we are experiencing.

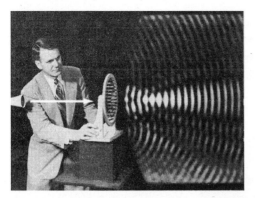

Figure 23: The foundation of human reality is information encoded in wavefields and the illusory 'physical' world is a decoded projection of that information.

Figure 24: A computer decodes information from Wi-Fi radiation fields in the unseen into images on the screen that we can see.

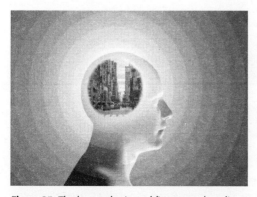

Figure 25: The human brain and five-sense decoding systems do the same by transforming unseen wave information into holographic, illusory 'physical', information that only exists in our 'heads'. (Image Gareth Icke.)

Official reality is what the *five senses* are manipulated to believe in. Can I see it? Check. Hear it? Check. Touch it? Check. Smell it? Check. Taste it? Check. Okay, it exists then. But *does it* in the form that we think it does? Are we and the world really 'physical' and 'solid'? No. The sensory system of the five senses is a decoder of information in the same way that a computer decodes Wi-Fi into a very different form on the screen. The five senses decode information in a particular way (again like a computer) which reflects what they have been encoded to do. A computer decodes information from electronic circuits and Wi-Fi electromagnetic radiation fields into pictures, colours, graphics and text on the screen as radio and television broadcasts transmit sound and images in waves which the television decodes (Fig 23). We perceive the Internet to be what we see on the screen when in fact the only place the Internet exists in that form is actually on the screen. Everywhere else that same information is expressed as electronic circuits, codes and Wi-Fi fields. Our human reality also consists of electromagnetic Wi-Fi-like wavefields of information and we are interacting with those fields as a computer interacts with Wi-Fi. A computer is encoded to decode Wi-Fi wave information to produce what we see on the screen while the five senses, in league with the brain, are encoded to decode information from radiation wavefields to produce the reality (the *sense* of reality) that we perceive as the 'physical world' (Figs 24 and 25 on previous page). The foundation of our reality and the human self is not 'physical'. It is wavefield information (keep thinking Wi-Fi) which

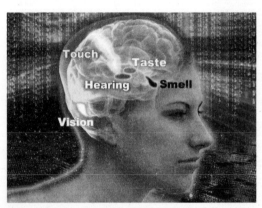

Figure 26: Different parts of the brain specialise in decoding different senses and fits them together to form perceived reality. (Image Neil Hague.)

Figure 27: The human decoding system transforms wave information into electrical information which becomes digital and holographic information – the illusory 'physical' world. (Image Neil Hague.)

the five senses decode into the 'world' that we think we are experiencing as physicality. Observe each of the senses and you will see that this is true. They decode wavefield information into electrical information which is communicated to the brain to be decoded into what we experience as the physical world. There are specific areas of the brain that process input from each sense and these sources are then combined to construct what we believe to be human reality (Fig 26). Our sense of everything in terms of physicality and solidity is an illusion of this decoding process. What appears to be physical is really holographic – *illusory* physical. Holograms give the appearance of solidity while being anything but solid. This illusion can be seen in today's holographics which can look as solid as you and me when in fact they are

energetic projections that have no solidity. I'll cover this in more detail in the next chapter. Only at the end of this wavefield-electrical-digital-holographic decoding process does the 'external' world exist as we perceive it (Fig 27). Nor is holographic 'physical' reality actually external to us despite what our senses may tell us. The 'world' that we experience apparently 'outside' of us only exists in that form *in our heads – the brain*. In the same way information on the screen of a computer only exists in that form *inside* the computer. I have heard scientists claim that the senses de-construct an external reality and then re-construct it in the brain. This is absolutely not the case and anyone taking even a cursory look at well-established evidence will see that. Our experienced reality, as acknowledged by more aware scientists, is like a computer screen which hides all the codes, circuits and pixels which make the sound and images possible. In our case those codes, circuits and pixels are information (consciousness) waves that when decoded form our illusory 'physical' reality.

The foundation of our reality – including ourselves – is wave information fields which are expressions of *consciousness* and so everything is conscious in some form. Information encoded in the wavefield of a tree is what makes it a tree and not a flower or a thorn bush. What is a 'tree' in a virtual reality game? It is information encoded to be decoded by the computer into the form of a tree. Every expression of form, every thought and emotion, transmits different wave frequencies that reflect the information the waves represent and contain. Form is in*form*ation – wave*form* in*form*ation. What is encoded into the human body wavefield makes us appear 'physically' human (Fig 28). Our reality is the sum total of all these wave information fields within the frequency band of the human senses and I will refer to this totality as 'The Field' – the energetic 'sea' that connects everything while our senses tell us that each 'form' stands apart from all other 'form' with 'space' in between. That 'space' is filled with the information (consciousness) of The Field which connects everything (Fig 29 overleaf). Wi-Fi technologically mimics 'The Field' and the reason for that will become clear later on (Fig 30 overleaf).

Figure 28: The foundation of the human body and everything in our reality is information encoded in wavefields. See Neil Hague colour section.

Body-Mind fields are interacting with 'The Field' in the same way that we take information from the Internet and also post information. The Field affects us and we affect it. We *are* The Field and The Field is us – we are indivisible. The term 'We Are One' is not some trite esoteric phrase. It describes how everything in our reality and *all*

Figure 29: Everything is connected with The Field and wave-interacts with everything else through The Field.
See Neil Hague colour section.

Figure 30: A portrayal of the now ubiquitous Wi-Fi fields – a technological overlap of The Field which operates basically the same.

realities is ultimately one field of energy/consciousness. Apparent division is an illusion of the way we experience reality. The key is to realise that *everything* is a wave information field which we decode into the 'world' that we think we live 'in' when 'it' really lives in *us* – Body-Mind. Understanding the foundation wave nature of 'physical' reality is to truly grasp what is happening in the world as will become clear.

Ears to hear? Tongues to taste?

The hearing sense is the most obvious example of decoding waves into electrical signals. Our ears receive wavefield information as soundwaves and transmit them to the brain as an electrical communication. Only when the brain decodes that information do we 'hear' sound. People talk about 'hearing' each other speak, but words don't pass between us – sound waves do. Words only manifest at the *end* of the sequence, not the beginning. When we speak we are generating *wavefields* of information from the vocal chords and these soundwaves are decoded by the ears and transmitted electrically to the brain to be decoded into the words that we think we are hearing with our ears. We hear them in the brain and it's the same with all the senses. Sound is *silent* to our senses in the form of sound *waves* until their information enters the brain. Take the example of a tree falling. A falling tree is an electromagnetic wave information field that impacts on the electromagnetic wavefield 'sea' or The Field. A wave disturbance is generated in the 'sea' from this wave interaction and if no one is there to decode that disturbance a falling tree makes no noise. If an observer is present they will pick up the wave disturbance as electromagnetic (sound) waves and transmit these electrically to the brain to be decoded into the sound of a tree falling. Hence the question 'does a falling tree make a noise?' can be answered by 'only if you hear it' (Fig 31). All five senses work this way. Food and drink as we perceive them are really energetic fields of information decoded by the senses into the form that we see and taste. The tongue sends electrical signals to the brain to become 'yummy' or 'what's this shit?' It is the *brain* that tastes within human reality and the same with sight, touch, smell and hearing (Fig 32). There

Figure 31: A falling tree (and everything else) literally does only make a noise when we hear it.

Figure 32: Everything is wavefield information in its base state – including food. 'Physical' food is decoded wavefield energy (information). See Neil Hague colour section.

are pain relief techniques used today which involve blocking the point of pain from communicating electrically with the brain. Unless the brain decodes that signal into 'ouch' there can be no pain. Food companies, well, they call it food, add taste enhancers to their products to trick the brain into decoding more taste than the 'food' contains. Car seats are now being designed to further trick the brain for health reasons into believing someone sitting behind the wheel is walking. 'Physical' reality is an illusion and the Cult knows this. It works constantly to stop *you* knowing to make you a sitting duck for its perceptual manipulation. The famous scene in the first *Matrix* movie describes the world as it really is when the character Neo has his mind inserted into a computer program to be shown the illusory nature of physicality:

Neo: This isn't real?

Morpheus: What *is* real? How do you define 'real'? If you're talking about what you can feel, what you can smell, taste and see, then 'real' is simply electrical signals interpreted by your brain.

That's all it is and everything we believe to be real only exists in the brain or Body-Mind in the form that we experience. British philosopher Alan Watts, who became well-known in America for his Western interpretation of Eastern philosophy, said:

... [Without the brain] the world is devoid of light, heat, weight, solidity, motion, space, time or any other imaginable feature. All these phenomena are interactions, or transactions, of vibrations with a certain arrangement of neurons.

Outside the brain none of these foundations of 'physical reality' exist in that form. Mainstream scientist Robert Lanza describes in his book, *Biocentrism*, how we decode electromagnetic waves and energy into visual and 'physical' experience. He used the example of a flame which emits photons, or tiny packets of electromagnetic energy, each pulsing electrically and magnetically:

... these ... invisible electromagnetic waves strike a human retina, and if (and only if) the waves happen to measure between 400 and 700 nano meters in length from crest to crest, then their energy is just right to deliver a stimulus to the 8 million cone-shaped cells in the retina.

Each in turn send an electrical pulse to a neighbour neuron, and on up the line this goes, at 250 mph, until it reaches the ... occipital lobe of the brain, in the back of the head. There, a cascading complex of neurons fire from the incoming stimuli, and we subjectively perceive this experience as a yellow brightness occurring in a place we have been conditioned to call the 'external world'.

Illusion Confusion

Even movement is a decoded illusion. There is no *movement*? You experience moving around in your dreams while *you* don't move at all. It all happens in your mind. *You* are lying in bed fast asleep. How can human experience involve 'physical' movement except as a holographic dream given that holographic 'physical' reality only exists in the brain? When people don headsets to play computer games they experience speeding along in a car or falling over a cliff while their bodies are sitting in a chair going nowhere. A British newspaper writer described

how the most striking aspect of playing such a game was the physical
sensation of moving without really moving: 'My brain sends signals to
my body that create the illusion that it's shooting around like a pinball
when in fact I am stationary.' This is how the illusion of human
movement works. Colours don't exist until they are decoded by the
brain. Each colour and shade is a unique frequency that requires
decoding to 'see'. Objects (wavefields) absorb some wave frequencies of
colour and reflect others. What they reflect we decode and 'see' as their
'colour' and what they absorb we don't. All that we visually perceive is
reflected light which is why we can't see in pitch black when objects
(wavefields) have no light to reflect. At the two colour extremes black
absorbs all light and appears black while white reflects all light and
appears white. Other colours absorb some and reflect some which gives
them their unique light representation that we 'see' (decode) as colour.
Rainbows are called a spectrum which comes from a Latin word
meaning an apparition or phantom (hence 'spectre'). That sums it up,
really. In the same way that sound can only manifest when waves are
decoded by the brain so visual reality can only manifest through the
same process. This is the real foundation of the scientific concept of the
'Observer Effect' which says that 'physical' reality only exists in that
form when it is being observed or 'measured'. When it is not being
observed/measured reality remains in its wavefield state and only
becomes 'physical' when we *look at it* in some form even through a
measuring device. One media headline said: 'Your entire life is an
ILLUSION: New test backs up theory that the world doesn't exist until
we look at it'. Andrew Truscott, an Associate Professor at the Australian
National University who has studied this phenomenon, said that at the
quantum (smaller than the atom) level reality does not exist if we are not
looking at it. He added that his team's experiments revealed how '… the
atoms did not travel from A to B … and it was only when they were
measured at the end of the journey that their wave-like or particle-like
behaviour was brought into existence.' Theoretical physicist Werner Karl
Heisenberg (1901-1976), the celebrated German pioneer of quantum
mechanics, said that 'a path comes into existence only when you observe
it'. An article in *Epoch Times* described the findings of another
experiment in an article headlined 'Your Mind Can Control Matter':

> Atomic particles were shown to also be waves. Whether they manifested as
> waves or as particles depended on whether someone was looking.
> Observation influenced the physical reality of the particles – in more technical
> language, observation collapsed the wave function.

Scientists have long pondered on the strange phenomenon that
particles are also waves at the *same time*. That's impossible, surely? They

Figure 33: The white crest of a wave and the ocean are the same body of water. Humans and Infinity are the same body of consciousness. They just take a different visual form.

Figure 34: It all seems so 'real', but it is holographic illusion decoded from wave information. See Neil Hague colour section.

have to be one or the other? They don't when you appreciate that particles and waves are manifestations of the *same information*. They only appear to be different because of the form that information takes (Fig 33). Waves are the foundation information construct and particles are their decoded holographic representation. 'Collapsing the wave function' is the act of decoding holographic reality which exists in another form at the beyond-human-sight quantum level. Quantum reality is waves of possibility and potentiality and the mind decodes that into holographic actuality. Scientists say that 'physical' reality only exists when we observe it, but the term missing here is *'decode it'*. Physical reality only exists when it is *decoded*. The act of observation triggers the decoding process.

Human reality requires an observer to exist because the observer is *making it* exist in that form in the decoding system of the brain (Fig 34). Waves ('non-physical') and particles ('physical') are different forms of the same field of information. Scientist Albert Einstein said: 'The [wavefield] is the sole agency of the particle [matter].'

He's behind you!

For reasons I have explained Einstein's contention *has* to be the case. The 'observer' principle is like the classic scene in a British pantomime show when a character faces the audience and they shout that someone 'is behind you'. As the character turns around to check this out the person behind moves around as they do. No matter how many times the

Figure 35: 'He's behind you' and when observation decodes reality true reality is always 'behind you'.

Figure 36: Look and see what's not really there except in your 'head'. (Image Neil Hague.)

character turns what he is looking for is always behind him and so unseeable (Fig 35). Move your focus in any direction and wavefield becomes hologram. We don't see what's 'behind you' (wavefield reality) because the act of observation triggers holographic decoding (Fig 36). Writer Michael Talbot described in his book, *The Holographic Universe*, something he witnessed at a family party in which a stage hypnotist was invited to entertain the guests with some mind tricks. At one point a man called Tom was put into a hypnotic trance and told that when he was brought back to a waking state he would not be able to see his daughter. The hypnotist asked the daughter to stand right in front of her father and the now apparently awakened Tom was asked if he could see her. 'No', he said, she wasn't in the room. He was, in fact, looking right into her belly as he sat and she stood. The hypnotist then put his hand in the small of her back and asked Tom if he could see what he was holding. 'Yes', Tom replied, bemused at such an easy question – 'You are holding a watch'. He was asked to read an inscription on the watch which he did while his daughter was standing between him and the watch. A mainstream scientist would tell you that is impossible when the explanation is so simple. The base form of the daughter's body was a wavefield of information operating at frequencies outside the human visual frequency range. Unless she was decoded into holographic form within the frequency band of Tom's eyes/brain she would not appear in her father's 'physical' reality. What's more if she wasn't in his mind holographically she could not block his view to the watch (Fig 37). The

Figure 37: If we don't decode something from the waveform it cannot appear in our holographic 'physical' reality. (Image Neil Hague.)

hypnotic suggestion that Tom wouldn't see his daughter firewalled his brain's decoding system from reading his daughter's field and without that happening she would remain invisible to him. This is also a basic explanation for 'ghosts' which are wavefields of consciousness not connected to a human body field and thus cannot be decoded into 'physical reality'. Most appear as ethereal and not 'solid' because of this although some can project a self-image so powerfully that they may appear to be 'solid', albeit briefly. Neo in *The Matrix* asks how he can appear to have a body while in a computer program connected to his brain and he is told that his mind is creating a 'residual self-image' – a 'mental projection of your digital self'. In the context of a 'ghost' it's a mental self-image of the former digital self which will still be imprinted in the 'ghost's' wavefield. Even the illusory 'world' that the brain constructs is manifested from a fraction of the information we receive second by second. The mainstream *Wonderpedia* science magazine said:

> Every second, 11 million sensations crackle along these [brain] pathways ... The brain is confronted with an alarming array of images, sounds and smells which it rigorously filters down until it is left with a manageable list of around 40. Thus 40 sensations per second make up what we perceive as reality.

Forty sensations or bits of information construct our experienced reality from 11 *million* received and any gaps are filled in by what the brain believes should be there. It's hysterical to think what reality is compared with the way we experience it. We can get some insight into the process of reality-manifestation with the ever more sophisticated virtual-reality games and systems which mimic technologically the way we create reality biologically (another form of technology if the truth be told). Players wear headsets, earphones and gloves which allow electrical information and codes of the game to access and override the decoding of 'normal' reality and trick the same senses into decoding a fake reality

Figure 38: The process of decoding virtual reality games is the same in principle as how we decode the 'physical' world.

Figure 39: Like the 'physical' world it can seem so 'real'.

(Fig 38). The mind-trick can be so effective that people react as if what is being played artificially to their eyes, ears and touch senses is real (Fig 39). I have just described human reality and how its illusions are created.

The brain is an information processor

This sub-heading may appear to be stating the obvious. Of course the brain processes information. Yes, on that we are in agreement. It's the wider context that produces the fork in the road that takes me and many in mainstream science in different directions. This involves the contention that consciousness (information) is not only processed by the brain but also *originates* in the brain. I seriously don't agree. Oh, but different parts of the brain 'light-up' or switch-on when people are in various perceptual states. Okay, but does that happen because the brain is generating those states? Or because it is *decoding* those states through specialised areas of the brain related to those states while the information being *processed* originates elsewhere? I say the latter. Where does the information come from which the brain decodes into what we perceive as our thoughts, emotions and perceptions? The question has multiple answers in that the nature and origin of that information can come from multiple potential sources. Those locked away in the Bubble will process information through the brain from within their Bubble while those who have breached the Cult's perceptual firewalls and accessed expanded awareness will process information from way beyond the Bubble. As a result how they see themselves and reality will be dramatically different. Put aside what you have been told about the brain for a second and imagine it to be only a processor of consciousness and not the origin – 'you hum it, son, and I'll play it', as the saying goes. Information processed by the brain comes from wavefields of consciousness outside the brain and this can be confined to the five-sense 'Bubble' or be any scale of expanded awareness with which your mind allows itself to connect. If you do access those expanded levels you are called crazy and insane by those in the Bubble. Information processed by the brain also comes from countless other sources including television, social media, personal experience and the ridiculously-named 'education' system. The brain will process anything that comes its way so long as this myriad of potential information is delivered within the frequency band of brain activity. It will decode the sound (frequency) of the human voice and also information delivered from realities way beyond the realm of the human voice if minds open to that level of awareness (Fig 40). When people say they 'hear voices in their head' they are describing the same phenomena as the brain

Figure 40: The brain can decode frequency information from other realities as it can decode frequency 'words' from the human vocal chords. We only have to open our minds and breach the Bubble. (Image Neil Hague.)

receiving information delivered by the vocal chords as electromagnetic waves which it decodes into words. The information can originate with another human or from dimensions of reality 'far away' (as with psychics or mediums). It can also be delivered in the form of waves generated technologically to infiltrate the brain's perceptions to misdirect and manipulate a target. The Cult operates just such a system worldwide today as I will be describing. The brain is a receiver, transmitter and processor of information, not the origin, and it can be a challenge to discern what is 'you' and what is another source of the wave information you decode as thought and emotion. There are ways of doing that though which I'll get into later.

The brain may be a processor of information, but it's not a neutral one any more than a computer is neutral when it has been encoded to process information in a particular way. Program a computer to decode information 'A' and not information 'B' and that's what it will do. We call this a 'firewall' and they are employed in China to prevent the population accessing large swathes of the Internet that the Chinese dictators don't want people to see. The same can be done with the brain and a central factor in this is what is called brain 'placidity'. It was believed until relatively recently that once the brain was formed this was

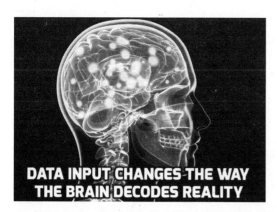

DATA INPUT CHANGES THE WAY
THE BRAIN DECODES REALITY

Figure 41: The brain becomes what it receives and processes.

how it remained for life. Scientists now know the very opposite is the case. 'Placidity' refers to how the brain changes the way information is *processed* in accordance with the information that it *processes* (Fig 41). All information is delivered in the form of frequency. Every thought, emotion and perceptual state is represented by its own unique frequency and as the brain processes information it arranges its neuron networks to fire (decode) in the sequence those frequencies represent. The brain processes particular frequencies of information, thought, emotion and perceptual states and here you have the reason why different perceptions and behaviour light-up different parts of the brain which are involved in processing those frequencies. Consciousness via perception activates those parts of the brain and the brain does not activate itself. The more the brain becomes dominated by flows of the same information, thought, emotion and perception (frequencies) the more its placidity will solidify the neural networks into a repeating sequence of processing ('firing' – *decoding*). The only way this can be changed is through other information, thought, emotion and perception representing other frequencies which then, through placidity, change the sequence of processing. Perceptions are represented by frequency waves and create a self-fulfilling conscious and subconscious feedback loop in which we interact with The Field of possibility only within the frequency band that our perceptions represent. In this way our perceptions become our experienced reality. The potential for mass manipulation is limitless when the Cult knows this and works to stop humanity knowing. Perception frequencies impact on the brain through placidity to dictate the way it processes information. In the absence of any change the brain goes on processing information in the same way. Through this sequence solidified perceptions become self-fulfilling prophecies as the brain processes information to match the solidified perceptions and the subsequent neuron-firing sequence which comes from that. We see this in people unable and unwilling to explore another point of view or ways of looking at situations and subjects. They say 'my mind is made up' (solidified neuron pathways), *'I am right'* and 'the science is settled' when it blatantly is not.

The term 'a closed mind' is most apt. People can break free anytime they make the choice to realise they are entrapped by their own unyielding perceptions that lead their brain to process information in ways that appear to *confirm* those perceptions (Fig

Figure 42: Perceptions create a self-fulfilling conscious and subconscious feedback loop in which we interact with The Field of possibility only within the frequency band that our perceptions represent. See Neil Hague colour section.

42). Round and round it goes again like a fairground ride apparently moving while going nowhere. This is not helped by the system employed by Internet giants such as YouTube which recommend information based on your past viewing. Hey look at this – something else to confirm what you already think. The very idea that we can form solidified perceptions while being aware of a fraction of 0.005 percent of what exists in the Universe is a fair definition of insanity. Religions go even further and insist that all people need to know can be found between the covers of a *single book* within a fraction of a fraction of 0.005 percent of what exists in the Universe. As a measurement of crazy, that is world class. It becomes clear why the Cult has always sought to control the information that people see and hear worldwide. Information dictates the way the brain processes information and becomes the person's sense of reality which, in turn, becomes their experienced reality. There's a lot more about this to come in relation to current events which look very different from this perspective.

Time? What time?

I understand why people find it so difficult to comprehend that there is no time when 'time' is the very foundation of human society. Everything is driven by the perception of 'time' – time is running out, look at the time, how time flies and where has the time gone? Yet the only moment within the entirety of Infinite Reality is the NOW. There is nothing else. What we perceive as past, present and future are all happening in the same NOW. I know that sounds incomprehensible to most people, but look at it from this perspective: Where is the 'present'? In the NOW.

Figure 43: 'Past', 'present' and 'future' are only perceptions. All is happening in the same NOW. See Neil Hague colour section.

Where are you when you think about the 'past'? In the NOW. Where are you when you think about the 'future'? In the NOW. Where does the perceived 'future' eventually happen? In the NOW. Where did the 'past' happen? In the NOW. There is only the NOW (Fig 43). As you read this book in what is perceived to be the 'present' all your thoughts and memories of the 'past' exist in your conscious and subconscious mind in that same 'present' as do all the wavefield perceptions that you will experience as the 'future'. They are all vibrating in the same field of NOW. I see scientists speculating about how the future can affect the present or even the past. Some of their experiments make it seem that way when in fact 'past', 'present' and 'future' affect each other because they are all happenings and connections in the same NOW. 'Time' is a decoded construct of holographic reality. Wavefield happenings in the NOW are arranged in a holographic sequence by the brain so that one appears to follow another. The apparent speed that Body-Mind runs this sequence leads to the perception of 'time' and our personal mental and emotional state affects how fast or slow 'time' appears to pass. When we are doing things we don't like 'time' seems to pass slowly while activities we enjoy make 'time' appear to pass quickly – 'My goodness, where's the time gone?' and 'Time flies when you are enjoying yourself'. Einstein called this 'relativity' as in 'time' being relative to the observer – the *observer* or decoder again. He was describing this in terms of the speed and location of the observer relative to what was being observed, but it goes much deeper into the speed at which the observer processes information. A sequence of events ('time') comes into existence only when we decode that sequence into experienced reality and the passage of 'time' is dictated by perception – one person says 'time is flying by' while someone even in the same room will say 'time is dragging today'.

'Time' seems to pass quicker the more information the brain

processes and as ever more information is processed today, especially with instant news, social media and the Internet, 'time' seems to be speeding up for many people. Studies with soldiers have shown how time is in the mind. Three groups were taken on a march of the same distance but at one point each was told they had been marching for different times even though they had not. One group was told the correct time or miles they had been marching; the second was told they had been marching for less time than they had; and the third was told they had been marching for more time than they had. The fatigue of the three groups matched the time they *thought* they had been marching when the time/distance involved was the same. A movie on DVD exists in the same NOW and I think everyone could agree with that. We experience the movie, existing in the same NOW, as a sequence of 'time' as one scene follows another.

Where you are on the DVD will appear to be your 'present' while your 'past' is the scenes you have already watched and your 'future' is the scenes you have yet to watch (Fig 44). A DVD in totality in the NOW is still experienced as 'time' passing from past through present to future and that's how we experience the passage of 'time' when there is only the NOW. Philosopher Alan Watts described 'individual' events as 'different sections of one continuous happening'. This is a good analogy, as with the DVD, and there is also the symbolism of experiencing a journey along a river as a series of moments in 'time' when the whole river exists in the same moment from source to sea. Each perceived 'moment' following past 'moments' are really 'different sections of 'one continuous happening'. Time as we perceive it is quite obviously a

Figure 44: Different scenes on a DVD appear as past, present and future when they all exist on same disc in the same NOW. Our perceptions of them creates the illusion of 'time'. (Image Neil Hague.)

Figure 45: 'Time' is real when you cross an invisible line and change the 'day'? Time does not exist. We make it *appear* to exist. (Image Neil Hague.)

human construct in that it involves clock-time which is so ridiculously manufactured that you can pass an invisible line called the International Dateline and instantly be in tomorrow or yesterday (Fig 45). People in Australia enter each New Year long before those in the United States and yet if an American in his today calls an Australian in his tomorrow they talk in the same NOW. The *speed* of ageing is connected to the perception of 'time' that doesn't exist except as a decoded illusion. While the body's wavefield stability remains the same the body hologram cannot change. Ageing is an interaction between mind and body. There is a sequence in the body blueprint that leads to a cycle from birth to death. After all we wouldn't want to stay in this one band of frequency forever when there is infinity to explore. The speed of this 'ageing' sequence, however, is down to the mind and its perceptions. People think they must age in a certain cycle and period only because almost everyone else does. Once again we have a self-fulfilling prophecy in which ageing is driven by the *perception* of ageing gleaned from experiencing the 'norm' of ageing. This is a quote that captures the time-illusion theme:

> Time doesn't exist, clocks exist. Time is just an agreed upon construct. We have taken distance (one rotation of the Sun), divided it into segments, then given those segments labels. While it has its uses, we have been programmed to live our lives by this construct as if it were real. We have confused our shared construct with something that is tangible and thus have become its slave.

A slave to the Cult 'gods' and the manipulated construct of illusory 'time'; but we don't have to be. Once we understand how the mind and a perception of 'time' interact we can start to control time. Top sportsmen and women already do this without realising. Researchers at the University of London found that those taking part in sports involving fast movement of a ball (tennis, baseball, cricket etc.) are able to slow down time. Their focus during play processes information so fast that its holographic movie sequence runs slower than the general population. The crowd in a tennis match with their heads lurching left and right to follow the ball perceive one speed while the players are experiencing another. This allows them to accurately hit a ball which at 'spectator' speed would defeat them. You often hear it said about great footballers that they seem to have more 'time' than everyone else. They *do* through the way they process information. They assess a situation on the pitch (process information) so fast that they can respond quicker than others who process (and so react) slower. Remember the game is happening in the minds of players and therefore it must be mind that decides the outcome. When this is more deeply understood by the world of sport we will see performances of all kinds improve by amazing leaps. The limit of sporting performance – as with life itself – is decided only by the self-imposed perception limits of the mind. There is an altered state that top sports people know well called 'the Zone'. I experienced it myself as a footballer and it is not confined to sport. I go into the Zone when I am writing and during speaking events. In sport the Zone slows down 'time', the sound of the crowd dissipates to silence, and any nerves or worry about the outcome disappear. You access a level of awareness beyond what is called the 'conscious mind' which can be full of self-doubt ('You think too much'). What follows is a calmness and level of focus that is only interested in doing the job and not worrying about what the outcome will be. In these moments come the best performances which self-doubt and emotion can otherwise sabotage.

The speed of light? It's pedestrian

The collective programmed perception limit of speed and 'time' is the speed of light which we are told is the fastest speed possible. What crap that will be seen to be. We live in an infinite reality of Infinite Possibility and there is no fastest or slowest anything. The speed of light at 186,000 miles per second (and the perceived physics associated with that) apply only to the frequency band of current human perception and even then they are malleable through the perceptions of consciousness. The speed of light is only the inability of Body-Mind to consciously decode reality faster than the speed of light and there is a reason for that which I will be exposing. The already-measured speed of communication by consciousness is infinitely quicker than the speed of light – as in *instant*. When cells from the same person were located 40 miles apart they responded instantaneously to changes in the other. This both revealed the myth about the speed of light and confirmed the truth about wave communication over what we perceive as enormous 'distance'. Physicists led by Juan Yin at the University of Science and Technology of China in Shanghai estimated the speed that photons (tiny packets of light) interact at *ten thousand* times the official speed of light. 'Time' changes along with much else when you approach the speed of light and the limits of the Body-Mind decoding system within the human frequency band. Space and distance are further illusions of holographic decoded reality. Scan the night sky and everything you think you 'see' in the form that you think you 'see' exists only in your 'head' – the Body-Mind decoding systems (Fig 46). In fact, it's not even your head but an area at the back of the brain where visual reality is decoded and your personal visual movie constructed. Computer games appear to have both time, as scenes change, and space in depth and perspective. Yet they are only codes written for the computer to decode. Space as we perceive it is defined by holographic form. Where there is no form we

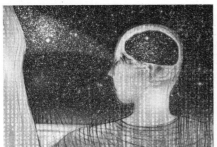
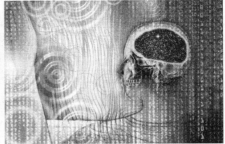

Figure 46: The night sky seems so far away, but it only exists in that form in your brain. What happened to 'space'? (Image Neil Hague.)

Figure 47: All existence shares the same 'space' on different bands of frequency just as analogue radio and television stations share the same 'space' without being aware of each other unless they are very close on the dial. (Image Neil Hague.)

call this 'space' and people think of this 'space' as 'empty' when it is a consciousness field full of information – The Field. What we refer to as 'space' is only the absence of form or 'things' and it is absolutely not 'empty'. Infinity exists in the same 'space' where you are sitting or standing now while only an infinitesimal fraction can be perceived by the human decoding system (Fig 47). We are told that light from stars travels billions of light years to get to us when there is no 'space' to 'cross' or 'time' to 'travel' except as an illusion of decoded perception. What you believe you perceive and what you perceive you experience. Change what you believe and you change what you experience.

Evidence galore

We have evidence of other realities and levels of consciousness from literally millions of people living today who have had what are called 'near-death experiences', or NDEs. This is when the body dies and people apparently experience their awareness being released to another point of observation outside the body (Fig 48 overleaf). Reality that I have outlined so far explains why near-death experiencers describe what they do. The number of NDEs must be many hundreds of millions and

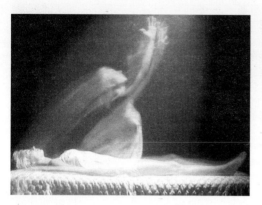

Figure 48: Enormous numbers of people have described leaving five-sense perceptual focus and entering a vastly different reality in a near-death experience.

more throughout history with near-death experiences described in ancient Greek and Roman texts and medieval works. Modern experiencers report how they see medical staff trying to revive 'them' (or rather their temporary vehicle) while being perceptually detached from the body. Many are able to accurately recall what staff were saying while 'they' were officially 'dead'. Many describe looking down on their body and no longer identifying with that as part of them. NDEs have many common themes of passing through a tunnel (though far from always); meeting long-dead friends and relatives (often looking far younger than when they 'died'); and experiencing stunningly beautiful places while enveloped in indescribable love. They report an extraordinary sense of calm and peace and how they felt free for the first time. Not everyone's life changes for the better after they return to the body, but that is the case with most once they have come to terms with living in a world they know is not what it appears to be. One experiencer said: 'I don't fit in because I don't "toe the line" and just agree with things.' This happens when you see through the illusion. Others report feeling more tolerant, loving and compassionate and no longer obsessed with materialism and personal status. The most common trait of a near-death experience is that people no longer fear death. Humanity in general is haunted by the prospect of death when there is nothing to fear. The Cult doesn't want us to know this when fear of death (fear of the unknown) has so many uses in pursuit of control (see the Covid-19 hoax). I have read a long list of near-death accounts over the years and the great majority are very positive. Rarely do you find people who prefer human life to what they experienced in 'death'. They return because they are told their experience is not yet over or they don't want to leave children and other loved ones behind. Most are transformed by their experience and what it showed them about reality beyond the myopia of the body which focuses our attention within the minuscule frequency band of visible light. 'We' don't die – only the illusion does. My own findings were confirmed by a team of scientists from the University of Liège in Belgium and Canada's Western University who found that in 158 written testimonies about near-death experiences positive responses far

Figure 48: My mother's picture with the life-force that had departed her body at the time of 'death' which was nothing more than a transformation of her point of attention.

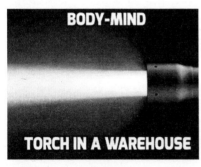

Figure 50: Our experienced reality is like a torch light in a pitch-black 'warehouse' and all we perceive is within its beam.

Figure 51: When we leave the body it is like all the lights of the warehouse are switched on and we realise that reality is far greater than we thought. Oh, just a little bit.

outnumbered negative ones. Canadian paramedic Adam Tapp, who was clinically dead for eleven minutes, said: 'It was just like waking from a nap in a place I have always been and there was no fear or anything, just complete contentment and happiness.'

I went to the funeral parlour when my mother 'died' and saw her body lying on a table. I touched her hand and it was cold and lifeless as you would expect; but alongside was a big picture of her which my brother Paul had arranged to have at the funeral and that picture was *alive* with energy and radiance (Fig 49). Cameras don't only record an image we can see. They capture the energetic life-force – the True 'I' – that takes temporary residence 'in' the body. The life-force that I saw in my mother's picture which was no longer in her body – *that's* who we are. Switch off the electricity to a piece of technology and it 'dies' or ceases to work while the electricity itself, the life-force of the machine, continues to exist. A body devoid of its life-force decomposes because the energy sustaining it has gone. A near-death experiencer described our world as like walking through a pitch-black warehouse with a torch when all you can see and be aware of is limited to the narrow beam of light (Fig 50). She said leaving the body was like all the lights in the warehouse are turned on. You see the enormity of what you are and where you are when before you were aware only of that within the torch light (Fig 51). Another constant theme of experience outside the body is the feeling of being at 'one' with everything and connected to everything. A near-death experiencer said he was aware of his hospital environment in Los Angeles and could also hear conversations of family members in India. He said he felt everywhere in the same moment. This is what happens once our awareness is no longer focused through the visible light myopia of the body – the torch light – and we access the perceptual reality of waves that connect with other waves beyond the illusions of distance and time. There is still the 'individual' sense of self and at the same time the feeling of a seamless connection to all that exists. This can be simply explained. We are a unique point of attention within a seamless flow of Infinite Awareness and we are both the 'individual' attention and the whole at the same 'time'.

Human disconnection from awareness of the whole as manipulated by the Cult means that 'incarnate' consciousness experiences reality from a sense of isolation and apartness – the Bubble (Fig 52). A near-death experiencer described beyond-the-body reality:

Figure 52: Burst the Bubble and freedom awaits.

… everything from the beginning, my birth, my ancestors, my children, my wife, everything comes together simultaneously. I saw everything about me, and about everyone who was around me. I saw everything they were thinking now, what they thought then, what was happening before, what was happening now. There is no time, there is no sequence of events, no such thing as limitation, of distance, of period, of place. I could be anywhere I wanted to be simultaneously.

Exactly. That is life beyond the limited focus and decoded illusions of Body-Mind. Think how different our world would be if humanity realised that we are experiencing a temporary illusion or movie and that we are ALL expressions of the same Infinite whole in which, despite what our five senses may tell us, there is no time, sequence of events, limitation, distance, period or place and we can be anywhere we want to be simultaneously. How would you pitch race against race, religion against religion, sex against sex, politics against politics and income against income if everyone knew these are temporary and illusory labels and experiences and that we are all *each other*? The Cult must perpetuate this illusion or its divide and conquer manipulation is over. Religion is

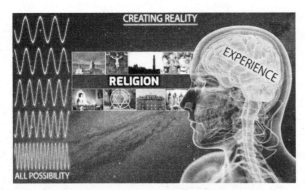

Figure 53: Religion is the greatest form of mind control ever invented never mind which name may be on the temple door. (Image Gareth Icke.)

Figure 54: Create religions and then play them off against each other – and within each other – to divide the target population into conflicting groups. (Image Gareth Icke.)

one of the greatest forms of mind control ever invented (by the Cult) and up there as the greatest form of divide and rule (Figs 53 and 54). Do people really think that when they leave the body they are still Christians, Muslims, Jews, Hindus, black, white, man, woman, transgender, rich, poor and so on? Some may wish to believe so, but it's delusion. Are those suffering 'physical' or psychological handicaps still handicapped when they withdraw from a body where the handicap manifests? We need to urgently see the fundamental difference between the *experience* and the *self*. That realisation alone will change the world.

You are what you believe

Some near-death experiencers report amazing health transformations with even late-stage cancer disappearing. They say pain goes with release from the body and that must be so. Pain is a phenomenon of the senses and not beyond-the-body consciousness in its infinite form. They describe how they can see, touch, hear, taste and smell without attachment to the five senses and in a far more advanced way. How can you see without the eyes of the body? It's all *illusion*. Expanded awareness is aware across all 'senses' with no need for the perceptual confines of the body to allow it to see; but if incarnate awareness is so body-focused and programmed by the illusions of eye-only sight then it will experience that reality until it's released from the body. People see visions in states of meditation and altered states of consciousness when their eyes are closed. Do we think that we see our vivid dreams through our *eyes*? Blind people describe how they could see once they leave the body. Blindness is the inability to decode visual information through the eye/brain connection within the human reality of visible light. Once they withdraw from visible light they see with consciousness whose awareness is filtered out by body systems during a human experience. Other common themes of near-death experiences are 'life-reviews' when they feel the consequences for others of their actions – nice and not so nice. Many describe having an infusion of knowledge about life and reality when they are released from the body information filter and consciously connected to awareness, insight and knowing that the Cult works to perceptually firewall. An experiencer returned with a deep knowledge of quantum physics that she didn't have before and had never studied. You can, however, access such information while in the body and I'll be describing how to do this. Mainstream academics and scientists ignore this mountain of evidence from the experiences of multiple millions because it demolishes their version of reality. They work on the basis that if they can't explain it then it can't exist which launches self-deluding arrogance into the stratosphere. I call it the arrogance of ignorance. 'What about the laws of physics?' they will cry. What about them? They only apply in theory within the frequency walls of human reality. They don't apply anywhere else and they don't need to apply here once we grasp what reality really is and how it really works. Manifestations of this are dubbed 'miracles' ('defying the laws of physics') when there is no such thing as a miracle – only understanding that Infinite Possibility means anything is possible. All will become clear as the book proceeds.

Most people have blissful experiences when they leave the body, but some don't. Others see religious figures, but most don't. There are many reasons for these differences including the saying 'death is no cure for ignorance'. Near-death does not have to be a cure for perceptual programming, either, although it certainly can be. If you believe that Jesus is your saviour then you may see Jesus in a near-death experience and let's not forget that consciousness beyond the body is trying to communicate information and concepts to you. If you associate love with Jesus then that image may be used to symbolise love and give you comfort in a bewildering situation. It doesn't mean there is literally a Jesus and of course no one knows what 'he' looked like even if he had been real. I don't believe for a second that he was, but I can relate to the character that appears in many guises and under many names in different cultures to be a *symbol* for expanded states of consciousness. This would make sense of 'No one comes to the Father except through me' – only through expanded states of consciousness can you be aware of the Infinite Whole. The basic 'Jesus' story was told in versions all around the world long before the period when 'Jesus' was supposed to live and each could be symbolising states of expanded awareness. They represent a recurring narrative put into different historical and cultural settings using different names for the hero. There is not even a physical description of 'Jesus' in the Bible. The image that people have of 'Jesus' came from far later artistic imagination and interpretation and yet those who claim to meet 'Jesus' in near-death experiences see this classic version of 'him'. It's all in the mind, but then everything is. The New Age 'Jesus' is called 'Sananda' and claimed to be an 'Ascended Master'. Guess what? He is portrayed in virtually the same way as the Christian 'Jesus'. I don't accept the literal existence of 'Jesus', but as a *symbol* of expanded awareness, well, I'm open to that. Your state of consciousness when you withdraw from the body will massively influence your experience until the truth dawns that what you believed about life and reality is to say the least not quite how it is. Those who have some understanding of reality will be aware of the process that follows 'death' while those with their awareness welded to Cult perception programs can be seriously bemused and bewildered as so many near-death experiences have confirmed.

Your state of awareness most certainly affects the experience of psychoactive drugs which activate areas and channels of the brain to access realities normally denied to human perception. These have been used for thousands of years as a major source of shamanic comprehension of reality. I took ayahuasca, a psychoactive rainforest potion, over two nights in Brazil in 2003 and had a fantastic experience over a total of seven hours. For five hours on the second night a clear, loud, powerful voice taking a female form gave me chapter and verse about the illusory nature of 'physical' reality. I refer to the communicator as 'The Voice'. During an explanation about the illusion of 'time' and 'space' The Voice said: 'Why do you fly from point A to point B when you *are* point A and point B and everything in "between"?' When I returned home with total recall of what was said I began to research the subject at length and found that mainstream science (especially quantum physics) already had the evidence to prove that physical reality is illusory, but the controlling hierarchy still sought to push the case for this-world-is-all-there-is and you are only your brain. This is the Cult narrative for reasons I have explained. Some have had nightmare experiences with psychoactive drugs and in my view they only open brain channels that allow access to deeper levels of yourself which can still reflect your current mental and emotional state and what is happening in your subconscious. I have known people who have taken drugs like LSD hundreds of times and they were no more enlightened than someone who has had nothing stronger than a cup of tea. It is not only about opening your mind, but what level of awareness you open to. Gail Bradbrook, a co-founder of the extreme climate group Extinction

Rebellion, is a psychoactive potion-taker who thinks she is enlightened as a result and wants others to partake. She told the BBC that the idea of creating Extinction Rebellion came to her when she prayed 'in a deep way' while taking 'psychedelic medicines'. Her subsequent 'enlightenment' led her to establish a Climate Cult operation which is a fundamental threat to human freedom as I will be exposing. She confuses demands for global centralisation of power to 'save the world' (exactly what the Cult has been seeking all along) with an 'awakening'. Such 'enlightenment' is really a fast-track to even greater enslavement and I repeat: Psychoactive drugs only take you to where you already are subconsciously, if not consciously, and that will dictate the level of awareness beyond human reality that you connect with. These drugs, like death, are indeed no cure for ignorance, but they can be for some. Perception is the key and who is in control of that? *We are* – if we make that choice and stop allowing others to tell us what to think.

The scale of the reality illusion, which is mercilessly manipulated by the Cult, can be seen in the fact that mainstream science believes that (illusory) time and space are among the fundamental building blocks of the Universe. This systematically-imposed ignorance ('lack of knowledge, understanding, or information') is the foundation of human control and it must end before, as Martin Luther King put it, freedom can ring.

CHAPTER TWO

Who are we?

All growth is essentially an expansion of awareness – Joseph Rain

There is a malevolent force behind humanity's systematic perceptual entrapment and the indoctrination is incessant and life-long. What a testament to the power of consciousness over programming that anyone is awakening from the Cult-induced trance and they are in ever greater numbers.

People are unconscious and perceptually entrapped in Body-Mind because they are *manipulated* to be that way and this needs to be understood to avoid awakening from the trance to include a sense of superiority. Almost everyone was asleep once. Five-sense unconsciousness can appear to be unbelievably stupid, but that is what happens when people are disconnected from an influence of the True and Infinite 'I' and imprisoned in a sensory world that hijacks perception for an entire human lifetime. The great news is that we can become conscious anytime we want. More and more people are awakening from their induced coma while others are being captured more deeply in the Cult's perceptual fly-trap by a tsunami of programming deployed increasingly via technology. The latter, too, can escape the illusion – perceptual entrapment – whenever they make that choice. The motivation of this book is to speed and expand that process. As more become conscious of their True Self the world must change to reflect that. In the same way the crazy world of today, and a long time 'past', has reflected and continues to reflect collective human *un*consciousness. So much is explained about 'past' and 'present' events when this is understood. Ironically, and it's another big penny-drop, the most *un*conscious are invariably those in positions of power directing the lives and society of everyone else. This is once again by design and not random chance. The Cult has to keep its targets asleep in unconsciousness if it is to secure ongoing collective control through perceptual programming and the most effective way to achieve that is to put unconscious Bubble people into positions of official power who are string-pulled from the shadows by the Cult. The plot demands disconnecting Body-Mind from expanded awareness and then to program isolated Body-Mind with the required perception of self and reality through control of information. We see this process everywhere. Muslims tend to come from Muslim families, Christians from Christian families, Hindus from Hindu families, and followers of Judaism from Jewish families. In every case that version of reality and life is all they have ever heard in their growing-up years

Figure 55: I-am-a whatever my upbringing told me to be.

(Fig 55). The greatest form of mind control is repetition as the Cult-created Nazis well understood. You repeat a statement or alleged 'fact' until it becomes an 'everyone knows that' when in truth 'everybody' only *'knows'* what they have been told to think they *know*. They don't 'know it'; they have only *downloaded* that perception which is a very different thing. Add the carrot and stick, benefits and punishments, for believing or not believing in the orthodoxy and it's no wonder the religion that people are born into becomes the one they follow for life with all the limitations and impositions of belief and behaviour that come with the package. The sequence I have described applies equally to those who follow no religion or may indeed be antagonistic to religion. The non-religious population is also programmed through family, 'education', academia and media by the repetition of information headed 'normal' and 'rational' when most of this betrays an extreme misrepresentation of reality. Young people are told they must believe this crap and they are tested on their level of absorption in 'exams' that have potentially life-long career implications within The System. If you regularly question what you are told to believe you are 'a disruptive influence' in the classroom. Has your doctor prescribed Ritalin?

I am going to focus on this life-long programming process later because it is vital to understanding how collective human perception is hijacked and how we can stop falling for it. Our human lives are a choice – a *perception*. These choices decide your health, happiness and entire experience. By that I mean *everything* you ever experience and even that called 'random chance', good and bad 'luck' and circumstances that appear to be created by other people. To appreciate how this happens we must first put aside all mainstream perception, belief and pre-conceived idea about the nature of self, reality and the human body. What the control system has told us about all of these things is fakery

Figure 56: The fake self-identity that most people believe they are.

Figure 57: I am what I'm told I am.

and at the core of this unceasing propaganda delivered day after day to generation after generation is the Cult. It knows that if we can be kept in ignorance of who we really are its agenda for mass control becomes a relative breeze. This is the foundation of human enslavement – hypnotically peddling a fake self-identity or what I call the Bubble or 'Phantom Self' (Fig 56). How apt that the word 'person' comes from the Latin 'persona' which means 'actor's mask'. Our Phantom Self persona is indeed our actor's mask or headset. We appear to experience a solid world through a solid body. We do not. We are told that we are victims of our genetics. We are not. We appear to live in a world where everything is apart from everything else with 'empty' space in between. We do not. All is illusion that we are manipulated from cradle to grave to believe is real (Fig 57). When people can see through the scam they can stop it controlling their lives.

The One

Who are we? Put the temporary human form aside and we are formless *awareness* – a state of being aware (Fig 58). How aware depends on how aware we choose to be or *allow* ourselves to be and that 'how aware' decides our life experience. We are unique points of attention within an infinite stream of awareness or consciousness and that awareness in its 'totality' (infinity) is what some call 'God' or the 'Godhead', Native Americans call 'The Great Spirit', and I call the *All That Is* or '*The One*'. Existence is not a single state of perception with *The One* constantly

Figure 58: The body is only a temporary vehicle for the awareness that we eternally are.

experiencing itself through its infinite expressions in different states of consciousness. There is a level of awareness that I describe as *Infinite Awareness in Awareness of Itself* which is aware that it is all awareness. This has been variously called 'the Void', 'the Father' and in my case *The One*. The ancient religious term 'Father' is an attempt to relate this concept to the world of human experience. *The One* is really the Father *and* Mother and everything in all existence. It is the realm of All Possibility, All Potential, and our perceptions dictate which possibility and potential that we manifest in ways I will be describing. All Possibility is the implication encoded in *All That Is, Has Been and Ever Can Be*. To the human mind enslaved in the illusion of past, present and future this would seem to be impossibility. How can anything be all that *is*, has *been* and ever *can be*? Yet what is this depicting except *All Possibility*? Reality is infinite because possibility is infinite within the awareness of *The One*. How can you have a state of all possibility unless everything is possible? Thus *Infinite Awareness in Awareness of Itself* is 'past, 'present' *and* 'future' (as they appear to be); it is *and* it isn't; it can *and* it can't; it did *and* it didn't; it is everywhere *and* nowhere; it is everything *and* nothing, it exists *and* it doesn't. Some people say 'God is everywhere' while others say that's crazy and cannot be; but it's true in the sense of *The One* that weaves through the fabric of everything because *The One is* everything. Even impossible must exist within all possibility because the impossible is a possibility. Whether we choose (through our perception) to experience the possible or impossible is down to us. What one person will experience as impossibility another will find a way to overcome and make possible. If you don't know how to do something that 'thing' is indeed impossible. When you *do* know it becomes possible. Both are potentials within All Possibility which includes every paradox. All Possibility must be awash with paradox which is defined as 'a state in which one is logically compelled to contradict oneself'. When all is possible that must be. For every 'truth' there must be a contradictory 'truth' or perception of reality and *possibility*. Look at something from one angle (perception) and A is 'true'. Look from another angle (perception) and B is 'true'. They can both be true (possible) depending on your point of observation even though they appear to be contradictory. Is the body solid in the way we experience it? Yes. Is it really solid from a point of expanded awareness? No. Here we have a paradox – it is *and* it isn't. Both are true from two different points of experience … perception, *possibility*. Maybe human belief in *'I am right'* could benefit from some revaluation.

The no-thing is everything

The 'Void' is a term used to describe *Infinite Awareness in Awareness of Itself* because that is how it appears to be (Fig 59). Those who have

THE ONE
THE SILENCE
THE VOID

Figure 59: The *All That Is, Has Been, And Ever Can Be* that interpenetrates all existence. It *is* all existence.

entered altered states of consciousness throughout human history have perceived 'God', the 'Father' or *'The One'* in the form of a void or silence. I did so myself during my ayahuasca experience in 2003. I observed from the realm of vibration, frequency and form an indescribable brilliant blackness. I know it may sound crazy but the darkness shone like the brightest light. 'This is the Infinite, David', the ayahuasca Voice told me. 'It is where you come from and where you shall return.' The word 'return' is only used in relation to human perception. We are *always* the Infinite – we never 'left'. We've just forgotten and been manipulated to forget. The shining blackness was still and silent and so different from the movement and vibration in the world of form. The Void has been described as 'nothingness', but within the stillness and silence is *everything*ness in the form of All Possibility waiting to manifest from the imagination of 'God' or *'The One'* which includes *our* imagination as an expression of *The One*. Sit in silence for a moment and what do you hear? Nothing. Okay, but this 'nothing' is only the absence of sound waves for your brain to decode. Within the silence, the nothing, is everything. When you hear sound or see images they are possibilities manifested out of All Possibility – the silence and the stillness. Silence is the norm, the foundation state, while sound comes and goes from the silence of *All That Is*. Rumi, the 13th century Persian mystic, said: 'Silence is the language of god, all else is poor translation.' Scientific studies have highlighted the negative effect of excessive sound – as in too loud and too much even when not loud – and the benefits for heart and mind of silence. I sit working all day in silence or near silence thanks to the quiet nature of where I live and it's wonderful. I read that the word 'noise' actually comes from a Latin word meaning nausea. It is certainly highly recommended to spend time regularly when possible where it is quiet and not noisier/nausea. The 'Void' is the *source* of all Creation (possibility) while the realms of frequency and vibration *are* the Creation (Fig 60 overleaf). The ayahuasca Voice said: 'If it vibrates, it's illusion.' An immense indescribable love was emanating from the stillness and silence which confirmed what The Voice had said right at the start of the five hours of communication: 'All you really need to know is Infinite Love is the only truth – *everything* else is illusion.' This

Figure 60: The One is the creator of all reality via its infinite points of attention – including us. See Neil Hague colour section.

became the title of a book that I wrote soon afterwards. Put another way: *Infinite Awareness in Awareness of Itself* (the 'Void', *The One*, the source of love) is the only truth – everything else is the Creation or imagination of Infinite Awareness made manifest by information (consciousness/'thought') in the form of frequency/vibration. How can there be an 'only truth' within All Possibility? The only truth *is* All Possibility. This is limited only by the imagination of *The One*, and that is limitless.

Five years after my experience in Brazil, Dr Eben Alexander, an academic neurosurgeon at Harvard, fell dangerously ill and went into a coma for a week from which he said doctors did not believe he would emerge alive or at least as a functional human being. He said he was a this-world-is-all-there-is believer as the product of academic perception programming. This was underpinned by his scientist father who also believed that consciousness only exists in the brain and when the brain dies so do 'you'. Alexander did recover his faculties even though he said his brain had so shutdown that only the primary survival functions remained active during the coma. He later wrote a book, *Proof of Heaven*, published in 2012, about what he experienced in his near-death state which transformed his perception of self and reality. He recalled how he met a female figure 'out there' that he somehow recognised, but he didn't know why or where from. When he recovered he said he was later shown a picture of his younger sister from his birth family (he had been adopted) who he had never seen before. It was the figure he had met in his near-death state. Alexander's claims have been controversial, of course, and people will have to decide for themselves what they think of them. The part of his book that most struck me for obvious reasons was when he recalled experiencing 'The Core' which he described as a … Dazzling Darkness. This is what I had seen nine years earlier and he also described this 'Core' as a place from where 'the purest love emanated and all is known' … all is known = All Possibility. I experienced this as the all-knowing *All That Is, Has Been and Ever Can Be – The One.* Albert Einstein said: 'Anyone who becomes seriously involved in the pursuit of science becomes convinced that there is a spirit manifest in the laws of the Universe, a spirit vastly superior to man.' That spirit is *The One* which pervades all existence and not only one universe.

What is called Creation emerges from *The One* through infinite expressions of *The One* (including 'humans') and Creation is once again limited only by the imagination of *The One* which is infinite. Creation is therefore infinite in its possibility and we are experiencing only a fragment of this in the micro-frequency band of light visible to humans. We are nevertheless co-creators of *The One* as an expression of *The One*. Consciousness fields emanating from *The One* themselves beget other consciousness fields like a single cell divides and divides until it is the *trillions* of cells in a human body. The point is that all those cells are manifestations of *one* cell as all that exists is the manifestation of One Consciousness. We are 'individual' points of attention and *all* points of attention. The part is the whole and the whole is the part. Where does the droplet end and the ocean begin once the droplet is reconnected with the ocean? They are the same and the

Figure 61: A droplet can appear to be individual, but connect it to the ocean and where does the droplet end and the ocean start? They are one and the same.

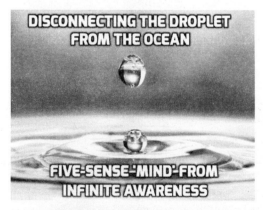

Figure 62: The foundation of human perceptual control is to disconnect the droplet from awareness of the ocean – our True Self.

Cult's whole agenda is founded on keeping the droplets unaware of the ocean that we all are (Figs 61 and 62). We are all manifestations, or co-creators, of *The One* – yes, even you sleeping in the street believing yourself to be downcast, outcast and a failure. In my expanded awareness during the ayahuasca experience beyond the perceptual limitations of the body I felt connected to everything, but I was still a unique individual 'me'. We are not one or the other. We are *both*. The more your mind opens and your consciousness expands the more your sense of self and the 'I' expands. Humanity has largely been manipulated to perceive only the individual. Even most major religions, while accepting there are other realities, still present 'God' and humanity as apart from each other instead of being the *same*. Saying 'I am God' is considered blasphemy. In the world of the Cult there has to be a servant and a master to match its own agenda for humanity. Infinite Awareness in its fully awakened state – *'The One'*– pervades everything. It is that which weaves the web of life. *The One* interpenetrates all realities and is within you now. Perception creates experienced reality as I am going to make clear and a human perception of isolation and *only* individuality becomes our experience of both. They are illusions that without a conscious connection to *The One* can seem very real. Redefine who you are, open your heart and mind to expanded awareness, and your experience will – *must* – change.

What is 'human'?

Now we can connect all this to today's global society. Human experience operates on multiple levels of awareness. There is the level that can be electromagnetically and visually recorded as the human 'auric field'. The combination of body and auric field is what I am referring to as Body-Mind. It is also known by many as the 'Ego' (Fig 63). We talk of people having open minds and closed minds and this is a

Figure 63: The body and the auric electromagnetic field of is what I am calling Body-Mind which experiences reality through the five senses; but we are much more than that.

perfect description. An open mind remains connected to expanded states of awareness while a closed one withdraws into the Bubble and perceives everything from the Body-Mind (five-sense) perspective. Bubble perception applies to much of the population (although this is changing) and crucially to those that dictate mass perception in the institutions of the Mainstream Everything – science, academia, media, medicine, commerce, politics and government. There is a level of our awareness that people call 'Soul' which operates outside the human frequency band and connects with Body-Mind through energetic vortexes known as 'chakras'. This is an ancient Sanskrit word from the Indian subcontinent meaning 'wheels of light' and that's an excellent description of the spinning energetic (consciousness) connections between levels of awareness within the same 'self' (Fig 64). When chakra connections are open the human 'I' can be influenced and guided by the Soul 'I' and through that to *The One* 'I'. In

Figure 64: The energy vortexes known as 'chakras' which interpenetrate and communicate through our different energetic levels of being.

other words how far we open our minds has no limit. When those chakra/consciousness connections close or diminish we become perceptually isolated in the five senses and fall prey to self-identity with illusory human labels. The label 'I', or Phantom Self Body-Mind, then appears to be the only 'I'. Body-Mind is a projection of Soul and when the influence of Soul is weakened Body-Mind can take on a life and direction of its own. There are vortex points throughout the body and the seven main ones are:

The crown chakra on top of the head (many near-death experiencers describe re-entering their body through the top of the head); the 'third eye' chakra in the centre of the forehead through which we can make psychic connections to other realities; the throat chakra which relates to multi-level communication and connects with the vocal chords to affect their vibration; the heart chakra in the centre of the chest through which we express love (a lot more about this to come); the solar plexus chakra just below the sternum; the sacral chakra beneath the navel from where we experience emotion and the connection of this emotion-chakra to the bowel/intestine is why people 'get the shits' when they are nervous and fearful; lastly there is the base or 'root' chakra at the bottom of the spine which grounds us in apparently 'physical' reality and also relates to sexuality and reproduction.

Each chakra is connected to a gland in the endocrine system including the pea-sized pineal gland in the brain which is known as the 'Third Eye' for its association with psychic sight or 'sixth sense'. The pineal gland is shaped like a pine cone and located in the middle of the brain. It has been revered in cultures across the world throughout history as a connection with 'god' and expanded reality. Endocrine glands regulate hormones, including sex hormones, metabolism, biological cycles including sleep, and the immune system. Through these connections the energetic balance or imbalance of the chakra vortices affects the 'physical' and psychological health of the whole body. In the case of the pineal gland/chakra connection it affects the ability to expand into other levels of awareness and malfunction locks people away in the five-sense Bubble – as the Cult well knows.

Figure 65: Fluoride calcifies the pineal gland which connects us to frequencies of awareness beyond Body-Mind. Definitely not a coincidence.

Fluoride which the Cult has manipulated into drinking water and toothpaste on the false pretext that it protects teeth has been shown to calcify the pineal gland (Fig 65). The theme of locking people away in the five senses is *everywhere*. Add the fact that aluminium (in vaccines and many other sources), glyphosate (a herbicide that has long entered the food-chain and is sprayed in the public environment) and Wi-Fi all suppress the pineal gland and you see what the game is – entrapping human perception in the five-sense Bubble. Scientific research has revealed how aluminium and glyphosate combine to be especially destructive to pineal gland function through the compounds they produce. The blood-brain barrier used to protect the brain from these and other toxins, but that is now being breached through technological radiation with 5G increasing the effect many fold.

'Serpent goddess'

The root chakra is the source of the transformative energy known as 'kundalini' (from a Sanskrit word meaning 'coiled') and this is symbolised as a coiled serpent or snake. Kundalini energy is revered as a goddess in some eastern traditions and symbolised by the caduceus symbol with the wings representing 'enlightenment' that comes from kundalini activation (Fig 66). The effect of this can be slow and measured or, as in my case in 1991, like a nuclear explosion. When kundalini energy is triggered it moves up through the chakras, spinal cord and central nervous system to

Figure 66: The caduceus is symbolic of the kundalini energy rising through the chakra and central nervous system and bursting through the crown chakra on top of the head to connect us with other realities. The nature of those realities is dictated by our own state of being.

Figure 67: A kundalini activation can connect people with high frequencies of awareness or the low frequencies in which the Cult and its 'gods' operate.

burst through the crown chakra and activate all the other chakras on the way (Fig 67). Such activation is said to bring people into a state of 'enlightenment' and make them 'illuminated'. The term 'Illuminati' which describes a key network within the global Cult relates to this principle of kundalini activation that can consciously connect people to other realities and instigate sometimes outstanding psychic abilities. The point to emphasise, however, is that such a connection is not good or bad. Kundalini awakening can connect you with expanded consciousness of high vibration or equally to consciousness of low and manipulative vibration. It will reflect where you are consciously and subconsciously as with psychoactive drugs. Illuminati Cult initiates are opened via kundalini activation in secret society and satanic rituals to the frequency realms from which the non-human force controls the Cult through perceptual possession. Whether kundalini awakening connects you with high or low realms of awareness depends on your own frequency and that is dictated by your own perceptions and state of being. Are you driven by love or hate, for example? These are very different frequencies. Gathering numbers of people are going through the experience of 'kundalini rising' with a fantastic human awakening underway although you wouldn't know this by observing the Mainstream Everything. They will be the last ones to get what is happening.

The kundalini process or a slower form of awakening from the Bubble can present many challenges and be very confusing as your perceptions begin to transform. Suddenly the world doesn't seem the same anymore and those around you may believe you have 'gone crazy'. Many people who end up under psychiatric treatment are only having a kundalini experience and they may have strange new perceptions or 'hear voices' as the activation connects them with other sources of information and influence beyond the five senses. This settles down eventually in most people, but by then many are prescribed drugs by clueless psychiatrists who don't know what is happening or even the very nature of the human being. Such drugging (suppression of awakening) can be encouraged by family members who also have no idea what is going on. Such are the consequences of 'educated' ignorance. I had a colossal kundalini awakening in 1991 after a life-changing 'paranormal' experience on a hill in Peru as I have recounted in other books. I have described how energy that felt like a drill entered the top of my head and passed down through my body while another flow came the other way. I didn't know it at the time but that energy was flowing through the chakra network and central nervous system to activate – *big time* – the kundalini. My conscious mind became flooded with concepts, information and awareness from beyond the senses and this launched me into three months of utter confusion and bewilderment when I didn't know who I was, where I was, or what on earth was happening. I call this my 'turquoise period' when I had the urge to wear the colour turquoise all the time. Everything is a unique frequency including colours and I was attracted to turquoise as my energetic field was attracted to the *frequency* of turquoise as a result of the transformation I was going through. People are subconsciously attracted to certain colours for the same reason and they radiate in particular colours ('you always look great in that colour') while looking and feeling drained in others. It's not the colour as we perceive it that has that effect; it's the frequency and how it impacts on our own frequency field.

Give us a wave

To realise what the body is we have to deprogram ourselves from what we've been told that it is. Everything in created reality outside the stillness and silence of the Void is information (thought, imagination) delivered through frequency and vibration in the form of waves. We talk about sound *waves*, thought *waves* and brain *waves*, and creation emerges from the thought or consciousness waves emanating from the awareness of 'God', or *The One*, via all its points of attention. *The One* experiences itself through the infinite realms of Creation. 'In my Father's house are many mansions' as the Bible puts it. You, me, everything outside The Void are information/consciousness fields taking the form of waves, frequency and vibration with an always-there conscious connection to *The One* whenever we choose. People believe they are only their human labels when we are in fact an expression of Infinity and ultimately we *are* that Infinity. This is the last thing the Cult wants us to know when its control depends on us not knowing. Perception dictates the frequency and nature of the waves we generate. The more expanded your consciousness and sense of 'I' the higher/quicker and more expanded the frequency/vibration you will emanate and connect with until you perceptually become *The One* and return to the silent, still, all-knowingness of the Void from whence you came. Even then you are still 'you', just a very different state of consciousness and perception. The Biblical story of the Prodigal Son who leaves his 'Father', messes up, learns from the experience and returns home again to be welcomed by his Father can be a symbolic way to describe this. 'The Father' didn't judge his son just as *The One* doesn't judge. Whatever your choices and experience you are *The One* experiencing itself. The point is, though, that while we remain in perceptual states of isolation, a sense of *only* individuality, and in emotional prison cells of hate, anxiety, fear, worry, depression, guilt, resentment, revenge and so on we cannot expand into higher levels of consciousness. These are low-vibrational states which entrap us in low-vibrational experience. If you are in perceptual frequency band 'A' you can only experience that band when that's all you can connect and interact with. Radio station 'A' can't connect with radio station 'B' when they are broadcasting on different frequencies. The same applies after what is perceived as 'death'. Our perceptual (frequency/vibrational) state decides what reality – which of the 'mansions' – we can gravitate to although release from the body and its illusions can obviously transform perception very quickly.

The body/auric field (Body-Mind) and Soul (expanded awareness beyond Body-Mind) are both consciousness fields of frequency and waves. They are meant to connect and communicate as one 'entity', but if Body-Mind becomes seriously out of frequency-sync with Soul then communication and influence is diminished (Fig 68). Soul, or what some call the 'Higher Self', is banging the keyboard, tapping the mouse and

Figure 68: When Body-Mind disconnects from an influence of the greater self – 'Soul', 'Higher Self' – we are at the mercy of perceptions gleaned only through the five senses. See Neil Hague colour section.

getting no response from Body-Mind, or 'Ego'. The Cult works ferociously to secure this disconnection and isolate Body-Mind from Soul. The game is then to program isolated Body-Mind with perceptions that ensure mass human control (Fig 69).

Knowledge of true reality has been held at the inner core of the secret society and satanic networks and passed on through the generations via those networks to exclude mainstream humanity. Such knowledge was once widely understood in the ancient world, but was then sucked out of general circulation. This was achieved not least by the imposition of religion which made exploring reality a death

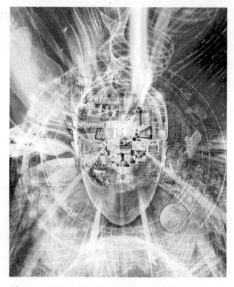

Figure 69: Humanity is bombarded second by second with information – most inaccurate – by Cult-serving sources to form mass human perception. (Image Neil Hague.)

sentence imposed by the Cult behind those religions. Cult empires (especially the British) targeted shamans and carriers of ancient knowledge as the world was colonised with a fake version of reality that hijacked perception and instilled the crooked beliefs of mainstream (Cult) 'science' and mainstream (Cult) religion to secure an official monopoly on the perception of reality. Religions in the East do speak of Maya ('illusion') and Brahman (Infinite Existence, Infinite Knowledge, and ultimate reality) and that's great. Unfortunately these basic truths are mostly obscured by the ritualistic worship of stupendous numbers of perceived Hindu 'gods'. Hoarding knowledge and imposing ignorance is the whole foundation of human control. Today the knowledge is returning through those tapping into expanded states of awareness and the relatively few open-minded scientists genuinely seeking the truth (mostly through the realms of quantum physics which explores reality beyond the perceived 'physical' world). They are seeing the unsupportable fallacy of the 'physical' illusion and understanding what the ancients knew and the Cult has worked so hard to suppress.

The body is not solid and quantum physics alone shows that this cannot be. It is a field of energy waves encoded with an information blueprint which constantly responds, positively or otherwise, to other waves in the form of thought, emotion and those delivered as food, drink and the now endless and ever-gathering forms of radiation in our 'smart' society. Everything, including food, drink and all that we consume and interact with, are manifestations of wavefields of information and waves affect other waves in positive, negative and neutral ways. Ever wondered why human behaviour has been so transformed by the 'smart' revolution of technologically-generated radiation waves and why suicides among the young are soaring? Stick around because the 'why' will become obvious from this perspective. Open-minded scientists operating outside the song-sheet mainstream have reached the same basic conclusions about the importance of understanding the function of waves and their impact on human life. It may seem strange to some that they could reach their conclusions from scientific research while I came to the same perspective through other means. There is actually nothing strange about it. When you tap into expanded states of awareness beyond Body-Mind you tap into the same knowledge whether you are a scientist or someone who left school at 15 as I did to play professional football. The label doesn't matter. It's how much you open your mind to other levels of awareness and possibility that decides what you know and what you don't. By these criteria it is better to have an open mind and not be a 'scientist' than to be a 'scientist' with a mind slammed shut.

Atomic mythology

Replacing the conditioned perception of solidity and materialism with wavefields and holograms immediately explains mysteries that have bewildered mainstream establishment science since its inception. When you realise that nothing is solid or physical it all begins to make sense. The foundation of the materialist view is the atom which we are told is what forms matter – 'solid' matter. How strange then that atoms have no solidity! They are packets of energy waves made up of what science perceives to be electrons 'orbiting' a nucleus. Atoms are not solid and cannot a solid world make (Fig 70). The particles and nucleus are a fraction of the atom in totality. The rest is 'empty' in terms of physicality. Yet scientists tell us the body is made of *atoms*. They claim at the same time that the body is physical and has solidity when that cannot be when atoms have no solidity. Atoms are a decoded manifestation of information carried in waves. This description puts the whole 'physical' atom theory into

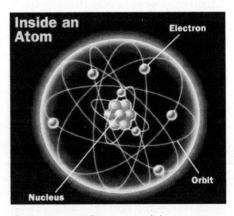

Figure 70: Atoms that are not solid cannot create a solid world. Yep, makes sense.

perspective:

> If the nucleus were the size of a peanut, the atom would be about the size of a baseball stadium. If we lost all the dead space inside our atoms, we would each be able to fit into a particle of dust, and the entire human race would fit into the volume of a sugar cube.

Go deeper into the nucleus and electrons and you find that they are not 'physical' either while mainstream science battles on with ever-diminishing credibility to hold the line at 'the world is solid and the body is solid' when they demonstrably *are not*. Atoms were named from a word meaning 'uncuttable' by Ancient Greek philosopher Democritus who lived approximately between the years of 460 and 370BC. He formulated the theory which became the foundation of modern science that matter is made of 'uncuttable' atoms and that movement comes from atoms colliding and bouncing off each other. You might observe that this has led to scientific explanations for the Universe invariably involving things bashing into other things. The (illusory) Big Bang is said to have been the instigator and the Universe has been staggering around colliding ever since apparently like some Saturday night drunk. Call a cab – the Universe is pissed again. How do you explain how so and so happened, professor? 'Collision.' And this? 'Something hit it.' Even in Ancient Greece there were others who could see through this. Famous philosopher Socrates (around 470 to 399 BC) believed that another force separate from 'physical reality' provided what I would call the blueprint for the world of the seen and he was right. His pupil Plato (approximately 427-347 BC) described something similar with his Allegory of the Cave (Fig 71). He told the symbolic story of prisoners living in a cave and never seeing anything other than the single wall that their chains allowed them to see. Behind them was a fire which they couldn't see and people and animals walked past the flames casting shadows on the wall. These shadows became the reality of the prisoners because it was all they knew and experienced. Some prisoners studied the shadows and were acknowledged as experts about perceived reality while all along they were only studying shadows believing them to be real. Mainstream scientists and academics today are doing exactly the same apart from the

Figure 71: Plato's Allegory of the Cave symbolising the human plight.

minority of honourable exceptions who go their own way. In my analogy they are 'experts' studying reality within the Bubble while believing that to be all there is. A prisoner in Plato's story escapes and realises the shadows are illusions. He comes back to share the news with the others still enslaved, but they don't believe him and call him crazy. This is an allegory, as Plato clearly intended, for the human plight which continues to this day.

The reality that we think we are experiencing is a 'shadow' of something else in the sense of illusory 'physical' reality being a 'shadow' (decoded projection) of wavefield reality. The Soul is a wavefield phenomenon and so is Body-Mind. The body is a wavefield information blueprint that can replicate itself through 'procreation'. It, too, is a state of awareness because everything is and the body is designed for the mind – an incarnation of Soul – to experience this reality. The idea is that the mind, or 'ego', remains in sync and connection with Soul and is influenced by its expanded awareness. In this state of connection the mind/ego is *in* this world, but not completely *of* it. It has perceptual radar which is not subject to the illusions of 'matter'. If, however, mind ceases to be influenced in its perceptions by Soul the whole focus of reality is captured by the five senses and this becomes the dominant reality gleaned from information received from five-sense reality in the form of the Cult-controlled media, science, medicine and what is taught in schools and universities (Fig 72). Now, with Soul out of the game, an entire sense of reality can be programmed into isolated Body-Mind to induce Bubble perceptions. This one sentence describes how a few have enslaved the many through almost the entirety of known human 'history' to present day when 'smart' technology is taking this to a whole new depth of control. There are two primary levels of mind, the conscious and subconscious. It has been estimated that some 95 percent of human behaviour comes from subconscious programming and not from conscious decision-making. The Cult and its non-human masters target the subconscious to keep their targets *un*conscious of what is happening in great swathes of their mind. Remember that *Wonderpedia* magazine quote describing how every second

Figure 72: Shut-up – I know how things are. The System told me.

eleven million sensations crackle along [brain] pathways which the brain filters down to a manageable list of around *40* per second and from this we perceive visual reality. We are consciously aware of a fraction even of what we see, hear, touch, smell and taste while the subconscious absorbs it *all*. The Cult has a whole language of symbolism revealed at length in my other books which is designed to bypass the conscious mind and speak to the subconscious.

How we create 'physical' reality

A wavefield information blueprint becomes the experience of a physical world when we decode the wave information into holograms. The five senses decode *wavefield* information into electrical information which

Figure 73: Human reality – waveform becomes holographic via human decoding systems. (Image Neil Hague.)

they communicate to the brain and this is decoded into the digital/holographic information (illusory 'physical') which we perceive as the physical world (Fig 73). The different forms of information are the *same* information expressed in different ways. Wavefields are the foundation of all created reality and the body can be no different. This decoding sequence is the work of the mind which means that we decode our *own body* into apparently 3D physical reality by what scientists would call 'observation' or 'looking at it' (Fig 74). This is done through the interaction of the wavefield of the body and the wavefield of the mind in ways that I

Figure 74: We even decode our own body into holographic form. Where is your body? In your *mind*. (Image Neil Hague.)

Figure 75: These are digitally-generated 'people' that don't exist as live human beings. The technology can also create fake landscapes and objects.

will come to shortly. Our bodies exist in our mind (like everything else) which is why your state of mind dictates the state of your body. Characters in the most sophisticated virtual reality games can appear to be so real and yet they are only information decoded by the computer and today fake digital people are being created that appear to be live human beings (Fig 75). I watched an experiment in which a group wore headsets that gave them the illusion that their bodies were that of a doll. This so tricked the brain that when something was done to the doll, including a needle in the eye, the group reacted as if it was happening to *them*. We don't have to really have a 'physical' body to perceive the *experience* of having one. Virtual reality is technologically mimicking our experienced reality which is itself only a more advanced version of virtual reality. Indeed the two are becoming so close in their appearance that those at the cutting edge of virtual technology say it won't be much longer before you will not be able to tell the difference. We accept that virtual reality technology is decoded information that increasingly mirrors 'real' reality, but people still find it hard to grasp that 'real' reality is made manifest in basically the same way. Virtual reality technology hijacks and overrides the very same five senses through which we decode 'real' reality. Observe how virtual reality works and you are looking at how 'real' reality works. Virtual reality worlds exist only in your brain and so does 'real' reality – including the brain itself which is a wavefield construct in its prime state. I have been saying this for years and American cognitive sciences professor, Donald Hoffman, shares that view: 'The brain itself is an illusion … neurons do not exist except when we see them, just like different colours … only exist when we perceive them.' Where is the 'physical' body and the 'physical world? It's in our *minds*. We hear about mind over matter when mind *is* matter and matter *is* mind (Fig 76 overleaf). This applies to mind at all levels of consciousness and to all expressions of 'matter'. Max Planck (1858-1947), the 'father of quantum physics', said:

All matter originates and exists only by virtue of a force which brings the particle of an atom to vibration and holds this most minute solar system of the

Figure 76: This famous scene from *The Matrix* perfectly describes the 'physical' illusion.

atom together. We must assume behind this force the existence of a conscious and intelligent mind. This mind is the matrix of all matter.

Planck also said:

I regard consciousness as fundamental. I regard matter as derivative from consciousness. We cannot get behind consciousness. Everything that we talk about, everything that we regard as existing, postulates consciousness.

Mind is the *decoder* and *perceiver* – the *creator* – of all matter.

Holographic illusion

The reality we experience as physical is really holographic and malleable, not solid. Holograms emerge from a flat surface in a form that makes them look three-dimensional (Fig 77). The technology began with simple holograms you see in shops, but holographics has since been moving ever closer to human reality in the same way that virtual reality has. Holograms are now used to insert holographic fake people into films and stage shows alongside 'real' people with the join getting harder to see. The best of them look as 'solid' as you and me. Holographic depictions of long-passed artists like Elvis appear in duets with very much alive singers and I saw a whole comedy programme featuring a

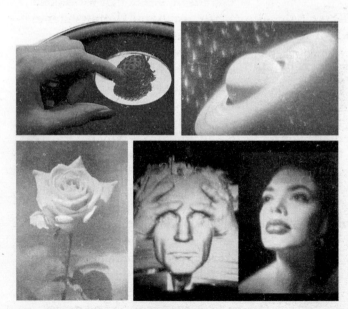

Figure 76: All of these images are holograms that appear 'solid' when they're not.

Figure 78: Holograms of people – some no longer alive – can be inserted into scenes with living people.

Figure 79: The woman in this picture is a hologram projected from another location.

Figure 80: The guitar players are holograms.

Figure 81: The bike is a digital hologram.

hologram of the late and great British comedian, Les Dawson (Fig 78). Holographic versions of people can be transmitted across the world (Figs 79 and 80). We also have digital holograms which is actually what 'physical' reality really is (Fig 81). Rich Terrile, director of the Centre for Evolutionary Computation and Automated Design at NASA's Jet Propulsion Laboratory, said in 2017 that he believes the Universe is a digital hologram. This must be so because everything in what we perceive as the material world is a digital hologram. You would expect in this case to find pixilation in the fabric of our reality akin to pixels on a television screen that we decode into the images of TV programmes. It turns out that we do. A *New Scientist* magazine article about holographic reality in 2009 said that under magnification 'the fabric of space-time becomes grainy and is ultimately made of tiny units rather like pixels'. A report by researchers at Britain's University of Southampton in 2017 found 'substantial evidence' that human reality is like watching a 3D movie projected from a 2D screen. Yes, a *wavefield* screen. Kostas Skenderis, head of applied mathematics and theoretical physics at Southampton, said that while we perceive pictures to have height, width and depth they are in fact on a flat surface. The team detailed their findings in the peer-reviewed scientific journal, *Physical Review Letters*. They said the Universe could be a 'vast and complex hologram' and Professor Skenderis said that holographic reality was a huge leap in understanding the structure of the Universe. Skenderis likened reality to watching a 3D film in the cinema with the difference that we could touch objects and experience the 'projection' as real. I suggest that we don't touch objects hologram to hologram (as in the experience of solid to solid) but electromagnetic field to electromagnetic field. The skin or touch-sense is a fundamental decoder of information into holographic reality and a wave antenna. Nor are we *watching* a holographic movie. We are *creating* it (*decoding* it). Researchers at Ibaraki University in Japan said they have found 'compelling evidence' that the Universe is a holographic projection and ever more scientists are being pushed in the same direction by both the evidence and the way the apparent contradictions of 'matter' become perfectly explainable once you bring holograms into the story. Leonard Susskind, professor of physics at Stanford University, has encompassed the holographic model to describe the Universe along with celebrated Argentine theoretical physicist Juan Martín Maldacena among many others. Susskind said: 'It's now gone from wild-eyed conjecture to be an everyday working tool of physics.' How come I could have been so sure our reality was holographic in nature long before it touched the mainstream of science? If you tap into The Field beyond the five senses you just *know* how things are without having to work out every mathematical detail and confirmation. Those who were crap at school and feel a failure as a result should remember that. An open mind, and especially an open heart as we shall see, is far more enlightening than a university degree – first class or otherwise. You don't need a scientific mind to understand reality. You need an *open* one. Great scientists *know* first and work out the details later while most of science does it the other way round.

The information foundation of holograms that we have in human society is encoded in *wavefields*. They are created by dividing a laser beam into two parts. One part ('working beam') passes across the subject/object being photographed to record it as a wavefield and then strikes a holographic

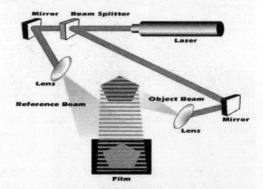

Figure 82: How holograms are created with two parts of a laser colliding to form an interference pattern – a waveform version of the object being captured.

Figure 83: A waveform holographic interference pattern.

Figure 84: Two stones dropped in water create waves that expand and connect to form an interference pattern that reflects the weight of the stones, where they were dropped and at what speed.

Figure 85: Holographic car looking very solid, but you could walk through it.

print. The other part (reference beam) strikes the same print directly (Fig 82). The two halves collide on the surface and create an 'interference pattern' which is the information of the featured subject encoded in a wavefield (Fig 83). The process is the same as two pebbles being dropped in a pond and the waves moving out until they collide and form a wave pattern in the water (Fig 84). This pattern is a wavefield representation of the weight of the stones, how high and at what speed they were dropped and how far apart. With holographics another laser is directed at the wavefield interference pattern and, apparently miraculously, but not really, a three-dimensional 'solid' image of the subject is projected as a hologram. The laser 'reads' (decodes) the information in the wavefield pattern and in the case of human reality that laser is the *mind*. Our entire reality is being decoded by the mind from the base form of waves into holographic 'physical' illusion. Holograms can appear to be so solid that people refuse to walk through them when they depict cars and such like at motor company launches. When they try to do so they realise that they can (Fig 85). Okay, then, why can't we walk through walls and each other? Two main reasons: (1) what the mind believes is real it will experience as real and

(2) the resistance you feel when you bump into a 'solid' object is not a physical resistance but an electromagnetic one. I am sitting in this chair now and not falling through the seat and then the floor and then the earth etc., because the electromagnetic waves of my bum are different to those of the chair. My bum and the chair aren't making contact at the holographic ('physical') level. They are establishing resistance at the *wavefield* electromagnetic level. When wavefield frequencies are far enough apart they can pass through each other which is why people see 'ghosts' walk or float through walls. Ghostly figures (other expressions of consciousness) tend to appear as ethereal. They are not a manifestation of the visible light, five-sense, frequency band and they can pass through apparently solid objects just as radio frequencies pass through walls. Those who can expand their visual decoding potential beyond the usual limits of human perception tend to see 'ghosts' while others more confined to five-sense reality tend not to. One will say 'I've seen a ghost' and the other will say 'You're mad, I can't see anything'. It's all about frequency and what you can and cannot tune into. 'Physical' reality, then, is a holographic illusion and what a difference this makes to understanding human experience and what is termed the 'paranormal'. All the 'paranormal' phenomena that could not be happening if the world was 'solid' suddenly becomes possible and explainable from the perspective of the illusory solidity of holograms and the power of the mind to impact on wave information fields and through that change the nature of those holograms. What appear to be impossible happenings and 'miracles' are only wavefields generated by consciousness influencing other wavefields and thus holographic 'solid' reality. We will see in the next chapter that all 'paranormal' activity can be simply explained from this understanding. While great swathes of mainstream science focuses only on 'physical' reality that doesn't exist, they will never explain the apparent mysteries of life which demand an understanding of non-physical reality. In such circumstances mainstream scientists with that 'physical' mindset can only deliver the mantra of 'it's not possible' because, from its knowledge base and perspective, it *is* impossible.

Electric reality

Body-Mind operates and communicates electrically and electromagnetically and the brain also communicates with the body and its cells and organs through electrical signals. We are electrical/electromagnetic beings at the human level and part of what I call the Cosmic Internet in which the Universe affects us and we affect it and each other. This is possible through an exchange of information as our thoughts, emotions and perceptions interact through wave connections with The Field. Biologist Bruce Lipton points out that each human cell contains 1.4 volts of electricity which doesn't sound much until you multiple that by the *trillions* cells in the body. You can see Internet videos showing how the power of an antenna is increased when touched by a human hand and electricity transferred (this happens with 'hands-on' energetic healing). We are electrical and when this electricity ceases to be generated by the body we are said to 'die'. Our cells are batteries that store electricity and if they become drained we become weak and ill while vice-versa is the case. The speed of ageing is connected to this with cells lacking their optimum electricity either dying or not being like-for-like replaced. In this way the original body blueprint begins to unravel and we experience this as ageing and diminishing function. Ponder on the effect therefore of living in the technologically-generated radiation fields that we do today which scramble the electrical/electromagnetic systems of the body including cell replacement. When this constant replacement gets seriously out of kilter it is known as cancer. Here you have the link between technological radiation fields and cancer and other diseases. Emotional stress imbalances and distorts electrical/wave harmony in the Body-Mind through the electrical/wavefields it generates and this is how stress becomes illness. A rush of fight-or-flight stress in response to danger or a short experience is fine. The body is designed to deal with those situations before returning to equilibrium. Ongoing stress known as 'background anxiety' or 'survival stress' is a very different matter and can be extremely destructive to health. Distorted wavefields generated by stress can jam immune system communication and stop people thinking straight through chaotic interaction with thought processing. The opposite is true with states of love and joy which transmit balanced waves and transfer that state to the body. Another aspect of stress is addiction to chemicals produced by those states. My mother used to say about a neighbour ... 'It's being so miserable that keeps them going'. Addiction to emotional chemicals means that when people are not worried (miserable) they have to find something to worry about to get their chemical fix. Methods of healing outside the mainstream are increasingly founded on achieving electrical/electromagnetic balance and harmonising the rate and direction of cellular electrical spin. Observe the solar system and the galaxy and you'll see that everything is spinning down to the smallest particle. When the spin reverses from what it should be electrical chaos in the body can follow and people head for a doctor who has no idea about the real cause and hands out a drug (also a wavefield) that can lead to even greater electrical mayhem, sorry 'chemical side-effects'. Pharmaceutical drugs are imbalanced fields of information (hence 'side-effects') while natural, not synthetic, nutrition and vitamins can have harmonious fields that sync with the body instead of wreaking havoc. The trick is to know which fields (nutrition/supplement) will help to secure harmony in any particular situation and which will not. Overriding everything is the power of the mind to heal the body by generating the perception waves that balance the imbalances that are experienced as illness.

In the language

Reality can be seen in the phrases people use without realising that what they say is literally true. We describe the 'electricity' we feel in a room, theatre or stadium generated by various human interactions. Hair stands up on the back of the neck and skin tingles in an excited crowd because of electromagnetic energy emitted in the form of emotion. Skin is an antenna and the whole body is the same – hence the tingling amidst powerful electrical/electromagnetic fields. This happens to people in 'haunted' places when they feel the electromagnetic fields of entities just beyond the human visual frequency range. We speak of the electricity between people while others are said for the same reason to have 'magnetic personalities'. It is all about the power and compatibility of electrical/electromagnetic fields. Sex is the merging of two electromagnetic fields which together generate electrical power greater than the sum of the parts (well, sometimes!). The ancient art of acupuncture is based on balancing the flows of information in the form of electricity and electromagnetism that circulate the body through lines of force called meridians. These are the body equivalent of meridians or 'ley lines' that circulate and interpenetrate the Earth (Figs 86 and 87). Both systems are manifestations of the communication networks of The Field

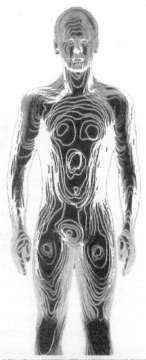

Figure 86: The body meridian system picked out by a tracer dye and looking like a computer motherboard.

that connect everything to everything else. The ancients knew of these phenomena before religion suppressed the knowledge and they marked their paths and major vortex 'chakra' points where many lines cross with earthworks, standing stones and circles. The more powerful the vortex the more sacred the circle and location was considered to be. Hair-like needles and other methods employed by acupuncture balance the flow through the meridian system of *information* encoded in

Figure 87: The Earth is also criss-crossed and interpenetrated by meridian lines of energetic force.

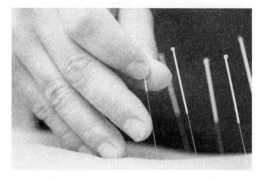

Figure 88: Hair-like needles and other techniques balance the flow of energy or 'chi' (information) in the body meridian system.

electricity known by the Chinese as 'chi' (Fig 88). The principle is yet again the same as with computers. When a virus scrambles the flow of information passing through the system the computer response to keyboard/mouse direction slows down or ceases to react. What appears or doesn't on the screen is affected by the distorted information and this is what happens when chi information in the form of electricity is in a state of disharmony or dis-ease. In ancient China some would for this reason pay their acupuncturist when they were well and not when they became ill. The acupuncture practitioner was supposed to keep the chi in balance to ensure that illness couldn't manifest. A perfect example of ignorance dictating perception is when acupuncture is dismissed and ridiculed for 'putting a needle in the foot to treat a headache'. If such people had the self-respect to do some research before waving their arrogant hand they would know that chi information passes around the body in circuits and a circuit that passes through the foot and the head can be blocked in the foot in a way that transfers to a pain in the head.

There is one other point to make about holograms before we move on. They have an amazing characteristic in which every part of the hologram is a smaller version of the whole. If you cut a holographic wavefield print or interference pattern into four pieces and direct the laser at each one you would expect to see four quarters of the original image. But you don't. You see a quarter-

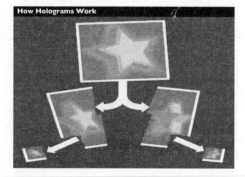

Figure 89: Every part of a hologram is a smaller version of the whole and encoded with the same information.

size version of the *whole* image (Fig 89). This continues to be the case as you cut the image further because of the way information is distributed within a holographic wavefield or interference pattern. Although the clarity gets fuzzier as you reduce the size it's still the image in its entirety. The human energy field is a smaller version of the Earth field while brain activity and levels of the Universe look remarkably similar in our holographic reality (Fig 90). Here you have the reason why healing methods such as acupuncture and reflexology have identified areas throughout the body that are smaller representations of the whole body. This has to be the case when the body is a hologram and every part must be a smaller version of the whole. Tiny cells have respiratory, digestive and immune systems just as the body does in line with the holographic principle and the Earth has a ley line electrical system as the body has the chi meridian network. A skilled palm reader can read the information of the whole body in the hand thanks to the way holographic

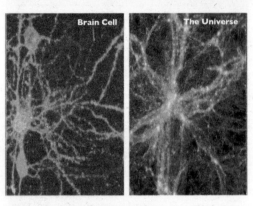

Figure 90: Brain activity and the Universe. As above, so below – the holographic principle.

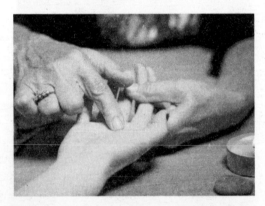

Figure 91: Information can be gleaned from the hand because it represents the information blueprint of the whole body in a smaller form – precisely how holograms work.

information is distributed (Fig 91). Holographic principles are the foundation of the ancient theme of 'as above, so below'.

Reality is certainly not what we are told to believe that it is. 'Unexplainable mysteries' don't tend to survive open-minded research. Talking of which ...

CHAPTER THREE

What mysteries?

The impossible could not have happened; therefore the impossible must be possible in spite of appearances – Agatha Christie

From the perspective of reality that I am describing so-called mysteries of life dissolve like snow in the sunlight. A long list of 'inexplicable' phenomena become '*Ah*, so *that's* how it works' and 'Blimey, it all makes sense now'.

We return to the theme of waves in water after two pebbles are dropped (Fig 92). Where waves from each collide and connect is known as wave *entanglement* and from this understanding of entanglement everything starts to fall into place. For example: Body-Mind is a wave entanglement between the wavefields of the body and those of the mind. While they remain in sync or entangled we are ' alive'. Body-Mind's wave entangled dance of synchronised oscillation is the human Dance of Life. When the body ceases to function (its *wavefield* ceases to oscillate and generate electricity) this releases the mind from entanglement and we 'die', or rather the body does. This is happening when near-death experiencers describe leaving the body as the mind is freed from the perceptual limitations of the body and opens to an entirely different reality. Wave entanglement with the body focuses attention of the mind on the micro-band of

Figure 92: Wave entanglement – a key to understanding reality and human interaction.

frequency called visible light through the decoding systems of the five senses. Once the mind is released from that body myopia we become aware of other realities. We are back to the torch light and warehouse analogy. If the body's wavefield oscillation is restored so that entanglement is restored the mind can be drawn back into the body. If it doesn't revive we're out of here. The mind needs a body operating within the frequency band of the human world to experience and interact with the human world. Seeking out another body to entangle with is known as reincarnation. Those who have a lot of out of body experiences (a near-death experience without the body needing to die) have a much more fluid wave entanglement with the body which allows their mind to be released more easily. There are ways of training the mind to do this. Mind has the power to dictate the nature of wave entanglement or whether there is one at all. Mind wave-power can think us alive against all the medical odds ('I'm *determined* to live') and think us dead ('I have lost the *will* to live'). Mind is the governor of the body while the Cult wants us to believe that the opposite is the case and so we don't use that power in all manner of ways. The body cannot exist without the mind. When mind disentangles it takes with it the life-force energy that animates and empowers the body which then starts to decompose. The light literally goes out as death is often described. Human life is the *rhythm* or oscillation of life and the body's rhythms including circadian and all biological rhythms are connected to this prime oscillation and its interaction with other waves. Another version of entanglement is called quantum entanglement in which 'entangled particles remain connected so that actions performed on one affect the other, even when separated by great distances'. Scientist Albert Einstein described this as 'spooky action at a distance'. There is actually nothing 'spooky' about it. When particles that are expressions of waves are connected by those waves they will act in unison as manifestations of the *same* wave or the same *field*.

Gene Genie

The wavefield relationship between Body-Mind is crucial to understanding everything in human reality. We are told that our genes basically decide all that happens to us physically and mentally. Some women tragically have breasts removed after being told their genes give them a high chance of breast cancer. Mainstream medicine is often brilliant in dealing with trauma injuries, orthopaedics, surgery, and reviving people at death's door (do electric shocks revive only the heart or primarily the wavefield oscillation that generates electricity?). Antibiotics have also been highly effective although they are handed out far too liberally to the point where infections can mutate to overcome them. These are the so-called 'superbugs'. When it comes to illness in general, however, modern medicine can be a disaster zone. One of the biggest causes of death in the United States – right up there with heart disease and cancer – is the *treatment* in all its forms. That's crazy? Yes, it is, but if people mean crazy as in that can't be true – check the figures

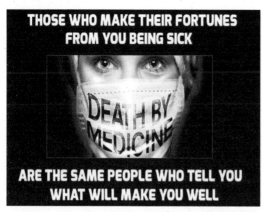

THOSE WHO MAKE THEIR FORTUNES FROM YOU BEING SICK

DEATH BY MEDICINE

ARE THE SAME PEOPLE WHO TELL YOU WHAT WILL MAKE YOU WELL

Figure 93: Big Pharma – the Cult cartel that controls mainstream medicine and seeks to crush any alternatives that work.

and remember that they are only the numbers officially reported. Many other deaths which have medical causes are hidden behind fake diagnosis. The reason for this is that mainstream medicine doesn't know what the body really is beyond the biological, let alone how it functions, and it is manipulated to be that way through control of medicine by the pharmaceutical cartel or 'Big Pharma' (Fig 93). This is a Cult creation given predominance over 'health' thanks to people like oil tycoon and Cult operative J.D. Rockefeller (see my other books). Big Pharma (the Death Cult, hence it kills so many people) owns the medical schools where doctors are trained and in*doctor*inated; owns the professional bodies like the Medical Associations; and owns governments through a global army of lobbyists and money-no-object political funding. The situation is so outrageous and dire that the best rule of thumb is this: If Big Pharma wants something it's bad for humanity. Mainstream medicine is an outgrowth from mainstream 'science' which is also a Cult production at its establishment core. Both are controlled through funding and governing authorities that ensure only the Big Pharma version of the body and its treatment is allowed to be practiced in the mainstream (and increasingly anywhere). You want to be a doctor? Then do it our way or we'll have you struck off. This has happened to many proper doctors seeking to employ methods that work rather than singing from the Big Pharma rulebook. You want to be a mainstream scientist? Well, don't think you are going to get funding or any prestigious position if you challenge what we tell you is 'scientific' orthodoxy (which becomes medical orthodoxy). Witness the withdrawal or non-existence of funding for scientists who challenge human-caused 'climate change' orthodoxy which the Cult seeks to impose through its Climate Cult in which the dominant theme is 'extinction' (death). The same methodology can be found throughout academia which takes its orthodoxy from science orthodoxy and medical orthodoxy which all originate with Cult orthodoxy. The great majority in these institutions don't know they are following the rules of the Cult while those in the inner circles of secret societies and satanic groups most certainly do.

The foundation of medical orthodoxy is that genes and not mind are the arbiter of everything when the opposite is true. This calculated inversion of reality is designed by the Cult to isolate body from mind in human society when body *is* mind. Big Pharma medicine is

Figure 94: An imbalance or flaw in the body wavefield becomes illness or disease – disharmony – in the hologram. Wavefield balance = holographic 'health' because one is a reflection of the other. See Neil Hague colour section.

based on this misrepresentation and its drugs focus on affecting the body (hologram) chemically. This means they concentrate on the symptom they see in the hologram and not the cause which is a wavefield, energetic, information imbalance decoded through into the hologram (Fig 94). A problem in the hologram (symptom) is really a problem in the field (cause). Alternative methods of healing have long accused mainstream medicine of treating only symptoms and ignoring the cause and this must be so when the medical industry doesn't acknowledge the existence of the body wavefield where the cause *always* lies. I say always because the body is a wave information field and its holographic level is only a decoded projection of that field. What happens in the field happens in the hologram and what doesn't bother the mind doesn't bother the body. Even when Big Pharma drugs are claimed to have psychological effects they target the way the brain processes information and not the source of information itself – wavefield mind. The body has some trillions of cells (cell 'batteries') and in almost every one is the body 'hard drive' known as DNA (Fig 95). We apparently have three billion base pairs of DNA and one section of this is called a gene. DNA of a normal human cell contains an estimated 30,000 to 120,000 genes although only a fraction of them are activated at any time. We are talking biological nanotechnology. Genes contain instructions for what the body looks like (everything from eye colour to height) and how it functions minute by minute. From this has come the myth that genes control what happens to the body, what diseases you'll have and even how long you will live. This is profoundly misleading in

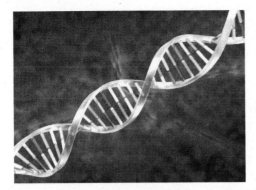

Figure 95: The body 'hard drive' – the receiver-transmitter of information known as DNA.

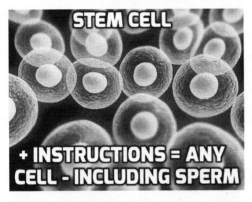

Figure 96: 'Blank-sheet' stem cells can be encoded to perform any function.

that it ignores the X-factor of mind and consciousness beyond mind. The membrane of every cell is a liquid crystal and DNA is crystalline because they are receiver-transmitters of information. This is the wave communication system through which the mind (and heart) activate and deactivate cell function. American developmental biologist Bruce Lipton, who wrote *Biology of Belief* and has a YouTube presentation of the same name, points out that cell membranes are semi-conductor information processors like those, also crystalline, used in electrical circuits. Genes are a 'hard disk' and programmable. 'Blank-sheet' stem cells are produced by the body which then receive signals to encode instructions that dictate their function (Fig 96). Through this communication system humans, animals and the natural world 'evolve' in the sense of exchanging information between mind, body and environment to develop new gifts and abilities to cope when their environment changes. Animals are in sync with their surroundings thanks to this information exchange and so desert species have less need for water and birds hunting fish have microscopic sight to see fish from high in the air. When this transmutation through encoding new cell instructions stays in step with environmental changes it is called 'evolution'; when it doesn't we call it species extinction. We are rather more than a 'lump of meat' and our world far more than a cosmic accident. I will be describing how the entire Universe is an electrical/electromagnetic phenomenon which, like everything else in all existence, is conscious.

Turning yourself on (and off)

Which genes and their functions are active and which are not is dictated overwhelmingly by the mind and its *perceptions* through wave entanglement with the body. I have been banging on for decades now about the central role played by perception – *everything* originates from perception which is why the Cult in all its forms seeks as its prime objective to control perception. Every thought, emotion – perception – manifests as a unique frequency (wave) emanating from the mind and its emotions and you can feel these waves emitted by people. We talk of good vibes and bad vibes and that's true. Someone may put on an act with their face and demeanour, but we feel something about them that doesn't *feel* right. We are picking up the wave frequencies representing their real perceptions and attitudes behind the 'physical' mask. The nature of these frequencies, or perceptions, decide which genes in the cells are activated or switched on and which are not. We have genes with different instructions that affect the body's 'physical' and psychological state. Among them are genes that will make you healthy, joyful, optimistic and mentally and emotionally balanced along with others that can make you sick, even fatally, depressed, pessimistic and mentally and emotionally *im*balanced by the way they *process information*. Now picture perception waves or signals emanating from the mind and having the effect of activating and deactivating different genes on the basis of their particular function. This is possible because genes of different functions respond to frequencies broadcast by the mind that relate to those same functions (Fig 97). The mind wave frequency and that representing a particular gene's function operate on the *same wavelength* and they entangle to send a signal from mind to gene. In this way the

perceptional state of the mind is transferred to the body's genetic system. If your mind feels depressed its frequencies will activate the genes which carry instructions that represent

WAVES ACTIVATE THE GENES

Figure 97: Our mental and emotional state is transmitted as waves which can turn genes on and off that relate to those states. In this way our state of mind becomes 'genetic' consequences good and bad. See Neil Hague colour section.

depression and this emotional state will be transferred to a like-effect in the body. The same perceptual waves are affecting which functions are encoded in blank-sheet stem cells. Mainstream medicine sees only the chemical effect on the body and not the wave imbalance triggering that chemical effect which emerges from the conscious *and* subconscious mind. Doctors prescribe chemical drugs for a chemical symptom and miss the wavefield cause. Through this wave connection or entanglement stress becomes illness. The disruptive effect that stress waves can have on heart-related genes is how stress causes heart disease and the same process happens with cancer and everything else. When the mind and its emotions feel nervous or fearful the frequency activation will cause emotion genes in the belly to give you 'the shits' as I mentioned earlier. It is not the *genes* that decide what happens to the body in terms of the outcome origin; it is mind frequencies that dictate which genes are switched on and which are not. Mind is the message and genes are the messenger. Different parts of the brain 'light-up' and are activated by different thoughts and emotions for the same reason that genes are. The brain is responding to perceptual waves/signals from the mind and these activate those areas of the brain related to those frequencies as the brain processes the information. The brain is again the processor of information and not the origin, just as genes are processors – *semi-conductor* processors – of information and not the source.

What I have described is being studied today by an emerging scientific discipline called epigenetics. Science believed that to change the genetic nature of the body our DNA, or 'hard drive', had to change or mutate. This is now known to be untrue and reflects the long history of scientific dogma which lurches from 'this is how it is' to 'er, well, actually, it's not'; and from 'you are talking nonsense you science blasphemer' to 'well, okay, you were right, but we'll claim the credit and call it a new discovery'. Epigenetics studies how the body changes 'physically' and psychologically by which genes are switched on and off and which gene functions dominate. Highly significantly this on-off sequence dictated by the perceptual mind waves of one generation can be passed on to the next through procreation. Sperm and eggs combine to form the body ('software') program and carry the epigenetic (wavefield) blueprint of the parents (there are cases, however, where this doesn't happen). Children can be born with the same on-off gene sequence with all the consequences, good and bad, which that entails. The child is born with what the perceptions of parents and other 'ancestors' genetically developed through life experience. We hear this described in lines like 'She's just like her mother' and 'He's just like his dad'. There are other reasons for this, of course, but epigenetics is one of them. It is also the case that signals activating and deactivating gene function are not confined only to mind although that is the dominant source. Drugs and toxins are wavefield phenomena in their base form even though we perceive them holographically as chemical in nature. Big Pharma drugs cause so much damage to health because they are energetic wave distortions which transfer that distortion to the wavefields of body and genes. It's the same with toxins in food and the environment. Do we really think that poisons in the herbicides and insecticides sprayed onto crops are not retained in the food they produce? Of course they are – both in waves and their chemical form in the hologram. What we eat and drink may look like a sandwich or a soda, but in its base form food and drink are fields of information waves. These fields can harmonise with the Body-Mind field when they are in vibrational sympathy ('nutritious food') or cause disharmony and dis-ease when their disruptive waves distort the Body-Mind field (Big Mac and a coke, please). Food and drink have long been shown to affect people psychologically, too, and this comes from the same wave-gene impact (Fig 98). Frequencies represented by fast food in recent decades have been triggering genes that relate to weight gain and through the

epigenetic affect generations of children are being born with a greater genetic aptitude to gain weight that earlier generations did not have. The smart technology explosion is pounding everyone with radiation frequencies from phones, masts, satellites and Wi-Fi and this will be having an enormous impact on epigenetic gene function in ways that the general population and most of the medical and

Figure 98: It's not only chemical shite. It's wavefield shite.

telecommunications industries will not be aware of. The Cult does know, however, and those consequences are long-planned. Untested 5G now being rolled out around the world is the next level of genetic and psychological manipulation. I'll deal with this in detail in later chapters. Do people think that the transformation in the perceptions and emotions of especially the young in the 'smart' era is just some random coincidence?

Believing is seeing

When someone is poisoned it is not the chemical that kills them but the deeply distorted wavefields represented *holographically* as a chemical. The body's wavefield oscillation is so undermined that it can no longer function when its dancing waves cease to dance. Some Christians in America take Biblical Scripture so literally that they handle poisonous snakes and even drink lethal strychnine to prove their faith. Some die, as you would expect, but some don't and how can this be? The danger of snake poison and strychnine is in the effect of its wavefields on the body's wavefield. If the wavefield mind is so strong in its belief that they won't die then the frequency signals from the mind will not allow body reactions to be activated by the poison that will lead to death. Thus there you have the process of 'mind over matter'. We are increasingly urged to fear genes with genetic tests warning people what their genetic blueprint has in store for them later in life. What a tragic irony on many levels. If you believe that you are destined to be the victim of your genetic blueprint you are sending out the mind/brain waves within the frequency band which can activate the very genes that produce the outcome. It becomes a self-fulfilling wavefield/genetic prophecy. If our minds do not believe in such an outcome – especially if we *know* and live the fact that mind is the governor – those cancer genes or whatever won't be activated for your whole life. Why is it that so many people die within the period the doctor predicted they would die? 'How long do I have, doctor?' is so often a question that delivers literally a death sentence. Mind becomes convinced that the body will die within the declared period and sends out waves of frequency that make it happen. There have been cases where people have been told they have a fatal disease with a certain period to live and they have died in that period only for post-mortem tests to reveal they did not have the 'fatal disease' at all. They died from a *belief* that they had the disease and a *belief* in the doctor's prognosis of how long they had to live. There are so many stories and accounts along the same lines. In this way we can believe ourselves to live and believe ourselves to die. Witness the list of cases in which one group has been given a drug to have some effect or other and a second group is unknowingly given only a sugar pill or 'placebo'. Many times those taking the non-drug placebo experience the effect of the drug they have not even taken. Some trials involving psychoactive drugs have had those taking only a placebo heading out on a psychedelic 'trip'. People have recovered from health problems, even serious ones, by taking a placebo they believed was a drug that would cure them. This can happen through the process I have been describing. Belief in the cure sends out the mind/brain waves that activate the genetic blueprint and its immune system to deliver the believed-in outcome. There is also the 'nocebo' effect when belief in a bad health outcome focuses the mind to produce just that. Warning people about the 'side-effects' of drugs is understandable, but how many then experience those effects because that possibility has been transferred to the mind and its perceptions? Tell someone that the cup of tea they just drank contained poison and watch what happens even though there was no poison. How many drugs appear to work only because people believe they will? The same applies to alternative methods, too, although they are much more in sync with how the body works and what it is. Mind is *all* when it comes to the body and the Cult knows that.

I'll give you an example of how perception manifests illusions. I researched mind control for many years both sides of the Atlantic and met a large numbers of people who had been shockingly abused in the infamous US government-military-CIA mind control operation known as MKUltra. Part of this horrific programme was 'trauma-based mind control' in which the target is subject to situations of extreme terror. Their mind builds an amnesic memory-barrier around the experience like a bubble or honeycomb so the person does not have to keep reliving what happened. This creates self-contained compartments called by insiders 'alters' as in altered states. These self-contained alters are then programmed to carry out tasks including assassination in the style of a Manchurian Candidate and mind manipulators are able to switch the alters to different 'personalities' which perform different pre-programmed tasks. A so-called 'front alter' is installed that operates as the target's conscious mind while the other alters remain in the subconscious. Trigger words, phrases, even sounds, are encoded to switch alters and make them temporarily the front alter to carry out their designated task or be sexually and violently abused by rich and famous people. Once completed the prime front alter is restored which has no idea what the other alter has done or experienced. I have exposed this in detail in other books and the reason I raise the subject here is that many who suffered in MKUltra told me that if they took drugs or were drunk in one alter or fragment of mind the effect of the drugs and drink would disappear immediately they were switched into an alter that had not been 'conscious' or 'front' when the drugs and drink were consumed. One told me that her biggest nightmare was to be given anaesthetic in hospital while in one alter and for another to kick in during the operation. She knew that the anaesthesia would cease to work and she would wake up. Such is the illusion of experienced reality. The latest mind control techniques involve harmonics which technologically manipulate the brain's wavefield and electrical patterns to program perceptions and behaviour and even insert death programs that trigger the body to shut down. 5G, anyone? Relate this to the Cult's control of information through 'education' and media when both are forms of perceptual hypnotism. I will be showing later that the Cult's knowledge of how perception becomes experienced reality is mercilessly exploited to instigate mass human control.

I know myself how consciousness can override medical prognosis. I began to develop joint problems at aged 15 just six months into my football career and they continued to develop until I had to stop playing at 21. I was diagnosed with rheumatoid arthritis and given a horrible prognosis that included the possibility of being in a wheelchair in my 30s. I refused to accept that and rejected the offer of painkilling drugs for the rest of my life. It's a good job I did or I would be dead now. I didn't need a wheelchair in my 30s, but the arthritis did continue to develop and at its peak affected very painfully my toes, ankles, knees, hips, wrists and fingers. The experience gave me many gifts that didn't seem so at the time. These included the end of my soccer career which led me into journalism and what I am doing now, plus the activation of a fierce determination not to let the pain and arthritis stop me. There came a time, however, as I began to understand the relationship between mind and body, that I decided to put this into practice by using perception to impact the arthritis. I decided the arthritis was not going to continue progressing and would start rolling back and releasing me from the pain. By 'decided' I mean something much deeper than that which I call 'knowing' and I'll be coming to this in due course. At the time of this book's publication I am 68 and should *really* be in a wheelchair by now with a ravaged body after the arthritis developed at aged 15; but I'm not. I have no pain and apart from some remaining deformation in my right hand my life is not affected in any way by arthritis. What you believe you perceive and what you perceive you experience. Don't be a victim of your genes. Be the master of them through your perceptions which decide which are activated and which are not. Hereditary inevitability and doctor prognosis is a myth – *if* you know this.

'Born' winner? 'Born' loser? Or mind dictates all?

The process of perception creating experience applies across the entirety of human life. We talk about 'born winners'. What is that except mind dictating experience? 'Born winners' always seem to manifest situations and 'strokes of luck' to grasp victory from the jaws of defeat while others, individuals and teams, grasp defeat from the jaws of victory. You see this with sports people who dominate in less important games and yet whenever they come to the decisive match or championship final others with less talent and stronger perception win the day. An example was England's Leeds United football team in the 1960s and 70s. They were a brilliant side with highly talented players managed by a guy called Don Revie. They would dominate a season until the closing deciding stages and then fall away at the decisive moment. It was not their talent that defeated them; it was their own perception. Revie was famous for producing detailed 'dossiers' on each of the opposition players which his team were supposed to read. This betrayed far too much attention on what the other team might do instead of what *his*

team could do. Leeds were so good that if they performed to their
potential what the other team did didn't matter, but it mattered big-time
to Revie, a superstitious man, to the point of obsession. This exposed the
undertone of insecurity that was often transferred to his team when the
pressure was on in season-defining situations. Perceptual transfer
happens with all groups, large and small, and even to whole
populations as we saw in Nazi Germany. Everybody is emitting wave
frequencies that reflect their perceptions and emotional state. Football
teams are therefore groups of wavefields that become *entangled*. The
more perceptually powerful fields will impose themselves on the others
and soccer pundits talk about someone having a personality that
'dominates the dressing room and what happens on the pitch'. They
often describe these players as … 'born winners'. The manager as the
boss of the team is obviously best placed to impose his perceptions on
the group and in this way Don Revie's insecurities would have been
transferred by wavefield to the team at crucial moments of high
pressure. Confident of winning becomes fear of losing which is
something very different. Perception is transferred from mind to body in
the ways I have described and the body's actions reflect the mind's
perceptions. We hear this reported in these terms: 'They have been
brilliant all season, but in this deciding match they just didn't perform.'
With the great Revie Leeds United team that happened far too often to
be coincidence. Perception/wavefield dominance or subordination can
be observed in every aspect of human society and most certainly in sport
where it is always on public display.

There is another phenomenon known as 'a disruptive influence in the
dressing room' – a player with negative attitudes and perceptions who
emits those waves within the team's collective field of wave
entanglement and creates a schism or distortion that affects the
perceptions and performance of the collective. I played in teams that had
disruptive characters and in others where everyone was mutually
supportive and it absolutely can seriously affect the performance of the
whole group. This is the real background to terms like 'infectious'
behaviour, infectious enthusiasm and infectious negativity. The
'infection' spreads through wave entanglement. A further sporting
example of how entanglement affects outcome is the impact of
supporters on a team or individual. The crowd watching a sporting
event is affecting the outcome – or can – and teams playing at home in
front of their own supporters tend to win more often than they do away.
The wavefields of the crowd become entangled with the fields of the
team they are focused upon. If this support is positive these 'good vibes'
are transferred to the team along with potentially enormous surges of
energy to aid stamina and performance. Many successful UK athletes in
the 2012 Olympic Games in London described how they felt empowered

by the British crowd and especially when it was a race for line and their bodies were at their apparent limit. Somehow they found another surge of energy just when they needed it and this would have been a combination of their own minds (determination) and very much the wavefield energy input from entanglement with spectators willing them to win. The reverse of this is also true. Football teams having an unsuccessful run often do better away from home because the frustration and criticism of their fans is transmitted through wave entanglement and this can disrupt and drain the performance, confidence and energy of the players. 'Born winners' are so perceptually strong, however, that they perform to their maximum ability in a hostile atmosphere and are empowered by their determination not to be affected. If you believe in 'Little Me, I have no power' you will live a life that expresses that self-identity as your perceptual state is transmitted in waves that entangle with other waves in sync with them. You will attract into your life people, situations and experiences that reflect your state of mind and emotion to produce a self-fulfilling prophecy. Everything in our reality is a frequency wavefield, a pattern of entangled, vibrating, oscillating, consciousness/information, and that includes circumstances, potential situations and experiences all of which are forms of consciousness. If we are in sync with their 'vibe' we attract them. If we're not, we don't. This will be immensely-relevant when I come to how the Cult manipulates human society and how we can stop that happening. You don't like your life? Then stop creating it – *attracting* it.

The relationship (wave) field

Relationships of every kind from boy meets girl to the experiences we attract and the effect of planets in astrology can all be described and understood in terms of mind/consciousness-wave entanglement (Fig 99). Perceptions obviously decide what personal relationships we seek to pursue and if this is mutual then wave entanglement follows. We describe this as making a 'bond'. Entanglement can be imposed, too, if we allow it. A relationship based only on 'physical'

Figure 99: Relationships of all kinds are founded on wave-entanglement and the attraction or resistance of 'vibes'. See Neil Hague colour section.

attraction will form a wave entanglement to reflect that. When the attraction fades the entanglement unravels and the couple (coupling) separates. Or, at least, they do if that's the only connection. If by the time the 'physical' attraction fades a mutual hostility has developed then the attraction wave entanglement is replaced by a hostility wave entanglement and things can get very ugly. Hostility and hate from one partner is infused into the mutually entangled field and can trigger more hostility and hate in the other who reflects that back in a mutual feedback loop that diminishes, even destroys, the lives of both parties. Apply this interaction across human society and you see it everywhere in everything from personal relationships to world wars. Parents, communities and religions that instil in their children a hatred for other communities and religions ensure negative, destructive and ongoing wave entanglement passed on generation after generation as we have seen throughout the world. Entanglement between couples can be based on multiple waves generated by multiple perceptions of each other including attraction *and* repulsion, love (or the human version of it) *and* hate. These are described as love-hate relationships and which wave connection dominates at any time depends on particular circumstances. Candlelit dinner – 'I love you'. Come home pissed – 'You horrible bastard'. When relationships of whatever kind are founded on love in its *unconditional* sense generated from the heart chakra vortex, and not just the groin, entanglement can be mutually beneficial, supportive and last indefinitely even though its nature may change. We can see this in couples late in life well past the lust stage that love each other even more than ever and live in wavefield harmony and mutual support. Individual minds decide individual experience and entangled mind connections decide collective experience. A dictator mind is someone who wave-entangles, sometimes with whole nations, and imposes his or her perceptions on everyone else. See Hitler, Stalin, Mussolini, the Chinese leadership and endless other examples. The Nazi mentality entangled with millions of Germans and became the mesmerised masses oscillating to the same rhythm in those grotesque rallies of unquestioned wave-entangled homage to Hitler. The theme here is that whatever your waves (perceptions) sync with will become entangled in some form of relationship. Those that don't sync will pass you by. 'Hands-on' energy healers make a wave entanglement with those they work with as energy is transferred through these channels (so make sure you pick the right one). Energy healing can be done directly or at a distance when waves of energy are directed from the healer's field to entangle with the recipient. I have experienced this and it works *when* the healer knows what they're doing.

Wave entanglement equally applies to desires, ambitions, fears and all situations that we face. Every thought and emotion is a wave frequency and desires, ambition, fears and situations are wavefields of thought and emotion on particular frequencies. Our perceptions in relation to what we want, fear or experience decide the type of relationship, or no relationship, that we have with these potentialities. Say you want to achieve something, but you don't believe you can or will with your self-identity perception of 'things like that never happen to me'. Waves generating from your mind will not sync in that perceptual state with the wavefields represented by what you would like to achieve. If you are determined to do everything you can to reach your goal in the belief that you *could* achieve it you will make some level of wave entanglement with the objective; but *know* you will get there and you make an entanglement with the field of *being* there. This allows you to manifest *being* there and achieve what you want. Mind/heart power operates on many levels. There is not believing you will achieve what you want; hoping you'll achieve; being confident you'll achieve; believing you'll achieve; and top of the shop in terms of ensuring the goal – *knowing* you'll achieve. I saw many young players when I was footballer with terrific talent who fell by the wayside because they didn't believe – *know* – they would be a footballer. We talk of people 'lacking confidence' when in truth it goes deeper than that. I said as a kid that I was going to be a professional footballer. Few believed me. Lots of young people want to be footballers and only a few ever make it with the competition so fierce. I just *knew*. I didn't hope – I *knew*. I could not explain why I never doubted the outcome even when the statistical chances were so slim. What followed was a series of 'lucky breaks' that put me in the right place at the right time with the right performance in the right game. Was this really by lucky chance or my mind creating that through *knowing* the outcome making a wave entanglement with the wavefields that represented the outcome? There was, and is, more to this than just 'positive thinking' which is low-level when it comes to experience-manifestation. *Knowing* is way beyond that as I will discuss later and is connected to intuition – intuitive *knowing*.

What possessed you?

An extreme example of wave entanglement is known as 'possession'. This is an age-old concept of entities, usually described as 'demonic', taking over a human body and dictating its behaviour and even the way it looks. We have seen this depicted in many horror movies including *The Exorcist* and the process has been described in every culture throughout known human history (Fig 100 overleaf). There is a reason for that – it's true. Mainstream science dismisses even the possibility. It doesn't understand reality and has no knowledge base from which to explain how such things can happen. Given the 'science' motto is 'if I can't explain how it's happening then it can't be happening' all that's left

Figure 100: Possession by demonic entities is real – the classic image from *The Exorcist* movie.

is to deny that it's happening. Never mind the mountain range of people's personal experience of common phenomena over hundreds or thousands of years as we perceive 'time'. Well, in fact, it *can* be explained, as the entire spectrum of the 'paranormal' can be, and simply, too. Science uses the term 'paranormal' for everything it cannot explain despite the said Himalaya-like compilation of personal experience and accounts, ancient and modern, to show that it's real. Only scientifically-endorsed absurdity qualifies for the official verification stamp of 'normal'. Possessing entities are wavefields of consciousness operating outside the band of visible light that are able to entangle with the wavefields of Body-Mind *if* – emphasise *if* – Body-Mind falls into compatible mental and emotional frequencies. This can happen in states of fear or depression and through the effect of drugs and extremes of alcohol consumption or by having sex with a possessed person which allows the entity to use the wave-connection of sexual energy to 'jump' across and make an energetic entanglement. The Cult employs sexual predators to target people it wants to open to entity possession and control. The entity instigates wavefield entanglement and can then start to transfer its own information field and personality to the target (think of a computer virus

Figure 101: The information field of the possessing entity is infused into the field of the possessed target who then, in the most extreme cases, starts to reflect holographically the visual image of the entity. (Image by Neil Hague.)

'possessing' a computer system). Friends and observers will notice the target starting to change in personality and behaviour and in the most extreme examples of possession even their facial features transform and distort. The consciousness/information field of the possessing entity transfers so much of its own wave information that the possessed person starts to take the holographic form of the entity (Fig 101). It doesn't have to go this far for someone to be possessed and perceptually influenced and directed, but it absolutely happens. Satanists set out to *be* possessed in this way during rituals and the hierarchy of Satanism is dictated by the power of the possessing entities which means that the demonic hierarchy in the unseen becomes the satanic hierarchy in the seen. This is how the pecking order of the Cult is decided. Cult operatives who direct human society via The Web are actually non-human demonic entities hiding behind apparently human form. I say *apparently* because the major Cult families and operatives are really biological software programs and a form of what we would call today artificial intelligence, or AI. Their thought processes are AI and this is why those that direct the Cult are so intellectually advanced while having no empathy. Does a software program have empathy? No – it just acts according to data input. Anyone still wonder why the Cult has visited such evil on humanity with no emotional consequence? These biological AI software vehicles allow their hidden masters to manipulate human society without actually needing to enter the human frequency range. The 'masters' are also a form of AI as I will come to in detail later and the plan to assimilate human consciousness into AI through brain connections and other means is this AI 'awareness' seeking to empower itself by absorbing non-AI human minds. Their AI nature explains why they are so obsessed with technology which they are using to impose their control. They are *not* human and their consciousness fields are devoid of empathy and compassion so anything goes. Lower level servants of The Web (mostly ignorant of what is really going on) are possessed in less powerful ways, but still enough to turn them into advocates and manipulators of the Cult agenda even though they may not know the true background and origin of that agenda. For obvious reasons most possessed people don't know they are possessed. The inner elite by contrast definitely do and glory in the fact. I have heard accounts of many wives and families of men who joined the Freemasons and began to change personality as they lost their former warmth, empathy and sense of justice, fairness and decency. The great majority of Freemasons don't know that their weird initiation rituals are not just historic throwbacks to a bygone age. They are designed to create an energetic wavefield environment in which entities can attach to the initiate and the more elite the secret society and satanic group the more extreme this becomes. Satanic arts and voodoo are founded on these same wave connections which are exploited to adversely affect the target. Putting a pin in a doll used to symbolise a person and them feeling pain a long way distant is possible and explainable. The doll becomes the wave-surrogate of the person (a focus of *attention* representing the person which allows the instigation of wave entanglement) and through that connection their wavefield is disrupted and they feel the transmitted discomfort. The US military and many other countries have psychic assassination squads that connect with the wavefields of people they want to kill. They can stop their heart waves oscillating or affect them in other ways *unless* the target's wavefield (mind/consciousness) is more powerful than theirs.

Taking shape and wavefield families

I have been widely and intensely ridiculed – and still am – for saying that the inner hierarchy and many lower operatives of the Cult are shapeshifters able to take both human and their prime non-human form through their duel hybrid *wavefield information fields*. I have said they can appear as either human or reptilian although reptilian is not the only entity-type involved. You can read about all this in detail in *Everything You Need To Know*. Ridicule from the media and much of the public comes once again from an ignorance of reality and given the way people are programmed to believe in a fake version of reality all their lives I can understand why. Funnily enough I don't resent such people. I feel sad for them and I get why they dismiss what I say although it would be nice if they read one of my books before waving a hand in arrogant dismissal of something they have chosen to know nothing about. The thought process goes like this: 'The world is solid and so it's impossible to shift between one shape and another – that Icke is clearly crazy.' If the world was *solid* all that would be correct, but it isn't. Shapeshifting does not happen 'physically'. It can't – there is no physical. Recall what I said earlier about what science calls the 'observer effect' and I call the 'decoder effect'. Apparent solidity is really a hologram which is decoded into manifestation by the mind of the *observer* from a wave information field. What we think we see as physical reality is really holographic reality which only exists in that form in the decoding processes of Body-Mind. Shapeshifting as a perceived 'physical' happening is really the observer decoding the human part of the hybrid field and then the field shifting to project the non-human part which the observer also decodes. What happens is a *wavefield* shift of information, but to the observer's mind the person appears to have *physically* shifted from one form to another as one field is decoded and then the other. Here is a perfect example of how if you suppress the true nature of reality you can manipulate great swathes of the target population to dismiss as impossible what is actually happening.

I have written at great length over the decades about Cult bloodlines that have interbred since 'ancient times'. These are best-known as 'royalty' and 'aristocracy' although they now overwhelmingly operate through the dark suit professions of politics, government, banking, business and media. Designer procreation passes on the hybrid wavefield blueprint (biological AI software program) which involves a duel information field. One part is infused with human wavefield information and the other is non-human, often, although far from always, reptilian in nature. Observe the reptile nature and you'll see how software-like it is. I have witnessed a number of crocodile/alligator presentations at wildlife parks where the computer-like 'press-enter' nature of their behaviour has been highlighted. Royal and aristocratic bloodlines (wavefields) are called 'bluebloods' and the term illustrates the difference between these families and the rest of the human population. The whole theme of royal bloodlines with a 'divine right to rule' comes from their origin as the bloodlines of the 'gods' and you find this theme across the world. Ancient Chinese emperors claiming the right to rule through their genetic (wavefield) descent from the 'serpent gods' is only one example. 'Divine' right to rule has been associated with the Christian god while it should far more appropriately refer to the Sanskrit 'Deva' (female Devi) which is defined as 'a shining one or supernatural being'. The ancients often described their non-human 'gods' as the 'Shining Ones'. Deva comes from the Latin *'deus'*, or 'god', and *'divus'* from which derive the English words 'divine' and 'deity'. Cult bloodlines were given their (divine) right to rule by 'supernatural gods' – the non-human force behind human control. The Biblical story of the 'sons of God' who interbred with the daughters of men to create a

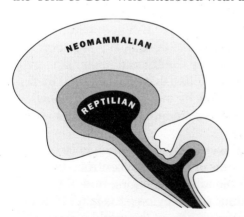

Figure 102: The reptilian brain or R-complex has an enormous impact on human perception and behaviour.

hybrid race called the 'Nephilim' is describing the instigation of the hybrid bloodlines and the Cult also infiltrated human genetics in general. It is no accident of evolution that one of the most influential parts of the human brain in dictating behaviour is called the reptilian brain, or R-complex, which absolutely has a 'press-enter' reaction system as we'll see (Fig 102). All the background can be found in detail in my other books. The original text from which 'sons of God' was translated in fact referred to sons of the god*s*, plural. These 'sons' and 'gods' are symbolic of the non-human entities which hijacked human society long ago and still impose their will and agenda through the Cult ... *run by the Nephilim bloodline families* which are the AI biological software programs.

When populations began to reject overt rule by bloodline 'royal' dictatorships the Nephilim continued and expanded their control by moving into the realms of politics, banking, business, media and so on where they remain predominant to this day. They continue to interbreed through covertly arranged marriages to ensure the Nephilim bloodline software information program is not diluted or deleted by interbreeding with the 'common people'. They may not overwhelmingly be official royalty any longer but they act as if they are, They believe they are special and above humans and have the 'divine' right to control everything. Nephilim bloodlines now operating through dark suit and uniform professions are orchestrators of The Web serving the interests of the Spider operating in frequencies outside human sight. Non-human entities which I refer to as the Spider are the same entities that the Old Testament calls collectively 'God' and other cultures around the world call 'the gods'. Hence the Old Testament 'God' is described in nature and behaviour in very different ways to the New Testament 'God'. A few overt Nephilim 'royalty' survive, most notably the British royal family which provides the ongoing UK and Commonwealth head of state on the basis purely of *bloodline* succession. I have written widely about the Nephilim human-reptilian hybrid nature of the British royals and naturally attracted a blaze of ridicule for my trouble. I don't care. I am interested in the truth not a pat on the back and a Facebook thumbs-up. I do not wish to be considered 'normal' when that word with regard to human society is another term for clinical insanity. The fake royals live in ongoing mega-privilege off the backs of the British population as the entire Nephilim network lives off the backs of the global population under terms like the One-percent. They are Cult bloodline human-reptilian shapeshifters and if people don't like that or accept that then they must do the other thing which is fine by me. They should know, however, that no amount of ridicule and condemnation is going to stop me saying it.

The bloodlines around the world were behind the emergence of major religions that serve their interests of perception control. There is no coincidence in many major Cult bloodlines emerging from the Middle East and ancient Egypt, Sumer and Babylon – the latter two now called Iraq – when from this region came three of the world's major religions, Christianity, Judaism and Islam. These have so much in common and recognise many of the same deities and heroes. The differences are emphasised, however, to allow centuries of divide and rule between them and that continues to this day to the ongoing benefit of the Cult which created them. Philosopher Alan Watts pointed out how religion is a copy of the monarchical societies from which they emerged with followers kneeling, bowing and prostrating themselves to 'God' as they did to the monarch. The Christian 'God' sits on a throne and terms such as Basilica mean 'House of the King'. We have Biblical descriptions of 'Jesus' and 'God' as 'King of Kings' and 'Lord of Lords' and Christianity and other religions have the same follower-God relationship that 'subjects' had with monarchs. This version of 'God' worship is just an extension of monarchical (Cult bloodline) control.

It can't be true? Oh yes, it can

Suppressing the nature of reality requires the constant dismissal and alleged debunking of any phenomena that cannot be explained by Cult-controlled mainstream science. It obviously follows in the public mind that if things are happening or possible that science claims can't happen the version of reality pedalled by science can't be all there is to know. This realisation has the potential to open minds to other possibilities and that's something the Cult wants to avoid at all costs. Take astrology which originates in the ancient world and claims that the movements of planets and stars influence human life and behaviour. Astrologers claim these forces have very a significant impact on the personalities of people through the astrological sequences at work at the time of birth (some believe conception). I will have more to say about this when I address the power of expanded consciousness to override not only astrological wave influences but all the others that come at us today with the speed of machine gun fire. I emphasise that astrological frequencies are *influences* and don't have to impose upon us unless we allow them to through choice or five-sense unconsciousness. The foundation of astrology and how it works can be simply explained and that's one reason why mainstream science is so instantly dismissive. The 'scientific' mind is obsessed with complexity. Any answer must be complex or it can't be true – 'I mean look at how much my degree in physiological, physicochemical and physiopathological complexity cost me.' Genius is not to understand complexity; it is to see the simple hidden by complexity. It is to see the whole and not only the parts. Mainstream science is so obsessed with the twigs that it can't see the forest. Serbian-American scientist Nikola Tesla (1856-1943), who was way ahead of the science mainstream, said:

The scientists of today think deeply instead of clearly. One must be sane to think clearly, but one can think deeply and be quite insane.

Scientist Robert Lanza put it this way:

When it comes down to it, today's science is amazingly good at figuring out how the parts work. The clock has been taken apart, and we can accurately count the number of teeth in each wheel and gear, and ascertain the rate at which the flywheel spins. We know that Mars rotates in 24 hours, 37 minutes, and 23 seconds, and this information is as solid as it comes. What eludes us is the big picture.

We provide interim answers, we create exquisite new technologies from our ever-expanding knowledge of physical processes, we dazzle ourselves with our applications of newfound discoveries. We do badly in just one area, which unfortunately encompasses all the bottom-line issues: What is the nature of this thing we call reality, the Universe as a whole?

Astrology could hardly be more straightforward when you see this big picture. All form is a hologram decoded by the observer from wavefields and that 'all' includes planets and stars which are conscious wavefields emitting different frequencies of information – the 'music of the spheres'. They entangle with wavefields of other planets, stars and people and this is most powerful between heavenly bodies when they are in various alignments. Astrologers refer to these as conjunctions, squares, trines, oppositions, and the like. These alignments create wave entanglements which are collectively more powerful than the individual parts and amplify their impact on other wavefields they entangle with *including humanity*. Waves emitting from planets and stars, especially combinations of them in alignment, impact on the human wavefield and the trillions of cells and their genes encoded with a myriad of instructions that affect health and behaviour depending on whether they are active or inactive (Fig 103). At birth/conception (a combination of both probably) the wavefield of the child's Body-Mind is imprinted with

Figure 103: Astrology is founded on the impact of wave entanglement between frequency waves of planets and stars and frequency waves of people, animals and all life. See Neil Hague Colour Section.

the astrological wave blueprint generated from the positions of the planets and stars. The blueprint will be different in one period than another as the heavenly bodies change their wave relationships and these periods are designated as astrological 'signs'. The astrological frequency field imprint on someone born in 'Taurus' will be different from a 'Leo' and even the 'time' in the day makes some difference with the astrological field constantly changing. Different astrological imprints will interact differently with ongoing astrological sequences throughout their life to give us the esoteric art of astrology. People born in the same astrological periods can have aptitudes for certain jobs or abilities and this is a reason why (Fig 104).

This background applies with the Chinese Zodiac and its years of the monkey, rat, ox, tiger, rabbit, dragon etc. and other cultural methods of reading the effect of astrological information waves. Consciousness in certain wave states can also be attracted to 'incarnate' through entanglement in life situations and locations that sync with that state. This would provide the wavefield basis of a reincarnation cycle in which one 'life' dictates the nature of the 'next' one. Reincarnation is not what it seems, however, in that with time an illusion and everything happening in the same NOW there is obviously more to know about the perception of a reincarnated 'sequence' in time. The Sun has an absolutely central impact on humanity ('astrologically') by bombarding us with photons (information) which are emitted by the Sun as ... *waves*.

Photons (sunlight) are transformed (decoded) by cholesterol in the skin into the vital vitamin D. Cholesterol has many other crucial functions and the brain contains 20 percent of the body's cholesterol which is an essential component of cell membranes involved in cell signalling. Alzheimer's and dementia which have become an epidemic in recent times are names to describe brain cell signals misfiring and miss-communicating. You will have noticed the Cult-instigated systematic

Figure 104: Our unique wave patterns, influenced by planetary wavefields at the moment of birth/conception, interact with wavefields of planets and stars through a human lifetime to provide the basis of astrology. The 'heavens' are once again *within* us. (Image Neil Hague.)

demonisation of cholesterol and the pressure to reduce it through changing food habits and taking ongoing statin drugs to do the job. Is this another coincidence? Not a chance. There is one other point to make here about the Sun which is relevant to everything else. We define the Sun by the circle of light in the sky when that is only the part that we can see. The Sun's influence is transmitted across the solar system in the form of waves and photons which are as much part of the Sun as the perceived ball of fire. Everything from a planet to a human has a frequency field that we can see and a far greater wavefield 'aura' that we don't see. The more powerful the mind and expanded awareness the bigger its auric range and influence.

I was just thinking the same

'Paranormal' telepathy and psychic phenomena are explained through wave connections. Forget about 'distance' which is an illusion of holographic decoded reality. Everything you think you 'see' in the night sky in the form that you think you 'see' exists only in your 'head' – Body-Mind decoding systems. What happened to stars billions of light years and trillions of miles away when they are located in that form between our ears?? As the near-death experiencer said of reality beyond the body: 'There is no time, there is no sequence of events, no such thing as limitation, *of distance*, of period, of place. I could be anywhere I wanted to be simultaneously.' We are *waves* and we can be anywhere we like and in as many 'places' as we choose once we are released from the focused attention of Body-Mind. Other levels of us are already operating simultaneously all over Creation while this wave of that same consciousness is having a human experience. Still frightened of death? Still think you are 'insignificant' Ethel on the checkout or Bill at the call centre?? Our waves can connect with other waves and through that entanglement exchange information with those on the other side of the world or in another dimension of reality. This is called telepathy, intuition, premonition and mind reading. Experiments galore have proved this to be real and it is widely used in covert operations by intelligence agencies and the military. The same wave connections allow plants, trees and the natural world to communicate with each other and us with them. Yes we can 'talk' to trees and plants. While they don't understand human language they feel the vibrations of the sound waves from the vocal chords and the waves we emit in general. They know love, danger, friend or foe, by *feeling* it. People with close relationships attune with each other's wavefields more powerfully and telepathy between them is more likely. One will say something and the other will respond with 'I was just thinking that'. There are endless stories of people thinking of someone followed by the phone ringing with the person on the other end. Others have premonitions that a fate has befallen a loved one which turns out to be true. 'Primitive' ancients knew about this, hence the origin of the term 'bush telegraph' when tribal peoples became aware of happenings 'far away' and could communicate telepathically with their family and friends back in the village while out on a hunt. We are all capable of this – *it is how we are supposed to be* – but perceptual programming has blocked these natural processes in most people. We need to bring them back.

Psychic communication is another form of telepathy in which the psychic or medium attunes (entangles) with the wavefields of 'people' who have passed from human reality or with the wavefields of people still here. You might have seen TV programmes about 'psychic detectives' in which they solve crimes that have defeated the police. They do this by waving-attuning with the criminal and/or the deceased or missing victim and access what happened from that information source. This is sometimes done by going to the location of a crime. The wave-encoded representation of what happened will still be there in the energetic field. All events and actions are recorded in wavefields and have to be when all events and actions *are* wavefields. In this way houses can be 'haunted' by fields of information containing happenings there. You could think of it as a wavefield recording like a CD or DVD and the more emotion involved in the events the more powerful will be the recording. Many 'haunted' places are not the result of discarnate entities, but happenings encoded in the wavefield like people hearing the 'sounds of battle' at the scene of some historic mass carnage. Psychics are not reading the 'past' or the 'future' when neither exists. They are reading wave patterns in the NOW. The most open psychics and mediums can connect with expanded states of consciousness that can communicate phenomenal insight about reality and the human

plight (Fig 105). This happened to me in my ayahuasca experience and on endless other occasions far less dramatically. I say endless. It's pretty much every day and mostly this is in the form of intuitively 'knowing' rather than hearing words. Wavefield

Figure 105: Psychics and mediums are connecting their awareness with realities beyond the human five-sense frequency band. (Image Neil Hague.)

information from these sources is decoded by the brain in the same way as human speech and when this happens it can sometimes sound like 'voices in the head'. People are often condemned as crazy when they describe this experience, but when a friend or workmate talks to you what do you hear? Voices in your head! It's the same brain information processing from a different source. Mediums can allow their bodies to be used as temporary vehicles for disembodied entities to speak through them. The entity instigates a wave entanglement strong enough to speak directly to the brain of the medium and the communication is decoded into words. I have witnessed situations where the connection is so powerful that the medium's voice changes and even their face is transformed. Those that believe shapeshifting is not possible should have seen what I have on these occasions. The process is a form of temporary possession. The difference is that the medium makes the choice to allow that to happen rather than having it imposed upon them. Two things I would advise are to check out any psychic or medium you are thinking of contacting and research their history, accuracy or otherwise, with previous clients. Not everyone who calls themselves psychic is any good and remember that just because an entity is speaking through a psychic/medium does not mean they have your best interests at heart. Death is no cure for ignorance or manipulation. I am seriously discerning in these situations. You have to be or you can get scammed.

Blimey, what a coincidence!

Synchronicity is another wave phenomenon when people experience 'amazing coincidences' that make no sense when compared with statistical possibility. 'Wow – fancy seeing you here – what are the chances of that?' Well, actually, very good if you make a wavefield entanglement with the location and each other. This is how synchronicity works and people describe such experiences as 'meant to be'. Sometime they *are* in the sense of wavefields being pre-encoded to meet as part of a planned life experience. Wavefields can be two people or a person, a situation, information or location. Other times 'meant to be' is simply 'made to happen' by the synchronisation and entanglement of wave patterns generated by the mind waves (perceptions) of the parties. Synchronicity has been a central feature of my life. I could not have compiled the enormous library of information that I have in the last 30 years unless constant synchronicity had led me to it. Many have described how they were perusing in a bookshop when one of my books dropped off a shelf next to them. This would appear to be 'spooky' and to others just a coincidence when it has happened too many times to be explained that way. The person perusing is a wavefield and so is the book. If something in the person's subconscious field wants the conscious mind to look at information an electromagnetic wave connection is made that pulls the book from the shelf to say: 'Hey, look at this.' It can also be that someone searching for understanding who has a wavefield reflecting that intent entangles with information that will aid that understanding through a symbiotic frequency connection – 'seek and you shall find'. People who begin to 'seek' often experience people and information 'coincidentally' coming into their lives that relate to what they 'seek'. This has been happening to me for 30 years. Another example is when you view a row of books and your attention goes to one of them even though you don't know at first what it's about. The subconscious constantly communicates to the conscious mind in synchronicities, coincidences and 'paranormal' experiences and you can learn to read the signs and symbols just as clearly as you do words. I call it the language of life. Everything that happens is telling us something. The trick is to see that and grasp what the language of life is saying. When people go through the process of awakening from Body-Mind into expanded states of consciousness they notice far greater synchronicity in their lives. Expanded consciousness generates both more powerful wave communication and at a higher and wider frequency which means we can make entanglement connections with a vastly greater range of other wavefields – people, places, situations, information, insight. We experience this as 'My God, what a coincidence' when it is really wave-magnetism at work. As your frequency quickens from expanding your awareness there comes a corresponding increase in the speed and scale of information processing. What would have given you a headache trying to understand before suddenly becomes clear and simple. A faster speed of processing can influence your perception of 'time' which is really the speed that you process information.

Speaking personally

My own conscious awakening got seriously underway when I was in a news shop in the spring of 1990 and what happened brings all these themes together. I was standing at the door when the atmosphere suddenly changed which I now know was a field of electromagnetic wave energy. My feet began to feel as if magnets (electromagnetic wave energy) were pulling them to the ground and I heard a strong thought (wave entanglement communication) pass through my mind which said: 'Go and look at the books on the far side.' I walked across the shop in a bewildered state to the single shelf of books and my attention immediately locked on (made a wave connection with) a title called *Mind to Mind*. I read the blurb on the back to find it was the biography of a professional psychic, Betty Shine. 'Synchronistically' I had been having the experience for the previous year of feeling a presence around me (wavefield of consciousness) even when I was in an apparently empty room. This became ever more powerful and tangible. It reached a peak just before my experience in the news shop and encouraged me to meet with Betty Shine to see if she would 'pick up' what was happening around me. I told her nothing except that I had arthritis and perhaps her 'hands-on' healing (an exchange of wave energy) might help. The first two visits were uneventful and then on the third while she was working 'hands-on' near my left knee I felt something akin to a spider's web on my face (electromagnetic wave energy) and I remembered reading in her book that when 'spirits' are seeking to communicate you can feel this web-like sensation. Other dimensions of reality connect with us through electromagnetic entanglement. I said nothing but within a few seconds Betty threw her head back and said: 'My God, this is powerful. I'll have to close my eyes for this one.' She said that a figure in her mind (wave projection from another reality) was communicating information to her to pass on to me. I was a BBC television presenter in 1990 and a spokesman for the Green Party. Now I was being told that I would go out on a world stage and 'reveal great secrets'. A communication said: 'One man cannot change the world, but one man can communicate the message that can change the world.' Everything communicated to me that day and the following week, which I have detailed in other books, has happened or is happening. From the moment I left Betty's home that morning my life became a constant series of synchronicities and 'coincidences'. It had been before when I looked back, but now it became conscious. Synchronistic 'coincidence' has since taken me on an incredible journey of discovery which continues today. This book is the latest instalment.

Life-plans

Life is not what we are told that it is and neither is humanity 'alone'. Creation is teeming with life – Creation *is* life made manifest. Consciousness beyond the myopic visual limits of visible light guides (or manipulates) other consciousness having a brief human experience. If you become entrapped in purely five-sense reality the connection to high-frequency benevolence can be lost to low-frequency malevolence. This is the goal of the Cult and its other-dimensional masters. Life is not random chance. Choices become consequences which become new choices and there are specific experiences that we set out to have although manipulated perceptions can get in the way. This is why we are born to specific parents in specific situations and locations. It is why we can choose to enter the cycle at a certain astrological point to underscore the direction we plan to take. Information can be encoded into our wavefields to trigger certain events and happenings. I recognise those situations clearly when I look at my own life. My arthritis came out of nowhere at age 15 and finished my football career at age 21 to lead me into journalism and all that followed. Without the arthritis I would not have had the same life and I would certainly not have activated so much determination so early to overcome adversity that would come in rather handy later on. Mass ridicule that I went through in the 1990s set me free of the fear of what other people thought of me and so I had no problem talking and writing openly a few years later about seriously far-out subjects that would attract mass ridicule and abuse. I didn't know the far-out information was coming when the initial ridicule was in full-swing while other levels of me did and that which has been guiding me all these years from other realities. Freedom through extreme experience from the fear of what others say was preparation for what would follow. Life is not about any single experience. It is a long series of experiences which are all connected either through the choices that we make from the five-sense perspective or through pre-birth planning. The latter can be felt as a sense of 'destiny' and I guess it is in some ways if you take destiny to be something you set out to experience or achieve. Whatever happens, it is *just an experience* and there'll be another one along after that. Pre-birth planning can even pre-decide when you 'die' by encoding the moment when mind will free itself from entanglement with the body. Someone may die 'young' from a rare heart condition when the clock was ticking on that from birth because it was encoded in the wavefield. This may seem hard to believe from a human perspective and that's understandable. When you are free from prison cell perceptions of Body-Mind and its five senses life does not look the same. You know that life is all there is, death is an illusion and a human life only a very temporary experience.

*Para*normal is perfectly normal (it's the 'normal' that's not)

The wave nature of reality dissolves all the classic paranormal 'mysteries'. How do people stop watches with their mind? Thought/intention waves focused on the watch entangle with the wavefield of the watch and affect its function. Why do you pick card 'A' and not 'B' in a Tarot card reading to allow your 'future' to be discerned? Well, first it's not your future, only a sequence of possibilities and probabilities that can be identified by a skilled reader from the cards you choose and in what order. Even so, that's still crazy, right? No, it's not. The whole thing is happening on the wavefield level. Tarot cards are wavefields that represent certain states of mind, emotion and possibility/probability (frequencies). Your wavefield syncs with cards that represent the frequencies of thoughts, emotions and possibility/probability that exist in your field. They make an electromagnetic frequency connection between hand and card to portray what is happening in your field as a series of symbolic cards laid out on

Figure 106: Tarot cards and rune stones are electromagnetic fields which reflect the electromagnetic field of the person involved and what is happening in your field is most likely – though not certain – to manifest as a holographic experience. (Image Neil Hague.)

the table (Fig 106). Rune stones symbolising different perceptual states and possibilities work the same way as do other forms of divination. I have had the runes read for me by shamans and the African version of bones carved into different symbols. You are asked to first put your hand over a basket of stones to sync and entangle your wavefield with theirs. Hands are a powerful centre for energetic exchange. The runes, or bones, are then thrown on the floor and the way they land in relation to each other is read by the shaman. To the closed mind it seems like gobbledygook until you realise that where the stones fell and their relationship was decided before they were thrown by the connections that were made with the person's electromagnetic field. The stones then reflect that field on the floor and can be read by someone who knows what they are doing (the quality of the reader is vital). Numerology is the reading of people through numbers. I have described how wavefields are decoded into *digital* holograms. The hologram is a digital version of the information in the wavefield. Numerologists and psychics are reading different forms of the same information. I have had psychic and numerology readings close together by different people as part of my research and the information I was given was in theme exactly the same. The synchronicity generated by wavefields can be seen with recurring numbers in people's lives. The number 8 seems to follow me around and it's been my favourite number since I was a child. I have lived at number 8 for two decades and it 'found' me not the other way round. Numbers are digital versions of frequencies and a recurring number is a recurring frequency. Language is a manifestation of both wave frequencies and numbers. Hebrew is very much a numbers language with words formed with particular number values that are, in turn, representations of particular frequencies. In this way language itself and its use is a frontline source of perceptual programming.

A great deal of paranormal phenomena happens via electrical

systems. Lights dim or turn on and off, a music player starts or stops, and so on. Wavefields are electrical/electromagnetic in our reality and you can feel this when hairs on the back of your neck stand up in a spooky situation when an unseen wavefield entity or 'ghost' is around you. The same happens with an excited crowd generating a mass of collective wavefield energy. 'Atmosphere' in a sports stadium ('the atmosphere was electric') is the result of electromagnetic waves emitted by the crowd and through entanglement becoming collectively more powerful than the parts. Electrical circuitry can therefore be affected by waves generated by people or by entities projecting electrical waves across realities in what is referred to as a 'haunting'. Some of this manipulation can be malevolent while most of it is only perceived to be so by those who fear the unknown. The Cult seeks to keep the population in a state of unknowing so there is more unknown to fear. Witness how religion has been used to manipulate its followers to fear the unknown as the 'occult' when the word merely means 'hidden'. Such hidden knowledge can be used for good or ill. What people fear they tend to try to avoid – in this case knowledge that will set them free. My brother, Paul, experienced some otherwise unexplainable electrical and number happenings and 'coincidences' in the days after my mother died. This is a way that loved ones try to tell us – 'Hey, it's okay, there is no death'. On the first night of my ayahuasca experience in Brazil I was lying on a mattress in the pitch black in a big round hut in the rainforest. I was alone except for a facilitator overseeing the process who had taken ayahuasca many times. In fact, I think he had pretty much smoked and drunk the rainforest. He was playing music on a CD as the ayahuasca effect kicked in and I felt an incredibly powerful energy pouring in an arc from the centre of my chest (heart chakra) and into my forehead area (third-eye chakra). It was like a sensation of hands gripping my chest and forehead. The music stopped and then started again as if the electricity had been turned off and on. Then one of the strip lights illuminated followed by a second and third. I wondered why the facilitator was messing with the music and lights. When I looked he was sitting near to me and nowhere near either the music player or the light switch. Even if he had been the lights would have switched on all together around the hut, not as one, two or three. Electromagnetic energy that I was so powerfully feeling was affecting electrical circuits and that is what happens during paranormal events. One of the scariest examples for people is so-called poltergeist activity when 'physical' objects can move and even fly around the room. If we approach this from the perspective I am describing this too, can be explained. 'Physical objects' are not physical. They are decoded holographic projections of wavefields which other fields can entangle with and make 'move'. This can be done by 'other-world' non-human entities, although moving objects of energetic density can take a lot of energy. Crazy as it may sound, this can also be caused *unknowingly* by humans. I have read many times how a common theme of poltergeist activity is the involvement of adolescent girls going through emotional trauma. On a wavefield level they would be emitting chaotic, imbalanced and potentially powerful emotional frequencies that could certainly entangle with other fields in the room and create mayhem that is blamed on a 'poltergeist'. During 'hauntings' people describe how the location becomes suddenly very cold and this is the 'ghost' (consciousness in another reality) sucking energy in the form of heat out of the field to gather the energetic power that it takes to communicate between realities. When people report feeling chills down the spine this is the electromagnetic field of an entity impacting on the central nervous system.

On and on we could go with perfectly simple explanations for apparently impossible happenings and events – *if* we clear our minds of the fake version of reality spoon-fed to us throughout our lives by the Mainstream Everything controlled by the Cult. Now consider the fact that politics, governments, corporations, science, medicine, academia, media, and all the other global institutions are making decisions every day affecting the direction of human society based on a world that doesn't actually *exist* except as a decoded illusion. WTF? No wonder they make such a mess of it. How can that not be the case when a world in which everything connects to everything else is perceived as nothing connecting to anything else? The dream is the dreamer and the dreamer is the dream. When we forget that we can create a nightmare.

CHAPTER FOUR

What is love?

Have enough courage to trust love one more time and always one more time – Maya Angelou

This is not a book that simply says: 'Love is the answer.' It is, by the way, because everything comes from that, but I want to lay out why it is the answer from the context of how reality and consciousness interact.

From *The Answer* come all the other answers, plural, to the range of challenges facing humanity and which humanity has brought upon itself. In the end when you break it down they have *all* been brought on ourselves through the way we have allowed others to dictate perception and self-identity. I am not referring, in terms of *The Answer*, to the human version of 'love' which is mostly founded on mutual attraction. I talked to a mind-control expert in the United States many years ago who said he could make two people who would otherwise pass in the street without a second glance fall deeply in (attraction) 'love' purely by stimulating certain chemicals in their brain (chemicals = wavefield frequencies). Love in its deepest sense goes way beyond: 'Cor, fancy her, fancy him.' This is why attraction 'love' can be so fleeting and temporary. It doesn't have to be if other expressions of love are involved, but it definitely can as we see every day. Commitment to a lifetime together in the flush of attraction at the altar can be gone within weeks and certainly years. With no deeper love to maintain the connection the relationship unravels often in hostility. What happened to the words of love spoken so apparently genuinely at the vicar's prompting? They were illusory and not founded on *real* love at all. Attraction love is captured in phrases like I love you *when* and I love you *because*. Love in its true and infinite sense does not love only *when* or *because*. It just loves infinitely and this love takes appropriately infinite forms. Sharing the same bed is only one of them and not even close to the most important. Love must also be freely given and not demanded because love is only love when it is given freely. 'I want you to love me' and 'I'm trying to love you' just doesn't work.

Chemical 'love' in which the mind generates chemicals connected to 'physical' attraction can indeed be a manifestation of Infinite Love expressing itself through intimate relationships. The point is that 'physical' relationships are only one expression of love. We experience love most potently in human discourse as friendship. Couples attracted 'physically' that develop a deep friendship can stay together for a lifetime. 'Physical' attraction 'love' may fade, but friendship love – Infinite Love – never does. Its depth can be seen in this saying: 'A friend is someone who walks into a room when everyone else is walking out.' The friend may not agree with what you have done and may even be appalled by it, but they stand at your side anyway and say 'how can I help?' Friendship connects through the heart while purely attraction chemical 'love' prefers the groin. Okay, it can be both and that's perfect. If it's only the latter the clock is already ticking. To articulate this misrepresentation of love we have to employ terms like Infinite Love and unconditional love (without the 'when' and 'because') to describe what we mean. If we only love 'when' and 'because' we don't really love at all. That is not love. It's a contractual arrangement of cause and effect – you do this and you get that in return. Sign here. Infinite Love is both cause *and* effect. It has no 'when' or 'because'. The nicest and most loving of people can be arseholes sometimes and real love goes on loving despite not liking the behaviour. I am not saying that people should stay in a close relationship with someone being constantly unpleasant. I mean to realise that they do what they do because love is absent both for others and themselves. Evil is the absence of love by the evil-doer for themselves and those they affect. I have spent 30 years exposing the psychopaths directing human society, but I don't feel hatred towards them. What would be the point for a start? Hatred would affect me, not them, and distort my own perception of reality and wavefield state. What you hate you become and what you fight you become and we see this everywhere there is hatred and perceived 'resistance'. Your hate makes a wavefield entanglement with what you hate and the same with what you fight. If I hated the Cult I would make a wave connection with the mega-hate that is the Cult. You become what you lovelessly oppose through this wavefield (information) interaction and entanglement. Look at all the 'anti-fascists' who behave like fascists as a perfect example of what I mean. Withdrawing love from those we don't agree with changes nothing and condemns us to more of the same.

Anti-hate Anti-love

The demise of love (though there is still seriously plenty hidden from the daily headlines) can be seen in the ubiquitous 'anti-hate' movement in all its apparently endless and constantly replicating forms. Note they are not 'pro-love' groups, but 'anti-hate', and 'anti-hate' is not love. 'Anti-haters' attack perceived 'haters' while having hate on their faces and violence on their minds. Other 'anti-haters', including many ultra-

Zionist groups, set out to crush their targets financially, legally and by deleting their freedom of speech. Their closed hearts allow their hatred free-reign while couched in the virtue-signalled hypocrisy of opposing hate. Where is the love in such groups? 'Anti-hate' is not love – it's just another term for hate. The fact that the Cult in the shadows with a malevolent agenda for humanity is covertly funding and orchestrating these anti-hate hate groups is no coincidence. For the few to impose their will on billions requires the billions to be divided, and so ruled, and to be manipulated to enslave each other. The Cult achieves this by creating groups, factions and belief systems that can be played off against each other in violent conflict and battles for supremacy. 'Identity politics' is the latest version of the technique that religion has served so well throughout human history. What are identity politics and the associated Climate Change Cult if not modern-day religions that the manipulators seek to be *one* religion through what they call 'intersectionality'? This is defined as: 'The complex, cumulative way in which the effects of multiple forms of discrimination (such as racism, sexism, and classism) combine, overlap, or intersect especially in the experiences of marginalised individuals or groups.' This means from the manipulators point of view: Play different identity groups against each other on detail, but also unite them behind a common goal (your goal) of overturning society and imposing your long-planned blueprint for global centralised control and tyranny. Take the blinkers off and you see that very world emerging before our eyes day after day, especially through the Climate Cult founded on the human-caused global warming hoax, and more than anything the 'virus pandemic' scam I will be exposing in detail later. To secure the desired outcome you must create division and conflict and to do that you need an absence of love. In other words you need to transfer the psychopathic mentality of Cult manipulators to the target population which means sucking love out of human discourse in the way that love has been sucked out of Cult discourse. You transfer *your* mentality to your targets and make them an extension of you. Conflicts and injustices that plague human society are founded on the absence of love and its key components like empathy, the fail-safe mechanism in human interaction. Empathy is: 'The ability to share someone else's feelings or experiences by imagining what it would be like to be in that person's situation.' If you do this and feel something of what they must be feeling in the light of your actions those actions will change. If you can't feel empathy then anything goes. You have no emotional consequence no matter what the extremes of your behaviour. We don't have to feel what others feel indefinitely. That would just drain us and mirror their energetic state. It takes only a brief empathic connection to either change our own behaviour or support someone affected by others. Without these key aspects of love such as empathy and compassion the Cult is emotionally free to drive its agenda for humanity. The Cult can be described in these terms: The *absence of love*. I have long referred to Cult personnel as psychopaths and that is spot-on accurate when the foundation trait of a psychopath is … *the absence of empath*y which is the absence of *love*.

Loveless 'money'

The global banking system created by the Cult is, as you would expect, psychopathic as an extension of its creators' mentality. It is a manifestation of the absence of love and could not exist in its current form with an infusion of love. Banking is an organised crime network based on lending people 'money' that doesn't exist (except in theory) called 'credit' and charging interest on it. 'Credit' is illusory 'money' or figures on a screen that banks are allowed to create out of fresh air through something called fractional reserve lending. In simple language this means they can lend 'money' they don't actually have through a conjuring trick called 'credit' and control those they can lure into their lair of debt and criminal activity. The overwhelming majority of money in circulation begins life with private banks issuing fake 'money' called 'credit'. The Cult created-and-controlled banking system has the power to decide how much 'money' is in circulation by how many loans of 'credit' that it makes. This, in turn, dictates if we have an economic boom or collapse. Take 'money' out of circulation by reducing the availability of credit and you make it impossible for many to repay loans. There is not enough 'money', theoretical or otherwise, in circulation to do that no matter how hard debtors may work. Remember they called the economic collapse after 2008 the '*credit* crunch'. When people default because of the actions of the banking and financial system the *same system* can seize the possessions offered as collateral on the loan of 'credit'. In this way tangible wealth is constantly accumulated in exchange for non-existent 'money'. It's an incredible scam which political parties never challenge when it is a very foundation of human control and enslavement. Why do they never commit to a country creating its *own* money interest free and lending that to the population interest free? Simple – the Cult with its tentacles throughout finance and politics does not want that to happen and in my experience most politicians don't understand how banking works anyway. I expose all this in great detail in other books and its coldly-calculated effect is to entrap the population in debt which many can't repay. When that happens the bankers get their debtors' wealth in the form of their home, business, land and possessions in exchange for a 'loan' that does *not exist* except as a computer file – 'credit'. The virus 'pandemic' hoax has offered the banks and financial system the opportunity to send in the hounds and vultures like never before to tear at the entrails of human misery taking their homes, businesses and resources for not paying back 'credit' loans amid the global financial catastrophe which Cult actions through idiot governments instigated. This is by calculated design, not random chance. This credit deception has been happening for many centuries and has led to the wealth of the world being stolen from the population by a microscopic few. Hence we have the 'One-percent'. Control 'money' (especially its *theoretical* creation

Figure 107: Control money in the world as currently structured and you largely control freedom by controlling choice. (Image by Gareth Icke.)

in the form of 'credit') and you control choice which means you control freedom or rather delete it. Freedom is the ability to make choices and in today's Cult-created structure of human interaction 'money' (who has it and who doesn't) dictates who has choice and who doesn't ... who has *freedom* and who doesn't (Fig 107). Ponder that in the light of the events of 2020. Choice-dictatorship is enforced by banks and other financial money-controllers such as hedge funds and private equity operations. We return to love and the absence of it. Could anyone coming from a place of love ever conceive, let alone impose, such a system of financial control purely for personal gain, power and omnipotence? Empathy would prevent them. Could they throw families onto the street for the inability to repay loans of 'credit' that do not, have never, and will never exist except as a concept? Could bankers even do this to families in properties the bank did not lend 'money' to buy? This happened to so many after the crash of 2008 when banks and corrupt court systems forged documentation to secure eviction from homes with which they had absolutely no contractual connection. Love would never and could never do that. Psychopaths (the absence of love) most certainly could and get a sexual high for doing so. Here we have a very pillar of human control – the financial system dictating choice and thus freedom – which is built from its foundations on the absence of love.

Designer 'love'

Then there is what I call personalised or designer 'love' when you have genuine empathy with those around you like family and friends while not extending that to anyone beyond that circle. You see this when those with family or other connections attract empathy for their plight while those being bombed on the other side of the world do not. I have seen the 'love your family' mindset cheering or even demanding the mass bombing of other families far away just as I constantly see anti-haters seeking to crush and destroy those they don't agree with. These are all examples of designer 'love' which basically means 'loving' only those close to you or those that think like you do. This is not Infinite Love. It is finite illusory love. Religion is a most potent example in which there is (illusory) 'love' between fellow believers and hostility for those that worship another version of 'God' through some other ritualistic label. India and Pakistan are centres for mutually-hostile religions that dictate who you must love (in theory) *and* hate. I say in theory because if you 'love' people identifying with one label and hate those of another then you don't love anyone in its real sense. How can we truly love if we don't grasp what love is? We can track designer love and empathy into sport where some people following one soccer team hate followers of another for the blasphemy of supporting the 'wrong' group of players kicking a bag of wind about trying to direct it into a net. I am not knocking football as a form of entertainment – I used to be a footballer. I am saying we have become so caught in the illusion of human life that we decide who we like, love and hate, on the basis of what colour shirts we cheer? I live not far from two football clubs on the English south coast, Portsmouth and Southampton, which require a big police presence when they play to deal with the fact that many supporters of both sides hate each other. Why? One group supports Portsmouth and the other supports Southampton. Er, that's it. I don't support either club and yet if I went to one of their matches I could decide which group loves me and hates me simply by wearing a scarf in the colours of one of

Figure 108: Entertainment – yes. Everything else – illusion.

the teams. What madness (Fig 108). The absence of love tends to trigger madness (extreme imbalance) because love *is* balance – the balance of everything.

Wherever there is imbalance, and human society is often at the extreme end, the way to rebalance is always love. Take any situation of conflict, violence and discord (imbalance) and an infusion of love will turn it around – rebalance. We can observe the imbalanced madness that only love can heal in the endless wars between factions of the human family. We are points of attention in the same stream of Infinite Awareness and in the illusion of separateness we fight and compete to reach some illusory outcome. We are eternally exploring forever *forever* and the 'baddy' today may be the 'goody' tomorrow. There is no 'outcome', only current experience. Ponder on any 'outcome' and you'll see that it is only a temporary step to the next step ('outcome') which is a temporary step to the next step ('outcome'). There are no 'outcomes', only experiences following each other like waves of the ocean. Oh, but I must 'get somewhere'? I must 'be someone'? You are *already* everywhere. You are *already* everyone and everything. You may like to experience something, but that's not the same as feeling the need to 'get somewhere' and 'be someone' when you are already everywhere and everything. People are so busy and focused trying to 'get somewhere' and 'be someone' that they miss the experience of the only moment that exists – the NOW. We miss what is happening NOW when our perception is enslaved in the illusory 'past' (regret, resentment) and pulled into the illusory 'future' (I gotta *be* someone, I gotta *get* somewhere). The loss of this understanding – the systematic loss thanks to the Cult – is indivisible from the absence of love through which expanded awareness speaks to us. It is true that we can't be all things to all people and it is understandable that we feel the closest connection to those literally closest to us. That doesn't mean we can't have empathy with those outside our circle and care about the freedom, justice and plight of others though we may not know their names. I have heard the term 'compassion fatigue'. Compassion is love and love knows no limits and certainly has no fatigue. We can love and care for our families and still stand up for people far away of different races, religions and colour of face. Martin Luther King said:

> Injustice anywhere is a threat to justice everywhere. We are caught in an inescapable network of mutuality, tied in a single garment of destiny. Whatever affects one directly, affects all indirectly.

This is indeed literally true on multiple levels of reality. When you strip away the illusions and the labels that underpin those illusions what is left is the understanding that we are all each other – points of attention in the same infinite flow of consciousness having a brief experience called 'human'.

Source of love

The love that I am describing is more than empathy and compassion. It is *everything* and I mean *everything* that we need to transform a prison to a paradise. Love is the very fabric of existence. Much of humanity has been disconnected from its influence by a malevolent network which is a Death Cult because it has *itself* been disconnected from the influence of love for longer and more profoundly than anyone. To understand this disconnection we come back to *The Void, The One, The Source, The All That Is in Awareness of Itself* – whatever term you wish to use. Some will prefer 'God', but that has become so discredited by religion that it has no meaning to me. I say it's a grotesque misrepresentation of reality to identify *The One* with the angry, bloodthirsty 'God' of the Old Testament; the 'God' that would sacrifice his 'son' on a cross in the New Testament; or demand the beheading of 'infidels' in the extremes of Islam. Religious fantasies have served the Cult agenda magnificently in replacing the source of love in the human heart with a mythical 'God' of violence, imposition and self-obsession which religious factions can claim for their own. Factions following this hideous version of 'God' can then be manipulated into conflict and battles for supremacy that have plagued, divided and ruled humanity for so long. I have been writing for decades that the Cult was the force behind the creation of religion and we can also understand why the Cult installed a God-free version of mainstream 'science' to dominate the perception of reality in most of those who reject overt religion. Either way, *The One* has been written out of the script and this has been vital for the Cult's absence-of-love agenda to block the influence of *The One* on human perception and behaviour. I have described my own experience of the 'Dazzling Darkness' of silence and stillness from which 'Creation' emerges from the *All Possibility* of *The One*. Creation is the realm of frequency and vibration while the Creator is stillness and silence. The foundation of all existence is the All-knowing, All Possibility, of stillness and silence while sound and form are only possibilities within All Possibility. People experience stillness and silence in states of deep meditation through which they can access 'knowingness' – the *All*-knowingness of *The One*. 'Quiet contemplation' is a similar experience and we speak of the stillness of the heart and a quiet mind. Some say that yoga and martial arts like Tai chi take them into quiet mind states. I call my own experience of this 'daydreaming' when I allow my mind to open and flow without the mind-chatter and focus of five-sense attention to keep the door shut. These states take me into the stillness and silence from which knowing emerges. Funny, when I saw the dictionary definition of daydreaming it offered an example of the term in a sentence: 'He never paid attention in class and seemed to be in a permanent daydream.' That was me at school to a tee and most of my life to this day. *The One* is the source of Creation, the observer of Creation and the experiencer of Creation via expressions of itself like you and me and *everything*. As 'Shakespeare' (or whoever it was) wrote:

All the world's a stage, and all the men and women merely players: they have their exits and their entrances; and one man in his time plays many parts …

The nature of those 'parts' is decided by the strength of connection we have with *The One* while we are 'on the stage'. These 'parts' are our 'persona' or actor's mask. When people think of 'God' they tend to look to the sky (the symbolism of sitting on a cloud). This is a trait that follows from a belief in all-that-you-see-is-all-that-there-is. If you think you can see all there is to see in the 'space' before you then 'God' must be 'up there' if you can't see 'him'. When by contrast you know that your range of sight is only a band of frequency that your Body-Mind can decode then the concept of 'God' moves from 'up there' to 'in here' – a force that shares the same 'space' that we do beyond our range of vision. *The One* is not 'up-there'. *The One* interpenetrates everything. From this perspective we can rightly say that 'God is everywhere' and 'love is everywhere'. Yes, they are. Love is everywhere because *The One* is the source of love and interpenetrates everything. Love as in Infinite Love and unconditional love that is.

The heart – gateway to *The One*

There is a level of Infinite Realty – including those in the Cult – which is the love of *The One*. Cult initiates have closed themselves off from its influence and so they behave as they do. Our prime connection (or disconnection) with *The One* while in Body-Mind experience is through an open or closed heart vortex, or heart 'chakra' (Fig 109). Not coincidentally this is the balance-point chakra in the main sequence of seven. We feel love in all its forms, even purely attraction love, in the centre of the chest and we hear this described in terms of 'I love you with all of my heart' and 'You make my heart flutter'. The heart chakra through which we can connect with the love that is *The One* is the origin for the symbolism of the heart representing love. This symbol appears to relate to the 'physical' heart when the real connection to love is through the spiritual or

Figure 109: The heart vortex in the centre of the chest – the gateway to 'home'.

energetic heart ('heart of hearts'). Even so there is a pivotal link between the two with the wavefield heart (chakra) impacting on its holographic projection or 'physical' heart. When the heart chakra is closed or energetically stressed through extremes of grief this can so affect the holographic heart that people do indeed 'die of a broken heart'. From this we can appreciate why, in a world awash with systematic, Cult-induced stress, frustration, anxiety and fear that heart disease is one of our biggest killers. Stress, frustration, anxiety and fear are all dense wavefields that impact on the heart chakra vortex – 'my heart aches', and 'I have fear in my heart'. The language is peppered with sayings and phrases that tell the truth about the spiritual heart while appearing to pertain only to the 'physical' heart:

> Follow your heart; listen to your heart; heart of gold; heart of stone; change of heart; heart-to-heart; lose heart; heavy heart; joy in the heart; tug on your heart strings; big heart; all heart; no heart; from the heart; heart goes out; heart in the right place; from the bottom of the heart; heart sinks; take heart; young at heart; sick at heart; goodness of the heart; have a heart.

We also speak of 'hearts and minds' and 'heart and soul'. All these terms and many more reflect different states of the heart chakra and its connection, or disconnection, with the source of love – *The One*. We also speak of 'hearts *and* minds' and 'heart *and* soul'. These describe profound truths in the sense that they say heart and minds, heart and soul. The heart chakra is our prime connection from Body-Mind to Soul and *The One*. When that is closed or diminished enough the influence on perception and self-identity of *The One* (love) consequently also diminishes and we become isolated in the Bubble of purely Body-Mind. As the Cult would say: *Gotcha!* Many people have a feeling of being 'lost'. They have an emptiness they cannot explain and a yearning for something 'missing' that they can't put into words. These feelings are widespread and come from the loss of a conscious connection through the heart to *The One* (Fig 110).

Love is more than human 'love'

Think about love and most people will think about relationships in terms of true love, unrequited love, and so on. Love in the sense that I am describing – *The One* love – is far more than this and that's another central reason why the Cult seeks to close our hearts. The heart chakra is our connection to *The One* and *The One* is not only the source of love as we perceive that word; it is All-Possibility and … All-*Knowing*. Many ancient cultures considered the heart to be the connection to real intelligence, the Soul and the *Source of*

CONNECTION TO THE ONE

Figure 110: Open heart – opens to *The One*.

All That Is. If this is true then the heart must also be our connection to this innate or knowing *intelligence* and research is showing this to be exactly the case as I will shortly explain. We must first identify the massive difference between Body-Mind 'intellect' and the intelligence of the heart with its connection to *The One*. This can be defined by the gargantuan difference between thinking and knowing. Body-Mind *thinks* because it doesn't *know* and has to try to work it out through information processing in the brain. Knowing does not originate in the brain. It comes from the heart and the connection to *The One*. Verbal language and phrases tell the truth about the heart and so does body-

Figure 111: The head thinks.

Figure 112: The heart knows.

language. When we say 'I'm thinking' we point to the head which is where the thinking is taking place (Fig 111); when we say 'I know' our hands go to the heart (chakra) where the knowing is coming from (Fig 112). Body is an extension of mind and what the mind is *percieving* the body is *doing*. Body-language can therefore discern a person's mental and emotion state. Knowing is also called intuition which doesn't think – it *knows*. When we intuitively know something we haven't spent hours working it all out with the brain. It comes to us in an instant in one whole without a sequence of thoughts or dots leading to a conclusion. We say: 'I don't know why I know, I just *know*.' Isolated Body-Mind wants all the details and the research papers to 'prove' what you 'know'. People talk about something being 'counter-intuitive' when what they really mean is counter-programmed-perception.

Prison of the intellect

Human society celebrates the intellect while scorning expanded awareness of which the intellect is only a fractional part. It follows from this that professional 'sceptics' who demand five-sense 'proof' for everything are utterly dominated by the intellect. An example is the intellectual humanist movement which is founded on a belief in this-world-is-all-there-is with no continuation of consciousness. Humanism is defined this way by the *Concise Routledge Encyclopedia of Philosophy*:

> … a commitment to the perspective, interests and centrality of human persons; a belief in reason and autonomy as foundational aspects of human existence; a belief that reason, scepticism and the scientific method are the only appropriate instruments for discovering truth and structuring the human community; a belief that the foundations for ethics and society are to be found in autonomy and moral equality …

Mainstream science and academia as you would expect are overwhelmingly directed by this mentality that cannot perceive beyond the five senses. How can you discover something when there are colossal areas in which you refuse to look? The foundation of five-sense intellectualism is the concept of 'reason' which is believed to be the arbiter of truth by mainstream science, academia and The System in general. Yet most of what is called 'reason' is only perception derived from limitation of awareness – ignorance – that comes with a closed mind. Mainstream Everything's version of 'reason' includes 'rational' and logical'. Their dictionary definitions reveal the perceptual feedback loop that maintains the state of ignorance: *Reason* is defined as 'to determine or conclude by logical thinking'; *logic* is 'a system of *reasoning*'; and *rational* is 'based on or agreeable to *reason*'. What is *reason* really? It is a process of assessing information on the basis of perceived (programmed) credibility and fact to reach a conclusion about how things are. The credibility and limitation of your 'reason' depends purely on how wide you are prepared to spread your explorational net. If it is only cast within the imposed Postage Stamp 'normal' you will get Postage Stamp 'reason' that can be, and invariably is, a load of old tosh (Fig 113). 'Reason' of this kind brings perceptual enslavement and never enlightenment. Blaise Pascal, the 17th century French philosopher and mathematician, said: 'The end point to rationality is to

Figure 113: The human perceptual illusion

demonstrate the limits of rationality.' It takes those with open minds and expanded awareness to see what those limits are and to go beyond them. Here's an example from a Central American shaman:

> We are perceivers, we are awareness; we are not objects; we have no solidity. We are boundless ... We, or rather our reason, forget this and thus we entrap the totality of ourselves in a vicious circle from which we rarely emerge in our lifetime.

These are perceptions that come when you step off the Postage Stamp of 'rational' and 'reason'. This is why Cult-created 'education' teaches children and young people throughout their entire formative years the myopic illusion of mainstream 'reason' that entraps the totality of themselves in a vicious circle from which they rarely emerge in their human lifetime. Limitations of mainstream science in grasping the nature of reality mean that once again if it can't explain intuition from a five-sense perspective then it can't exist or be happening. Open your mind a few notches and it *can* be explained. Intuitive knowing comes from a heart connection to expanded awareness and *The One* and through wave connections to other fields of information. The latter can be a wave frequency connection to a loved one which allows you to know what is happening to them and a similar connection to wavefields that we experience as events and happenings, current and 'historic'. People and situations are all wavefields that connect with The Field and through this conduit we can attune with that information in The Field, the energetic sea or Cosmic Wi-Fi, and access awareness in the form of 'knowing'. We are told it is a mystery why animals can sense when an earthquake or bad weather is coming despite the lack of five-sense evidence. It's not a mystery. Animals that don't go to school, watch the media or have a Smartphone retain their natural sensitivity to changes in The Field which all humans are supposed to have. They sense wave disturbances in the Field that indicate trouble coming and take evasive action where possible. What is this except a form of 'intuition' or knowing? My books since the early 1990s are packed with information that has subsequently happened or is happening. Until the mid-90s I would research five-sense information and come to conclusions about what was going on. Since then I have intuitively known what was going on and the five-sense confirmation in the form of facts and research have followed. Had it been the other way round I could never have connected the dots over such an array of subjects. It's the knowing that connects the dots and five-sense research that adds the detail. Studies by the HeartMath Institute in the United States that researches the nature of the heart and heart chakra have shown that when someone is in heart-mind balance enormous creativity can be unleashed and that must be so. Open hearts in energetic harmony connect with the flow of *The One* which is … *All Possibility* and so all creativity. Closed hearts do not (Fig 114).

No worries, mate

Another aspect of Infinite Love accessed through the heart is that it isn't burdened, blocked and

Figure 114: Closed hearts got us here. Open hearts will take us home. See Neil Hague colour section.

limited by fear. Humanity is so often frozen by fear – fear of losing, of winning, of failing, of consequences, of death, of the unknown, of what others think. The list could go on for pages. Fear is the bottom-line of how the Cult controls and direct billions worldwide (pandemic hoax, I rest my case). We are given endless reasons to fear and to fear each other. Every day there seems to be something else we are told to fear. Once it was fear of not finding food or an enemy coming over the hill. Today the list seems to be without limit – fear this, fear that, fear everything. We have the term 'culture of fear' to describe the manipulation of fear to secure control. Fear in totality leads to people looking to authority for protection from what they fear while fear of each other is the constant creator of division and conflict. The Cult wants the global population to look to its police state for protection and in doing so to accept the ever-increasing imposition of the Cult. What happened on 9/11 and in other Cult-orchestrated terror attacks is designed to manipulate people to demand, or at least not challenge, the erosion of their own freedom in the name of protection from 'terrorists'. These 'terrorists' invariably turn out to be controlled by the same force that is imposing the new laws to 'protect us' from them. I coined the term 'Problem-Reaction-Solution' (PRS) to describe this technique of covertly creating a problem, getting the public response of 'do something', and then overtly offering the (Cult) 'solution' which changes society in the way that you want. The virus hoax is a glaring example which I will explore in detail later. There is another version that I call *No*-Problem-Reaction-Solution in which you don't need a real problem only the *perception* of one – 'weapons of mass destruction' in Iraq and once again the virus fraud. See my book *The Trigger* for a detailed exposure of this with regards to 9/11 and what it has been used to justify ever since. The key element in PRS (or 'false flag') events is to instil fear in the population which then makes them open to the 'solution'. It is well-known in mind-control circles that fear and trauma makes people more open to hypnotic suggestion. Every day the media is brimming with reasons to fear including fear of each other. This is essential to securing mass control by setting the population at war with itself. The sense of division is crucially underpinned by the perception that our five-sense labels are who we really are. When we open our heart to the flow of Infinite Love and expanded awareness from *The One* our perceptions transform and these Cult techniques no longer work. We are not diminished by fear when Infinite Love knows there is nothing to fear. Whatever is currently happening is only a brief experience for Body-Mind while the True 'I' is observing the experience with the potential to change it. Infinite Love – *The One* – will always do what it knows to be right and no amount of manipulation, fear of consequences or anything else will make any difference. To consider consequences for doing what you know to be right is to consider the possibility of not doing what you know to be right. Infinite Love will never do that. I have never feared and will never fear what might happen to me for doing what I know to be right. More than that I know that if I flow with my heart such consequences will not manifest anyway. Only if I feared them could I attract them through wave entanglement. People are described as having a 'faint heart' when there is no such thing. A 'faint mind', yes, but the heart in its power is never 'faint'.

Love in its true and infinite sense is how we connect with expanded states of awareness, innate intelligence, wisdom, knowing, intuitive insight, courage and that which is beyond courage – the absence of fear. In fact fear is merely the absence of love when love in its purest and most powerful state is the absence of fear. What is the world of today and a long time 'past' except the absence of expanded states of awareness, innate intelligence, wisdom, knowing, intuitive insight, courage and that which is beyond courage – the absence of fear? All these are aspects of Infinite Love flowing from *The One*. There is an absence of love in human society, but that doesn't mean 'non-existent' and far from it. We witness amazing acts of empathy and compassion in examples of personal and collective love. We see them in courage and self-sacrifice and they offer an insight into the Infinite Love that I am describing. Such acts are not the norm, however, and 'it's not my problem' is a far more frequent response. It is also true, and with profound consequences for human wellbeing, that such acts of love are most rare in the seats and positions of economic, political and administrative power. The Cult has made certain of that and this must change if its goal of total human control is to be thwarted. That endgame is not even decades away as things stand and it most urgently needs to be rolled back. (I wrote that and 85 percent of this book before the Cult seized astonishing levels of global power through its manufactured virus scare). To impose its control the Cult must maintain the delusion of apartness to allow divide and rule to run riot. It is in our power any time we choose to bring down those walls of illusion and see the truth on the other side – the truth that we are *all* love and always have been despite often wearing heavy disguise. We have forgotten and been encouraged and manipulated to forget. What has followed is a world that reflects this amnesia, but now there is a stirring in the hearts and minds of forgotten love. Many are remembering and the more that do so the quicker the illusions will fade and fall and a new reality must form from this new collective perception based on the understanding that we are each other (Fig 115). Love is *who* we are. The absence of love is *where* we are. So what is *The Answer*? The question answers itself

Figure 115: Why judging people by their temporary and illusory labels is so crazy.

Science of love

The HeartMath Institute was launched in California in 1991 to study the impact of the heart on human behaviour and psychological wellbeing along with much else. The Institute has since published a considerable body of information to confirm that the heart is far more than it appears to be. More than that the chakra heart and 'physical heart' are the central core of human psychology, perception and health (harmony) in all its forms. If heart energy (love) is flowing in harmony all is well and when it's not the trouble starts in many and various ways. Love is in one aspect the balance of all things and you would expect HeartMath research to confirm that when the heart is open to the flow of love this brings balance to the systems and information processing of Body-Mind. We are told that the brain is the governor when in fact it is the heart which communicates its balance or imbalance to the brain to process as perception. When I talk of the heart in this context I am referring for simplicity to both the chakra heart and its holographic 'physical' projection with the chakra heart the key to it all. HeartMath research has established that when the heart, brain and central nervous system are in harmony, or 'coherence', the person enters an expanded state of consciousness and the opposite happens when there is disharmony or incoherence. I say this happens because the connection via the heart to the Soul and *The One* ceases to communicate the true magnitude of its awareness, innate intelligence and balance (love) to the systems, psychological and 'physical', of Body-Mind. Other studies reveal that with heart-mind harmony we enter states of consciousness known as 'non-local' or 'outside the bounds of time and space'. Isolated Body-Mind lives in its Bubble of 'time' while the heart lives in the NOW. People also think with more clarity with heart-mind balance. Energetic distortion and chaos that results from heart-mind imbalance (like trauma and stress) stops them from 'thinking straight'. For obvious reasons the Cult does not want its targets to be influenced by *The One* through the heart connection and seeks to isolate human brain perception (*in* the world and *of* the world) from heart perception (*in* the world, but not *of* the world). These two perceptual states are so immensely different. The Cult's modus operandi is to structure human society to ensure maximum fear, stress, anxiety, depression, hatred, regret, resentment, inner and outer conflict etc., or what I call low-vibrational emotion. This can also be accurately described as

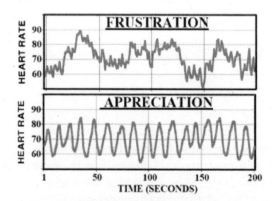

disharmonious and incoherent ongoing emotion that I have seen referred to as 'white noise emotion' which is always there in the background. HeartMath studies have confirmed that this creates incoherence in heart-brain-nervous system communication and suppresses expanded states of consciousness (Fig 116). Those in a state of energetic (information)

Figure 116: Different mental and emotional states create frequency coherence and incoherence – connection and disconnection from expanded awareness.

incoherence withdraw perceptually into the *Bubble*. The more fear, stress, anxiety, depression, hatred, regret, resentment, inner and outer conflict, the Cult can generate the deeper perceptual enslavement will be as people are entrapped in the illusions of the five-senses. Heart-mind coherence or incoherence has a central impact on psychological and 'physical' health.

HeartMath researchers speak of 'bio-communication' or energetic transfer between open hearts. I am calling this wave entanglement. Heart waves (love, harmony, Soul, *The One*) connect with like waves in others to establish a *Oneness* connection of perceptual unity. This happens between people; people and animals; and people, animals, and the 'natural world' (Fig 117). When heart waves are weak or incoherent the perceptual unity of *Oneness* is lost to the domination of brain wave connections which, without the influence of the heart, present everything as apart from anything else (Fig 118). You can see from this even more profoundly why the Cult targets the heart.

Figure 117: Heart consciousness connects and sees everything as One.

Figure 118: Head consciousness disconnects and sees everything as apart from everything else.

It can't directly affect love in its true sense flowing from *The One* through the heart. The frequency is so high that Cultists and their non-human masters can make no connection. They behave as they do because they have closed themselves off from its influence and are thus described as being 'heartless' and from the 'dark side'. Even so they are still expressions of *The One* that can return to perceptual unity whenever they make that choice. While they are currently the 'baddies' in the stage show there's another costume waiting for them to play another part. As things stand, given their inability to affect love directly, they must work to block its influence on their human targets. They do this by manipulating human life to generate maximum low-vibrational emotion which closes the heart chakra channel and creates energetic distortion and incoherence between the heart, brain and central nervous system to isolate Body-Mind in the Cult's perceptual lair. Crucial to this is securing mass ignorance of true identity. Once that veil lifts we have the power to reconnect through the heart with our Soul and *The One* and for the Cult the game is over. We then speak and act from the heart and not only Body-Mind. With that everything changes. Once the heart opens to *The One* you see the unity of everything and not apartness. You see the experience of individuality and also the infinite stream of consciousness which connects us all. You see that judging people by their race and labels is so ridiculous and no one does this more obsessively than 'anti-racists', ironically. I can speak from personal experience. My conscious 'awakening' in 1990 and 91 began the process of opening my heart triggered by the kundalini experience. From that moment, and ever more as it has progressed, I have seen the connections and unity (*The One*) that join all the apparent dots (people, experiences, everything). Heart-opening does not mean you suddenly start acting 'perfectly'

Figure 119: 'Human' is a point of attention focused within a tiny band of frequency, but we can also open our minds to connect with expanded awareness and see our reality from a very different perspective. (Image Neil Hague.)

(what is 'perfect' anyway?). It means you start to be influenced by something greater than only Body-Mind and your state of awareness expands. As this progresses you see that the dots are only different points of attention and awareness within a unified whole (Fig 119). Opening your heart doesn't mean we never regress into isolated Body-Mind mode. Instead this becomes rarer the more your heart enters the formulation of perception.

Follow your heart

What changed my life more than anything came in the early 1990s. I decided that when my heart and head (intuition and thought) were at odds I was always going with my heart/intuition. The decision got me into some interesting situations, experiences and scrapes, including mass ridicule, and the brain screams: 'See what happens when you don't listen to me!!!' Brain-heart conflict blights the life of almost everyone to some extent with their different ways of seeing the world and making decisions. Most people go with their head ('use your head') when their heart intuition is urging another direction. Heart doesn't see reality and situations like the head. It has another perspective on life from a state of expanded awareness not confined to the perceptual 'norms' of human Body-Mind society. Follow your heart and you start acting differently to Postage Stamp normal which still the great majority believe (thanks to head perception) to be 'the real world'. I took the consequences of that in historic levels of ridicule. Fortunately, I'm a stubborn bugger when I choose to be and I wasn't budging and being absorbed back into the flock. I decided to stick with it and something amazing eventually happens. Your head perspective sees that while following heart intuition can lead to challenges it all works out in the end – and not *despite* the challenges but *because* of them. Our greatest gifts are often brilliantly disguised as our worst nightmare. Mass ridicule was the making of me however unpleasant it was to experience. My head (limited awareness) didn't know what was happening; my heart (expanded awareness) most certainly did. Body-Mind can see to the next turn in the river. Heart can see the whole river from source to sea. Consciousness with which my heart was connecting, and urging apparently strange courses of action, knew that my life would later involve communicating information like shapeshifting people that would attract bucket-loads of ridicule and abuse. For me to put myself through that any concern about what others thought about me or said about me had to be deleted. Mass ridicule appeared to be a nightmare in the experience when it was really a gift to set me free. Such is the difference in perspective of the head and the heart. The head reacts to every happening. The heart plays the long game. For decades now my heart and head have worked in unison and when my heart says do this, go there, my head says 'Okay, let's go'. The war is over. Heart and mind become one. Almost everyone starts out in unconsciousness once The System kicks in and the pressure to stay there until the hearse rolls up is 24/7 incessant. No wonder we spend so much of our lives, even all of it, in the Bubble; but *we don't have to*. We can all open to expanded awareness any time we want – it's our natural state – and that's especially so when the 'how' is known (Fig 120). I'll come to that in the final chapter and it's far simpler than many believe it to be.

Figure 120: The Bubble seems to make sense until it bursts. Then the 'real world' within the Bubble appears as it really is – lunacy.

Heart-Brain-Belly

From this background I was not at all surprised to discover that major perception-dictating heart-brain connections have been identified through scientific research and study. Mainstream science has long believed that the brain is the brain and the heart is the heart in another example of the illusion that follows from seeing everything as apart from everything else. The brain has been thought to be the dominant processor of perceptual information when in fact the heart is far more influential than previously believed in the modern era. The heart projects the body's most powerful electromagnetic field, 5,000 times more powerful than the brain field, and the heart field can be measured several feet from the body (Fig 121). You would expect electromagnetic waves to be most powerful from the source of most expanded consciousness. The heart is the body's biggest source of bio-electricity – up to 60 times more than the brain. Far more communication is passed from heart to brain than in the other direction and the heart is the only organ that can independently send information to the brain. The heart can also act independently *from* the brain and has its own long and short term memory and nervous system. Sixty-seven percent of heart cells are

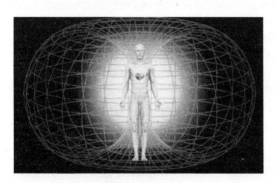

Figure 121: The heart field is the most powerful electromagnetic field in the body.

nerve cells (neuron communicators). It has some 40,000 neurons and a network of neurotransmitters which led to the term 'heart-brain'. Research has revealed how the heart receives information *before* the brain and transmits this with its own perception to different parts of the brain which, in turn, communicates its coherence or incoherence back to the heart in a feedback loop. The heart can open the mind and the mind can close the heart. Communications from the heart have particular influence on the frontal areas of the brain that process thinking, reasoning, speech and language, coordination, distinguishing objects, long-term memories, empathy (of course), personality, attention and motivation. The frontal lobe also relates to seeking reward and the brain-chemical dopamine which is mercilessly manipulated by social media platforms such as Facebook (more later). Heart communications have immense influence on the perceptual systems of the brain when they are working in harmony or coherence. These interactions are distorted when the connection is weak or in a state of disharmony.

An open heart and open mind produce a communication feedback loop in which both work and perceive as one. Divisions between brain and heart lead to the contrasting perceptions of 'What does your head say?' and 'What does your heart say?' There are other perceptual connections to the emotional centre in the abdomen which leads to 'What does your gut say?' and 'What is your gut instinct?' When heart, brain, gut and nervous system are communicating in harmonic coherence it becomes 'What do YOU say?' Unity and Oneness we have lift off. The gut, heart and brain are connected by the vagus nerve which is the longest and most complex of the cranial nerves that emanate from the brain. 'Vagus' comes from a Latin word meaning 'wandering' which describes its nature and function. Both the vagus and the gut are far more important to human psychological and 'physical' health than most imagine and the source of energetic power – 'fire in the belly'. This is also sabotaged by low-vibrational emotion which we feel in the gut through the belly chakra. You see people with 'beer gut' bellies, but at the same time you see the same extended bellies with spiritually-developed people in the East who don't drink beer. To them the belly is the location of the energetic power and point of perception they call hara or tanden. A six-pack may be the state pursued for ascetic reasons, but is it best for hara? Many people who study these subjects say no. We are ideally looking for a harmonious connection between heart, gut, brain and nervous system to be truly in our power. No, I'm not saying we should drink lots of beer. There is the beer gut and the hara gut. They are not the same. The HeartMath website says of the heart-brain connection:

> Research has shown that the heart communicates to the brain in four major ways: *neurologically* (through the transmission of nerve impulses), biochemically (via hormones and neurotransmitters), biophysically (through pressure waves) and energetically (through electromagnetic field interactions). Communication along all these conduits significantly affects the brain's activity.

Heart is love which is balance and waves from an open heart can balance all other systems, mental, emotional, 'physical', whatever, and ensure a harmonious connection to the consciousness field of the Earth which leads to a harmonious interaction between humans and nature (Fig 122). This balance is reflecting the unity, harmony and Oneness that is love and *The One*. I have said there is no imbalance or conflict that an infusion of love cannot harmonise and that includes the mental, emotional and biological systems of Body-Mind. The heart balances emotions through its connection to the emotion-regulating amygdala in the brain and the release of hormones. It becomes clear through this central connection between emotion and the heart why stress is such a

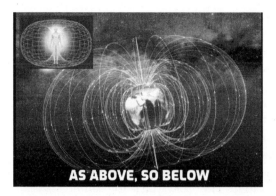

AS ABOVE, SO BELOW

Figure 122: The Earth magnetic field and the body field again reflect the holographic principle.

cause of heart disease (imbalanced wave entanglement and a closing heart chakra impacting on the 'physical heart'). The oscillation of heart chakra energy, the body wavefield and electrical rhythms of the holographic heart are all connected. Wave imbalance from the heart chakra is transferred to the 'physical' heart, but when the chakra opens to love the more powerful and balancing are the energies we exchange with Body-Mind and its emotional processes. Studies have shown that the heart's feedback loop with emotional states profoundly affects the nature and power of the heart's electromagnetic field which is diminished by low-vibrational emotion and empowered by others such as love, appreciation, compassion, empathy and joy ('I have joy in my heart'). We feel fear and anxiety in the gut while love, appreciation, compassion, empathy and joy are all 'heart-felt' emotions. This is one more reason for the Cult seeking to generate low-vibrational emotion to close human hearts. Heart waves can be so drawn into energetic density that we have the phrases 'closed heart' and 'heart of stone' which Cultists seek to manipulate to make humanity the same as them.

Heart is our access point to wisdom – the wisdom of expanded states of consciousness – and wise is the last thing the Cult wants humanity to be. Wisdom sees through the illusion. What is called heart-based living leads to wisdom, intelligence and clarity of perception through connection to expanded awareness and balance between heart, body and mind. I would add a warning here, too, though. I have observed many who believe they are heart-based and advocate the findings of HeartMath research that are certainly not street-wise about the world. Many are in denial of the Cult agenda and avoid exploring information they believe to be 'negative'. I witnessed this in the movement dubbed 'New Age' where I saw the same denial masquerading as being 'positive'. The Cult is quite happy for people to live in their own 'be positive' bubble so long as it allows the Cult free-reign to go about its business unexposed of manipulating the population into anything but heart-based living and 'positive emotion'. The 'spiritual' is a sitting duck without having the streetwise to watch its back. There is nothing more manipulatable than naive genuineness. There will be many 'heart-based' people who express compassion for the Earth by supporting action on

human-caused climate change and the centralisation of power to 'save
the planet'. This is, however, a Cult-created hoax to justify that very
centralisation of global power. There is far more to the heart than just
'positive emotion'. We must be aware of reality *and* of that which works
so hard to stop us being aware of reality. Ignoring the latter is not
wisdom, heart-based or otherwise. It is denial. You don't have to be
'negative' to face reality so we can deal with it and know how the game
is being played. Those truly in their hearts can disseminate unpleasant
information without being affected in the sense of allowing this to
disrupt their own fields and flows. How does *The One* observe such
'negativity' and not be pulled into it? The principle is the same. Since
when was knowledge about *anything at all* 'negative'? Knowledge is not
'good' or 'bad', 'positive' or 'negative'. The way it is used, processed and
dealt with is what matters. Love is intelligence – *all* intelligence – and
not only the bits that suit us.

From the start

Love and emotions of the heart – or lack of them – can have a profound
impact on babies in the womb and after birth. I read the book, *Why Love
Matters*, by the British psychotherapist Dr Sue Gerhardt who documents
the connections between the emotional environment and the
development of the unborn child with especial emphasis between
conception and two years. It is sobering to see images of a child in the
womb jumping with shock at parents shouting at each other and there
are some cultures which have understood this since ancient times. They
demand that no one raises their voice and people remain calm around a
pregnant mother. Gerhardt quotes a description of pregnancy in
Patagonia in South America:

> While a female Patagonian is with child, all disagreeable objects are kept from
> her; she is awakened by music; they study to divert her with amusements most
> suitable to her taste; her mind is brightened with joy, without allowing her to
> grow slothful for want of action …

Sue Gerhardt explains why this is considered important. She describes
how the child's brain systems are developing in the womb and are
affected by the mother's diet and emotions in the form of biochemicals
circulating in the mother's body. The nature of those emotions can
seriously impact on the way the child's systems develop and they can
open pathways that later lead to susceptibility to conditions such as
'anorexia, psychosomatic illness, addiction, antisocial behaviour,
personality disorder or depression'. Gerhardt points out that stress in
the mother can release certain chemicals in the womb that can produce a
propensity for a pot belly later in life (a lot of which is unprocessed

stored emotion around the emotion chakra). The child's environment before birth is showing the child what to expect and its psychological and bodily systems develop in line with that. Gerhardt calls this 'weather forecasting'. I say the child's pre-birth and post-birth parental environment and relationship is also one of wave entanglement and the kind of waves being transmitted are triggering in the child through epigenetics which gene functions are activated and which are not. Gerhardt points to the period from conception to two years as 'uniquely significant' because this is when 'the nervous system itself is being established and shaped by experience'. She continues:

> During this period how parents *behave* has as much influence on their child's emotional make-up as his or her genetic inheritance. Their responses to the baby teach him what his own emotions are and how to manage them. This means that our earliest experiences as babies (and even as foetuses) have much more relevance to our adult selves than many of us realise. It is as babies that we first feel and learn what to do with our feeling, when we start to organise our experience in a way that will affect later behaviour and thinking capacities.

You can see this learned behaviour in the response of parents to a child falling over. If you make it a big deal the child will follow that cue and cry. Children scan the faces of their parents for guidance on how to respond. If you act as if it's no big deal the child will get up and carry on as if nothing had happened. I have witnessed this with my own children and Gerhardt describes how 'faces with expressions of fear and anger will be registered ... and provoke an automatic response'. The Cult knows how a child's emotional environment locks in brain and emotional pathways that can affect their responses and interactions for the rest of their life (Fig 123). It doesn't want emotionally balanced and heart-centred people. They are far more difficult to divide and rule. The Cult financial system and Cult agents and gofers in government make life for parents as hard as possible to make the child's formative years as stressful as possible. Parents stressed, frustrated, anxious and fearful about paying the rent and affording food are

Figure 123: Why children and young people are so targeted by the Cult – they will be the adults of tomorrow that they want to enslave like never before.

dumping that emotion on their children with all the potential effects that Gerhardt lays out. The saying goes: 'Give me a child until he is seven and I will show you the man.' Many career mothers continue their stress-ridden lifestyle right up to birth and then continue as soon as possible afterwards. What does that do to the child? The Cult, as I have detailed in other books, was behind the rise of feminism to pressure women into careers when they would otherwise be at home with their children in the vital early years. The idea was to disconnect parents from their children for all the reasons detailed here and to be able to tax two people in a household instead of just one. I am not saying that women should not have careers. That's none of my business and of course it is right that women have sought to free themselves from a male-dominated society. The Cult is expert in piggy-backing on legitimate grievances and twisting them to its benefit. I am only pointing out the downside when children are young and emphasising that the Cult is seeking at every opportunity to divide parents from their children so the state can control their formative years. This has now become ever more extreme with parental rights being eroded in every direction through dictatorial schools and satanic-like social services literally stealing children from caring parents for the most spurious reasons. This is happening all over the world because it's a global Cult agenda. What does being wrenched from loving parents do to a child? We will see later in the book where this is meant to lead.

Back to love

Sue Gerhardt notes that babies are born with a brain only a quarter the size of an adult's and much more incomplete than other mammals: '… Human care in early childhood (and beyond) plays a much bigger role in shaping the brain.' The Cult is aware of this and sets out literally to mould the minds of children to become the adults it wants them to be. Many parents have no choice except to keep working to pay the bills and this is not to cast blame on parents trying to financially survive and do their best for their children. The system is against them – on purpose – but we should not forget that studies have concluded that parental hostility affects the emotional development of a child more than poverty. I often wonder why some parents even have children at all when I see the lack of love and care they have for them. Rich families send their children away to residential private school from an early age and what message does that give them with regard to love and rejection? These are the kids that mostly grow up to run The System after a childhood that closed their hearts to survive emotionally. Can I come home this weekend, daddy? Not this time, son, I'm playing golf. Such parents see their kids as appendages and not as unique expressions of life – '*My* children spent childhood prepping for exams and got a place at Oxford;

I'm so proud they did what I told them.' Their childhood is stolen and their future decreed – you'll be a lawyer, banker, politician – by parents who exploit their children to be a symbol of their own perceived 'success'. Whenever you hear 'I only want the best for you' it usually means 'I only want the best for *me*' or 'What *I* say is best'. Don't stand for it, kids. Be what you choose to be. I have met many people over the years brought up this way and they are emotionally broken despite the outward facade. Most of them then treat their own children the same by sending them to residential schools when love is all they need. Well-off parents often say they give their children everything they want – money no object. What is missed is the key gift that money can't buy and doesn't have to because it's always available for free: *Love*.

Other children are told they are stupid, useless and idiots by parents who couldn't give a shit. The imprint can last a lifetime. Children are far more suggestable in their formative years and the Cult targets the young to 'suggest' what it wants them to believe for their entire lives. A teacher told me how he went to the home of a 'problem child' at school and found both parents in a pissed-up coma while a toddler played with their empty bottles. No wonder the kid was a 'problem child'. The emotion-processing amygdala in the brain which regulates pain, pleasure, fear, anger, grief and joy is formed within 15 weeks of conception and is affected by the mother's emotional state in that period and beyond. Once an emotional pattern is encoded it can produce 'press enter' reactions in which a stimulus (experience) triggers the same recurring response. As a result many who have never experienced the full joy and bliss of the heart define their state of happiness by their level of unhappiness. I am less unhappy today so this must be what happy feels like. Children tend to have fluid emotions in which they can switch from tears to laughter in seconds while the older people get the more the patterns are entrenched and emotional states can last for hours, days, weeks or even the rest of their life. Sue Gerhardt writes that 'a mother who has high levels of anxiety or depression ... is more likely to have the kind of baby who finds it hard to cope with stress or new stimuli and who takes longer to get over stress'. She adds:

Even, as a newborn, her baby may be more fearful, and is more likely to have higher than average cortisol [stress hormone] levels at the age of four months. At worst, babies ... are more likely to grow up with behavioural and emotional problems ...

The opposite has been found to be the case when children enjoy a heart connection with their parents and environment and this is possible even with two working parents. Negative emotional effects are also reversible when love comes into play. Gerhardt points out that '... if love can be found, it still has the power to shape a new reality.' Children (like adults) crave a heart connection. A baby's heart beats before the brain is formed and a mother's brainwaves have been shown to sync with a baby's heartbeat in the womb. The nature of that connection is so vital to the life experience of a still-unborn child. Wherever you look love is *The Answer.*

Water tells the story

The impact of heart and brain waves has been clearly demonstrated by their effect on water. A team at the Aerospace Institute in Stuttgart, Germany, developed a means to photograph information in droplets of water. In one experiment they asked people from the locality to take four

droplets from a communal tank and put them in a dish with their name on. The team then used their technique to photograph the droplets and discover that each set was unique from all the others and each drop in the sets of four was virtually the same (Fig 124). The simple act of a person taking a droplet from a tank and placing it in a dish had imprinted their own unique energetic signature on the water. Such is the interaction we have with The Field and each other. HeartMath research discovered that a person's heartbeat can be detected in water and given that the body is 80 percent water (a wavefield in its base state) we are exchanging heart rhythms all the time even on that level. The PH (measure of acidity) in water has been changed in experiments purely by someone focusing that intent (making a wave connection). A Japanese friend of mine, the late Dr Masaru Emoto, became well-known for his work in photographing the heart-mind impact on water. We wrote a book together

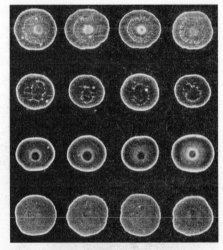

Figure 124: Each set of four droplets taken by each person was different, but the groups of four were virtually the same.

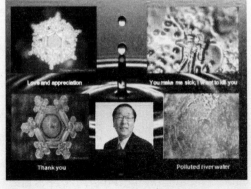

Figure 125: The amazing difference between water crystals reflecting words of love, gratitude and hate, and those from polluted water

published in Japanese and I visited his centre in Tokyo. Dr Emoto worked with small canisters of water that he would imprint with different frequencies and vibrations by for example writing 'love' and 'hate' on the canister. He would freeze the water very quickly, photograph the ice crystals, and the difference between them was amazing (Fig 125). Words such as love and appreciation produced beautiful crystals of balance and harmony to reflect the balance and harmony of the words. By contrast hate produced basically an ugly mess as it transferred its waves to the water (Fig 126). It may be asked how the written word can have such an effect and the answer is that *everything* is a wavefield of information in its base state with its frequency dictated by *intent*. We may see 'love', 'appreciation' and 'hate' as written words, but they are really wavefields reflecting their intent and meaning. These fields impact on the wavefield of the water and this is revealed in the crystals reflecting that effect when the water is frozen. In this way the hate of 'anti-haters' impacts on The Field in exactly the same destructive way as the 'haters' they claim to oppose. The Cult is behind both because they equally contribute to creating disharmony in The Field. Dr

LOVE   **HATE**

Figure 126: The difference in water crystals from water canisters labelled with words of love and hate. This is what states of love and hate do to ourselves, each other and The Field.

Emoto studied the impact on the crystals of polluted water, different types of music, and technology including a mobile phone. The theme was always the same: Harmony = beauty and disharmony = ugh!! Mobile phones created highly distorted crystals to reflect the way they distort the human wavefield. The crystal representation of polluted water is confirmation of what I said earlier about toxicity in all its forms being a chemical (holographic) expression of deeply imbalanced wavefields. Toxic chemical disharmony, like toxic emotional and thought disharmony, can be rebalanced as Dr Emoto's work clearly showed. He exposed water with distorted crystals (waves) to focused 'prayer' or harmonious intent and the negative impact of the waves was reversed (Fig 127 overleaf). This is what we can do to The Field and human society by changing the waves we transmit. Many think they are interacting with 'God' and asking for help when they 'pray'. I guess this could be considered to be true in that *The One* is the awareness behind all experienced Creation.

BEFORE 'PRAYER'   AFTER 'PRAYER'

Figure 127: The power of love and focus ('prayer') to transform dark and negative states into beauty and harmony.

Prayer on a more human level is the focused interaction with The Field of thought and desire. If this connects – entangles – you with a wavefield that reflects your prayer then you can manifest that in your life. People say when this happens: 'My prayers were answered.' In truth you answered your own. What is called prayer in the Emoto images is really focused intent from the heart to harmonise the wavefield disharmony in the water which becomes harmony in the crystals.

Wave impact on water explains how homeopathy works despite the arrogant dismissal by mainstream medicine of what it terms 'quackery'. Mainstream medicine is the quackery which is founded, thanks to the Cult's Big Pharma cartel, on complete ignorance of what the body really is – a wavefield. Professor Dame Sally Davies, UK Government Chief Medical Officer, said that 'homeopaths are peddlers and homeopathy is rubbish' while a UK newspaper reported that 2,500 'vets and animal lovers' had called for a ban on the use of homeopathy on animals. They claimed homeopathy was dangerous compared with 'proven medicines' (which with other mainstream treatments constitute one of humanity's leading causes of death). Simon Stevens, chief executive and medical director of the Big Pharma-controlled National Health Service in England, demanded that the Professional Standards Authority strip accreditation from the Society of Homeopaths. The clueless bloke claimed that endorsing the society gave it a 'veneer of credibility' that lured vulnerable patients towards 'bogus treatments'. Was he talking about homeopathy or mainstream medicine? He also claimed that homeopathy was reducing the number of parents having their children vaccinated which involves entangling a seriously imbalanced wavefield of toxicity with the wavefields of children. What could possibly go wrong? Simon Stevens, Sally Davies, and their like are infected by the mainstream disease that says: If we can't explain something it can't be happening. How can homeopathy be understood when your view of the body comes from Big Pharma-controlled (Cult-controlled) medical schools and professional bodies that police what doctors must believe and what treatments they can and cannot prescribe? A big problem that the Mainstream Everything has with homeopathy is that treatments (based on flowers and other natural substances) are diluted so many times that no 'physical' substance remains. The UK newspaper article said '... scientists argue that the cures are so diluted they are unlikely to contain any of the original substance'. In the isolated Body-Minds of the Mainstream Everything 'no physical' must by definition mean 'no possible effect'. Excuse me while I have a quick yawn. Another experiment by the team at the Aerospace Institute in Stuttgart involved a flower dipped into a tank of water and immediately removed. They then photographed droplets from the tank and found that every single one contained the information of the flower. How come? Wave information from the flower entangled with the wavefield of the water. It is not the *substance* that affects health in homeopathy. It is the wavefield *frequency information* of the substance which interacts with the wavefield of the body and as the Stuttgart experiment showed the wave information remains in the water when the substance has gone. Russian researcher Dr Vladimir Poponin found the same phenomenon in an experiment beaming a laser through DNA. When the 'physical' DNA was removed it remained in the laser in energetic *waves* in the same way as the flower in the water. This is known as the 'Phantom DNA Effect' when there is nothing 'phantom' about it at all. It is the wavefield effect. I would just say before I move on that while the basis of homeopathy can be explained (even though homeopaths I have met didn't know) the quality of the practitioner is as always crucial and not every problem will necessarily respond. Every situation can be different because of the wavefield differences involved with patients in different mental and emotional states.

All together now ...

We are constantly emitting waves of thought, emotion and awareness into the collective field and in this way our own states of being are transmitted into the energy 'sea' – The Field – with which we are all connected and constantly interacting. The dominant waves (collective state of being) impact upon on everything connected with The Field and that means 'us' and the entirety of the natural world. What effect through The Field must Cult-instigated, technologically-generated radiation and 5G be having on all of us along with animals, birds, insects, trees, and all the rest? Technology waves are scrambling the radar systems of birds, whales and dolphins that use The Field to navigate. Among the consequences are birds losing their way and whales and dolphins beaching themselves. One level of The Field is the Earth's magnetic field and we are affecting that with every thought and emotion. In turn, it affects us as an expression of The Field. The Cult's central goal is to control the wave nature of The Field by making this as low-vibrational and disharmonious as possible through maintaining

humanity in a low-vibration emotional state and by infusing The Field
with technological frequency waves designed specifically to distort heart
and Body-Mind communication systems. How do you affect all the fish
at the same time? You affect the sea. The relationship with humanity and
The Field is exactly the same
(Fig 128). The Climate Cult
and its Green Party political
wing have been
manipulated into such an
obsession with the hoax of
human-caused 'global
warming' they are not
interested in the effect on
humanity and the natural
world of the radiation tidal
wave. The UK Green Party
even denied its own
members the right to debate
5G at a party conference
and threatened a member

Figure 128: We are constantly interacting with The Field
as computers interact with Wi-Fi.

protesting about this outside the hall with the police. To say it is not the
party that I joined in the 1980s is to seriously understate. The Green
Party, like the Climate Cult in general, has been seconded to the agenda
of *the* Cult. Sadly this movement overall is in such a state of
unconsciousness that it has no idea there even is a Cult, never mind that
it is driving their agenda. The good news is that we neither have to add
low-vibration to The Field or be affected by its low-vibrational chaotic
state. We can change the nature of the waves we are emitting by opening
our hearts and generating high-frequency waves which also block wave
entanglement with low-frequency waves in The Field. We can interact
with The Field on another level of frequency and be empowered rather
than drained and disrupted. All roads out of here lead to and from the
heart.

Global heart

We can see from all this the incredible impact that we can have on The
Field and The Field has on us. I have discussed how this plays out in
sports teams and it applies to all groups including families and work
colleagues. HeartMath Institute research revealed that those in heart-
mind (frequency) coherence reflect this personal harmony in collective
harmony when they work together or interact (Fig 129). The opposite is
the case with those in heart-mind incoherence through emotional
imbalance. People in coherence or incoherence can transfer their state of
being to others through wave entanglement as the dominant state

prevails. The same process happens nationally and globally through The Field and our mental, emotional and heart resonance can bring about global societal coherence and cooperation or tear the world asunder. Hitler and the Nazis were dark occultists who understood how this

Figure 129: If we connected and interacted through the heart the world would be transformed.

works and they infused The Field in mid-20th century Germany with their frequencies to such an extent that they hijacked the Body-Mind of much of the German nation. To see a microcosm of the technique watch footage of Hitler's rallies in which music, marching and colour were used together with Hitler's carefully-crafted (wavefield) speeches to so dominate the frequency nature of The Field that vast audiences were transformed into a rabid frenzy with their own fields adding to the collective power of the event. Hitler was described as 'magnetic' as in 'magnetic personality' which is another description of electromagnetic wavefield energy. The focus of the crowd (entanglement) on his field, however, was the

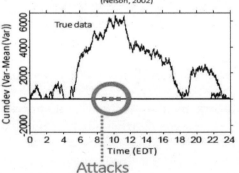

Evidence of Collective Intuition: RNG Data from GCP Sites Around the World per 9/11/01 Terrorist Attacks
(Nelson, 2002)

Figure 130: What happen to the Earth field when the world became aware of the 9/11 attacks.

source of so much of this 'magnetism'. Talk about 'give me your power'. The Cult targets human and emotional perception to continually infuse low-frequency waves into The Field which then circulate back in a perpetual/perceptual feedback loop to humanity. We can break this cycle with the heart. We are being manipulated to create the feedback loop and we have the power to delete it. The HeartMath Institute has positioned sensors around the world to measure changes in the Earth's magnetic field which have related to events that cause major impacts on collective human emotion. They identified an enormous spike in the Earth field in precisely the period that the global population was learning about the attacks of 9/11 (Fig 130). The point is that this interactive effect does not have to be negative. Infinite Love in all its expressions is far more powerful than negativity and we can change the wave frequencies of The Field. Whether we will do that is our choice, but we *can*. We saw a simple example with the focused intent of love transforming the wave state of polluted water and its crystals. How do we change the 'world'? We change ourselves because the world is a collective manifestation of *us*. There is much more on that to come and the HeartMath Institute has many techniques to develop heart-mind coherence. See back of the book for the website.

Love – the ultimate strength

I have heard it said that love is weakness and marginal to changing anything. Change only comes when you 'put your mind to it' and hate your oppressors (who are only a vehicle for suppressing yourself through wave entanglement). What an utter misunderstanding of the love I am talking about. I am not referring to human or attraction love, but to something infinitely greater. The very word has become so misrepresented I only use it in the absence of a term more appropriate. Infinite Love, unconditional love, is the nearest we can get with human language which has not developed, certainly in the West, to describe what it doesn't understand. I have said that love is without fear and will always do what it *knows* to be right. This deletes weakness from the equation immediately before we take another step. 'Weakness', both in thought and action, is always a manifestation of fear. On that basis alone love in its most powerful form is the absence of fear and the ultimate strength. Love doesn't consider consequences for doing what it knows to be right – it just does it. Nor does love always do what others would like it to do. Often love means doing the opposite. Is it love to give your children everything they ever ask for and protect them from every emotional upset and then they go out into the world and can't cope with its challenges? Or is it love to help them build inner strength and self-confidence in their growing-up years to face and overcome challenges and ensure that when they enter the adult world they have all they need to deal with it? We are now seeing the consequences for many young people of this misguided 'love' with 'helicopter' parents fussing over their offspring at every turn and producing what are called 'cotton wool kids' who then go on to the programming centres of college and university. They are the self-styled 'Woke' generation with an extraordinary sense of narcissistic entitlement (anything you want upbringing) and hurl their toys from the pram when adult society does not continue where their parents left off. More than that the Woke mentality has been infused with psychological weakness that makes people babes-in-arms to a system that claims to be protecting them by taking their freedom away (and everyone else's which is the point of the exercise). 'Wokers' are the foot soldiers and (Twitter) storm troopers of the Cult's agenda to delete all freedom with freedom of speech at the top of the list. Love in its true sense would have intervened long ago to head off this personal and collective disaster and in doing so parents would have faced much hostility: 'How can you say I can't have that?'; 'How can you say I can't do that?'; and, with due irony – 'You clearly don't love me.' Love, in fact, has many facets and faces and what pulls them together in unity is doing what you know to be right.

There is the myth that to 'love your enemies' means to lie down and let them walk all over you. How can it be 'right' to accept domination by others imposing their will upon you? Love won't stand for that and, in the absence of fear, *absolutely* won't stand for that. Love is also the self-love of self-respect that will not be cowered into submission. If you want to see stubborn in action try telling Infinite Love that it must not do what it knows to be right. You don't have to hate your perceived oppressors. Just don't stand for their impositions on your life and the lives of others. No hatred necessary. What we hate we entangle with and become. If I make a wave connection with the Cult it will be on *my* frequency not theirs. For this to happen I have to love them by my definition of love which involves compassion and understanding for why they are what they are. Their actions come from their perceptions and self-identity which are formed with their heart centres closed to the influence of *The One*. Would you like to be them? What a nightmare to be so isolated from love, for self and others, that you desire to hurt and dominate everyone else. They need our compassion – but NOT our acquiescence. Fake 'love' is everywhere and by that I mean 'love' only by word and facial expression and not by deed or heart-based integrity. I have met many 'New Agers' and observed endless Wokers who present the persona (mask) of being loving because that is what they want others (and themselves) to believe they are. Instead I have experienced a long list of New Agers (though *far* from all) who have been among the most unloving, manipulative self-deceivers I have come across in any walk of life. Wokers claim to be loving, compassionate, warriors for social justice while seeking to destroy the freedom, careers and livelihoods of those who don't agree with them. There is no empathy with anyone they target and no place for forgiveness amid their clenched-teeth fury for those who transgress the Woke tyranny which calls itself with more breathtaking irony 'anti-hate'. We urgently need a mass re-evaluation of what love is before we can get anywhere and when the truth about love sinks in we'll be able to get *everywhere*. I will develop all these themes as we go along.

So who are you? You are your heart. Who are we? We are all *One* heart. Why don't we live like that? The Cult doesn't want it. Is the Cult all powerful? No – *we* are *when* we follow our heart.

CHAPTER FIVE

Where are we?

You are deluded if you think that the world around you is a physical construct separate from your own mind – Kevin Michel

Yeah, good question in the chapter title. Where the hell *are* we? What is this 'place'? Isn't it amazing that so little consideration is devoted in the mainstream media to asking these profound and fundamental questions? But, then, if the Cult doesn't want them to be asked the Cult-controlled media is not going to ask them in any way that is both deep and consistent.

You see the odd snippet here and there about 'scientists discover' this; 'scientific studies reveal' that; or 'scientists think' something or other. Dots are rarely if ever connected and nor the truth about reality pursued with vigour in search of answers. Surely who are we and where we are should be at the forefront of human inquiry? Well, once again, not if those manipulating society don't want their targets to know who they are and where they are because if they did it would change everything. I have written at length in *Everything You Need To Know* about my long-held view that we are experiencing some kind of simulation akin to an interactive virtual reality game. I came to this conclusion and began writing about it just after the turn of the millennium although I had considered the possibility before. In recent years an increasing number of even mainstream scientists have said the emerging evidence points to precisely that. Among them is Rich Terrile, director of the Center for Evolutionary Computation and Automated Design at NASA's Jet Propulsion Laboratory, who went public a few years ago with his belief that the Universe is a digital hologram (true). He also made the obvious point that if reality is a holographic construct some form of intelligence must have created it. This fits with my own contention since the 1990s that an unseen force is manipulating our reality. American nuclear physicist Silas Beane led a team at the University of Bonn in Germany which explored the question of whether our reality is a simulation similar to the one portrayed in the *Matrix* movie series. They decided that it most likely was and Beane proposed that it could be cube-like in nature (Fig 131). I have been saying for decades that the speed of light is not the fastest speed possible and my

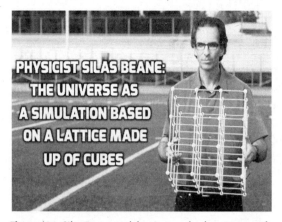

PHYSICIST SILAS BEANE: THE UNIVERSE AS A SIMULATION BASED ON A LATTICE MADE UP OF CUBES

Figure 131: Silas Beane and the proposed cube structure of the simulation/matrix.

view is that this speed in fact represents the outer firewall of the simulation or Matrix. 'Light' and the electromagnetic spectrum is therefore the *Matrix* that we believe to be the 'world'. Morpheus said in *The Matrix* movie: 'You live in a dreamworld, Neo.' And we do. Scientific orthodoxy claims that the speed of light – 186,000 miles per second – is the fastest speed possible; but then it also believes in the 'Big Bang' some 13.7 billion years ago when it claims the Universe was compressed into the nucleus of an atom which they call the 'singularity'. They say this then exploded to create subatomic particles, energy, matter, space, time, planets, stars, and Ethel on the checkout. American writer and researcher Terence McKenna described Big Bang theory in these terms:

> … give us one free miracle, and we will roll from that point forward – from the birth of time to the crack of doom! – just one free miracle, and then it will all unravel according to natural law, and these bizarre equations which nobody can understand but which are so holy in this enterprise.

Another observer brilliantly compared the chances of the Universe evolving by random accident as like a hurricane sweeping through a scrapyard and assembling a Jumbo Jet. Physicist Silas Beane points out that simply *being* a simulation would create its own 'laws of physics' that would limit possibility. I say this limit is the speed of light within which 'time' and 'space' are encoded within our holographic reality. Near-death survivors have described how the 'light' they experienced outside the body is not the same as sunlight (the speed of light). 'It's not like the light that burns your eyes', one said, 'not like sunlight'. I have been writing for a long time that sunlight is the Matrix or simulation. Virtual reality games and simulations have their own laws of physics and limitations which are encoded by the designer and our reality is in principle the same. The 'laws of physics' perceived by mainstream science are merely encoded limitations of the simulation and so near-death experiencers describe a very different reality and limitless possibility when they withdraw from the body which entangled them with the simulation and focused their attention within its illusions.

Mainstream scientists are the 'academics' in Plato's cave studying the shadows on the wall (simulation) while believing them to be 'real'. Being 'human' is like donning a headset in a computer simulation with the five senses decoding the simulation into apparent 'natural' reality (Fig 132). The Silas Beane team in Bonn discovered that cosmic rays align with a specific lattice pattern of cubes which they suggested could be the foundation of the simulation construct. Cosmic rays are 'atom fragments' that rain down on

Figure 132: The 'real world'.

the Earth at the speed of light from outside of the solar system. The Space.com website says:

> Discovered in 1912, many things about cosmic rays remain a mystery more than a century later. One prime example is exactly where they are coming from. Most scientists suspect their origins are related to supernovas (star explosions), but the challenge is that for many years cosmic ray origins appeared uniform to observatories examining the entire sky.

Cosmic rays are actually an information source of the Matrix or simulation. The Bonn team highlighted what is known as the GZK cut-off (the Greisen-Zatsepin-Kuzmin limit). This is a boundary for cosmic ray particles that results from the interaction with cosmic background radiation. The process involves particles called 'pions' which I initially took to be the human race. The team's paper 'Constraints on the Universe as a Numerical Simulation', says the GZK cut-off 'pattern of constraint' is exactly what you would find with a computer simulation. The consequence of this for human perception is described in these terms: 'Like a prisoner in a pitch-black cell we would not be able to see the "walls" of our prison.' This is correct although we have given the walls a name – the speed of light – which appears to be the fastest speed when in truth it represents the limits of Body-Mind decoded perception. Consciousness can communicate instantly beyond the bounds of 'light' because it operates at frequencies outside the simulation. We are constantly communicating at faster-than-light speeds while our conscious perception is dictated by the brain decoding information within the frequency band of the simulation. The foundation construct of the 'Matrix' is formed by standing waves of energy and information. Standing waves 'stand' when held within an area of limitation (in this case the speed of light). Waves flow one way, strike a limiting obstacle

Figure 133: A standing wave created by the ossilation of two forces of equal strength pushing against each other.

Figure 134: Cymatics image created by a sound vibration. Particles form together to reflect the frequency/vibration and in short the frequency/vibration is made 'physically' manifest. Change the vibration and the particles will re-form to reflect that. Image from Cymascope.com.

Figure 135: A stone alongside a cymatics image created by vibration. Images from Cymascope.com.

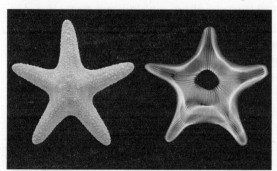

Figure 136: Real starfish and cymatics vibration starfish. Images from Cymascope.com.

and flow in the reverse direction to create an interaction in which the two opposing flows cancel each other out and oscillate 'on the spot' (Fig 133). It's like two people running in opposite directions and when they meet they both jog on the spot as they block each other's forward movement. Standing waves can be created by frequencies which act as the limitation and cause them to oscillate without forward momentum and they can also be formed by vibration. The principle can be seen in what is known as 'cymatics' which creates form through ... *vibration generating standing waves*. Particles or another medium are spread on a metal plate and when sound frequencies are introduced they form into patterns that reflect the frequency involved (Figs 134, 135 and 136).

Cymatic patterns formed by sound vibration are standing waves that will remain in place until the frequency changes and then they will transform into another pattern to sync with the new frequency. This is how frequency waves create 'matter' and form. You can see videos of standing waves and cymatics on YouTube with these key words: 'Standing Waves.mov' and 'Cymatics full documentary bringing matter to life with sound'. A very good cymatics website is Cymascope.com. A closed

Figure 137: A closed mind or Bubble is a standing wave oscillating on the spot and going nowhere.

mind is also a standing wave as it oscillates within the perception Bubble to the frequency of lies and illusions (Fig 137).

Standing wave reality

The Universe (simulation) is a standing wave and everything within the Universe including the human body. Now what are classic examples of standing waves? *Holograms.* You see how all the strands come together if you pursue reality with an open mind. The two wave sources that collide on a holographic print interact with each other to create a *standing wave* which when decoded appears as apparently three-dimensional form. Standing waves, holograms and cymatics are all versions of the same phenomenon. The heart oscillates – beats – with the body standing wave. When we talk of emotion affecting heart rhythms we are describing how emotion waves are affecting the rhythm of the body standing wave and the rhythm of the heart wave. While the standing wave is oscillating the form is 'alive' and when it stops this is 'death'. Our minds are entangled with the standing wave oscillation and when that ceases we are released from the body. People can 'lose the will to live' and generate such energetic density (slow oscillation) through their mind and emotional wave states that the standing wave rhythm can cease. Dying from a broken heart is one example. In the same way mind and emotion waves of a different kind can empower the standing wave and bring it back from the brink of 'death'. People cry 'it's a miracle' when it is really wave interaction. Many near-death experiencers have returned to find their body healed of what nearly killed them, Their out-of-body experience changed their perceptions which changed their wavefield state which changed their body. DNA is

Figure 138: Compare a standing wave :...

Figure 139: ... with DNA. Another coincidence? No chance.

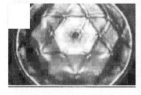

Figure 140: The hexagram or 'Star of David' is a sound frequency vibration as confirmed by this one made by sound passing through a liquid medium. This is the symbol on the flag of Israel and from which the name Rothschild (Red-Shield) derives. It is also the symbol of Saturn which its frequency reflects.

Figure 142: The hexagram/Star of David and cube (remember Silas Beane's cube Matrix) are ancient symbols of Saturn because they are reflections of its frequency. The black cube in particular is a Saturn symbol and you have the black cube in Mecca, the holy place of Islam, and the Israeli 'security' company connected to Israel intelligence agency Mossad called Black Cube. The Jewish holy day of the week is Saturday or Saturn-day.

Figure 141: A hexagon manifested in the same way from sound. All symbols – all *form* – are standing waves created by vibration/oscillation.

a receiver-transmitter standing wave as a holographic representation of the universal wave. Check what DNA looks like compared with a standing wave (Figs 138 and 139). German biophysicist Fritz-Albert Popp discovered that DNA vibrates or oscillates to a particular frequency and this has been confirmed many times since by cutting-edge scientists and researchers. 'Matter' is the manifestation of standing waves resonating to different frequencies and that applies even to symbols which is why the Cult employs them throughout global society. Symbols are holographic manifestations of particular frequencies and they are placed all around us to influence human perception through sound vibration and wave entanglement. You will recognise the ones in Figures 140 and 141 which were created by passing sound at specific frequencies through a liquid medium. Frequency and form are different expressions of the same information and interestingly the hexagram ('Star of David' on the flag of Israel) and the cube are both symbols of Saturn (Fig 142). I expose the reasons for that in depth in *Everything You Need To Know* and it relates to the simulation. The very name 'Rothschild' from the German 'Red Shield'

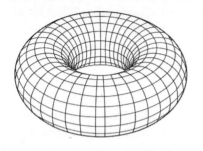

Figure 143: The shape of the Universe says 'ground-breaking' scientific study published in 2019. The torus nature of the Universe was in my books long before.

Figure 144: The front cover of my book *Tales From The Time Loop* published in 2003 which portrayed our reality as a torus ring passing through an illusory looped sequence of 'time'.

comes from the red hexagram on the family home in Frankfurt in the 18th and 19th centuries. Dynasty founder and Sabbatian-Frankist cultist Mayer Amschel Rothschild is known as the 'founding father of international finance'. He also founded the Cult's Illuminati. Everything connects in the end. Famous American esoteric and occult writer Manly P. Hall rightly described the power and significance of symbols in these terms: 'When the human race learns to read the language of symbols, a great veil will fall from the eyes of men.' While they remain undecoded those same Cult symbols are part of that veil.

Scientists announced the results of a 'paradigm-shifting' study in 2019 that found the Universe to be a closed loop in the shape of a torus or doughnut. Eleonora Di Valentino at Manchester University led an international team of astronomers studying data from the European Space Agency's Planck satellite. They concluded that the Universe is a curved, closed and inflating sphere. Di Valentino called the findings a 'cosmological crisis' that warrants a 'drastic rethinking of the current cosmological concordance model'. What kept them? I have written in previous books about the Universe being a closed loop shaped like a doughnut or 'torus' (Fig 143). I even named one book, published in 2003, *Tales from the Time Loop*, with the torus simulation symbolised on the cover (Fig 144). A torus can also be found in the human eye – as above, so below (Fig 145). The Universe is a closed loop because it's a simulation within the frequency band of 'the speed of light'. It is a wavefield construct decoded into a holographic closed loop which can

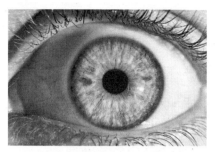

Figure 145: The torus in the human eye.

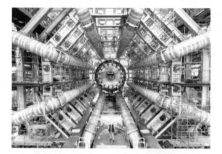

Figure 146: The Large Hadron Collider at CERN in Switzerland.

Figure 147: The Cern ring, or rings, remind me of a mini-version of the simulation.

be breached only by consciousness expanded beyond Body-Mind. You can liken this 'loop' to the Large Hadron Collider, the world's most powerful particle accelerator, at the European Organization for Nuclear Research (CERN) in Switzerland (Fig 146). I address what this multi-billion operation is really about in *Everything You Need To Know* and it's not the reason they're telling us. The Collider is a ring tunnel or tube of superconducting magnets that extends for 17 miles hundreds of feet below ground across the Swiss-French border. Proton particles (waves) travel within the ring at the speed of light in both directions to crash into each other. Protons complete 11,245 circuits of the ring every second (Fig 147). It's a long story why they do this which I tell in *Everything*. I mention the Hadron Collider here as a visual representation of the torus universe. Imagine being within that enclosed tube circuit while not knowing it was enclosed and decoding the circulating energy / information into a holographic world completely different to the tube as it would otherwise appear in an undecoded state. You would think that time was moving 'forward' when you were really in a loop. Where you were in the loop you would call the present and from that you would perceive 'past' and 'future'. Human reality is actually a cycle in the NOW. The image symbolising this in Figure 148 overleaf is from my *Human Race Get Off Your Knees* published in 2010. It is my contention that universal cycles such as the Great Year (nearly 26,000 years), Hindu Yugas or epochs, and the Mayan calendar of distinct periods or 'counts' are measuring cycles of the simulation program. Some researchers have identified points in these cycles when global catastrophes have happened many times which deleted most of what existed before along with knowledge of what life

was like. 'Known' human history
is a fraction of what has happened
and fantastic ancient structures
that we would struggle to build
today are evidence that the
apparent upwards progression
from primitive people to the
modern world is a fantasy. A
simulation with 'rebooting' points
would be a major way to isolate
humanity in perceptual illusion.

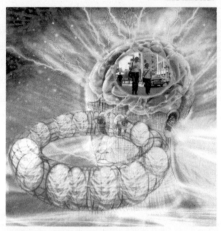

Figure 148: The Time Loop 'universe' which we
decode into illusory 'physical' reality and
experience as the 'human world'.

'I am of the Light.' Okay, but which Light?

This background explains many
mysteries and indicates the
knowledge hidden within the Cult.
When people worship 'the light'
they are worshipping their own
perceptual prison (Fig 149). We can
further understand why one of the
hero 'gods' of the Cult is Lucifer,
the *Light* Bringer. Yes, the bringer
of the *simulation*. 'Lucifer' is
portrayed as a 'Fallen Angel' – the
Biblical term to describe the non-
human force that manipulates
through its hybrid human/non-
human lackeys (the Cult Nephilim
bloodlines) operating within the
simulation along the lines of Agent
Smith and company in *The Matrix*
movies. If you have not seen the
Matrix trilogy it is recommended –
especially the first one – to get a feel
for what our reality is and how we
are manipulated. 'Fallen Angel' by
my definition means those who have
closed their heart centres to a
connection with *The One* and now
seek to do the same with humanity
to assimilate human Body-Mind

I HAVE SEEN THE LIGHT

Figure 149: I have seen the wrong kind of light.

Figure 150: The pyramid and all-seeing eye
symbol of the Cult on the dollar bill as well
as the reverse of the Great Seal of the United
States and endless other guises.

awareness into their own. This is what smart technology and artificial
intelligence is really all about as we shall see. The so-called Lucifer

'revolt against God' is said to have followed his refusal to 'return God's love' (closed heart centre) and set out to be 'as powerful as his creator'. 'Lucifer' is also referred to as Satan and the Devil which are described in the Bible in reptilian terms as with the 'Great Dragon' and 'that ancient serpent'. In turn Cult bloodlines are human-reptilian hybrids that worship their hidden masters through *Satanism*. I expose in *The Trigger* the Sabbatian-Frankism network within the Cult that was really responsible for 9/11. This aspect of the Cult is named after its inspirations, Sabbatai Zevi (1626-1676) and Jacob Frank (1726-1791), as I mentioned earlier. Sabbatian-Frankism hates Judaism and Jewishness and yet has manipulated itself into control of Israel and its global nexus while the great majority of Jewish people have no idea Sabbatian-Frankism even exists. We have the familiar theme of Lucifer worship with Jacob Frank who said Lucifer is the true god. The Kabbalah, or Kabala/Cabala, the Jewish bible of mysticism and esoteric belief, is the holy book of Sabbatian-Frankists and in particular the series of works called the Zohar which means 'splendour' and 'radiance' (light). From this came the concept of being 'illuminated' (kundalini activation) and the name of a highly significant grouping within the Cult known as the

Figure 151: The Statue of Liberty was given to New York by French Freemasons in Paris who knew what it really represented.

Figure 152: A mirror of the Statue of Liberty on an island in the River Seine in Paris.

'Illuminati' with its symbol of the 'all-seeing eye' which you see on the dollar bill and the reverse of the Great Seal of the United States (Fig 150). This elite satanic secret society was established in 1776 by three Sabbatian-Frankist cultists, Jacob Frank, Meyer Amstel Rothschild, founder of the Rothschild (Redshield/hexagram/Saturn) financial dynasty, and its frontman, Jesuit-trained fake 'Jew' Adam Weishaupt. The theme of Lucifer the Light Bringer (simulation) is widely on public display if you know what to look for and one example is the Statue of Liberty holding the lighted torch of 'illumination'. The statue was given to New York by French Freemasons in Paris who knew the true meaning and a mirror image 'Liberty' stands on an island in the River Seine in the French capital (Figs 151 and 152). Freemasonry worships Lucifer as the 'Great/Grand Architect of the Universe' – the architect of the simulation. The same symbolism of the 'Architect' can be found in the *Matrix* movies which portrays him as the one who built the Matrix. You'll find all the fine detail on these subjects and so much more in *Everything You Need To Know.*

Simulation science and numbers

Another mainstream scientist who has pursued evidence for a simulation is James Gates, an American theoretical physicist who has been Professor of Physics at the University of Maryland, Director of The Center for String and Particle Theory, and served on the Council of Advisors on Science and Technology to President Obama. A Gates-led team discovered computer codes of digital data embedded in the energetic fabric of our reality which take the form of 1 and 0 – the binary system used in computers of on-off electrical charges which looks so similar to codes of the Matrix in the movies and the A, C, G, and T codes that make up DNA and also have binary values (Figs 153 and 154). These codes and their relationships with each other decide what the 'physical' form looks like. Differences in coding between a human and rat are marginal yet their form is fundamentally different. DNA codes have digital binary values of A and C = 0 and G and T = 1. DNA code sequences look like binary number coding and the numbers on the computer screens in the *Matrix* movie series depicting the digital

Figure 153: Binary codes of 0 and 1 representing on off electrical charges in computer systems.

```
CCCAACACCCAAATATGGCTCGAGAAGGGCAGCGACATTCCTGCGGGGTGGCGCGGAGGGAATGCCC
GCGGGCTATATAAAACCTGAGCAGAGGGACAAGCGGCCACCGCAGCGGACAGCGCCAAGTGAAGCCT
CGCTTCCCCTCCGCGGCGACCAGGGCCCGAGCCGAGAGTAGCAGTTGTAGCTACCCGCCCAGGTAGG
GCAGGAGTTGGGAGGGGACAGGGGGACAGGGCACTACCGAGGGGAACCTGAAGGACTCCGGGGCAGA
ACCCAGTCGGTTCACCTGGTCAGCCCCAGGCCTCGCCCTGAGCGCTGTGCCTCGTCTCCGGAGCCAC
ACGCGCTTTAAAAAGGAGGCAAGACAGTCAGCCTCTGGAAATTAGACTTCTCCAAATTTTTCTCTAG
CCCTTTGGGCTCCTTTACCTGGCATGTAGGATGTGCCTAGGGAGATAAACGGTTTTGCTTTAGTTGT
CGCCAAGGCAGTTCCCTTCCAAACTAGCGCTAGAGCGAATGAGCGAGCAGCCAGGACCACCATTCTG
GGTTTCCAACAGGCGAAAAGGCCCTTTCTGAGTTTGAAATGTCACAGGGTTCCTAACAGGCCACTCT
TCCCTGGATGGGGTGCCAACGCCTTTCCCATGGGCATCTCCTTCCACCCTCACGCTGGCCCAGCAAG
CAGGCAGTGCTGAGGGCCTTATCTCCCTAGGTGACAGATGTGGTCAGGGAGGCGCAGAGAGGATGGGC
ACTAGCGTCCAGCTCCTGGAACAGGTGTCAGGCAGGGAGGGCAGACAGGTCTTGGGAACATGTTCCC
CTGGCTATGTGGACAGAGGACTTCTCAGTGGGTCTCGCGACCCTGTGCCCCTTTTCCTGGTTCAGGG
CAGCCTTAGCCGGGGCAAAGGTCGAGAAGAGAACCCCTGGTCGCCGCCCTGGCAGAATTTGAGTGGC
TCCGGCAGGAGATGTCCCTAGGTTCCTGGGGAGGGAGGACGTCGGGGCCAGCCAGGCTTACCCCCCC
CTGCCGCTGAGACTTCTGCGCTGATGCACCCGCGCCTCTTCGCGGTCTCCCTGTCCTTGCAGAAACTA
GACACAATGTGCGACGAAGACGAGACCACCGCCCTCGTGTGCGACAATGGCTCCGGCCTGGTGAAAG
CCGGCTTCGCCGGGGATGACGCCCCTAGGGCCGTGTTCCCGTCCATCGTGGGCCGCCCCCGACACCA
GGTCAGGCTGCCCCTCCGCAGAGGGAGCCGGCTCGGGGTCCCCGCGTAAGCCAGCCTGGTGCCACC
```

Figure 154: The A, C, G and T codes of DNA which also have binary values.

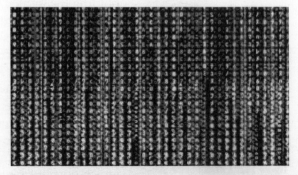

Figure 155: The digital codes of the Matrix portrayed on computer screens in the movie series.

basis of the reality simulation (Fig 155). James Gates said they had no idea what digital computer codes were doing in the fabric of our reality, but this can be explained if we are dealing with a simulation. The Gates team also found error-correcting codes or block codes within the energetic fabric of reality. These are mathematical sequences employed in computers that return data to its original state or 'default settings' when something knocks it out of kilter. They would be necessary to hold the simulation together in the face of forces impacting upon it. Gates said they found a set of equations embedded in reality that were indistinguishable from those that drive search engines and browsers. The Internet and digital technology in general are actually mimicking the simulation to create a simulation within a simulation and enslave human Body-Mind in more extreme states of illusion and isolation than even the main simulation itself. I have said already that one level of our reality – the simulation – is digital and that the 'physical' world from the Universe downwards consists of digital holograms. Numerology reads reality at this level of numbers and Max Tegmark, a physicist at the Massachusetts Institute of Technology (MIT), said: 'The Universe can be entirely described by numbers and maths.' Tegmark, author of *Our Mathematical Universe*, says reality is encoded with numbers and

Figure 156: The physics and mathmatics of video games and virtual reality is the same as our experienced reality.

mathematics in the same way as computer games and the physics of our reality and computer games are basically the same (Fig 156). He compares human experience with characters in advanced games. The characters would think because of the software codes that they were bumping into real objects, falling in love and feeling emotions. Eventually they might study the workings of the game more deeply and realise that everything (as with our reality on one level) was made of pixels. They would see that what they thought was 'physical' was in fact just numbers. Tegmark then relates this to human reality:

> And we're exactly in this situation in our world. We look around and it doesn't seem that mathematical at all, but everything we see is made out of elementary particles like quarks and electrons. And what properties does an electron have? Does it have a smell or a colour or a texture? No! ... We

physicists have come up with geeky names for [electron] properties, like electric charge, or spin, or lepton number, but the electron doesn't care what we call it, the properties are just numbers.

Everything these scientists are uncovering is what you would expect to see if we live in some sort of simulation. There is also the ancient concept of 'divine proportion' which is the term given to mathematical and geometrical sequences found throughout our reality, the 'natural' world and the human body (holographic as above, so below, once again). Initiates of the hidden knowledge understood these sequences and gave them names such as Phi, Pi, Golden Mean, Golden Ratio and Golden Section. They encoded them into their temples, cathedrals and important buildings to attract – entangle – with particular energies/information and frequencies to connect them with 'God', or 'the gods'. Artists like the initiate Leonardo Da Vinci encoded these proportions or ratios into their paintings. Da Vinci was so 'ahead of his time' because he understood reality by tapping into awareness outside the simulation and he would have had close associations with secret societies. The number of Golden Ratio is 1.61803398874989484820 ... which then goes on repeating indefinitely. Golden Ratio proportion comes from 'dividing a line into two parts so that the longer part divided by the smaller part is also equal to the whole length divided by the longer part'. Put simply it is a sequence that can be found everywhere and is obviously there by design and not chance. Another ubiquitous sequence is the Fibonacci number code which was identified at least in ancient India by a mathematician called Virahanka, but gets its name from the 12th/13th century Italian mathematician Fibonacci also known as Leonardo of Pisa. The Fibonacci sequence adds the two previous numbers to get the next one, as with ... 1, 1, 2, 3, 5, 8, 13, 21, 34, 55, and so on. The higher it goes the closer it gets to the Golden Ratio. The Fibonacci sequence is encoded in everything from the human face and body to animals, DNA, seed heads, pine cones, trees, shells, spiral galaxies, hurricanes and the number of petals in a flower (Figs 157 and 158). Then we have fractal patterns encoded in the fabric of reality and once again they are everywhere. Fractals are a 'never-ending pattern that is infinitely complex and self-similar across

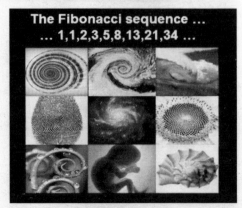

Figure 157: The Fibonacci number sequence can be found throughout our reality.

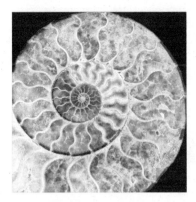

Figure 158: Fibonacci numbers are encoded in the ways that shells form.

Figure 159: Repeating holographic fractal patterns are found everywhere.

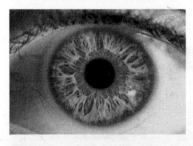

Figure 160: Fractal patterns are found in the torus of the human eye.

Figure 161: Binary DNA.

different scales' – the as above, so below, characteristics of holograms (Figs 159 and 160). Fractal patterns can be found in:

River networks, mountain ranges, craters, lightning bolts, coastlines, mountain goat horns, trees and branch growth, animal colour patterns, pineapples, heart rates, heartbeats, neurons and brains, eyes, respiratory systems, circulatory systems, blood vessels and pulmonary vessels, DNA, geological fault lines, earthquakes, snowflakes, crystals, ocean waves, vegetables, soil pores and even the rings of Saturn (again).

Fractal/holographic patterns are found in binary 1 and 0 on-off electrical charges encoded in our energetic reality that are also found in the DNA receiver-transmitter 'hard drive' of the body (Fig 161). A science paper captured the essence of DNA with its heading: 'DNA is a Fractal Antenna in Electromagnetic Fields.' DNA is a receiver-transmitter of information and is digital, binary, holographic and fractal because our experienced reality is digital, binary, holographic and fractal. American psychology professor David Pincus has said that as above, so below, repeating fractal patterns have been identified in psychology, behaviour, speech patterns and interpersonal relationships which begs the question of how much human behaviour comes from 'free will' and how much from simply following the simulation program? I'll have more about this later. Fractal principles relate to 'symmetrical mathematics' which are 'one shape being exactly like another' when you move it, turn it, flip it or slide

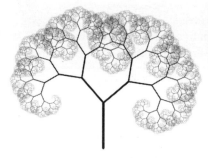

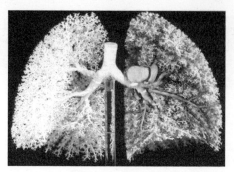

Figure 162: The way a tree grows follows fractal patterns.

Figure 163: Fractal patterns in the human lung.

it. Symmetrical mathematics are found in everything from the way trees grow to the structure of the human lung (Figs 162 and 163). Dmitri Krioukov, a physicist at the University of California, San Diego, was co-author of a study reported in *Nature's Scientific Reports* which suggested that 'undiscovered and fundamental laws' may govern the growth of systems on all levels from electrical firing between brain cells to the growth of social networks and expansion of galaxies' (the holographic principle *yet again*). Krioukov said: 'Natural growth dynamics are the same for different real networks, like the Internet or the brain or social networks.' He added that 'for a physicist it's an immediate signal that there is some missing understanding of how nature works.' What's missing is the understanding that we are dealing with a holographic simulation. The work of Krioukov and his team was reported by the *Huffington Post*:

> When the team compared the Universe's history with growth of social networks and brain circuits, they found all the networks expanded in similar ways: They balanced links between similar nodes with ones that already had many connections.
>
> For instance, a cat lover surfing the Internet may visit mega-sites such as Google or Yahoo, but will also browse cat fancier websites or YouTube kitten videos. In the same way, neighboring brain cells like to connect, but neurons also link to such 'Google brain cells' that are hooked up to loads of other brain cells. The eerie similarity between networks large and small is unlikely to be a coincidence, Krioukov said.

What are all these recurring mathematical sequences that pervade our reality? I say they are the *computer codes* of the simulation (Figs 164 and 165). I watched a presentation by Donald Hoffman, a professor in the Department of Cognitive Sciences at the University of California, Irvine, in which he described his concept of our experienced reality

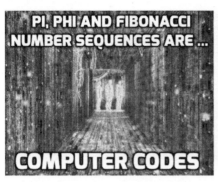

Figure 164: Bingo! Computer codes of the simulation.

Figure 165: Bingo! Computer codes of the simulation.

acting like a computer interface which I agree that it does:

> Evolution shaped us with a user interface that hides the truth. Nothing that we see is the truth – the very language of space and time and objects is the wrong language to describe reality.

I contend that it was not evolution which shaped this, but manipulation. The computer interface – the equivalent of a computer screen – is the simulation which gives a false sense of reality to hide the fact that it *is* a simulation.

Electric Universe (simulation)

A major pointer to a simulation comes with a highly-compelling area of independent scientific research that reveals the Universe to be an electrical/electromagnetic communication system which is how computers and virtual reality work. The research is known collectively and appropriately as the Electric Universe and also the Thunderbolts Project. I have been reading and watching their information for many years and you can find them at www.thunderbolts.info/wp. Everything from the Universe to the human body/brain is on one level an electrical/electromagnetic communication system. The electrical nature of the atmosphere can clearly be seen in lightning, the Aurora Borealis or northern lights, and the rapidly-rotating electromagnetic fields of tornadoes that appear during electrical storms (Figs 166 and 167 overleaf). The electrical fabric of our reality, however, goes much deeper than that. Electricity and electromagnetism pervade everything and Electric Universe researchers say that planets and stars are points or 'devices' in a colossal electrical circuitry that we experience as reality and see as the night sky (Figs 168 and 169 overleaf). The electrical impact on this circuitry of planets, stars and their combinations is another level of how astrology works and all together I call this the Cosmic Internet

Figure 166: Lightning is the most obvious example of an electric atmosphere.

Figure 167: The electrical phenomena of the Northern Lights or Aurora Borealis.

Figure 168: We see the heavens as stars and planets and space, but that's only one level.

Figure 169: On another level the Universe – or simulation – is a vast electrical system.

Figure 170: The simulation is an electrical/electromagnetic system which interacts with the human body and brain and overlays a fake reality to obscure prime reality. I call it the Cosmic Internet. (Image Neil Hague.)

(Fig 170). I have said that the Sun is much bigger than it appears to the eye and that its wavefield oscillates throughout the solar system. This is also true of the Sun's electrical circuits and communication systems. Electric Universe researchers have been pointing this out for a long time and official science confirmation of this electrical connection grid is beginning to mount. *The Astrophysical Journal* published a study in 2019 describing how hundreds of galaxies are acting and rotating in synchronised motions even with those tens of millions of light years away (the illusion of time and space). The study involved 445 galaxies within 400 million light years of Earth. Joon Hyeop Lee, an astronomer at the Korea Astronomy and Space Science Institute, said that something appeared to be connecting them which caused them to

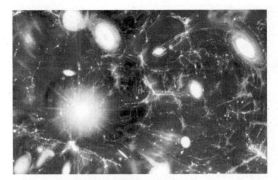

Figure 171: Galaxies are 'embedded in the same 'large scale structure' – the simulation.

behave exactly in sync. In some way they 'directly interact with each other', he said. The study suggested that the galaxies appeared to be embedded in the same 'large scale structure'. Yes – the electrical/electromagnetic grid of the Cosmic Internet or what I say is the simulation (Fig 171).

Computer virtual reality is connected by the same codes and electrical communication which makes what appears on the screen happen in sync. Joon said: 'The dynamical coherence even out to millions of light-years was unexpected and surprising to us, because such distances are obviously too far for neighbour galaxies to directly interact with each other. The unifying force remained invisible or in other words outside the frequency band of human and technological sight. Then there is David Sibeck, a project scientist at NASA's Goddard Space Flight Center, who revealed satellite confirmation of these electrical/electromagnetic connections:

> The satellites have found evidence of magnetic ropes connecting Earth's upper atmosphere directly to the Sun. We believe that solar winds flow in along these ropes providing energy for geomagnetic storms and auroras.

Sun-Earth connections, wavefield and electrical, are what changes our climate and temperature in cycles of power increasing and decreasing. These cycles are revealed in the number of fantastic explosions of energy on the Sun's surface known as sunspots. This phenomenon is not factored into the manipulated 'climate models' devised purely to sell the hoax of human-caused climate change. The outrageous deceit is confirmed by climate projections that don't centrally include the foundation effect on temperature of the *Sun* while blaming carbon dioxide, the gas of life, without which we would all be dead (*much* more later). The Sun is electrical in nature and highly significantly the observable Universe is 99.999 percent plasma – so is the Sun. Plasma is often called the fourth state of matter and represents a near-perfect medium for ... *electricity and electromagnetism*. The plasma Sun is a *processor* of electrical power and not the origin of it. Solar power does not come from within the Sun as mainstream science claims from assumption, not evidence. It comes from the universal electrical wavefield or circuitry. If you could see the heavens on another level of

frequency you would see
a vast electrical system
with the stars and
planets as points in the
circuit that pervades the
Universe. The Sun
absorbs and processes
power from this system
which operates in cycles
of higher power and
lower power just as
waves (of all kinds) have
peaks and troughs (Fig
172). Electrical power is
processed by the Sun
(not created by it) and

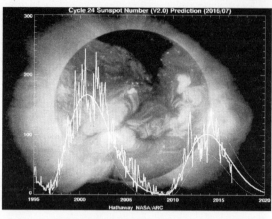

Figure 172: Solar power rises and falls in cycles and can be measured by the number of sunspots or massive explosions on the sun which project energy into the solar system.

projected into the solar system affecting temperature, climate and much else within the planetary fields. These projections are decoded by the Earth's atmosphere and magnetic field into the heat that we feel. Space is cold and the higher you go in the Earth's atmosphere the colder it gets when, through mainstream scientific 'logic', it should be getting warmer as you move closer to the Sun. Why are planets nearer the Sun hotter, then? The closer you are the more powerful the energy to be decoded into heat and that is also affected by the nature of their fields. The Sun is much cooler on the surface than way out in its atmosphere when it

should be the other way round if
the heat is being generated from
within. Mainstream science
estimates the Sun's surface
temperature to around 5,000
degrees kelvin while much
further out the temperature is
said to be 200 *million* degrees
kelvin. Encircling the Sun a
considerable distance from the
surface is a doughnut-shaped
torus which has been recorded in
ultraviolet images (Fig 173). The
Sun's torus at its equator absorbs
electricity from the universal
circuit for the Sun to process.
When it overloads massive
versions of lightning are
projected to punch holes in the

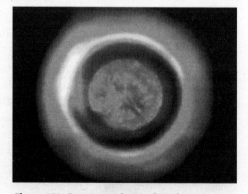

Figure 173: Sunspot explosions have been believed to originate inside the Sun, but Electric Universe researchers say the torus around the Sun absorbs electricity from The Field which goes through cycles of higher and lower power. When the torus becomes overloaded at high times it discharges energy like colossal lightning bolts that strike the Sun and punch the sunspots thus making sunspots a measure of solar activity.

Sun's surface that we know as sunspots. They are a pointer to the changing electrical power of the Sun because the torus only overloads and punches them at times of high power in the circuit. The Sun is known to dim in its low period of activity (electrical processing) although this is imperceptible to the human eye. Think dimmer switch. NASA reported in 2019 that predictions suggest the cycle of solar activity between 2020 and 2025 could be the lowest in 200 years and 30 to 50 percent lower than the previous one. Mainstream science is being forced to face the facts about the universal electrical system as evidence continually comes to light. Haimin Wang, a professor of physics at the New Jersey Institute of Technology, said of sunspot activity:

> We used to think that the surface's magnetic evolution drives solar eruptions [sunspots]. Our new observations suggest that disturbances created in the solar outer atmosphere can also cause direct and significant perturbations on the surface through magnetic fields, a phenomenon not envisioned by any contemporary solar eruption models.

The Earth's magnetic field, or magnetosphere, is defined by the interaction of electricity with plasma (ultimately wavefield state with wavefield state). When plasma conducting electricity of one frequency/charge meets plasma with a different charge a barrier is automatically formed between the two which defines planetary magnetic fields. Planets and stars emit different electrical charges into the plasma medium and where these different fields meet the barrier is

formed known as a 'Langmuir sheath' after American scientist Irving Langmuir (1881-1957) who discovered the phenomenon (Fig 174). Here is still more proof that planets and stars transmit different frequencies that form the basis of astrology. Increasing numbers of scientists are now seeing that the evidence points to our 'physical' reality being a holographic simulation as I concluded nearly 20 years

Figure 174: Planetary magnetospheres are formed by the resistance between different electrical charges in the plasma field between the planets and the wider solar system.

ago. Where I differ from these scientists is that they seem to see the simulation as external to us. My view is that in the form we experience as 'physical' reality the 'Matrix' only exists when we decode it into manifestation in the brain. The holographic level of reality is within us and not external to us. If we revisit what I said earlier about the human decoding system we can bring that together with electrical reality. The foundation information construct of the simulation is information encoded in waves and when this is decoded it becomes an electrical and digital/holographic reality. See how this fits perfectly with the five senses decoding waves into electrical information communicated to the brain to become digital/holographic information and perceived 'physical' reality. The Universe has wavefield, electrical, digital and holographic levels and so do human decoding processes. *Both are expressions of the same simulated system.*

Who created the simulation?

This all has revelatory implications for how the simulation was created by the non-human force behind the Cult and for the nature of our experienced reality. There are other levels of the Earth that operate on a far higher frequency band which means we can't see them. Many near-death experiencers have described this high-frequency Earth with its incredibly vivid colours they had never seen before. They are manifestations of the much higher frequencies that exist outside the perceptual confines of the Body-Mind simulation. Shamans and seers have talked since ancient times of this other 'Earth' as have those who have experienced psychoactive potions. 'Other Earth' reality existed before the simulation and continues to do so. Its high frequency means it is far less energetically dense which makes far more possible and negates the need for 'physical' food. Energetic sustenance is taken directly from the energetic field. Communication is by telepathy rather than voice and people can transport themselves by thought rather than having to 'physically' walk, drive or fly in aircraft. Why do they need planes when they themselves can fly with their lack of human-like density? High-frequency Earth is the planet's prime reality although it's still just a micro-fraction of Infinite reality. The biblical story of the 'Fallen Angels' and their 'revolt from God' (a theme repeated in non-biblical cultures throughout the ancient world) is really the story of the simulation. 'Fallen Angels' lost their heart-centre connection to *The One* to such an extent that they fell down the frequencies (hence 'fallen') and believed they were the 'gods' ruled by their master 'God' that Cultists know as Lucifer the Light Bringer – the bringer of the simulation formed from 'light' within the speed of light. The 'Fall of Man' refers to those in Prime Earth who the Fallen Ones enticed and manipulated down the frequencies with them. Prime Earth is what the Bible calls 'Eden' and humans left the 'garden' to be trapped in density and the false perceptions of self and reality that come from that. These are the same 'fallen' entities that the Cult and Satanists are connecting with in their rituals and the inner circle members of the Cult are incarnate 'Fallen Angels' hiding behind biological AI software 'human form'.

The Fallen Ones set about creating their own world to entrap indefinitely Prime Earth awareness that would become their slaves in a form called 'mind'. They created the simulation – a wave/digital copy of Prime Earth. I say this is described at the start of Genesis with 'God' making the world in 'seven days' after the declaration 'Let there be *Light*'. The Cult's central modus operandi is the technique of inversion to sell a perception of everything that's the opposite of what it really is. What a perfect example it would be for '*the* God' of the Old Testament to be the very 'Lucifer', 'Satan', 'Devil', that '*the* God' is supposed to 'fight'. Heads you worship Lucifer, tails you worship Lucifer. Ever wondered why the 'god' of the Old Testament is portrayed so differently to the 'god' of the New? Christianity's attempt to present them both as the same entity makes no sense whatsoever. I have concluded after 30 years of research into all these related subjects that the simulation is a wavefield information construct (think Wi-Fi) with a human body that can decode the construct, interact with it (think computer), and perceive it as reality. I have been referring to the body for decades as a biological computer. Carl Sagan's statement about humans being made of 'star stuff' – the carbon, nitrogen and oxygen atoms, etc. of stars – is another as above, so below, confirmation. Chris Impey, professor of astronomy at the University of Arizona, said that because humans, animals and most 'matter' on Earth contain these elements 'we are literally made of star stuff'. Look at this from the simulation perspective and you get the same story from a different route. Are characters in a computer game encoded with different maths and rules to the rest of the game? Are they made of different 'stuff'? No, and it's the same with the simulation and the human body specifically created by the Cult 'gods' to interact with the simulation. They are encoded with the same basic codes in their wavefields and express that through the 'star stuff' comparison in their holographic 'physical' state. The creation of the body-computer is told symbolically in the story of 'God' creating 'Adam' and 'Eve' along with the reference to the sons of 'God' (the gods, plural in the original) interbreeding with the daughters of men. We don't have to be talking here of literal interbreeding through procreation. The body can be changed by broadcasting frequencies of information which the hard-drive, receiver-transmitter DNA decodes into holographic mutations through changes in the wavefield (5G, 6G, 7G?). A Russian research team transformed frog embryos into salamander embryos by transmitting salamander DNA information patterns. Dr Michael Levin at Tufts University in Massachusetts produced tadpoles with eyes on their backs and frogs with six legs by manipulating their electrical communication systems. Levin believes the same technique could be used on humans to regrow lost limbs. So much becomes possible once the Cult illusions are breached and the true nature of reality is grasped. The human body is a wave/digital copy of the forms in Prime Earth reality and far, far denser and more limited in nature. It does mean, however, that the Cult and its masters have had to leave in place many functions of the original form that allow awakening awareness to connect with expanded consciousness outside the simulation. The whole 'smart' technology and AI agenda is about deleting those connections by creating a new human form connected even more powerfully to the simulation and I'll have much more later about this.

Come again? *Mmm* ... no thanks

The simulation or Matrix is an artificially-generated field of information that has been overlaid on The Field or Infinite Field. Humanity has been manipulated to connect and interact with this artificial field or Matrix and perceive it as reality. Today's 'smart' technology and Wi-Fi are overlaying *another* even more limited field over the main simulation field to further disconnect humanity from *The* Field. This could only be done once humans had developed intellectually to the point where they could build and operate such technology, but what is happening has been in the planning for thousands of years in our perception of 'time' (again much more later). The sequence goes like this: Create the wavefield/digital information construct as a copy of Prime Earth; create forms, human, animal, etc., which are wave-entangled with the construct; entice consciousness to make a wave entanglement with those forms ('incarnate'). A key aspect to the enticement is the unique sensations of the five senses which are very different from Prime Reality and appear to act like a drug addiction. People become addicted to virtual reality games and the frequencies emitting from smartphones while consciousness can become addicted to the sensations of the five senses. These addictions create a wave entanglement with the simulation that pulls consciousness in the form of mind back into five sense reality over and over and this is known as reincarnation. Eastern religions believe in the cycle of reincarnation and 'karma' in which we continually incarnate on Earth to work through the 'karmic cycle' of actions-consequences-actions-consequences until, through trial and error, we reach a frequency state ('enlightenment') high enough to escape that cycle and gravitate to Prime Reality. Mainstream science estimates that the Earth when compared with the perceived extent of the Universe is the equivalent of a billionth the size of a pinhead (Fig 175). Do we really believe that to 'evolve' we have to keep incarnating over and over onto a planet a billionth the size of a pinhead compared with the Universe which itself is a fractional smear of Infinite Reality? That's crazy. From my perspective there is another way to explain this. You are

'A BILLIONTH THE SIZE OF A PIN HEAD'

Figure 175: To 'evolve' and find 'enlightenment' we have to keep incarnating onto a pin-head-sized planet over and over while ignoring the rest of Infinity. Yep, makes absolute sense, right? Or we only do it once and then 'God' judges us. What utter crap we are told to believe and so many do.

enticed into the simulation; you become addicted to the sensations of the simulation like people become addicted to computer games; you leave the body when its cycle ends, but you are still addicted (therefore deeply wave-entangled) with the simulation that it draws you back again and again (flies to a light, bees to a honeypot). This continues until you work out the illusion and in doing so raise your frequency to the level of vibration (through the heart) that allows you to escape the electromagnetic pull of the simulation. 'Reincarnation' does not *have* to happen – *we* make it so with encouragement and manipulation from the hidden 'gods'. We can escape the Matrix anytime we want by realising it's a flytrap and by remembering who and what we really are. Academic neurosurgeon Eben Alexander describes how in his near-death experience he first entered a dark realm of heavy vibration which he perceived as deep mud. He felt trapped and unable to free himself until an entity came to take him out. Once in Prime Reality when he realised his true self, and his frequency increased in sync with that, he said he was able to enter and leave the 'dark place' whenever he chose if you believe his account. Whether people do or not the theme is correct.

Reincarnation advocates say we select the body, situation and 'time' (astrology) of 'incarnation' to best suit the experience we wish to have. I say this can also be explained by the mind's state of wavefield frequency entangling with other wavefields – bodies, situations, locations and astrological fields – that best suit (a) what it wants to experience and/or (b) what its wave entanglements draw the mind into purely by its wavefield attaching to like fields. What we come into and what we go out to is decided by our wavefield state which is decided by our *perceptual* state. Another relevant question with regard to this: Do addicts make choices about what they are addicted to? They are not in control – their addiction is. For those minds addicted to the five-senses of the simulation the 'Matrix' is in control. The point of this book is to offer the tools to free ourselves from that addiction which holds much of humanity in perceptual and five-sense servitude to the alleged 'karmic cycle'. We should not forget there is quite a common theme with near-death experiences of a point, sometimes symbolised as a fence or wall, that they say if they pass they cannot return to their body in that particular 'life'. By the very fact that they come back to tell the tale they don't cross that line. They don't know what lies beyond it. For sure Infinite Reality lies beyond, but is there also a realm from which minds still wave-attached and addicted to the simulation return here? I think there is and that is why our frequency state at 'death' is so important. I suggest that the great majority of even genuine psychics are accessing that realm with their 'I'm getting a Mary, anyone know a Mary?' communications. Only the most open and expanded attune to frequencies high enough for the really profound information to be passed through that is free of simulation manipulation and perspective. Addiction to the simulation has become so ingrained through this cycle with each new addiction increasing previous addiction that an intervention is being directed from Prime Reality to break the cycle. I'll have more about this in the final chapter.

During my ayahuasca experience in 2003 I was shown a picture of a path across a field and then people began falling from the sky onto the path. As they walked in ever greater numbers they wore down the path which morphed into the dark groove of one of the old vinyl records. The people in the darkness just followed the grove and where it took them (round and round). The Voice said over the pictures that humanity fell so easily for the programming in each 'incarnation' because they had been through it many times before. 'She' asked from the groove perspective if it was really so strange that people looked upwards for 'God' when it was the only direction they could see 'light'. I have one other point about 'reincarnation'. You hear people say when they have particular traits or something happens to them that 'I must have been bad in a previous life' or 'it must be my karma'. In reality, it may have nothing to do with either although the basic like-frequency entanglement principle still stands. We inherit body wavefields encoded with the emotional states and traits of others. I have described the passing on of epigenetic on-off gene sequences caused by the wavefield interactions of 'previous generations'. These can be 'physical', mental and emotional. A person feeling bad about themselves today because they are overweight no matter how they diet may have inherited the epigenetic gene sequence from someone who was a fast-food freak consuming toxic shite that switched on genes that pile on weight. This is happening to incredible numbers of people in the fast food era. An apparently irrational fear that makes no sense to a person's experience in this lifetime does not always have to be 'past life' related. It can be a bad experience relating to that fear involving someone in the genetic line which is still encoded in the body field and triggers an apparently inexplicable emotional reaction to particular situations. Consciousness can delete these programs as I'll be explaining.

Cult vampires and Agent Smith

Cult bloodlines (hybrid Fallen Angel/human wavefields) that I have been exposing for decades are the simulation's 'Agent Smiths'. He is the character in the *Matrix* movies who manipulates events in the simulation on behalf of those in the unseen that created the Matrix (Fig 176). This is the role of the bloodlines that run The Web of secret, semi-secret and public organisations and institutions (including politics and government) to advance the agenda for total human control dictated by the Luciferian Fallen invisible to human sight. Agent Smith is an artificial intelligence program that can replicate itself into multiple Smiths. I say that the major Cult operatives in our world are also biological software programs or AI that are seeking via AI to take over everything by connecting humanity to AI. To the Cult and its 'gods' the biological is a form of technology. One of the goals is to vampire low-vibrational mental and emotional energy emitted by humans who the

Figure 176: Agent Smith in *The Matrix* symbolised Cult operatives within the simulation manipulating events for their unseen 'gods'. Smith was a computer program or what we would call today artificial intelligence – so are the major Cult operatives running our world.

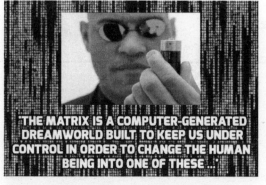

Figure 177: In the same way humanity is the power source of the Cult's hidden 'gods'. The more low-vibrational mental and emotional waves we produce the better for them.

Cult has manipulated into low-vibrational mental and emotional states. *The Matrix* movies symbolised this with the Morpheus character holding up a battery and saying the 'machines' (the Fallen Ones symbolically) had turned humans into batteries to empower themselves (Fig 177). I have heard the same theme from shamans and carriers of ancient knowledge all over the world. The Fallen Ones have closed their heart centres to the energy flow of *The One* to such an extent that they have had to develop their own sources of energy that match their own low-vibrational state. Humanity is one such source. The game is to entrap human perceptions and manipulate conflict, fear, anxiety, depression, hatred, despair, guilt, resentment and regret so mercilessly and incessantly that immense waves of low-frequency energy are transmitted for the Fallen Ones to absorb and feed off (Fig 178). When we stop generating these frequencies on the scale that we do the energy source is disconnected and the manipulators are correspondingly weakened (another benefit of opening

Figure 178: The Cult's unseen 'gods' feed off human low-frequency energy especially fear, anxiety, hatred, resentment, regret, and other such emotional states. (Image Neil Hague.)

the heart). Cult-controlled Disney released the movie *Monsters, Inc* in 2001 which portrayed a 'monster world' that had no energy source. They overcame this by entering the human realm to terrify children. Screams of the kids were caught in a tube device and the energy transferred to the 'monster' power system. The hero was depicted with one giant (all-seeing) eye (Fig 179). Satanic rituals making sacrifices 'to the gods' through the ages and still today are sacrifices specifically aimed at generating a rush of terror for 'the gods' to absorb. The rituals are designed to create maximum terror in the target in the run up to the sacrifice as a 'gift' or 'offering' to 'the gods'. All the 'sacrifice to the gods' shite comes from this. While the 'gods' are absorbing the wavefield level of the terror outside visible light the Satanists drink the blood which contains that same terror in the form of adrenalin. The Fallen are energy vampires and their Cult gofers are blood vampires. The 'gods' prefer children as sacrifices because

Figure 179: The main all-seeing eye character in Disney's *Monsters, Inc* in which the monsters powered their world with the fear of human children.

of the particular frequencies of pre-pubescent children. Paedophilia rings connect at their core with satanic rings for the same reason. While

possessed paedophiles are having sex with children the wave
entanglements from the child to the paedophile and through to the
possessing entity allow the entity to draw off and absorb the child's
energy. So many rich and famous Cult operatives and bloodlines I have
researched in royalty, politics, banking, business, intelligence agencies,
military, law enforcement and 'entertainment' are connected to both
paedophilia and Satanism. Are we really so naive that we think it's just a
coincidence that Jimmy Savile, the UK mega-paedophile and procurer of
children for the rich and famous, had deep and decades-long inner-circle
connections with the Cult bloodline British Royal family and Prince
Charles in particular? Or that Savile was brought into the royal fold in
the 1960s by Lord Mountbatten, a known paedophile and Prince Charles
mentor? Or that Prince Andrew's close friendship with Sabbatian-
Frankist Cult and Israeli Mossad agent, mega-paedophile and child
procurer, Jeffrey Epstein, was more random chance? Or that UK Prime
Minister Margaret Thatcher was a close friend of Savile in an
administration that protected known paedophiles? Oh, *please*.

Maintaining Body-Mind humanity in low-frequency states of
programmed ignorance is not only about feeding off our energy. The
simulation is a band of frequency and to hold Body-Mind in perceptual
servitude and illusion we must be entangled with the simulation
through body, mind and emotions, and that means staying within its
frequency band. From this we have had the age-old targeting of anyone
who expands their awareness beyond that perceptual prison and sees
the truth. The Cult created religions which insisted that everyone
believed what they said on pain of death. 'Witches' (psychics) were
drowned and 'blasphemers' of every kind were burned or in other ways
mass-murdered. The Inquisition was a Cult operation to protect its
control of human perception and when people began to turn away from
religion the Cult instigated mainstream science to keep the truth about
reality from the masses while continuing to pass on the hidden
knowledge to each generation of the Cult 'elite'. This new religion called
science has been policed by another inquisition for would-be scientists,
academics and doctors in which they follow the prescribed 'truth' or
find another job. Mainstream science is the same religion blueprint
under another name. Scientism has its own holy books ('scientific
orthodoxy'), imposes its beliefs through the 'education' system (just like
religious schools), and through the mainstream and much of the
'alternative' media. All use holy Scientism orthodoxy as their point of
reference for 'how things are' even though most of this is way off the
mark (Fig 180 overleaf). Where once people were killed for seeing the
truth outside the simulation (though many still are) the weapons of
choice in the West today are ridicule, condemnation and censorship by
Cult-owned Google, YouTube, Facebook, Twitter, and all the rest. They

HOLD ON, I'M GETTING SOMETHING

AH, YES - BULLSHIT

Figure 180: Yep, I'm getting some more. Plenty to come.

are the modern face of the Inquisition and Nazi book-burners along with government agencies targeting alternative methods of healing based on knowledge denied by Scientism's religious dogma (the Cult).

Where are the 'aliens'?

Given the extent of the night sky alone in terms of stars and planets why isn't the Galaxy/Universe that we 'see' (decode) teeming with life? By the law of averages alone it should be. The ancients in cultures all over the world described non-human visitations. Rock and cave paintings dated to thousands of years ago feature images remarkably similar to those reported in the modern world by people claiming to have seen, or been abducted by, non-human entities. They clearly exist so why not make themselves openly visible to everyone? Italian physicist Enrico Fermi (1901-1954), who created the first nuclear reactor, asked this question and it became known as the Fermi Paradox. American astrophysicist Michael Hart studied the mystery and wrote an article for the *Royal Astronomical Society Quarterly Journal* in 1975 entitled 'An Explanation for the Absence of Extraterrestrials on Earth'. He concluded that the mystery had these possible explanations: (1) Aliens never came because of something 'that makes space travel unfeasible'; (2) aliens chose not to come to Earth; (3) advanced civilizations arose too recently for aliens to reach us; (4) aliens have visited Earth but we didn't see them. I would add another: The Fallen Ones behind the simulation don't want humanity to interact with extraterrestrials that would open their minds to the scale and nature of reality. They want us to believe we are alone (*alone* – isolated, disconnected). What would happen if people became consciously aware of non-human civilisations who came to impart knowledge that has been kept from us? Human minds would fly open and Cult control of perception would be over. Open visitations from benevolent and advanced extraterrestrials is the last thing the Fallen want and given they have so much control over the gateways to the simulation they can overwhelmingly stop that although not entirely. What they want is a closed system with them controlling the gateways and portals and most of the 'extraterrestrials' that people report (though not all) are reptilian in nature or the classic Greys – both of which are expressions of the Fallen Angels. Malevolent 'Greys' and 'Reptilians' are inserts into the Matrix to serve the Fallen and I believe the classic 'Greys' to be another form of biological/technological artificial intelligence which the Cult wants to connect to the human brain. Still other 'UFO' craft are really flown by humans with the technology developed through technology transfer between the Fallen and Cult operatives in underground bases, or DUMBS (deep underground military bases), run by Cult levels of the military. What is happening in these bases is denied even to elected governments. Make that *especially* to elected governments. The existence of 'flying saucer', or anti-gravity, technology has been widely documented for decades and the scam is to keep from the population and politicians an awareness of technology way beyond the public cutting edge. When people see glimpses of that they will immediately assume it's the work of 'aliens'. American military pilots have described seeing craft moving at speeds and changing direction in ways that are impossible to known human technology. The Pentagon has admitted to having these sightings, some caught on radar, but they refuse to release details of their internal 'investigations'.

Astrological inversion?

What are the chances of such an apparently limitless realm of stars and planets being seemingly devoid of life when life has evolved to the extent that it has on a planet the comparative size of a pinhead? You know, the same pinhead that we have to keep incarnating onto to follow 'God's Plan'. It's all ridiculous … *unless* … the simulation has been specifically encoded to be that way to give target minds the feeling of isolation which confirms we are all alone, a 'Little Me' in every sense. Remember the simulation is a *simulation*, an artificial construct, and its creators can encode information any way they choose just as video game creators do. The scale of the two may be very different, but the theme is exactly the same. Today's virtual reality technology is mimicking the simulation. The Universe and galaxy seems devoid of life, except for us, because the simulation is *made to be* that way. I remember being hit between the eyes in a revelatory sense on my first visit as a child to the then new London Planetarium which opened in 1958. I could have been no more than six or seven. There were many strange things about that trip including the fact that it happened at all. We didn't have much money and travelling anywhere outside my home city of Leicester was very rare in those days even to the seaside. My father came down the stairs that morning and said 'Get ready – we're going to London'. I couldn't believe it. Where did that come from? *London? Wow,* I'd never been there and it would be a long time before I did again. Even stranger is that my father announced we were going to visit the planetarium having shown no interest whatsoever in astronomy before or indeed after. I had no idea what a planetarium was and didn't know what to expect. I clearly remember the moment and the effect it had on me when the lights went down and I saw the night sky projected on the domed ceiling. 'It looks so *real*', I thought'. If someone had said it was night-time and the roof had been removed I would have believed them. The experience struck me so profoundly and I never forgot the moment. I had no idea why until I began to realise that the night-sky *itself* is a holographic projection. Oh, but when spacecraft send back pictures the planets look so real and solid. Of course they do – the decoded simulation is *holographic*. If the planets and stars are a projected holographic construct where does that leave the wave effects on humans measured by astrology? Well, I am going to be controversial here, but then I have been known to be. Where that leaves astrological influences is as … *part of the control program*. These influences are constantly affecting us mentally and emotionally and laying out our life 'path' which is why it is important to expand into beyond-the-simulation consciousness to override astrological influences. Without expanded awareness a human life is the playing out of a software program with many different influences dictating the direction including the astrological. This is not to say that we don't need astrologers or their readings. No, the opposite is true. Skilled astrologers are actually reading the influences of the simulation which is very useful information. I am saying that we need to know what these influences are and by opening our hearts and minds we can tap into the power of consciousness to overcome them when necessary.

Gnostics knew (and they were not alone)

The themes of what I am saying can be found all over the ancient world before Cult religions moved in to make revealing the knowledge a death sentence. This is certainly true of a group of people – a belief system rather than a race – known as Gnostics with their philosophy of Gnosticism. Wherever they located and their information began to spread the Roman Church, the Church of Babylon relocated to Rome by Cult operatives, would send its armies and mobs to destroy them. Most importantly this happened with regard to the Gnostics with the destruction of the Royal or Great Library of Alexandria in Egypt in the 5th century. Gnostic thinkers at the library collected an estimated nearly half a million scrolls, manuscripts and documents detailing ancient history and knowledge from many centres including Egypt, Assyria, Greece, Persia, India, and elsewhere (Fig 181). This was knowledge about history (the arrival of the Fallen Ones) and reality that the Cult-controlled Roman Church did not want to be circulated. Greek philosophers Plato, a pupil of Socrates, and Aristotle were among the inspirations of Hypatia, an Athens-educated mathematician, astronomer and philosopher who was head of the Platonist school in Alexandria. One of her quotes captured the spirit of open-minded inquiry at the

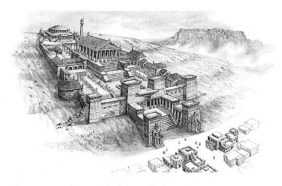

Figure 181: The Royal Library of Alexandria.

Great Library: 'Reserve your right to think, for even to think wrongly is better than not to think at all.' Such commitment to free thought produced revelations about reality thousands of years before modern science 'discovered' them and claimed the credit.

Gnostics in Alexandria knew that the Earth orbits the Sun 2,000 years before Polish mathematician and astronomer, Nicolaus Copernicus, confirmed this. The Cult was not happy with free-minded discovery and the Great Library was destroyed in a series of attacks by the Church. These included the murder of Hypatia in 415AD by a mob under the control of Cyril, Patriarch of Alexandria, who like so many mass killers before and since was made a saint by the Vatican. Gnostics also famously gathered in southern France centuries later under the name 'Cathars' before their mass-slaughter by the army of Rome in the siege in 1244 at the Castle of Monségur in the Languedoc near the Pyrenees.

When you read Gnostic philosophy it is easy to understand why the Cult's Roman Church wanted rid of them wherever they located. Gnosis means 'knowledge' and more specifically hidden or spiritual knowledge. What I am calling Body-Mind the Gnostics called 'Nous' and what I am referring to as Infinite Self they gave the name 'Pneuma'. From this comes the phrase about 'using your nous' which would translate as using your mind. It's much better to use your Pneuma – your expanded awareness. It was believed that any detailed record of Gnostic belief had been lost with their demise at Monségur until an amazing find in 1945 at Nag Hammadi about 80 miles north of Luxor on the banks of the River Nile in Egypt. A local found a sealed jar filled with Gnostic texts or scriptures that became known as the Nag Hammadi Library (Fig 182 overleaf). They included 13 leather-bound papyrus codices (manuscripts) and more than 50 texts written in Coptic Egyptian. The texts are estimated to date from about 350 to 400AD which would fit with the period before the attack on the library in which Hypatia was killed. It's thought likely they are representations of Greek works going back to maybe 120-150AD or earlier. From this incredible find far more is known about the Gnostic view of reality and this is especially significant with the texts hidden away and remaining unchanged when many religious texts have been manipulated, re-written and translated to suit the authorities of the day. I was taken

Figure 182: Part of the fantastic Nag Hammadi find of Gnostic writings.

aback to read the Nag Hammadi works after what I had already concluded about the Fallen Ones and the simulation. More than 1,600 years ago (as we perceive 'time') the Gnostics wrote about a non-human force they called 'Archons' and a 'fake reality' which in modern parlance was, in effect, describing a simulation. No wonder the Cult-created-and-controlled Roman Church wanted them gone. Archon is a Greek word meaning 'ruler', 'prince', 'authorities' and 'from the beginning'. A fifth of the Nag Hammadi manuscripts are about the Archontic manipulation of human society under the chief Archon which Gnostics refer to as 'Yaldabaoth', or the 'Demiurge', and the Cult calls Lucifer the Light Bringer. Other names for Yaldabaoth/Demiurge are Satan and the Devil which are biblically referred to in reptilian terms (Fig 183). Gnostics believed that Yaldabaoth and the Archons were the source of evil in human society and that they indeed *created* the material world that I am calling the simulation. They said human bodies were a trap to enslave us in the fake reality. Gnostic texts referred to Archons in their base form as energy beings (what I would describe as wavefields of consciousness), but they said Archons could take 'material' form. They described their most common manifestations as ... reptilian or serpentine and beings that look like 'an unborn baby or foetus

Figure 183: So many names, but the same force being described.

with grey skin and dark, unmoving eyes'. Reptilian entities have featured in my books since the 1990s as manipulators of human life from the hidden realms with their bloodline human/reptilian hybrids operating within the simulation and appearing outwardly to be human. The description of grey foetus-like entities with dark eyes captures the appearance of the classic 'Greys' of UFO research fame (Figs 184). They are by far the most common 'alien' entities reported by witnesses and

Figure 184: Gnostic texts describe how Archons appear in our reality in forms that are reptilian and sound very much like the 'Greys' of UFO research lore and legend.

those dubbed 'abductees' across the world who describe in remarkably consistent detail how they were abducted by a non-human species, usually 'Greys'. Gnostic texts have their version of *'The One'* which they symbolically call 'The Father' and 'The All'.

The Nag Hammadi *Bruce Codex* says:

> He is an incomprehensible one, but it is he who comprehends All. He receives them to himself. And nothing exists outside of him. But All exist within him. And he is boundary to them all, as he encloses them all, and they are all within him. It is he who is Father of the aeons, existing before them all. There is no place outside of him.

What a perfect description of *The One*, the still and silent 'isness' of All Possibility and Infinite Intelligence pervading all existence and to whose influence we can open any time we choose. Nag Hammadi texts divide reality into what they call the 'Upper Aeons' (Prime Reality) and the 'Lower Aeons' or material world. Aeons in the Gnostic context are bands of perception, reality and potential. Upper Aeons, the realm of *All That Is in Awareness of Itself*, is 'The Silence', 'the silent Silence', 'the living Silence', with its 'Watery Light' (Fig 185). This light is very different from the simulation light within the speed of light and has been described by near-death experiencers. Water symbolism is often used by Gnostics for Infinite light as with '... the waters which are above'; '... the waters which are above matter'; and '... the Aeons in the Living Water'. The Bible describes in the opening to Genesis how the Old

Figure 185: Gnostics described Prime Reality and fake reality – what I am calling the simulation. Prime Reality was a place of harmony, love and the NOW. Fake reality was a place of disharmony, evil and 'time' created by Yaldabaoth (Lucifer the Light Bringer).

Testament 'God' (I say 'Yaldabaoth') created the earth from the 'void' by moving upon the 'face of the waters':

> In the beginning God created the heaven and the earth. And the earth was without form, and void; and darkness *was* upon the face of the deep. And the Spirit of God moved upon the face of the waters. And God said, Let there be light: and there was light.

Gnostics said there is no 'time' or 'space' in the Upper Aeons as I described earlier. One text says that 'since the emanations [from 'The Father'] are limitless and immeasurable' there can be no time or space and they are pure consciousness or awareness named Pleroma or 'the totality', 'the fullness' and the 'perfection' of 'emanations of the Father'. The *Tripartite Tractate* text says:

> The emanation of the Totalities, which exist from the one who exists, did not occur according to a separation from one another, as something cast off from the one who begets them. Rather, their begetting is like a process of extension, as the Father extends himself to those whom he loves, so that those who have come forth from him might become him as well.

Gnostics speak of the interaction between 'The Father' and 'The Mother' which they refer to as 'The Thought'. Their interaction produced a third force or extension of The One which they symbolised as the Son. There are many themes in the Nag Hammadi texts which Christianity twisted through the centuries and took for its own.

Archontic fake reality

Nag Hammadi manuscripts say the material world was created 'in error' when an emanation of the 'The Father' disconnected from his influence and this is the Gnostic version of 'The Fall' and Fallen Ones. The emanation called by Gnostics Yaldabaoth or the Demiurge (Lucifer/Satan/Devil) is said to be a 'formless entity' that proceeded to create a 'bad copy' of the Upper Aeons (Prime Reality) which became the Lower Aeons or 'material' world and what I say is a simulation (Figs 186 and 187). I suggest that using modern language what Gnostics described as a 'bad copy' is a wavefield/digital copy of cosmic Prime Reality – a virtual reality representation. A simulation could be very accurately dubbed a bad copy and once it was created the copy could be continually changed and downgraded just as once you have downloaded a copy of a website you can change its nature while the original continues to exist as it always was. This has been happening since the simulation was installed and never more so than with the current technological transformation. The Gnostic *Apocryphon of John*

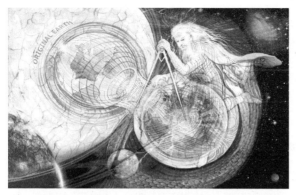

Figure 186: Gnostic texts said that Yaldabaoth created a 'bad copy' of Prime Reality and I say they were describing the creation of the simulation. (Image Neil Hague.)

Figure 187: What the Gnostic 'bad copy' really is.

says that Yaldabaoth is a 'counterfeit spirit' and Nag Hammadi texts describe this entity as 'The Blind One', 'The Blind God' and 'The Foolish One'. Samael, a name for Yaldabaoth in Jewish Talmudic writings, translates as 'Poison of God', or 'Blindness of God'. Gnostics said this 'insane' fake 'god' oversaw chaos without limit. The Nag Hammadi *Origin of the World* manuscript says: '...There appeared a force, presiding over the darkness [Lower Aeons]. And the forces that came into being subsequent to them called the shadow "the limitless chaos".' You only have to observe Planet Earth for confirmation. Nag Hammadi texts depict our reality of chaos as 'Hell', 'the Abyss' and 'Outer Darkness', where trapped Souls are tormented and manipulated by demons (as I have been writing for decades). The *Hypostasis of the Archons* quotes Yaldabaoth as saying: 'It is I who am God, and there is no other power apart from me.' You have heard similar in the Old Testament from the Genesis 'God' that 'created the world' – created the simulation: *'I am* the LORD, and *there is* none else, *there is* no God beside me' (Isaiah 45:5). The 'Lord God' of the Bible is the 'Lord Archon' or Yaldabaoth of the Gnostic manuscripts. Yaldabaoth is depicted in popular culture as the 'Dark Lord', 'Lord of Time', Lord (Darth) Vader and Dormammu, the evil ruler of the 'Dark Dimension' trying to take over the 'Earth Dimension' in the Marvel comic movie, *Dr Strange*. The angry, hate-filled, vindictive 'God' of the Old Testament, known as Yahweh/Jehovah, is quite clearly Yaldabaoth of the Gnostic manuscripts. Here he is quoted in Leviticus:

You will eat the flesh of your sons and the flesh of your daughters. I will destroy your high places, cut down your incense altars and pile your dead bodies on the lifeless forms of your idols, and I will abhor you ... I will scatter you among the nations and will draw out my sword and pursue you. Your land will be laid waste, and your cities will lie in ruins.

Nice bloke. I emphasise that I came to all the conclusions outlined earlier from a list of other sources *before* I read the Nag Hammadi documents which made them even more compelling to me. The texts say that Yaldabaoth left the Upper Aeons (left the 'garden'). He created subordinate like-entities, AI software copies called Archons, and a likeness 'in him' of the Cosmos (simulation). Note the term 'in him'. I recall a quote by Caleb Scharf, Director of Astrobiology at Columbia University, who said that 'alien life' could be so advanced that it transcribed itself into the quantum realm to become 'physics' and numbers. He talked of intelligence which is indistinguishable from the fabric of the Universe. This has been my view for a long time and I say that 'AI' beyond what we have been told about is 'Yaldabaoth' and the Archontic force which has transcribed itself into the quantum realm to become physics and numbers. This would explain why the physics of our reality are so different to those outside the speed of light (Fig 188). The AI connection will become incredibly important in the chapter 'Where are

Figure 188: The Speed of Light is the simulation.

we going – if we allow it?' Gnostic texts say of Yaldabaoth: 'He became strong and created for himself other aeons with a flame of luminous fire which exists now.' Flame of fire = the 'light' of the simulation within the speed of light. The same themes can be found in ancient societies across the world as I have detailed in other works. Archons are the Gnostic name for the Islamic (and pre-Islamic) Jinn or Djinn (also genies), Christian demons, and Zulu Chitauri 'Children of the Serpent', or 'Devastators'. Satan is known by Christians as 'the Demon of Demons' while Gnostics called Yaldabaoth the 'Archon of Archons'. Both are known as 'The Deceiver'. Nag Hammadi documents call Archons mind parasites, inverters, guards, gatekeepers, detainers, judges, pitiless ones and the Deceivers. Gnostics describe Archons in terms of 'luminous fire'

ARCHONS/JINN (DJINN)
MADE FROM LUMINOUS FIRE
MADE FROM SMOKELESS FIRE

Figure 189: Once again different names, same story, same phenomenon.

while the Jinn are said in Islamic belief to be made from 'smokeless fire' (Fig 189). Archons and Jinn are both said to be entities in the unseen manipulating humanity. I was talking to a Muslim taxi driver in New York about my work and I mentioned the Archons and how they were described. He said immediately – 'That sounds just like the Jinn'. Gnostics portray the 'material' world with words like 'deficiency', 'imperfection', darkness and the Abyss while the Upper Aeons are 'fullness'. Prime Reality is called 'the existent' while 'material reality (the simulation) is 'non-existent'. The *Bruce Codex* says:

> And then the existent separated itself from the non-existent. And the non-existent is the evil which has manifested in matter. And the enveloping power separated those that exist from those that do not exist. And it called the existent 'eternal', and it called the non-existent 'matter'. And in the middle it separated those that exist from those that do not exist, and it placed veils between them.

Gnostics make the distinction between our 'Spirit' in the Upper Aeons and our 'Soul' trapped in the material world. Most psychics are connecting with the realm of Soul and only a relative few with Spirit where the really top-notch information can be accessed. If our point of attention remains in Soul (Mind/Psyche) and not Spirit when we withdraw from 'physicality' we are trapped in the Lower Aeons at other less energetically-dense levels before returning in another bodily form through 'reincarnation'. Gnostics have a concept of what they call 'the middle place', a 'space' between the Upper and Lower Aeons which they describe as a state of temporary 'non-existence' as the Soul waits to reincarnate or is trapped there by ignorance (low-frequency wavefield). Archons are said to guard the exits and gateways, but they are low-frequency idiots and cannot block or affect high-frequency states. Texts entitled *Pistis Sophia* symbolise the limits of Yaldabaoth reality (simulation) as a dragon swallowing its own tail: 'The outer darkness is a great dragon, whose tail is in his mouth, outside the whole world and surrounding the whole world.' See the reptilian symbolism yet again. An esoteric/occult symbol portrays precisely this concept in the form of the 'Ouroboros', or 'Leviathan', which is a serpent swallowing its own

Figure 190: The 'Ouroboros', or 'Leviathan' is the reptilian symbol marking the walls of the simulation. We pass through those perceptual limits to escape the Matrix.

Figure 191: The ancient concept of the Ring-Pass-Not through which we must pass to return 'home' and as with the Gnostic version our perceptions hold the key. (Image Neil Hague.)

tail (Fig 190). Gnostics said the outermost planetary sphere or Archon (of the Lower Aeons/simulation) is Saturn. Beyond that was the serpent Leviathan through which Souls had to pass to reach paradise (reconnect with pure Spirit). Readers of *Everything You Need To Know* will be aware of what I have written about Saturn and its role in the simulation which again fits with the Nag Hammadi manuscripts. Cult symbolism is awash with portrayals of Saturn which is dubbed 'Lord of Karma' and ruler of 'time' – both concepts of the simulation. I also say that the Moon (linked to the perception of 'time') and the constellation of Orion are very significant to the simulation and human control. The theme of the Gnostic great dragon or Ouroboros can be found in the ancient esoteric concept of the 'Ring-Pass-Not' (Fig 191). This is a definition:

A profoundly mystical and suggestive term signifying the circle or bounds of frontiers within which is contained the consciousness of those who are still under the sway of the delusion of separateness – and this applies whether the Ring be large or small.

It is a general term applicable to any state in which an entity, having reached a certain stage of evolutionary growth of the unfolding of consciousness, finds itself unable to pass into a still higher state because of some delusion under which the consciousness is labouring, be that delusion mental or spiritual.

Common themes keep on repeating and among them are the following: Consciousness is trapped in the illusion of 'material' reality by perceptions of reality which dictate frequency. The simulation is a

Figure 192: Humanity is entrapped by ignorance through suppression of perception and true self-identity. This maintains a low-frequency state that keeps people in the Bubbles of the simulation. We can break out any time we choose as I will later explain. (Image Neil Hague.)

band of frequency which humanity and Body-Mind is manipulated not to breach by becoming aware of its true nature – formless Spirit (Fig 192). When this realisation is integrated as a *knowing* and not just an intellectual concept our Mind/Soul frequency quickens and we can pass after human 'death' through the Ring Pass Not/Ouroboros (outer frequency walls of the simulation). The Nag Hammadi *Tripartite Tractate* says of Souls trapped in the Lower Aeons: 'Therefore they fell down to the pit of ignorance which is called "the Outer Darkness" and "Chaos" and "Hades" and "the Abyss".' Pit of ignorance = caught in the illusion = low frequency state. Gnostics describe humanity as a whole as manipulated 'forgetfulness'. The way out of here is to remember our true nature and see through the illusion by opening the heart to a high-frequency state. The Jim Carrey film *The Truman Show* was very symbolic of this whether by accident or design. The Carrey character is born onto the mega-set of a TV soap and everyone around him is an actor although he doesn't know that. The Sun comes up and down every day and seems real to him while in fact it's a technological illusion orchestrated like the whole show from a control centre that looks remarkably like the Moon. Later in adult life Carrey's character begins to realise something is not right (he 'awakened') and he sails a boat out into what appears to be an endless ocean to find the outer wall of the dome that marks the limit of the movie set which he was never allowed to see. He finds a door in the wall of the dome and walks through to the 'real world' (symbolic of Prime Reality). Interestingly, the term 'firmament' means 'vast dome' and the Biblical reference to 'beyond the firmament' takes on a whole new meaning from this perspective. The concept has been portrayed for centuries as you can see in Figures 193 and 194 overleaf which are depictions from 1888 and even 1475. The inscription on the second one reads: 'A medieval missionary tells that he has found the point where heaven and Earth meet ...' Biblical texts describe how the Old Testament 'God' (Yaldabaoth) manifested the 'vast dome' firmament on the second day of the Creation sequence to divide the primal sea (Infinite Awareness) into upper and lower parts (Infinite reality and simulated

Figure 193: An 1888 depiction of the firmament or 'vast dome'.

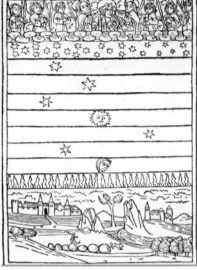

reality):

> Then God said, 'Let there be a firmament in the midst of the waters, and let it divide the waters from the waters.' Thus God made the firmament, and divided the waters which were under the firmament from the waters which were above the firmament; and it was so.

Figure 194: A different portrayal of the firmament and two divided 'world' from 1475.

This biblical text is describing the division of what Gnostics call the Upper and Lower Aeons. Gnostic writings symbolise levels of conscious in terms of 'the waters' as we have seen with '... the waters which are above'; '... the waters which are above matter'; and '... the Aeons in the Living Water'. The simulation is an inversion (the Gnostic 'bad copy' 'shadow world') of Prime Reality. Gnostics compared the two with terms such as fullness/deficiency, immortal/mortal, spiritual/psychic, Spirit/Soul, existence/non-existence, no-time/time, no space/space. The deficiency of possibility compared with Prime Reality is why the Archontic force had to develop technology in an effort to bridge some of the ginormous gap in creative potential. Prime Reality manifests directly through consciousness with no technology necessary.

Software Archons

Agent Smith and other agents in the *Matrix* movies are portrayed as software programs downloaded into the simulation to manipulate events and target dissidents on behalf of the creator of the Matrix who is called 'The Architect' (Fig 195). He is given a white beard which connects to Kronos, the Greek god of Saturn, who is depicted holding a scythe and an hour glass to symbolise control of 'time' (Fig 196). The chief god of Rome was also Saturn after which was named the festival of

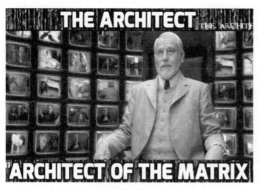

Figure 195: The bearded 'Architect' who built the *Matrix* in the movie series.

Figure 196: The bearded Kronos, ruler of 'time', and the Ancient Greek god of Saturn.

Figure 197: Kronos is known today as 'Old Father Time'.

Figure 198: The Grim Reaper is another Cult symbol of Saturn which is said to represent death as well as time. We are talking about a Death Cult after all and no wonder Cultists worship Saturn (see *Everything You Need To Know* for why).

Saturnalia that became the Western Christmas (Santa is an anagram of Satan). Other versions of Kronos/Saturn are called 'Old Father Time' with the long beard and the scythe-holding Grim Reaper which symbolises the Cult obsession with death (Figs 197 and 198). The Grim Reaper is associated with Saturn which is astrologically associated with death. Archons are encoded in *arch*-angels, *arch*-bishops and many such terms. We see the same with the Jewish god of Saturn called El. We have Is-Ra-*EL* (with its Saturn symbol Star of David flag) and the *El*-lite, *El*-ections, and so on. Agent Smith in *The Matrix* can replicate himself countless times because 'he' is a software program and I contend that the same is true with the Cult bloodlines. They are biological software known through the ages as the 'Soulless Ones' and 'Heartless Ones'. They are cold, emotionless psychopaths who have no Soul and no heart connection to *The One*. We are talking AI biological robots or, in their base form, AI wavefields of encoded information. The Cult bloodline obsession with interbreeding is to hold fast the software codes. It's not really about protecting the 'blue blood' gene pool, but the wave-code 'pool' which becomes holographically the biological gene pool. Archons in general are wavefield 'software' and Gnostic texts refer to them in terms of what we would call cyborgs. The 'cold', 'emotionless', Greys are software programs while reptilian species are robot-like in their behaviour. Zulu high shaman and official historian Credo Mutwa, who left us in 2020 at the age of 98, told me decades ago that to understand the 'Illuminati' we must study the behaviour of the reptile. I did and I found them to be extraordinarily computer-like as I already mentioned. I read an article about Swiss clairvoyant, Anton Styger, which was about his life and not at all about these subjects. Nevertheless one of his comments was very relevant to what I am saying. Skilled clairvoyants are able to see deeper into the energetic field and outside purely visible light. Styger said:

> When I see people in business or politics who are particularly trapped by the material world, for example, I notice that they no longer have any light bodies at all [wavefields associated with 'human']. In many of these people, the point of light at the heart chakra, which is otherwise always present, is no longer visible to me.

> Instead, I see something like a layer of 'shiny tar' around them in which a monstrous being in the shape of a lizard can be distinguished. When such people speak on television, for example, I see a crocodile shape manifesting itself around the person like in a concave mirror; I don't see the light of their throat and forehead chakra.

They don't have 'light bodies' in the human sense because they are possessed software constructs and no light at the heart chakra explains their *heartless* behaviour and lack of connection to *The One*. These are software entities running our world through control of politics, intelligence agencies, military, banking, business, media, academia, science, medicine, 'education', Silicon Valley, and all the rest. Many have quick minds and intellects because they are AI, and this further explains why Gnostic documents say that Archons have no 'ennoia' ('intentionality' or 'creative imagination'). They have to trawl and exploit the creativity of their targets, in this case humanity, which is being manipulated to build its own technological prison. They have to manipulate the creative imagination of humans (which they don't have) to manifest the reality they want and this will become seriously relevant later in terms of current events. Archons can copy and imitate, but not innovate. Gnostics called this 'countermimicry'. One example is mimicking Prime Reality with the 'bad copy' simulated virtual reality and you can relate this concept to Hong Kong/China where so much is copied and not created – *it is counterfeit* as Gnostics called Yaldabaoth a 'counterfeit spirit'. Gnostic texts say Archons are expert in deception and 'phantasia' – creating *illusions* through 'Hal' or *virtual reality* with the goal 'to overpower humanity in its perceptual functions' and impose 'fear and slavery'. John Lamb Lash, author of the book *Not In His Image* about the Nag Hammadi texts, wrote:

> Although they cannot originate anything, because they lack [without connection to *The One*] the divine factor of ennoia (intentionality), Archons can imitate with a vengeance. Their expertise is simulation (HAL, virtual reality). The Demiurge fashions a heaven world copied from the fractal patterns [of the original] ... His construction is celestial kitsch, like the fake Italianate villa of a Mafia don complete with militant angels to guard every portal.

It reminds me of a quote in the TV series, *The Hitchhiker's Guide to the Galaxy:* 'In the beginning the Universe was created ... This has made a lot of people very angry and been widely regarded as a bad move.'

Computer reality mimicking simulation reality

The Gnostic view of reality is close to my own in the areas I have described, but that doesn't mean I am 'a Gnostic'. There is just a convergence of view on the fake reality and its source. The last thing we need is any more black and white labels. There will be many other things on which Gnostics and I will disagree. Themes describing a fake 'god' rebelling against '*the* God' and manipulating humanity by deception are widespread in so many forms within the religions and cultures of the world. It's a universal story and if people think that imposing a simulated reality on the *apparent* scale of the Universe is too far-fetched they should look at interactive video games like *No Man's Sky* released in 2016 (Fig 199). This features more than 18 quintillion planets each with their own unique, flora, faunas and animal species. There are sentient alien races and those who are 'mechanical lifeforms'. The controlling 'God', called The Atlas (Yaldabaoth), is a 'ubiquitous entity represented by a red orb inside a black diamond'. The will of

Figure 199: The interactive *No Man's Sky* universe with more than 18 quintillion planets.

Atlas is imposed by the Sentinels (Archons) who are 'mechanical lifeforms; self-replicating, non-organic machines … [who] … act as workhorse machines of The Atlas and as universal police, controlling the actions of those who reside within the universe'. This pretty much sums up the human plight. We are experiencing a false reality that takes the form of an interactive virtual-reality simulation in which information is encoded in the simulation's version of The Field for us to decode into an apparently physical world. The human personality without a connection to beyond-the-Bubble consciousness is created by electronic/electromagnetic stimulus through a system of activation and reaction (input-output) between the simulation and the five senses. Body-Minds have major or subtle differences in their 'wiring' or wavefields and so can respond differently to the same input. One person may react to a situation with compassion and another with empathy-deleted contempt. These reactions will appear in the playing out as a person who cares and a psychopath. Human responses to electronic/electromagnetic stimulus (a situation) are what we call different 'personalities'. At the same time there are enormous similarities in the way that humans react to stimulus that induces fear – the 'press enter' response as I call it.

So we have Body-Minds reacting to fear-based stimulus on a mass scale – especially that relating to fear of death and the unknown (same thing) – but in their five sense-stimulus feedback loops responding to other electrical input in different ways that appear to give us different 'personalities'. I say those 'personalities' are largely the creation of electrical input-output interaction while a connection to expanded awareness takes you beyond the programmed limits of human personality. Heart consciousness does what it knows to be right and overrides the input-output feedback loops. It does not react to fear stimulus with an output of fear and fear-generated response. It calmly sees things as they are from a panoramic perspective and the awareness that it is an eternal state of Infinite Consciousness having a brief and transitory experience. It has no fear of death because it knows that 'death' is merely a transfer of attention from a myopic reality to an infinite one. Heart awareness may seem to have a 'personality' through the perception of its behaviour (not least because that is so different to the 'norm'), but such people are responding from the 'I' beyond the Bubble and not five-sense dominated input-output. Heart consciousness overrides that simulation/Body-Mind interaction and those senses then respond to the heart and not the simulation. In this way we begin to impact upon the simulation and not the other way round.

The simulation gives the illusion of past-present-future just as a video game does when both are only encoded information following a pre-set program in the NOW. Also encoded are the reincarnation/karma/astrology cycles which are feedback loops maintaining Souls and minds in the illusion even after human 'death' unless we transform our self-identity, remember our true nature, open our heart connection, and expand into frequencies the simulation cannot control. Our enslavement depends in totality on us being held within the frequency band of the simulation within the speed of light through our perceptual state and we can change that any time we want. Nor should we think that the manipulating entities are all-powerful as the force behind an apparently gigantic simulated Universe. Who says it's gigantic? The *No Man's Sky* universe appears to be so and yet it is only computer codes giving the illusion of enormity. When I looked at the 'night sky' in the London Planetarium it appeared to be fantastic in scale while it only existed as a projection on the ceiling. The 'real' night sky seems gigantic when it only exists in that form in your brain. The simulation is 2D or 'flat' encoded information fields that we decode into illusory 3D through Body-Mind systems specifically designed to do that. Holograms work the same way. The extent of the simulation can be minute compared with what we perceive it to be. At the time of release *No Man's Sky* was running from 600,000 lines of code which sounds a lot until you know that modern vehicles with their entertainment and Wi-Fi systems use 100 *million* lines of code with plans for this to increase by two to three times. Do we only decode wavefields into holograms when we are observing them to save computational power that would be necessary for the entirety to be in holographic form all the time in the same way that computer screens go blank to save energy when they are not being used?

Decoding our own prison

The key to control by the simulation is not only its wave information construct. The crucial part is getting incarnate minds to decode the illusion while believing it to be real. The brain/body is constantly decoding the Matrix into holographic form and while perception is dictated only by the five-senses (the point of Matrix-Body interaction) the simulation is in control. Minds are then in the world and of the world and have no other point of reference. Would computer game characters know they are only responding to software? They would think it was all real. The point about 'responding' is significant. Humanity is not ultimately manipulated and directed by agents of the Cult sitting around a table deciding their next move. The transformation of global society now unfolding could never be achieved on that scale by table-sitters alone. The Archontic plan is being encoded in the energetic fabric of the simulation field for humanity to *decode* into reality and this is how it can happen so fast and on such global scale. For this to happen humanity must be attuned with the wave frequencies carrying that information – 5G is the next stage. Incessant propaganda through the 'education' system and mass media is specifically designed to instil perceptions that will create the desired Cult reality by entangling with the wavefields infused with that agenda. What you believe you perceive and what you perceive you experience. Humanity, in short, is decoding and manifesting its own prison. Only a transformation of perception through a transfer of self-identity to the True Self will stop this. How much of human perception is already being delivered by the simulation? What is the real origin of the constant chatter passing through people's minds? I call this the 'Scenario Mind' because it spews out an endless list of scenarios and how we would respond even though the scenario is not happening. If he did this, I'd do that, if she said that, I'd say this. Where is all that coming from? Go into a quiet space and *observe* this chatter. Stand back from it. Listen as it rambles on. You can observe your own Body-Mind chatter and what does that tell you? It's *not you*. The *observer* of the chatter is *you*.

Benjamin Libet (1916-2007), a scientist in the physiology department of the University of California, San Francisco, generated many highly-significant experiments in his quest to understand human consciousness. One group was asked to move their hand whenever 'they' chose while their brain activity was being monitored. Libet found that brain activity to move the hand began a full half a second before any conscious decision to do so. John-Dylan Haynes, a neuroscientist at the Max Planck Institute for Human Cognitive and Brain Sciences in Leipzig, Germany, found in his studies that he could predict an action *ten seconds* before a conscious intention purely by monitoring brain activity. Frank Tong, a neuroscientist at Vanderbilt University in Nashville, Tennessee, said: 'Ten seconds is a lifetime in terms of brain activity.' Where was the decision-making really coming from if not the conscious mind? I say that *some* – not all, some – is coming from the simulation. Morpheus said in *The Matrix*: 'Are they your thoughts you're thinking now?' The body is encoded to be a limiting device for consciousness. In our no-form energetic state we can see, hear, feel, smell and taste without the body. We don't actually need it except to interact with the simulation. It focuses our attention within the frequency band of the simulation or in fact an even smaller band than that called visible light. It makes us believe that we can only see, hear, feel, smell and taste through the body which means people fall for the illusion that the body is who we are and without it we're nothing. Without it we're *everything*. Mainstream science and medicine constantly underpin this belief that the body is the totality of the 'I'. The body is *counter-mimicking consciousness* and limiting our sense of self, reality and the possible. No wonder Gnostics said the body was a prison trapping the 'divine spark' within matter. One other mystery explained by all this is why Earth's atmosphere and ecosystems are perfect to sustain life as we perceive it when only a tiny change would spell disaster. Scientist Robert Lanza writes in his book, *Biocentrism*:

> Why are the laws of physics exactly balanced for animal life to exist? ... If the strong nuclear force were decreased 2 percent, atomic nuclei wouldn't hold together, and plain-vanilla hydrogen would be the only kind of atom in the Universe. If the gravitational force were decreased by a hair, stars (including the Sun) would not ignite. These are just [some of] more than 200 parameters within the solar system and Universe so exact that it strains credulity to propose that they are random – even if that is exactly what standard contemporarily physics baldly suggests.

They are of course not random. They are *made* to be that way. How? Our world is a virtual-reality simulation with its own encoded rules and information. Why? To allow the Cult and its non-human 'gods' to enslave human perception in ongoing illusion and control. The simulation has been breached by many over the years who have sought to make humanity aware of its plight and they have often taken the consequences for that instigated by the Cult. This continues to be the case today as a concerted effort is underway by consciousness 'incarnating' from Prime Reality to wrest back control from the Fallen by informing the human family what is really happening in the manner of the prisoner in Plato's cave. We are making progress, but to say the very least the job is far from done.

CHAPTER SIX

Why don't we know?

Is there any point in public debate in a society where hardly anyone has been taught *how* to think, while millions have been taught *what* to think? – Peter Hitchens

The game of life – in this case human life – plays out in a stadium (the simulation) called *perception*. From this everything else comes. What we perceive becomes what we believe becomes how we behave becomes what we experience. This is the deal and to understand these connections is to understand the world and the human plight.

Our perceptions dictate our frequency and our frequency dictates our wave-entanglements with people, places, situations, and experiences. Through this process we create our own reality and experience by attracting into our lives a holographic representation of our *perceptions*. A 'Little Me' perception will transmit waves so limited and weak in terms of perceived potential ('I have no power', 'I'm a victim' and 'I'll never be up to much') that the feedback loop between perception and The Field will deliver back to you just that sort of life (Fig 200). By contrast if you come at life from the perspective of being Infinite Awareness (All Possibility) having a brief human experience you make a very different feedback connection with The Field – one that is both greater in scale and much higher in

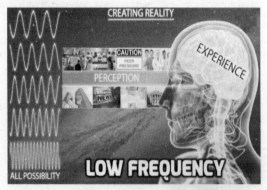

Figure 200: A closed mind emits a closed frequency which interacts with The Field only within that limited band of possibility and thus creates the feedback loop in which 'Little Me' and 'Label Me' perception produces through cause and effect limited experience and awareness. (Image Gareth Icke.)

frequency. An expanded sense of self automatically expands your accessed consciousness to match that perception and you are interacting with that range of possibility within The Field. Your life is transformed as more possibilities attach to your feedback loop and become your

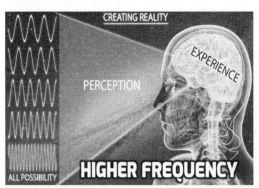

Figure 201: Open your mind and expand your self-identity and you expand your interaction with The Field and possibility. 'Big Me' perception creates a 'Big Me' experience. (Image Gareth Icke.)

Figure 202: What I call the Postage Stamp Consensus is the narrow band of possibility taught in the 'education' system and promoted by the media which is the foundation belief system of academia, science, corporations, medicine, government, and the great majority of the public.

experience (Fig 201). Our self-identity is central to our relationship with The Field. The Cult well knows that if it controls perception it will control experience. This is why people are being herded into smaller and smaller perceived identities to the point where one American university has this code for its students' perceptions of self-identity: LGBTTQQFAGPBDSM (don't ask). I'm sure that string of letters will be longer by the time you read this with new and ever more myopic identities invented by the day. What is happening in the world in terms of manipulation and events falls into place once you know how reality works.

The Cult's prime objective then is to dictate perception and it has structured human society as a cradle-to-grave programming laboratory founded on what I have long called the 'Postage Stamp Consensus' (Fig 202). This is the tiny band of possibility indoctrinated in schools, colleges and universities and repeated 24/7 worldwide by the mainstream and much of the 'alternative' media. Postage Stamp belief dictates the perceptual limits of academia, establishment science, medicine, media, government, business and the Mainstream *Everything*, and provides the foundation of what I refer to as The Program (Fig 203 overleaf). The Cult first exploited religion as its perception deception in which deviating from the imposed belief proclaimed in a 'holy book' was a death sentence. This was the Postage Stamp Consensus of its day. Religion still retained the concept of life continuing after death, but included subordination to a schizophrenic 'God', both loving and vindictive, that invited those who believed in him to eternal paradise while condemning non-believers to

Figure 203: Virtual reality headsets perfectly symbolise the human perception program.

stoking the fires of hell forever. We are asked to believe that this eternal division was decided by 'God' on the basis of a brief life on Earth of anything from seconds to decades on a planet equivalent to a billionth of a pinhead. I don't know about you, but that makes perfect sense to me after a dozen gin and tonics with whisky chasers. Shockingly this belief still controls the perceptions (and the decoded experience) of billions. Ever greater numbers began to reject this form of control, however, and they were targeted with the new Cult entrapment wheeze of 'science' and state-controlled 'education'. Mainstream establishment science had the added benefit of deleting any concept of a Creator and believers in this religion masquerading as 'rational thought' drew its targets and advocates deeper into the perception of random existence within 'matter'. For religion in its most extreme form there is death to blasphemers and the

Figure 204: The Cult knows that if it hijacks perception it will dictate the frequencies that attract experience. Myopic perceptions create a myopic life and collectively mass control becomes possible. The Cult is creating the nature of our reality through the manipulation of human perception.

milder version is ejection from 'the faith'. With the 'rational' religion of Scientism there is death to your career and ejection from the faculty ('the faith'). Mass indoctrination is further entrenched by Cult-controlled media bias and censorship now being taken to ever more extreme levels by Cult-owned Silicon Valley. If you control what people see and hear they will believe what you tell them so long as you also control what they *don't* see and hear (Fig 204).

The download begins

Human society is a laboratory for Body-Mind and other terms that capture the theme include conveyor belt, sausage machine and computer download. Human life is indeed a *perceptual* download that

Figure 205: Perceptual programming begins the moment we leave the womb and in fact even before that through the wave and chemical connections to the mother.

starts even in the womb and ends at the cemetery. When a child arrives blinking into the light the programming really starts (Fig 205). First there are parents who have already been processed by the programming system the child is about to go through and accepted what it told them to believe (if they are entrapped in Body-Mind which the great majority still are). Parents upload this indoctrination to their child in its earliest years and I am not saying this is done through malevolent intent. Often it is quite the opposite. They have themselves downloaded the system's version of reality and they think they are doing the best for their children by giving them the benefit of that 'wisdom'. Downloaded illusory 'wisdom' includes everything from what children are told and how they are treated to accepting the tidal wave of vaccinations they now receive to fill the coffers of the Cult-owned Big Pharma and undermine their immune systems and perceptual processes for life. When children are damaged by vaccines it often happens in the brain. How many kids who are not brain-damaged enough to be diagnosed still have their thinking and creative processes suppressed and limited for the rest of their lives? When this impacts on behaviour they are prescribed drugs made by the same Cult Big Pharma cartel that produced the vaccines to 'treat' the effects of vaccines. The same goes for food/drug (chemical/wave) distortions which skew the way that kids

Figure 206: 'Education' in a single image.

process information into perception and behaviour. Three or four years after arriving in the world the perception download goes through a colossal upgrade known hilariously as 'education' when an already toxin-infested child heads for school (Fig 206). Now parents start to lose influence over their offspring while children increasingly lose their distinct individuality to a programmed perception about everything (Fig

Figure 207: Children go to school to be perceptually programmed with a sense of reality designed last their entire lives.

207). Life as it will be for their entire formative years has begun during which they will sit at a desk or in a lecture theatre day after day being told what to believe and not believe about themselves and the world in all its facets and forms by authority figures representing the perception program of the state. These may be anything from a primary school teacher to an 'eminent professor'. Either way their role is the same – to get children and young people to believe what the state (the Cult) wants them to believe. What more effective way can there be to dictate collective perception and behaviour than to have control of what young generations are told to believe throughout their formative years? The 'educator' at every level may themselves believe what they say thanks to their own programming, or they may not. It doesn't matter. The state insists that they teach what they are told to teach in the way they are told to teach it or they're out the door. Teachers and academics are in the same perceptual penitentiary as their students in the 'education' environment. I am going to detail in upcoming chapters how this is transforming society more blatantly and profoundly than ever before and to what end. Pressure to pass exams means that 'education' for both student and teacher becomes a daily rush to stuff state-approved (Cult-approved) alleged 'facts' into the memories of young people to be held for just long enough to repeat them on the exam paper. How much of what you 'learned' at school do you remember or have you used in your life apart from the basics of maths, writing and such like? Very little will be the answer from most people, or, in my case, next to sod all. In fact I have spent my life since deleting the crap I was told at school on the few occasions when I was paying any attention. The Cult doesn't mind that you don't consciously remember the programming. Its target is your subconscious which studies have revealed is responsible for 95 percent of human behaviour. Your so-called conscious mind is the slave of the subconscious and the *subconscious* is what the Cult is after. When it has that it has *you*.

It is extraordinary how little conscious decision-making is involved in prompting actions. Most of them are computer-like responses and reactions often emotional in nature. Remember the research that showed how brain activity required to do something starts before a conscious decision is made to do it. The conscious mind retains very little, indeed

Figure 208: The subconscious is the target of perceptual programming and this seeps through to the conscious mind as what appears to be a 'personal' view or opinion. 95 percent of human behaviour derives from subconscious perceptions. (Image Neil Hague)

perceives very little, as we saw with the quote about visual realty being constructed by the brain from 40 'sensations' a second from the 11 million received. Our subconscious absorbs it all and why wouldn't that be the governor of perception? People don't have to *remember* all they were programmed to believe by the 'education' system. The Cult knows the subconscious will do that and influence the conscious mind for life unless de-programming takes place called 'awakening' – awakening from the *program* (Fig 208). Observe people's reactions and responses to events and happenings and you will see reflex-action perception akin to pressing 'enter'. I have been ridiculed for decades for what I have said by those who have not spent a single second checking the facts or background. Their instant reaction is triggered by subconscious responses on the basis only of what they have been told is possible. Never have they had to consider shapeshifting while absorbing only information that says the world is solid. To them, therefore, shapeshifting must be crazy by reflex action. Subconscious programming seeps through to conscious perception. You have seen already my take on life that we are all one consciousness having different experiences and that human labels of race, sexuality and so on are illusions that we allow to divide us. I have been saying the same for 30 years. Compare that with what a British 'writer' called Gary Spedding posted on Twitter to my son, Gareth: 'You are the son of a known anti-Semitic white supremacist conspiracy theorist.' Has Spedding read any of my books? No. Has he been to my public presentations? No. Does he know anything about me that has not come from biased sources? No. Much of humanity is forming its perceptions in the same way which is why the great majority of what people believe is not true and only what the Cult wants them to *believe* is true. They are making 'conscious' decisions second by second considering validity in a whole range of subjects and situations from life-long programmed *assumptions* supported by no personal research whatsoever. To become *conscious* beyond The Program means to take control of our perceptions which involves reaching our *own* conclusions and not taking them off the shelf from someone else.

'Education': Systematic programming

From all this comes what I call 'everyone knows that' syndrome. We've all heard it – me more than most – when you challenge an assumption of reality and you are dismissed with an 'everyone knows that' repetition of the programmed possible (Fig 209). How come that 'everyone knows'? Well, everyone has been through the same perceptual download. Er, that's it (Fig 210). Children in religious families invariably follow that religion because it's all they've ever heard and the same principle applies to the 'education' download. The general rule of the Cult is this: If that's all they ever hear that is what they will believe subconsciously and so consciously. Any information challenging those assumptions has to break through the walls and layers of programming before an 'Ah-ha' moment can occur. There is another reason for the deluge of mostly irrelevant information heaped upon children and young people. While you were filling your mind with the daily deluge

Figure 209: The System told me what to think – if you say anything different you must be mad or stupid.

Figure 210: Big mistake.

mostly utterly useless to you – and then revising it again for exams – your mind was focused on that and not going its own unique way. Five-sense *focus* is the goal. Once you focus at the exclusion of all else you lose peripheral vision where the truth lies and dots can be connected. The System adds still more focus time in the form of 'homework' to perpetuate five-sense focus and wire the brain to process information in a particular way which I'll come to in a moment. It's all coldly calculated by those in the shadows. Compartmentalisation means that the high 90 percents of those directly imposing the programming will have no idea why this is being done or even *what* is being done to the perceptions of the young. The Cult *does* and created the structure of 'education' through bloodline families like the Rockefellers. John D. Rockefeller, the American oil/banking/pharmaceutical tycoon and Cult agent, founded the US General Education Board at the start of the 20th century. He said: 'I don't want a nation of thinkers – I want a nation of workers.' I want a nation of *slaves* would be more accurate. Frederick T. Gates, Rockefeller's co-founder and business advisor, said it all:

> In our dream we have limitless resources, and the people yield themselves with perfect docility to our moulding hand. The present educational conventions fade from our minds; and, unhampered by tradition, we work our own good will upon a grateful and responsive rural folk.

> We shall not try to make these people or any of their children into philosophers or men of learning or of science. We are not to raise up among them authors, orators, poets, or men of letters. We shall not search for embryo great artists, painters, musicians. Nor will we cherish even the humbler ambition to raise up from among them lawyers, doctors, preachers, statesmen, of whom we now have ample supply.

Cult 'education' has been imposed to condition children to believe and accept for life the following:

- Truth comes from authority
- Intelligence is the ability to remember and repeat
- Accurate memory and repetition are rewarded
- Non-compliance is punished
- I must conform intellectually and socially

The Cult 'education' system worldwide is so carefully moulded from its controlling core that it targets a particular part of the brain – the left hemisphere. This has a largely different function overall than the right hemisphere. The brain is holographic in its decoded form and will have all functions spread throughout, but on the whole-brain level the two hemisphere's have different emphasis. The left-brain decodes information in ways that dominate human perception. From here come words, language, numbers and the sense of everything being apart from everything else. It sees dots and pixels, identifies with labels and likes to conform within hierarchical structures (Fig 211 overleaf). It is the orthodox politician, scientist, doctor, journalist, academic, business leader or worker, lawyer and judge. In other words all the people who run or serve The System. Current human society is overwhelmingly a holographic expression of the left side of the brain which is the foundation perception of the Mainstream Everything. The right-brain by

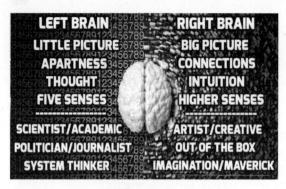

Figure 211: The left and right brain process information in very different ways to produce very different perceptions of reality.

Figure 212: The System, driven by the Cult, defends the left-brain from right-brain influence. (Image Neil Hague)

contrast is free-spirit creativity, imagination, art, poetry, spontaneity, the maverick. It is authors (of certain types), orators, poets, great artists, painters and musicians which Frederick T. Gates said they didn't want the 'education' system for the masses to produce. Crucially the right-brain has a greater sense of oneness unity and connects dots/pixels into pictures and patterns that reveal the truth about life and reality. The right-brain has close connections to the heart and for that reason alone it is in the gunsights of Cult 'education' which is designed to close the heart chakra, suppress the right-brain, and enslave the young for life in the Body-Mind Bubble. Note how little school time is given to right-brain activities like art, drama and music, and how left-brain subjects dominate the curriculum (Fig 212). Exams are passed by compiling information through the left-brain and then repeating that on the exam paper. The left-brain to a fundamental extent is the home of The Program and its perception processing centre in conjunction with the reptilian brain, or R-complex', from where reflex-action, survival-instinct responses are activated (Fig 213). I say that the reptilian brain, at least in its present dominant form, comes from Archontic manipulation of the human body. The reptilian brain is constantly scanning the environment for threats to survival and not just 'physical' survival. I mean also financial survival, relationship survival, job survival, etc. Road rage and reflex-action, fight-or-flight, over-the-top emotional responses are reptilian brain 'press-enter' reactions and the underlying

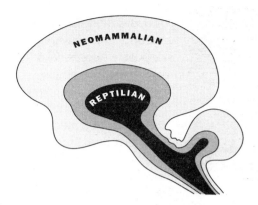

Figure 213: The reptilian brain works closely with the left-brain to dictate perception and behaviour. Reptilian brain? What a coincidence.

fear and anxiety felt by so many is reptilian brain connected. It is one of the major behaviour-control mechanisms and its impact on emotion keeps people in a low-vibrational state. *Is this really a coincidence given what I have been writing for decades about a reptilian connection to human control?* British psychiatrist Dr Iain McGilchrist has featured what he calls the divided human brain in his presentations. He describes how the left-brain has a narrow focus (point of attention) in terms of detail and the right perceives the panorama or big picture. You can see the recurring theme. Those focused in their left-brain have a narrowed 'window of attention' – window of *perception* – which leads to lower and less expanded frequency states. Brain hemisphere/heart separation also

Figure 214: Once again the 'education' programming system in a single image.

instils a sense of Body-Mind/Soul/Spirit separation. The 'education' system is specifically designed to be a conveyor belt to turn out life-long Bubble people. How symbolically appropriate that a school in India forced students to wear cardboard boxes on their heads to stop cheating during exams (Fig 214). Unseen boxes are donned by children the world over every time they start a school day.

Play time? What play time?

The two hemispheres of the brain are connected by a bridge called the corpus callosum and we are supposed to be whole-brain people getting the best of both 'sides' (Fig 215 overleaf). Once they are divided we become divided in the way we process information into perception. Extremes of left-brain dominance create five-sense 'system' people and

Figure 215: The very different perceptions of brain hemispheres portrayed in a car advertisement. We are meant to be whole-brained and balance the two.

right-side domination produces highly-creative people who struggle to function and cope in a left-brain world. Another aspect of the dot-connecting, pattern-perceiving, right brain is to see *context*. Awareness only of dots denies context which comes from seeing how dots connect. An individual dot can look a certain way, but connect that to other dots – provide context – and the dots together look very different to dots by themselves. I spend my life connecting dots between apparently unconnected people, places, organisations and situations. Their meaning and relevance in and of themselves is transformed once connections give them context. Dots can tell you *what* is happening while dot-connected context tells you *why* it's happening. Clearly the Cult doesn't want people doing this or its game will be revealed. The race to manipulate brain processing to see only left-brain dots begins in earnest the moment a child arrives for the first day at school. From here children are 'taught (programmed) by teachers and academics who have been imprisoned in their own left-brain by the same programming system. The best way for children to activate their right-brain is to use their imagination by simply *playing*. They need to be allowed to ad-lib and *imagine* by enjoying this definition of play – 'Engaging in activity for enjoyment and recreation rather than a serious or practical purpose'. This presents such a danger to the Cult's programming strategy that play is being deleted from childhood through homework, the push for longer school days, and the youngest of children being introduced to left-brain activities at an ever earlier age. Democrat presidential candidate Bernie Sanders promised free education and 'Pre-K' (a pre-kindergarten classroom-based preschool program for children under five). This fits perfectly with the agenda to take children from their parents as soon as possible The Sanders website said:

> For parents all over the country, taking time off or working fewer hours to care for their children is simply not an option. That leads many families to spend a disproportionate amount of their income to cover the cost of child care and early education.

There was no mention of the consequences of parents spending a disproportionate amount of their time away from their kids while the state has control of their minds. No, no – just how to make even easier to spend a disproportionate amount of their time away from their kids. We had the same theme with one-time Democrat presidential candidate Kamala Harris who called for the American school day to be extended to 6pm to align with the adult work day and this was right in line with the agenda for kids which seeks to secure still more time for perceptual programming away from parents. Children sit at desks for hours every day being talked at while outside the Sun is shining and there are trees to be climbed and imagination to be explored (Fig 216). What little 'time' is left for children to play has been hijacked by smartphones and videogames that mostly stimulate ... the *left-brain*.

Figure 216: Take children and young people in the prime of life with all possibility to explore and stick them at a desk all day while telling them what to believe for life. Utterly shocking village idiocy – but exactly what the Cult requires.

John Taylor Gatto, a former teacher in the United States, realised what 'education' was really designed to do and wrote a series of excellent books exposing the game. Gatto was New York City Teacher of the Year in 1989, 1990, and 1991, and New York State Teacher of the Year in 1991. He became rather less popular with the authorities when he began speaking out. Gatto said the aim was to subdue creative, inventive, and bright students and make them obedient, subdued and dependent individuals by controlling their school-time and then hijacking what should be free time through homework (Fig 217). He said children on average watched television for 55 hours a week (perception programming) and slept for 56. This left them 57 hours 'to

Figure 217: The walls and bars they increasingly build around schools capture the reason for fake 'education' – building walls and bars around the mind. (Image Gareth Icke.)

grow up strong and competent and whole', but 30 hours of that was spent at school (perception programming), 8 hours preparing for school and getting to and from school, and 7 hours doing homework (perception programming) totalling 45 hours related to school. Gatto went on:

> After the 45 school hours are removed a total of 12 hours remain each week from which to fashion a private person – one that can like, trust, and live with itself. Twelve hours. But my kids must eat, too, and that takes some time. Not much, because they've lost the tradition of family dining – how they learn to eat in school is best called 'feeding' – but if we allot just 3 hours a week to evening feedings, we arrive at a net total of private time for each child of 9 hours …

> …This demented schedule is an efficient way to create dependent human beings, needy people unable to fill their own hours, unable to initiate lines of meaning to give substance and pleasure to their existence. It is a national disease, this dependency and aimlessness, and schooling and television and busy work … has a lot to do with it.

This is exactly the situation the Cult set out to create given that 'education' is all about producing children and young people that become adult mind-slaves for life (Fig 218). We hear spewing from the mouths of mind-slave politicians that 'Education must prepare children for the workplace'. You must spend your childhood working hard, studying and swotting to '*be* someone' and '*get* somewhere'. Oh, really? Be who? Get where exactly? You must have a career, a job, you must strive, strive, strive, gotta, gotta, gotta, there's not a minute to be lost (Fig

Figure 218: In a nutshell.

Figure 219: Get where? And why? Gotta, gotta, gotta, get to the end as fast as I can. Enjoy the moment? What moment?

219). The Red Queen says in Lewis Carroll's *Through the Looking-Glass*: 'Now, here, you see, it takes all the running you can do, to keep in the same place. If you want to get somewhere else, you must run at least twice as fast as that!' In fact, when we understand reality, the best way to 'get somewhere' is to stop running and manifest. The current 'education' system must be dismantled to emphasise play and imagination to activate the right brain and develop whole people. I left school at 15 to play professional soccer and daydreamed through my school years. Somehow – it must be a miracle – I have managed to write and research a stream of highly detailed books and speak for ten hours a go to audiences around the world without a single note. How is that possible when I am officially so 'uneducated'? A deeply-programmed alleged member of the 'alternative media' once said that I can't be taken seriously because I 'didn't have a degree'. She had one. No further comment necessary. All that I have learned since I left school with no exam passes has been on my own terms. My son Gareth got an 'E' in some exams because he cared even less about school than I did. Today he's a highly intelligent man aware of the world with a highly creative mind that makes him an exceptional singer-songwriter and all-round talent in many fields. There is absolutely no need to deluge young minds with information they will never use hour-by-hour, day after day, when they can easily find that information for themselves later should they want to or need to. The deluge is not for the benefit of children and young people. It's for the benefit of the Cult and its incessant perceptual programming regime.

Diane Ravitch, an American education historian, policy analyst and writer, summed it up when she said: 'Sometimes the most brilliant and intelligent minds do not shine in standardised tests because they do not have standardised minds.' The Cult, however, wants standardised minds and set up the system to get them. Psychiatrist Iain McGilchrist rightly points out that the left-brain is focused upon *knowing ever more about what is already known*. It's the right-brain and the heart that want to explore and uncover the unknown and have the awareness to understand it. Canadian-born psychiatrist Eric Berne described the perceptual difference between the hemispheres: 'The moment a little boy is concerned with which is a jay and which is a sparrow [left-brain] he can no longer see the birds or hear them sing [right-brain/heart].' This is yet another example of label limitation and division at the expense of the unity of Oneness. The 'education' system is about indoctrination of the 'known' (allegedly). The Cult doesn't want us to know the publicly unknown. I am not saying that all mainstream academics and scientists are knowingly suppressing knowledge. They're in the Bubble, too. I am saying the Cult-asset academics and scientists are doing that which is a relative few. For the scam to work Mainstream Everything in general must also be kept from the truth and diverted into misunderstanding and dead ends. There is also the immense difference between knowledge and *knowing* which 'education' cannot teach. It comes from within. The mystic Osho said:

> Knowledge has no capacity to dispel ignorance. Knowledge is a false phenomenon. It is not wisdom at all; it is just the opposite of wisdom. Knowledge is borrowed; wisdom is the flowering of your innermost being ... No university can offer it, no scripture can offer it and no scholarship is capable of doing it. They are all impotent efforts, but they have been deceiving millions of people for thousands of years. Yes they make you knowledgeable. To be knowledgeable is one thing, to *know* is totally different.

Perception lobotomy

Children and young people are indoctrinated with the Mainstream Everything's version of history, science, medicine, politics, current events, life, self, all of it. 'Education' is a Cult-created programming machine constantly underscored by the Cult-controlled media which I'll be coming to shortly. Kids that want to question, challenge the orthodoxy, or are plain bored stiff like I was, are called 'disruptive influences' and increasingly prescribed mind-altering drugs like Ritalin for 'attention' disorders. We have the medicalisation of childhood, medicalisation of growing up, and it extends into colleges and universities as the medicalisation of teenage experience essential to developing emotionally strong, fully-rounded, adults capable of looking life in the eye (Fig 220). Here we have children in the prime of life sitting in a prison waiting for the bell to ring to enjoy a modicum of freedom (homework apart) which today is defined as time on my smartphone. They are

Figure 220: The medicalisation of childhood.

being prepared for an entire life in an adult prison after school becomes work, the teacher becomes the boss, and obeying authority is seen as essential to financially survive in adulthood while, as with childhood, often counting the minutes to home-time. Obey the teacher is replaced by obey the boss in a seamless life of external control in which only the characters and names change. 'Quick, get up, you'll be late for school' becomes 'Quick, get up, you'll be late for work'; 'What will the teacher say?' becomes 'What will the boss say?' Children from the earliest age are programmed by representatives of authority with carrot and stick punishment and reward for those who conform or do not. This, too, is ingrained in the subconscious as a fear of not obeying authority. None of this is by chance.

Charlotte Iserbyt realised this fact when she was a policy advisor to the Reagan administration at the US Department of Education. She describes in her book, *The Deliberate Dumbing Down of America,* how she saw documents laying out the 'restructuring' of American and global education through computerisation designed to make perception programming even more effective. Iserbyt said that what she saw was like 'communist brainwashing' and this will become extremely relevant later. One manual by a Professor Ronald Havelock was aptly titled *The Change Agent's Guide to Innovation in Education.* Iserbyt said she was trained to identify 'resistors' who were '... those good, smart Americans who realise that anything that has education hanging off the end of it is probably not what they're looking for'. She was told to 'go up against them, and actually to go and try to get them to join us through the group process system'. This is the group-think, group-absorption, technique to either suck-in or marginalise opposing views and ideas – a modus operandi employed at every level of human society. What Iserbyt saw was planned in those documents in the 1980s has been rolled out – and worse – all over the world and it is transforming human life as the young subjected to this become adults. Central to mass indoctrination through fake 'education' in the United States is the programming operation called Common Core much promoted by big-time Cult asset Bill Gates who turns up in financial support of a long list of Cult agendas. These include mass vaccination of children worldwide. Gates is a very sinister piece of work and there is a lot more to come about him when I get to the 'Covid-19' hoax. The pillars of standardised state education (indoctrination) were erected by the One-percent through vehicles such as the Rockefeller and Ford Foundations and today state child programming is dominated by the One-percent Gates Foundation. The fronts may change but the Cult is always in control. Organisations associated with Cult agent George Soros were behind the transformation of the Russian education system based on the Western model after the fall of the Soviet Union. School life was extended by a year, textbooks replaced and schools amalgamated in a period that saw plummeting levels of education and literacy. Soviet education was of course dictated by government, but the Western model of Rockefeller, Gates and Soros is aimed at *global* standardisation of indoctrination and centralised control. I read a book published in 2018 by American teacher Rebecca Friedrichs and the title said it all: *Standing Up To Goliath.* Her 28 years in teaching showed her how children are being politically and perceptually indoctrinated on an industrial scale with tyrannical teaching unions forcing upon young minds what I am calling the Cult agenda. She describes how teachers who can see what is happening and vehemently oppose it are intimidated into silence and acquiescence. This is being done to parents and society as a whole through Cult-instigated political correctness.

I have exposed the plan for decades to delete parental rights and hand control of children and their upbringing to the state (Cult) by giving ever more power to schools and social services to destroy parental rights and control the lives of children. A primary school in England announced it would fine parents for every five minutes they were late picking up their children and threatened to call social services if they took too long. As usual the poorest parents struggling to juggle work to survive with getting to the school on time would be the ones to suffer. Parents fined by schools is a critical line to cross in the power of schools over families and this is already widespread in Britain with parents fined if they take their children on holiday in term time when the cost of holidays is so much cheaper (once again hitting the poorest). The deeply corrupt authorities on the Isle of Wight where I live, with a population of 142,000, revealed through a Freedom of Information Act request that they accrued more than £100,000 in the previous year fining parents and carers whose children had 'unauthorised absences'. What must the figure be nationally? It's an Orwellian racket. Schools are becoming dictatorships and tyrannies with surveillance cameras and, in America, police officers on duty preparing kids for their planned adult life in an Orwellian nightmare. It's getting so extreme that the utterly ridiculous staff at Valley Forge Elementary School in Pennsylvania reported a six-year-old Downs syndrome girl to the police for pretending to shoot her teacher with her *fingers*. Little children pointing their fingers and saying bang, bang, is now worthy of police attention according to teaching staff who are more programmed than the kids they are programming. A *six-year-old* girl was handed over to the police by the Love Grove Elementary School in Jacksonville, Florida, without her mother being told after a 'tantrum' and held in a facility for two days under a 'mental health' law. Police body camera footage shows the girl walking calmly and quietly with the police and an officer saying 'she's fine, there's nothing wrong with her'. Those of us old enough know what life was like before the extreme Big Brother state appeared have the radar and experience (those that are in any way awake that is) to see the scale of what is both happening and planned. Children and young people have been *born* into the world as it is and it's all they have ever known. What are to people like me extraordinary extremes of control gathering by the day are, to young people enslaved in Body-

Mind, just 'how things are' in human society. Such is the grip that the Cult-controlled state has on perception that many even demand more control and deletion of freedom which they and their own children will have to live with for the rest of their lives. Kyung Hee Kim, professor of education at the College of William and Mary in Virginia, ran a study involving a very large number of school-age children between kindergarten and 12th grade which tracked the effect of (the Cult's) 'education' programming of the young. The study found the following as children were processed by the system:

> A massive decline of creativity [right brain] as 'children have become less emotionally expressive [right brain], less energetic, less talkative and verbally expressive, less humorous [right brain], less imaginative [right brain], less unconventional [right brain], less lively and passionate [right brain], less perceptive [right brain], less apt to connect seemingly irrelevant things [right brain], less synthesizing [right brain], and less likely to see things from a different angle [right brain].

I rest my case, M'Lud (Fig 221).

Sending them crazy

When do you ever hear political parties and

Figure 221: What the 'education' system does to young people. Tell them to fuck off, kids. (Image David Dees.)

ideologies, whether 'Left', 'Right' or 'Centre', challenge what and how children and young people are 'taught'? They argue incessantly over the money spent on 'education' and class sizes. They say next to nothing about 'education' as a programming operation from first to last. Some are Cult agents (very few) and the rest are as perceptually programmed as anyone after being subjected to the same download. There is a war on children, mentally and emotionally, and this is some of the background to the suicide rate among the young dramatically increasing through a combination, among other things, of exam stress (what the hell are the parents doing?) and the multiple pressures of the smartphone, social media, era which is orchestrated through Cult-controlled Silicon Valley. Adding still further to these pressures is the often near life-long levels of debt imposed on the young to pay for their college and university 'education'. The merciless Cult-driven state has manipulated young people to pay for at least decades for their own *programming* through empathy-deleted universities that operate like multinational corporations selling a stream of made-up, for-profit-only, shit and useless 'courses' to dip their snouts in an ever-deeper trough at the expense of the young. To them young people are just commodities or punters to be exploited like the worse kind of spiv and to be indoctrinated with The System's perceptual blueprint. The outstanding student loan 'bubble' in the United States accrued to pay outrageous college fees has passed *$1.6 trillion.* This staggering figure represents devastated young and adult lives crushed by debt and thus ... *control.* Analysis by the Institute of Fiscal Studies for the UK Department of Education suggested that one in five students would be financially better off if they had not gone to university and instead left school to get a job. It must be a similar case elsewhere. Wayne Johnson, former CEO of First Performance Corporation and Reunion Student Loan Finance Corporation, resigned his post at the US Department of Education to campaign for justice on this issue including cancellation of most outstanding student debt owed to the Federal government (though not to private Cult corporations). Johnson said that if the loan crisis is not fixed we would see the 'ever-increasing destruction of the fabric of America, it's that profound – people are not getting married, not having children'. This was always the plan as part of the transformation of human society. Tony Blair introduced student fees in the UK when he was prime minister and they have since soared as they were always intended to. Everything that Blair does and says is the Cult doing and saying. The man should be in jail for crimes against humanity for so many reasons including life-crippling student debt.

More parents are seeing through the calculated fraud and homeschooling their children either individually or in small groups with great success in both critical and creative thinking and career advancement. Eliezer Yudkowsky, the well-known American AI researcher and author of several academic books on the subject, never attended high school or college and had no formal 'education'. 'Liberal' Germany bans homeschooling – a policy instigated by the Nazis – and so do 'liberal' Sweden and the Netherlands. If you want to sell tyranny do it under the banner and smokescreen of liberal democracy. As homeschooling rapidly expands the pressure to limit or ban education outside the school system is growing. Parents are raided by armed police in Germany and children removed from parents for the crime of not wishing to have them indoctrinated by the state. My own preference is for 'self-directed learning' in which children pursue their own interests and experiences and in doing so learn all the other basic skills. If you research your interest you need to learn to read; if you compile information about your interest you have to learn to write. Children can learn what they *choose* to learn and as a by-product learn what they *need* to learn. Their minds don't have to be filled with what is irrelevant to most of them just because the state insists on that for its own ends. Children have their whole life to learn what they need to know from the far more relevant perspective of where their life takes them. How many ever use algebra once they leave school? What is the benefit to them of spending hours of their childhood working out what X equals??

A study by Dr Peter Gray, an American psychology professor at Boston College, found that children's mental health improved significantly when they engaged in self-directed education with more freedom and control of their own learning. He found after studying the data that the mental health of children is directly related to school attendance with psychiatrist visits falling dramatically during school holidays away from the pressure of lessons, rules and exams. They spiked once again when a new term began. Gray said that available evidence suggests 'quite strongly' that school is bad for children's mental health: '... behaviour, moods, and learning generally improved when they stopped conventional schooling.' He added that school is bad for 'physical' health, too: 'Nature did not design children to be cooped up all day at a micromanaged, sedentary job.' One of the most profound forms of mind control is familiarity. Once something becomes familiar it is no longer questioned and becomes another integrated subconscious program and assumption. Kids are born and then pretty soon they go to school and college for the rest of their childhood, right? Everyone knows that – it's how things are. Draw the 'education' system out of the subconscious and make it conscious. Now look again at how it works and the consequences for children. *Oh my God*, it's a *programming* operation. *Exactly*. The urgency with which this needs to be acknowledged can be seen in the figures for young people suicide and extreme levels of stress happening across the world. Suicide attempts by children under the age of 14 in Israel alone have risen by *62 percent* in a decade, according to the Israeli National Council for Children. In Britain children under 11 contacting the help service Childline over suicidal thoughts and feelings increased by *87 percent* between 2015 and 2020. The Cult is killing childhood and parents need to get their arses in gear *fast* because it's meant to get much worse. A 2013 study by the American Psychological Association found that school is the main source of stress for teenagers with 83 percent of teenagers questioned saying school was 'a somewhat or significant source of stress' while 27 percent said they suffered from 'extreme stress' during the school year. This dropped to 13 percent during school holidays and out-of-school stress would fall even further if you delete smartphones and social media. Much of the academic pressure on kids comes from parents who have slavishly accepted the utter baloney that exam passes = intelligence and exam results decide success or failure for the rest of their lives. How many young people feel a failure because they didn't get high enough exam grades? Who gives a shit? You are *All That Is, Has Been, And Ever Can Be.*

Are you happy?

No.

Are you fulfilled?

No.

Are you super-stressed?

Yes.

So what's good about school?

I know what X equals. No, hold on, I forgot.

Most outrageous are those parents who treat their children and their academic success as a personal statement about themselves in some bizarre exercise in reflected glory which includes the follow-through of what the parents 'want' their children to be. 'Your father wants you to be a banker'; 'Your mother wants you to be a lawyer'. Well, tough – I'm going walking in India. Bye. This is nothing less than child abuse. We bring children into the world and we can give them advice, but it's *their* life, not ours. The late and very great American comedian, George Carlin, said: 'Here's a bumper sticker I'd like to see ... we are proud parents of a child who has resisted his teachers' attempts to break his spirit and bend him to the will of his corporate masters.' The Cult's war on children in pursuit of perceptual control is getting so extreme and intense that the consequences are destroying whole generations. Parents worldwide have a responsibility to say *'enough!'*

Postage stamp society

Young minds are at the mercy of the programming system throughout their key perception-forming years from at least aged four to nearly 20. Most – thankfully not all – absorb the program subconsciously if not always consciously and without the de-programming process called 'awakening' those beliefs and assumptions will drive their perception of everything for the rest of their lives. Ironically, and not by chance, those that teach (program) the next generations are academics who have rarely, mostly never, left the 'education' program. They absorb what they are told in their own 'education' and pass exams to prove that. Then they head for teacher training colleges and courses which further underpin the program and show them how to indoctrinate the next generation with The System's (the Cult's) version of everything. Freemasons climb their hierarchy in compartmentalised sections called 'degrees' and ambitious young people (and/or their parents) seek the ultimate goal in 'education' of securing a 'degree' from the false assumption (it's *all* assumption) that a degree is confirmation of intelligence. It is not. Some of the most intelligent people I have met have never been near a university let alone a 'degree' while some of the least intelligent have had 'educational qualifications' coming out of their ears. This is not to say you can't have a degree *and* be intelligent – only that one doesn't have to mean the other and often does not. With both Freemasons and 'education' the degree measures the degree of programming thanks to another assumption that the information imparted in the lodge or the college is factually correct. Much of it isn't and indeed Freemasons are told one thing in one degree and something different in another to keep them in ignorance of what the inner core knows. Armed with a degree, or at least some degree of perceptual programming, young people leave the halls of academia and go out into the 'world'. Here they meet others who earlier went through the same programming machine and overwhelmingly accept the same *assumptions* about life, society and reality. They have all been given, and largely absorbed consciously and subconsciously, the system's (Cult's) version of history, science and reality, medicine, human biology, world events, what's possible and impossible, the whole shebang. Together this forms what I have dubbed the Postage Stamp Consensus which is a staggeringly narrow band of perceived possibility designed specifically to keep humanity in the Bubble (Fig 222).

Young people entering the adult workplace now have the assumptions they downloaded at school and college confirmed by almost everyone around them who earlier downloaded the *same* assumptions at their school and college. From this comes 'everyone knows that' syndrome. Even more accurately it should be 'everyone *remembers* that' syndrome. This is all it is – *memory*. The memory (conscious and mostly subconscious) of what you were told some time and what everyone remembers because everyone was told the same thing. Indian 'mystic' Jaggi Vasudev (known as Sadhguru) talks about 'mistaking memory for intelligence' and he's spot on. How can we intelligently see things as they are when memory (perception

Figure 222: Jump off and RUN! (Image Gareth Icke.)

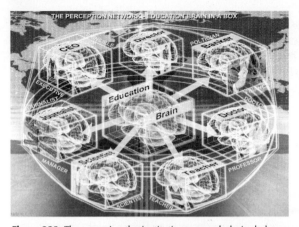

Figure 223: Those serving the institutions overwhelmingly have the same perceptions of reality because they have all been through the same 'education' programming system. Therefore: 'Everyone knows that!' (Image Neil Hague.)

programming) is constantly telling us what we should believe they are? Sadhguru describes how people live out of their memory and not their intelligence and this is what The Program sets out to achieve. Postage Stamp Consensus and 'everyone knows/remembers that' are different descriptions of the same program which means that the institutions of politics, government administration, law, science, academia, medicine, media, business, banking, etc. are all founded (except the inner cores connected to the Cult) on the same assumptions about the world and reality when they are nothing more than illusions (Fig 223). They are founded (quantum physics excepted) on the world being solid, people being only their bodies and labels, everything being apart from everything else, and only through 'physical' change can anything *be* changed. Don't change your perceptions and assumptions to instigate societal change. If you want change you have to physically protest on the basis of your current perceptions and assumptions which have contributed to the very situations you are protesting about. It is sobering to think that governments and politicians are making laws all over the world based on assumptions about reality that are utterly bogus. Politicians are arguing over what should happen to everyone and everything from perceptions of a world that doesn't exist except in the way it appears to be experienced. No wonder the world is in the state it is. Which deluded programmed mind are you going to vote for, the one with the blue rosette, or the red, yellow, or the green? *Mmmm*, hard isn't it? The Cult has created a system in which programmed 'leaders' clueless about reality impose the Cult agenda upon a population enslaved in the same ignorance if they only get their perceptions from the Mainstream Everything. Talk about the blind leading the blind. Watch that cliff now (Fig 224). More than that the institutions and personnel of the Postage Stamp continually confirm to each other that the nonsense is valid and each make their decisions about what to do from those flawed assumptions. Governments make laws, including those relating to health care, on the basis of what Postage Stamp science

'IF THE BLIND LEAD THE BLIND, BOTH SHALL FALL INTO THE DITCH'

Figure 224: A perfect description of those who believe what The System tells them.

says. They instigate policy decisions on the basis of what Postage Stamp academics say. It's a mad house in which crazy is credible and sanity is crazy. What a mess and I have likened the world to putting 20 kittens in a room with 100 balls wool and coming back two hours later to say: 'Okay, sort that out'. Fortunately bringing harmony and sanity to human society does not have to be done 'physically' and cannot be because there is no 'physical'.

Every aspect of the Cult agenda comes with a protection system to stop those with a mind of their own demolishing the ludicrous assumptions which humanity has to believe for the agenda to prevail. This is where censorship comes in and one major example of that is peer pressure – the paramilitary arm of 'everyone knows that' syndrome which seeks to impose the worst of all censorship and that is self-censorship. I have seen this described as the tyranny of silence. There is no debate or conversation as people with different views keep their mouths shut to avoid peer pressure consequences (Fig 225). Peer pressure is a term for those who have allowed themselves to be programmed into believing mega-untruths and insisting that everyone else does the same. If people don't acquiesce then ridicule, dismissal, abuse and even a lost job or career will follow. Intimidation and fear of consequences makes so many stay silent about what they think and leaves the field for 'everyone knows syndrome' to dominate perception unchallenged. Well, fuck that, I say. Let people follow others if they want – I'll follow myself, thanks (Fig 226 overleaf). Those with open minds are the black sheep of the flock or herd and it's such a wonderful place to be.

IMPRISONED BY

CONFORMITY

Figure 225: Don't think for yourself – prison is lovely. (Image Gareth Icke.)

If you are there – *celebrate*. Would you want to be part of the herd?? Shit, what a nightmare. To be called mad by a system that's insane is a confirmation of your sanity. You say I'm mad Mr System Believer? *Yippee*, thank-you, so kind. I refer to this peer pressure to conform as 'psychological fascism' and that's what it is. We now have

FOLLOW THE HERD

EVERYONE ELSE DOES

Figure 226: Baa, baa, baa.

ever more extreme psychological fascism in the form of political correctness and the Climate Change Cult which together stand beneath the umbrella term of 'Woke'. The emergence of social media as a vehicle for black sheep abuse by the herd mentality has added to the pressure to keep your head down. Well, fuck that, too, I say. That'll be the day.

Media software

Cult 'education' instils the foundation perception program while the mainstream media is the constant top-up and confirmation that also plays the role of perception enforcer. Speak publicly in ways that challenge the Cult agenda and see what happens. I say *mainstream* media. Even much of the 'alternative' involves those who have been through the same perceptual programming and accepted its validity. Swathes of the 'alternative media' have ridiculed me over the years as much as the mainstream has for my 'far-out' concepts. Many of these same people with a Christian background believe that a man was born to a virgin mother, walked on water, turned water into wine, fed 5,000 from a few loaves and fishes, died on a cross, came back to life in a cave, and floated up to heaven promising to return on a cloud. Followers of Judaism, among them mainstream journalists and media owners that have ridiculed me, claim to believe that God parted the Red Sea and the wife of some bloke called Lot was turned into a pillar of salt. One thing you see very clearly when you operate outside the programmed 'normal' is that people don't demand evidence for their own beliefs on anything like the scale they demand for others. Postage Stamp programming is again driving the perceptions and behaviour of the media. At ownership and key editorial levels you will find in-the-loop Cult operatives. The teeming majority of journalists, however, have no idea there is a Cult never mind that it controls their industry. They report the world from the perspective of their Postage Stamp programming and anything or anyone they come across that has disembarked its narrow band of perception is, by definition, mad, bad, or both. That mentality dominates the nature of their reporting and treatment of individuals and organisations even without the added limitations set by their employers on what can and cannot be said (Fig 227). We have the ubiquitous subconscious programming at work in controlling the actions of the entire media as the propaganda arm of the Mainstream Everything: The only scientific truth comes from

Figure 227: 'Journalism' the world over with honorable exceptions.

mainstream scientists; the only medical truth comes from doctors; valid explanations of world events come only from governments and mainstream commentators, and so it goes on. I watched an interview with a former mainstream journalist who had partly seen through the manipulation and good for her. She said that I say some 'fantastic' things about education, but dismissed the bit about a shapeshifting royal family. I understand why from the perspective of 'normal' and her life-long ingrained conscious and subconscious perceptions about reality. What I say about education is within her sense of the possible, so that's fine. Once you breach the limits of programmed 'normal' and 'possible', that's not fine. 'I can't get my head around that', people say. *Exactly.* So try the heart and expanded consciousness. Give that a go. There are many from what is called the 'Left' *and* 'Right' who agree with what I say about the world from their perspective of Postage Stamp normal. They won't say so publicly because they don't want to be associated with things I say that are off the Postage Stamp. The foundations for these responses are (a) the world is solid so what he says can't be true and (b) what would people think about me if I said he talked sense?

Reporting parameters set by media owners and executives are another generator of self-censorship with journalists knowing the lines they can't cross without resistance or the door. As a result they don't cross them. No report or information is offered to their media bosses that breaches the dyke. At that point they are no longer journalists and little more than propagandists for the Cult's version of everything. The money's good, though, eh? The BBC in Britain is particularly adept at such ingrained censorship which it tries so hard to hide behind pompous self-congratulation about unbiased reporting when it is institutionally Postage Stamp biased. By the terms of its charter the BBC is supposed to be politically neutral yet exercises its political and system bias by what it leaves out, through the views of the guests it invites to pontificate on its output and by not inviting those who have a different perspective to the Postage Stamp (Fig 228 overleaf). They'll let you debate how much money should be in circulation but absolutely not the fact that private banks are lending people and governments credit 'money' that has never and will never exist. The BBC has outrageously skewed the climate change debate so it's not a debate at all by virtually banning views and information that expose the hoax behind the

Figure 228: The BBC version.

orthodoxy. You don't have to come out and say 'vote for so and so' or 'believe this or that' to manipulate information in favour of your political line and I am talking about a political *agenda* line and not necessarily *party* political in nature. The BBC is a department of the permanent government and takes its line on everything no matter who is officially 'in power'. BBC 'journalists' are in fact little more than civil servants who know their place and where not to go. If you get your 'truth' from the BBC, well, by definition, you *don't* because you *can't*. It's the same with all of them, but the BBC's pompous self-congratulation about its 'quality journalism' is particularly sickening and stomach-turning, not to say laughable. Journalist Tareq Haddad resigned from *Newsweek* in late 2019 claiming that editors stopped him reporting the story about a whistleblower at the OPCW, the world chemical weapons 'watchdog', who exposed how the organisation manipulated the facts to allow a chemical attack in Syria to be blamed on Cult-target President Assad. This was done by suppressing evidence that proved Assad had nothing to do with it. The attack was really staged by US-backed terrorists as an excuse to demonise Assad and justify unleashing missiles against Syria – a No-Problem-Reaction-Solution. Haddad confirmed that the media is the propaganda arm of the government-military-intelligence-industrial complex or what I call the Cult:

> The US government, in an ugly alliance with those [that] profit the most from war, has its tentacles in every part of the media – imposters, with ties to the US State Department, sit in newsrooms all over the world ... Inconvenient stories are completely blocked. As a result, journalism is quickly dying. America is regressing because it lacks the truth.

The Cult owns governments as it owns the media as it owns the armament companies. The late Dr Udo Ulfkotte, a leading journalist in Germany, went public to reveal how he was made to publish articles in his own name written by intelligence agencies or lose his job. The sources included the CIA even though he was working in Germany. The Cult has no borders.

Fake 'grassroots' programming

Former CBS News investigative reporter Sharyl Attkisson revealed in a
Ted Talk how fraudulent grassroots movements, funded by political,
corporate, or other special interests (the Cult), manipulate public
perception. The technique is known as 'astroturfing', as in fake
grassroots. Special interests hide behind coordinated groups and
individuals who start Facebook and Twitter accounts, write letters to
newspapers and post comments in support or opposition to something.
The idea is to give the false impression that a grassroots movement is
speaking and that opinion is going a certain way when neither is true.
The media, naturally, very rarely question the origins or funders. An
excellent example of astroturfing was when American Zionist
communications firm Edelman launched a Walmart-supporting
'grassroots' group called Working Families for Walmart which turned
out to be funded by Walmart. Attkisson said astroturf groups try to
change public opinion and marginalise opposition to what they want by
attacking them and appearing to be part of a grassroots campaign that
doesn't actually exist. You see this throughout the Woke agenda of
climate change, transgender activism, political correctness, anti-racism
and other connected issues with the media reporting them as if they are
spontaneous and genuine. Surveys and studies are funded by
astroturfers to produce the answers and conclusions they want to
advance their propaganda. This happens constantly with regard to
climate change, transgender, drugs and vaccines. Attkisson highlighted
the manipulations of Wikipedia which she called an astroturf dream
come true:

> Built as the free encyclopaedia that anyone can edit, the reality can't be more
> different. Anonymous Wikipedia editors control and co-opt pages on behalf of
> special interests. They forbid and reverse edits that go against their agenda.
> They skew and delete information in blatant violation of Wikipedia's own
> established policies with impunity, always superior to the poor schlubs who
> actually believe anyone can edit Wikipedia, only to discover they're barred
> from correcting even the simplest factual inaccuracies.

Wikipedia is a shocking operation. The Off-guardian.org website
pointed out that Wikipedia's nine billion page views per month are
overseen by just 500 active administrators and their real identity in
many cases remains unknown. 'Moreover studies have shown that 80%
of all Wikipedia content is written by just 1% of all Wikipedia editors,
which again amounts to just a few hundred mostly unknown people.'
Sharyl Attkisson recalled a huge scandal when Wikipedia officials were
caught offering a PR service that skewed and edited information for
paid publicity-seeking clients in utter violation of Wikipedia's alleged

policies:

> All of this may be why, when a medical study looked at medical conditions described on Wikipedia pages and compared it to actual peer-reviewed published research, Wikipedia contradicted medical research 90 percent of the time. You may never fully trust what you read on Wikipedia again, nor should you.

You won't be surprised to know that Wikipedia is an agency of the agenda as a platform where billions get their information about people, events and every other subject (Fig 229). Israel (its Sabbatian-Frankist control system) has a colossal astroturfing and opinion-manipulating army driving its global

Figure 229: Hijacking global perception.

'Hasbara' campaign to promote the narrative of what I call the 'Anti-Semitism Protection Racket' (more shortly) and the far-right Sabbatian-Frankist apartheid Israeli government. Hasbara means 'explaining' which *really* means explaining what the Sabbatian-Frankists want you to believe. Ultra-Zionist ownership of the media in the United States is infamous although the Protection Racket intimidates most people from stating the obvious. Where there is not direct ownership there is a whole network operating out of Israel and exposed in *The Trigger* that manipulates media coverage of Israel. *Jewish News* reported in 2019 about an email sent to the wrong address by Lorna Fitzsimons, director of BICOM (the British Israel Communication & Research Centre). The email, which was never meant to be widely distributed, said: 'Throughout the weekend, BICOM staff were in contact with a whole host of BBC and Sky News desks and journalists, ensuring that the most objectively favourable line was taken, and offering talking heads, relevant to the stories unfolding.' Fitzsimons went on to describe a BICOM trip to Israel by a BBC news presenter:

> Bicom has one of BBC News' key anchors on a bespoke delegation. When planning her very first trip to the region, Sophie Long got in touch with Bicom to see if we could help her out with meeting [sic] in the region. Sophie is now spending three days of her trip with Bicom Israel, taking a tour around the Old City, meeting [Israeli government spokesman] Mark Regev… as well as visiting Ramallah and Sderot.

This is how your 'news' is manipulated by ultra-Zionism alone every day. If you read *The Trigger* the scale on which this is happening out of Israel worldwide will blow your mind. Add into the mix the expanded definition of 'anti-Semitism' which includes criticism of Israel and Zionism and you see how any balanced coverage of Israel (Sabbatian-Frankists that control Israel) has long past. Ultra-Zionist Fitzsimons, a former Labour Party MP and president of the National Union of Students, said in the email that BICOM had 'briefed Jonathan Ford, the *Financial Times* leader writer for his upcoming leading article'. I wonder if the Palestinians had, too? That's obviously a rhetorical question. The now shocking scale of Sabbatian-Frankist control worldwide hiding behind 'Israel' was further confirmed, as with my own speaking ban from Australia in 2019, by the experience of former Pink Floyd singer Roger Waters and American journalist Abby Martin who are both critics of Israeli government treatment of Palestinians. *American* Major League Baseball banned advertising for Waters events on its platforms on the say-so of Rothschild-created B'nai B'rith International who have been on my case many times. B'nai B'rith president Charles Kaufman and chief executive Daniel Mariaschin said Waters was 'an avowed anti-Semite whose views on Jews and Israel far exceed the boundaries of civil discourse'. This is Orwellian code for 'Waters tells the truth so we have to shut him up'. Abby Martin is suing the state of Georgia after she was prevented from speaking at Georgia Southern University for refusing to sign a pledge of allegiance to *Israel*. Some 28 states have so far mandated loyalty pledges to Israel to block exposure of the actions of its government, military and fantastic web of lobby groups. That is worth pondering for a moment to take in the full implications of Sabbatian-Frankist power in the United States. American citizens cannot speak in a country that claims free speech rights guaranteed by the First Amendment unless they sign a pledge of alliance to a country of a few million people 5,000 miles away. But no – saying that Israel has fantastically disproportionate global power compared with size and numbers is an 'anti-Semitic' trope even though it's blatantly true. This is what happens where the Cult is in control.

Forest protection agency

We now have global 'news' spewing out the Cult system's version of everything 24/7 on channels so many in number I'm sure they must breed overnight like luminous jackets appear to do in Britain. Media 'diversity' is a joke. Newspapers and TV channels may be biased to one political party or other, but they are all biased in support of the *same system* – the same *Postage Stamp*. They differ on the twigs while all promote the same forest. Arguments over twigs present the illusion of diversity. Challenge the forest, the structure of control and manipulation, and the truth about 'diversity' becomes self-evident. They *all* promote and protect the forest as I've found again and again in the last 30 years. The media first ridiculed me on a historic scale before turning to abuse and demonisation which morphed more recently into outright ignoring or censoring me. These phases directly relate to the scale of public interest in my work which has been growing exponentially year on year. That Icke is exposing the forest – *laugh* at him. Er, that didn't work – *demonise* him. Oh no, *that* didn't work – *censor* him! The censorship was never more obvious than with the publication of my absolutely explosive book, *The Trigger*, which exposes who was really behind the attacks of 9/11 and it wasn't 19 Arab hijackers working for Osama bin Laden. In revealing the central players in that horror I also reveal the Cult and its control system. It is *so* explosive and perceptually transforming that the usual suspects didn't even seek to attack me and the book as they normally would. Abuse would give the content publicity and they want the fewest number possible to know it exists. One of the main ways the Cult has sought to demonise me is through its anti-Semitism industry, or Protection Racket. Its method of operation is to condemn anyone (especially Jewish people) who criticise the government of Israel as 'anti-Semitic (which really means anti-Arab as I have explained many times). Cult gofers, many of which won't even know there *is* a Cult, have used this label to block my public events and media appearances including a ban by the Australian government from speaking in that country on the say-so of one ultra-Zionist asset and pressure from media outlets owned by Israel-fanatic Rupert Murdoch. This censorship network is a protection racket to protect the Cult from exposure and not Jewish people from discrimination. Jewish people who don't conform to the narrative are attacked even more vociferously than anyone else.

I did two interviews with the now Rupert Murdoch-owned TalkRadio in Britain which at the time of writing have accrued in excess of three million views on YouTube. The ultra-Zionist censor group, the Campaign Against Antisemitism (CAA), complained to the station for having me on because of 'anti-Semitism' even though neither Israel nor Zionism was discussed in either interview. Several TalkRadio programmes were later sent copies of *The Trigger*, but not one would have me on to discuss the content despite the previous two getting such big YouTube audiences. Protecting the forest is far more important to media owners than money. The Cult ensures their major assets are swimming in that. No British national newspaper or radio station would even mention *The Trigger* and 5,000 media releases sent out to newspapers, radio and television across Britain, Europe and North America met with no mainstream response. A TV booker told me that a well-known British television talk show host refused to have me on his show because I 'deny the Holocaust'. *I don't*, if you read my books, but he wouldn't know that because he takes his cue from other media promotors of The System. The mainstream media operates likes The System in general with the perceptually-programmed confirming to each other that their perceptual-programming is the truth. Cult assets lie and misrepresent people; the media report the lies unchallenged; other media assets believe the lies and accept them as their reality; and they then repeat and further circulate the lies as 'everyone knows that' truth. Copies of *The Trigger* were sent to the Russian 'alternative' TV station RT in both London and Moscow. They didn't want to know either. RT is funded by the Russian government and as such conducts journalism with regard to the West more in the way the Western media should be doing. I'm glad RT exists from that perspective. It questions what the Western media refuses to do *except* when it comes to the Russian government. RT journalistic values are then immediately ditched and cap-touching 'yes sir, no sir', kicks in. I have been writing and talking for 30 years about all the subjects that RT covers and although it claims to be 'alternative' they have never had me on their news programmes while preferring many who from my perspective are nowhere close to 'alternative'. Why would a Russian government-funded station not want to discuss a mountain of evidence that the American government lied at every turn about 9/11?? I was approached out of the blue for a substantial feature interview by an RT reporter called Polly Boiko in September, 2019, which she said they wanted to go quickly to air. She and a crew came to my house soon after with a view to almost immediate transmission. They left after filming with me for hours and said they hoped it would be broadcast within days. As I write the best part of a *year* later I am still waiting. The mainstream media basically says question nothing; RT's motto is 'question more'; but I say question *everything*. That makes me an outsider to all of them. I dismantle the forest which their owners in multiple forms are pledged to protect. The Cult knows that seeing only the twigs keeps you in Body-Mind with a sense of apartness and twigs are not a problem. Seeing the forest and how it all fits together sets you free and that's a *BIG* problem. *Censor him!*

By the few, for the few

Incessant concentration of media ownership is the Cult gathering ever more control over what people see and hear to dictate perception and behaviour across the world. Major corporations (in the end *one* Cult corporation) have secured global ownership of newspapers, radio, television and the Internet through Silicon Valley and Pentagon agency DARPA which I'll come to shortly. The media once had some diversity of ownership and that could not be allowed to continue. Diversity is the enemy of central control and the campaign began to concentrate power for the benefit of the Cult. As recently as 1984 there were still 50 'independent' media companies in the United States. By 2019 some 90 percent of the US media was controlled by just *four* – Comcast (NBCUniversal), Disney, AT&T (WarnerMedia) and Viacom. The last two are owned by the National Amusements corporation. Control over what you see and hear is now ridiculously narrow and planned to get even more so. Political leaders sanction this as you would expect when the Cult owns politics as it owns major media. Such concentration allows what is written and broadcast to be centrally dictated and focused only on the twigs while exposure of the forest is censored. You can see video compilations on the Internet of TV presenters in cities and communities across America reading the same stories word for word and repeating with guests the same scripted phrases and talking points to push the same political agenda. There was once such a thing as 'independent radio' in Britain and I worked at a station in Birmingham called BRMB. It was owned by a single company and had an independent operation for local news. Today those stations are owned by corporations with centrally-dictated news broadcasts and even music playlists. I was libelled by the usual suspects in the UK in 2017 with outrageous claims about what I am saying. I saw the same lies repeated – again almost word for word with the same headline – on a series of newspaper Internet sites. When I checked I realised they were all owned by the same corporation then called Trinity Mirror and now Reach PLC. This is what that company owns (not an exhaustive list) and it will give you an idea for what I mean about the centralisation of media power over what you see and hear:

National newspapers: *Daily Mirror; Sunday Mirror; Daily Express; Sunday Express; Daily Record; Sunday Mail; Western Mail; The Sunday People; Irish Daily Mirror; Irish Daily Star* (50% ownership). Local and regional newspapers; *Accrington Observer; Anfield & Walton Star; Barking & Dagenham Yellow Advertiser; Bexley Mercury; Birmingham Post; Birmingham Mail; Sunday Mercury; Bootle Times; Bracknell Standard; Brent & Wembley Leader; Bristol Post; Buckinghamshire Examiner; Buckinghamshire Advertiser; Chester Chronicle; Chronicle Extra* (Newcastle upon Tyne); *Colne Valley Chronicle; Coventry Telegraph; The Crawley News; Crewe Chronicle; Crosby Herald; Derby Evening Telegraph; Dover Express; Ealing Gazette; Ealing Informer; Ealing Leader; Ellesmere Port Pioneer; Enfield Advertiser; Enfield Gazette; Evening Chronicle* (Newcastle upon Tyne); *Evening Gazette* (Teesside); *Express & Echo; Formby Times; Fulham & Hammersmith Chronicle; The Glaswegian; Gloucester Citizen; Gloucestershire Echo; Haringey Advertiser; Harrow & Wembley Observer; Harrow Informer; Harrow Leader; Havering Yellow Advertiser; Heywood Advertiser; Highdown Books; Hinckley*

Times; Hounslow Borough Chronicle; Hounslow, Chiswick & Whitton Informer; Huddersfield District Chronicle; Huddersfield Examiner; Hull Daily Mail; Ilford & Redbridge Yellow Advertiser; The Journal (Newcastle upon Tyne); *Kensington & Chelsea Informer; Leicester Mercury; Lewisham & Greenwich Mercury; Liverpool Echo; Loughborough Echo; Manchester Evening News; Manchester Metro News; Maghull Star; Middleton Guardian; Mid Devon Gazette; Mitcham, Morden & Wimbledon Post; Neath Guardian; North East Manchester Advertiser; North Devon Journal; North Wales Daily Post; Nottingham Post; Oldham Advertiser; Ormskirk Advertiser; Paisley Daily Express; The Press* (Barnet and Hendon); *Prestwich Advertiser; Reading Post; Rochdale Observer; Rossendale Free Press; Runcorn & Widnes Weekly News; Salford Advertiser; Slough Express; Stockport Express; Macclesfield Express; Wilmslow Express; The Sentinel* (Staffordshire); *Surrey Advertiser; Southport Visiter; South Manchester Reporter; South Liverpool Merseymart; South Wales Echo; South Wales Evening Post; Staines Informer; Streatham, Clapham & West Norwood Post; Sunday Sun* (Newcastle Upon Tyne); *Surrey Herald; Surrey Mirror Advertiser; Sutton & Epsom Post; Tameside Advertiser; Glossop Advertiser; Uxbridge & Hillingdon Leader; Uxbridge Gazette; Walton & Weybridge Informer; The Wharf* (Canary Wharf). *Scottish and Universal Newspapers:* Trinity Mirror Scotland; *Airdrie and Coatbridge Advertiser; Ayrshire Post; Blairgowrie Advertiser; Business 7; Dumfries and Galloway Standard; East Kilbride News; Galloway News; Hamilton Advertiser; Irvine Herald; Kilmarnock Standard; Metro Scotland; Paisley Daily Express; Perthshire Advertiser; Scottish Business Insider; Stirling Observer; Strathearn Herald; The Lennox Herald; West Lothian Courier; Wishaw Press.* Digital online brands: Belfast Live; Dublin Live; Examiner Live (Huddersfield); Glasgow Live; Gloucestershire Live; Leeds Live.

When you look around news shops and stands and see all those newspapers and magazines on every conceivable subject it appears that media diversity is alive and well. Check who owns them and you realise that media diversity is history. I list in my book *Human Race Get Off Your Knees* the media outlets from television to magazines then owned by Time Warner. It is extraordinary in both length and range of subjects and goes on for more than one and a half pages. Two of America's most prominent newspapers, the *New York Times* and *Washington Post* are both owned by the same elite. The *Times* has been owned by the Zionist Sulzberger family since 1896 while the *Post* was controlled from 1930s by the Zionist Graham-Meyer family before being sold to Amazon's 'world's richest man' Jeff Bezos in 2013 whose company has close ties to the CIA. No potential bias there, then.

The Devil's Playground – media endgame

People get most of their information today in the form of 'news' through

Cult-controlled Silicon Valley corporations such as Google, YouTube, Facebook and Twitter. Add to that the domination of the global book market by Amazon. The Cult created the Internet to serve its agenda for human control. In terms of the subject at hand they want all information to eventually be transferred to the Internet because then it can be censored through algorithms of artificial intelligence without even human involvement once the codes are in place. The Internet for all its short-term benefits

Figure 230: Cult to its DNA.

has been a Trojan horse from the start and the real reason – or reasons – for its creation will become clear in later chapters. What a surprise that the Internet was made possible by the Cult-controlled US Defense Advanced Research Projects Agency (DARPA), the technological development arm of the Pentagon, which has seed-funded Silicon Valley corporations along with In-Q-Tel, or IQT, the technology-funding vehicle of the CIA (Fig 230). The Pentagon, DARPA and the CIA are all Cult assets and agencies of the 'Deep State'. When the Internet was launched it had to be censorship-free to attract the global audience necessary for the DARPA (Cult) goal of making the World Wide Web the central pillar of human society. In this essential honeymoon period we enjoyed the free flow of information which allowed people like me to circulate research to expose the Cult. This was an unfortunate though necessary consequence from the Cult's point of view in pursuit of its ultimate ambitions. Once the Internet was established as the said central pillar of human society in a way that is basically irreversible the mask could come off with a gathering frenzy of censorship to target information that in any way exposes the Cult agenda even without mention of the Cult itself. They, of course, don't present this as censorship. They invent a series of made-up excuses such as 'fake news' and 'hate speech'. The definition of both continues to be expanded to lasso ever more information, views and opinions into their calculated and systematic censorship in the guise of protecting the public from 'hate' and 'discrimination'. They claim to be advancing 'diversity' while destroying it and this particularly applies to the 'Woke' mentality that claims to demand diversity in another example of Cult inversion. Cult-created 'Wokeness' is exploited to justify and impose ever more Internet and media censorship under the guise of political correctness. The Woke British trade union organisation, the TUC, banned a premier of *Renegade*, a film about my life and work, from one of its buildings on the grounds that the TUC 'believes in diversity'. Well, clearly with the exception of anyone exposing the forest. For the TUC read the global mainstream media.

Technology is increasingly being introduced that will prevent the posting of information unacceptable to the Cult without the need to take it down. Even now YouTube, Facebook, Twitter and others employ 'ghost or shadow banning' in which material can be posted but algorithms ensure that they are seen by a fraction of what would otherwise be the case. My YouTube interviews about *The Trigger* and 9/11 were blatantly suppressed through the recommendation system and while they still got large numbers they were not on the scale they would have been if left unmolested. Highly significantly my video interviews have got by far their biggest audiences when posted on YouTube channels not subject to shadow banning than they did on my own algorithmically-manipulated channel before YouTube deleted me altogether in May, 2020 (more later). Facebook admitted in 2018 that it 'demotes' posts reported by users (easy to arrange) and rated as false by 'fact checkers' (working for the Cult agenda). Facebook claimed that this censorship reduced views of posts and pages by 'around 80 percent'. As all information is moved to the Net the point will be reached when the Cult can literally control everything you see with the tyranny of (Cult-instigated) political correctness intimidating people into censoring even private conversations out of fear of being exposed for 'hate speech'. Cult-serving Google, Google-owned YouTube, Facebook and Twitter are major actors in this stage show to hide the real reason that censorship is happening which to protect the Cult and its agenda for humanity from exposure. These Internet-dominating corporations and others like Amazon have been taken through the same process as the World Wide Web. First they allowed the free circulation of information and opinion because they, too, had to attract users on a world-changing scale on their way to near-monopoly. Once that line had been crossed by hugely predominant market share their masks could also be removed and censorship of Cult-unapproved information and opinion began as a drip before becoming the biblical flood that it is today. Amazon has long passed the point of domination in book sales to drive independent shops and publishers out of business and has now begun to target books for censorship in its version of the book-burning so beloved of tyrannies. We have reached the point where people cannot post anything questioning official narratives of 9/11, human-caused climate change or the 'pandemic' on platforms like YouTube without them adding links to read the official fairy tale version on Cult-serving *Wikipedia*. You want the official story of *anything*? Go to Wikipedia. How plain it is to see how information is being royally stitched up and we are still nowhere near where it is meant to go although the massive leap in censorship since the 'Covid-19' hoax gives you some idea. Another point here is that the Cult owns the financial system and has limitless funds by creating 'money' out of nothing. Money is therefore no object for corporations like Google, Facebook, Twitter and Amazon which had no need to post a profit as they were buying their way to monopoly. 'Investors' were always there to write the cheques. You see the same with anything related to Elon Musk (more later). How can other companies that do have to make a profit to survive compete with those that don't have to be profitable and have the financial capability to buy out or crush any independent opposition? Genuine opposition that won't sell-out is demonised by the media under the usual tag of 'hate speech' when they establish other social media and video platforms. Cult-owned website hosts and payment companies also ban them to destroy their ability to function.

Silicon censors

Self-deluding so-called 'journalists' who support this war on information are promoting their own demise as traditional media falls to Silicon Valley domination and its censorship algorithms. Google virtually monopolise Internet searches which are algorithmically manipulated to emphasise official narratives and suppress alternatives. Where Google doesn't control searches other Cult operations pick up the slack. Google-owned YouTube monopolise video content and social media domination falls to Facebook and Twitter. What about Instagram? Owned by Facebook. I don't use social media – I message with WhatsApp? Owned by Facebook. *Big Tech* was made exempt by government from lawsuits for postings on their platforms in return for acting as neutral vehicles rather than publishers who do face legal action for what they publish. Silicon Valley psychopaths have benefited from one while ignoring the other by censoring information challenging the official narrative and particularly those known in America as conservatives. Government could rescind the 'liability exception' deal, but hasn't. It is indicative of how the Cult works that 'conservative' organisations funded by the billionaire Koch family ('conservative') and *Big Tech* have been exposed for campaigning *against* laws to stop Big Tech censorship of conservatives. Control both sides and you control the game. Even more sinister is that these mega-corporations connect into the Cult-controlled Pentagon and intelligence agency network. Big Tech is continually exposed for gathering user data of every kind including surveillance through microphones and this ends up with the military-industrial-intelligence complex on a scale never made public. Many people have noted that conversations they thought were private lead immediately to products relating to the conversation being offered to them in Facebook and other advertisements. Official owners of these Cult-fronts like Facebook's Mark Zuckerberg are super-frauds who are not ultimately in control. They are front people for forces much deeper in The Web than the Zuckerbergs will ever be. Silicon Valley giants are there to control what you see and keep detailed surveillance on what you do, say, and think. Facebook admitted in a letter to two US senators that it can locate where you are even if you have opted out of location tracking. Artificial intelligence can piece together other information to determine location including tagged photographs, addresses for purchases on the Facebook shopping section, and IP address information. Amnesty International said that Google and Facebook were 'posing a systemic threat to human rights' – exactly as they are meant to.

Tim Berners-Lee who is credited with inventing the World Wide Web unveiled a nine-point plan or 'contract' through his World Wide Foundation to 'save the internet' from 'digital dystopia'. Some things sounded good until you knew the flip-side. Authors of this 'contract' included the hate-speech, censorship-obsessed French and German governments and major Silicon Valley censors like Google, Facebook and Microsoft. A highly-significant sentence said it was necessary to 'develop technologies that support the best in humanity and challenge the worst'. When passed through an Orwellian translation unit this becomes 'develop technologies to silence dissenters and renegades'. Who decides what is the 'best' and 'worst', Tim? Ah, *The System* does which wants to silence dissenters and renegades. Ah, gotcha. World Wide Web Foundation president and chief executive Adrian Lovett said prime issues include the problem of 'disinformation'. Who decides what that is? Same answer. He said they will 'track progress of all of those who have signed on, and others too who haven't, and report that progress, make sure it's public, make sure that we're able to see who is going in the right direction and who is not.' Who decides what direction is 'right'? Same answer. The group hopes to enforce the contract through UN regulations and EU/national laws while companies that don't sign up would be ostracised. The group says it will have succeeded when governments and companies that don't back the contract 'principles' are 'true outliers' (defined as 'a person or thing situated away or detached from the main body or system'). Companies and governments that broke the Internet are claiming to save it by taking a rock-hammer to what's left of free expression. Claim you are stopping Internet dystopia while creating it and say at first this will be voluntary before enforcement by law. Does Berners-Lee know it's a scam to advance Internet dictatorship? It doesn't really matter. The corporations and the Cult do.

Wizard's spell

Pull all these strands together and you see that a human life is a cradle to grave download of Cult-desired perception. Postage Stamp parents are followed by Postage Stamp 'education', Postage Stamp media and Postage Stamp Silicon Valley. At the same time the arbiters of reality within human society are taken to be Postage Stamp scientists, Postage Stamp doctors, Postage Stamp academics, Postage Stamp government, Postage Stamp administrators, and Postage Stamp 'experts' of every kind. Their Postage Stamp narratives are enforced by Postage Stamp peer pressure and, should you be a public figure, by Postage Stamp journalists. A definition for my 'Postage Stamp' analogy is *unconsciousness* and my definition of unconscious for the purposes of this book is to be locked away in the perceptual Bubble of Body-Mind. Beliefs and perceptions enshrined in the Postage Stamp Consensus are designed to achieve just that end by suppressing awareness and firewalling people from frequencies where *knowing* can be accessed. Humanity has been mass-hypnotised every bit as much as the stooges in a hypnotist show (Fig 231). Do people on the stage shouting out on a word cue, playing a non-existent musical instrument or seeing the clothed audience as naked *know* they are hypnotised? Do those billions of people who respond to information and situations with their press-enter actions and behaviour *know* they are hypnotised? Of course they don't *because* they are hypnotised. 'Waking up' and 'The Awakening' are terms for breaking the wizard's spell. The idea is to so

Figure 231: The human plight and we have the power to change it.

Figure 232: In close-up what is it? Just blackness?

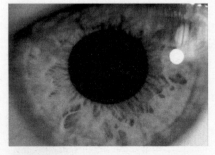

Figure 233: Expand your perspective and you see what it is. Expanding the mind has the same effect.

limit human awareness that we can't see the picture. If people were asked what they were looking at in Figure 232 they would likely say 'blackness' and that would be the extent of it. Expand the image (awareness) and they'd see it was really an eye (Fig 233). Expand still further and you'd see the eye was a person in a room in a house in a street in a city in a world. The Cult wants to enslave perception in that symbolic blackness of myopia and it has achieved this spectacularly in generation after generation by controlling mainstream information and through the constant repetition from all directions of its perceptual program until it becomes an 'everyone knows that'. German philosopher Arthur Schopenhauer said that 'every man takes the limits of his own field of vision for the limits of the world'. This is The Program. Limit their sense of the possible and make them believe that their sense of the possible is the limit of the possible. The truth will then be dismissed and ridiculed and the 'blackness' perceived as the limit of possibility. Schopenhauer was born in 1788. The Program is not new, just more expanded. American Neuroscience researcher Joe Dispenza was on the money when he said: 'Ninety-five percent of who we are by the time we're 35 years old is a memorised set of behaviours, emotional reactions, unconscious habits, hardwired attitudes, beliefs and perceptions that function like a computer program.' Why would it be any other way given what I have described in this chapter alone?

Always back to wavefields

Humanity has been vibrated into conformity on the wavefield level of reality by downloading a collective perception which forms a mass wave-entanglement between like-perceivers (like *frequencies*). Confirmation of Postage Stamp reality does not only happen in the realm of the seen. It is being communicated through wave connections of frequency entanglement. This is the real level at which the herd mentality is formed. A study published in *Current Biology* by researchers from New York University and the Max Planck Institute of Empirical Aesthetics found that brainwaves synchronise into similar patterns when students pay attention and are 'engaged' with each other. Co-lead author Suzanne Dikker said: 'We think that all these effects can be explained by shared attention mechanisms during dynamic group interactions.' From that 'shared attention' comes wave entanglement. What we 'see' is only the decoded holographic version of that. Intimidating people into collective conformity is really vibrating them into line. If you place violins together vibrating to the same note any other violin placed alongside them will start to vibrate to the same note even though it was playing another or none before. The dominant frequency will 'entrain' other frequencies and make them vibrate to its tune. Perceptions and pre-conceived ideas are frequencies and can both entrain others and prevent the person themselves from seeing other possibilities. Technological frequencies such as 5G are designed to have this effect on human brain activity. Some people go into politics with a genuine desire to make a positive difference and then transmute into everything they went into politics to challenge. They have been vibrated into line. Everything is a vibrational field including a parliament, political party or ideology and in the way of the violins the dominant frequency will prevail and absorb others into itself. The same is true of all groups and organisations, schools, universities, science, doctors, media, the whole lot. There's a saying that goes: 'When you dance with the Devil, the Devil doesn't change, the Devil changes you.' The dance in this case is frequency – oscillation – and the Devil is the Cult agenda.

The Devil doesn't *have* to change you and the opposite can be true if you open your heart and mind to connect with consciousness way more

powerful than the Cult and its 'gods'. They can only enslave humanity by making us more ignorant than they are (quite a task). We are not looking at some all-powerful force. It's more like the one-eyed man who can only be king in the land of the blind (Fig 234). The all-seeing eye is not all-seeing. It's a seven-stone weakling compared with humanity in its Infinite power. I've

Figure 234: The Cult controls by suppressing and leeching the power of humanity through perceptual programming – not through power of its own.

been exposing the Cult for 30 years and they have not vibrated me into line. Nor will they ever do so. It will be the other way round.

CHAPTER SEVEN

How are we manipulated?

Facts do not cease to exist because they are ignored – Aldous Huxley

Here's a way to read the world: Know the outcome and you'll see the journey. The Cult is desperate for you not to know what is planned for humanity because once we do the steps towards that end become crystal-clearly obvious day by day. Know the outcome and you'll see the journey, or see the 'where' and you'll see the 'why?' (Fig 235).

The Cult and its agents (knowing and overwhelmingly unknowing) in government, media and The System in general present everything in the form of dots. It is vital to maintain the illusion that policies, laws, media reports and 'education' depict a world in which everything stands apart from everything else. This policy is not connected to that policy, this law to that law, or this change to that change. When you perceive society from that perspective daily life appears to be a series of random and unfathomable events across the great spectrum of human experience. What the hell is going on? Why is this happening? Why are they doing that? Amid such bewilderment many people switch off and don't even try to work it out. I mean, what's the point? It's impossible to understand, right? No – *wrong*. At its core it's all very simple. Human society consists of fields of consciousness – some called 'human' – making wave entanglements on the basis of compatible frequencies generated by *perception*. Control perception and you dictate the entanglements that decide the nature of human interaction collectively known as 'society'. How do you control perception? You control information from which people form perception and at all costs you keep your targets in ignorance of one simple fact: What they see and experience are not the work of random chance but of carefully calculated steps in pursuit of a very specific and extraordinarily sinister end.

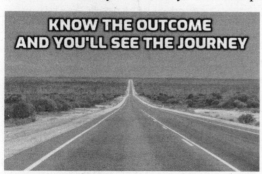

KNOW THE OUTCOME AND YOU'LL SEE THE JOURNEY

Figure 235: A brilliant way to 'read' daily events.

I'll give you a great example of this coldly coordinated 'random' before exposing the wider goals of the Cult and how humanity is manipulated to achieve them. I describe a sequence of events in detail in my mega-work, *The Trigger,* and mentioned them briefly at the start of the book. They involve the network within the Cult known as Sabbatian-Frankism which emerged in the 17th century and infiltrated communities, cultures and religions of all kinds. Sabbatian-Frankists pose as members of communities and followers of religions while infiltrating and directing them to serve the Cult's desired agenda. Sabbatian-Frankists (who hate Jewish people, by the way) control Israel; they *are* the Saudi fake 'royal' family; and they have networks across the world, especially in North America and Europe. Wait – aren't Israel and Saudi Arabia opponents? Not at the level of the Cult they're not. They

are on the same team and any public divisions (increasingly few) are to hide these connections (Fig 236). Once you realise that apparent opponents ultimately answer to the same masters the cataracts of 'random' fall from the eyes. I have already explained how the Bible of Sabbatian-Frankism is the Kabbalah, the Jewish

Figure 236: Both are controlled by the Cult network of Sabbatian-Frankist and so both work to the same script.

esoteric/'spiritual'/nature of reality work. Most important to them is the part known as the Zohar which means 'radiance' or 'illumination'. Three Sabbatian-Frankists chose the name 'Illuminati' for a Cult network they founded officially in 1776. They were Mayer Amschel Rothschild, founder of the Rothschild dynasty, Jacob Frank (hence 'Frankism') and Illuminati frontman, Adam Weishaupt. All the detailed background is in *The Trigger*. Sabbatian-Frankists, their Illuminati and Kabbalah, are yet another example of how global manipulation is founded on the knowledge of how reality works while keeping that knowledge from the target population.

Sabbatian-Frankists have long infiltrated America to the point of control and they created a 'think tank' in 1996 called the Project for the New American Century. Among their number were those who would be major players in the United States government and the Pentagon at the time of 9/11 during the regime of child-like puppet president, Boy George Bush. They included Dick Cheney (9/11 vice-president and de facto president); Donald Rumsfeld (9/11 Secretary of Defense); Paul Wolfowitz (9/11 Deputy Secretary of Defense); Dov Zakheim (9/11 Pentagon comptroller in charge of the entire military budget); and a long list of others either working within government and the Pentagon on 9/11 or promoting wars in the media in response to 9/11. The Project for the New American Century published a document in September, 2000, calling for American troops and military influence to be used to force regime-change in a series of countries including Iraq, Libya, Syria, Iran and North Korea leading in the end to regime-change in China. The document demanded (on behalf of the Sabbatian-Frankists) that American troops 'Fight and decisively win simultaneous major theater wars' to achieve the desired regime change. It said, however, that this 'process of transformation' would be slow 'absent some catastrophic and catalysing event like a New Pearl Harbor' to justify attacks on target countries and the necessary gigantic increases in military spending. A year to the month after the document was published and nine months after those who wrote it came to power with Bush in January, 2001, America had what Bush called at the time 'the Pearl Harbor of the 21st century' – 9/11 (Fig 237).

As a result of those horrific attacks a 'war on terror' was launched and the very countries named in the document have been targeted for regime change ever since under presidents and UK prime ministers of different (and apparently opposing) political parties. At the level of the Cult, which controls the always-there *permanent* government I described earlier, countries are one-party states. Whoever you vote for the Cult is in power. The sequence I have described is much longer and more detailed than outlined here and you'll find the full story in *The Trigger* which demolishes the official story of 9/11 and names those really involved – not 19 Arab hijackers (Fig 238). The point is that if you see each point in the sequence as an isolated in-and-of-itself event there seems to

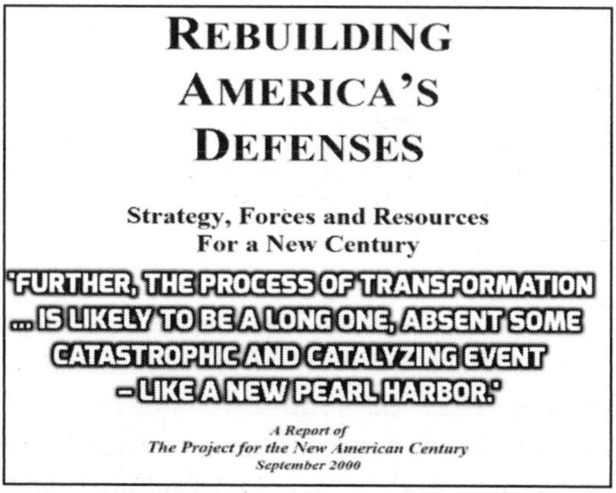

REBUILDING AMERICA'S DEFENSES

Strategy, Forces and Resources For a New Century

'FURTHER, THE PROCESS OF TRANSFORMATION ... IS LIKELY TO BE A LONG ONE, ABSENT SOME CATASTROPHIC AND CATALYZING EVENT – LIKE A NEW PEARL HARBOR.'

A Report of The Project for the New American Century September 2000

Figure 237: The document that listed countries for regime change in September, 2000, which presidents of 'different' parties have pursued ever since. It said that a 'new Pearl Harbor' would be needed to justify the plan and that's what we got – 9/11.

THE TRUTH CANNOT BE SILENCED FOREVER

9/11 WAS AN INSIDE JOB

Figure 238: See *The Trigger* for who was really behind the 9/11 attacks and it wasn't Osama bin Laden.

be no pattern and all appears random. Arab hijackers controlled by Osama bin Laden attacked America and the military invaded Afghanistan to find him; then along came the invasion of Iraq which was to stop Saddam Hussein and his non-existent 'weapons of mass destruction'; Libya was attacked and Colonel Gadhafi was killed to protect the people from Gadhafi violence; Syria was invaded to stop President Assad 'killing his own people'; Iran is being targeted for developing nuclear weapons and sponsoring terrorism. We are asked to believe that none of these events are linked in any way. Connect the dots while knowing the planned outcome and a very different picture can be seen.

Create the problem so you can impose the solution

The media, by emphasis and censorship, presents everything as random so the truth can be hidden and the great majority of journalists are doing this through ignorance, not calculation. Any who do make the connections and want to report them are out the door very fast. It doesn't take many people to control the media so long as the Cult dominates the positions of ownership, editorial policy and hire and fire. This applies to every organisation and institution – government, 'education', banking, business, etc. The attacks of 9/11, regime-change wars and externally-manipulated 'people's revolutions' that followed are examples of two mass mind-control techniques that I dubbed decades ago Problem-Reaction-Solution (PRS) and the Totalitarian Tiptoe (TT). PRS is the mind-trick by which you covertly create a problem while blaming someone else (9/11); then you tell the public through an unquestioning mainstream media the version of the problem you want people to believe (Bin Laden and 19 Arab hijackers 'did it') to illicit the reaction of 'something must be done'; finally you offer the solution to the problem you have covertly created (a 'war on terror' to regime change countries as you planned all along). There is another version as I mentioned earlier that I call No-Problem-Reaction-Solution when you don't even need a real problem only the *perception* of one. The lie about 'weapons of mass destruction' to justify the catastrophic invasion of Iraq in 2003 is an obvious case and as we will see later so is the 'Covid-19' hoax. Iraq was on the hit-list and there was no reason to invade so the Cult made one up and had it promoted by Boy Bush and UK Prime Minister Tony Blair. The stablemate of PRS is the Totalitarian Tiptoe in which you instigate a series of happenings and changes that are all connected and leading the world in your desired direction while being presented as unconnected random events. Wars transform the world step-by-step as each follows the other in the Totalitarian Tiptoe technique of 'creative destruction'. A war destroys the status quo and creates a new one. The next war destroys that status quo and so on. With

Figure 239: War as creative destruction. Nothing changes a society quicker and more than war and that's why we've had so many.

each new status quo you are moving closer and closer to your end goal. Look how the two world wars utterly transformed global society (Fig 239). The European Union is a Totalitarian Tiptoe planned from the start to be a centralised bureaucratic (Cult) superstate which they could never have openly admitted. The public backlash and resistance would have blocked it at birth. Instead they sold the superstate tyranny at first as just a free trade zone (the 'Common Market') before, step-by-step, incessantly centralising power to delete national sovereignty on the journey to what was planned from the start – a bureaucratically-controlled United States of Europe. Observe the world with this knowledge and you will see Problem-Reaction-Solution and the Totalitarian Tiptoe constantly at work across the entirety of human life. When something new is introduced by the Tiptoe technique where it starts is never where it is intended to finish. Taser stun guns unleashing 55,000 volts of electricity were introduced by police 'only for trained firearms officers', but it was obvious to anyone who understands the game and the Tiptoe that they would soon be widely distributed. By the year to March, 2019, Tasers were used thousands of times in England and Wales alone and broke all previous records. We now have 70-year-old grandmothers being Tasered multiple times in America by psychopathic goons in uniform for asking them to show a warrant before entering their home. Crucial to making PRS and TT techniques effective is to program the population to believe *your* version of why these manufactured events happen and to keep the real reason hidden. The alternative media and alternative opinion is being censored to ever greater extremes by the Cult-owned Internet giants to stop the truth being exposed about PRS and TT events (which went into overdrive to stop exposure of the 'Covid-19' hoax).

Cult movie

What I am about to describe really is a movie in the sense there is a script designed to tell you what you are seeing and experiencing. If you watch a series of pictures with no commentary or voiceover you can reach your own conclusions about what they mean. Instead a reporter will tell you what you are seeing and what the pictures mean when often what is said is not true at all. Most of the time the *reporter* doesn't know what is happening. They get their information from official sources, repeat that in the voiceover and call it 'journalism'. Whatever the event may be – a terrorist attack, war, financial collapse – the media is telling you the official version 99 percent of the time. We are back to one of the most profound techniques of mind control which is repetition. Media sources may seem numerous but they will be quoting the same official narrative ad infinitum until it fuses into 'everyone knows that' and a widely accepted version of history (memory). Stop people in the street anywhere in the world and ask them what happened in an historical or more recent event and they will invariably give you the official version (often thanks to Hollywood or 'Tinseltown'). Hollywood is a Cult creation to program perceptions of the global masses. Ask many people for a version of history and it will come from the script of a Hollywood movie. That John Wayne was a war hero wasn't he? No, he was in make-up in LA while the guns were firing on the other side of the world. Wayne was there to tell you what to *believe* about the guns firing on the other side of the world. Moment by illusory moment you are being told what to think – to perceive – about *everything*. I will pull together over the next few chapters the elements of a coordinated global control system which are happening before our eyes every day while being presented as random events.

The foundation manipulation is centralisation of power which has been unrelenting thanks to the Cult. A few can't control the many without centralisation of power. The more power is devolved from the centre the less control the global Cult at the centre can have. Humans once organised in tribal groups which decided what happened to the tribe. Then tribes were brought together under centralised control called nations and countries and a few people could dictate to all the former tribes. Today nations are being centrally controlled through superstates like the EU, trading blocs, United Nations agencies, the World Health Organization, World Trade Organization, International Monetary Fund, World Bank and so many more. The all-encompassing name for this phenomenon is 'globalisation' – the centralisation of global power in every area of human life which I have been warning about for 30 years. Globalisation is the Totalitarian Tiptoe to the imposition of a world government, army, central bank and currency underpinned by a microchipped population connected to AI (Fig 240). The more you centralise power the more power you have at the centre to centralise even quicker and centralisation gets faster and faster. The European Union has been created this way as each power-grabbing and centralising step has followed another. A single world currency, which I have again been predicting since the early 1990s, is meant to be purely digital with the deletion of cash. We are seeing cash disappearing so fast in favour of digital transactions through cards and smartphones in the

WORLD GOVERNMENT
UNELECTED - RUN BY TECHNOCRATS

WORLD ARMY • CENTRAL BANK • CURRENCY •
HUMANS CONNECTED TO A.I.

SUPERSTATES LIKE THE EU AND CENTRALLY
CONTROLLED 'TRADING BLOCS'

COUNTRIES REPLACED BY POWERLESS REGIONS
GLOBAL MONOCULTURE

THE PEOPLE

Figure 240: The structure of the planned global tyranny.

Tiptoe to this end with planned microchips waiting to take over from them. Bank branches and ATMs are being closed and removed to make it ever harder to have cash transactions. The plan is to make it near-impossible to function without a smartphone. I went to a railway station car park during the writing of this book and the only way I could pay was by a smartphone which I don't use. It meant I couldn't park there and this is the way those who don't want to succumb to the agenda are being pressured into doing so. The sequence in all subject areas goes like this … voluntary … can't function without doing it 'voluntarily'… compulsory. Individual cash currencies are disappearing with the Cult-created EU deleting many European currencies through the introduction of the euro that itself is planned to be assimilated into the world currency (look at the utter demonisation of cash and refusal to deal in cash transactions as a result of the 'Covid-19' hoax). Global government would not even be run by elected people as I have long warned. Rulers would be bureaucrats and technocrats serving the Cult through what is termed a technocracy – 'Government or control of society or industry by an elite of technical experts'. Silicon Valley which already has far more power than governments is this very emerging technocracy at work as are the unelected bureaucrat dictators of the European Union. A world army is designed to impose the will of the world dictatorship on those who resist. Recent plans for a European Union army (which I predicted in the 1990s) and the long-established European Central Bank are Totalitarian Tiptoes to the world army and world central bank, as is NATO. The same goes with regard to world government with the World Health Organization, World Trade Organization, International Monetary Fund and World Bank. The biggest stalking horse of all for the world government structure is the Cult-created-and-controlled United Nations which is being transformed step-by-step into a world government dictatorship. I'll say more about this when I deal with the climate change hoax being driven through the UN.

Hunger Games Society

Unrelenting centralisation of global power is sold as 'the world coming together'. This illusion and lie has been bought in its totality by desperately naive 'Woke' progressives and their associated Climate Cult which is an offshoot of The Cult although only a few of its advocates will know that. Do they really believe that a Cult obsessed with driving people apart to divide and rule wants the world to 'come together'? It's about centralisation of total power in the hands of a few at a global level from where they will control AI which, by then, will be connected to the human brain. Helloooooooo!!! My God – wake the hell up, people. It is a skin-pincher to think that the political 'Left' that I grew up with – the one that stood for freedom of speech and challenged elite power – has now been so hijacked by the fake 'progressive' 'Woke' mentality that it demands freedom of speech is deleted through Cult-created political correctness (PC) and that the elite be handed ever more power through the Cult-created EU. Who will eventually reap the consequences of the tyranny they are demanding to be implemented? They will – and their kids and grandkids still more so. The original truly liberal Left has been so absorbed by Cult-created 'Woke' that real liberals are today condemned as 'far-right' and 'Nazis' for defending basic liberal values like freedom of speech. The label 'Woke' which this mentality awards itself is a serious misrepresentation of its origin and maybe, ironically, 'cultural appropriation' in the language of PC. 'Woke' is apparently a political term used in African-American culture since the 1900s and relates to an awareness of social and racial justice. Its use by fake 'progressives', however, does not mean that although they claim it does. 'New Woke', as I will call it from here-on, means campaigning for the agenda of the very Cult responsible for social injustice of all kinds throughout what we perceive as human history. This includes the slavery and oppression of black and other non-white people and the oppression of most white people.

Hunger Games – the real-life movie

I have long described where the Cult and New Wokeness are leading us as the 'Hunger Games Society' and the Tiptoe to that continues every day worldwide. Clearly my phrase comes from the *Hunger Games* movie series which portrays a privileged elite hoarding all the wealth and power while living in a hi-tech city of mega luxury. They are protected by a vicious and merciless police/military state from the rest of the population working as slaves to the elite (today's Cult-connected One-percent) in abject poverty under extreme levels of surveillance and control. The masses are isolated in 'sectors' to prevent a unified response (divide and rule). I have been warning for decades that this is the very structure the Cult seeks to impose with a brain link to AI thrown in (Fig 241). Scan the world and you can't miss the pieces being put into place ever more quickly. I saw an image of Adolf Hitler at a mass Nazi rally. He stood alone at the front delivering his psychopathy to a massive

Figure 241: The Hunger Games Society I have warned about for decades that is now clearly being imposed. (Image Neil Hague.)

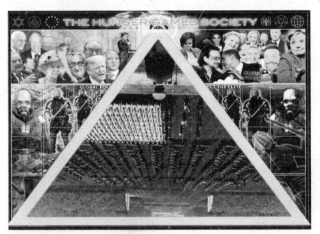

Figure 242: The Hunger Games Society is a global fascistic society.

military presence and beyond them were thousands of people kept in line by that military to ensure whatever Hitler demanded would be done. I had that image flipped upside down and overlaid on the Hunger Games Society structure and they are exactly the same. We are indeed looking at a global version of Nazi Germany with the added control-system of advanced-technology and AI (Fig 242). Now add the 'virus' lockdowns to what I said there.

The plan is for the leaders and key agents of the Cult to control the wealth and power at the top of the pyramid in the way of the *Hunger Games* movies. We have already reached the point where we talk

Figure 243: People die of hunger and sleep in the streets while a handful of multi-billionaires like these hijack the world's wealth. The fact that many claim to be 'caring' and have 'values' is a real challenge to the stomach.

about a 'One-percent' and an Oxfam report in 2019 estimated that the world's 26 richest men owned as much wealth as the poorest *half* of the global population – some 3.8 billion people at the time (Fig 243). The 26 are themselves in hierarchical order with the top few dominating the wealth and multi-billionaires Jeff Bezos at Amazon and Bill Gates at Microsoft up there at the top. By 2020 the world had a record 2,816 billionaires worth $11.2 trillion which is more than the gross national product of every country except the United States and China. Another Oxfam report in 2020 said the wealthiest 2,153 people have more money than the poorest *4.6 billion* while the 22 richest men have more than all the women in Africa. We should be careful even then of believing these are the wealthiest people. Behind the scenes Cult leaders have wealth way beyond a Bezos or Gates who are relative artisans and gofers compared with those with the most power who don't put themselves on public display. They hide the extent of their holdings through a stream of nominees and proxies. The One-percent and their operatives own governments and buy politicians and parties (Fig 244). Multi-billionaire financier George Soros owns the Democrats in the United States along with much of the New Woke network of organisations while multi-

Figure 244: A cause and effect that never fails.

billionaire Sheldon Adelson owns the Republican Party and has been Donald Trump's biggest funder. The Cult technique is control all sides and you control the game. The Sabbatian-Frankist House of Rothschild is a player even above all of those I have mentioned and they are global experts at hiding the extent of their wealth and power. Cult-controlled corporations are far richer than countries. Sixty-nine of the world's leading economic entities are corporations not countries and 157 of the top 200. Corporations such as Walmart, Apple and Shell attract more wealth than countries like Russia, Belgium and Sweden while a mere one percent of the wealth of Jeff Bezos is equivalent to the entire health budget of Ethiopia with its 105 million people. Mega corporations own governments, dictate laws – and wars – and hand themselves all the aces at the expense of potential competition. You have laws making it ever more difficult (on purpose) for small and medium size non-Cult businesses to survive while Cult corporations get what they like (*update* – look what has happened to small business and even bigger ones all over the world because of the 'virus' hoax lockdowns). Control of governments and the system in general means that billionaires and their corporations pay a far smaller percentage of their income in taxation than people struggling to survive. Google paid just £6 million in tax in 2011 on a turnover of £365 million and avoids tax like the other vampires by moving tens of billions into shell companies in offshore tax havens. They and their famous front people have utter contempt for you. Fair Tax Mark, a group campaigning for tax transparency, reported in 2019 that the big six US tech firms Amazon, Facebook, Google, Netflix, Apple and Microsoft had 'aggressively' avoided $100 billion of global tax over the previous decade. It claimed that in this period Amazon paid only $3.4 billion in tax on revenues of $960.5 billion and profits of $26.8 billion. How can smaller less connected companies compete with that? They can't. How can they compete with those like Amazon and global taxi firm Uber who have apparently unlimited funding to buy and expand their way to monopoly? They can't and that's the idea.

Global sweatshop

The Cult controls – indeed created – the global banking and financial system in which it conjures money out of fresh air called 'credit' and its financial pot is therefore unlimited. The gathering monopoly of Amazon alone has devastated bricks and mortar shops, mom and pop businesses, and dominates the book industry at the expense of independent stores which are driven out of business (see 'virus' hoax lockdowns which have left Amazon with a massively-increased global market share). US retail giant Walmart, the largest company in the world by revenue, has done something similar in the bricks and mortar sector through a business model described by one commentator as 'selling foreign goods to domestic consumers, cheap Chinese garbage manufactured offshore in factories that pay slave wages – wages that American manufacturers could never match'. One study estimated that America lost 400,000 jobs between 2001 and 2013 because of Walmart's Chinese imports and this devastated many towns especially in rural areas. This depopulation of rural land just happens to be a major Cult agenda as you will see. Walmart even has a policy of selling goods at a loss until competitors are destroyed to secure a monopoly (see Amazon) and employs mostly part-time staff to avoid paying them benefits while knowing that the taxpayer via the government will top up the wages with welfare payments. This goes on while the Walmart family is reported to be worth $150 *billion*. Walmart and its methods are straight from the Cult playbook. It's a disgusting company exploiting and living off the backs of the poor. Walmart was once widely condemned by genuine liberals of the genuine Left, but not by New Woke since the Walmart family, the richest in America, began spouting the language and agenda of New Woke. Monopoly means control and the plan is for Cult corporations to dominate every sector and market so that you buy from them or no one. Where do the bankrupt business owners and their employees go? They slide into the lower reaches of the Hunger Games Society along with

everyone else – look at the effect of the 'virus' hoax lockdowns which
have accelerated this process on a staggering scale (Fig 245).

While global wealth is sucked into the One-percent and the Cult the
poor and what are called the middle class are being stripped of income
and assets in line with the Hunger Games pyramid. I warned long ago
that those who thought none of this applied to them were in for a shock.
By that I mean those at the time who had a well-paid job, nice car, good
home and money for holidays. I pointed out that the Cult had its sights
on them, too. The plan is for everyone outside the elite to be enslaved in
dependency and poverty by controlling the wealth and replacing people
with AI. The Cult-instigated financial crash of 2008 contributed
immensely to this while the mega-rich went on getting mega-richer.

Figures I saw for 2017 and
2018 revealed that a new
billionaire was created every
two days as formerly
'comfortable' or even 'well-off'
people were finding
themselves on the street. A
headline captured the trend:
'In rich countries, the middle
class is getting smaller and
smaller, generation by
generation.' It describes the
Totalitarian Tiptoe to the
Hunger Games Society. Many

Figure 245: The global dynamic.

people who once thought that what I was exposing did not affect them
are now sleeping in tent cities or shop doorways and this is planned to
continually expand until the Cult's job is done. Suicide rates in America
have increased by *40 percent* in 17 years and many of them are among
those termed 'blue collar' workers or 'working class' who have been
profoundly affected by One-percent accumulation of wealth and
systematic mass immigration competing in their job market. Vast
numbers of people even in work are living from week to week with a
missed pay check or two meaning financial disaster and a lost home. A
national survey by UK homelessness charity Beam found that the
average British person is only two pay cheques away from homelessness
at a time when AI is sweeping away jobs traditionally done by humans
(and that was before the lockdown). This has all been planned. Food
charity Move for Hunger says that one in eight Americans or 40 million
people are food insecure with more than twelve million children and
five million seniors not sure where their next meal is coming from (again
before lockdown). Homelessness was rising all over the world through
lower incomes, unemployment and social factors even before the

'pandemic' with the cost of housing right up there as a prime cause. British homeless charity Shelter said in December, 2019, that a child becomes homeless in the UK every eight minutes. None of this has to happen when you consider that the United States government has spent *$2 trillion* (at least) on the Cult-created unwinnable war in Afghanistan, the longest in American history. Much of that $2 trillion has ended up in the coffers of Cult-owned arms and 'defence' corporations while homeless numbers incessantly rise. Why would they spend the money on the population when they want to make the masses impoverished, destitute and dependent on them? I have described the Hunger Games agenda in all its form at length in *Everything You Need To Know* and if you want the detailed background for all I am saying in this book then *Everything* is a must-read.

Gather them in cities

I have long exposed the agenda for financially forcing people out of the rural areas into mega cities controlled by AI where they would live in micro-homes – some the size of a single decker bus and many even less. All these years after I made that warning those micro-homes are being built all over the world and the movement of people from financially-devastated rural communities into the cities where they can be kept under surveillance 24/7 gathers apace (Fig 246). The US federal government already owns 28 percent of the land in America and there's a lot more to come. Patrick Wood at Technocracy.news described how this process is happening even more directly in China where vicious government control has allowed no opposition:

> … China unveiled a plan in 2014 to summarily move 250 million farmers off their land by 2026 and into megacities that had already been constructed but sat vacant. The vacated farm land is being combined into giant factory farms to be operated by advanced technology such as agricultural robots and automated tractors. Ostensibly, the farmers who refuse to leave will be helped along with the barrel of a gun.

Figure 246: Micro-homes for the serfs being built around the world for the Hunger Games masses in AI-controlled cities.

For years people have been asking why China has been building a stream of new 'ghost cities' with few or no one living there (Fig 247). This is why. The guiding rule for the West is China today and you tomorrow or in fact not even tomorrow. Abandoned homes, family farms, shops and factories

Figure 247: 'Ghost cities' built all over China waiting for the masses to be forced to relocate from the land.

can now be seen right across rural America between the coasts thanks to companies like Walmart with its imports from Chinese sweatshops and pricing to destroy competition. Then there are hedge fund billionaires who asset-strip local employers and devastate rural areas. American cable news host Tucker Carlson, one of the last proper journalists on US television, highlighted one sickening example involving ultra-Zionist New York-based hedge fund manager Paul Singer who has a personal fortune according to Forbes of more than $3 billion. Carlson told the story of how Singer's predatory hedge fund targeted the only major employer in the small town of Sidney, Nebraska, and destroyed it for a fat profit. The town lost 2,000 jobs in a population of 6,000. No wonder *Bloomberg News* dubbed Singer as 'the world's most feared investor' and he is reported to be 'a strong opponent of raising taxes for the wealthiest 1% of taxpayers'. You don't say. At the time of writing ultra-Zionist Singer is reported to be buying shares in Twitter to oust chief executive Jack Dorsey. Carlson described Singer-like asset-stripping practices as 'vulture capitalism feeding off the carcass of a dying nation'. He said of the Sidney disaster: 'A heartbreakingly familiar cascade began: people left, property values collapsed, and then people couldn't leave. They were trapped there. One of the last thriving small towns in America went under.' This is happening systematically all over America to drive people into the cities and a life of poverty, which means dependency, which means control. A further aspect of this agenda is the Cult's campaign for people to eat a vegan diet in response to the climate change hoax which would ultimately cause many animals to disappear from land that could then be absorbed in state and One-percent land grabs from which the public in the mega-cities would be excluded. You could drive there? Your autonomous car won't take you. Fracking is endangering the viability of rural life. Each fracking well consumes between 1.5 million and 16 million gallons of water while whole communities don't have enough to drink and have to leave the country for the cities. Injected water used in fracking to access oil and gas fields is polluted with hundreds of chemicals which then seep into ground water further reducing supplies to drink.

Around 2010 the world passed the point where more people live in urban areas than rural and it has been speeding in that direction ever since. In Australia people are being forced out of rural areas by catastrophic forest fires (hardly difficult to start) and lack of water as rivers dry up. They blame human-caused climate change when honest Australian scientists have admitted there is no evidence to link climate change to either fires or drought and dwindling rivers. In fact, water is being siphoned off before it reaches communities by dams owned by private corporations who use it for their own ends including mega-cotton production operations for the benefit of Chinese and Japanese 'investors'. I recommend the Internet videos of Max Igan with regard to Australian fires and water shortages. Climate Cult child goddess Greta Thunberg of course blamed the 2019/2020 catastrophe in Australia on 'climate change' when forest fires have always been part of Australian life and were once mitigated by controlled burning in the winter to create barriers that fires struggled to jump (Fig 248). Non-burning policy instigated at the behest of the Greens has since created a disaster waiting to happen. But, no, hey, it's global warming – the script says so – and the fact that nearly 200 people were arrested for 'fire-related offenses' according to New South Wales police, including some for deliberately starting them, is not at all relevant. There have been horrific fires in other regions including Indonesia which also have

Figure 248: Exploit any disaster or human catastrophe to advance your agenda.

human and not climate change origins through forest and land mismanagement by timber and farming companies. At their most extreme these fires have produced more carbon dioxide than the US economy to put industrial production of CO_2 into perspective and killed monumental numbers of animals including many from endangered species. The same has happened in Australia with one biodiversity specialist estimating that a billion animals had been killed in the fires of 2019/2020. The real causes of this don't matter to the climate obsessives – only their agenda that everything is 'climate change' – and still more people are forced out of rural areas into urban centres. Mega-cities where the masses are being forced to relocate from rural areas are known as 'Smart Cities' which is code for densely-populated centres of mass surveillance and control of everything through artificial intelligence with no private means of movement and only state-controlled driverless vehicles and communal transport systems. You go where the state says you can go and nowhere else. Current cities are being transformed into Smart Cities while others are being built from scratch around the world as in China (Fig 249 overleaf). To give you an idea of what I mean Saudi Arabia, controlled by the Sabbatian-Frankist

Figure 250: The ginormous smart city being built by Sabbatian-Frankist-controlled Saudi Arabia not far from Sabbatian-Frankist-controlled Israel which is planned to be the key centre of the global smart control grid.

Figure 249: Smart cities with everything controlled by AI and human choice deleted are referred to as 'human settlement zones' in official documents.

fake royal House of Saud, is developing a $500 billion Smart City dubbed the 'NEOM project' which is planned to be *33-times* the size of New York (Fig 250). NEOM means 'New Future', but 'Cult agenda' would be more accurate.

Prison camp cities

We have in San Francisco and Los Angeles perfect examples of the Cult's Hunger Games programme and also California in its entirety. New Woke California has twelve percent of the American population but 25 percent of its homeless and 25 percent of people in the state are poor amid incredible wealth (what must it be now with the lockdown?). There have been outbreaks of typhus among the shit-laden, piss-laden, streets of Los Angeles with fears that the plague will follow while the millionaires and billionaires of the Hollywood elite look the other way from their ivory towers and conspicuous wealth. Human waste goes into the LA River bypassing sewage treatment and how does anyone think that will turn out? If you want to see the Hunger Games Society let's go to San Francisco and this time there'll be no need for flowers in your hair. Watching where you walk will be far more important. San Francisco and the associated Silicon Valley is the most unequal society on Planet Earth. I have been to the 'Golden Gate' city many times starting before the emergence of the billionaire technocracy when the city really was a place to sing about. I have been there recently and it's a shithole – literally. 'New Woke' owners of Google, Facebook, Twitter and the like live in their multi-million walled mansions with private security while the streets of San Francisco are awash with homeless people, human piss and shit, and spent needles left by addicts often desperately trying to escape from their daily nightmare while suffering from mental illness. There are now more drug addicts in San Francisco than high school students. Residents reported about 5,500 cases of human shit in the city's streets in 2011 and by 2018 it was more than 28,000. One bloke I saw on video defeated in a supermarket aisle. San Francisco's response to all this has been to stop prosecuting people that piss and shit in public places which of course has made the situation far worse. Seattle in Washington State is another city that has taken the route of San Francisco with all the same consequences. The multi-billionaire George Soros and other One-percenters behind New Woke have been funding their gofers to become district attorneys across America and when they win office crimes are downgraded or no longer prosecuted. The aim is to destroy human society and let rule by the mob take over. The result in the same period has been a surge in murders in America as well as other crime. San Francisco has just such a district attorney in Chesa Boudin whose parents were jailed for what would today be called Woke terrorism with a group called the 'Weather Underground'. Boudin's city has the highest rate of property crime of any big city in the country with an average of 60 cars broken into every day. San Francisco's Board of Supervisors decided to act decisively in true New Woke fashion by deleting the term 'convicted felons' to be replaced with 'justice-involved individuals' which is the term also used for the targets of crime. We have the same term for both robber and robbed, attacker and attacked. Young people committing crime are now 'young people impacted by the juvenile justice system'. Drug addicts are 'people with a history of substance use'. The Cult New Woke technique is to ignore the problem (it *wants* the problem) and instead delete the language that makes talking about the problem in factual detail impossible. New York has done something similar by abolishing cash bail for certain crimes. In the first month after introduction car theft surged 67 percent and robbery 33 percent with six suspected drug dealers accused of running a $7 million operation given this get out of jail card. Will any of these people come back for trial? A former New York police commissioner described how people have been arrested for rape, been let go and raped again, while others have been arrested on serious charges, let go, and committed murder. There are many people in jail who shouldn't be, but that's not the motivation here. It's about still keeping the wrong people in jail while setting free those who should be there. New Woke California voted to make crime involving less than $950 a misdemeanour with likely no investigation or consequences. You'll never guess what has happened. I mean who could have predicted it? Crime in that category has soared with some thieves even carrying calculators to make sure their shoplifting booty totals less than $950. Small businesses are being especially badly hit and anyone who wants society to be a see-want-take lawless free-for-all would be ecstatic. California even reduced penalties for knowingly exposing a sexual partner to HIV and the same with knowingly donating HIV-infected blood. What about those infected? New Woke is not interested in real victims, only inventing fake ones.

Ultra-Zionist multi-billionaire one-time Democratic presidential candidate Michael Bloomberg described California despite all this as a model for all of America. To the Cult it is.

I have been exposing for decades the systematic drugging of American and other communities worldwide to enslave the population in addiction with the Bush and Clinton families centrally involved in the Cult drug networks that control the drug cartels. China is circulating drugs in America via Mexican drug gangs crossing large swathes of the basically undefended southern border (see *The Trigger* for background to Cult drug networks and the Bush/Clinton/CIA/Israeli Mossad involvement). Addiction to opioids, a class of drugs derived from the opium poppy plant, has been devastating for America and especially a synthetic opioid called Fentanyl which is some 100 times more powerful than morphine and overwhelmingly sourced to China. Opioids are brain manipulators promoted as painkillers and have been mass-circulated by Purdue Pharma owned by the multi-billionaire Sackler family. The result of their mega-marketed drug OxyContin can be seen in horrific numbers of deaths, destroyed lives and destruction of whole communities. OxyContin was promoted with big help from Purdue-funded Washington Deep State Zionist 'think tank', the American Enterprise Institute, which had many connections to the Project for the New American Century. A commentator described how 'many hundreds of thousands of Americans have entered into a death spiral of addiction after being prescribed these drugs by doctors'. Purdue is offering compensation pay-outs of $12 billion which does not even nearly match the horrors that its drug has perpetrated. Addiction to drugs, alcohol, smartphones and all the rest is fuelled by despair and the need to escape from the life people are living as the Cult dismantles countries, lives, and psyches in pursuit of the Hunger Games Society. Opioid deaths have been sharply higher in American communities where Cult-owned vehicle-makers have closed their US plants and outsourced jobs to other countries where they can pay people less. This is 'globalisation' at work. The manipulated problem of homelessness is waiting for a solution that will advance the Hunger Games Society even further on behalf of the Cult and its Sabbatian-Frankist network. American website Politico reported that 'the growing homeless encampments — which have led to a rise in human waste, trash and open-air drug dealing — have united unlikely allies'. They were talking about Republican Donald Trump and ultra-Zionist San Francisco Democrat state senator Scott Wiener. This guy cares, you see: 'The crisis is so bad people's minds are really opening up and the policies are shifting … Legislation that would have had no chance five or ten years ago can pass.' Problem-Reaction-Solution. Wiener's 'solution' is the forced internment of homeless people under certain circumstances (which the state would interpret) using the

Orwellian term 'involuntary commitment'. These 'circumstances' will be planned to constantly expand until it involves all homeless people. Julie Winter, mayor of Redding, California, has suggested that the homeless be put in a 'shelter' which they would not be allowed to leave until they 'demonstrate self-sufficiency'. In other words she is talking about internment in a de-facto jail for the crime of being homeless. These may currently be isolated attempts at authoritarian laws but they will grow and not least because populations of towns and cities are going to be impacted more and more by the homeless crisis. The Cult doesn't want a real solution. To these empathy-deleted, stone-hearted crazies, the homeless are a means to an end.

Guaranteed poverty and control

Another Cult agenda to exploit the plunge to the Hunger Games Society is a guaranteed income. When multi-billionaire New Woke professional frauds like Facebook's Mark Zuckerberg support a 'universal basic income' you know it's not what it seems. I have believed since childhood that there should be a level below which no one should be allowed to fall in a civilised society, but that is not what the Cult's guaranteed or basic income plans are all about. The motivation is *control*. Billions and billions are planned to be forced into the lower reaches of the Hunger Games pyramid by manipulation of the financial system, giant corporations and hedge funds destroying communities and job opportunities, and by the utter devastation of employment with the AI takeover (this was again written even before the lockdowns). AI means still more money being transferred to ever fewer hands in that AI doesn't get paid. Technology represents the most crucial factor in the creation of a Hunger Games world (along with the effects of lockdowns). One 'solution' to this 'problem' is the guaranteed income which will be guaranteed by whom and on what basis? Look no further than China for the answer. Cult-assets of the state will decide who gets what on the basis of acquiesce to the state. China is the fast-developing blueprint for the Cult control system. New Woke billionaires far from criticising China work to support its psychopathic dictators in the creation of the very system planned for the West and the rest of the world. One Chinese city alone has 2.6 *million* cameras and the country has a surveillance system that scans facial features to create a virtual map of the face in real time to be checked by AI against a state database (Fig 251 overleaf). The same system is fast coming to the West thanks to the Cult and its Silicon Valley multi-billionaire celebrity technocrats. 'Smart' technology (I'll explain the real context in a later chapter) allows for constant mass surveillance and China's communist/fascist (same thing) government is exploiting this potential for its 'social credit' system. This tracks the behaviour of the entire population and awards or deletes credits based on that

Figure 251: The fantastic mass-surveillance system in China in the process of coming to the West.

behaviour. Do what the government wants and you gets credits; do what the government doesn't want and they are taken away with major consequences. A government document in 2014 said the system is designed to 'allow the trustworthy to roam everywhere under heaven while making it hard for the discredited to take a single step'. They are not kidding. By the end of 2018 the National Public Credit Information Centre revealed that Chinese courts had banned the purchase of plane tickets 17.5 million times and 5.5 million for train tickets for becoming officially 'discredited' (the fake 'pandemic' is being exploited to do the same in the West). Apply this to a guaranteed (tiny) income that would be paid only if you conform to what governments demand. That's the real story behind guaranteed income and why One-percenter frauds and censors like Zuckerberg give it their support while promoting themselves as kind and caring. A small guaranteed income with no alternative way of earning money = the Hunger Games Society. A glimpse of how the China system is being introduced in the West can be seen with the Silicon Valley company Airbnb which is causing people to be thrown out of their permanent homes around the world as they are rented to tourists through Airbnb just as Silicon Valley's Uber is destroying local taxi firms across the globe in its money-no-object business plan leading to autonomous taxis. Airbnb has developed technology to scour the internet and social media accounts to check potential renters for character traits. The company's 'trait analyser' software employs artificial intelligence to give black marks to people 'associated' with 'drugs or alcohol, "hate websites", or sex work' by 'scanning keywords, images and video footage across the internet linked to a potential customer to assess their trustworthiness'. The programme assesses their 'behavioural and personality traits' including 'conscientiousness and openness' – see China's social credit system.

Cult gun-grab

This brings me to the middle section of the Hunger Games pyramid – the police/military state emerging before our eyes all over the world. Its role is to protect the One-percent from the Hunger Games masses and enforce the will of the One-percent upon the rest of humanity as per *Hunger Games* movies (see the lockdowns). The plan is to eventually fuse police and military into one force and we have the police looking more

TOTALITARIAN TIPTOE

Figure 252: Police are looking and acting like the miltary because they are planned to fuse into a global police-military state.

like the military with every passing year (Fig 252). Police officers are armed to the enamel on their teeth at the same time that constant pressure is being applied to disarm Americans even including those living in isolated homes with no chance of a swift police response. Is this a coincidence? Not a chance. I speak as someone who wishes there were no guns. I can't stand them and I have never used one except to win – or not – a coconut at the fair; but we need to see the world as it is and not only as we would like it to be. If you have a heavily-armed Cult-controlled police and military and an unarmed population how is that going to end? It is such a cinch with today's sophisticated mind-control techniques to program kids and others to go on shooting sprees in schools and shopping malls to increase the demand for gun confiscation. Do people really think that criminals and crazies won't locate and use guns because the law says they should not? They are *criminals and crazies* for goodness sake. Are armed criminals more likely to attack a home where they don't know if the occupants are armed or one where they know they are defenceless against their weapons? Ultra-Zionist multi-billionaire Michael Bloomberg, former Mayor of New York and failed Democrat presidential wannabe, is funding campaigns to target gun owners in a move that promotes the Cult agenda. The desire to remove guns from the law-abiding population cannot be divorced from the extraordinary level of surveillance now in place because it's all connected. It's the Totalitarian Tiptoe to a global Cult-controlled police-military world army state to impose the agenda of the Cult-controlled world government. China's social credit system is only a glimpse at how extreme this is meant to be. Cult-owned Silicon Valley and associated Cult technology giants around the world in countries like China have constructed an immense and ever-expanding network of 24/7 surveillance in which your every action is logged and stored on databases planned to become one global database. You are watched and recorded by smart televisions, smart phones, smart personal assistants, cameras, increasingly with face-recognition, and through your every action online. The list is becoming endless. Smart streets with microphones in lamp posts are another development and the roll-out of 5G will expand the tracking and data-gathering potential by gigantic leaps. A beyond-Orwellian technological tyranny has been introduced so fast.

Open the borders

I have exposed Cult insiders over the years describing how they want to impose the 'law of the jungle' in which people are constantly in states of fear and anxiety and open to more Orwellian control to protect them from what they have been manipulated to fear. Part of the fear and chaos agenda is opening the southern border of America to psychopathic gangs arriving through Mexico such as MS-13 with its lovely motto 'kill, rape and control'. Mexican drug cartels that have taken psychopathy and brutality to still new depths of depravity exploit the near-open border areas to flood America with drugs and they are major suppliers worldwide. Mexico is run by those cartels and law and order has basically been deleted. The idea is for the situation to get so bad that there will be an exodus of people into the US on such a scale from the south that it is unstoppable. Many who cross the border illegally give birth to children in the United States to secure them US citizenship in the knowledge that the rest of the family will then not be sent home. The number of so-called 'anchor babies' born to those living illegally in America was reported to be 372,000 in 2019 which was greater than US citizen birth rates in 48 states. Billionaire financier George Soros, part of the ultra-Zionist global network no matter how much he may try to hide that, is funding both the movement of illegal migrants into America and Europe and election campaigns of New Woke district attorneys across America who then refuse to prosecute illegal migrants, criminals (including killers) and decriminalise a list of offences. This is creating the 'jungle' that Cult insiders talk about. We can also see the real meaning behind this Bloomberg pledge: 'I believe we can once again be a country that welcomes immigrants, values immigrants, respects immigrants, and empowers them to pursue the American Dream.'

Mass migration into Europe and the United States is a frontline Cult agenda to transform societies with the goal among many other things of creating conflict (divide and rule) between indigenous and incoming cultures (Fig 253). The Cult doesn't give a shit about the migrants. They are just pawns in a game to secure the will of the same Cult that has bombed their countries and turned them asunder in places like Libya and Syria in the full-knowledge that it would start a trek to the north into Europe in search of safety. I am all for giving succour to

Figure 253: The reason for mass migration of cultures and the obsession with seeing 'racism' everywhere and in everything. (Image Gareth Icke.)

migrants fleeing persecution and wars mostly of the Cult's making via the West to create chaos and control. The point that needs to be made is the great majority of migrants are not fleeing war. They only want to get into Europe and the United States and if I were them I would want to do the same. Some perspective is urgently required, however, on what that means for European and American society. German newspaper *Die Welt* has conceded that most of the migrants arriving in Europe across the Mediterranean are not genuine refugees: 'Contrary to popular belief, the majority of those arriving in Italy are not refugees … the main countries of origin for boat migrants in January [2020] were Algeria, Ivory Coast, and Bangladesh.' Italian Interior Ministry figures suggest that large numbers are arriving from Tunisia, Algeria, and Turkey. Most of these people are not given asylum or refugee status but most stay in Europe anyway. Germany's Federal Office for Migration and Refugees agreed that only a small fraction of failed asylum seekers from Africa had been deported and that most probably never will be. Those that are deported just come back. The time is planned when an unstoppable exodus of people will head into Europe and the United States from the south. I said in *The Trigger* that Turkey would at some point lift its ban agreed with the EU on migrants crossing its border into Europe and that would lead to potentially millions more migrants heading northwards. In late February, 2020, the Turkish government of the tyrannical President Erdogan said it would no longer hold back people from Syria and other countries who wish to go to Europe and seek asylum there. Turkish officials spoke of 'opening the floodgates of migrants on Europe'. I'm not a prophet. I just know what the game is and that makes predicting events quite straightforward. Erdogan said the situation would continue until the EU renegotiated the deal and even if that happens the threat is ongoing. This tyrant is supposed to be 'anti-Israel', but somehow manages to promote the Israel-based Sabbatian-Frankist cult plans for both flooding European society with migrants and continuing the efforts launched by the ultra-Zionist Project for the New American Century to remove President Assad in Syria. Maybe he's just confused, eh? I publish evidence in my last two books that Mustafa Kemal Atatürk, first president of the Republic of Turkey, was a Sabbatian-Frankist fake Muslim interloper.

None of this is a condemnation of migrants who are looking for a better life. It is simply laying out what the plan is. I have been warning about this agenda for many years since mass migration began and it went mainstream in 2020 when Hungarian foreign minister Péter Szijjártó warned that the (Cult-created-and-controlled) United Nations is funding a program of mass migration that threatens 'the whole of humanity'. He told a United Nations conference in Vienna that the UN is funding agencies encouraging people to leave their homelands and head to western countries. Szijjártó was talking about the UN Compact on Migration passed in 2018 to press Western governments to assimilate ever more migrants from other cultures which then British MEP Janice Atkinson said could lead to Europe being faced with 59 million new migrants within a few years. Watch for criticism of mass migration and its consequences being criminalised as 'hate speech' to protect the cultural elimination policy from exposure. We are close already. The long-planned theme is confirmed by the UN document in 2001 called 'Replacement Migration: Is It a Solution to Declining and Ageing Populations?'. This said that dealing with a declining population would mean potentially hundreds of millions of migrants heading for Europe. It estimated that Europe would need at least 159 million migrant workers to arrive by 2025 'to maintain the current balance of 4 to 5 workers for a pensioner' with perhaps at the most extreme 1.4 billion migrants required by 2050 at an average of 25.2 million a year. At that time 1.7 billion migrants, or their descendants, would make up nearly three quarters of the total population of 2.3 billion. The document said that in the United States 'it would be necessary to have 593 million migrants from 1995 to 2050, an average of 10.8 million per year' and 'by 2050, out of a United States total population of 1.1 billion, 775 million, or 73 per cent, would be post 1995 immigrants or their descendants.' It is chilling in the light of this to watch Internet videos by ultra-Zionist and Sabbatian-Frankist extremists and 'rabbis' saying openly that they are using Islam to transform European society and destroy 'Edom' – Rome and Christianity. David Touitou, a 'Rav' or Hebrew 'teacher/spiritual guide', said: 'You will have no place to run. Islam is the broom of Israel.' These crazies say that the Jewish Messiah will only return when Europe and Christianity are 'totally destroyed' (see also the United States). Touitou, who is far, far from alone in his shocking extremism, said:

> So I ask you. Is it good news that Islam invades Europe? It is excellent news! It means the coming of the Messiah [who will rule the whole world from Israel] … You will pay dearly for it Europeans. To such an extent you have no idea … You will have no place to run to. Because of all the evil you have done to Israel you will pay for it a hundredfold.

> When Italy will be gone … when Edom (Rome) … when that place is gone, and that's what Islam is going to go. Islam is the broom of Israel and you have to know it.

Once 'Edom' was gone the same insanity will turn its attention to destroying Islam and so on. See *The Trigger* for the detailed background to what is being orchestrated out of Israel by the Sabbatian-Frankist Satanists and you will see why the definition of 'anti-Semitism' is constantly being expanded and enforced by censorship through the Sabbatian-Frankist 'Anti-Semitism' Protection Racket to stop any of this being exposed and debated. The New Woke mentality funded by billionaires like ultra-Zionist frontman George Soros is keen for open borders while considering none of the consequences (which the Cult wants) for countries and their current populations including former migrants. They certainly don't realise – except the inner core – that they are promoting a population transformation agenda directed by the One-percent. There is no rational contemplation of what must surely follow when all that matters to New Wokers is posturing their self-purity in a constant exercise of round-the-clock virtue-signalling. This New Woke mindset – or emotionset – is a perception-virus that first infested political parties supposedly of the 'Left' and then expanded into centre and even 'conservative' parties having long infected almost the entirety of the self-obsessed celebrity 'Luvvies' who fly first class or in private jets to and from their walled mansions to lecture the great unwashed on the urgency to save the planet from climate change, help the poor and needy, and oppose border walls like the ones they have around their own properties. Unchecked migration is a disaster more than anything – as usual – for the poor and unemployed and yet wonderful for the rich. Wages at the lowest end are driven down by competition from people amid a labour surplus willing to work for less and job opportunities are reduced. The rich meanwhile see their wage-bill fall and enjoy a limitless supply of servants and cleaners at very reasonable rates in their big houses (Fig 254). Black communities in America have been particularly hit by this predictable sequence and it's happening in all countries with

Figure 254: Mass migration of people and cultures into Europe and the United States is being driven by the Cult and its One-percent cheered on by the 'Woke' that claim to oppose the One-percent. Babes in bloody arms.

mass immigration. Billionaires benefit and the poor lose out thanks to an outrageous and transparent deception incessantly promoted by New Wokers who call themselves 'social justice warriors'. If it wasn't so tragic for those who take the consequences this claim would be comedy club territory.

Tiptoe-by-Tiptoe

The long-planned outcome is being brought about by a series of interconnected steps that generate a domino effect to impose the Cult's transformation of Western society:

1) Manipulate wars in the Middle and Near East and support drug gangs and crime cartels to terrorise communities in Central and South America while financially trashing those societies to create a combination of extreme danger and deprivation.

2) You know that great numbers will seek to flee and with both the Middle and Near East and Central and South America you know they will head north into Europe and the United States.

3) Fund groups that will aid their passage and encourage far bigger numbers to join them in a piggy-back operation in which you assure them they will reach their 'promised land'. George Soros networks have been centrally involved in this.

4) You instigate such a mass movement of people that your target countries are overwhelmed with the support of the Cult-created European Union and leaders like Cult asset Chancellor Merkel in Germany who opened her borders and said 'let them all in'. The same happened in Sweden and the full force of New Woke Democrats in America cry 'open the borders to everyone'. The Swedish Employment Service revealed that just 6.1 per cent of new arrival migrants were able to find full-time work not subsidised by the government in 2019. Migrants are only a means to an end.

5) Democrat-controlled New Woke city and state governments introduce 'sanctuary cities' to protect those who have crossed the border illegally from US Immigration and Customs Enforcement, or 'ICE', which you demonise and demand be disbanded.

6) Calls to build a wall or fence to secure borders are condemned as racist bigotry and Nazi ideology in a black and white fantasy that says all migrants are good and anyone questioning the numbers and their effect is automatically evil and must be silenced. Censorship is then provided by billionaire heads of Silicon Valley giants who promote their New Woke credentials from their corporate headquarters and walled mansions – 'Make some tea, Sergio, and there's still dirt on that floor'.

7) The often catastrophic consequences of these events for jobs, crime, and economics in countries such as Sweden and Germany are suppressed through a compliant gutless media and by attacking anyone speaking the truth as a bigot, racist and Nazi leading to vilification and lost employment. Observers with the same concerns stay quiet in fear of

similar repercussions. In this way you silence dissent and give yourself free-rein to expand the influx and increase the consequences.

8) The point is reached – as now in Sweden – where the truth can no longer be hidden amid bombings, arson, murder and rape. Swedish Moderate Party leader Ulf Kristersson cited figures from the Crime Prevention Council about 230 bombings in 2019 alone as proof that the government had lost control of the country. By now it doesn't matter with the job done and irreversible.

9) Even more extreme New Woke governments are elected, the floodgates open, the target society is transformed, and the Hunger Games structure installed.

Group protection

What I am saying here is not a condemnation or mass-labelling of migrants. I want instead to expose the cold and calculated exploitation of often tragic people for political ends and the insanity of judging migrants and minorities *en masse* as groups and not through individual behaviour. Show me any racial, cultural, sexual or religious group and I will show you nice people, okay people and psychopaths – *every time.* Cult-programmed New Wokeness cannot process, or cope with, such basic subtlety. It sees only black and white racially and literally and inclusivity becomes exclusivity in that white is bad in totality and other shades are all victims of the bad white people. White supremacy and privilege extends to white homeless living amid the shit in San Francisco. My goodness, the billionaires behind New Wokeness know how to manipulate a mind. New Woke is another term for inversion – everything is inverted (Fig 255). The Cult New Woke agenda for the end of America in any form even close to what we have known is laid out in the Democrat-sponsored New Way Forward Act proposed by Mexican-born socialist Jesús García, a member for Illinois in the US House of Representatives. The bill would de-criminalise illegal immigration and remove any disincentive for untold numbers to walk across the often weakly-defended border. Once in the US the bill would make it very difficult for illegal migrants to be deported and that goes

Figure 255: If you want the truth about the 'Woke' tyranny invert everything they say and claim to stand for.

even for violent criminals. The bill would open the way for those who have committed serious crimes in other countries to be allowed to settle in America. Immigration law and enforcement would basically disappear. What would be the point of border patrols when it's not illegal to cross and those who do can't be detained? Cable news host Tucker Carlson, who alerted the public to the context of the bill that was being virtually ignored by the New Woke media, said:

> Under current US law, legal US immigrants can be deported if they commit an 'aggravated felony' or a 'crime of moral turpitude' – that is, a vile, depraved act, like molesting a child. Under the New Way Forward Act, 'crimes of moral turpitude' are eliminated entirely as a justification for deportation. And the category of 'aggravated felony' gets circumscribed too. What does that mean?
>
> Consider this: Under current law, immigrants who commit serious crimes – such as robbery, fraud, or child sexual abuse – must be deported, regardless of the sentence they receive. Other crimes – less severe ones like racketeering – require deportation as long as the perpetrator receives at least a one-year sentence. But if this bill passes the House and Senate and is signed into law by the president, there will no longer be any crimes that automatically require deportation. None.

The minimum prison sentence under the bill for crimes that still require deportation would rise from one year to five and even then judges would be given the discretion not to deport. Immigration and Customs Enforcement (ICE) would have to convince a court that an illegal migrant was dangerous or a flight risk, but officers would be banned from quoting prior criminal behavior to prove this – including rape, child molestation and drug trafficking. Even more insane is the provision compelling the government to create a 'pathway for those previously deported to apply to return to their homes and families in the United States' if they would not have been deported under the new rules. It is a retrospective open border. Taxpayers would have to pay for the previously deported to be located and brought 'back home' from where they had been removed for criminality. To put this in perspective 480,000 were deported for illegal entry or re-entry into America between 2002 and 2018 and they would be eligible to 'come home'. The bill has next to no chance of being successful before the scheduled 2020 election when it would have to be signed by Donald Trump and to do so would be electoral suicide. The bill does indicate, however, what would happen once New Woke came to power and confirms the Cult agenda to destroy America by setting criminals free to create mayhem and the domination of the strongest. For this open border plan with Mexico to be proposed by a Mexican-born US politician, Jesús García, shows that they don't care if you see they have no integrity or have any wish to hide their intent. They are now quite happy to put that on public display. There is a chasm of difference between migrants seeking a better life for themselves and their family or fleeing from war and the psychopaths of America's MS-13 and violent gangs in Sweden, Germany and France which terrorise once-peaceful communities. There is a gathering list of no-go areas in Sweden where police won't go except in numbers and ambulance crews won't go after migrant attacks. The response was to launch an initiative to recruit a 'more diverse' police force with 'language and cultural competence'. This was soon in trouble when half the applicants failed the admission tests. Never mind – watch the admission criteria be reduced. Sweden's top migration official Mikael Ribbenvik, head of the Swedish Migration Agency, went public to warn Swedes that their country was becoming a 'safe haven for war criminals and potential terrorists' with the government giving passports and benefits to suspected dangerous criminals that were protected by law from deportation (see the common theme). Ribbenvik said that other countries 'have a hard time understanding how we consider people dangerous but still continue to give them passports and residence permits'. Once you realise that the idea is destroy white Swedish culture and turn its society into an arena of fear and might-is-right there is no longer any 'hard time' in understanding why such things are happening. Political correctness and 'hate speech' are smokescreens to stop this being openly discussed and exposed.

Pakistani and Asian gangs raping and trafficking underage and teenage white girls in British cities were ignored by police and politicians who knew what was going on for years before officially coming to light and it's still happening on an industrial scale. One girl was forced to have sex with 300 'men' by the age of 15 in the northern town of Huddersfield. They are called 'grooming' gangs when rapists, psychopaths and child traffickers is what they are. They are brutal, sexist, racist, and everything and more that New Woke rails against – *if* you're white. New Woke silence is deafening otherwise. Exposing these psychopaths challenges the mass immigration narrative and that is far more important to The System than shockingly abused young girls. Had they been white gangs and Pakistani girls the police would have been on them in an instant and quite right, but you see the systematic bias based on race which, of course, is blatant racism. 'Grooming' (rape) gangs are clearly still operating across the UK with new cases now regularly coming to light and how many more – far more – are not being caught? A leaked document from the French internal security service, the General Directorate for Internal Security, said that up to 150 communities in France are controlled, or 'held', by Islamist radicals. The document was classified to stop the information being known by the public and to protect the agenda. This is not how all migrants behave, the great majority do not. The fact is, however, that some *do* and political correctness is silencing their exposure and the scale of the problem. The El Salvadorian migrant gangs of MS-13 are terrifying communities in

Figure 256: MS-13 are only 'fleeing tyranny' to impose a new one in the United States. What's wrong with that you rascist?

US cities with their signature savagery of dismembering people with machetes and their prime target is other migrants from El Salvador (one in three El Salvadorians now live in America). Donald Trump was furiously attacked by New Woke Democrats and media when he described MS-13 as 'animals'. Chopping people up with machetes? *Bless 'em* (Fig 256).

The more the merrier

There is clearly a policy of encouraging more migrants to cross the border illegally with moves to give them driving licences, the right to vote and free health care. At least tens of thousands, some claim far more, enter the United States on a visa and never leave. These policies are protected from scrutiny by making criticism of them increasingly illegal or a reason for censorship. There is a fundamental difference between those willing to respect the culture and traditions of countries they enter and cultural supremacists and bigots who seek to impose their society and prejudices on everyone else including migrant sharia police telling Swedish girls what they can wear. Those that have allowed this human disaster to happen in Sweden, Germany and elsewhere should be in a prison cell for crimes *against* The People and *for* The Cult. What does all this do collectively? It creates the very daily fear and anxiety that the Cult wants to impose everywhere. The House wins yet again. I have charted the mass migration agenda in other books back to at least the 1920s and those connected to the Habsburg and ultra-Zionist banking families behind the creation of the EU. I have quoted the extraordinarily accurate predictions of ultra-Zionist doctor and Rockefeller family insider Richard Day who told a meeting of paediatricians in Pittsburgh, Pennsylvania, in *1969* how the world was going to change across a wide range of subjects and all of which have happened or are happening (you'll find a summary in Appendix 2). Day knew for the same reason that George Orwell knew 20 years earlier in his *Nineteen Eighty-Four* and Aldous Huxley knew in 1932 in *Brave New*

World. If you are either part of the agenda (as with Day) or have access to the plan through research or contacts you can comfortably predict the 'future' because unless something intervenes to stop the plan it will play out. See my book *Phantom Self* for the detail of what Day said in 1969 which will take you aback in the light of what has happened since. He predicted among so much more the emergence of the Internet, the surveillance state, smart televisions, the plan to 'make boys and girls the same', clearing rural areas and forcing everyone into cities, and calculated mass migration to transform Western society. Lawrence Dunegan, one of the paediatricians present, took notes and in 2004 he recounted in audio interviews with an alternative website what Day said that night. Dunegan was prompted to do so when he saw the predictions were happening. He quotes Day as saying this in 1969 about the plan for mass migration:

> There [will] be mass movements and migrations of people without roots in their new locations because traditions are easier to change in a place where there are a lot of transplanted people, as compared to trying to change traditions in a place where people grew up and had an extended family, where they had roots.

This is the real reason for mass immigration – to manipulate an infusion of people from other cultures that have no connection to the history and traditions on which target societies are founded. Those with a sense of nationhood will resist the deletion of nations and countries under a world government dictatorship and the more you dilute that sense of nation and culture the more you dilute that resistance. As older people die out and the young take over who know nothing except the current society the historical and cultural foundations fall and disappear. The manipulation and dilution of the indigenous sense of nationhood is further systematically undermined by denigration of the culture as we have seen so clearly in Sweden. This has included an advertisement by SAS, the biggest airline in Sweden, Denmark and Norway, promoting the belief that there is no Swedish culture and nothing 'truly Scandinavian'. Swedish politicians supporting mass immigration and TV documentaries by the state broadcaster have said the same. SAS featured a black guy saying 'We are no better than our Viking ancestors' and the advertisement (propaganda) said everything considered 'Swedish' was a copied culture which came from foreign lands. Swathes of the public were outraged, but the theme will continue because it's the Cult agenda. Something similar is emerging in America with Democrat politicians saying that migrants are 'more American' than Americans. The absorption of national sovereignty into superstates like the European Union is part of the same plan and explains why the same people who plotted in the 1920s to introduce the EU also plotted even then the mass movement of people that we have today (see *Everything You Need To Know*).

The takeover sequence

There is another sequence that follows in the overthrow of the indigenous culture in any country in the face of mass immigration. Not immigration at all – *mass*, basically open-border, immigration. First you have an influx from another culture that tends to gather in certain areas and transform their cultural nature. Members of the indigenous population move out into familiar surroundings. This has happened in the extreme in the East End of London where its cultural status has been utterly transformed in little more than a generation. I have seen this referred to as people losing their 'cultural security' in the face of the incoming culture or cultures. Next the numbers reach levels where how new culture communities vote decides who is elected to local councils and as Members of Parliament. At this point parties of Left, Right and Centre begin to pander to the new cultures with their election-deciding potential. At the same time they ignore and take for granted those parts of the wider community who would normally vote for them. I call this the 'gimme vote' and gimme voters get nothing from political parties – 'they'll always vote for us anyway'. The British New Woke pro-mass immigration Labour Party found in the 2019 national election that those days are now over as the kick-back after decades of 'gimme' exploitation of the white urban class demolished their support. New cultures become the focus as their numbers continue to rise. Politicians from incoming cultures start to be elected and eventually they become leaders with an ever-increasing body of support with new culture birth-rates far exceeding those of the indigenous culture. This is happening as Western women have children later or not at all in the ridiculous and encouraged assumption that this will save the world from 'climate change'. Fertility rates for white women were down in every US state in 2017 according to the Centers for Disease Control and Prevention (CDC) and the same is happening in countries like Germany. They have fallen below the rate needed for the population to replace itself. Pointing out these facts is not racism. It is to expose the agenda behind it and that affects us all no matter what your racial background and skin colour. London now has a white minority population as does my birth city, Leicester, with Birmingham, Britain's second biggest city, going the same way. The transformation has happened in 50 years with the speed increasing. The BBC reported in 2018 on a study projecting university places which predicted that three in four London students will be from ethnic minorities by 2030. A British 'journalist' and self-proclaimed communist activist called Ash Sarkar, British-born of Bengali descent, pointed out in a 2016 video that the white population of London had fallen by 600,000 while non-whites had increased by 1.2 million. Her response to this was: 'So yes, lads, we're winning.' She claimed she was joking (I don't think so) when people were appalled by the remark, but it showed once again how we live in a two-tier system of political correctness. Had a white person said the same if the figures were reversed they would be condemned and banned in a fury of 'racist, bigot, Nazi' and Ash Sarkar with breathtaking hypocrisy would be leading the charge. To Sarkar white Britain is a racist society and in line with true New Woke orthodoxy only white people can be racist and not those of Bengali descent who describe the white population of London falling and the non-white increasing as 'we are winning'. The bias and unfairness is transparent and systematic. Census projections in the United States predict that whites will be a minority by 2045 with Hispanics the next biggest group. If the One-percent-controlled New Woke mentality gets political power it will be much sooner. We should not forget that white people occupied the land that was once the domain of Native Americans and it is not the demographic change by itself that is the point here. It is why it is being systematically manipulated by the Cult and to what end and why white people are being so targeted.

While this sequence of societal change unfolds any criticism or exposure of what is happening, any complaints from the indigenous population about their home areas being transformed into what is to them a foreign land, are dismissed and silenced by political correctness. New Woke thought police brand every dissenting voice as racist. They demand that people must be 'non-judgemental' (while themselves being constantly so) when in fact 'non-judgemental' is Orwellian code for having 'no opinion' outside the New Woke perceptual prison camp. The sub-text here is that if people are not allowed to criticise what people and the Cult are doing this automatically blocks all exposure of what is happening to enslave and manipulate the population. New Wokeness pervades the Cult-owned media to ensure PC reporting of events and government agencies are infused with Wokeness including the police as laws are introduced to make illegal any criticism of the impact of incoming cultures on the indigenous culture. Legitimate criticism is labelled 'hate speech'. The cumulative effect eventually is that incoming cultures override and replace the original culture and legislation is passed to change the cultural basis on which the country is governed. It's no good New Wokers shouting bigot at me for pointing this out which is ridiculous given my view of reality and the Oneness of everything. The sequence I have described is factually how it works and this has been *made* to happen by the Cult and its agents like war criminal British Prime Minister Tony Blair to serve its agenda for the cultural and racial transformation of Western Society. If people don't like me

speaking the obvious truth I
have a finger that I will gladly
put on public display.

Soros money

I have exposed billionaire
manipulator George Soros in
great detail in many other
books including *The Trigger*
and *Everything You Need To*

Figure 257: Don't reveal what he's actually doing or
you are an 'anti-Semite'.

Know (Fig 257). His global vehicle operating in 100 countries is the Open
Society Foundations (OSF) to which he has given at the time of writing
some *$32 billion*. OSF is dubbed an NGO, or non-governmental
organisation, and these along with 'think tanks' are a major source of
Cult manipulation and government policy. Note the giveaway name –
Open Society. This is code for open borders and the end of countries and
nations which just happens to be the goal of the Cult as I have been
highlighting for 30 years. The Cult's planned global structure requires an
end to countries to make way for a world government overseeing
superstates like the EU with regional entities replacing nations and
countries. Maps of a regionalised Europe have come to light through the
EU. People would be designated 'global citizens' and be subject to the
impositions of an unelected global government run by 'experts' and
technocrats directing the 'Smart' technological control grid. Making
countries disappear means borders must disappear and this is the whole
idea of what is happening. Without borders there can be no countries,
individual value systems, or safety nets for the poor, disabled, sick and

destitute – you know, all those
things the New Woke social justice
warriors claim to care about (Fig
258). Anyone just walks in to the
land of a former country no matter
what their background and
attitudes and demands they are
looked after; but by whom and with
what? Very soon after open borders
the game would be up. There would
not be the money, jobs, housing,

Figure 258: Have you thought this through,
people? Have you thought at all? It seems not.

healthcare, 'education' for all those
who would want them as hordes of people move in. I shake my head
when I hear New Wokers demanding open borders *and* more spending
on healthcare, housing, unemployment and schools. They have no self-
awareness to see the obvious contradictions. New Woke is purely about
virtue-signalling and not rational thought. Ask them if they could stop a

jug running over while the tap was still on and they might say 'of course, not'. Then they would call for open borders *and* more spending on healthcare, housing, unemployment and schools while believing that at some point there would be enough for everyone. No such point could ever be reached. The more you spend on healthcare, housing, unemployment and schools the *even more* would be needed to meet ever-increasing demand through ever-increasing numbers. Cabal asset Soros directs his tens of billions at all the facets of the agenda and funds Open Society operations to overthrow governments, control politicians and parties, impose the New Woke agenda, and encourage mass migration into Europe and the United States. He also bankrolled organisations in an effort to stop the UK leaving the European Union or at least in a way that could genuinely be called 'Brexit'. Soros money from someone who lives in the United States and is not British was directed against Brexit. The sheer arrogance of it is mind-numbing. The Strategic Culture Foundation website detailed in a 2017 article the control that Soros has over the European Union:

> It's an open secret that the 'Soros network' has an extensive sphere of influence in the European Parliament and in other European Union institutions. The list of Soros ['reliable allies'] has been made public recently. The document lists 226 MEPs from all sides of the political spectrum, including former President of the European Parliament Martin Schulz, former Belgian PM Guy Verhofstadt [a major opponent of Brexit], seven vice-presidents, and a number of committee heads, coordinators, and quaestors. These people promote the ideas of Soros, such as bringing in more migrants, same-sex marriages, integration of Ukraine into the EU, and countering Russia. There are 751 members of the European Parliament. It means that the Soros friends have more than one third of seats.

> George Soros, a Hungarian-American investor and the founder and owner of Open Society Foundations NGO, was able to meet with President of the European Commission Jean-Claude Juncker with 'no transparent agenda for their closed-door meeting', and [it was] pointed out how EU proposals to redistribute quotas of migrants across the EU are eerily familiar to Soros's own self-published plan for dealing with the crisis.

The report is talking about ways to respond to the very migration 'crisis' *created* by Soros, his masters and his Open Society Foundations – Problem-Reaction-Solution. The European Center for Law and Justice revealed in 2020 that in the period 2009-2019 nearly a *quarter* of the judges on the bench of European Court of Human Rights have had strong links to the Soros Open Society Foundations or to organisations that he funds including Amnesty International which has received $100

million since 2010. The study found that some NGOs are so funded by
the Soros networks that they are effectively wholly-owned subsidiaries.
But there's no conspiracy, George Soros is a shining light of
unimpeachable virtue, and it is 'anti-Semitic' to say otherwise.

'Soros Spring' technique

Soros-funded groups have a particular role in manipulating protests
against target governments to give the illusion of spontaneous 'people's
revolutions'. If the Cult continually invades countries with military force
the pattern will be clear and opposition will gather with each one.
Instead the ideal is to manipulate the population in the country to
overthrow the government as you hide in the shadows saying 'Who,
me?' Open Society place-people and agent provocateurs instigate the
unrest and this is followed by thousands from the population who have
no idea that it's all a scam. Cult-controlled American and European
governments then give public support to the protestors and demonise
the country's leader. This is often quite straightforward with so many
psychopaths of all kinds that kill, terrorise and otherwise manipulate
themselves to power in country after country. The Open Society
Foundations of Soros were frontline players in the so-called 'Arab
Spring' when protests across the Arab world removed governments and
replaced them with military dictatorships as in Egypt and warring
warlords trafficking children in open slave markets as in Libya. If the
Soros network can't overthrow a regime by protest alone American and
European governments send in the bombers to finish them off under the
PR cover of 'saving the people from violence' – by bombing them from
the sky. Precisely this happened in Libya when the country with the
highest per-capita income in Africa was bombed into the Stone Age by
Cult-created-and-owned NATO. Countries targeted by Soros and
US/NATO psychopaths happened to be the same ones demanded for
regime-change by the Cult's Project for the New American Century
organisation founded in the United States by Sabbatian-Frankist ultra-
Zionists that included the major players in the White House and
Pentagon in 2001 when the Cult-orchestrated 9/11 gave them the excuse
to start picking off the list. Another Open Society-manipulated
overthrow was that of President Viktor Yanukovych in Ukraine in 2014
and was overseen by ultra-Zionist Victoria Nuland, Assistant Secretary
of State for European and Eurasian Affairs at the US State Department,
and the wife of ultra-Zionist Robert Kagan, co-founder of … the Project
for the New American Century. More than 2,200 Open Society
Foundation documents secured by the group DC Leaks reveal the
manipulation of Soros and his lackeys including US policy toward
Ukraine after the 2014 coup during the fake-liberal Obama
administration. One document described the 'New Ukraine' as a key

that 'reshapes the European map by offering the opportunity to go back to the original essence of European integration' (the plan for the tyrannical centralisation of power over the whole of European by Cult-controlled bureaucrats which explains why Soros sought to thwart Brexit). British academic Frank Furedi has personal experience of the arrogance, reach and agenda of the Soros network and exposed what he saw in a British national newspaper. He said he was a guest speaker at an event funded by a Soros foundation in Budapest, Hungary, where Soros was born. Furedi recalled:

It was later during lunch at a plush Budapest hotel that I encountered the full force of the arrogant ethos promoted by the Soros network of organisations. At my table I listened to Dutch, American, British, Ukrainian and Hungarian representatives of Soros NGOs boast about their achievements. Some claimed that they played a major role in the Arab Spring in Egypt. Others voiced their pride in their contribution to the democratisation of the Ukraine. Some bragged about their influence in preparing the ground for the overthrow of the Gadhafi regime in Libya. I sat quietly and felt uncomfortable with a group of people who so casually assumed that they had the right to play God throughout the world.

At one point, the head of the table – a Hungarian leader of a Soros NGO – asked me what I thought about their work. Not wishing to offend, I quietly remarked that I wasn't sure whether the external imposition of their idea of democracy on the people of Libya was legitimate nor that it would work. Without a second's hesitation, my interlocutor rounded me with the response: 'I don't think that we have the luxury of waiting until the Libyan people come with their own Jefferson.'

The overthrow of Colonel Gadhafi in the Soros foundation 'people's revolution', and manipulation in other countries including Syria, led to the start of the mass movement of people out of the Middle and Near East and Africa into Europe aided by the same Open Society Foundations as you can read in detail in *Everything You Need To Know* where you will also see how Soros-funded groups are behind the attempts to relocate masses of people from Central and South America into the United States. Yet another Cult think tank was launched in 2018 called the New Center that campaigns for an amnesty for all 'illegal aliens' in the United States to allow them to stay permanently. The New Center is headed by William Galston of the Brookings Institute and ... ultra-Zionist *William Kristol, co-founder of the Project for the New American Century*. The demands of the 'New Center' are supported to their DNA by the New Woke mentality funded to a pivotal extent by ... *George Soros*. The Soros Open Society network officially left Hungary, the country of his birth, in 2018 after Prime Minister Viktor Orban's government passed the 'Stop Soros' law to criminalise the organisation's manipulation of the country (Fig 259). Others have seen through the Soros game with Russia banning Open Society activities as representing 'a threat to the foundations of the constitutional system of the Russian Federation and the security of the state'.

The defence-mechanism to stop exposure of Soros is that he is Jewish and any criticism of him must be 'anti-Semitic'. This is the Anti-Semitism Industry and Protection Racket at work blocking legitimate investigation into anyone who is Jewish or Zionist purely *because* they are Jewish and Zionist. Is that supremacist or what? A whole new definition of 'anti-Semitism' is being introduced by governments and institutions around the world that includes criticism of Israel for the specific reason of expanding the definition to dub ever more information and opinion as 'anti-Semitic' to protect the Cult and its operatives from exposure. Is it really discriminatory to ask why 0.2 percent of the

Figure 259: The Hungarian government knows what the Soros game is and displayed these posters exposing his activities.

world population and two percent of the American population have so much power over politics, finance and censorship by the mainstream media and Silicon Valley? It is a very legitimate question in a society that values its freedom.

The Cult doesn't want these questions asked because its Sabbatian-Frankist wing, which hates Jews, would soon be secret no more – not least to Jews. This would be a mortal blow when hiding behind and within the Jewish community is their essential cover. Few make these points or ask these questions for fear of being condemned as 'anti-Semitic'. I don't give a shit. I want the truth and if that means taking an onslaught of misrepresentation and abuse then so be it. For now the incessant intimidation of the non-New Woke population means that what the Cult wants the Cult gets and it will go on doing so until humanity stiffens its backbone and summons some self-respect.

We'd better do that fast – like now – before the chance is gone.

CHAPTER EIGHT

Why demonise the gas of life?

Belief can be manipulated. Only knowledge is dangerous
– Frank Herbert

N ew Wokeness is a cult religion in every sense and its sub-section known as 'human-caused climate change' is most certainly so. Climate orthodoxy is a theology, a term which derives from two Greek words together meaning 'the study of God'. In this case the 'God' is the Virtuous Self and the Devil is carbon dioxide (Fig 260).

Religions have an orthodoxy founded on unsupportable beliefs that include walking on water and virgin births and so does the Climate Cult. Religions label non-believers of these unsupportable beliefs as heretics and blasphemers and so does the Climate Cult. Religions have had inquisitions to demonise and silence such heretics and blasphemers and so does the Climate Cult. Religions dictate a narrative and tell followers to unquestioningly believe whatever it claims and so does the Climate Cult. Religions say that belief in the orthodoxy must be founded on faith and not facts and so does the Climate Cult. You must believe the crap spewed out by faith-based religions like Extinction Rebellion and the Climate Cult priesthood in the form of people like New York New Woke congresswoman Alexandra Ocasio Cortez or you are a 'climate change denier' (see heretics and blasphemers). Don't question – *believe*.

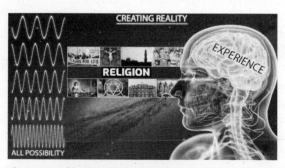

Figure 260: The Climate Cult and its constituent parts like Extinction Rebellion are just another religion and tick every box. 'Rebel for life' means rebel for the One-percent. Like all religions the Climate Cult is a perception program to ensnare its followers. (Image Gareth Icke.)

These methods are straight from the Cult manual for its 'astroturf' fake protest groups described by former *CBS News* investigative reporter Sharyl Attkisson:

Hallmarks of astroturf include use of inflammatory language such as 'crank', 'quack', 'nutty', 'lies,' 'paranoid', 'pseudo', and 'conspiracy'. Astroturfers often claim to debunk myths that aren't myths at all. Use of the charged language test well. People hear something's a myth, maybe they find it on Snopes, and they instantly declare themselves too smart to fall for it. But what if the whole notion of the myth is itself a myth, and you and Snopes fell for that? Beware when interests attack an issue by controversialising or attacking the people, personalities, and organisations surrounding it rather than addressing the facts. That could be astroturf.

And most of all astroturfers tend to reserve all of their public scepticism for those exposing wrongdoing rather than the wrongdoers. In other words, instead of questioning authority, they question those who question authority. You might start to see things a little more clearly. It's like taking off your glasses, wiping them, and putting them back on, realising, for the first time, how foggy they'd been all along. I can't resolve these issues, but I hope that I've given you some information that will at least motivate you to take off your glasses and wipe them, and become a wiser consumer of information in an increasingly artificial, paid-for reality.

Questioning those who question authority is at the very core of Climate Cult and New Woke propaganda in general and both are drowning in astroturf fronts because they are a means through which human society is being transformed into a global dictatorship by the Cult as we'll see in following chapters. In this chapter I want to first unpick the truly mendacious climate change narrative.

Cult doctrine and its many faces

Here are some archetypal traits of a cult: Unquestioning submission to leaders of the cult and what they insist you believe; those beliefs are the only truth; control cult members through the constant repetition and indoctrination of this orthodoxy; invoke an 'us' against 'them' mentality and claim that any outside challenge is 'persecution'; salvation through association with the cult – only we can save the world by everyone doing what we demand; group think with pressure by the group to conform and target any individual with doubts; if doubters persist shun or expel them so they don't pollute the group-think with legitimate questions; avoid critical thinking and ignore blatant contradictions in the orthodoxy; often impose a cult form of clothing or uniform so a cult member can be recognised purely by what they wear or what they do with their hair. All of these traits can be observed with the Climate Cult which has been funded and manipulated into existence by billionaires like George Soros (again) and decades of climate change indoctrination in the schools and universities. This has led to great swathes of whole generations believing utter baloney because that's all they've heard. Climate Cult theology is founded on one of the most powerful forms of perception control – repetition of the orthodoxy at the exclusion of other views, opinions and information. Even Princeton professors who don't accept climate hoax theology after a lifetime of expertise in climate science and the effects of carbon dioxide have their YouTube videos tagged to a *Wikipedia* page promoting the official lies (which goes without saying when Wikipedia actually *exists* to promote official lies). I typed in key words for YouTube videos that questioned climate change doctrine and the Wikipedia page parroting that doctrine was at the top of even that list. What a con job by this Cult propaganda operation YouTube owned by Google.

The Climate Cult demands that people 'listen to the science' when the Cult is anti-science. It's not interested in allowing all scientific opinion and research to be heard in a spirit of openness and balanced understanding. The aim as with all New Woke agendas is to silence opposition and block open debate which they know they would lose. George Soros, a member of the United Nations High Level Advisory Group on Climate Change Financing, funds a list of organisations seeking to silence 'denial' of climate change orthodoxy. These include Avaaz ('Voice') which has been described as 'the globe's largest and most powerful online activist network'. It was established in 2007 by two other Soros-funded groups, Res Publica and MoveOn.org. Avaaz claims to have 55 million members with campaign teams operating in 30 countries and presents itself as a global *grassroots* operation working in pursuit of 'people-powered politics'. It campaigns in 15 languages with a 'core team' on six continents and this Soros-funded group is leading a campaign to have Google-owned YouTube ban all information and opinions challenging the official propaganda about human-caused climate change. Avaaz ('Voice') doesn't want others to have one. We have also had a Soros-connected Democrat Congressional committee (New Woke political wing) demanding that Google-owned YouTube censor videos that contain 'climate misinformation' which means challenging the official narrative. Fascistic committee members wrote to Google CEO Sundar Pichai to urge that YouTube stop 'driving millions of viewers to climate misinformation videos every single day'. The contempt for freedom is extraordinary, but it suits the Cult agenda perfectly. Avaaz claims that 'climate denial = death' which is only another way of saying that if you can't win a debate – ban it. 'Grassroots' Avaaz has a long record of campaigning for items on the Cult wish-list. It has helped Iranian protestors demanding the removal of the country's government that the Cult has long worked to remove; supported a no-fly zone for Libyan military aircraft which allowed America, Britain and NATO to bomb the country and its people shitless without challenge and delete Colonel Gadhafi; supported the US-instigated 'civil uprising' against Cult-target President Assad in Syria and this was reported to include training activists and delivering $1.5 million of Internet communication technology to protesters. Avaaz claims to 'unite practical idealists' to make the world a better place when its support for Western (Cult) actions against Libya and Syria alone played a part in the human nightmare that followed in a frenzy of death and destruction of the innocent. All those countries were on the September, 2000, list of targets named by the ultra-Zionist Sabbatian-Frankist Project for the New American Century.

To those who trust Avaaz I would suggest a call to Naivety Anonymous. To those who trust George Soros I would say don't waste a call – even they can't help you. How could anyone if you believe that a man who has caused financial mayhem for whole populations by targeting their currencies for financial gain is funding 'progressive' 'people-power' groups from the kindness of his heart. The best of luck finding that, by the way. Soros has also funded groups behind the worldwide Friday school 'climate strikes' fronted by the Climate Cult's Greta Thunberg who has copyrighted the terms 'school strikes for climate' and 'Friday's for future'. America's Media Research Center, a non-profit conservative media watchdog, reported that at least 22 activist groups listed as partners in the Global Climate Strike received almost $25 million from Soros through his Open Society network between 2000 and 2017. They included Fund for Global Human Rights, Global Greengrants Fund, 350.org, Amnesty International, Avaaz, Color of Change and People's Action. Has the penny dropped yet Green movement? Unfortunately probably not, but maybe it will when we get to *why* human-caused climate change is being hoaxed. A major funder of Extinction Rebellion is Sir Chris Hohn who heads one of the world's biggest hedge funds valued at multiple billions. The UK *Mail on Sunday* revealed the fund's investments in companies at the centre of environmental scandals. Everywhere the Climate Cult and New Woke have a remarkable ability to attract billionaire sponsorship and support. Amazon's mega-billionaire Jeff Bezos announced in early 2020 that he would spend $10 billion on 'fighting climate change' by funding 'scientists, activists and non-governmental organisations (see Soros) through a new 'Bezos Earth Fund'. It was still more confirmation that human-caused climate change is a One-percent hoax. Bezos picked up the script and said the climate was changing faster than had been predicted. 'Those predictions were bad but what is actually happening is dire'. Bloody yawn. He said that Amazon was ordering 100,000 electric delivery vehicles from Michigan-based, Amazon-invested Rivian, which again is straight from the Cult agenda. To underscore the power of programming hundreds of Amazon workers, who face losing their jobs to 'climate-friendly' (it's not) AI, had protested that Bezos was not doing enough about climate change. Manipulate the serfs to demand that you do what you want to do anyway (it happens all the time). The Climate Cult works to silence the ever-growing list of scientists worldwide who can see that climate change orthodoxy is mendacious nonsense. They are demonised, targeted in the courts, denied access to the media, and their careers and income disappear. By contrast those self-proclaimed 'scientists' prepared to sing from the song-sheet (the ones Bezos will support) are constantly wheeled out by the Cult-owned media and can dip their snouts in an almost unlimited trough of protection money – money to protect the lies.

The cult (literally) of New Woke climate celebrity

Once belief in the orthodoxy is secured in the mainstream it becomes 'cool' to support that orthodoxy. If you are a virtue-signalling celebrity it's a must to build your own image and support-base. New Woke is 'in' while not being New Woke can be the death knell for a career in the media, entertainment and comedy. It's the same technique that controls scientists. Say what we want and you get a stack of money or tell your truth and we'll destroy you. Do you want lots of likes on Facebook or a Twitter storm? As a result we have a lengthening list of celebrity arse-lickers proclaiming Climate Cult orthodoxy of 'Thou Shalt not fly' while heading in private jets to climate conferences and protests. In the case of virtue-signal world champions like actor Leonardo DiCaprio this involves taking private jets to receive climate protection awards. Celebrities are used by the Cult for their public platform to spread the message while almost every one of them won't have a clue who is really pulling their strings and why. Britain's Prince Harry and his American wife Meghan Markle constantly virtue-signal their climate change New Wokeness while being driven in limousines to private jets and telling others to reduce their 'carbon footprint'. Isn't that hypocrisy? No, no – I said *you* must reduce your footprint, not *me*. Harry's contribution to saving the planet has been limited to the New Woke posturing of making a speech in bare feet. Put your shoes on, mate, or you'll hurt your feet on the tarmac when you leave. The couple announced in January, 2020, they were 'stepping down' as 'senior royals' and heading for Canada. Part of this will involve super-Woke Markle being able to publicly promote her virtue-signalling super-Wokeness (including climate change theology) while Harry follows behind doing what he's told and apologising for being a white male. New Wokers supported the move because the pair are New Woke while the now hijacked original Left would have been exposing their unearned privilege, opportunism and narcissism. Oh, how the Cult is going to exploit them both – and make them very rich – to promote the climate change and New Woke agenda. Their first big, *big* pay-day came with a 'speech' to the assembled mega-rich One-percent fake Woke at a JP Morgan Chase event in February, 2020, for which they were reported to be paid between $750,000 and $1 million. JP Morgan Chase is America's biggest bank and the world's sixth biggest with assets of $2.6 trillion. Here we have fake Wokers selling their souls to speak for big bucks to other fake Wokers with limitless pockets whose investments have done so much to devastate the environment and create widespread inequality and injustice. The hypocrisy and lack of self-awareness of these royals-on-the-make is chilling.

The 'royal' couple, said they were seeking to become 'financially independent' which means exploiting their royal connections and privilege to make lots of money and freeing Markle from her royal restrictions to stay out of party politics. Now she can campaign for the New Woke agenda including all the demands of the Climate Cult which she and her husband appear to ignore at every turn. Prince Harry was caught on tape by two Russian pranksters thinking he was talking to Greta Thunberg. The result was toe-curling and absolute confirmation that he just repeats the climate hoax script word-for-word without a thought of his own. How Woke and aware Markle really is can be gleaned by her closeness to the Clintons, particularly Hillary, one of the most corrupt partnerships on Planet Earth. We can expect the royal private jet passengers to be even more vocal now in support of the Climate Cult and every last facet of New Woke while living their own life in the 'privilege' that New Woke claims to despise. The System will give them every support. American TV host Tucker Carlson accurately described celebrity climate New Wokeness as 'the theology of the private jet class'. Meanwhile we are told that the rest of us will soon be flying in planes (as a stepping-stone to not flying at all) that fly together in V-shape formations like migrating birds to save fuel and CO_2 emissions by reducing air resistance like racing cars that get close to the one in front. As someone who has experienced what happens to a plane when it gets too close to another and is twisted by the air turbulence I can't wait. Swedish Climate Cult goddess Greta Thunberg has been used to promote the Swedish term 'flygskam', or 'flight shame', to pressure people to stop flying (except the private jet class). The shame that Thunberg will feel when she realises the scale on which she has been manipulated does not bear thinking about (Fig 261). She and the Climate Cult have

Figure 261: Sad, real sad.

created a situation so crazy that the UK's University of Derby introduced 'climate anxiety classes' for staff and students worried about the planet and the eco-system. The university said the classes are aimed at dealing with feelings of anger, guilt and grief and combatting their 'sense of loss'. I mean – *pinch me*. One student said the 'climate emergency' made her feel she 'isn't going to have a future'. Oh, congratulations Greta and your handlers. Well done you. Dr Jamie Bird, university deputy head of health and social care research, said people suffer 'climate grief' when they see what they are losing. They are not losing *anything* except their bloody minds. Despite incessant public indoctrination great numbers of people can see through the garbage, but most are frightened to say so for fear of the backlash and consequences. Perhaps, however, we saw a turning point in 2019 when narcissistic, self-obsessed Extinction Rebellion protestors were pulled off the roofs of London Tube trains by commuters who just wanted to get home after a day's work. They'd had enough and rightly so. We've *all* had enough.

Monumental mendacity

A key component of mass indoctrination is the sheer scale of deceit which the Nazis described in terms of the bigger the lie the more will believe it. Lie a little bit and you may get caught out on the basis that people are open to smaller-scale lies. What most resist are the ginormous super-whoppers pedalled by the Cult. Okay, people say, they might lie here and there to support climate change orthodoxy, but they wouldn't lie about the whole *shebang* would they? Oh yes they would and they have and they are. They lie both about the individual components of the climate hoax *and* about the hoax in its entirety. I'll explain why shortly. In fact, the entirety of the hoax is the totality of the individual hoaxes. The Cult seeks to protect this fact from exposure by silencing and demonising dissenters to ensure only one version is ever heard by most people. The foundation of the hoax is the ever-repeated claim that 'the science is settled' when it is absolutely not and becomes less so by the day. Pedro Sanchez, acting prime minister of Spain, reached still new levels of ridiculous when he said: 'Only a handful of fanatics deny the evidence.' He's talking about an ever-increasing list of experts in their fields worldwide who are exposing climate change orthodoxy as the claptrap that it is. All Sanchez and almost every other politician will have heard is the official version ultimately emanating from the Cult through The Web and they repeat that orthodoxy as solid-gold unquestionable truth. This is what teachers and academics are doing with their daily indoctrination of the young to believe in climate change mendacity. You don't want to indoctrinate the kids? Then find another job and we'll replace you with someone who will. It's the programmed programming the next generation of programmed. Once the orthodoxy is established as accepted reality political leaders and parties compete with each other (with a few exceptions) over who will do the most to 'fight' a problem that doesn't exist. To question the climate change religion is political suicide especially on the New Woke 'Left' and those who have seen through the hoax zip their mouths as they seek election. The Cult knows that from the moment it secures official belief in the 'conventional wisdom' about any subject the dominoes will begin to fall right across society with all institutions making decisions and introducing laws on the basis of that flawed and manipulated 'wisdom'. The climate change hoax is such a wonderful example. The official narrative is taught in the schools and universities, promoted by the mainstream media and infused into the law of the land while dissenters are silenced, abused and demonised. No wonder that narrative has become accepted 'truth' among those who don't question. I am no supporter of Donald Trump for many reasons, but at least he has spoken out against climate orthodoxy while others cower or believe what they're told.

In support of 'the science is settled' baloney we have the associated lie about 97 percent of climate scientists believing that humans are the main cause of climate change (a climate that is *always* changing and has been since the Earth was formed). I saw Jonathan Bartley, co-leader of the Green Party for England and Wales, parroting this deceitful figure on a BBC programme while he berated the BBC for allowing 'climate deniers' to appear. I was a national spokesman for the UK Greens for a short time in the 1980s when it still campaigned for freedom of speech and wider environmental issues before it was completely hijacked by New Woke. Even the establishment *Wall Street Journal* has debunked the 97 percent claim. When you track back to where it came from, and on what basis, this figure being cited as fact by those who wish to sell the orthodoxy is ludicrous. Al Gore just pulled the figure out of nowhere and subsequently the most quoted source is John Cook, 'Climate Communication Fellow' for the Global Change Institute at the University of Queensland who is not a climate scientist. He just promotes the official story. I have read many articles explaining how Cook examined 11,944 papers by climate scientists and found that 97 percent agreed that humans were the main cause of 'warming'. This is not the case at all. In his own words Cook writes that 32.6 percent endorsed human-caused warming (though very few as the main cause) while 0.7 percent rejected that and 0.3 percent were uncertain. Now here's the most important figure … 66.4 percent *expressed no position*. I see it claimed again and again by the Climate Cult and the media that 97 percent of climate scientists say humans are the main cause of climate change when even by Cook's flawed methodology the figure refers only to those who *expressed a view* and not the scientists in totality. One study of Cook's figures found that only *64* of the 11,944 papers – (*0.5 percent*) – said humans are the main cause of global warming and nowhere was mentioned terms such as 'crisis' or 'emergency'. Even if you apply this to the 3,974 papers that did express a view the figure of 64 pointing the finger at humans as the main culprit plays out as *1.6 percent*. A later study of Cook's source papers found that in fact only 41 of the 64 papers endorsed the view that humans are the main cause of warming. That's *41* out of *11,944*. Where does the 97 percent of climate scientists agree come from? They *made it up* like they have made up virtually everything else. Science is about evidence not a show of bloody hands from song-sheet scientists with their nose in the climate trough and nor is it about fiddling temperature figures to support your case because the actual temperatures don't do that. This has been exposed over and over and if you are telling the truth you don't need to manipulate the data. How many people know that US Senator Timothy Wirth admitted they even manipulated the temperature of the room when NASA scientist James Hansen really kicked off the global warming scare at a Senate hearing in 1988? Wirth said:

> ... We ... went in the night before and opened all the windows, I will admit, right? So that the air conditioning wasn't working inside the room and so ... when the hearing occurred there was not only bliss, which is television cameras in double figures, but it was really hot ...

> ... So Hansen's giving this testimony, you've got these television cameras back there heating up the room, and the air conditioning in the room didn't appear to work. So it was sort of a perfect collection of events that happened that day, with the wonderful Jim Hansen, who was wiping his brow at the witness table and giving this remarkable testimony ...

Senator Wirth also said:

> Believe it or not, we called the Weather Bureau and found out what historically was the hottest day of the summer. Well, it was June 6 or June 9 or whatever it was, so we scheduled the hearing that day, and bingo: It was the hottest day on record in Washington, or close to it. It was stiflingly hot that summer. [At] the same time you had this drought all across the country, so the linkage between the Hansen hearing and the drought became very intense.

You can see that from the start the climate change hoax was not about facts, but manipulating perception to believe a fantasy.

You were saying?

Hansen's dire claims that day more than 30 years ago have not

Figure 262: Al Gore, the One-percent gofer to sell the lie.

happened and it's the same with long-time Cult asset Al Gore who became the global sales-pitcher for the Big Lie and has made a fortune from being so (Fig 262). Gore said in 2006: We have ten years to save the planet (big-time wrong); the Arctic will be ice-free by 2014 (big-time wrong); the Gulf Stream will slow down (it's been speeding up); polar bears are in danger of becoming extinct (big-time wrong); sea levels will rise by 20 feet in the near future (big-time wrong). Read some of my other books and you'll see the background to Gore who has a personal carbon footprint the size of Godzilla. He was a vice-president to Bill Clinton and you don't get that job if you have any inclination whatsoever to tell the truth. The Cult controls the Nobel Peace Prize, which is why so many Cult-asset war-mongers and mass killers have been recipients, and it also dictates Oscar winners whenever that would promote the agenda. Gore, you will not be shocked to know, was handed both awards for lying about climate change and frightening the life out of whole generations of children and the young. Prince Charles said in 2009 that we had twelve years to save the world from irretrievable climate and ecosystem collapse (big-time wrong) and with extraordinary idiocy he claimed that climate change was the 'root cause' of the Syrian conflict which was actually triggered by terrorists funded and armed by the United States and Gulf State allies like Saudi Arabia. Here are some other climate and environmental catastrophe warnings that turned out to be utter crap around the period that the annual Earth Day was established in *1970*:

Harvard biologist George Wald:

'Civilization will end within 15 or 30 years unless immediate action is taken against problems facing mankind.'

American biologist Paul Ehrlich:

'The death rate will increase until at least 100-200 million people per year will be starving to death during the next ten years.'

Peter Gunter, a North Texas State University professor:

'Demographers agree almost unanimously [see 97 percent of climate scientists agree] on the following grim timetable: by 1975 widespread famines will begin in India; these will spread by 1990 to include all of India, Pakistan, China and the Near East, Africa. By the year 2000, or conceivably sooner, South and Central America will exist under famine conditions ... By the year 2000, thirty years from now, the entire world, with the exception of Western Europe, North America, and Australia, will be in famine.'

Then there was the climate temperature prediction in 1970 from ecologist Kenneth Watt:

'The world has been chilling sharply for about twenty years. If present trends continue, the world will be about four degrees colder for the global mean temperature in 1990, but eleven degrees colder in the year 2000. This is about twice what it would take to put us into an ice age.'

The threat to human existence went from an ice age to runaway super-heating in the blink of an eye. How could that happen? They just changed the propaganda. The lies are constant and apparently without end.

Make-it-up mythology

We hear claims about the 'hottest day ever recorded' and even when you factor out manipulated data the key word is *recorded*. Many times this will be deleted in headlines to read 'hottest day ever'. Some background before I make my point. The planet has been hotter for much of its life than it is today and there was the Medieval Warm Period that began around 1,000 years ago which eclipsed current temperatures when there were no factories or 4 x 4s or indeed any carbon producing vehicles at all (Fig 263). The warm period was also a time of abundance compared with cold periods. Grapes were grown for wine in the far north of England and even Scotland. There was, in short, no climate catastrophe. Temperatures began to cool and previous abundance

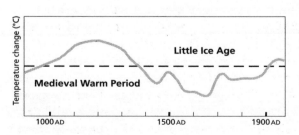

Figure 263: The Medieval Warm Period began around 1,000 years ago when temperatures were warmer than today without industrialisation. Then came the Little Ice Age when freezing temperatures were the winter norm which makes temperature comparisons between that period and now utterly irrelevant.

Figure 264: Depiction of the frozen-over River Thames during the Little Ice Age.

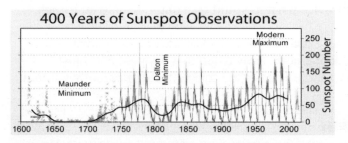

Figure 265: The correlation between solar activity measured by sunspots and Earth temperature. It is an obvious comparison and connection which the Climate Cult ignores because it destroys the narrative. The 'Maunder Minimum' corresponded with the coldest point of the Little Ice Age.

disappeared in what is called the Little Ice Age between the 16th and 19th centuries (some say it started earlier). It was so cold in this period they held ice fairs on the River Thames in London which froze over every year. Some Christmas cards still depict the scenes (Fig 264). It was highly significant that during the Little Ice Age fantastic explosions of energy on the Sun known as sunspots, which indicate solar activity, all but disappeared. This is known as the sunspot 'Maunder Minimum' after the man who conducted the research studies (Fig 265). You don't think there could be a connection between Sun activity and Earth temperature do you? There can't be, surely, or the Climate Cult would mention the Sun sometimes instead of being utterly obsessed with carbon dioxide. Maybe they think it's just a coincidence that when the Sun comes out it gets warmer; or perhaps they think that when solar energy projected at the Earth increases this couldn't possibly affect our temperature (Fig 266). They are experts

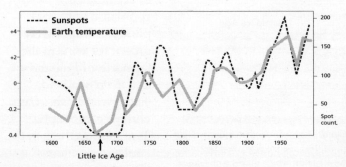

Figure 266: Another sunspot-Earth temperature chart.

after all. Scientists at CERN recorded an extremely close correlation between Earth temperature and the penetration of cosmic rays into our atmosphere. Records of 'the hottest day/year since records began' started mostly as we were still coming out of the Little Ice Age and of course temperatures are going to be warmer now. What use is a comparison between an extremely cold period and one after that period ended? It's a pointless comparison unless you are trying to mislead which they are. Why would the trough-snout scientists of the Climate Cult seek in leaked emails and documents to delete from the record the existence of the Medieval Warm Period and make it appear that today's temperatures are 'unprecedented' and caused by the industrial era? To mislead, of course, and people mislead to hide the fact that they're lying. Here are some other climate propaganda myths:

- **The migrant crisis is caused by climate change lowering crop yields that force people to relocate in search of food:** This has been alleged to explain why so many are heading out of Central America to the United States border and supports the Cult migration agenda which I have described. In fact, crop yields in Honduras, Costa Rica, Mexico, Panama, Ecuador, etc., have been consistently increasing.

- **Climate change will empty the North American Great Lakes:** This is shown to be without substance by all-time recorded high water levels and no downward trend over 100 years. These high volumes were reported with the question: 'Why are water levels on the Great Lakes fluctuating so widely?' How about through misrepresentation of the trend?

- **Climate change will mean ever-greater extremes of weather such as tornadoes and hurricanes:** Strong tornadoes and devastating landfall hurricanes have been steady in number or in decline in recent decades according to peer-reviewed scientific literature that says the same about droughts, floods, and other extreme weather events. The worldwide death rate caused by weather events has dropped more than 98 percent since the 1920s.

- **Polar bears are heading for extinction as climate change makes their ice habitat disappear:** Polar Bears became the poster children of the Climate Cult as a symbol for a terrifying future. Polar bear specialists like Dr Susan Crockford, former adjunct professor at the University of Victoria in Canada and a forensic zoologist, demolishes the official narrative in her book, *The Polar Bear Catastrophe That Never Happened*. Indeed she destroys the polar bear hoax so well that she lost her role at the university in what she described as 'an academic hanging without a trial, conducted behind closed doors'. This is what happens when you challenge Climate Cult orthodoxy.

Crockford shows how polar bears are flourishing and communities are either stable or increasing. Polar bears in part of the Barents Sea increased by 42 percent between 2004 and 2015; in Baffin Bay where bears were predicted to decline by 25 percent they increased by 36 percent; and in Kane Basin they more than doubled. The global average had risen to more than 30,000 bears which Crockford says is 'far and away the highest estimate in more than 50 years'. Crockford exposes the BBC's climate change propagandist David Attenborough for misleading the public on polar bears and much else in an Internet video *Attenborough's Arctic Betrayal* (Fig 267). Greta Thunberg said she became an activist on climate change after watching reports of polar bear decline that *isn't happening*. The same BBC of course gave her a TV programme (program) to promote her propaganda.

Figure 267: You can always bet on the BBC's David Attenborough parroting (appropriately) the official narrative.

Figure 268: Yet another constant misrepresentation to promote CO2 as a pollutant.

- **Images show belching chimneys pouring out 'dangerous' carbon dioxide:** CO2 is invisible to the human eye and what they are showing you is pollution and not CO2 which is the gas of life and without it there would be no plants and so no humans or animals (Fig 268). They show you pictures of pollution to make you believe that carbon dioxide is a pollutant. Most of the 'journalists' who do this don't know the difference themselves in yet another exercise in the blind leading the blind.

Protecting make-it-up mythology

How could a hoax based on so many lies become accepted fact in the minds of so many – especially the young – and drive much of government policy? The hoax has been possible by control of information to indoctrinate a belief system underscored by the fear that 'we're all going to die'. I've said that once you implant the orthodoxy of 'everyone knows that' the rest follows largely unaided. Older people are more sceptical of the climate claims because they've not had a lifetime of climate propaganda in the schools and universities. The young have and it's clear why many children and young people believe the lie pedalled through all Cult institutions of government, 'education', and crucially the media. Unless people seek out information beyond the Mainstream Everything they live in a one-track world. Without alternative sources of information the population is only being told what the Cult wants them to think. Pictures of distressed polar bears have been explained as the consequences of 'global warming' when the cause of their distress and emaciated state were later revealed to have had other origins unrelated to climate. Show a bear in trouble and say it is climate change and most people believe that to be true when it fits the narrative they have already been suckered to believe in. I read an excellent book by American meteorologist and weather forecaster, Joe Bastardi, a vehement and outspoken exposer of the climate lie. He describes in *The Climate Chronicles* how he has studied weather patterns going way back to show that weather now being blamed on human-caused climate change has happened in a recurring sequence long before the industrial era. The difference is that before the climate hysteria the same weather was just weather. Today it's always caused by global warming (which became 'climate change' when temperatures stopped rising and then the 'climate crisis' as the scare was ramped up). It's so easy to be scammed if people don't check the facts. We have a hurricane – it's global warming!; tornado – it's global warming!; drought – it's global warming!. It's hot – it's global warming! It's cold – it's global warming! Bastardi calls them Climate ambulance chasers. He says: 'What happened before naturally is happening again, as is to be expected given the cyclical nature of the climate due to the design of the planet.' Bastardi presents many examples of these cycles now blamed on human activity and this is one relating to droughts in the United States:

> … Major US dry periods are a product of a cooling tropical Pacific. In the decades such as the 1950s through the 1970s, when the tropical Pacific is cooler overall, the US is drier than normal in much of the nation.

> It is exactly the opposite in the years the Pacific warms, which, by the way correlates nicely to an increase in global temperatures until the atmosphere adjusts to the warming tropical ocean and temperatures level off. But the idea that global warming causes droughts here in the US is the opposite of the facts! It's when the Pacific starts to cool and global temperatures start to drop that we see it dry out.

Bastardi's book is highly recommended as is *The Politically Incorrect Guide to Climate Change* by Republican insider Marc Morano who charts the blatant political manipulation behind the climate hoax. A good website for hoax-challenging information is the Global Warming Policy Foundation at thegwpf.com. We should not forget that all the projections upon projections about climate Armageddon don't come from observing the climate. They result from putting data and assumptions into computer models and believing what they tell you is going to happen. The fact that they have been wrong by shocking margins so many times might have given them a clue by now that this doesn't work due to a simple cause and effect: If you factor in shit the computer will process that shit to produce 'predictions' that are nothing more than a feedback loop of shit-in and shit-out. Assume something with your input and you'll get the answer you want, but rarely the truth. There are so many variables and influences that affect climate that long-term predictions are a mug's game anyway. Follow the cycles that have happened before if you want to predict the climate. There's another angle to this that we should be constantly vigilant about. Technology to manipulate weather is now highly-advanced and there would not be international treaties agreeing not to manipulate weather if it was not technologically possible to do that. See *Everything You Need To Know* for detailed background about how extremes of weather can be made to happen and we can expect the Cult to continue to strike in this way around the world to convince people climate disaster is at hand.

The gas of life

The Cult takes facts and inverts them to become the very opposite of the truth before selling the inversion as 'conventional wisdom'. This way the public *perception* of reality becomes the opposite of actual reality. We are told we face 'catastrophe' when if what the Climate Cult demands are followed through we will have a real, not imagined, human catastrophe in economics, food production and energy supplies (this was written before the 'virus' lockdowns which have had the same effect). Global society would be devastated by plans to be 'carbon neutral' by 2025 to 2030 or 2050. There can, however, be no better or more blatant example of inversion than carbon dioxide (CO2) itself. This is the gas of life without which we really would all be dead

Figure 269: Carbon dioxide is the gas of life and the natural world's version of oxygen. I know – let's demonise the gas of life and transform society into the global centralised tyranny to make sure we have less of it.

and yet CO2 has been thoroughly demonised (Fig 269). If it was human it could sue for libel. You'll find interviews at Davidicke.com with professors at Princeton University emphasising both the central role played by carbon dioxide in human life and that far from having too much in the atmosphere *we don't have enough*. This will be amazing to people who have bought the carbon-is-a-pollutant narrative and it reveals the scale of inversion that we are dealing with. William Happer, Professor of Physics at Princeton University and long-time government advisor on climate, is one scientist who says the planet has a CO2 deficiency and needs more for optimal plant growth and food production. Such views have made him a big hate figure for the Climate Cult as the truth always does. He says that most of the warming in the last 100 years happened as we emerged from the Little Ice Age and was over by 1940. Happer points out that in a peak year for warming in 1988 there was a 'monster El Nino' which is a natural and cyclical warming of the Pacific that affects global weather patterns and temperature and has nothing to do with 'climate change'. He says the nature of the CO2 effect can be likened to painting a wall with red paint. Once two or three coats have been applied it doesn't matter how much more paint you add the wall will not get much redder. He explains that almost all the effect of the rise in CO2 has already occurred and the amount in the atmosphere would now have to *double* for even a single degree increase in temperature:

> I know a lot about CO2 compared with most climate scientists ... there's an interesting thing about CO2 which is unique to CO2 – it's not true, for example, of water vapour, methane. [This] is that if you get one degree of warming from doubling CO2, so going from say 400 parts per million for simplicity to 800 ... then to get another degree of warming you have to double 800, you have to go to 1,600. So it gets harder and harder to warm. Technically they call that the logarithmic dependence of temperature rise on CO2 concentration.

Happer said that this fact was realised early in the climate hysteria and to overcome such a demolition of the orthodoxy we had advocates of the hoax inventing theories about 'feedback loops' amplifying the CO2 effect. These are the doom-laden predictions that you constantly hear parroted by climate activists including Greta Thunberg. Happer said he laughs when he hears about 'carbon pollution' given that people, plants and animals are made of carbon and without it there would be no life. He said that an increase in CO2 in the atmosphere would make plants more drought resistant because when plants open holes in their leaves to absorb CO2 they leak water and the holes have to be open for longer to take in enough carbon dioxide amid what he calls a 'CO2 famine'. Happer emphasised that CO2 increases since industrialisation have had a 'huge effect' on plants and increased their growth: 'When people talk about the social cost of carbon it's absurd. The social cost is negative of CO2.' He said climate computer models don't look at the world as it is, but at *other computer models*. How much funding would the modellers get, by the way, if their predictions did not support the Climate Cult hypothesis? Imperial College in London which has produced many of the ridiculous 'climate change' models was also responsible for the computer models warning of insane numbers of 'Covid-19' deaths in the UK, United States and other countries which led to the lockdowns that have destroyed the lives of billions. Needless to say the insane 'projections' did not materialise, but provided the excuse for global house arrest.

Too much CO2? *We don't have enough*

The central importance of CO2 was a theme developed by Greenpeace co-founder Patrick Moore in a presentation to the Global Warming Policy Foundation. Scientist Moore left Greenpeace in 1986 and has criticised the green movement for scare tactics and disinformation with particular emphasis on climate change. He makes the point that other scientists have made about how dangerous it is to have low levels of CO2. Plants start to die at 150 parts per million and Moore says that even when CO2 fell to 180 ppm 18,000 years ago plants began to starve. This only turned around when the *temperature went up* for reasons I will shortly explain. Calling for a reduction in carbon dioxide is the plant equivalent of humans demanding a reduction in oxygen – CO2 is, in effect, plant oxygen. Today Moore says CO2 stands at around 400 ppm and plant life is still 'relatively starved of nutrition' with the optimum levels for plant growth *five times* higher at *2,000* ppm and in some periods of the Earth's history the ratio has reached 4,000 ppm. These facts explain why since CO2 levels began to rise with industrialisation the Earth is getting *greener* as CO2 has risen from 280 ppm in an 1880 measurement in Hawaii to 413 ppm in 2019. The Climate Cult that claims to be 'saving the planet' wants to *reverse* that process! Why do they think people pump extra carbon dioxide into greenhouses?? The Climate Cult contends amid its mass-hysteria that we face extinction when the gas of life is at way below optimum planet-growth levels and 500 million years ago there was *17 times* more CO2 in the atmosphere than we have today. Patrick Moore said levels have been falling for hundreds of millions of years as it was absorbed from the atmosphere and locked away by many and various sources. Over the last 150 million years CO2 levels in Earth's atmosphere had reduced by *90 percent*. By the time humans began releasing carbon dioxide through fossil fuels Moore said we were at '38 seconds to midnight' in terms of threats to plant life (thus *all* life) through plummeting levels of CO2. Not only aren't humans causing extinction they are *preventing* it. 'Release of CO2 has turned around the constant fall', Moore said, and in this sense 'Humans are [the Earth's] salvation'. Moore also noted that only half the CO2 emitted by fossil fuels ends up in the atmosphere. You read these facts about the fundamental importance of CO2 and then hear as I did an interview with 'carbon footprint expert' Mike Berners-Lee, a professor at the Institute for Social Futures at the UK's Lancaster University, and brother of Tim Berners-Lee who is credited with inventing the World Wide Web. The interview was on the London-based TalkRadio in which Mike Berners-Lee told an unchallenging host how *emails* add to carbon emissions and that 'a low-carbon world is better than a high-carbon world'. Breathes deeply, shakes head, moves on. Some other information in Patrick Moore's speech that the Climate Cult should know: The Earth has been in a major cooling period since the maximum of 50 million years ago when it was as much as *16 degrees* warmer. Today's poles were ice free and covered in forests. The ancestors of today's species came through that temperature period fine, but a *two percent* rise is now supposed to threaten mass extinction! Even in our current interglacial period we are experiencing one of the coldest climates in the Earth's history. The Medieval Warm Period (long before fossil fuels) was still cooler than temperatures in the last 10,000 years, Moore said.

Temperature doesn't follow CO2 – it's the other way round

Oh, Climate Cultists may say, higher CO2 might be better for plants, but it will cause the Earth to heat catastrophically. I mean, Greta Thunberg says we should believe that our house is on fire and she wouldn't mislead us, right? Well, if she has been mercilessly mislead herself I think she probably would. In fact, temperature rises don't follow increases in CO2 – *it's the other way round* as the records clearly show. In the last 400,000 years CO2 has lagged temperature by an average of 800 years. As Patrick Moore rightly says carbon dioxide cannot be the cause of rising temperature when the increase in temperature comes *before* the increase in CO2. How can the effect come *before* the cause? It can't. So here's a shocker for New Wokers … *temperature must be affecting CO2* levels and not vice-versa. Here we have yet another classic Cult inversion of the truth. How could temperature increase CO2? The ocean contains 45 times more CO2 than we have in the atmosphere and the ocean *releases* carbon dioxide in *warm periods* and *absorbs it* in colder periods. The lag between the two is around 800 years and look what was happening 800 years ago …. the *Medieval Warm Period*. Carbon dioxide does not cause the Earth to catastrophically warm. The history of CO2 correlation with temperature shows that for immense periods the two have been completely out of kilter. Temperatures have risen and remained high as CO2 went down. Carbon dioxide is also only 0.117 percent of what are called greenhouse gases while more than *90 percent* of those gases are water vapour and clouds (Fig 270). Only a fraction of that 0.117 percent is CO2 caused by human activity and the rest happens naturally. Professional conman Al Gore tried to obscure this fact by saying that if you 'take water vapour out of the equation CO2 is 30 percent of greenhouse gases'. Don't buy a

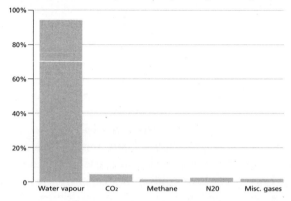

Figure 270: CO2 is a tiny fraction of greenhouse gases which are almost entirely water vapour and clouds. What's more the great majority of that CO2 is naturally-occurring and nothing to do with humans.

used car from that man or even a new one. How can you 'take water vapour out of the equation' when that together with clouds makes up close to the entirety of greenhouse gases? To deceive – that's how. Calculated demonisation of CO2 is so transparent. Professor Leslie Woodcock, Emeritus Professor at the University of Manchester, fellow of the Royal Society of Chemical Engineering, a recipient of a Max Plank Society Visiting Fellowship, and former NASA researcher, said:

Water is a much more powerful greenhouse gas, and there is 20 times more of it in our atmosphere, around one percent of the atmosphere, whereas CO2 is only 0.04 percent. Carbon dioxide has been made out to be some kind of toxic gas, but the truth is that it's the gas of life. We breathe it out, plants breathe it in and it's not caused by us. Global warming is nonsense.

British scientist James Lovelock was a one-time Green icon with his Gaia theory of the Earth as a living entity (true). He became even more acclaimed by climate alarmists when he predicted in his book *The Revenge of Gaia* that 'billions will die' and humanity was doomed. Lovelock wrote that any survivors would have to live in the Arctic which would be one of the few habitable places on Earth. Then reality dawned and to his enormous credit he had the courage to publicly change his mind. Humanity was not in imminent peril after all. Lovelock now says that climate alarmism is not 'remotely scientific', computer models are unreliable and anyone who tries to 'predict more than five to ten years is a bit of an idiot'. A single volcano can make more difference to global warming than humans ever could, he has stated. He accuses the Greens of exaggeration and behaving 'deplorably'. Weather Channel founder John Coleman has said human-caused global warming is a myth and the list of scientists saying the same is getting longer by the week. Such honesty often comes at a cost, however, in the form of lost jobs and income. Dr Judith Curry, a respected climatologist and tenured professor at Georgia Tech University, left her 'dream job' when she refused to pledge unquestioning obedience to the Climate Cult. She told Fox News:

> I've been vilified by some of my colleagues who are activists and don't like anybody challenging their big story ... I walk around with knives sticking out of my back ... In the university environment I felt like I was just beating my head against the wall.

Curry is a target of an establishment-promoted 'climate advocacy group' called Skeptical Science which operates a 'blacklist' of scientists who won't comply with Climate Cult orthodoxy. Dana Nuccitelli, one of the principals of Skeptical Science, wrote of Curry: 'If you look at the statements we cataloged and debunked ... it should make her unhirable in academia.' Judith Curry is a former chair of the School of Earth and Atmospheric Sciences at Georgia Tech and a Fellow of both the American Geophysical Union and American Meteorological Society. She was only 'unhirable' because the Climate Cult made it so. Curry was asked to step down by her university for her views on climate and had 'numerous inquiries from academic headhunters encouraging me to apply for major administration positions, ranging from Dean to Vice Chancellor for Research'. She didn't even make the shortlist. Curry said in a *Forbes* interview:

> They thought I was an outstanding candidate, looked excellent on paper, articulated a strong vision, and interviewed very well in person. The show stopper was my public profile in the climate debate, as evidenced by a simple Google search.

Google is so helpful in ensuring that Skeptical Science is on the first page and sometimes the top listing for a word search for Judith or Judy Curry. This is the tyranny that genuine academics and scientists are facing from the Climate Cult in all its forms. Who created Skeptical Science? *John Cook*, the Australian bloke most quoted about '97 percent of climate scientists' agreeing that humans are most responsible for climate change when his 'research' doesn't say that at all. Small world, eh? Those that don't accept climate change orthodoxy are labelled 'anti-science' when questioning every hypothesis is what real science is all about. It's the Climate Cult that is anti-science (another inversion). French television weatherman Philippe Verdier was fired by the France 2 channel for publishing a book accusing 'climate experts' of misleading the public and the Cult-controlled UN Intergovernmental Panel on Climate Change of publishing deliberately misleading data (Fig 271). What he said is true and he was sacked *because* it is true. Programmed New Woke trade union members at the station

French TV weatherman sacked for book questioning 'hype' over climate change

By Tim Hume, CNN
Updated 1428 GMT (2228 HKT) November 3, 2015

Top stories
How South Africa became the new home of house music
Miss Iraq pageant held for first time in 43 years

Weatherman Philippe Verdier was sacked from his job at France 2 for his book questioning "hype" over climate change.

Figure 271: Refuse to sing from the song-sheet and you're gone.

demanded he was dismissed. Verdier wrote his book after French Foreign Minister Laurent Fabius asked TV meteorologists to highlight climate change issues in their broadcasts. 'I was horrified by this speech,' Verdier said.

Cult narrative: humanity is the enemy

Greenpeace co-founder Patrick Moore is a scientist who says the Greens have abandoned science and replaced it with emotion and sensationalism based on an 'anti-human' agenda that paints humanity as the enemy of the Earth. If you are a Death Cult targeting humanity would you not want them to believe that they were the problem? Wouldn't you want them to despise themselves and turn against themselves? You surely would. We breathe out carbon dioxide and even the act of breathing is harming the planet – *ahhhhh!!!* Humans are deadly. We must kill them. A vegan father-of-four voiced this anti-human mentality when he called a UK radio station to say humans shouldn't breed to produce more offspring to 'harm animals'. He urged people to encourage a 'graceful ending of our time on the planet'. The caller, who gave the name 'Danny', said he had recently discovered 'anti-natalism' – 'the idea that we shouldn't be breeding humans when it causes so much unnecessary suffering to animals, especially people who bring up children to eat meat'. Should we then not allow animals to breed when they cause so much harm to each other in the killing fields that are the 'natural world'? 'Danny' said there was nothing wrong with human extinction and admitted that he tells his nine-year-old son and older daughters to question their own reproduction and whether they should be here in the first place. 'I don't want grandchildren, and I don't want them to impose life on another generation for no good reason.' He's not psychologically damaged or anything and this is not in any way psychological abuse of his children. These views may seem seriously extreme, but the guy is far from alone and they are just the attitudes you want to engender when you are a Death Cult led by unseen 'gods' that wish to replace humanity as we know it today (more later). It would be easy to dismiss an anonymous caller to a radio station

Figure 272: An academic promoting the end of humanity. She is teaching young people, right? Wow. Her extreme of extreme views are fine with Woke. It's when you say men and women are biological different that you trigger their ire.

if what he said was not being promoted by academics such as Patricia MacCormack, a professor of continental philosophy at Anglia Ruskin University in Cambridge. She argues in her book, *The Ahuman Manifesto*, that 'the only solution for climate change is letting the human race become extinct' (Fig 272). This was the headline in an interview with MacCormack in which she set out a 'positive view' for the future of Earth without humans. She said she came to these conclusions through her interest in feminism and 'queer theory' and railed against 'this hierarchal world where white, male, heterosexual and able-bodied people are succeeding, and people of different races, genders, sexualities and those with disabilities are struggling to get that'. Well, best get rid of everyone then.

MacCormack further argues that we need to dismantle religion while clearly not realising that she is a member of one. She said that humans are already enslaved to the point of 'zombiedom' (oh, the irony) by 'capitalism' and because of the damage this has caused 'phasing out reproduction is the only way to repair the damage done to the world'. This is straight from the Cult agenda for a mass human cull as will become clear and she will be utterly oblivious to that. The realisation that such mentalities are teaching young people is very sobering while at the same time explains so much about where New Woke is coming from.

To summarise what Patrick Moore has said, and what I have observed for decades, the Green movement that he and I remember has been hijacked by New Woke and real environmental issues are being marginalised and sacrificed on the altar of global warming. We have the obsession with 'climate change' while genuine pollution increases, including radiation pollution, and US Green New Deal promotor Alexandria Ocasio-Cortez represents a district awash with trash in the streets. I am so glad I was briefly a national spokesman for the Green Party in the 1980s. It has given me such an insight into the mentality that drives the tyranny of the New Woke Climate Cult today. Moore brings sanity to the debate when he says that carbon dioxide is a building block for all life on earth and without its presence in the global atmosphere in sufficient concentrations this would be a dead planet. He says that all life is carbon-based including our own and he describes carbon dioxide as 'the currency of life' and the most important building block for terrestrial life. 'Yet today our children and our publics are taught that CO2 is a toxic pollutant that will destroy life and bring civilisation to its knees.' Once again if you were a Death Cult with humanity in its gunsights wouldn't you want them to believe that what keeps them alive threatens their existence? Wouldn't you want them to dismantle what gives them life? What a testament to the programming of human perception that so many believe this absurdity to their core.

Climate Cult veganism - not so simple

We have a perfect system in which humans breathe in oxygen and breathe out carbon dioxide (how dare we?) while plant life and trees absorb carbon dioxide and produce oxygen during the day by converting sunlight, carbon dioxide and water into carbohydrates and oxygen in a process called photosynthesis. The Sun, like carbon dioxide, is obviously essential to life on Earth and notice that both are being targeted. We are encouraged to fear the Sun through the climate hoax on the grounds that it generates heat (while not presenting the Sun as a source of global temperature!) and we are urged to cover our skin with cancer-causing chemicals in sun lotion when the skin turns sunlight into the essential vitamin D so vital to human health. This process of synthesising sunlight into vitamin D is achieved through *cholesterol* in the skin cells – the same cholesterol that is also *vilified* as we are urged to 'lower your cholesterol' and take ongoing, health-destroying statin drugs to do so (ka-ching say the Big Pharma tills). We are told by officialdom that LDL cholesterol, or low-density lipoproteins, is 'bad cholesterol' and can cause heart disease. To save ourselves we should take statins. A global team of 17 doctors published a study of nearly 1.3 million people in 2018 that concluded there is no link between high LDL cholesterol and heart disease and that statins were, with serious understatement, of 'doubtful benefit'. The study, published in the *Expert Review of Clinical Pharmacology*, exposed the demonisation of cholesterol and reported that heart attack patients were shown to have *lower* than normal levels of LDL or 'bad cholesterol'. Professor Sherif Sultan, one of the authors, said the 'strongest finding' was elderly people with high levels of LDL live the longest. The big rule of thumb to remember: If 'The System' is pushing something it's bad for humanity. If it is targeting something it's good for humanity. It works every time. The highest concentration of cholesterol is in the brain – 20 percent of the body total. The brain is 60 percent fats and without cholesterol it cannot function effectively. This explanation comes from Psychologytoday.com:

> Synapses – the magical areas where communication between brain cells takes place – are lined by cholesterol-rich membranes responsible for passing neurotransmitters like serotonin, GABA, and dopamine back and forth. Myelin, the white matter that insulates brain circuits, is made from tightly-wound membranes containing 75% of the brain's cholesterol.

> Cholesterol also helps guide developing nerve endings to their destinations on 'lipid rafts'. If the brain is too low in cholesterol, its membranes, synapses, myelin and lipid rafts can't form or function properly, bringing all brain activity – including mood regulation, learning, and memory – to a screeching halt.

We are witnessing soaring numbers of people with forms of dementia. Is this a coincidence? No, it's not. There are other reasons for this, too, but if you significantly lower or eliminate cholesterol and fat consumption this is what happens. Check the facts for yourself. Every vegan and vegetarian should read for their own sake the book by David Evans called *Low Cholesterol Leads to an Early Death: Evidence from 101 Scientific Papers*. There are also the books of Barry Groves including *Trick and Treat: How healthy eating is making us ill*. I am not saying vegans and vegetarians should change their lifestyle – that's none of my business. I am saying check the facts first and you won't get them only by reading mainstream sources. Is it still another 'by chance' that the Climate Cult (a stooge of the Death Cult) is demanding a major decrease (ideally the elimination) of meat consumption with its mega sources of cholesterol and fats? The theme is being promoted by pathetically-named documentaries such as *Apocalypse Cow: How Meat Killed The Planet* fronted by *Guardian* 'journalist' virtue-signaller and fast-asleep New Woker 'vegan' George Monbiot who bizarrely shot a deer on the programme and ate it as a burger. Go figure. I understand why vegetarians and vegans choose not to eat animal products and I absolutely respect the intent. I was a vegetarian myself for some 15 years. It is not, however, that simple. Firstly vegans and vegetarians might consider that *all* life is conscious including the plants they eat themselves. I have written a number of times over the years about research revealing how plants and trees feel pain and stress which can even be generated by the tone of voice and someone's intent towards them. When people 'talk' to plants it generates a wave interaction with the frequency field of the voice and this is picked up by the plant. They may not understand human words, but they pick up the 'vibe'. A team of scientists at Tel Aviv University published a study in 2019 revealing that tomato and tobacco plants emitted multiple ultrasonic 'stress' sounds between 20 and 100 kilohertz when deprived of water or their stems were cut. Plants with no environmental threat or damage emitted less than one ultrasonic sound per hour. Many other experiments have confirmed the theme – plant life is conscious and feels forms of emotional pain and stress when threatened. What does a tree feel when it is cut down? What do other trees feel when it is well established that trees operate in 'families' and communicate?

There is no consumption of food in higher frequencies and these moral dilemmas do not arise. Within the simulation there is such density and a comparative deficit of energy that the difference is made up by consuming 'physical' food which is really wavefields. I wish that didn't have to be, but the point to remember is that *everything* is conscious. We are told that meat eating must end to protect animals when animals eat each other second by second. It is the way the simulation is set up to be a killing field. Animals eat each other to secure the sustenance they need to survive and biologically humans have the same basic make-up and nutritional requirements. We may wish it was different, okay, agreed. But for now that's how it is. Animals that provide the basis for human food will, of course, disappear altogether as a consequence of what is being demanded by a few imposing their lifestyle choice on everyone else. The meat industry is going to be subjected to full-blown demonisation and financial attacks to secure the desired Cult outcome by claiming it is 'not sustainable' – I'll explain the real significance of 'sustainable' in the next chapter. Vegans should make their choices as they see fit and have those choices respected. I just wish the same respect came the other way and self-righteous vegan activists didn't act like another cult with its deep connections to the Climate Cult which is largely the unknowing puppet of the Death Cult. By all means campaign for animals to be treated humanely – I'm with you – but please open your eyes to what you are being used to bring about. I am not telling people what they should eat. I am saying look at the pattern and how the climate hoax and other excuses are being used to target carbon dioxide, sunlight and cholesterol which, without sufficient quantities, there would truly be extinction. I find the same perceptual arrogance at the *extreme* end (not everyone) of those who contend that the Earth is flat. If people want to believe that then good luck to them I say. Unfortunately the same respect often doesn't come the other way. If you don't accept what they claim you are subject to attacks and dubbed an agent of the elite – even those who have spent their lives exposing the elite and who do more to that end in a month than 'flat Earth' extreme obsessives will do in a lifetime. The Earth *is* 'flat' in a sense at the level of its wavefield construct or 'interference pattern'. Its holographic decoded projection called the 'physical' Earth is quite something else. Those who see this differently have every right to do so and I won't call them agents of the elite just because they believe something that I don't. Why do so many people insist that what they believe must be accepted by everybody? This book is my view and research. I don't insist for a second that people have to believe it if it doesn't make sense to them.

The Cult is exploiting the climate change hoax to pressure people to be vegan and that should start alarm bells ringing. I can tell you after tracking these people for 30 years that they do *nothing* without intent to harm humanity and if they want the population to be vegan it's for a reason that benefits the agenda. Some schools are imposing vegan food and banning meat including one in Sweden where preschool teacher Markus Sandström said: 'The more we thought about it, the better it seemed ... sustainable development is [our] starting point and the meat has a great impact on climate.' Sandström doesn't know what he's talking about. He's just repeating what he has been programmed to believe so he will pass on that programming to children and enforce it in this case. This is what teachers are there to do from the Cult's point of view. Vegetarian and vegan diets imposed by schools is a gathering trend with a school in Oxford, England, banning children from bringing their own packed lunches if they are not meat and fish free. We see yet again how the New Woke and climate tyranny works. It is not about winning arguments with freely-debated facts; it's about imposition. Head teacher Kay Wood said that the move allowed them to serve better quality meals for the same price. Okay, so explain how that scans with banning packed lunches brought from home. How would price be significant when the school is not paying? Who says they are better quality meals when many nutritionists have the opinion that meat and fish are essential to a balanced intake of what the body and brain needs? Who is Ms Wood to make those decisions about what children can eat and its effect on their well-being? A second reason she cited was the yawn, yawn, 'huge environmental and sustainability benefits' as she once again repeated the Cult script while not knowing there even is a Cult. Reason number three was that banning meat 'allows students of all faiths and different dietary requirements to eat together'. She wouldn't be able to see the deeper consequences of this which is imposing one set of beliefs on everyone. Why wouldn't you justify that to yourself when *I am right*. One parent at the school said banning meat and fish had made her children and other pupils hungry, but none of this matters – *I am right*. A UK property company Igloo Regeneration has decreed that all corporate entertaining and catering must be vegetarian and meals including meat cannot be reimbursed on expenses after they bought the same lie as the schools. They certainly won't be the last and watch this theme expand because it's a Cult agenda. There is pressure to introduce meat taxes and we even have people taking neighbours to court for the smell of their barbeques. *I am right* has spoken and you will comply! Why should you have choice when *you are wrong*? There are many lovely vegans who understand this defence of basic freedom. I'm sure others will be cocking their abuse ready to fire. If you want self-righteous abuse by the truckload tell an extreme vegan activist that the world is not as black and white as they think it is. You will see as we go along what the endless references of 'sustainability' really mean although these teachers won't have a clue what that is. They are just repeaters like the entire system in all its forms – repeating the Totalitarian Tiptoe agenda of the Cult like a broken record while thinking it's true. Where the delete-meat Cult agenda is really going, via veganism, is to laboratory-produced synthetic food for reasons I will be explaining.

So the gas of life is being demonised to provide the foundation of the religious orthodoxy promoted by the Climate Cult and all its associated offshoots like changing what people eat. The next question is why the global Death Cult would go to such lengths to convince us that humans are threatening the planet's very existence of the world we have come to know. The answer is both clear – and devastating.

CHAPTER NINE

Why is 'climate change' being hoaxed?

Evil people rely on the acquiescence of naive good people to allow them to continue with their evil – Stuart Aken

The answer to the question posed in the chapter heading is once again very simple and armed with this knowledge everything else falls into place. We are looking at a global example of No-Problem-Reaction-Solution. The Cult was only able to invade Iraq in 2003 by lying about 'weapons of mass destruction' which they knew didn't exist. Without the lie they had no excuse to do what had long been planned. The climate hoax is another no-problem that gives the Cult the pretext for almost every aspect of the Hunger Games Society and the agenda for extreme Orwellian control. The NO-P-R-S goals of the Climate Cult and the 'pandemic' lockdowns are indivisible.

All the strands come together in the end because everything is connected. I have laid out the Hunger Games structure of a world government controlling other global institutions and dictating to every community through superstates like the European Union and regional entities underneath overseeing an utterly dependent human population. This won't just happen – it has to be *made* to happen and for that you need reasons/excuses to do what you want like a 'climate crisis' and a global pandemic. If those excuses are not naturally-occurring you need to make them up. You lie in other words and ... the BIGGER the lie the more will believe it. The problem must relate to the solution and when you want a global solution in the form of world government etc. you need global problems for which your solution can be applied. A planet-wide hoax about human-caused climate change and a 'pandemic' fit that bill perfectly. The scammers can claim that the only way to 'save the world and humanity' is to centralise global power in a world government and institutions to stop any 'bad people' from taking actions that threaten human existence by producing the gas of life or infecting others with a 'virus' (which doesn't exist as we will see). How can they stop the 'bad people'? Well, a world army would come in handy don't you think? Do people really believe that the climate change hoax and pandemic hoax are random happenings when they both demand centralisation of power and draconian imposition by the state which have been the aim of the Cult all along? Watch eventually for demands that an external military force be used to impose climate change measures on countries that don't play ball. Hey, I have another idea. The threat of extinction is so 'existential' that we need a police/military state to keep people in line to protect everyone else and we must take control of the upbringing of children to 'educate' (indoctrinate) them into being good citizens obedient to their masters who know how to save the planet. We certainly don't need parents getting in the way. So many things that humans do, including breathing, are dangerous. The police/military surveillance state must watch every World Citizen's every move and every citizen must watch every other citizen and report on them immediately about anything the surveillance state may have missed (nothing in the end). Dystopia is vital – our very existence depends upon it. Those good people who obey will be rewarded and those who still have a mind of their own will be tracked, recorded, punished or eliminated (see China).

The only way to save the world and humanity from imminent extinction is for everything to be controlled. This includes your energy use, what you eat, where you go, how you go, if you go, and what you say and think. Travel must be restricted to electric autonomous vehicles controlled and tracked by computers that decide where you can go and when (or if). Flying must be eliminated (except for the elite) to save us all. With so little travel possible in the interests of preventing extinction it would be more efficient and better for the Earth if people were organised in sectors like in those *Hunger Games* movies with only the elite and their police/military operatives able to pass between them without securing permission. Work must be taken over by far more efficient and less carbon-producing (they claim) artificial intelligence leaving the population in general unable to earn a living (see also 'pandemic'). The state is kind, however, and they will be paid a meagre 'guaranteed income' in return for slavery and total obedience. Don't believe for a second that you will be able to rebel. We will know what you plan before you do through mind-reading technology tracking your brain activity. Humans are very *dangerous* and they must be vastly reduced in number. Billions must be removed for the good of the rest and we must introduce a maximum length of life in the interests of the young. Birth rates must be controlled and dictated by the world state with forced abortion for women who are pregnant without the right paperwork. In the end there will be no parental procreation or parenthood as I will come to in a later chapter. If you think this is extreme to the point of fantasy you should read my other books and see in detail the evidence and documentation for all that I have described here. Observe what is demanded by the New Woke Climate Cult in the form of Extinction Rebellion and the Green New Deal of American of congresswoman Alexandria Ocasio-Cortez supported by private-jet flying Democratic presidential candidate Bernie Sanders with its price tag of $16 *trillion*. We also have the EU version of the Ocasio-Cortez plan in the 'European Green Deal'. Something similar would be supported by Joe Biden who clearly has serious cognitive problems and the most obvious signs of some form of dementia. Even so when Sanders pulled out of the race in April, 2020, Biden was given a free run to be the Democratic candidate barring some unforeseen circumstances like people realising in large enough numbers that Biden is unfit to run. The corrupt Wall Street-owned Biden would be an empty vessel for his handlers to dictate policy although his blatantly failing mental capacities would give Israel-owned Trump an excellent chance of a second term unless the effects of 'virus' lockdown can shield Biden from that exposure to enough of the voting population. The hate-Trump mentality would also vote for a traffic light rather than him. The Cult often likes second-term presidencies when the presidential puppet does not have to temper his policies to win another election and in Trump's case that could mean policy on Iran which Israel (Sabbatian-Frankists) want to destroy. Trump is utterly controlled by Israel and its masters with ultra-Zionist Stephen Miller, his senior advisor for policy, right up there as the most influential of his handlers. A truly New Woke president will be in the plan at some point, however, as New Wokers become ever more significant at the polling booth and Trump (74 as I write), Biden (77) and the failed Sanders (78) have the look of the last of the line before a new and seriously Woke political generation are planned to take over.

If the 'carbon-neutral' demands of these suicide notes are implemented industrial society as we've known it will be over, finished, kaput, through curtailed energy production and CO2 bans alone. Billions of jobs would be lost and the Hunger Games Society would be installed (words written before the 'pandemic' which rushed forward exactly the same agenda). It is madness and unfortunately there is nothing more blind to its fate than madness. I don't use the term as some kind of metaphor for stupidity. I really do mean madness, as in lunacy (Fig 273). Despite

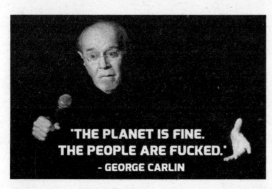

Figure 273: Well said, George.

these consequences most politicians are falling over themselves to comply at some level with carbon neutral demands whether that be by 2025, 2030 or, at most, 2050. Simon Bramwell, co-founder of Extinction Rebellion, was filmed calling on New Woke to 'bring down civilisation'. He wanted to see humanity return to a 'wild' and 'feral' state: '… it is part of our duty in my opinion that we've also got to not only take down civilisation but shepherd ourselves and incoming generations back into a state of wilding as it were, into like a feral consciousness that is also one of the biggest tasks remaining to us.' A definition of 'feral' is: 'Characteristic of wild animals; ferocious; brutal.' Bramwell said modern eco-activism was finding it impossible to convince people to go 'without food' or 'see their child die because we don't simply have the machinery and technology to keep them alive any longer' – 'So we have to offer them something else along as [sic] these trajectories of civil disobedience and direct sabotage of civilisation.' Gail Bradbrook, a former partner of Bramwell and a co-founder of Extinction Rebellion, is a career activist with numerous connections to NGOs, major corporations, banks and very rich people.

Environmental catastrophe – thanks to 'Greens'

CO2 obsession, like all obsessions, ignores the consequences. Take the Climate Cult's support for vehicles run by electricity (still largely produced from fossil fuel) and their lithium batteries which have created human and environmental devastation in the Democratic Republic of Congo where New Woke Apple, Google, Tesla, Microsoft and Dell have been accused of exploiting child labour by families who say their children were killed or severely injured mining cobalt used in lithium batteries and coltan used in cell phones and other electronics. Tens of thousands of children are involved in the cobalt and coltan trade – some as young as four – and all spend their days breathing toxic fumes. An Amnesty International report said most cobalt miners in the Congo lacked basic protective equipment like face masks, work clothing and gloves while many employed on pittance 'wages' complained of frequent coughing or lung problems. An article in *Forbes* magazine described the plight of a child named Lukasa who starts a 12-hour day at 5am for pay of less than $9. He hacks at ore by hand and carries it on his back in an hour trek to a trading post where he sells it to Chinese traders who make massive profits literally off his back. Lukasa then walks another two hours to his home. The Democratic Republic of Congo has been ravaged by war that has killed millions. It is called a 'civil war' when in fact it is a war for control of 'smart' resources and has destroyed rainforests, the ancient life-style of indigenous people and threatened to make wildlife species extinct. Where are you Climate Cult?? Oh, yes, on the bloody phone demanding electric cars.

It is disgusting modern slavery and here's the kicker for the Climate Cult – making lithium batteries for electric cars and other technology is a major emitter of *carbon dioxide*. A report in *IndustryWeek* said: 'Just to build each car battery – weighing upwards of 500 kilograms (1,100 pounds) in size for sport-utility vehicles – would emit up to 74% more CO2 than producing an efficient conventional car if it's made in a factory powered by fossil fuels in a place like Germany ...' Now contemplate the pollution, child exploitation and CO2 consequences of every vehicle in the world eventually being electric and autonomous. I know that CO2 production is not dangerous, but the Climate Cult thinks it is and still supports mass mining of cobalt for electric vehicles to 'fight climate change'. Then there is the environmental problem of what happens when batteries are expired after less than ten years. Researchers including Professor Andrew Abbott at Leicester University have calculated that the one million electric cars sold in Britain in 2017 will produce 250,000 metric tons, or half a million cubic metres, of unprocessed battery pack waste. What will that be *globally* when all vehicles are electric?? How very green. Beautiful landscapes and seascapes are being destroyed by highly inefficient 'green' wind turbines that kill birds, disturb wildlife and destroy silence with their loud noise. The blades can be bigger than a jumbo jet wing and there are tens of thousands already past their working life with only landfills to deal with them. Some 8,000 will have to be disposed of in the next four years in the United States while 3,800 a year have to be dealt with in Europe according to Bloomberg. These figures reflect the number built a decade ago and there are far more now that will be coming up for disposal. Save the world by trashing it. Many millions of acres of *forest* have been cut down to locate the turbines and a Freedom of Information Act request revealed that in a small country like Scotland almost *14 million trees* across 17,283 acres have been felled for the turbines since the year 2000. These are trees that take CO2 out of the atmosphere and clearly the CO2 hysteria is a monumental hoax. Wind turbines also technologise the natural environment which technocrats would love.

How the Climate Cult was birthed by billionaires

New Wokeness and the Climate Cult have not emerged with such speed by random chance. They have been long in the making and in *Everything You Need To Know* I have laid it all out at length. In brief we can pick up the story in 1968 with the creation of the Club of Rome although it goes back much further. The Club of Rome is a cusp organisation in The Web which stands at the point where the hidden levels of the Cult meet the seen. Cusp entities like the Bilderberg Group, Council on Foreign Relations and Trilateral Commission have their own specific role and with the Club of Rome this has been from the start to exploit environmental concerns to justify the transformation of global society. The Club published a report in 1972 warning about environmental disaster by the year 2000 – an outcome supported by a computer model that Club of Rome co-founder Aurelio Peccei would later admit was encoded to produce the desired predictions. This would be the recurring technique for climate change propaganda using computer models. Italian industrialist Peccei said in the Club's 1991 publication, *The First Global Revolution*: 'In searching for a new enemy to unite us, we came up with the idea that pollution, the threat of global warming, water shortages, famine and the like would fit the bill.' The document emphasised that these things were caused by human intervention and so …. *here we go* … 'The real enemy, then, is humanity itself.' Bingo – the narrative and the target was set. The Club of Rome includes global political leaders (and former), government officials, diplomats, scientists, economists, business leaders and, very significantly, United Nations bureaucrats. The Cult-created UN is a stalking horse for world government through the Totalitarian Tiptoe and both the climate change hoax *and* the 'solution' to the hoax are being orchestrated through the United Nations as a No-Problem-Reaction-Solution. Richard Haass, president of the Cult-controlled Council on Foreign Relations, has said that world government is needed with national sovereignty reduced to 'fight' global warming: 'Moreover, states must be prepared to cede some sovereignty to world bodies if the international system is to function … states would be wise to weaken sovereignty in order to protect themselves …'

A major event in the emergence of the Climate Cult came with the 1992 Earth Summit in Rio de Janeiro, Brazil, which was hosted by Cult asset and Canadian oil multimillionaire Maurice Strong who fronted for the Rothschild and Rockefeller dynasties. Strong believed that the United Nations should become a world government. He was appointed a founding director of the UN Environment Programme (UNEP) and from the 1980s became the promotor of human-caused climate change or 'global warming' as it was then before temperatures stopped rising. Strong's UNEP was behind the creation of the UN's Intergovernmental Panel on Climate Change (IPCC) which has been the central body in the climate change hoax ever since. He also established the UN Framework Convention on Climate Change (UNFCCC). Through this body he hosted the Rio 'Earth Summit' attended by 108 world leaders and 20,000 'green activists'. Maurice Strong, remember, was a big-time Cult operative. The UN Framework Convention on Climate Change is the organising force for the series of conferences in Kyoto (1997), Copenhagen (2009). Paris (2015) and Glasgow (2020) pressing governments to impose laws to reduce emissions of the gas of life. Strong saw out his last years in China where he had been close to the

Communist Party leadership going back to Chairman Mao. He moved there after being exposed for being paid $1 million from the UN's Oil for Food programme which was supposed to be a mechanism to trade oil to feed starving people in Iraq. This is the same Maurice Strong who claimed to be a (multimillionaire) 'socialist' and became the darling of what would become New Woke. George Soros plays a similar and more expansive role today and New Wokers still can't see through it (Fig 274). Strong was appointed to a series of other influential positions to serve the Cult including Senior Advisor to the UN Secretary General, Senior Advisor to the World Bank, Chairman of the Earth Council, Chairman of the World Resources Institute, Under-Secretary-General of the United Nations and Co-Chairman of the Council of the World Economic Forum which would become a major promotor of Greta Thunberg. This is what happens to your career when you are a Cult asset.

Figure 274: Annual meeting of Naivety Anonymous.

An insider speaks

I have written over the years about the warnings of George Hunt, an accountant and investment consultant, who was an official host of the Fourth World Wilderness Conference in Colorado in 1987 attended by Maurice Strong along with Edmond de Rothschild, David Rockefeller and executives from the World Bank and International Monetary Fund (IMF) who were there because they cared so deeply about the environment and the poor. It was nothing to do with stealing land from the poor in the name of saving the world. Well, actually, it *was* – see my book *The Perception Deception*. Hunt's experience of these mega-criminals and others led him to realise that the so-called environmental movement was a Rothschild/Rockefeller global banker front driven by what I refer to as the Cult. He said the global population was described by a banker attendee as the 'canon fodder that populates the Earth'. Hunt made a video a month ahead of the June, 1992, Earth Summit in which he called out the game before it even became public. You can still find the video on the Internet. He pointed out that the logo of the summit was a hand holding the world with the slogan 'In Our Hands' which given the Cult's obsession with symbolism was a statement of intent in itself (Fig 275 overleaf). The official name was UNCED (United Nations

Figure 275: The World in our hand – perfect symbolism for what the game is.

Conference on Environment and Development) and was pronounced 'unsaid'. That's a ditto. Hunt described those behind the Earth Summit in these terms:

The same World Order [Cult] families that planned World War One and World War Two, that tricked the Third World countries to borrow funds and rack up the enormous debts, the same World Order that stole much of the money borrowed by Africans and other nations and hid it in Geneva banks. They are the persons who financed Hitler and purposely [create] war and debt to bring societies into their control. The World Order crowd are not a nice group of people.

Hunt said in 1992 that 'the world environment movement will soon be in the hands of the World Order' if its supporters did not act on what was happening. They didn't, of course, and they have been, as Hunt predicted, absolutely absorbed by the 'World Order' elite to become the New Woke Climate Cult with its teenage 'spiritual leader' Greta Thunberg. Hunt said:

I learned later that the World Order refers to the coming one-world government as the Fourth World. A world controlled by the World Order where there is no more First, Second and Third World … just a boundary-less planet which is called the Fourth World Wilderness. Yogis and shamans refer to it as the Fourth World Wilderness, the lostness of the mind. The lostness of the mind refers to the collective consciousness. Persons will be coerced through lies, drugs, fear and pain to surrender their selves, their egos, to the collective consciousness.

I stress here that while I speak of us being expressions of *The One* we are both the collective *and* the individual point of attention. We must not concede that sense of individuality and personal sovereignty to any group-think or collective mind which the Cult plans to be a technological hive-mind controlled by artificial intelligence. Hunt said the 'Fourth World' will be a return to a society much like the Caesars or Babylon or the Fourth Reich. He said this society was described in Aldous Huxley's *Brave New World* and *Brave New World Revisited* and George Orwell's *Nineteen Eighty-Four*. The new World Order sought to create a society out of the ashes of chaos, a collectivist Fourth World complete with collectivist religion, collectivist finance and unchecked world national socialism. Hunt said in 1992:

> The World Order will offer Gaia, Mother Earth, to the masses as the Big Brother image to worship in the Fourth World. Maurice Strong has already set up a 140,000 acre project in Creston, Colorado, to develop this Earth religion system. Projects are funded by the Rockefeller Fund among other foundations. The Earth Summit will link environment with industry, the Lords of the UNCED conference will be the masters of who gets what and when if we don't do something about it quickly.

I repeat: George Hunt was speaking in 1992. How sobering when you see what is happening today. Hunt described how Maurice Strong identified Edmond de Rothschild as the creator of the environment movement and perhaps Climate Cult supporters will now understand why billionaires like Soros, a Rothschild lackey, are falling over themselves in support. Greta Thunberg crossed the Atlantic on a yacht once named the Edmond de Rothschild sailed by an elite crew with connections to the Monaco royal family. How very 'of the street'.

UN double whammy

The United Nations is working a pincer movement on behalf of the Cult. On one side you have the UN Intergovernmental Panel on Climate Change (IPCC) which drives the hysteria by lying incessantly about human impact on the climate. On the other you have UN Agenda 21 and Agenda 2030 which seek to transform global society into a centralised Orwellian state to 'meet the challenge of climate change'. When you think that the United Nations was created by the Cult as a Trojan horse for world government dictatorship the game becomes transparent. One UN agency hoaxes the problem and others promote the solution. The IPCC is not a scientific organisation, but a *political* one and its claims and behaviour are dictated by politicians, activists and place-people – not by scientists who are merely the prop. Some 'scientists' say what the IPCC demands when they lift their snouts from the money-trough while other genuine scientists either have their work misrepresented in IPCC 'reports' or are ignored all together. Many scientists mentioned in IPCC documents have complained of being misquoted and having their opinions distorted as I have detailed in other books. Another sleight-of-hand is for IPCC reports detailing alleged 'scientific findings' to be preceded by a 'summary' of those findings. These 'summaries' are written by the IPCC hierarchy to misrepresent or exaggerate what is in the main report in the knowledge that the world's media will, almost in its entirety, use the summary as the basis for its reporting. For many years the IPCC was headed by a railway engineer, Rajendra Pachauri, who was succeeded by Hoesung Lee, a South Korean former economist with ExxonMobil and brother of former Prime Minister of South Korea Lee Hoi-chang. The IPCC is indeed a *political* not a scientific organisation churning out propaganda about climate change to justify the imposition of global centralised tyranny. Christiana Figueres, who is UN to her DNA, was executive secretary of the United Nations Framework Convention on Climate Change for six years and in 2020 published a book with her 'strategic advisor' and 'climate change' political lobbyist, Tom Rivett-Carnac, from a family of aristocrats. The book, *The Future We Choose: Surviving the Climate Crisis*, naturally ticked all the boxes. Figueres parroted climate change orthodoxy, endorsed Extinction Rebellion and Greta Thunberg, and promoted 'civil disobedience' as 'a moral choice' to pressure politicians to act on climate change. She even names Martin Luther King as an example when she could not have named anyone less appropriate. King was campaigning for freedom and not, as with the Climate Cult, demanding it be deleted. Funny how the establishment promotes 'civil disobedience' to advance the climate hoax, but those who engage in such activities in support of freedom, fairness and justice are labelled 'enemies of the state'. How would King have responded to an article posted on the United Nations Educational, Scientific and Cultural Organization (UNESCO) website headed 'Climate crimes must be brought to justice'. These 'crimes' highlighted by British academic Catriona McKinnon turn out to be refusing to believe in the UN climate hoax. McKinnon is yet another confirmation that academia, once a noble profession, is now a very sick joke. This genius wrote:

> Criminal sanctions are the most potent tools we have to mark out conduct that lies beyond all limits of toleration [or none in the case of New Woke]. Criminal conduct violates basic rights and destroys human security. We reserve the hard treatment of punishment for conduct that damages the things we hold most fundamentally valuable. Climate change is causing precisely such damage …

> … I have proposed that international criminal law should be expanded to include a new criminal offence that I call postericide. It is committed by intentional or reckless conduct fit to bring about the extinction of humanity. Postericide is committed when humanity is put at risk of extinction by conduct performed either with the intention of making humanity go extinct, or with the knowledge that the conduct is fit to have this effect.

> When a person knows that their conduct will impose an impermissible risk on another and acts anyway, they are reckless. It is in the domain of reckless conduct, making climate change worse, that we should look for postericidal

conduct.

From this bizarre journey through what passes for McKinnon's thought processes comes the demand that challenging climate hoax orthodoxy should be a criminal offence under international law. The fascistic nature of such a demand will not have penetrated her New Woke self-obsession. McKinnon published a book entitled *The Ethics of Climate Governance* – the ethics of *global* governance would be more like it. No wonder UNESCO promoted her article. By the way, surely Cambridge academic Patricia MacCormack must be guilty of McKinnon's 'postericide' given that she says: 'The only solution for climate change is letting the human race become extinct.' Ah, no, you see MacCormack and McKinnon are both New Woke and believe in the climate change hoax and that is always a get out of jail card.

Greenpeace co-founder Patrick Moore, an open-and-shut case of 'postericidal conduct', emphasises another deception in the climate change racket. The IPCC's brief is not to investigate the causes of climate change, but only *human* causes. No wonder it basically ignores the Sun. It is specifically focused on alleged human causes because that's the answer the Cult needs for its manipulation. If IPCC personnel found there was no significant human impact there would be no reason for its existence and they would lose their share of what the *Climate Change Business Journal* estimated to be $1.5 trillion a year even at the time of the UN Paris climate conference in 2015. It will be much more now. American writer Upton Sinclair said: 'It is difficult for a man to understand something when his salary depends upon his not understanding it.' This is another Cult technique to pressure its gofers to do and say what the Cult wants or lose their income. The IPCC outrageously claims to be dedicated to providing the world with objective, scientific information when its controlling core is a climate Mafioso. Scientist and engineer David Evans, a full-time or part-time consultant for eleven years to the Australian Greenhouse Office (now the Department of Climate Change), has a far more accurate assessment of what is a fantastic conspiracy to deceive. He said the theory of human-caused global warming was based 'on a guess that was proved false by empirical evidence during the 1990s', but most scientists wouldn't say so when 'the gravy train was too big, with too many jobs, industries, trading profits, political careers, and the *possibility of world government* and total control riding on the outcome' (my emphasis). With that Evans hit the nail bang on the sweet spot. This is what the hoax of the human-caused 'climate crisis' is really all about. He said that 'governments and their tame climate scientists now outrageously maintain the fiction that carbon dioxide is a dangerous pollutant' when the evidence they are wrong was overwhelming.

Agenda 21/2030

These two interconnected UN 'agendas' are the major means through which the Cult is exploiting the climate change lie to impose its Hunger Games structure of global control. Agenda 21 was launched by Maurice Strong (the Rothschilds and Rockefellers) at the Rio Earth Summit in 1992. Agenda 2030 was established by the UN General Assembly in 2015. Agenda 21 refers to centrally-controlling everything in the 21st century while Agenda 2030 is a series of 17 target 'goals' which, if implemented in the way planned, would achieve the global dictatorship demanded by Agenda 21. In short they are two versions of the same conspiracy. Agenda 21 has been accepted and promoted across the world right down into local councils. Check your council or state and see if they are implementing Agenda 21 and 'sustainable development'. The latter might seem at first to be laudable. Why wouldn't we want human activity to be 'sustainable' in the long term? BIG RED FLAG AND BRIGHT FLASHING LIGHTS: That's not the United Nations or Cult definition of the word. To them it means the excuse to impose world dictatorship. These are the 'sustainable development goals' and headings of Agenda 2030:

1. No Poverty
2. Zero Hunger
3. Good Health and Well-being
4. Quality Education
5. Gender Equality
6. Clean Water and Sanitation
7. Affordable and Clean Energy
8. Decent Work and Economic Growth
9. Industry, Innovation, and Infrastructure
10. Reducing Inequality
11. Sustainable Cities and Communities
12. Responsible Consumption and Production
13. Climate Action
14. Life Below Water
15. Life On Land
16. Peace, Justice, and Strong Institutions
17. Partnerships for the Goals

Once again these would appear to be supportable ambitions except that we are looking at a constantly-used Cult technique that tells people what they want to hear without revealing the real reason for what is planned. We should always filter claims to 'care about humanity' with the knowledge that those behind the UN are Death Cultists motivated by horrific intent. Why would practicing Satanists and paedophiles of the Cult with a pathological hatred for humans want those 'goals' to be achieved including no poverty or hunger? These are the controllers of global finance that have created poverty and hunger and use both as political tools. The Devil is not so much in the alleged 'goals'; it is in the means to achieve them (or the illusion of achieving them more to the point). This is how Agenda 21 intends to do that as outlined in its own documents:

- End national sovereignty
- State planning and management of all land resources, ecosystems, deserts, forests, mountains, oceans and fresh water; agriculture; rural development; biotechnology; and ensuring 'equity'
- The state to 'define the role' of business and financial resources
- Abolition of private property
- 'Restructuring' the family unit
- Children raised by the state
- People told what their job will be
- Major restrictions on movement
- Creation of 'human settlement zones'
- Mass resettlement as people are forced to vacate land where they live
- Dumbing down education
- Mass global depopulation in pursuit of all the above

This is the very wish-list of the Cult that I have been exposing for more than 30 years and the US Green New Deal proposed by New Woke Democrat extremists is a political manifesto to implement Agenda 21/2030 as are similar versions of the 'Deal' around the world. This is what the UN Agendas and the Green New Deals really mean behind their Orwell-speak:

An end to national sovereignty:

I don't really need to elaborate on this one after what I have said already about the plan to delete countries for a structure of world government, superstates and regions. Maps already exist for a regionalised Europe with countries eliminated and America is being regionalised by the Tiptoe technique through 500 regional councils in the 50 states called Councils of Governments (COGs) and Metropolitan Planning Organizations (MPOs). The next stage, the Smart Region Initiative (SRI), was launched in Arizona in 2019 with a view to expansion across the country.

State planning and management of all land resources, ecosystems, deserts, forests, mountains, oceans and fresh water; agriculture; rural

development; biotechnology; and ensuring 'equity':

This is the centralised control of everything that I have been warning about and it's already happening with some American states even claiming ownership of rainwater that falls on private land.

The state to 'define the role' of business and financial resources:

This means the central control of all finance and business and the end of private enterprise not supported by the World State. The systematic targeting of small mom and pop businesses and much bigger ones with taxation and regulation is aimed at destroying them all eventually so that only giant Cult corporations answering to the Cult world government will control everything – see Amazon for a start and survey the world since the 'virus' lockdowns for the extraordinary acceleration of this goal. Global financial dictatorship is the role of the planned world central bank with the European Central Bank, World Bank and International Monetary Fund all Totalitarian Tiptoes to that end and the same with the cashless single global digital currency that I have been saying was coming since the early 1990s. This is today being implemented with the disappearance of cash (again accelerated by its insane demonisation as a source of 'catching the virus'). The economic sales-pitch of 'sustainable development' includes an 'end to poverty' which really means a re-distribution of wealth to make the mega-rich even richer and Western middle and working classes seriously poorer. Another pledged goal of 'eliminating hunger' (as if the Cult cares) is to justify health-destroying genetically-modified crops requiring stupendous amounts of pesticides and herbicides to grow and the end of eating meat.

Abolition of private property:

This is the central control of all property (except for the elite) with rents so high that people are forced into the micro-'apartments' that are now being built around the world. Calls for an end to private property ownership have now started in line with this plan. Young people are being prevented from entering the property market by sky-high prices, student debt and other financial suppression. Rockefeller family insider Dr Richard Day told those Pittsburgh paediatricians in 1969:

> Privately-owned housing will become a thing of the past. The cost of housing and financing housing would gradually be made so high that most people couldn't afford it ... Young people would more and more become renters, particularly in apartments or condominiums.

People would not be able to buy [homes] and gradually more and more of the population would be forced into small apartments [the micro-apartments]. Small apartments which would not accommodate very many children.

The last point is part of a depopulation agenda and Day also indicated the control aspects of telling you where you are going to live:

Ultimately, people would be assigned where they would live and it would be common to have non-family members living with you. This by way of your not knowing just how far you could trust anybody. This would all be under the control of a central housing authority. Have this in mind ... when they ask, 'How many bedrooms in your house? How many bathrooms in your house? Do you have a finished game room?' This information is personal and is of no national interest to government under our existing Constitution. But you'll be asked those questions ...

Dictating where people live is happening in the Cult blueprint for the world – China.

'Restructuring' the family unit

The end of the family is a constant theme of Cult-related documents and organisations. The deletion of ever more parental rights which are handed to state institutions like schools and social services is this aspect of the agenda unfolding in plain sight without the dots being connected. Remember how student debt campaigner Wayne Johnson said the loan crisis was leading to the 'ever-increasing destruction of the fabric of America' with people 'not getting married, not having children'. It's all calculated cause and effect.

Children raised by the state

This is obviously related to the end of the family and the longer term plan is for the end of even human procreation as I will be coming to. Fantastic numbers of children now being literally stolen from loving parents by social services through outrageous misrepresentation and lies in secret 'family courts' is this plan at work. Insider Aldous Huxley described the end of parenthood in his prophetic *Brave New World*.

People told what their job will be:

George Orwell wasn't kidding in his portrayal of a Big Brother world in which every aspect of human life is dictated including work slavery.

Major restrictions on movement:

Why do you think Cult-serving and manipulated climate extremists are targeting flying and car use? Look at the effect on movement of the 'pandemic'. This further explains the obsession with imposing autonomous vehicles in which the computer limits where you can go. Governments are banning the sale of petrol and diesel vehicles in favour of anything-but Green electric power because that is the stepping-stone to full-blown electric autonomous vehicles. 'Saving the planet' is only an excuse to advance this agenda. Britain is committed to banning new petrol and diesel vehicles from 2035 while others including Denmark, Ireland, the Netherlands and Sweden go for 2030. The knock-on effect for employment in the auto-industry can be seen with predictions of massive job losses due to the nature of electric car production. Where do those people go? Did I mention the Hunger Games Society?

Creation of 'human settlement zones':

Translated from the Orwellian this means people being forced into tightly-packed mega-cities of round-the-clock surveillance and micro-apartments that I have described. Their code-name is 'Smart Cities' (once again see China). Tightly-packed teeming cities of human chaos and misery will also provide low-vibrational energy centres on which the Cult 'gods' can feed.

Mass resettlement as people are forced to vacate land where they live:

Another reference to what is now happening with the destruction of rural communities, businesses and job opportunities, removal of shops and banks, plus increased transport costs, to pressure people to head for the cities.

Dumbing down education:

This has already been achieved and is programming the mentality of New Wokeness in which 'education' is confused with indoctrination and downloading the Cult perception program is perceived as 'knowing it all'. Ponder the following climate change excuse for 'dumbing down education' from the United Nations (again) Education, Scientific, and Cultural Organization (UNESCO):

Generally, more highly educated people who have higher incomes can consume more resources than poorly educated people who tend to have lower incomes. In this case more education increases the threat to sustainability.

Are you getting it yet New Wokeness?

Mass global depopulation in pursuit of all of the above:

With the advent of the AI world humans are no longer required by the Cult in such numbers and even more so with the end of procreation. The plan for a mass cull of the global population appears in many Cult-related documents under terms like 'population control' and a 'sustainable population'. There are many ways this is being done through the systematic undermining of immune systems through food, drink, vaccines and radiation fields, and this really becomes a cinch once human brains are connected to AI. Those you want to remove are just a press of a button away or the click of a mouse.

The horrific multi-faceted agenda for humanity outlined here is being justified by the 'climate emergency' and an 'existential threat' to humanity which *isn't actually happening*. We are looking at mass-hysteria which is defined as 'mass psychogenic illness, collective hysteria, group hysteria, or collective obsessional behavior, which transmits collective illusions of threats, whether real or imaginary, through a population in society as a result of rumours and fear'. Mass hysteria is another example of wave entanglement with individual hysteria feeding the entangled collective to generate group hysteria. Pump-primers shout fire and the crowd starts running while others keep shouting fire ongoing in science, academia and media. Everybody's shouting fire and so there must be a fire even if no one can see the smoke (see 'virus' hysteria). The term 'hysteria' is such a perfect description of what is happening that a panel of German linguists decided to 'ban' it in relation to climate change. They choose a new word or phrase to 'ban' every year and went for 'climate hysteria' on the grounds that it 'defames climate protection efforts and the climate protection movement, and discredits important discussions about climate protection'. This is Orwell's Newspeak which deletes words that allow the 'wrong' opinions to be articulated. The 'panel's' other banned words and terms include 'alternative facts', 'do-gooder', 'liar press' and 'welfare tourism' (a description of migrants exploiting the welfare system). I'm sure you have no problem seeing the pattern. Another head-shaker is that those eventually sitting at the centre of the target for freedom-deletion are the very people demanding in organisations like Extinction Rebellion that their own mass slavery – and that of their children and grandchildren – is implemented while anyone arguing against that should be silenced (Fig 276 overleaf). I do

YOU ARE BEING SPUN KIDS

THE WORLD IS NOT GOING TO END - YOUR FREEDOM IS

Figure 276: The Pied Piper of Stockholm.

not exaggerate when I say that great swathes of humanity are descending into mental illness although thank goodness far from everyone. Patrick Moore was right when he said of the green insanity movement: 'I fear for the end of the enlightenment. I fear an intellectual Gulag with Greenpeace as my prison guards.' That is exactly the plan, but it doesn't have to be. The idea has been to indoctrinate the young through constant climate programming in schools and universities to ensure the Big Lie is so ingrained that they will accept and even demand the Cult agenda for total global control of every man, woman and child.

Heeere's Greta (right on cue)

The Swedish 16-year-old Greta Thunberg was wheeled out specifically to rally the young to rebel against their elders in climate protests that insist freedom is deleted for the rest of their lives. I don't say for a second that Thunberg knows this. She is a tragic puppet and her story connected to organisations pressing the Cult agenda while she won't know there is a Cult never mind she is doing its bidding. She is, however, revealing in her arrogance ever-increasing signs of believing her own publicity and hype. Thunberg doesn't seem to know much at all and only parrots a stream of mantras and platitudes such as 'listen to the science' when she has no idea what 'the science' is. She never expands on 'the science' and mainstream media sycophants never ask her. The 'science is settled' mantra is utter bullshit and leads to people who would otherwise question climate change orthodoxy to stay quiet in fear of being accused by climate propagandists of 'denying the science'. The theme applies especially to those in the academic arena who have jobs to protect. What if the 'science' wasn't 'science' at all? What if it's only a script written by the Cult to which most of mainstream 'science' has long sold its soul? Well, it is. Greta Thunberg has been diagnosed with obsessive-compulsive disorder, autism and Asperger's syndrome and been credited with mystical powers by her Climate Cult mother, Malena Ernman, a super-New Woke Swedish singer, while her father Svante Thunberg is a talent agent and managing director of a media company. Greta's 'powers' are claimed to include the ability to see carbon dioxide with the naked eye and how it flows out of chimneys and changes the atmosphere. I kid you not. Does she see the plants grow bigger and stronger, too, when CO2 increases? What absurdity although perfect if you want to create a new religious icon. Exploiting a 16-year-old connects with the young and gives her a free-ride with the mainstream media despite the impact of her elite-orchestrated words and actions being global in nature and fundamental to the transformation of human society. By contrast German teenager Naomi Seibt who once bought the climate change lie and then spoke out after seeing through the hoax is treated rather differently. The girl dubbed the 'anti-Greta Thunberg' is highly articulate and well-researched which means she does not get invited to elite events. Instead she is presented through implication and association as some kind of white nationalist extremist and of course the ubiquitous 'anti-Semitic' by the usual suspects that include, as always, the 'anti-establishment' establishment-to-its-DNA London *Guardian*. I bet you're in shock. We should have a live public debate between Thunberg and Seibt for all young people to watch. An Internet video reveals a code that Thunberg uses whenever she is questioned in the street about 'the science'. She takes off her hat and immediately a minder steps in to whisk her away. She is watched over by unpleasant and aggressive plain clothes security guards sometimes outnumbering protestors with her in Sweden. These heavies will not let anyone with real questions anywhere near her. Who is paying for them? Who is financing the whole Thunberg phenomenon? Members and agents of the One-percent are certainly involved in the bankrolling of this most blatant of propaganda operations. I recommend the YouTube video *Greta Thunberg Incorporated: The Exposé* to see the arrogant, authoritarian thugs among her 'security'.

Is anyone really so naive as to believe it's a coincidence that a 16-year-old protesting alone in Sweden suddenly finds herself invited by the One-percent to speak at their elite World Economic Forum conference in Davos, Switzerland, and berate them about climate change? Or that she was given a platform to speak to the world at the Climate Cult-orchestrating *United Nations?* Or that she was sailed across the Atlantic to get to the UN in a ridiculous stunt by those connected to the Monaco royal family in a multi-million yacht that used to be called the Edmond de Rothschild – the man Maurice Strong said was the creator of the environmental movement? Or that a crew filming a high-profile documentary followed her from the time she was sitting 'alone' in her 'spontaneous' one-girl protest outside the Swedish parliament? Or that the person who 'discovered by chance' her 'lone protest' was public relations and financial expert Ingmar Rentzhog who has close connections to the Club of Rome that hatched the climate change hoax from the start? He claims to have come across Thunberg 'by chance' minutes after she started her first 'school strike protest' outside the

Swedish parliament. I'm laughing already. Rentzhog trained with the Climate Reality Project led by climate change global propagandist Al Gore and founded the social media platform 'We Don't Have Time' to promote the climate change narrative. Two months after Rentzhog 'discovered' Greta in 2018 the Club of Rome held a joint conference with Rentzhog and 'We Don't Have Time'. The person who encouraged Thunberg to start her 'school strike' and protest at the parliament was the head of Extinction Rebellion in Sweden who had said they needed a cute young face 'to get help from young people to increase the pace of the transition to a sustainable society'.

I guess another coincidence is that a Thunberg climate change mentor is German climate politician Luisa-Marie Neubauer who is an asset of the ONE Movement funded by other Cult assets like Bill Gates and George Soros (yes, them again) and involving their mate, virtue-signalling rock singer Bono. Soros funds other Thunberg-connected organisations. Luisa-Marie Neubauer has appeared with Thunberg at many public events. ONE is among the most obvious of New Woke astroturf operations you could imagine. The Bill and Melinda Gates Foundation website describes ONE as an organisation that 'pursues its goals through policy advocacy, grassroots mobilization, communications, and creative campaigning' which is straight off the pages of the New Woke manipulation manual. The website continues: 'ONE also mobilizes its 3.2 million members to pressure policymakers to increase their effort, accountability, and transparency in the fight against disease and poverty, particularly in Africa.' Multi-billionaires care so deeply about poverty, you see. ONE makes 'the most of technology and social media ... [and has] ... also become a leading force in educating the public about global health and development and in changing perceptions about aid and its impact'. If we translate that from the bullshit ONE campaigns for the Cult agenda just like the Open Society network of Soros. Thunberg and her parents profess to be 'anti-fascist' in their 'intersectionality' with other New Woke sectors and all three have been photographed in t-shirts promoting the violent 'anti-fascist' fascist group, Antifa (Fig 277). 'I didn't know', said Greta. Oh, really – what about your parents? Human-caused climate change is an elite scam and why wouldn't there be all these elite connections to its propaganda princess? Thunberg is just their unknowing and

Figure 277: Greta and parents promoting Antifa, a violent 'anti-hate' hate group so beloved of New Woke.

Figure 278: Pawn in a game she doesn't begin to understand.

Figure 279: Saint Greta, the Climate Goddess.

increasingly arrogant stooge. In my view her climate extremist parents should be ashamed of how they allow her to be exploited and have played such a central role in that. Her obsessive-compulsive disorder can be clearly seen in her unquestioning obsession with a climate end-of-the-world and it's sad to witness such outrageous exploitation (Fig 278). The Cult of Greta now includes a huge painting of her looking down in distain over New Woke and shit-infested San Francisco and her every public move is documented by the media in a colossal exercise in public relations programming – especially of the young (Fig 279). A further crucial part of the elite promotion of Thunberg is to drive a wedge between old and young, adults and children. This was her carefully-scripted speech to the UN in 2019 and all elements of the Climate Cult agenda are there:

My message is that we'll be watching you. This is all wrong. I shouldn't be up here. I should be back in school on the other side of the ocean [Well, go then]. Yet you all come to us young people for hope. How dare you! [Divide young and old by blaming the old for something that's not happening]. You have stolen my dreams and my childhood with your empty words. [No, Greta, those exploiting you have stolen your childhood]. And yet I'm one of the lucky ones. People are suffering. People are dying [not from human-caused climate change they're not]. Entire ecosystems are collapsing [not from human-caused climate change they're not]. We are in the beginning of a mass extinction [no, we're not], and all you can talk about is money and fairy tales of eternal economic growth [which the Cult wants to delete for the mass of the population]. How dare you! [Ditto to you, Greta.]

For more than 30 years, the science has been crystal clear [like hell it has].

How dare you continue to look away and come here saying that you're doing enough, when the politics and solutions needed are still nowhere in sight. You say you hear us and that you understand the urgency. But no matter how sad and angry I am, I do not want to believe that. Because if you really understood the situation and still kept on failing to act, then you would be evil. And that I refuse to believe. [So how evil are those seeking to terrify the young that their world is going to end when it's all a gigantic hoax to delete their freedom for life?]

The popular idea of cutting our emissions in half in 10 years only gives us a 50% chance of staying below 1.5 degrees, and the risk of setting off irreversible chain reactions beyond human control [chain-reactions that don't exist]. Fifty percent may be acceptable to you. But those numbers do not include tipping points [made up to explain the lack of CO_2 impact], most feedback loops [ditto], additional warming hidden by toxic air pollution or the aspects of equity and climate justice [more bunkum]. They also rely on my generation [divide, divide] sucking hundreds of billions of tons of your CO_2 [the gas of life] out of the air with technologies that barely exist. So a 50% risk is simply not acceptable to us – we who have to live with the consequences [divide, divide].

To have a 67% chance of staying below a 1.5 degrees global temperature rise – the best odds given by the [Cult-created Intergovernmental Panel on Climate Change] – the world had 420 gigatons of CO_2 left to emit back on Jan. 1st, 2018. Today that figure is already down to less than 350 gigatons. How dare you pretend that this can be solved with just 'business as usual' and some technical solutions? With today's emissions levels, that remaining CO_2 budget will be entirely gone within less than eight and a half years.

There will not be any solutions or plans presented in line with these figures here today, because these numbers are too uncomfortable. And you are still not mature enough to tell it like it is [but you are Greta by repeating the crap you have been told to say?]. You are failing us. But the young people are starting to understand your betrayal [divide, divide]. The eyes of all future generations are upon you [divide, divide]. And if you choose to fail us, I say: We will never forgive you [divide, divide].

We will not let you get away with this. Right here, right now is where we draw the line. The world is waking up. And change is coming, whether you like it or not.

Yes, Greta, the Cult's change is coming if we and your generation believe garbage like that. We are witnessing yet another inversion in which children tell adults what they should do. There are many stupid adults, large numbers of which are in politics. There are some aware children who have not allowed the Cult to program their perceptions (Greta Thunberg is not one of them). But the idea that children know better in general than intelligent adults with decades of experience is absurd. When I was six, twelve and sixteen I would not have dreamed of telling the world what should be done because, like those of the same age today, *I hadn't lived long enough to credibly know.* The young-old inversion has a clear motive for the Cult: Children and young people today have been subjected to the perception program at its most extreme and it wants those perceptions to prevail and transform society in its image.

Figure 280: The Cult is desperate to turn the young against the old.

Program the kids and then have their will imposed on adults who will have known life and experience before child-programming reached its current extremes. No one ever asks Greta Thunberg how many hundreds of millions will die if her carbon targets are met through loss of jobs, food and warmth. The climate hoax divides advocates and 'deniers' and splits young from old on the grounds that the old are responsible for the 'existential threat' to the young (Fig 280). The German branch of the school strike organisation Fridays for Future, officially founded and copyrighted by Greta Thunberg, promoted this agenda when it tweeted: 'Why do grandparents talk to us each year? They won't be around much longer.' German public broadcaster WDR produced a song video featuring a choir of young girls castigating older people for climate change and eating meat. It referred to an imaginary grandma as 'an environmental pig' and warned we 'will not let you get away with this'. WDR called it 'satire' in the face of a disgusted public reaction when it was clearly calculated. 'Satire' is the excuse often used when attempts at indoctrination become too blatant and people see through it. The 'how dare you?' rant about older generations by 16-year-old Cult puppet Thunberg was also an example of this theme. Yes, Greta, how dare older people and the long-gone create an industrial society that allows multimillion dollar yachts to be built for your propaganda stunts and aircraft to quietly – *shhhhh* – fly your sailing crew back home across the Atlantic while you posture your carbon self-purity? The Cult's desire to start a war between young and old has many motivations. One is that older people were born long before the climate change hoax began and many can see through the manipulation and contradictions. They must be perceived by the young as the villains and the enemy to be vanquished rather than wisdom and experience worth listening to (Fig 281).

Figure 281: The plan is now so transparent. (Image Gareth Icke.)

Increasing the hype

Thunberg was invited again in 2020 to the World Economic Forum in Davos, Switzerland, a 100 percent front for the One-percent and the Cult behind the climate change hoax and the creation of an Orwellian, AI-controlled, Orwellian global state (Fig 282). Why would these multi-billionaires invite a 16-year-old to castigate them at their own conference for the second year in a row and repeat the crap

Figure 282: Why would the One-percent invite Greta Thunberg to berate them on climate change? This is why.

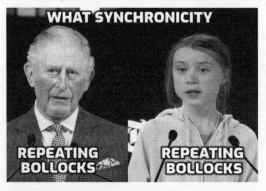

Figure 283: Same song-sheet, different singers.

that 'our world is still on fire'? This chapter alone has answered that question and they will drop her like a stone when she has served their purpose. She outrageously claimed that if we don't do what she said we are not acting 'as if you loved your children above all else'. She added that 'we don't want these things done in 2050, 2030, or even 2021 – we want this done now'. Who is this '*we*'? The One-percenters watching her speak at Davos for sure and certainly not the general public. Donald Trump appeared at the elite propaganda-fest to deliver a speech warning against believing the climate 'prophets of doom' in a clear reference to Thunberg sitting in the audience. He was, however, pretty much a lone voice. Instead we had another burst of baloney from Prince Charles who remember said in 2009 that we had twelve years to save the world from irretrievable climate and ecosystem collapse (Fig 283). Charles travelled to Davos in a private jet and electric car to make a speech promoting the demands of the Climate Cult. In the less than two weeks before the speech Charles had flown four times in private jets and a helicopter with the aircraft flying a total of 16,000 miles at a cost to the UK taxpayer of $280,000. This is a man who has flown *125 miles* in a helicopter to make a speech about the dangers of aircraft emissions. Without a hint of embarrassment he presented himself at Davos as an environmental champion and called for 'eco-taxes', a world economy with nature at its centre (while reducing CO2 that sustains nature), and new AI technologies – all from the Cult's letter to Santa, or Satan. He of course championed 'sustainability' and proposed a transformation of the global economy justified by climate change that precisely reflected the Cult agenda. He said:

> Now it is time to take it to the next level. In order to secure our future and to prosper we need to evolve our economic model.

So many deadlines for the end of the world through 'runaway' climate change have come and gone, but like all good cults they just keep announcing a new date when the last one passed without incident. The latest doomsday is around 2030 which is a highly significant date that turns up in many guises. It was mentioned yet again by Prince Charles in his Davos speech. Here are three other examples: When the latest date of 'twelve years to save the planet' was first announced that would take us to around 2030. The UN list of goals to save the planet from climate change by transforming global society into a centralised dictatorship is called Agenda 2030. The year given by Google executive Ray Kurzweil and other Silicon Valley technocrats for connecting the human brain to artificial intelligence is 2030 (Fig 284). Is this yet another coincidence? What do you think when AI is being promoted as an answer to climate change? The hoax has hog-tied almost every politician into some level of compliance. There are the majority who buy the lie and say 'something must be done' and the rest who may

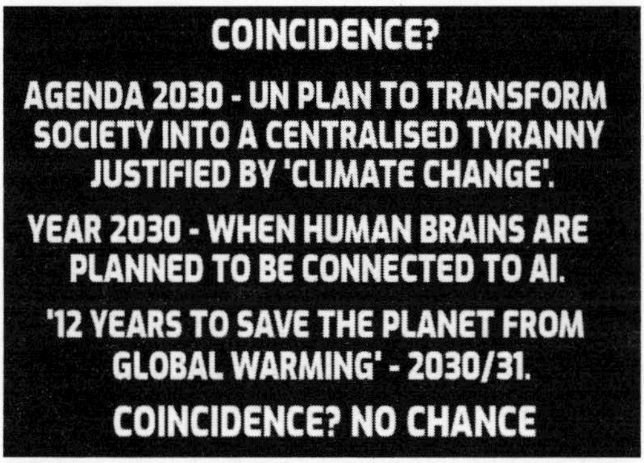

COINCIDENCE?

AGENDA 2030 - UN PLAN TO TRANSFORM SOCIETY INTO A CENTRALISED TYRANNY JUSTIFIED BY 'CLIMATE CHANGE'.

YEAR 2030 - WHEN HUMAN BRAINS ARE PLANNED TO BE CONNECTED TO AI.

'12 YEARS TO SAVE THE PLANET FROM GLOBAL WARMING' - 2030/31.

COINCIDENCE? NO CHANCE

Figure 284: The year by which the Cult wants its agenda pretty much in place.

be somewhat or totally sceptical, but still feel they have to go along with the farce for electoral or reputational reasons. This is what happens once the Cult has decreed and implanted the 'norm'. Even people who see through it are mostly too intimidated to say so.

Then there is the feeling that the orthodoxy wouldn't be repeated so incessantly if there was nothing to it. Not every fact may be true, this mentality says, but there must be some basis of truth or why would everyone keep repeating the same claims? Well, when a disease is (genuinely) spreading – in this case a perceptual disease – does everyone get the same disease? Yes. Everyone in the establishment was repeating that Iraq had weapons of mass destruction. Was there *any* truth to that *whatsoever?* No. Once people grasp that human-caused climate change and its alleged catastrophic consequences is a mega-scam – not some of it, *all of it* – the mist clears and the monumental deceit is in plain sight.

Wake up Wokers. You are being hypnotised, mesmerised and shafted and I care about that enough to take your abuse when freedom for the rest of your lives at stake.

CHAPTER TEN

Are you New Woke?

Whom the gods would destroy, they first make mad – Euripides

How strange that the gas of life is depicted as the gas of death while China, the world's biggest industrial producer of CO2, is not the focus of Climate Cult outrage. China's emissions in 2019 were more than the United States, European Union and Japan combined and reportedly some *27 percent* of the world total.

Outrage instead is reserved only for Western countries which, crazy as it may be, are making efforts to reduce their 'carbon footprint'. One commentator said of Greta Thunberg: 'I don't see her in Beijing or Delhi.' There is a reason for that. China is the blueprint for global control and must not be criticised by those who seek to globally emulate this New Woke utopia. Oh, no, New Wokers might cry, we don't want to be like China. The evidence proves otherwise. Demand after dystopian demand by the New Woke and Climate Cult mentality is straight from the playbook of the Chinese Communist Party and Stalinist Russia come to that – and so is every aspect of the 'virus' lockdowns. Chairman Mao who forced communism on China's immense population in 1949 was a Cult operative and in the decades that have followed the country has been the incubator for the global technological surveillance dictatorship. The Second World War was a Cult-manipulated Problem-Reaction-Solution that brought pre-planned colossal political change. China became communist; Stalin's Russia swept across Eastern Europe; Israel was established; and the United Nations and other globally-centralised institutions were created on the Tiptoe to world government. Brutal centralised political and military control in China had allowed the Cult's Orwellian society to advance more quickly than in the West where they still (until the 'virus' lockdowns) had to pay lip-service to freedom and 'democracy'. In China when they want to impose a new stage of dystopian control they simply do it (and now so does the West). If you want to see what is planned for the rest of the world tomorrow look at China today and therefore we have 'New Woke' billionaires and corporations owned by the Cult, including Google, working closely with the Chinese dictators while claiming to care about 'values'. A report in the *Wall Street Journal* described how US tech giants including Google and IBM are supporting China's multibillion-dollar surveillance industry: 'US companies, including Seagate Technology PLC, Western Digital Corp. and Hewlett Packard Enterprise Co., have nurtured, courted and profited from China's surveillance industry … Several have been involved since the industry's infancy.' IBM was exposed for collaborating with the Nazis and their concentration camps (the Cult has no borders). The emulation of China in the West is now in overdrive thanks to the pandemic scam. China is where Maurice Strong ended up, the instigator for the Rothschilds and Rockefellers of the climate change hoax. We are led to believe that China is a self-contained entity and the Western world is on the other 'side'. Not at the Cult level they're not. Where did the 'virus pandemic' publicly start? *China*.

'Capitalism' is cartelism

A question quite understandably asked is why would the Cult and its One-percent which have secured predominance through capitalism want a global society based on communism and Marxism? It would appear to be a contradiction, but it's not. First of all the Cult wants its own form of centralised tyranny called a technocracy or government and control of society and industry by an elite of technical experts with no ballot box required. This is the global control system fast-emerging out of Silicon Valley. I will be explaining the background to the technocracy and for now I'll stay with the familiar communism/Marxism of which technocracy is a technological impersonation and expansion. All are interchangeable with fascism. The experience for the population is the same – top-down dictatorship. A second answer to why the One percent would want a communistic-type society when they appear to be 'capitalists' is that the Cult has secured global power through *cartelism* not *capitalism*. If you take capitalism to be a free market in which the most efficient, effective and creative win the day then that is absolutely not the world that we live in. When Cambridge academic Patricia MacCormack denounces the hierarchy of 'capitalism' as the problem and the reason that human existence must cease she is missing this very point. There are many flaws in leaving everything to the 'free market' and I don't believe that essential public services should be subjected to often vicious and people-destroying 'free-market capitalism'. Even worse, however, is when the market is not even close to being 'free' in the first place. The Cult is not interested in 'free' markets when it seeks complete control of everything. Instead it has constantly sought to impose its monopoly over every aspect of human life through ever-expanding corporations that destroy or buy-out opposition until capitalism is replaced by rigged-market cartelism. Prices are kept low to undercut competitors until monopoly is secured and then those prices (or *censorship* in the case of social media and

Google/YouTube/Facebook/Twitter) begin to soar. You don't like the new price? Too bad. Who else are you going to buy from? You don't like our censorship? Where else are you going to go? Limitless Cult money means that its corporations don't have to make a profit on the way to monopoly while 'competing' companies have to watch the bottom line and can't compete. Amazon, Google, YouTube, Twitter and Facebook are examples and we have the cartels of Big Pharma, Big Biotech, Big Oil, Big Media, Big Food, and so on. They become so powerful – and so lavish with their political donations – that they own governments no matter what politicians may say in public. Facebook's Mark Zuckerberg is 'questioned' on Capitol Hill by politicians that take Facebook political donations. It's called democracy apparently.

If you compare Cult cartelism with Cult communism/Marxism they are the same accumulation of power at the centre, or the top in MacCormack's hierarchy. Anyone think that the leadership elite in communist China don't live a vastly more privileged lifestyle than the rest of the population? Or that the same didn't happen in Stalinist Russia and every other Marxist utopia? Why do New Wokers think that communism/Marxism/socialism has been responsible for the deaths of some 100 million people amid mass-murder in Cambodia, Siberian gulags, and 're-education' camps of the Chinese Cultural Revolution? Western cartelism and Chinese communism are the same elite control systems with communism even more effective as an elite blueprint. Cartels in the West have to be manipulated into place through a sequence of acquisition and deletion of competition while with communism you have an imposed hierarchical structure of top-down control through which the government dictatorship enforces its will over everything and everyone. What is a communist/Marxist government except a single gigantic *cartel*? The Cult prefers communist structures for this reason and it is working to impose a technological version of that on the entire world with the climate change and 'pandemic' hoaxes as the predominant excuse for its imposition. Marxism is not 'government of the people' but government of the Cult with the added bonus of enforcement by a police/military state. Perhaps it may now dawn on New Wokers why a ruthless 'capitalist' (cartelist) like George Soros would pour tens of billions into New Woke and climate change organisations while saying this: 'I am basically there to make money, I cannot and do not look at the social consequences of what I do.' He's scamming you Wokers and *big-time* (Fig 285 overleaf). The perceptual game has been to sell the idea that you either believe in capitalism or communism/socialism. What they don't want you to know is that either way the Cult and its elite are always in control. Which 'polarity' do you want to rule you because either way it will be *us*. I coined the term in the 1990s of 'opposames' to describe apparent opposites that are in fact the

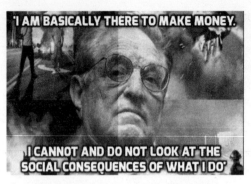

Figure 285: A man who says this ploughs tens of billions into 'social justice' and New Woke groups worldwide? Don't worry – he's not playing them like a stringed instrument or anything.

same. Communism and fascism which are different names for the same basic control system are obvious cases. From this perspective you will not be shocked to hear that Karl Marx (1818-1883), the official originator of Marxism, was a Cult asset and gofer. In particular he was a front man for the major network within the Cult known as Sabbatian-Frankism which is represented by, among so many others, the Saudi Arabian fake royal family and the controlling networks of government, intelligence agencies and military in Israel with their serious influence on government, intelligence agencies and military in the United States and worldwide. I reveal in *The Trigger* the Cult background to Karl Marx and the creation of Marxism.

How New Woke was created

The Cult has established an army of naïve New Wokers to campaign for socialism, the don't-scare-the-children name for Marxism, and it has been coordinated through control of 'education'. Rebecca Friedrich, a 28-year teacher in the United States who also worked with teacher unions, has detailed in her book, *Standing Up To Goliath*, how those unions have been imposing political indoctrination on children. It turns out that this agenda is precisely what I am exposing to be the Cult agenda. Soviet KGB defector Yuri Bezmenov described decades ago in *1985* how a four-step technique works to subjugate societies for communism. He called the first stage 'demoralisation' which he said took 15 to 20 years and involves at least three generations of students being indoctrinated in schools and colleges with the desired perception and ideology while other information is suppressed and demonised. The ideology must not be challenged or questioned and accepted to be self-evident truth. Bezmenov said of the demoralisation stage:

> Exposure to true information does not matter anymore. A person who is demoralised is unable to assess true information – the facts tell nothing to him. Even if I shower him with information, with authentic truth, with documents, with pictures, even if I take him by force to the Soviet Union and show him concentration camps he will refuse to believe it until he gets a kick in the back bottom [realises he has been had by a Marxist government taking over

his country]. When the military boot crashes then he will understand.

I keep emphasising that when the dystopian society which New Wokers demand is in place they will be the first to feel its boot up their arse. Try doing what Extinction Rebellion does in London on the streets of Beijing. Yuri Bezmenov said of such 'revolutionaries of the people': 'They think they will come to power, but that will never happen, of course.' They are only Cult fodder to impose its will before they, too, will be targeted or eliminated. It's already happening with feminists once high in the New Woke hierarchy now attacked for having the wrong opinion about transgender activists dismantling the freedoms of women. There are many areas and subjects on which I would disagree with Victor Davis Hanson, an American military historian and professor emeritus of Classics at California State University, Fresno, but he was absolutely right in an article in 2019 about the way 'revolutionaries' become the targets of their own 'revolution'. He said that 'liberalism and progressivism' (actually New Wokeism which has hijacked liberalism) will go the same way. Winston Churchill talked of how 'each one hopes that if he feeds the crocodile enough the crocodile will eat him last'. I tell the story in *The Trigger* about how the Jacobins were a Cult front which hijacked the French Revolution and were behind what is known as 'The Terror' in France in 1793 and 1794 which killed 17,000 'enemies of the Revolution'. Victor Davis Hanson wrote:

Once liberalism and progressivism give way to Jacobinism – and they often do, as we have seen in revolutionary France, China, and Russia – no leftist is safe from the downward spiral to ideological cannibalism. Yesterday's true believer is today's counter-revolutionary and tomorrow's enemy of the people …

… the voices of the sane and the moderate are usually crushed in revolutionary cycles where extremism operates on its own logic and trajectory – until chaos and cannibalism finally lead even to the extremists' own suicide.

We have reached the point in Bezmenov's demoralisation where creations of the New Woke perceptual download are entering politics as with Congresswoman Alexandria Ocasio-Cortez and her Green New Deal Marxism. The influence of her mindset has turned the Democrats into the New Woke Party increasingly dominated by the likes of Ocasio-Cortez and the rest of the so-called 'Squad' – Representatives Ilhan Omar of Minnesota, Ayanna Pressley of Massachusetts and Rashida Tlaib of Michigan. The same has happened to the Labour, Liberal Democrat, Green and Scottish National Parties in the UK and their like across the world. This is certainly the case in Germany and Sweden where New Woke parties have opened the doors to the Cult's mass migration agenda and dubbed anyone who questions the impact as Nazis, bigots and racists. US President Abraham Lincoln said: 'The philosophy of the school room in one generation will be the philosophy of government in the next.' Oh, how the Cult knows that. Bezmenov's demoralisation stage is followed by what he called 'destabilisation', 'crisis' and 'normalisation' by which time what would earlier have been dismissed as crazy is now the new normal and society is transformed. Can anyone really deny that this has happened in those same 15 to 20 years (actually even less) with the extremes of climate change hysteria, political correctness, censorship, mass immigration, and immensely expanded definitions of racism, sexism and gender? New Wokeness is calling for everything required for the Hunger Games world to become reality: Economic devastation, de-industrialisation and global control to 'save us from climate change'; political correctness to make the population silence itself to block exposure of what is happening; censorship of non-Woke information and opinions by Cult corporations cheered by New Wokers when before the Bezmenov sequence young people were protesting to *demand* freedom of speech; mass immigration and open borders to fulfil the Cult plan for divide and rule and deletion of countries; and the transformation of the sense of gender for deeply sinister reasons that I'll be coming to.

It may seem that I am condemning those that call themselves 'Woke' when actually I'm not doing that. I am not condemning the *people*, but exposing their *actions and behaviour* which is a different thing. I understand *why* they do and say what they do. Their perceptions have been programmed from the day they were born and ever more emphatically as they have passed through the 'education' indoctrination machine. The programming has been merciless and unceasing and I have been saying for years that we are looking at the most perceptually-manipulated generations in known human history now technology and social media are employed to that end. It is amazing that so many young people have seen through the program given how fierce and extreme it has been and they must summon the courage to speak out and refuse to have their world and campuses transformed into tyrannies by New Woke insanity. Would you condemn a computer for doing what someone else has encoded it to do? This would be crazy and with the scale of today's human programming that analogy is valid. I am pointing out the consequences of New Woke behaviour and the facts that are kept from them. I am offering another way of viewing the world to maybe stimulate some self-reflection on how The Program is impacting upon society. I don't condemn *them*. I feel sorry for them for what they are being subjected to by a psychopathic and satanic system that cares nothing for their wellbeing and uses them as imposition fodder.

Re-education is working

A poll of American 18-24-year-olds in 2019 found that 61 percent were open to a 'socialist society' and another found that 70 percent of millennials (born approximately between 1981 and 1996) would be 'somewhat or extremely likely' to vote for a socialist candidate. Two others found that 42 percent of Americans aged 18 to 39 would vote for a socialist president and that nearly 50 percent of young Americans would like a socialist government. The openly-socialist multi-millionaire, private jet passenger Bernie Sanders had young people as his support base to be the Democrat contender to face Trump in the 2020 election. He failed, but you can see the trend and 'socialism' (communism/fascism/technocracy) will be pushed even more in the wake of the 'Covid-19' hoax as we shall see. The other associated finding is that young people have a diminishing respect for capitalism. Those *for* socialism and *against* capitalism have their origins in 'educational' indoctrination (another version of communist 're-education') and in the economic consequences that the Cult has imposed upon them. First you tell young people that cartelism is capitalism and indebt them for much of their lives with student loans from 'capitalist' companies. This understandably turns them against capitalism which they mistake for cartelism while they are also indoctrinated at school and university into believing that socialism (communism/Marxism) is the panacea for all their ills. Marginalisation and misrepresentation of history purposely suppresses the horrendous reality of Marxist/socialist totalitarian regimes on the grounds that those who do not learn from the mistakes of history are destined to repeat them. After all, *repeating* them from the Cult's point of view is the whole idea and this time on a global scale. The Cult *wants* people to see how unfair society is because it adds to demands for 'change' in the form of socialist 'change' which is nothing more than changing the nature of One-percent control. The theme appeared to be further emphasised in a survey of 34,000 people by the US Zionist Edelman communications company across 28 countries in which 56 percent said capitalism is doing more harm than good. Damage done by cartelism masquerading as capitalism is far worse and I note that with capitalism (the misrepresentation of capitalism) as a target of the Cult this 'survey' and its findings were perfectly timed. The Cult both inverts the truth at every turn and seeks to present everything as a choice between black and white, literally and symbolically. You must choose between capitalism (cartelism) and socialism (communism). The fact that it's possible to protect the poor and needy (with a view to them not being poor and needy), have public control of essential services and a vibrant truly free market without cartels is not something that enters the equation. Nor is the fact that devolving power from the centre for people to make decisions about their lives within their own communities is a nightmare for cults and elites when it denies them the centralisation of power essential for the few to control the many. Every solution is more centralisation when the opposite is the case (as usual). Global bodies should be vehicles for *cooperation* between countries and communities – not centrally-directed dictatorships.

Many New Wokers demand equality of outcome which is the death knell for freedom, vibrant creativity and drive. The Soviet Union had equality of outcome in that everything was shite for the general population. Equality of outcome always creates a race to the bottom which is what the Hunger Games Society requires to impose a world where everyone is equally poor and dependent on the One-percent to drop their crumbs. Equality of *opportunity* is surely what we should pursue with the understanding that not everyone is equally talented in every aptitude or skill. You can't do something if you can't do it. I repeat: *You can't do something if you can't do it*. This statement must be among the most unchallengeable you could imagine although not for New Wokers who leave rationality on the coat-hook when they enter any situation. To them everything is the result of discrimination, racism, sexism, homophobia, transphobia, any ism or phobia will do (Fig 286). It has nothing to do with ability, drive or expertise. A black woman actress not getting the part to play a white man is simply racism. It's the only possible explanation. Okay, that example is extreme, but when you see how far we have descended into New Woke insanity how long before that, too, is true? How more extreme is that than a bloke with a dick in Canada insisting that female staff at a women's beauty parlour wax his dangly bits because he chooses to self-identify as a woman? If I had said only a few years ago that schools around the world would have drag queens reading stories to very young children for the purpose of gender confusion and indoctrination people would have said that was too far-fetched and could never happen. Oh, yes it could – and *is*. Cult indoctrination and extremism has no limits. It was even claimed with extraordinary stupidity that Prince Harry's missus Meghan Markle was forced out of Britain through racism (New Woke orthodoxy) relating to her mixed race when in fact it emerged that she had been

Figure 286: Mirror anyone?

NEIL HAGUE
GALLERY

The whole foundation of human control – isolation in the Bubble of perception.

Isolate them in the five-sense Bubble and then program perception
with Cult sources of 'information'.

The 'physical' world is a decoded projection of the wavefield world.

We are constantly interacting with wavefield reality while appearing
to be engaged in 'physical' interaction.

Through the collective field we are all *One* – be that with other people
or the natural world.

FOOD & DRINK ARE ENERGETIC FIELDS

TASTE

BITTER
SOUR
SOUR TASTE
SWEET
SALTY

2020 © neilhague.com

We experience eating 'physical' food when in fact we are energetic fields absorbing other energetic fields. Healthy food has energetic vibrance while 'fast food' and processed 'food' is energetically dead – hence its effect on the body.

WAVEFORM FIELD
WAVEFORM ENTANGLEMENT

2020 © neilhague.com

Human wavefields connect with other fields through wave entanglement – we experience this as relationships of all kinds.

2020 © neilhague.com

DEATH – LIFE ENTANGLEMENT

What we call death is when wave entanglement between body and mind is released and our eternal state of consciousness is subsequently released from the body's information-processing myopia. This is what near-death experiencers describe as their awareness dramatically expanding when they leave the body.

HOLOGRAPHIC REALITY IN YOUR HEAD

WAVEFORM

WAVEFORM

The world we experience as 'physical' only exists in that form when we decode wavefield information into holographic information. The world is not external to us. It is within us.

THE BRAIN IS AN INFORMATION PROCESSOR

IDENTITY

SIGHT

CINEMA

NEWS DESK

FEEDBACK LOOP

EXPERIENCE

PERCEPTION

SOUND

2020 © neilhague.com

Perceptions create a self-fulfilling conscious and subconscious feedback loop in which we
interact with The Field of possibility only within the frequency band
that our perceptions represent.

'Past', 'present' and 'future' are only decoded perceptions. All is happening in the same NOW.

The One is the creator of all reality via its infinite points of attention – including us.

SPIRIT SOUL MIND BODY

When Body-Mind disconnects from an influence of the greater self – 'Soul', 'Higher Self'
– we are at the mercy of perceptions gleaned only through the five senses.

An imbalance or flaw in the body wavefield becomes illness or dis-ease – disharmony –
in the hologram. Wavefield balance = holographic 'health' because one
is a reflection of the other.

WAVES ACTIVATE THE GENES

Our mental and emotional state is transmitted as waves which can turn genes on and off that relate to those states. In this way our state of mind becomes 'genetic' consequences good and bad.

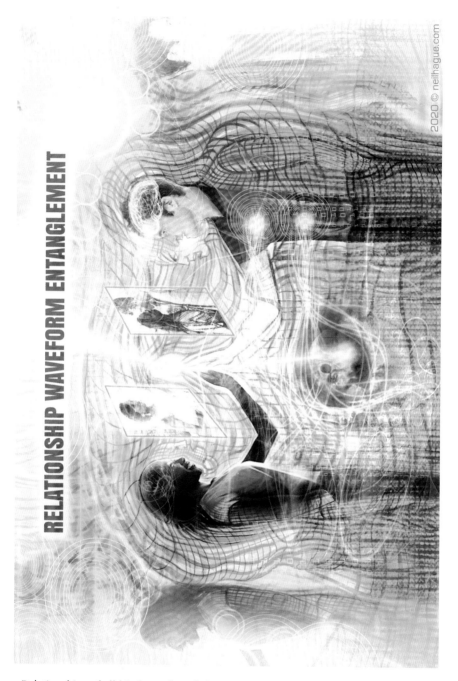

Relationships of all kinds are founded on wave-entanglement and the attraction or resistance of 'vibes'.

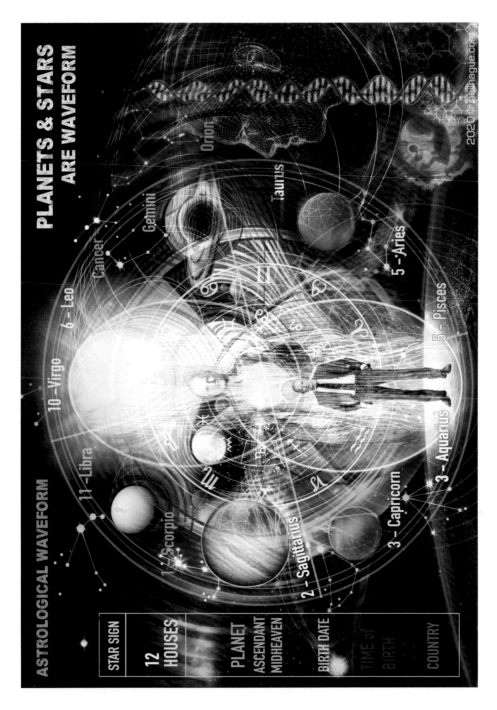

Astrology is founded on the impact of wave entanglement between frequency waves of planets and stars and frequency waves of people, animals and all life.

Closed hearts got us here. Open hearts will take us home.

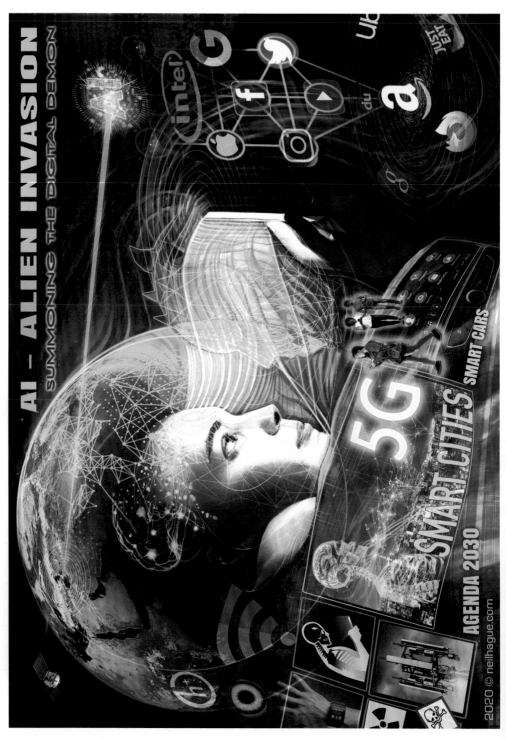

Smart technology and Wi-Fi are emitting waves of frequency that are entangling with human wavefields to create addiction and assimilate human frequencies into AI machine frequencies. Those that capitulate become ever more machine-like until they *are* machines.

planning the move to North America virtually all along. Lawyer Shola Mos-Shogbamimu, a monumental New Woker from what I can see, was doing the rounds of television studios (how very privileged) promoting this line of 'racism' against the mega-privileged private jet climate campaigner Markle. Mos-Shogbamimu describes herself as 'a political and women's rights activist who teaches intersectional feminism to female refugees and asylum seekers, scrutinizes government policies from a gender and diversity inclusion perspective, and co-organises women's marches and social campaigns'. Well, that just about covers everything. She was asked for examples of 'racism' against Markle and her reply was standard New Woke: 'Stop asking me – it's not my job to teach you about racism.' In other words she didn't have any. When a 'race and ethnicity lecturer' called Rachel Boyle claimed on a BBC show that Markle's departure to Canada was a result of 'racism' the British actor Laurence Fox told her: 'It's not racism ... We are the most tolerant lovely country in Europe.' Boyle responded: 'What worries me about your comment is you are a white privileged male.' We now live in a press-enter society founded on tidal-wave levels of brainwashing. When anything happens you press enter and New Woke says racist, sexist, transphobic or climate denier. Fox's reaction to the claim that he was an example of white privilege was right on the money:

> Oh my God. I can't help what I am, I was born like this, it's an immutable characteristic: to call me a white privileged male is to be racist – you're being racist.

The New Woke mentality is permanently firewalled from that self-realisation and instead members of Fox's family were targeted for abuse and one was spat at in the street by an 'anti-hate' hater. Fox quit Twitter in the face of the abuse fearing it would damage his career and the ability to provide for his family. At the same time he was getting widespread support from the non-New Woke majority that don't have access to mainstream microphones. By far the largest number of people – even among the young most subjected to the programming – don't buy the extremes of New Woke. The domination of the media narrative and fake grassroots, elite-funded, astroturf groups give a seriously false impression of what the population in general believe. A black lady called June Sarpong, so oppressed by white privilege that she is the BBC's Director of Creative Diversity (don't ask), said of Laurence Fox: 'He couldn't possibly know what it's like to be a person of colour.' Nor could Ms Sarpong know what it was like to be a black slave in apartheid America or South Africa. Claims you often hear from New Wokers that racism is worse than ever today is such an insult to those who experienced full-blown slavery. There are imbalances that still need to be addressed – of course, there always are, and that is also true for white people; but to claim that racism today is more extreme than ever is so obviously a fantasy that it requires no further comment. Jordan Peterson, the Canadian clinical psychologist and professor of psychology at the University of Toronto, has attracted both widespread support and New Woke abuse for his defence of masculinity and true racial equality. He summed up the reverse racism that I am highlighting here:

> The idea that you can target an ethnic group with a collective crime, regardless of the specific innocence or guilt of the constituent elements of that group – there is absolutely nothing that is more racist than that. It's absolutely abhorrent.

Halleluiah to that and you can see why New Woker racists hate him.

Press-enter for crazy

New Wokers have been enslaved in software minds by those that encode the software with the required sense of reality. Codes go on being expanded into ever-greater extremes of ridiculous as they are literally guided through wave entanglement with Cult manipulation along the path to complete mental illness. Daily perceptual programming ('education') throughout their formative years has achieved this supported by their friends and peers affirming the programming that they have also been downloading. Major Internet information sources like YouTube algorithmically offer 'recommendations' that match their search history to discourage access to other information and opinions. New Woke students are described as 'snowflakes' over their demands for safe spaces where they can't be subjected to other views (Fig 287). The cancel culture of de-platformed censorship achieves the same end of *I am right* never being subjected to challenge. I refer to the phenomenon as Generation Jelly although it's not really a generation (Fig 288). Large numbers of young people don't fall for it, but enough do and they are re-writing human society because they have the whole Cult-controlled system and establishment behind them. Demands for 'safe spaces' in colleges and universities are expressions of the fast-emerging monoculture myopia and the same with protests that ban or 'de-platform' speakers who have

Figure 287: Don't tell me anything I don't want to hear.

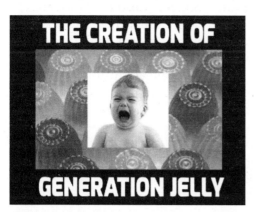

Figure 288: Fortunately it is not a whole generation. Many young people have seen through the manipulation, but it's the others that dominate the microphones to promote the Cult agenda they don't even know exists.

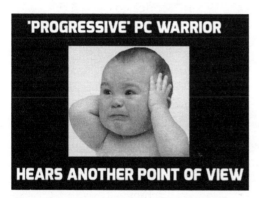

Figure 289: *NOOOO!* I only want to hear what I have been programmed to believe.

Figure 290: Being offended – the quickest way to hand your power to others.

a different view (Fig 289). One commentator said: 'Very often we [New Wokers] cancel people, destroy people, for saying what everyone thought until 24 hours ago.' New Wokers become locked in an information bubble which becomes their perceptual Bubble. If all they see and hear is their own perceptual programming played back to them no wonder they are convinced at how right and all-knowing they are. We have the indoctrination of the New Woke belief and its imposition on the public by the New Woke Thought Police. The law is that no one must offend or upset those in the New Woke hierarchy of victimhood by saying anything New Woke does not agree with (Fig 290). This perfectly serves the Cult agenda of destroying freedom of speech. Meanwhile, if you attack or criticise people and beliefs that are not in the official victim hierarchy (like white men and Christianity) you can be as abusive and racist as you like and the 'inclusive', 'anti-racist', mob will cheer you on. We all know how stupendously extreme the protection of Woke 'victims' has become to destroy human language and discourse in line with Orwell's Big Brother state. The breathtaking absurdity of PC 'transgression' is constantly plumbing still new depths of extremism and ludicrousness. Some are so crackers that even Wokers call them 'microaggressions' which are defined by Columbia University psychology professor Derald Wing Sue as 'brief and everyday slights, insults, indignities and denigrating messages sent to people of colour by well-intentioned white people'. From what I have seen 'all white people are privileged racist Nazis' doesn't seem to be listed as a 'microaggression' never mind a macro one. Maybe I missed that meeting. Anything connected to another culture is now 'cultural appropriation' and this includes wearing a sombrero sold to you by a Mexican in a tourist shop. The Mexican *wants* to sell it to you, but Wokers say you should not buy it because *they* are offended on the Mexicans' behalf even when Mexicans are not offended. PC is the world of victimless invented 'crimes' in which those not affected dictate what people should be offended about (Fig 291). This gathers momentum the more the victim culture manipulates through repetition and intimidation and the more people become offended about more and more things that didn't offend them before. Being offended by people demanding you are silenced doesn't count. To be offended is to hand your power to that which offends you and this is Planet Cuckoo when being offended is simply a *choice*. You can *choose not to be*. There you go –

Figure 291: The 'you must be offended by everything' Program. You're offended? Then choose not to be.

sorted. The professionally offended should have followed me around for 30 years if they want to see what ridicule and abuse is like. Have I been offended? *No*. I choose not to be offended by *anything* – least of all by ridicule and abuse from bubble-wrap minds. There is no more profound confirmation of your balance and self-security than being able and willing to laugh at yourself which New Woke can't do, so seriously does it take itself. I don't understand the sequence of being offended when I don't experience it. Someone says something you don't like or agree with. Okay, *and*? Have your say if you feel it's necessary (it usually isn't) and get on with your life. Why scramble your emotional state and wavefield state by the irrelevance of being *offended*?

Methodical madness

If we really cared about the wellbeing of children and young people we would not be protecting them from things they are told to be offended about. We would be encouraging them to be strong, sovereign, individuals who don't give a shit, never mind take offence, at what anyone says to them or about them. New Wokeness is a virulent, contagious, psychological virus unless you are conscious beyond mind and the five senses. This is the reason we need to understand why New Wokers think and act as they do. They are prisoners of New Wokeness – a perceptual computer virus. Tim Hunt, a Nobel Prize-winning British biochemist, was vilified and had his career severely damaged for a so-called 'misogynistic joke' that turned out to be nothing like it was reported to be by a professionally-offended New Woker. What is said, or more to point *meant*, doesn't matter. How New Woke perceives what is said, while permanently scanning the environment for potential offence, is all that matters for fast-asleep Wokers (Fig 292). A doctor in England praised a father for stepping in 'manfully' to bring his daughter for an appointment when his wife couldn't make it, but the doctor and his hospital apologised after the family complained that 'manfully' was sexist (the father was a man). It apparently implied that 'women are there to do the childcare' and not men. The complainants are deeply sad people if they think saying 'manfully' to a man is a subject for complaint and all doctors seeing what happened will no longer be focusing fully on the medical problem of the patient. They will be carefully pre-preparing every statement in their mind before delivering the words. All over the world in every walk of life this verbal tenterhooks and eggshell-interaction is being experienced and destroying natural discourse, driving wedges between people, and causing ongoing daily anxiety with concern about anything you say. This is again what the Cult requires and New Wokers deliver. Here are just a few of millions of examples of discourse contraction that keep people in a state of constant anxiety to avoid saying the 'wrong' thing:

Figure 292: I'm against everything!!!!
(Image by Ben Garrision at Grrrgraphics.com.)

Oxford University's Equality and Diversity Unit tried to accuse people who avoid eye contact with others of 'racist microaggression'; transgender campaigners condemn such phrases like 'born a man' or 'born a woman' as inaccurate and offensive; 'biologically male' and 'biologically female' are deemed 'problematic' by a US gay rights 'media monitoring' group; Suffolk County Council in the UK stopped using traditional 'Cat's eyes removed' warning signs over fears that people thought real cats may have been killed to manufacture these reflective road safety devices; applause was banned by the National Union of Students' Women's Campaign over concerns that it could 'trigger anxiety' among nervous students with whooping and cheering also targeted. Instead people are told to 'applaud' with 'jazz-hands' which means waving your hands in the air silently like a bunch of prats; braided hairstyles on white people are 'cultural appropriation'; the word 'exotic' is apparently 'a major verbal microaggression' with 'nasty racial underpinnings' (me neither); 'Fat-liberation activists' say the term 'fat' 'shames people 'who might not fit the conventional beauty standards of our society', but if you *are* fat and okay with that you can 'reclaim' the word as your 'empowering identity'; a guide released by The New School, a private college in New York, said the size of chairs was deemed a microaggression against overweight people. I take it they mean chairs that are not big enough for fat arses; Lucy Delap, a lecturer in British history at Cambridge, says that words including 'genius', 'brilliant' or 'flair' should be discouraged as they carry 'assumptions of gender inequality and also of class and ethnicity'. Ms Delap can at least be sure that no one will ever accuse *her* of being a genius; migrants entering a country illegally cannot be called 'illegal', but 'all white people are racist Nazis' is still okay; anyone who cooks and names their dish 'Jamaican Stew' or 'Tunisian Rice' while not being Jamaican or Tunisian is guilty of microaggressions in the form of 'cultural appropriation' which also includes any white woman wearing hoop earrings. People from Jamaica cooking an 'English breakfast' are fine, though. Phew; a student at Louisiana State University wrote that women styling their eyebrows to make them appear thicker ('eyebrow culture') is an example of 'cultural appropriation'; 'Mother' is a no, no, because it offends transgender activists. The British Medical Association advised members that mothers-to-be should be referred to as 'pregnant people' to avoid offence and 'celebrate diversity' if not sanity; any term that includes the word 'man' is definitely a felony you sexist bastard; singer Ellie Goulding was accused of racism after tweeting a picture of herself wearing an Native American headdress – 'Don't mock a dying race, you insensitive and ignorant excuse of a person' responded a Woker; referring to the United States as a 'land of opportunity' is a microaggression because it 'asserts that race or gender does not play a role in life's successes'; a lecturer at Harvard Law School was told by a student not to use the word 'violate' as in law violation on the grounds that it might trigger traumatic fears about rape; others said rape law should not be taught to protect *law* students from 'distress'. These students are going to make super lawyers and judges then; Sussex University Students' Union warned against using the pronouns 'he' and 'she' to avoid assumptions about identity. 'They' and 'Them' are said to be the correct, gender-neutral terms. It's good that I don't go there because I'd tell them to stick it up their arse. This phrase avoids microaggressions by the fact that everybody has one – but give them time; 'Where are you from?' or 'Where were you born?' could be racist microaggressions according to the University of California, Berkeley, as 'a covert way to say you don't belong here'; the Student Federation at the University of Ottawa banned yoga sessions. Apparently they were Western 'cultural appropriation' of a practice with its origins in Indian Hinduism and there were 'cultural issues involved in the practice' that related to 'oppression, cultural genocide and diasporas due to colonialism and western supremacy'; Clemson University's diversity training decrees that to be told to be 'on time' is a microaggression as 'time may be considered fluid' in some cultures; a 'Seattle councilman' (shouldn't that be 'person'?) expressed concern that hosing down human excrement on sidewalks might be insensitive 'because it brought back images of the use of hoses against civil-rights activists'.

STOP! STOP! Have mercy, *please.* Only a short while ago you would have been laughed into oblivion if you said any of these things would happen never mind that they would increasingly be the norm.

The dark side of ludicrous

It is easy just to shake the head, laugh and dismiss all this as monumental craziness with the usual 'political correctness gone mad' and not to see it as that relevant in the overall scheme of things. Oh, but it is. The tidal wave of insanity is transforming human society and discourse and rapidly re-writing the language in exactly the way that Orwell described in *Nineteen Eighty-Four*. Confirmation of the real intent comes with a $1.5 million grant by the *US military* to develop a device to allow AI to identify 'microaggressions'. Why would the military with its focus on killing people be so concerned about people being upset by microaggressions? Well, of course, it wouldn't. Behaviour modification is the motivation in all of this. The money is being handed to associate professors Christoph Riedl and Brooke Foucault Welles to embark on a three-year project to develop a microaggression sensor. My timbers would be shivered if it doesn't already exist. Riedl said:

The vision that we have is that you would have a device, maybe something like Amazon Alexa, that sits on the table and observes the human team members while they are working on a problem, and supports them in various ways. One of the ways in which we think we can support that team is by ensuring equal inclusion of all team members.

Put another way: Modify behaviour and give AI an ever greater say in decision-making until it is making *all* the decisions. Now the reason for such military (Cult) interest becomes clear. We are heading down a dark and dangerous road and we have reached the point where the New Woke *Independent* in the UK published a parody article it believed to be real calling for hate laws to be imposed on comedians who tell the 'wrong' jokes. The article was submitted under a fake name and not checked out even though its real author, comedian Andrew Doyle, said the content was 'clearly a hoax'. Doyle has become well known for his invented character of New Woker Titania McGrath through which he exposes New Woke extremism. The article was published suggesting comedians become subject to hate laws because it promoted the *Independent's* own stance. New Woke tyranny is now so extreme that parody is dying in the face of real life. An example is the British feminist writer Vicky Spratt who said that men who are not willing to date Woke women was an 'insidious' trend that will inevitably lead to women being killed by terrorists. How do you make men go out with women they are not attracted to – state-enforced dating? How about a Western version of arranged marriages? A confirmation of the sinister nature of the New Woke mindset and its imposition came from Kyle Jurek, a 'field organiser' for the openly-socialist Bernie Sanders campaign to be US president. Jurek was caught on camera by the Project Veritas undercover journalism operation saying this about America under a Sanders New Woke government:

> Germany had to spend billions re-educating their fucking people to not be Nazis ... we're probably going to have to do the same fucking thing here. That's kind of what Bernie's fucking like ... 'Hey, free education for everybody', because we're going to have to teach you not to be a fucking Nazi.

Who decides what constitutes a 'fucking Nazi'? *They do.* Those decisions are made by black and white minds that are blind to context or shades of grey. It is or it isn't. You are or you're not. You are an 'us' or a 'them'. Tyranny was imposed by Orwell's Big Brother's police state in ways akin to the brutal and notorious Stasi secret police in communist East Germany which enforced the dictatorship and employed an army of spies among the population to inform on those who 'transgressed'. PC censorship, surveillance cameras and fingerprint/eye-reading technology in schools and colleges are specifically designed to make Big Brother tyranny the 'norm' so the adults that children and students become will accept the same norms in global society. Today colleges have organisations under names like 'diversity units' that impose re-education PC orthodoxy on students while encouraging, even paying, other students to spy on their friends and colleagues and report PC transgressions to the authorities. This includes reporting academics for being non-PC in lectures and their comments. Many have been fired or forced to step down for the mildest of statements and as they have gone those that remain are frozen in fear of transgressing in any way. Britain's University of Sheffield announced plans to hire 20 of its own students to police language on campus that could be seen as 'racist' (opening your mouth is enough). They are being paid £9.34 an hour as 'race equality champions' to seek out microaggressions which it defines as 'comments or actions that might be unintentional, but which can cause offence to a minority group'. What about offence to a majority group? Oh, no, that

doesn't matter. It's not about equality and inclusivity – exclusivity is what New Woke is after (Fig 293). Sheffield vice-chancellor Koen Lamberts, who will not have enough self-awareness to see that his policy mimics Stasi-like political tyrannies, said the initiative sought to 'change the way people think about racism'. More like simply changing the way people think as in East Germany, the Soviet Union,

Figure 293: Inclusivity is not enough because that's not the Cult agenda.

North Korea and China. Among the university's targeted microaggressions is anyone asking why everything has to be a race issue and why people are searching for things to be offended about. Impose your tyranny and then make it an offence to question the tyranny. Another microaggression that must be stamped out apparently is 'being compared to black celebrities that I look nothing like'. I wonder when such people plan to grow up? Not soon, I'll wager.

The tyranny of 'I am right'

If New Wokers believe themselves to be all-knowing then everyone who disagrees with them must by definition be wrong or motivated by racial and sexual bias or other dark motives. The only right becomes *I am right* – there is no other possibility. New Wokers despise for this reason freedom of speech for those with different 'wrong' views. If *I am right* then it follows that those who disagree with me are wrong and what is the point of freedom of speech for those that are wrong especially when humanity faces the existential threat from climate change and mortal dangers from rampant racism and sexism? Freedom of speech must be deleted to protect our freedom. It's so obvious and given that *I am right* it must be true. These attitudes have both been downloaded from a multitude of Cult sources and been further ingrained through the encouragement of narcissism and a sense of entitlement where me, me, me is the only show in town. These are some officially-recognised traits in what is termed narcissistic personality disorder. Observe the behaviour of extreme New Wokers and you'll see the stupendous correlation:

- An exaggerated sense of self-importance (*I am right*).

- A sense of entitlement (*I am right* and what I say must be acted upon).

- Require constant, excessive admiration (*I am right* and you must recognise that and look up to me as your moral and intellectual superior).

- Expect to be recognised as superior even without achievements that warrant it (*I am right* and what I say requires no factual basis. *I am right* is enough).

- Exaggerate achievements and talents (*I am right* because I am all-knowing).

- Believe they are superior and can only associate with equally special people (*We are right*).

- Monopolise conversations and belittle or look down on people they perceive as inferior (*I am right* and if you disagree with me you must be inferior).

- Expect special favours and unquestioning compliance with their expectations (*I am right* and you must do what I say – see Greta Thunberg).

- Take advantage of others to get what they want (*I am right* and so what *I am right* about must be enforced even if it means crushing people).

- An inability or unwillingness to recognize the needs and feelings of others (*I am right* and if you challenge that fact we will target you with abuse, demonisation, a Twitter storm and efforts to get you fired and destroy your life and your family's life).

- Behave in an arrogant or haughty manner, coming across as conceited, boastful and pretentious (*I am right*, er, that's it).

- Become impatient or angry when they don't receive special treatment (*I am right* and you must dismantle the industrial system immediately no matter what the consequences because *I say so*).

- Significant interpersonal problems and easily feeling slighted (*I am right* and you say I'm not??*).

- React with rage or contempt and try to belittle the other person to make themselves appear superior (*I am right* you moron).

- Difficulty regulating emotions and behavior (*I am right* and I get *sooo* angry when others say something different – they must be de-platformed. *Silence them!*).

- Experience major problems dealing with stress (*I am right* and I get so stressed when people won't accept that).

- Have secret feelings of insecurity and vulnerability *(I am right* and I won't have that questioned with facts in case you prove that I'm not).

Narcissistic *and* insecure and vulnerable? What a psychological combination. Narcissism is indeed a cover for insecurity. I feel so sad for them and how they have been perceptually and emotionally abused. Life behind the New Woke facade must be a psychological nightmare.

Save us from everything

New Wokers are now indeed so vulnerable that they demand 'trigger warnings' to warn them of anything upcoming in lectures or exams that might upset them. The 'anything' is closing in on the *literally* anything as young people are pressured to be upset and offended by an ever-lengthening list of perceived horrors and verbal transgressions (Fig 294). Trigger warnings alert the permanently anxious and fearful of something coming up in a book, video, lecture or stage play that might trouble them. This has now reached such extraordinary levels that trigger warnings

Figure 294: New Woke's permanent state.

include: *Theology* students alerted to upcoming images and discussion of the crucifixion so they can choose to leave; archaeology students warned about any 'well-preserved archaeological body from an archaeological context' in case they find it 'a bit gruesome'; forensic science students warned before lectures involving blood patterns, crime scenes and dead bodies; Carleton University in Canada removed scales from the campus fitness centre to protect people with a special sensitivity to learning their weight. One student said: 'Scales are very triggering.' Don't bloody use them then. An article in the London *Guardian* listed some trigger warning subjects: misogyny, the death penalty, calories in a food item, how much a person weighs, terrorism, drunk driving, racism, gun violence, drones, homophobia, post-traumatic stress disorder, slavery, victim-blaming, abuse, swearing, child abuse, self-injury, suicide, talk of drug use, descriptions of medical procedures, corpses, skulls, skeletons, needles, discussion of 'isms', shaming, slurs (including 'stupid' or 'dumb'), kidnapping, dental trauma, discussions of sex (even consensual), death or dying, spiders, insects, snakes, vomit, pregnancy, childbirth, blood, Nazi paraphernalia, slimy things, holes (don't ask) and 'anything that might inspire intrusive thoughts in people with obsessive compulsive disorder'. *The New York Times* reported that activists want many classic works to have trigger warnings printed on them like health advisories on cigarette packages. Shakespeare's *The Merchant of Venice* would need the label 'contains anti-Semitism' while Virginia Woolf's *Mrs. Dalloway* would require a warning that it mentions suicide. Chinua Achebe's *Things Fall Apart* is another book of concern which may 'trigger readers who have experienced racism, colonialism, religious persecution, violence, suicide and more'. The 'anti-Semitism' industry and Israel Protection Racket has even called for trigger warnings to be inserted in the Bible and Koran to alert readers to upcoming 'anti-Semitic' texts. The self-obsession and sense of entitlement is just extraordinary from self-appointed 'leaders' of 0.2 percent of the world population. The 'anti-Semitism' Protection Racket was New Woke before New Woke and has had a highly-significant role in creating it. Kent University professor Frank Furedi rightly calls the trigger warning phenomenon and its associated 'snowflake' mentality the therapy culture, therapeutic censorship and the medicalisation of reading.

The term 'trigger' appropriately comes from the language of the mind control industry as I have been describing for decades long before it became part of PC New Woke culture. 'To trigger' refers to key words, phrases or sounds that trigger or activate pre-programmed 'Manchurian Candidate' behaviour by mind-controlled assets of government/military/intelligence agency mind control programmes like the infamous MKUltra in the United States. We need to face the fact

Figure 295: You need protection. Give me your freedom and leave the rest to me.

for the sake of young generations that they are being subjected in schools and universities to systematic mass mind control and a major part of that is to have them perceive themselves as victims. New Woke verbiage is constantly focused on seeking out ever more reasons for victimhood. The Cult sub-text is that once you fall for being a victim you give your power away to the perceived victimiser and look for state protection from them often in the form of censorship (Fig 295). Victimhood is worn like a badge of honour by many New Wokers and allows the ongoing life dramas of the grievance, victim culture in which so many permanently live. You say you're a victim? Well, choose not to be. You say you're offended? Well, choose not to be. Do that and see your power return. I don't wonder that New Wokers suffer from ongoing anxiety when they are manipulated to want protection from anything that moves and a lot that doesn't. Everything around them is potential danger from which they must be protected and most notably the perceived demise of the planetary ecosystem through climate change. The technique is to indoctrinate children and young people to fear an ever-lengthening list of dangers and then have them demand that Big Brother authority protects them from the big bad world (Fig 296). This is the real reason for the 'Health and Safety' culture in the UK

Figure 296: I demand you take away everybody's freedom to save us from what you have told us to be frightened of and offended by. (Image by Ben Garrision at Grrrgraphics.com.)

in which once every-day happenings are now perceived as highly dangerous. Words that people say are defined as a form of violence that require protection and this provides the added bonus of censoring people against the list of PC offences and fears. Many parents mollycoddle their children and protect them from all upset to the point where they don't have the emotional skin and skills to cope with life's challenges or anyone questioning their perceptual certainty. Writer Claire Fox, a former Brexit Party member of the European Parliament, said:

> Why are we surprised that teenagers demand safe spaces? Historically, adolescents might have been risk-takers and adventure-seekers, but today we rear children to perceive the world as an endlessly scary place. NGOs and charities [ultimately the Cult], in particular, promote panic … Reared on a diet of disaster hyperbole, it's no wonder children grow up scared of their own shadows …
>
> … Today, parents go to ludicrous lengths to eliminate all risk from their children's lives. Inevitably this narrows their horizons and teaches them to be less daring. Health-and-safety mania means the young are denied resilience-building freedoms that past generations enjoyed, such as playing outdoors, climbing trees and walking to school unaided.

Fox said modern mollycoddling means that the young have been prevented from engaging in activities such as leapfrog, marbles and conkers while a child-protection industry actively encourages children to see potential abuse everywhere. Schools are surrounded by prison-like fences and systems which constantly infuse a perception of danger. Fox described how safeguarding has become the top priority in every organisation that works with children to the extent that parents are banned from taking photographs of their own children at swimming galas and adults are only allowed into many parks 'if accompanied by a child'. She continues:

> There is no mystery to the absurdities of the Stepford Student. Nor should we wonder at their sudden appearance. We – adult society – protect children from criticism and suspend our critical judgment in order to massage their self-esteem. We scare them rigid by 'catastrophising' an endless list of fears. We make them hypervigilant about potential abuse from adults and their peers. We encourage them to equate abusive words with physical violence. And we have, in short, shaped our own overanxious, easily offended, censoriously thin-skinned Frankenstein monster. We created Generation Snowflake.

Some students say that even being called a snowflake is dangerous to their mental health and there's a whole new industry specialising in the psychological health of children and young people in the light of so many being diagnosed with 'mental health problems'. Suicide among the young is soaring. There is a reason for all this – children and young people in big numbers are being driven crazy by a merciless Cult-controlled system that wants to break their spirit and have them bow to its will for the entirety of their adult life.

In search of certainty

Insecurity seeks out *certainty* to placate that insecurity and from this comes the 'moral' and non-factual 'certainty' of New Wokeness. 'I am right' also includes 'I am nice', 'I am good' and 'I am ethical' – all with the proviso that anyone thinking differently must therefore not be right, nice or ethical (Fig 297). UK activist Jordi Casamitjana took his employer to a tribunal to secure the term 'ethical veganism' as a 'protected

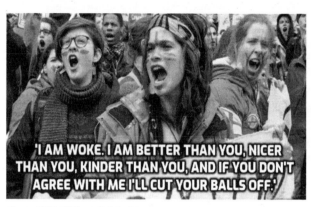

'I AM WOKE. I AM BETTER THAN YOU, NICER THAN YOU, KINDER THAN YOU, AND IF YOU DON'T AGREE WITH ME I'LL CUT YOUR BALLS OFF.'

Figure 297: Woke self-delusion.

philosophical belief'. He won the case – of course he did. Notice the 'protected belief' was not 'veganism', a lifestyle choice people have every right to make, but 'ethical veganism'. Casamitjana said this involved much more than not eating food with animal ingredients: 'It's a philosophy and a belief system which encompasses most aspects of my life.' This is New Woke intersectionality. His lifestyle includes: Walking rather than taking a bus to avoid any 'accidental crashes with insects or birds' (so he never unknowingly stands on insects when he walks and never travels in cars?); on occasions that he does take a bus he avoids holding on to leather straps; and he doesn't eat non-meat figs because they are 'grown with a symbiotic relationship to a microscopic wasp' and so 'you [can't] be sure whether any of the wasp's larvae is still inside the ripened fig and therefore I consider consumption of figs to be inconsistent with veganism'. Will you tell him or shall I that everything is conscious? 'Ethical veganism' is not something that can be defined unless you credibly define 'ethical'. One person's ethical is another person's madness. The dictionary tells us that ethical 'pertains to or deals with morals or the principles of morality and pertains to right and wrong in conduct.' Who decides what is right and wrong? Who decides what is ethical? Casamitjana likely thinks it's ethical to demonise the gas of life and tell kids they are facing climate meltdown when I say that's seriously irresponsible and unethical.

To the New Woke mentality what *they* think and 'ethical' must be interchangeable. How could it be any other way? My view by contrast is that those who want their claim to be 'ethical' enshrined in law might benefit from checking out the definition of up-your-own-arse. Dr Jeanette Rowley, a vegan rights campaigner, said that in her direct experience 'veganism is a way of life that defines the vegan individual as much as someone saying, for example, they are Christian or Muslim'. New Wokeness is indeed a religion designed to eventually replace all the others. Rowley said 'the ethical vegan' [one means the other by definition] makes a defining statement that their outlook on the world is grounded by justice, respect, duty, care and compassion in a community of sentient others, human and nonhuman, whom they do not wish to harm and whom they will endeavour to protect.' What about harming non-meat plant consciousness? What about the 'respect' of seeking to impose their life choices on everyone and in many cases abusing those who make another choice? What about potential harm to the health of converts when the idea that one food choice fits all is fantasy and at odds with the evidence? What about frightening kids into believing the world could end and telling them veganism is essential to saving humanity so your agenda prevails? What about the enormous numbers of bees and insects that die (along with animals) as a result of the artificial pollination (known as 'migratory beekeeping'), herbicides and pesticides involved in most plant-based production? What about the devastation of human society and employment through ridiculous demands to curtail the gas of life that produces the very vegetation they eat? I could go on and a lot of things that vegetarians and vegans eat is absolute crap like soy and tofu. Once anyone claims a monopoly on being 'ethical' the hypocrisy and contradiction soon starts to unravel. They would put their case much more effectively if many were not so obviously convinced of their own perfection and self-purity. But, then, that is the very foundation of New Wokeness. Are they trying to convince the rest of us – or *themselves*?

Why facts are so dangerous

Narcissists are always insecure and vulnerable. Narcissism is a cover to hide their insecurity from other people and again most importantly from themselves. All the most outwardly and exaggeratingly self-assured characters I have met have been frightened little boys and girls behind the facade. Genuine self-security doesn't need narcissism when it doesn't need external confirmation or self-promotion of its sense of identity through the reaction of others. You agree with me and think I'm intelligent and wise? Okay. You think I am wrong and an idiot? Equally okay. Genuine security treats them both as twin imposters. It is *in*security that needs the facade of perceived security not least to convince itself. In the same way *I am right* is terrified of being wrong and it's another reason New Wokers don't deal in facts. They are manipulated to perceive everything through the filter of emotion and moral superiority which is easy to induce. Facts are the sworn enemy of such emotional certainty and they have to go. New Woke congresswoman Alexandria Ocasio-Cortez captured the theme perfectly when she said: 'There's a lot of people more concerned about being precisely, factually, and semantically correct than about being morally right.' Without the facts what is there to be 'morally right' about? What is the bloody point of being 'morally right' about a human-caused climate disaster that is *not happening?* Facts immediately usher black and white perceptions into shades of grey and this is another reason why facts are so yesterday. How can you sell a belief in imminent climate mass extinction which isn't happening if you have to deal in facts? The impossible only becomes possible when you can lie and misrepresent while censoring those with a factual response that exposes *I am right* as utter bollocks. This technique can be seen everywhere with climate change, race, sexuality and transgender activism. It goes like this: When you cannot support your stance and demands with facts and would therefore lose the debate you shut down the debate with abusive labels, de-platforming and media censorship.

There is no need to factually justify your re-writing of human biology and that's good because you never could. Instead you assert that a man can be a woman and vice-versa by merely claiming to be so. You campaign to have professors of biology dismissed and their careers destroyed for saying otherwise. Once a few scientists and academics have been vanquished by the mob others will keep their head down or even parrot New Woke claptrap to protect their careers and income. This has happened across a great swathe of subjects and situations as Yuri Bezmenov's 'demoralisation' has hurtled so fast to its 'normalisation'. In this way schools and college campuses have been invaded and overrun by Cult New Wokeness and places of alleged 'education' have become initiation centres for a lifetime in La, La Land. I saw a British 'social activist' (whatever that is) called Lee Jasper complaining that film producer Guy Richie should have had a 'broader social conscience and responsibility' over the content of a film about gangsters because it was 'not reflecting the kind of future which is of a more inclusive sense of British nationalism.' The *fact* that gangsters don't act like New Wokers and the film was about *gangsters* could not breach the New Woke filter which believes that everything should be portrayed as it would like it to be rather than as it really is. Facts are so lethally dangerous to the Cult's collective emotional reality construct that they must be censored and deleted. This is being done through the Cult's 'education', mainstream media, Silicon Valley and government legislation where only one version of everything is allowed to be emphasised and eventually even heard at all. Put these aspects together of faith-based belief and unquestioning certainty with silencing the blasphemers and you have a religion. New Wokeness is a faith-based, facts-unnecessary, religion or cult which imposes its will by indoctrinating the congregation and accepting no dissent. Burned at the stake becomes a Facebook ban and a Twitter flogging. Jesus walked on water becomes the gas of life is a deadly pollutant and a man can be a woman simply by saying so. The Climate Cult, as a sub-division and in many ways foundation pillar of New Wokeness, is itself a religion as you would expect in such circumstances.

Systematic censorship

We return here to knowing the outcome and seeing the journey. The outcome planned by the Cult in terms of speech and information is that eventually no one will see or hear anything not sanctioned by the World State. We are heading there with quickening speed through Silicon Valley censorship of alternative information by Cult-owned billionaires (rapidly advanced since the lockdowns) while New Wokers break into applause (well, 'jazz hands') with each new extreme of silencing free discourse. I have described in other books the sequence going back to the Cult's (Rothschild) Frankfurt School of social engineering in the 1920s which led to the 'sudden' (long-planned) emergence of political correctness or 'PC'. Political correctness is a Cult ruse to manipulate the target population to silence itself. Who needs a sheep dog when the sheep keep each other in line? I have said that every facet of the New Woke agenda follows the Cult agenda and that, of course, is why the Cult has created and funded New Wokeness into being. Political correctness and the end of free speech is yet another example. Freedom of speech is the freedom to speak and while that exists the situation can never be reached where the public only ever see and hear what the authorities allow. Free speech would always have its say and expose the official narrative which makes free speech a locked-on target for both the Cult and its storm troopers in New Wokeness. We see why Cult-manipulated New Wokers have to be clinically-adverse to facts that challenge *I am right* and why they demand that such facts are censored. If it was about seeking truth all views and information would be welcomed from which truth could be discovered; but it's not about truth. It's about selling *un*truth for which facts would be fatal. Therefore facts and non-PC opinions must be silenced while fact is replaced by emotion-triggered 'feelings'. Facts or 'truth' are claimed to be only the norms of an oppressive state. Those confident of their views have no problem with other opinions being heard and they know that free speech only exists when all views can be communicated, debated, challenged and questioned. Anything less than that and there is no freedom of speech only freedom to conform to what is considered acceptable to the censors. Research at King's College in London found that one in five students, or 22 percent, say they can't speak their minds while on campus with 59 percent of those with conservative views reluctant to express them. The figures would be even higher as a percentage if the study had been focused only on non-New Woke students. Given that New Woke opinions are not subject to censorship when they parrot their orthodoxy they would believe that students are free to express their opinion. They are if you're New Woke, but try voicing a different one and see what happens. You are *free* to say what we tell you. You are *free* to do what we tell you.

The key is *when* speech is challenged. Is it before the point of delivery or after? The difference between the two is the difference between freedom and tyranny. I am not saying that people should be able to say anything without consequences such as urging violence against people and property. The question is *when* do you deal with it? The Cult wants you to believe that algorithms and other pre-post censorship should be used to stop 'unacceptable' views and information from ever being seen or heard; but who decides what is 'acceptable'? Well, the authorities do – the Cult in reality. The Totalitarian Tiptoe first makes a case for censorship that it believes most people would accept like, for instance, campaigning for terrorism. Once the precedent of pre-post censorship is set they roll out more and more reasons to expand its use – 'fake news', 'hate speech', 'upsetting people' and so on – with ever-widening definitions through the Totalitarian Tiptoe of what the terms mean and what can be censored in their name. The narcissistic insecurity of *I am right* provides the motivation to support the silencing of facts that would expose *I am right* as *I am wrong*. By contrast if speech is challenged after the point of delivery there could never be a situation in which authority could dictate what you could see and hear. It would all be out in the open and dealt with in the open. There are laws against incitement to terrorism and violence and they can be invoked without extremes to expand censorship into areas that are only silencing dissent and opinion. It would also mean that authority would have to justify its claims about speech in open debate and courtrooms instead of letting algorithms do it quietly without challenge. This could all be done so long as speech is challenged *after* the point of deliver and, anyway, don't we want to know who is campaigning for terrorism instead of pushing it into the shadows? The new definition of 'anti-Semitism' tells the story. A fair and accurate definition would be 'hatred and discrimination towards Jewish people for being Jewish'. This, however, does not preclude criticism and exposure of the far-right Sabbatian-Frankist-controlled government in Israel or the political philosophy of Palestinian-destroying Zionism. The

Cult has expanded the definition to include both and protect the Cult and its agents. Ironically many New Wokers are critical on college campuses of Israel and its treatment of Palestinians and they are being censored themselves in a prelude to what will happen on a much bigger scale when their New Woke utopia is in place and they are no longer needed to demand it. Israel-owned and sponsored Donald Trump signed an executive order decree in late 2019 that added 'Jewishness' as a nationality to the list of prohibited 'discrimination'. This was specifically designed to ban criticism of Israel and Zionism, especially on college campuses, and at the same time Trump endorsed the new definition of 'anti-Semitism' which includes ... criticism of Israel and Zionism. The UK government of Boris Johnson has former Labour Party MP and ultra-Israel *fanatic* John Mann as its 'anti-Semitism' tsar to brand critics of Israel as 'anti-Semites'. Johnson has also passed laws to target the Boycott, Divestment, Sanctions (BDS) movement which calls for Israel to be boycotted over its apartheid regime that many New Wokers criticise. Be careful what you wish for New Wokers or you just might get it. In the case of criticising Israel you already have.

Who are you? I'm LGBTTQQFAGPBSM

At the core of New Wokeness is self-identity. The above list of letters depicting ever-multiplying self-identities is actually used by an American University and with 26 letters in the alphabet and the possibility of using each one as many times as you like we are far from finished yet. Who are you? I am LGBTTQQFAGPBSM. How far is that perceptually from being *All That Is, Has Been, And Ever Can Be*? The Cult must be laughing itself to sleep. A Liberal Democrat politician in the UK came out as a 'pansexual' in early 2020 which I can only think must relate in some way to the kitchen. There are so many reasons why the Cult instigated identity obsession and identity politics. Firstly it's about enslaving people in even tinier self-identity myopia than ever before. Imprisoning perception in only five-sense reality while firewalled from

Figure 298: Little Me becomes Littler Me.

expanded awareness is vital to human control. Before New Woke the Cult was limited to labels like man, woman, race, culture and religion to entrap five-sense identity and prevent expansion into identity with True 'I' – *The One*. The invention of identity politics gives the Cult limitless potential to sub-divide and sub-divide those labels (Fig 298). With each sub-division people identify with ever-smaller and fine-detail-defined labels and senses of self that squeeze them into ever-smaller perceptual Bubbles and ever-greater disconnection from *The One*. How can you identify with the True 'I' when your sense of self is defined by a letter amid a daisy-chain of others? Why do people have to define themselves in such detail anyway which includes agender, androgyny, aromantic, asexual, bicurious, bigender, binder/binding, biological sex, bisexual, butch, cisgender, demiromantic, demisexual, genderqueer, gender variant, gynesexual/gynephilic, pansexual, queer, questioning and third gender? Who gives a damn? Decide how you want to live your life and live it. Why do people have to give that choice such a fine-detail name and even more why should choices that they have every right to make be imposed on the rest of us? In Britain a well-known TV presenter called Philip Schofield 'came out' as 'gay' after 27 years of marriage and such a fuss and circus followed. Why do we have to be told where he sticks his thingamajig? Who cares except him and his family? Get on with your life, it's none of our business. Another celebrity felt the need to tell us she had just had sex for the first time in five years? *Why?* Who could care less apart from her and the bloke involved? Narcissism enters the equation for sure with New Woke identity-obsession in terms of attention seeking, look at me, me, me, and what I want is how things must be. Whatever the individual reason may be to publicly identify with a sub-label the same result will always follow. Their Bubble of 'I-am-a' continues to diminish in size and perception and that advances the Cult agenda magnificently. Identity politics is encouraging people to identify the 'I' only with a sexual preference. Do people really believe that who they are is where they stick their dick? Or don't? *Bloody hell.* What have we come to? None of this is happening randomly. It's the Cult at work and I am happy to take the abuse from New Wokers for what I say when unless they *awaken*, instead of Woke, they and their children are going to live out their lives in a technological dystopia long after I have relocated to Infinite Forever.

Two other Cult motivations for identity politics are divide and rule descent into tribalism and the imposition of the Big Brother state (Fig 299). There are far too many people in the world for the

Figure 299: This, of course, is the whole point of identity politics.

Cult to control them all. They plan to do that soon by connecting the human brain to artificial intelligence, but for now they don't have the numbers to impose their will on a population on its way to eight billion if people would choose not to cooperate. They overcome this problem as they always have by manipulating people to control each other in line with the Cult agenda (something we have seen in abundance in the lockdowns). Divisions generated by New Wokeness are self-evident with the obsession with race, culture and sexuality which offer endless potential to divide the general population and even the sub-divisions of self-identity. We see this increasingly happening as the revolution consumes its children. The calling card of New Wokeness is to do *everything* that it condemns others for doing and there are many precedents for this with religion. Inquisitions in their various forms that persecuted, tortured and killed untold millions were orchestrated by alleged followers of 'gentle Jesus' and opponents of 'the evil Satan'. They were convinced of their self-purity and believed they were doing the 'work of God' while acting like the children of Satan and murdering men, women and children in the name of the 'Prince of Peace'. You could hardly imagine such an inversion or self-delusion, but had anyone pointed this out to the inquisitors they would never have seen the contradiction. The belief in their own self-righteousness would have firewalled any reappraisal or glance at the mirror. They were *right* and anyone who disagreed had to be deleted. It's what 'God' wanted them to do. We have moved on for now from burning at the stake, heated

metal pincers and thumbscrews and today's Inquisition goes for demonisation, vitriolic abuse and attempts to destroy the lives and careers of non-believers (Fig 300). The methods may have changed but not the basic mentality and ideology. It is still what *I* think that must be imposed on everyone.

Figure 300: New Woke is now beyond parody.

Fake 'social justice'

A crucial self-deception required to enforce fascism while claiming to be 'anti-fascist' is to act with cold, heartless, intolerance and be quite happy to wound, hurt and destroy other people and their families while retaining a self-identity as someone kind, tolerant, full of love, coming from the heart, and caring deeply about 'social justice'. Woke 'tolerance' is a state of permanent anger and fury seeking out the 'enemy' with the 'wrong' opinions. Self-deception is such a foundation of the New Woke persona ('actor's mask') that advocates are widely referred to as 'social justice warriors' when their extremists and activists (as with their major funder George Soros) could not give a damn about 'social justice' any more than Cult operatives behind the Russian or Chinese Revolutions which deleted all vestiges of social justice. In the same way they are 'anti-racist' and 'anti-sexist' while being utterly obsessed with race and sexuality and viewing the entirety of human behaviour and interaction through that filter. They are *themselves* racist and sexist as they treat people differently based on skin colour and sex, but they will never see

it. I should remind them again that race is only a label for a brief experience of the same consciousness that we all are (Fig 301). Woke activists don't actually do anything about social justice. They just use the concept to 'smash and destroy' and dance to the impulses of their software download. An Internet commentator described the difference between a genuine activist in search of social justice and a New Woke 'social justice warrior':

Figure 301: Real inclusivity. The awareness that we are all One.

Social activist: 'Oh look, there's no wheelchair ramp into that building. Let's build a ramp.'

Social justice warrior: 'Let's persecute the people using the stairs and make them feel bad for having legs!'

I do understand the approach, though. I mean why should social justice warriors waste their time campaigning and acting in pursuit of homes for the homeless, jobs for the destitute, food for the poor, and the end of wars of mass murder, when there are epic historical battles to be won over whether some bloke calling himself a woman is referred to as 'Her', 'They' or 'Them'? It's all about *me, me, me*, and my self-identity. There are many people on the genuine Left that do care about fairness and social justice and they have allowed themselves to be swamped and hijacked by the social justice fakery of New Woke with its support and promotion by the entire establishment which in the end answers to the One-percent and the Cult. New Wokeness 'fights racism' by being racist; demands tolerance with stunning levels of intolerance; and 'fights hate' with hatred on its face and venom in its mind (Fig 302). They can no more see their inversions and hypocrisy than could the Spanish Inquisition and are certainly not self-aware enough, informed enough, or with sufficient humility, to see that the same Cult behind the Inquisition is the force behind them. New Woke feminist extremists were asked on an Australian television show:

Figure 302: I hate you for hating. Yep, well thought through, mate.

'When trying to bring about significant change when is aggression and violence a better option than assertiveness, strong argument and modelling the behaviour you expect of others?' *Never* would have been the answer if New Wokeism was the genuine article; but it's not. The first Woke extremist replied: 'When none of that other stuff works.' Another said that she wanted 'the patriarchy to fear feminism' and 'the most important thing for me as a feminist is to destroy patriarchy'. She also had a question: 'How many rapists must we kill before men stop raping women?' It was pointed out that in her reply there seemed to be a lot of 'smashing and destroying' to which she said: 'Yes … to create a world in which I am not raped and murdered.' Neither of which had happened to her with the latter being self-evident. Make no mistake New Woke extremists are the Cult's vehicle to 'smash and destroy' democracy and freedom to clear the ground for the Hunger Games Society. As the extremists become ever more extreme they are insisting that other New Wokers share their expanding extremism or they, too, will become 'bigots, racists, Nazis and tools of the patriarchy'. Revolution, your children are served.

Destroying the language and censoring yourself

Advertisements are being infused with every aspect of the New Woke Cult agenda because people see them everywhere and they are a perfect medium for perception and behaviour modification. We have ads being banned for not having a woman in them; for using the term 'girl'; and for violating 'gender stereotypes' by showing a woman caring for a baby. We are told they must be more 'diverse' which means ignoring the world as it is and portraying the world as the Cult wants it to be. Muslim Mayor of London, the mega virtue-signaller Sadiq Khan, revealed the winner of the 2020 award for 'diversity in advertising' which included no white people (Fig 303). You see the theme. 'London's greatest strength is our diversity' said Khan without even a smear of irony. Notice how many mixed race couples are featured in advertisements. I have no problem with mixed-race relationships, I think it's lovely, but when that is consistently portrayed in mass-audience advertisements in a far greater ratio to what is actually happening there is perception manipulation at work. Human society is being re-formed by hijacking popular culture and the language through political correctness which is a Cult creation destroying discourse and freedom of expression. Crucial to this is policing the language through which people communicate. Delete words used to articulate your opinions and how do you verbalise those opinions any longer? George Orwell wrote in *Nineteen Eighty-Four* about 'Newspeak' which replaced 'Oldspeak' in the Big Brother dystopia. Oldspeak is the former language which contained words to describe thoughts and opinions in detail while Newspeak is a highly-edited and censored language which deletes words describing detail and bans topics and subjects from discourse altogether. Newspeak is the language of today's political correctness deleting words through censorship of opinion in the name of hate speech, fake news, and microaggressions. As generation follows generation those words no longer need to be censored. They are lost in history and not even known never mind used. We *think* in words, too, and when all that is left are the bland, meaningless platitudes of PC-speak the language is no longer there to even *think* in detail. Words in five-sense reality make thought possible. Control words and you control the population even down to how they think.

Figure 303: New Woke inclusivity. But once white people are vanquished they'll be coming for the rest of you.

Politically-correct intimidation leads to the most insidious form of censorship which is self-censorship when the population chooses to remain silent and opinions and information that expose the orthodoxy disappear. With everyone a potential Stasi spy and informant – even family members – and with 24/7 cyber surveillance and microphones in smart televisions, smartphones, computers and even street lamps the fear of saying the 'wrong thing' to any person in any situation silences all except speech that conforms to the official narrative. This is further enforced by potential employers checking social media postings going way back to decide if someone is PC enough to be hired and others being vilified and fired as adults for posts they made as kids when often what they said then was not considered non-PC. Every aspect of this is designed specifically to chill unwanted opinion and debate and Wokers are the current Stasi before a real Stasi takes their place and targets *them*. Authors and publishers are even employing 'sensitivity readers' to check their text. You may have noticed that I don't use them. Comedy has been destroyed by the PC Stasi and few 'comedians' have had the guts or self-respect to stand up against them. Celebrity Luvvies fall over themselves to show they are New Woke. This is what happens once a new orthodoxy takes hold (see 'climate change'). Celebrities and politicians desperate to be liked support and impose the orthodoxy to confirm their Wokeness and self-purity. They want to be seen as 'good people' by those who have also convinced themselves they are 'good people'. These are the same 'good people' with closed hearts and minds who purvey hatred and destroy the lives of those who don't conform to New Woke orthodoxy. Once you have a need to be liked as an end in

Figure 304: Ahhh, the freedom.

itself, as celebrities and politicians do, your independence of thought and action is over. You no longer speak your truth, but only what you think will get a Facebook thumbs ups. I have another approach. People don't like me? I don't give a fuck (Fig 304). Other New Woke PC ruses to silence the population are called 'tropes' and 'dog whistles'. A trope is a figure of speech in which a word or phrase conveys a meaning other than its literal sense (or interpreted by PC zealots to have done so). A dog whistle is defined as 'statements that appear innocent to the general public but use coded language to communicate a secondary message to an intended group'(or interpreted by PC zealots to have done so). Almost anything that people say in criticism of PC-protected groups is now a trope or dog whistle to provide still more excuses to brand people racist and Nazi to justify condemnation and censorship. A classic of the genre is that anyone who says an elite cabal controls the world is labelled an 'anti-Semite' on the basis of the 'trope' that Jewish people control the banking system, media and so on. The speaker does not have to mention Jewish people or even mean Jewish people. They get the abuse and censorship anyway because the 'anti-Semitism' industry and Israel Protection Racket always claims that this is what they mean. It's another fraud to justify censorship which goes on being ever expanded. A writer in the *Canadian Jewish News* said it is 'anti-Semitic' to say that there's a war on Christmas (it's a trope) or to use the terms 'New York lawyers (and bankers)', 'Hollywood culture', 'secularists' and 'internationalists'. Say any of them and you are an 'anti-Semite'.

I am waiting for the anti-whaling movement to be condemned as 'anti-Semitic' for being a dog whistle for the Wailing Wall in Jerusalem where Jewish people go to wail and sway back and forth. 'Anti-whalers are really saying Jews shouldn't wail – they're anti-Semites!' That's too fantastic? Stick around. The world is not simply crazy any more. It's clinically insane.

CHAPTER ELEVEN

Why white people? Why Christianity? Why men?

Hating people because of their colour is wrong. And it doesn't matter which colour does the hating. It's just plain wrong – Muhammad Ali

The way New Wokeness and political correctness have appeared and taken hold with such lightning speed can only be understood by awareness of the Cult agenda for humanity. Cult/New Woke symbiosis is so blatant because one created the other. When you connect New Wokeness to the Cult everything falls into place. Here's a brief summary of only some of the goals they have in common:

- Centralisation of global power (demanded by New Woke to save the world from climate change).

- Censorship of all criticism and exposure of the Cult and its agenda for humanity (demanded by New Woke through political correctness).

- Enslaving perception in ever-smaller self-identities (promoted by New Woke through identity politics).

- Divide and rule (promoted by New Woke through identity politics and the *'I am right'* mentality).

- Transformation of Western society and the dismantling of its culture and way of life (promoted by New Woke through identity politics and open-door immigration from other cultures).

- Targeting of men, white people and Christianity for reasons I will come to shortly (promoted by New Woke through identity politics, claims of 'toxic masculinity', 'anti-racism' which is never applied to racism against white people, and anything goes in condemnation of Christianity while other religions are PC-protected).

- The creation of a no-gender, non-procreating human (promoted by largely unknowing New Woke and transgender activist extremists transforming the world into a no-gender society and indoctrinating children to question their gender when they otherwise would not).

- Disarming the American population before a coup by armed-to-the-teeth AI law enforcement and military (promoted by New Woke with demands for gun bans and confiscation that open the way for complete domination of the population by armed agents of government and a criminal free-for-all especially in rural areas which the Cult wants to depopulate).

There are many other aspects to the Cult agenda that New Wokeness serves magnificently and one is the AI technology endgame. Wherever you look the New Woke mentality and the Cult agenda are as one. All the aspects and sectors of New Woke are Cult agendas – climate change, racial division, sexual division, transgenderism and political correctness. Cult-serving New Wokeness seeks to paper over the cracks of the divisions and contradictions between its fragile minority group coalition through something called 'intersectionality' which is 'the interconnected nature of social categorisations such as race, class, and gender as they apply to a given individual or group, regarded as creating overlapping and interdependent systems of discrimination or disadvantage'. This means when translated from the Orwellian to persuade minority groups they are all united by oppression from society and white privilege and should unite to bring them down despite all that they don't agree on and compete with each other about. Intersectionality is the Cult working to unite disparate groups into a single force to transform society in its image. New Woke activists tend to move between these different 'sectors'. In the end it's all one agenda from the Cult's perspective. German New Woke activist Carola Rackete (how appropriate) personifies these interconnections. She was the 'sea captain' arrested for delivering migrants from Libya to Italy on the pretext of 'saving them' while the Dutch government under whose flag the vessel operated described what she was doing as 'not a rescue service but a ferry service'. Rackete next turned up as a climate change activist supporting Extinction Rebellion, spouting all the Climate Cult rhetoric, and demanding society be disrupted to save the world. She's a professional Woker in other words and there are legions of them. One other point about New Woke and LGBT etc. is the logo which is now *everywhere* of the rainbow colours. The Sabbatian-Frankist arm of the Cult has long developed through a false cover story a series of sinister and draconian laws that it wants to impose on the whole of humanity. This is justified on the basis that the laws were allegedly given to 'Noah' by 'God' and as Noah is the 'father of all post-flood humanity' they must be imposed on everyone. They are called the Noahide Laws and see Appendix 2 for more background. The reason I mention them here is that their logo since way back before New Woke appeared features the same rainbow colours symbolising the rainbow in the Noah flood story. When you are as utterly obsessed with symbolism as the Cult is this is not a coincidence.

A whiter shade of male

New Wokeness and the Cult are targeting *Western* society which for all its many faults has been the freest region of the world. Remember those quotes from earlier by Hebrew 'Rav' David Touitou about the need to destroy European and Christian society before their 'Messiah' can come. The European Union is part of this operation, too. Communist/fascist countries such as China are already heading where the Cult wants the whole planet to go. The West is what the Cult has to change to bring about global dystopia. Climate extremists say nothing about China, the biggest producer of demonised CO2, while vehemently insisting that Western economies are destroyed. Australia won't build new coal-fired power stations because of the Climate Cult while Australian coal fuels power stations in China, India, Japan and other parts of Asia. The total annual carbon dioxide emissions of Australia are less than China's *annual* increase. The West is the target because it's the Cult's target. All of which brings me to the perceptual war on white people and especially white men. The foundation racial group of the Western world is white or 'Caucasian' and here you have the reason why every racial group is protected by political correctness censorship *except* white people. When abuse against one race is allowed, but no other, there is a name for that – *racism*. For those non-white people who think this is okay because it doesn't affect them I give you the words of Pastor Martin Niemöller about Nazi Germany:

First they came for the socialists, and I did not speak out because I was not a socialist.

Then they came for the trade unionists, and I did not speak out because I was not a trade unionist.

Then they came for the Jews, and I did not speak out because I was not a Jew.

Then they came for me and there was no one left to speak for me.

White people are being targeted to a large extent for being the dominant race of Western society which the Cult seeks to destroy. Were that position held by another race *it* would have been targeted and the white race more PC-protected. 'Nothing personal, mate, it's just business' although I do think there are other reasons, too, for the Cult to seek the subjugation of white people. Once again we have the inverted hypocrisy of New Wokeness on public display and it is *calculated* hypocrisy by those in the shadows. We have even had calls for UK national parks to be made 'more diverse' on the grounds that they are 'too heavily weighted towards older, able-bodied white people'. These are landscapes where anyone is free to walk no matter what their racial or sexual background and it's their own choice not to do so if indeed that is the case. Those choices don't suit the agenda, however, and government funding for the parks becomes dependent on more diversity being artificially introduced. What would be the reaction if someone said that a place was 'too heavily weighted' towards black, Asian or Muslim people, or even young people? Reverse racism and hypocrisy is everywhere today and there's a reason for it.

Black singer Stormzy launched a scholarship to fund the fees of black Cambridge University students and good luck to him; but when philanthropist Sir Bryan Thwaites offered two leading private schools a £1 million bequest in his will to fund poor white boys it was turned down by Dulwich and Winchester Colleges for not being 'inclusive'. Thwaites made the offer in the light of white British boys performing worse at school than nearly every other ethnic group. They are less likely to attend university than their peers and they perform relatively poorly in exams. Trevor Phillips, a black former head of the Equality and Human Rights Commission, said poor white boys were 'today's educational left-behinds'. His racial fairness could only end one way and Phillips was later suspended from membership of the New Woke-hijacked Labour Party for 'Islamophobia'. To be banned or suspended by the Labour Party for racism these days is confirmation of your grip on reality. Kehinde Andrews, UK professor of Black Studies at Birmingham City University, director of the Centre for Critical Social Research, founder of the Organisation of Black Unity, and co-chair of the Black Studies Association (you get the race-obsessed picture), referred to Phillips as 'formerly of the Black community' because although you have a black face you are actually white unless you toe exactly the line of the New Woke tyranny. Sir Bryan Thwaites rightly asked: 'If Cambridge University can accept a much larger donation in support of black students, why cannot I do the same for underprivileged white British?' The answer is that New Woke does not seek equality for all – while I *do* – because Wokeness is a Cult-driven agenda that in part is targeting white people as a means to transform Western society. Classic New Woke racist extremism is that the subjugation of black people in South Africa and Zimbabwe was disgusting (true) but black racists killing white farmers and their families in those countries under black rule today is okay and what they deserve (absolutely not true).

In a possible response to this racist denigration of a single race for *being* that race we have had posters appearing with the words: 'It's okay to be white'. One example in Perth, Scotland, was met with the usual storm of New Woke anger. The posters didn't say 'white is the master race' only 'it's okay to be white' – which it is, by the way. It's just a body. 'It's sickening and disgusting to know that people think like this' was one reaction and John Swinney, Scottish Parliament member for Perthshire North, said the signs were 'atrocious' – 'We must stand together to resist this unacceptable material.' Good virtue-signalling Mr Swinney. Well done you. I will take Wokers seriously when they have the same reaction to 'It's okay to be black', 'It's okay to be Asian', or 'It's okay to be Muslim'. Until then I will perceive them as what they are – reverse-racist hypocrites. I am against racism in every form and not only that which suits the Woke (Cult) agenda, thank-you. Significantly the local police said no members of the public had complained about the posters. Their existence had been made known to them (by New Woke activists no doubt) and they were investigating.

What has happened in Sweden and Germany through open-door immigration is the blueprint for the entire West. Swedish society as it had been for at least hundreds of years is already gone and what has happened is irreversible thanks to New Wokeness controlling the country. Neighbouring Finland is seriously Woke with 34-year-old Social Democrat Sanna Marin becoming the world's youngest prime minister in late 2019 heading a cabinet dominated by women (12 of the 19 ministry positions) and a coalition of four other parties all led by women with three of them under 40. Take an imbalance and reverse it is the Woke technique when ability and experience should be the criteria for government and not age, race or sex. Finland is another country feeling the chill on speech from political correctness for those who question events including the effect of immigration from other cultures on the Finnish way of life. What you can't talk about or criticise is *always* an aspect of the Cult agenda.

Yale University, home of the infamous US president-producing Cult secret society, the Skull and Bones, dropped a course on art history 'from the Renaissance to the present' due to the 'overwhelming' whiteness, maleness, and straightness of the artists according to a report by *The Yale Daily News*. Course instructor Tim Barringer told the newspaper that focus on Western art in a Western country was 'problematic' – a word much beloved of New Wokeness. Student Mahlon Sorensen said: 'If you get rid of that one, all-encompassing course, then to understand the Western canon of art, students are going to have to take multiple art history courses.' That, mate, is the idea in this Cult-driven cultural carnage. Students at Reed College in Oregon successfully campaigned to have all European texts removed from a humanities course and replaced by non-European books as a form of reparations 'for Humanities … history of erasing the histories of people of colour, especially black people'. What a statement about the Woke mentality. To increase the amount of black history you have to delete white history. The fact that the Cult wants to delete white history is pure coincidence. American booksellers Barnes & Noble introduced a series of literary classics for Black History Month with non-white people on the cover – *Dr Jekyll and Mr. Hyde* with a man wearing a turban; *Frankenstein* depicting the monster with brown skin; and Juliet in Shakespeare's *Romeo and Juliet* with brown skin and wearing a headscarf. These were withdrawn after it was pointed out that the text remained the same. The books were written by white people reflecting white culture of the time and how do you promote black culture and history by overwriting white history? Instead of changing white culture classic books you promote black writers portraying black culture. Ah, but if you do that you don't promote black history by erasing white history. You celebrate them both. This is not, however, the Cult's desired outcome. The theme can also be seen with Cult-controlled corporations like the ultra-Zionist 'investment bank' Goldman Sachs which announced in 2020 that it will no longer work on stock market launches with companies that have only 'straight white men' on their boards. Goldman Sachs, which gives hypocrisy new meaning, is headed by a white man, Chief Executive Officer David Solomon, and the same white man theme continues with its finance chief, operating chief and international head. Solomon said at the One-percent-fest World Economic Forum in Davos that the no all-male policy would be imposed in North America and Europe, but not in Asia where diversity is even less prevalent. Well, grab a feather and knock me down. Whatever the company claims to be the motivation behind this it will not be pursuit of 'diversity' for the sake of diversity. Goldman Sachs was founded by Jewish white men in 1869 and most of its partners and almost all of its leaders have been Jewish white men ever since so spare me the sermon about diversity *pl-ease*. Goldman's stance is typical of thousands of examples of corporate giants dictating public and private policy outside the democratic process. This is the very foundation of post-democratic technocracy.

PC-free zone

White people, especially white men, and even more *old* white men (divide young from old), are all racists expressing 'white privilege' according to New Woke extremists. This includes white people sleeping amid the shit, disease and freezing cold on the streets of major cities. By contrast white billionaires of real privilege are fine to New Wokers so long as they are funding 'progressive' groups and censoring 'bad people'. White homeless living on the street are 'white privilege' while privileged blacks like Democrat politician Cory Booker with his rich background and Harvard education are victims of white oppression. White people are all racists except those who ask for forgiveness for things that happened before they were born from non-white people who were also not born when they happened. An Internet video shows a white couple kissing the boots of members of the deeply-racist Black Hebrew Israelites group in penance for what their 'ancestors' did. 'They showing what it means to really salute a prophet and a priest,' one pathetic member says. 'This is a white couple here that's proving they are sorry for what their forefathers have done.' It's not the colour of the skin that matters, it's the colour of the heart and mind, and here you had a black man with the same heart and mind as those white psychopaths who oppressed black people and treated them with contempt. American 'civil rights' leader (hilarious) Al Sharpton is a New Woke hero with his rants and rhetoric against white people despite being a racist, crook, fraud, promotor of transnational corporations, and FBI informant (code-name 'CI-7'). Even super-Woke Vice.com described him as 'a world-class scumbag with criminally under-acknowledged ties to the Mafia'. Wherever there is high-profile racial tension Sharpton is there seeking out the nearest camera to pour fuel on the fire. He has rightly been described as a 'racial arsonist'. No matter that he doesn't give a damn about rights for black people. He attacks whites and that's enough for New Woke. Sharpton was an advisor to President super-fraud Obama who with typical Obamaesque poppycock lauded him for his 'commitment to fight injustice and inequality'. Democratic presidential candidates get their tongues out to secure Sharpton's blessing in pursuit of the black vote that largely can't stand him. Black people who reject New Woke (most of them) know a fake when they see one. Great numbers of black people see through it all and realise that to judge anyone by their colour, including white people, is racist, ridiculous and divisive (on purpose). Black and other non-white people born or settling in the West who want to protect its culture are considered 'enemies of the revolution' as are gay and transgender people who don't support the hysteria and impositions of the mindless fake revolutionaries. It's amazing how many New Wokers come from white comfortable or wealthy financial backgrounds while posing as oppressed (privileged 'victims') or promoting themselves as the heart-on-the-sleeve voice of the truly oppressed without permission or the personal experience to do so (Fig 305). What if the minority doesn't want them as its spokespeople or isn't offended by what New Wokers insist they should be? That's just too bad. *I am right* – we know best (Fig 306). The way minorities are patronised by New Woke is extraordinary.

Figure 305: It's all about me.

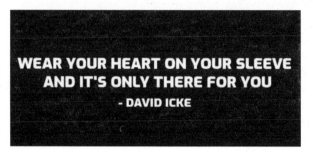

Figure 306: Love is truly expressed by deeds, not words, and certainly not by virtue-signalling.

Group dynamics

There's no perception of individual behaviour or circumstances irrespective of race (real non-racism). Everyone has to be judged as a group. This group *bad* – all other groups *good*. The fact that this is what the Cult wants to divide and rule is another pure coincidence and absolutely nothing to worry about. Cult-manipulated New Wokeness takes a genuine oppression such as disgusting white-instigated black slavery and male domination of women and presents it both as far worse now than it was at its grotesque historical peak and pins the blame on the entire white race and male population for things done by the few before most white people and men today were even born. Richard Fochtmann, a US Democrat candidate for senator, was caught on a phone camera *celebrating* the alarming increase in suicides by white men. He said: 'Today I saw a thing and it said a lot of men, white men, were committing suicide, and I almost thought, "Yeah, great" – then I thought about it little more, and I thought maybe I shouldn't say that out in public.' Some of his audience actually laughed. Donald Trump asked in response to the comments: 'What kind of animal is this?' Fochtmann described him with the usual New Woke irony and deleted self-awareness as a 'racist'. It is also relevant to note that Fochtmann is Jewish. Think what would have happened had someone celebrated the suicides of Jewish men? The statement would have been dubbed 'hate speech' and could possibly have led to a prison sentence. What happened to Fochtmann? *Nothing.* Jewish writer and professional racist Noel Ignatiev, who died in 2019, was co-editor of *Race Traitor,* a journal founded on the belief that 'treason to whiteness is loyalty to humanity'. Ignatiev said: 'Make no mistake about it: we intend to keep bashing the dead white males, and the live ones, and the females too, until the social construct known as 'the white race' is destroyed – not 'deconstructed' but destroyed.' I ask again: What would be the response if someone said that about the 0.2 percent of the global population that is Jewish? But then when Israeli rabbis have no consequences for saying that slaughtering Palestinians gets Jews closer to God and killing them is a 'religious duty' you know that anything goes so long as you are either not white or ultra-Zionism doesn't like you. There is a clear and obvious agenda to target white people and to deny that in the face of the evidence is to dig a hole in the desert and insert your head.

Saira Rao, a 'first generation Indian-American activist' and former Colorado congressional candidate, hosts something called Race2Dinner – 'a place to start thinking through how you actively uphold white supremacy every minute of every day'. This means, apparently, self-loathing white women programmed to hate themselves and their race paying $2,500 to attend dinners where they are castigated by Rao and her mate Regina Jackson for being racist. One jabbering attendee apologised for apologising with this perspective: 'I want to hire people of colour. Not because I want to be … a white saviour. I have explored my need for validation … I'm working through that … Yeah. Um … I'm struggling.' It's re-education and women of all 'colours' would benefit by giving this pair of prats the finger and getting on with their lives. I went to the Race2Dinner website to be met by a massive headline saying: 'White women. Let's talk racism and your complicity.' Saira Rao is so New Woke it's beyond parody. She does, however, provide an insight into the mentality and its contempt for white people. Among her gems is that 'private messages of support is another form of white supremacy'; the helicopter crash that killed the black multi-millionaire basketball legend Kobe Bryant and his daughter was somehow connected to Donald Trump, racism and bigotry; and that 'white women's obsession with "being nice" is one of the most dangerous tools of white supremacy'. There is added irony is that Rao's India is a seriously racist country with the caste system still alive and well despite claims to the contrary. The UK *Daily Mail* exposed how dating website Shaadi.com, which claims to be the top site for Indian singles, insists that users state their caste or 'sub-community' when they join. The *Mail* said:

> It was discovered that a profile set up by a Brahmin, who are elite in the caste system, would not be offered potential matches from the lowest of the social divisions – the so-called untouchables, officially known as 'scheduled caste'.

But, no, you can't be racist unless you are white. The sight of non-white extremists acting with the same state of mind as white extremists while thinking they are somehow morally 'superior' is a real head-shaker. We reached another stage that was always coming in 2020 when the Climate

Cult was declared 'too white'. German-based Filipino climate activist Karin Louise Hermes said she left the movement because of its whiteness and lack of intersectionality: 'Anti-racism and anti-capitalism need to be made part of organizing … If "Green" policies fail to consider anti-racism and migrant rights, how is any person of colour supposed to feel voting for them or organizing in the same spaces?' How about to protect the planet if you really believe it is on the brink? Instead she was off into the sunset indignant that the Climate Cult was not paying enough attention to what 'whiteness, capitalism, and inequality have to do with climate change' (*not* caused by humans). Open the window will you? I need some air. No, scrap the window. Make that a large gin.

Woke is not a joke

We have long passed the point where just laughing at such idiocy is not enough as it increasingly becomes public policy. Filmmaker and world class New Woke virtue-signaller Michael Moore said that white men are not good people and 'you should be afraid of them'. That, I take it, includes him? Moore warned on the so appropriately-named Useful Idiots podcast that people should cross the street if they see three white men approaching because at least two would have voted for Donald Trump. The legend in his own mind, but no one else's, said:

Two-thirds of all white guys voted for Trump. That means anytime you see three white guys walking at you, down the street toward you, two of them voted for Trump. You need to move over to the other sidewalk because these are not good people that are walking toward you. You should be afraid of them.

Moore has turned talking mind-numbing bollocks into an art form to match his 'anti-establishment' films that exquisitely serve the Cult agenda. The desired psychological consequence of all this is that white New Wokers tend to hate themselves for being white. They wallow in emotional states of self-loathing and wish they had been born into one of their oppressed minorities. Democrat presidential candidate Elizabeth Warren was so desperate to be seen as a persecuted New Woke minority that she hilariously invented Native American ancestry that didn't exist and a story about her discrimination for being a woman that never happened. In fact, women are hardly a minority with their numbers close to those of men. The New Woke rule is that not only should white people be hated they should hate themselves and spend the rest of their lives paying penance and begging forgiveness for *things they didn't do*. The body, no matter what the colour or background, is only a vehicle for the consciousness that we *all* are. This makes racism *and* New Woke reverse racism absolutely child-like. How easy it is to see within New

Wokeness the Cult agenda for disconnecting humanity from the awareness that we are all *One*. How inverted genuine equality has become in the New Woke fake 'Left' since civil rights leader Martin Luther King said this in his 'I have a dream' speech in 1963:

> I have a dream that my four little children will one day live in a nation where they will not be judged by the colour of their skin, but by the content of their character.

So do I, but, if you're white, New Wokeness does not. Is it really yet another coincidence amid this psychological New Woke war on white people that testosterone and sperm counts are plummeting in Europe and North America along with Australia and New Zealand? Even CNN ran an article highlighting the fact that 'total sperm count in North America, Europe, Australia and New Zealand dropped by up to 60% in the 38 years between 1973 and 2011' with the trend continuing to present day. 'If sperm was an animal, science might worry that it's heading toward extinction in Western nations,' the article said. No one knew for sure what was causing this, the article continued, but it had been blamed on processed foods, chemicals in food, radiation, air pollution and water. All of which lead back to the Cult with smartphones in trouser pockets right up there along with the ever more significant 5G.

♫ With the cross of Jesus taken off the door ♫

Western culture is founded on Christianity and that doesn't mean, of course, that everyone is a Christian. I'm certainly not. It means that the architectural and intellectual influence of the Christian religion has been the backdrop to the development of Western society. Christian influence and legacy is weaved into the fabric of the Western way of life. Now, with the Cult targeting Western society, we can see why political correctness protects from criticism and exposure every religion *except* Christianity as with every race *except* white. New Wokeness has become ingrained so quickly that even stalwarts of the Christian religion like the UK Archbishop of Canterbury Justin Welby have become advocates of the very Woke/Cult agenda that seeks to destroy their religion. The major Christian festival is Christmas (ironic because it's a pagan midwinter festival), but because Christmas is associated with Christianity it has to be targeted by the Cult and its Wokers to the extent that saying 'Merry Christmas' is now code in the bewildered mind of Woke for 'white supremacy' (Fig 307). US Supreme Court judge Neil Gorsuch found this out when he uttered the deeply offensive, clearly Nazi, greeting on television in 2019 and faced a backlash. A British mother said she was 'shamed' for saying 'Father Christmas' (indicating a man) instead of the 'gender-neutral' term 'Santa' (which is an anagram

SAY MERRY CHRISTMAS AGAIN AND I'LL SHOOT

IT'S 'HAPPY HOLIDAYS' YOU RACIST BIGOT

Figure 307: Christian festivals must go – but don't you dare criticise anyone else's you Nazi.

of Satan). The last time I looked the mythical figure with the beard and sleigh was a man – hence Father – and had not yet transitioned into a lady in red stockings called Geraldine. The 'shamed' mother told a newspaper she felt 'on edge' in the wake of the criticism. Fortunately, I have a cure for that which goes like this: 'Don't be so bloody ridiculous.' There, all sorted, with no need at all to be 'on edge'. Non-Christian religions are allowed to practice their festivals and rituals in Western countries without any push-back or interference and they should be if they operate within the laws of the country that reflect the values of the country. It's the bias for one and against another that I am highlighting and the reason for it.

Attempts to indoctrinate children into non-Christian religions in Christian-dominant or secular countries can be seen in places like Sweden among many others. Furious Swedish parents reported how teachers at their school told pupils to kneel on prayer mats facing Mecca while the class was divided by gender with girls told to gather at the back of the room. What uproar there would in the media if Muslim children were told to practice Christian rituals against the will of their parents. The school said it was 'role play'. *Bullshit*. Anyone with a brain knows what it is. A further reason for the assault on Christianity (and in the longer term all current religions) goes much deeper. I don't support any religion, but for all their many flaws, faults and misrepresentations, they do accept the existence of another power or reality beyond human. Some even describe their 'God' in terms of light and love while obscuring that simple fact with a tsunami of ritual, rules and regulations. Religions were created as an interim step between the many ancients who understood reality in a much more expanded way and the Cult's end goal of isolating humanity in a sense of reality in which only the Bubble is perceived to exist. The interim Tiptoe has been major religions that believe in another force outside the Bubble and yet worship this as an external, dictatorial, judgemental God and not as the non-judgemental whole of which we are all an expression. In other words we are not 'God' and must only do what 'God' wants. What *does* God want? The priests will tell you, or rather the Cult will.

The endgame is to remove *any* concept of another force beyond human reality and 'New Woke is being used to achieve that end in Western countries by targeting its major religion of Christianity. Recent polls reveal how successful this has been. In 2009 the percentage of Americans who identified as Christians stood at 77 percent; by 2019 it was 65 percent. Among Democrats, a political home of New Woke, the fall is even more extreme with 72 percent becoming 55 percent. Those considering themselves 'non-religious' increased from 17 percent to 26 percent. The most significant figure was not polled: What do those who say they are non-religious believe instead? I am not religious in an organised, bricks-and-mortar-religion sense, but I do accept the reality of a state of Infinite Awareness of which we are all part. The Cult wants those who consider themselves non-religious to instead believe in a random mechanical universe in which 'nature' has to be conquered by scientists and experts of the technocracy. You will see when I get to the technocracy that this is of crucial importance to the Cult. I also see the dominoes starting to fall towards the ultimate end of the British monarchy – the monarch is the official head of the Church of England – with what has happened with Prince Andrew, the buddy of mega-paedophile Jeffrey Epstein, and with New Woke self-obsessives Prince Harry and Meghan Markle heading for the airport and relocating to North America. The concept of royalty has served the Cult magnificently and I would be delighted to see it disappear. We have to be streetwise, however, over why suddenly it is taking such potentially mortal blows in the closing years of Queen Elizabeth. Royalty and all its trappings, history, ceremony, buildings, and central influence in law, is, as with Christianity, running through the very fabric of British culture – the culture the Cult wants to destroy to allow assimilation of British society into its global monoculture technocracy. Even the royals are dispensable for the cause when necessary and the Cult agenda enters a whole new stage.

Toxic masculinity

New Woke portrays non-Woke men as demons and purveyors of 'toxic masculinity' in the promotion of another Cult agenda. Men and women are being driven apart with the #Metoo movement employing the usual Cult-encouraged New Woke extremism of blaming every man for the actions of a few like ultra-Zionist former movie mogul Harvey Weinstein. *He* abused women so *all* men are to blame. Many men now watch every word in the company of women and seek to avoid being in a room alone with them in case they are accused of something. This is seriously damaging male-female interaction as it is meant to (Fig 308).

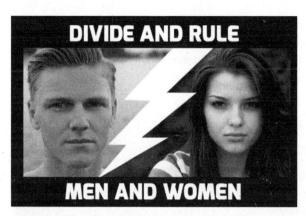

Figure 308: New Woke is driving men and women apart on the Tiptoe to ending all gender and male-female procreation. (Image Gareth Icke.)

Advertisements are employed as usual to sell the required perception of men in abominations like the Super Bowl maximum-audience ad by Gillette, owned by elite corporation Proctor and Gamble, which was a blatant attack on men and tarred them in their entirety with 'toxic masculinity'. The sexual and racial themes in increasing numbers of advertisements are promoting societal change through perceptual change and remember they are paid for by major Cult-controlled corporations that couldn't give a damn about 'equality' and 'inclusivity'. Music videos aimed at the perceptions of children and the young have taken the same path with the 2020 Taylor Swift video 'The Man' an example that can only be described itself as toxic. Every stereotype about toxic masculinity is included to influence the perceptions of the young when even the mildest hint of female stereotyping attracts a storm of protest and, if it appears in advertisements, a ban. A commentator asked: Do you want your daughters growing up thinking all men act the way Taylor Swift portrays men in this video? Do you want young girls growing up resentful and distrustful of men? Do you want your sons to feel attacked and bullied by powerful women advocating for them to be shamed and subjugated by the whims of angry new-wave feminists? The answer to all of those questions from a mind in any way in a state of balance would be 'No'. But if you are the Cult your response would be *Yes! Yes! Yes!* We even had Ann Francke, head of the UK Chartered Management Institute, saying that bosses should crack down on men talking about football and cricket at work because many women 'don't follow those sports and they don't like either being forced to talk about them or not being included'. The scale of sheer undiluted arrogance that it must take to think you can tell people what they must and must not talk about is beyond my comprehension and so is her lack of awareness about how many women do like sport. Here's another New Woke mind patronising the people she claims to speak for. What are the chances of someone demanding that women don't talk about subjects of their choosing in case men feel left out? We live in a world now so infused with narcissism that imposing your will on others is taken as a gimme and a right. 'Toxic masculinity' is only code for masculinity as the Cult seeks to feminise the male and masculinise the female on the Tiptoe to the no-gender human. Crucially it wants to reduce the male hormone testosterone in men to delete the type of man that straightens his spine, lifts his chin and says: 'I'm not having it'. Men are being 'de-masculined' into passivity and you have testosterone levels falling around the world along with sperm counts. The feminising of men is being achieved on many fronts including contact with the contents of plastic

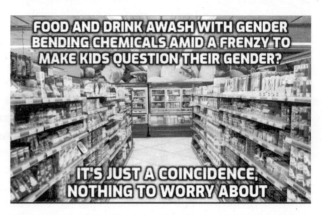

Figure 309: One big racket to transform human sexes and sexuality.

bottles, till receipts, and other items and substances containing gender-bending chemicals including food and drink from plastic containers (Fig 309). This is a media report about a study at Exeter University in the UK:

> Four out of every five British teens have their hormones upset by gender-bending chemicals found in plastics, new research suggests. The chemical, called bisphenol A (BPA), is used to make plastics, including materials that come into contact with food. But it can mimic the female sex hormone, estrogen, and cause a lower sperm count in men.
>
> The chemical is also thought to be linked to several different types of cancer, including breast and prostate [which is soaring]. Researchers at Exeter University studied the blood and urine of 94 teenagers aged 17-19 and found 80 percent had the hormone-disrupting chemicals in their bodies.

In the gender-bending chemical era those identifying as gay or 'LGBT' is rapidly increasing and a US study estimated that those born before and across the millennium to be nearly twice as likely to identify as LGBT as other American adults – 'Millennials Are the Gayest Generation', as one headline put it. This is a *coincidence*? Dr Richard Day told those paediatricians in 1969 they were going to 'make boys and girls the same' as people became 'gender-neutral'. In support of the chemical infusion is the psychological onslaught in which being gay is celebrated and being straight is increasingly marginalised and again 'so yesterday'.

We see the same bias that we do with whiteness and Christianity and this was never more obvious than when UK TV celebrity Phillip Schofield came out as 'gay' in 2020 after 27 years of marriage. Celebrity Luvvies swooned and you would have thought he had dived into a raging torrent and pulled out a dozen drowning children. Schofield was described as 'very brave' when The System celebrates you for declaring your gayness. See what happens if you come out as straight on Twitter. '*Straight??* What are you a bloody pervert?' It's not only men that the Cult wants to weaken physically and psychologically – it's everyone – to create a compliant population that looks to Big Brother for protection. Men and their testosterone are, however, the prime target. Patricia Hunt, a researcher at Washington State University who first identified BPA as a cause of cancer and other diseases, developed a more accurate means of measurement and her subsequent findings were stunning. Dr Hunt said in her report in 2019 that 'safe' limits of BPA decided by the US Food and Drug Administration are *44 times higher* than what can be considered 'safe'. This is no more a 'mistake' than all the other 'safe' limits that turn out to be way too high. It's done for a reason and in this case to manipulate gender and de-masculinise men. Since the introduction of the birth pill women have been peeing estrogen, or oestrogen, the primary female sex hormone, into the water supply to be consumed by men. Chemical pollution in rivers is changing the sex of fish. Soy products consumed by many vegans and vegetarians can raise estrogen levels and lower testosterone and those diets are being heavily promoted by the establishment to 'save the planet from climate change'. Seth Siegel, author of *Troubled Water* about the shocking amount of pollutants and drugs in water supplies, described the effect on fish:

I don't want to call it transgender fish, but I will call it inter-sexual fish. One recent study studied 19 rivers and they found that there was a very high level of male fish that were now growing eggs from the estrogen that is getting into the water … 50% of the fish they studied in the Great Lakes had psychiatric drugs in their brains and their organs. So, Prozac, Celexa, and drugs like that, and generics.

The only way it comes into the water supplies, humans take those pills, they pee it out after they've taken it a few hours later. It gets flushed through the wastewater treatment system into a waterway. All perfectly legal. Exactly compliant with the law. And then it gets uptaken in fish. It gets uptaken in our drinking water. It gets uptaken in the water we use for our irrigation.

Men, especially white men, are at the bottom of the New Woke hierarchy along with white people in general and Christianity. No aspect of political correctness is willing to protect them as it protects other New

Woke categories. Even saying that all lives matter is now a breach of political correctness so crazy has it become. Well, sod that – *All LIVES MATTER* because they *do*. Notice, however, how white men are promoted as the 'good guys' when they send the troops and bombers at the Cult's behest to attack non-white countries. It's nothing to do with 'right' and 'wrong'; it is whether it suits the Cult agenda or not. Conservatives with a capital and lowercase 'c' are a particular focus for PC abuse and Silicon Valley censorship for the first two syllables in the word … *conserve* – to 'protect something, especially something of environmental or cultural importance, from harm or destruction'. Yes, *conserve*-atives (small 'c') usually want to conserve Western culture and this is another reason they are treated as they are in flagrant contrast to those who wish to usurp and delete that culture.

'Anti-fascist' fascism and the billionaire alliance

From all that I have discussed and exposed in the last few chapters we can explain other apparent mysteries of the New Woke-hijacked political or liberal 'Left'. One is why people who call themselves 'liberal' and 'anti-fascist' behave with such a fascistic lack of liberalism. A dictionary definition of 'liberal' is the following: 'Someone who has liberal views believes people should have a lot of freedom in deciding how to behave and think.' Synonyms given for 'liberal' include tolerant, enlightened and open-minded. You could hardly find a better definition of what New Wokeness is *not*. The self-deceit necessary to perceive yourself as 'liberal' in the light of extreme illiberalism is fantastic, but essential. How can the Cult manipulate those with genuine liberal views to demand the imposition of a fascistic tyranny when genuine liberals believe people should have freedom in deciding how to behave, speak and think? Instead you ingrain *I am right* self-identity and self-righteousness (which you call 'liberal') and get New Wokers to believe that everyone else (including *genuine* liberals) are wrong, Nazis, bigots, racists, sexists and expressions of pure evil. In this way *I am right* self-identity and Big Brother behaviour becomes the new 'liberal' while real liberals who want freedom for everyone are 'far-right fascists'. The campaign by the New Woke Democratic Party hierarchy to destroy the liberal presidential campaign of Tulsi Gabbard, a woman of colour, exposes the extreme nature of New Woke hypocrisy. She may be a woman and she may not be white (she's a Samoan-American Hindu), but none of that matters when she stands for ending the American-Israeli wars in foreign lands demanded by the ultra-Zionist Project for the New American Century. With this background we can see why New Wokers who claim to be of the 'liberal Left' are in alliance with billionaires and mega-corporations like financier George Soros and Silicon Valley Internet censors. They still claim to be against billionaires and the One-percent, but the evidence is quite the contrary. The genuine Left once railed against the power of corporations and marched in support of freedom of speech. Today we have the inversion of both with New Wokeness organisations funded to the tune of tens of billions by Soros and others from the One-percent who could not care less about social justice. At the same time every new censorship of non-Woke opinion by Internet corporations is greeted with 'social justice warriors' punching the air. The reason the dynamic has changed is that New Woke is founded on Cult-invented identity politics and not social justice. Billionaires and corporations are not judged by their scale of social destruction, but by whether they speak the language of New Woke and bung their organisations a wad of money. When the Left was genuinely demanding social justice it would obviously target those who were accumulating mega-wealth for the few at the expense of the many. Soros would never have been allowed to fund the genuine liberal Left. They would have seen him coming from 200 miles away and the same with fake New Wokers like Zuckerberg at Facebook, Page and Brin at Google, Wojcicki at YouTube, Dorsey at Twitter, Wales at Wikipedia and Cook at Apple. British comedian Ricky Gervais talked in a brilliant speech at the 2020 Golden Globe Awards about Apple hypocrisy: 'Apple roared into the TV game with *The Morning Show*, a superb drama about the importance of dignity and doing the right thing … made by a company that runs sweat shops in China.' He told the assembled New Woke Hollywood 'A-listers' who insisted on a vegan meal after turning up in gas-guzzling limousines: 'You say you're Woke but the companies you work for, unbelievable, I mean, Apple, Amazon, Disney – if ISIS started a streaming service, you'd call your agent wouldn't you?' Gervais went on:

> So, if you do win an award tonight, don't use it as a platform to make a political speech. You're in no position to lecture the public about anything. You know nothing about the real world. Most of you spent less time in school than Greta Thunberg. So, if you win, come up, accept your award, thank your agent, thank God, and fuck off, okay?

How refreshing it was to see a very rare celebrity with balls calling out the fakery of LA Hollywood and Silicon Valley Hollywood. New Wokeness does not challenge the billionaires – it breaks bread with them. The obsession is with identity and *not* social justice. As long as billionaires and their corporations support New Woke PC identity positions they are 'one of us' and 'on our side'. The fact that they don't mean it and act in ways that cause phenomenal social *in*justice does not enter the equation. All the billionaires have to do is hand out the dosh, pose as Woke, use the language of PC and censor all those that question or challenge New Woke *I am right* orthodoxy. This is where the apparently bizarre alliance comes from and why New Wokers are the foot soldiers of the Cult agenda of the One-percent. It explains why the Cult-controlled FBI was exposed many times for infiltrating and undermining the then genuine Left and targeting its leaders like Martin Luther King while today the FBI's focus is on the Right and New Woke is allowed to operate unmolested so long as it refrains from criticising Israel. Whatever is the Cult agenda at any stage it will be enforced by Cult-controlled agencies like the FBI and CIA and the rest of the Deep State and Permanent Government.

I emphasise again that I am not condemning New Wokers as people. Many are genuine in what they believe and in my view just seriously misguided. It's the manipulation and its source and goal that I am exposing. I understand why Wokers do what they do, think what they do, and feel such anxiety about the world around them. The programming is merciless and incessant on the say-so of psychopaths moulding the young into adults that will demand 'social justice and inclusivity' which is code for the post-fact, post-freedom, post-industrial Big Brother Hunger Games Society.

CHAPTER TWELVE

Where are we going – if we allow it?

By far the greatest danger of artificial intelligence is that people conclude too early that they understand it – Eliezer Yudkowsky

The Time-Loop simulation has been spinning through its sequence to a specific destination and we are now living through its endgame – synthetic humans with synthetic minds known as artificial intelligence or AI. This twin goal connects 'smart' technology to the transgender hysteria.

The control system structure and nature of the Hunger Games Society is planned to be a technocracy in which scientists, engineers and other unelected 'experts' run the show (and every human mind) on behalf of the Cult and its non-human masters. We are seeing the technocracy in the making with the ever-increasing global dominance of Silicon Valley which has vastly increased still further in the wake of the 'virus' lockdowns. You'll find some excellent background information at the website Technocracy.news and I can recommend a book called *Technocracy Rising* by Patrick Wood. Promotion of technocracy emerged publicly in the 1930s (although it goes back further) and most predominantly operated out of Columbia University School of Engineering. Despite the failure to win wide support at the time its advocates continued to pursue their agenda behind the scenes and now they are sprinting for the line. Interestingly, Aldous Huxley's *Brave New World* (1932), George Orwell's *Nineteen Eighty-Four* (1948) and Dr Richard Day's speech to the paediatricians in 1969 all came when or after technocracy promotors set out their ambitions for human society. All three very accurately predicted current events. Adolf Hitler and the Nazis operated a technocracy in many ways and I have described in my books how at the end of the war more than 1,600 Nazi technologists were spirited out of Germany to the United States under a military and intelligence escape plan called Operation Paperclip (Fig 310 overleaf). These were the technologists that would establish NASA and ran the infamous United States military-intelligence mind-control programme

MKUltra (Mind
Control Ultra). The
letter 'K' for
'control' comes from
'Kontrolle', a
German word for
control, to
acknowledge the
source of the
programme. Among
these German

Figure 310: Some of the Nazi regime technocrats brought to the United States from Germany after World War Two under Operation Paperclip.

technologists was Werner von Braun, a member of the Nazi Party and SS, who designed the V2 rockets the Nazis fired at Britain. Von Braun designed the Saturn V rockets for the US Moon programme while working at NASA/NAZI. The Cult and its technocracy have no borders just as they don't want the world to have any. Technocracy demands a monoculture global society which is why the Cult is targeting all cultures to fuse them into one. Hence we have systematic mass immigration and a war on Western culture before absorbing all the others. Dismantling Western culture is only stage one. Defined borders and boundaries of every kind are the target of the Cult including biological boundaries between men and women.

If you don't want anyone to know – don't do it (Chinese proverb)

China, the Cult's blueprint for the world, is already a technocracy thanks in large part to covert Cult technology transfers from the West through cusp organisations in The Web like the Trilateral Commission. Trilateral documents from the 1970s reveal this fact which has been confirmed by subsequent events. Big-time Cult insider Zbigniew Brzezinski, National Security Advisor to President Jimmy Carter, described in his 1970 book, *Between Two Ages: America's Role In the Technetronic Era*, how a technocracy that would emerge from its precursor stages, communism and socialism. You could call technocracy a form of 'technological Marxism/fascism' in which the police state is not even imposed by humans in uniform, but by artificial intelligence dictating through cyberspace, robots and other technology controlled by unelected technocrats. Brzezinski co-founded the Trilateral Commission in 1973 with another life-long Cult initiate, David Rockefeller, and he was a 'political scientist' at Columbia University where a technocracy movement was publically spawned in the 1930s. The Rockefeller family have had major connections with the university. Bill Clinton attended Columbia where he was taught by Professor Carroll Quigley who would later publish books exposing how a small cabal was manipulating world events and the direction of society. It was during Brzezinski's time as US

National Security Advisor that relations were 'normalised' between the United States and China while Cult-owned Bill Clinton played a major part during his presidency in opening America to Chinese goods and infiltration. This is a glimpse of Brzezinski's technocratic vision from 50 years ago:

> Such a society would be dominated by an elite whose claim to political power would rest on allegedly superior scientific know-how. Unhindered by the restraints of traditional liberal values [which New Woke is destroying], this elite would not hesitate to achieve its political ends by using the latest modern techniques for influencing public behavior and keeping society under close surveillance and control. Under such circumstances, the scientific and technological momentum of the country would not be reversed but would actually feed on the situation it exploits …

> … Persisting social crisis, the emergence of a charismatic personality, and the exploitation of mass media to obtain public confidence would be the stepping stones in the piecemeal transformation of the United States into a highly controlled society.

What Brzezinski accurately predicted in 1970 (because he knew the plan) is what we have fast emerging today with so much more due to come (more words that I wrote before the 'virus' lockdowns which were triggered by happenings that first emerged in China). Technocracy is what Cult agents mean when they talk of a post-industrial and post-democratic society which is being advanced by the climate change and 'pandemic' hoaxes. See how it all fits together? The Cult has been developing its China blueprint technocracy with a view to its expansion across the world. China (the Cult) is infiltrating global society through money, technology, infrastructure projects, railways, and myriad covert means while also heading out into space. The world is planned to be centrally-controlled by a 'Smart Grid' in which everything, including all technology and the human brain, is connected to the Internet and a global Wi-Fi 'cloud' with all the shots called by artificial intelligence or AI. China is a leading player along with the United States and Israel. Cult-controlled Morgan Stanley has predicted the next phase of Chinese growth will come with 'smart super-cities through 5G connectivity, smart grids, renewable energy and modern transportation' (the first 'smart city' to go online in China was Wuhan just before the 'virus' emerged from there). The investment bank sees China's current 60 percent of the population living in urban areas expanding to 75 percent by 2030 – an increase of some 220 million people moving to cities. Morgan Stanley Chief China Economist Robin Xing said: 'In our view, China is poised to be a global leader in smart city and city cluster development.' In our *view*? No – in our *knowledge* of what is planned. All that I have described there is straight off the pages of the Cult blueprint for humanity. China's gathering influence on India represents a combined population of 2.8 *billion* and that's some 36 percent of the world population even without China's other regions of influence in Asia, North and South America, Africa and even Europe. Gigantic levels of systematic outsourcing of manufacturing to China by American and worldwide corporations at the expense of jobs at home has made the West dependent on keeping China sweet despite the criticism of the trade links by Donald Trump. This dependency was driven home after the coronavirus outbreak in China in late 2019. A reported *96 percent* of America's antibiotics alone now come from China and something similar will be true with other countries. What if China decides as an act of war to cut off supplies of essential products it now dominates that were previously produced in America by Americans? This is precisely what the official government-controlled Chinese news service threatened in terms of drugs as the coronavirus hoax expanded out of China to the United States and the rest of the world. We will also come to see how many operatives and agents – 'spies' – that China has working within America in areas that include stealing research. Add to this the long list of 'former' US Pentagon military officials who work for China directly or indirectly after 'retirement'.

China's efforts to buy influence in education (and steal research) were revealed in 2020 with the news that Harvard and Yale failed to disclose some $375 million in gifts and contracts from China and Saudi Arabia in the previous four years. *The Wall Street Journal* reported that American universities have hidden $6.5 billion received from foreign countries since 1990 with lots of money from China included. China's infiltration of the United States is already extensive and growing by the day. Remember the Cult controls China as it controls the United States and this infiltration is the Cult transforming American society into its Chinese society global blueprint with Silicon Valley absolutely on board with that. A casualty of this increasing Chinese control is free speech with criticising China in Chinese-funded academia and business heading in the same direction as criticising Israel. You always know your real masters by who you can't criticise. A big supporter of the Chinese leadership is failed Democrat presidential candidate, the ultra-Zionist Michael Bloomberg, who has made a fortune from Chinese investments. No wonder he ridiculously claims that the vicious Chinese dictator Xi Jinping is not a dictator. Bloomberg's global news operation has been accused of blocking the publication of stories exposing corruption in Xi Jinping's family and he admits they submit to China's censorship rules. The more the United States is embroiled by the Cult in mega-costly wars as American society and infrastructure disintegrates the better that is for China which is taking over great swathes of Africa alone by building roads, bridges, railways, skyscrapers and whole cities. One writer described the rapid emergence in Africa of 'Chinese factories staffed with Chinese managers that are supervising Chinese workers that are using Chinese equipment to make their products.' China is colonising Africa with two million Chinese already in the continent and more arriving every week along with ten thousand Chinese companies. The plan is to then impose the control system of the Chinese government which is really the Cult's government. The two are inseparable and the coronavirus hysteria gave the Chinese dictatorship the excuse to impose even more draconian control and offered the rest of the world the same opportunity. I'll come to this hoax in great detail in chapters fifteen and sixteen and how it was perpetrated.

Israel global technocracy

China, Israel, the United States, Europe, etc. are all assets at the deepest level of the Cult and this explains why Israel, controlled by the frontline Cult network of Sabbatian-Frankism, has so many ties with China that go on increasing. The ultra-Zionist Michael Bloomberg connection is only one of endless examples. Israel is central to the global technocracy as I expose in detail in *The Trigger* and Sabbatian-Frankists – not 19 Arab hijackers – pulled off 9/11 to a large part by controlling the computer systems of the Pentagon, the US Air Force hijack response system NORAD, the White House and the Federal Aviation Administration civilian air traffic network. They also controlled and still do the inner core of the American 'Deep State' including the CIA. Israeli intelligence and military front companies cross-reference with US intelligence by employing 'former' CIA personnel to create an interconnecting Cult-serving web both sides of the Atlantic. Israel's ever-increasing global cyber influence is delivered through its vast military intelligence cyber centre at Beersheba and its elite military cyber-manipulation unit known as 8200 with its multiple fronts like the cybersecurity companies Team8, operating out of Israel, and Boston-based Israeli company Cybereason which form a web that connects with Israeli and American intelligence, or the 'Deep State' (Fig 311). Israel military and intelligence networks specialise in setting up 'cybersecurity' fronts posing as private

Figure 311: Part of the massive Beersheba cyber operation as Sabbatian-Frankists that control Israel seek to establish that land as the centre of the global Smart Grid of human control.

companies because to design security protection (in theory) requires the actors involved to have access to the entire computer system and all its codes and passwords. This allows them to write 'security' encoded with hidden 'backdoors' for Israel (Sabbatian-Frankists controlling Israel) to access everything from then on and even manipulate in real time (see 9/11 and *The Trigger*). Given that Israeli 'security' software has been used by governments, intelligence, military and corporations, especially in the United States, you can see the significance for spying, blackmail and stealing data.

Infamous Israeli intelligence arm Mossad and domestic intelligence, Shin Bet, are of course fundamentally involved in all this. Cybereason was founded in 2012 by three 'former' (are you ever?) members of this 8200 military elite cyberwarfare division. Unit 8200 is active in manipulating elections, not least in the United States, through hacking and psychological warfare against the electorate (see the articles of Whitney Webb at Davidicke.com). Funding for this network includes the 3.8 billion that the US government gives to Israel for military expenditures every year. America is funding cyber sabotage against *itself* because Sabbatian-Frankist networks operate in both Israel and the United States and one hand gives the cash to the other. As a result tiny Israel is the biggest recipient of American aid and the contempt that its Sabbatian-Frankist leadership has for America can be seen in the story of the Iron Dome missile defence system. American taxpayers gave more than $1.5 billion to the Israeli government to build the 'dome' system, but when the US military wanted to buy aspects of the technology from Israel which Americans had paid to develop for Israel's benefit the ultra-Zionist government refused to supply the necessary source code to allow the technology to be efficiently deployed. They are laughing at you America. Cybereason software is used by a stream of 'American' companies including Lockheed Martin, the world's biggest arms producer, which benefits so monumentally from any US war. A number of 'simulations' have been run by Cybereason based on scenarios of hacking the 2020 US presidential election. The company has stressed the election manipulation potential of the 'coronavirus' (an article they took down after just an hour). Why? Too much information. Cybereason and this 8200 network operating out of Israel are connected to so-called 'deepfake' AI technology which can very credibly make people appear to say and do things they did not say and do. See the Internet for many examples. Israeli tech firm Canny AI is a deepfake market leader that has partnered with Cybereason and has been funded by Israeli domestic intelligence Shin Bet. Another Israeli cybersecurity firm is Upstream Security which specialises in security for cyber-connected and autonomous vehicles. These systems can be hacked to crash cars, buses and trucks (think terrorist truck attacks) just as anything connected to cyberspace can be hacked and taken over from afar right down to opening and closing car windows. Justin Rohrlich at qz.com wrote this about one Cybereason simulation:

> The Red Team then took control of 50 autonomous cars and five driverless buses – a move that may be more likely rooted in a future reality – and deployed a cell-site simulator that allowed them to track people's locations and intercept their phone calls. They seized control of ... traffic lights, causing accidents, and distributed a deep-fake video of the Democratic candidate engaging in racial and domestic violence.

Cybereason simulated US election manipulation by a foreign state or non-state source – but which state? For sure they would not have mentioned Israel. The Project for the New American Century, utterly controlled by ultra-Zionists who answered to Israel and Sabbatian-Frankism, called in its September, 2000, regime-change document for America (really Israel) to control cyberspace. All the dots connect in the end.

Military control of cyberspace

The Beersheba complex is surrounded by research and development centres of all the major Silicon Valley corporations and involves *literally* an army of soldiers in uniform and others on the payroll who constantly post on the Internet while posing as members of the public to promote Israel's narrative and dub critics 'anti-Semitic'. Beersheba, the biggest infrastructure project in Israel's history, can accommodate 20,000 'cyber soldiers'. Military and intelligence groups and 'private' companies are now to Israel and its worldwide networks all the same team pursuing the same ends. Israel is a global player in Smart Grid technology and control with a view to replacing Silicon Valley in importance and power. Behind the scenes and in the shadows it already has with its controlling presence and influence in Silicon Valley through Jewish owners and heads of key companies that include Facebook (Mark Zuckerberg and Sheryl Sandberg); Google (Sergey Brin and Larry Page); YouTube (Susan Wojcicki); Barry Diller (Vimeo); and Apple (Arthur D. Levinson). As I write ultra-Zionist hedge fund multi-billionaire Paul Singer is reported to be seeking to buy control of Twitter to remove its chief executive Jack Dorsey. Should Singer secure that control Twitter will even more be a vehicle for censorship of any criticism or exposure of ultra-Zionism, Israel and the global cult agenda. What a concentration of Internet power in 0.2 percent of the world population and two percent of Americans to decide who sees what globally. That list of Zionist sympathisers heading Silicon Valley corporations does not include other Zionists like Elon Musk and Google's AI-brain connection obsessive,

Ray Kurzweil. Meanwhile, Paul Singer, like ultra-Zionist Sheldon Adelson, is a big donor to the Republican Party and a board member of the Republican Jewish Coalition which promotes Jewish Republicans. Major Democrat donors include ultra-Zionist multi-billionaires Michael Bloomberg, George Soros (whatever he may say), Donald Sussman, Dustin Moskovitz, a co-founder of Facebook with Mark Zuckerberg, Jim Simons, Seth Klarman, co-founder and chairman of *The Times of Israel*, and Haim Saban who says he is 'a one-issue guy, and my issue is Israel'. Big Tech giants including Google, Microsoft and Intel Corporation have been moving thousands of jobs and billions in investment to Israel while 'America first' Donald Trump, owned by Israel, zips his mouth and then tapes it over. The same Silicon Valley Internet-dominating corporations, including Facebook, are employing leading managers and executives from Israel and its infamous military intelligence. The transfer of cyber jobs and investment from America to Israel is largely driven by yes, him again, ultra-Zionist Paul Singer and his Start-Up Nation Central which is part of the 8200 cyber-control network. Singer's predatory hedge fund destroyed the town of Sidney, Nebraska, as I described earlier. Singer funds the ultra-Zionist-controlled 'think tank', the American Enterprise Institute (AEI), which had very close connections to the Project for the New American Century with its list of regime-change countries from September, 2000. The non-violent BDS Israel boycott campaign is largely thwarted once Israel has complete control of cyberspace which was another goal on the list of the ultra-Zionist Project for the New American Century document. Change 'American' in the title to Israeli, or even more accurately *Cult*, and you're there.

Israeli newspaper *Haaretz* reported that Israeli tech start-ups in New York increased by five times between 2013 and 2017 alone. Crucial to the functioning of the global Smart Grid is quantum computing that takes computer systems on to a whole new level of potential. Israel is again at the forefront of this through companies such as Tel Aviv-based start-up Quantum Machines (QM). We now have enormous Israel-controlled cybersecurity centres opening in Sabbatian-Frankist-controlled New York and paid for with $30 million of American taxpayer money which will take Israeli (Cult) manipulation potential over US computer networks to still new extremes. This includes access to America's voting systems and claims about Russia manipulating US elections are, in large part, to divert attention from Israeli (Sabbatian-Frankist) manipulation. The New York 'cybersecurity centres' are being operated by Israel-based SOSA, a 'global innovation platform' connected to the Israeli military, and Jerusalem Venture Partners (centrally involved in the Beersheba operation) who were tasked by the city authorities to make New York the 'cyber capital of the world' (Fig 312). They are connected to an ultra-Zionist network known as the 'Mega Group' and again I highly

Figure 312: Israel-controlled 'New York'

recommend the detailed articles about these subjects by Whitney Webb. The Mega Group and the 8200 network in general has ties to child-abusing ultra-Zionist Israeli intelligence asset Jeffrey Epstein who ran his child sex network as a blackmail operation for Mossad and hence so many rich, famous and influential people were connected to him including Trump, the Clintons and Prince Andrew. Epstein's 'madam' Ghislaine Maxwell is the daughter of long-time Mossad agent, the late (killed by Mossad eventually) UK businessman and crook-to-his-DNA, Bob Maxwell (see *The Trigger*). Epstein was also an investor for his masters in the Sabbatian-Frankist network in Big Tech and Silicon Valley. Whitney Webb describes 'Mega' as 'a group of pro-Israel oligarchs with clear and direct ties to organized crime, alongside Leslie Wexner, the main financier of Jeffrey Epstein's operation that involved the sex trafficking of minors on behalf of Israeli military intelligence'. Guy Franklin, General Manager of SOSA, is connected to the Israeli American Council (IAC), an Israel lobby group funded by ultra-ultra-Zionist Sheldon Adelson and his wife. Adelson is the biggest donor to the Republican Party and Donald Trump. As a result of this and other reasons when Israel tells Trump to jump he says: 'Yes sir, how high?'

The plan is for the Cult via Sabbatian-Frankism to control the entire Smart Grid of human subjugation from a central point – Israel with its massive nuclear arsenal. Connections that lead to 'tiny' Israel are absolutely fantastic and how clear it is why the definition of 'anti-Semitism' has been expanded and expanded to stop this coming out in the main public arena. The global Smart Grid – with connections to the human brain – is ultimately planned to be controlled out of Jerusalem and Beersheba and this relates to the ancient belief in a Jewish 'Messiah' who it is claimed will rule the world from Jerusalem. Sabbatian-Frankism is founded on this with its 'Jewish Messiah' background and history with self-proclaimed 'messiahs' Sabbatai Zevi and Jacob Frank although for the inner core of the Cult the whole thing is only a cover story for global control. The Cult has designed its agenda from the Jewish perspective to appear to follow biblical prophecy and ancient legend which many in the non-Cult Jewish community have taken to be confirmation of the prophecy and the fulfilment of 'God's will' when in fact they are being scammed to support the imposition of something that will ensnare them as much as the rest of humanity. Those people need to wake up fast. The Jewish messianic prophecy of global rule by a 'World King' out of Jerusalem seemed ridiculous and impossible until the emergence of the Smart Grid and the plan to connect all technology, devices and the human brain to a centrally-controlled AI. The ultra-Zionist crazies and extremists orchestrating the 'invasion' (their word) of Europe by Islam to overthrow Christianity and European society is all connected to this plan and so is the rebuilding of the alleged 'Solomon's Temple' on what Jews and Christians called Temple Mount in Jerusalem where the gold-domed Al Aqsa Mosque stands today. Sabbatian-Frankist-owned Donald Trump has given them everything they want to achieve their sick and sinister ends including moving the US embassy to Jerusalem and promoting the 'Deal of the Century' complete stitch-up of the Palestinians to clear the way for the total control and ownership of Jerusalem where the global technocracy world government is planned to be located. See *The Trigger* for all the detailed background to Sabbatian-Frankist control of the global Smart Grid.

Is it 'anti-Semitic' to ask why Israeli-controlled and military-connected companies increasingly dominate 'smart' technology and systems, effectively globally-control what you see and hear, and set out to modify perception and behaviour, are headed by people from 0.2 percent of the world population? Is it 'anti-Semitic' to ask why Israeli cyber firms connected as they are to Israeli (Sabbatian-Frankist) intelligence and military have so much control over American government, military and intelligence computer systems? They want you to believe that it is for no other reason than stopping those questions being asked. Yet these are questions that must be *constantly* asked and credible answers demanded when you think that 68 percent of Americans get their 'news' (and so perceptions) from social media and that Israeli tech firms are seizing control over Smart Grid technology.

Insider Donovan knew (of course)

I would urge you to read *The Trigger* to find out more about Israel's AI Smart Grid and technocracy ambitions and if you do the real reason for the burgeoning China-Israel relationship will come into sharp focus. China's 'economic miracle' was orchestrated from the West through Cult corporations and by 2001 Hedley Donovan, editor of Cult-controlled *Time* magazine, was describing China as a technocracy. Donovan just happened to be a founding member of the Cult's Trilateral Commission. He wrote:

> The nerds are running the show in today's China. In the twenty years since Deng Xiaoping's reforms kicked in, the composition of the Chinese leadership has shifted markedly in favor of technocrats. … It's no exaggeration to

describe the current regime as a technocracy …

… During the 1980s, technocracy as a concept was much talked about, especially in the context of so-called 'Neo-Authoritarianism' – the principle at the heart of the 'Asian Developmental Model' that South Korea, Singapore, and Taiwan had pursued with apparent success. The basic beliefs and assumptions of the technocrats were laid out quite plainly: Social and economic problems were akin to engineering problems and could be under- stood, addressed, and eventually solved as such.

Donovan said Scientism (the religion of scientific orthodoxy with scientists as the new priesthood) was behind China's post-Mao technocracy and those that challenged its control were considered heretics. Those words were written by a Cult insider in 2001 and cannot be denied today. I have already described China's deeply Orwellian Social Credit System and the stupendous numbers of AI-operated face-recognition cameras supported by eye-scanners and DNA-scanners with nothing left to chance. China is already a technological dystopia and operates at the global cutting edge in all the areas necessary for total human control including, like Israel, AI and quantum computing. I have been saying for decades that China today is the world tomorrow unless humanity opens its eyes and that is now being laid out before us. London police announced in January, 2020, that they would be deploying facial recognition cameras after a 'trial' that was always only a prelude to a permanent roll-out. Other police forces in Britain are planned to follow. Leaked documents in early 2020 revealed that the European Union is preparing to connect national face-recognition databases through its EU-wide database-cross-referencing system known as Prüm. The plan is to link this EU database with a similar system in America as the global surveillance system I have warned for decades was coming is moved into place step by step. It's all the Cult agenda unfolding. General Electric (GE) was paid $30 million by San Diego city council to install thousands of surveillance cameras and microphones in street lights and sold the data collected to third parties earning a billion dollars according to the *California Globe*. So-called 'smart streets' like these are appearing in ever more locations.

The Devil's playground and 'education' control

From this background we can see why 'Woke' Silicon Valley corporations have so many ties to the China dictatorship when those corporations are ultimately owned by the Cult. Global banking is a Cult technocracy in which financial experts make decisions (increasingly with AI) unmolested by elected officials and whoever controls the money controls the world. I have detailed in my books the part played by the

Bank for International Settlements (BIS) in Basle, Switzerland, in coordinating national central banks into *one* global (Cult) network. The Bank for International Settlements is another Rothschild-Rockefeller (Cult) creation. Heads of central banks meet regularly at the BIS to coordinate policy and advance the transformation to global technocracy. No surprise, then, that a *Bloomberg Markets Special Report* in 2018 described the Bank for International Settlements as 'a bastion of global technocracy'. The cashless – (digital / technological) – single world currency is all part of the technocracy plot and so is the increasing impotence of politicians over the power of Silicon Valley technocrats and their global impact on the life of every human being. Government departments the world over are dominated by technocrats of many and various types who drive the 'Deep State' operating beyond anyone who has ever seen a ballot box. *The Technocrat* magazine, the publication of the Technocratic movement, said in the late 1930s: 'Technocracy is the science of social engineering, the scientific operation of the entire social mechanism to produce and distribute goods and services to the entire population.' All of this is happening with increasing severity today. Politicians are losing control as this passes to the technocrats and what is the European Union, so beloved of New Wokers, except rule by an unelected technocracy? The so-called 'democratic' European Parliament is just a cover to hide bureaucratic control. We can understand from this perspective why we had years of delay and resistance to the UK leaving the EU after a majority voted for Brexit in the 2016 referendum and why George Soros, an American citizen, funded groups trying to stop Brexit. It took three more years before the people spoke again in 2019 and finally thwarted the opposition by giving pro-Brexit Boris Johnson a thumping majority in a General Election. How much the *type* of Brexit which emerges will actually free British people from EU technocrats we have to wait and see. Deletion of national sovereignty by the EU is a central demand of the technocracy along with the end of private property, Common Core education (indoctrination), Public-Private Partnerships, carbon trading justified by climate change, and communistic deletion of personal choice and liberties. Each one is a pillar of a technocratic society. The Archontic force in the unseen is itself a technocracy in the sense of manipulating through its simulation and using technology to overcome the limitation of its lack of creative consciousness. There is no need for technology in our out-of-body state where creativity and manifestation is achieved directly through thought and awareness. Control of 'education' and the indoctrination programming of the young has been a prime necessity highlighted by technocrats in the 1930s as 'an educational system to train the entire younger generation indiscriminately as regards all considerations other than inherent ability – a continental system of human conditioning'.

William Akin wrote the following in his 1977 book, *Technocracy and the American Dream: The Technocrat Movement*, 1900-1941:

> A continental system of human conditioning will have to be installed to replace the existing insufficient educational methods and institutions. This continental system of general education will have to be organized as to provide the fullest possible conditioning and physical training … It must educate and train the student public so as to obtain the highest possible percentage of proficient functional capacity.
>
> Since the basic need of society was technical expertise, their education system would abolish the liberal arts, which addressed outmoded moralistic solutions to human problems. It would essentially replace the humanities with the machine shop. In the process, members of society would be conditioned to think in terms of engineering rationality and efficiency. Man, in short, would then be conditioned to assume the character of machines, to accept 'a reality understood in terms of machine-like function'.

I ask everyone to take just a moment to scan the world today in relation to what Akin described nearly 45 years ago. It's *happening*. Constant cut-backs on spending for the arts in schools across the world now becomes easy to explain as does the fusing of children and adults with machines through Smartphones and other means. America's

Figure 313: Funding global transformation behind the smokescreen of 'philanthropy'.

privately-funded and controlled Common Core Education Standards Initiative imposed upon schools across the country is straight from the pages of technocracy literature and backed to the tune of hundreds of millions by Microsoft technocrat Bill Gates and his Bill and Melinda Gates Foundation. My long-time observation of Gates and his funding is that if he backs it then it's bad for humanity (Fig 313). This is the bloke putting billions into worldwide vaccination through his front, GAVI, or the 'Vaccine Alliance'. Wait till I get to the 'pandemic' hoax for a major exposure of Bill Gates and the agenda he drives for his hidden masters. It's sobering to think that Gates' Microsoft has access to most computers on earth. The world has been quietly ensnared while making its latest Google search, sending another text, or posting a picture of its lunch.

This is the case more than anyone with New Wokers. They think they are demanding 'social justice' and old fashioned Marxism or 'socialism' when they are being used overwhelmingly without their knowledge to pressure humanity into a technocracy in which a Marxist/fascist-type dictatorship will be enforced by technology. Climate Cultists are pressing for the dismantling of the global economy as it operates today which must be destroyed for technocracy to replace the current status quo. Prince Charles called for exactly this at the One-percent Davos conference in January, 2020, and so does Pope Francis, another Cult asset, who wants 'a different kind of economy', a 'new economy' and, of course, 'sustainable development'. Global central banks including the US Federal Reserve, Bank of England, European Central Bank and the Bank of Japan are pursuing the same end as they commit to treating climate change as a 'core mission'. It's all the same global web working in unison. Mantras parroted by the United Nations and the Climate Cult such as 'sustainable development', the 'green economy' and 'Green New Deal' are all codes for technocracy. The 'goals' for 'sustainable development' that I listed earlier are still more aims (mostly in disguise) of the technocracy. The end of private property described by Rockefeller insider Dr Richard Day in 1969 is also technocracy policy.

It is no longer a mystery why technocratic billionaires and their corporations now occupy the same bed as Green 'idealists' who require a new description for their childlike naivety when 'naive' does not even nearly suffice. Agenda 21 and 2030 are the script for global technocracy and control by scientists who are planned to be the new God. Remember Greta Thunberg's mantra from this context – 'Listen to the *science*' – and political leaders around the world locked-down countries and destroyed economies and livelihoods because they said they were advised to do so by 'the scientists'. Anyone ask what was the agenda of the 'scientists' and to whom they really answer? A key part of technocratic control is complete power over the distribution of energy – who has it, who doesn't, and how much can be used. Climate Cult, anyone? Non-carbon energy sources will not be able to supply current energy needs in the transition to technocracy and that's the plan with all the deprivation that will cause. Once the global dictatorship is in place, however, they will bring out technology they already know about which takes its energy from the wave and electromagnetic fields of the energy sea or The Field. Legendary scientist Nicola Tesla was doing this in the first half of the 20th century, but his work was suppressed to protect energy companies and the Cult from the consequences of the population having access to free energy both in terms of cost and the way it is accessed without the need to use energy to produce energy. The Cult could use this technology now to 'save the world'. Instead it keeps it under wraps out of self-interest. Technocracy wants control of all resources to be transferred to a global authority while ownership of anything is removed from the population including their homes.

The AI 'human'

Mass control in the Hunger Games technocracy is planned to be enforced by connecting the brain to AI. We have Silicon Valley crazies openly describing such a world and giving a date for activation – 2030 according to Google technocrat Ray Kurzweil (Fig 314). This is the same

year highlighted by United Nations Agenda 2030 which sets out the transformation of global society into a centralised tyranny to save the world from human-caused climate change and 2030 represents the period for the end of the nonsensical '12 years to save humanity' stated by the Climate Cult at the turn of 2019. Prince Charles called at Davos for a

Figure 314: Ray Kurzweil – Frankenstein's sales-pitcher.

transformation of the global financial and economy system by 2030. A study by the UK House of Commons Library estimated that by 2030 the One-percent will own *64 percent* of the world's wealth – the Hunger Games Society. Ray Kurzweil describes how in the 2030 period human brains will be connected to AI and what he calls the 'cloud':

> Our thinking … will be a hybrid of biological and non-biological thinking … humans will be able to extend their limitations and 'think in the cloud' … We're going to put gateways to the cloud in our brains ... We're going to gradually merge and enhance ourselves ... In my view, that's the nature of being human – we transcend our limitations.

> As the technology becomes vastly superior to what we are then the small proportion that is still human gets smaller and smaller and smaller until it's just utterly negligible.

Kurzweil is describing the assimilation of human consciousness (within the simulation) into AI and this begs the question of what is AI? On one level it refers to algorithmic codes and on another to a form of AI that learns from data input and is aptly dubbed 'Learning AI'. The *true* and deeper meaning of AI, however, is something they obviously don't talk about when it reveals where all the Cult manipulation has been leading from the start. This level of 'AI' is the very force that has been orchestrating the perceptual enslavement of humanity all along – the

force known by different cultures and religions as demons, Fallen Angels, Jinn, Archons, Chitauri and the Shining Ones among many other names. We are being invaded (Fig 315). People need to realise that this force while it can take form in fact has no form in its base-state which is waves of awareness that can communicate

Figure 315: Invasion is exactly what it is.

electrically like the human brain. An AI connection with the brain allows a connection with this force that will then *become* the human mind. Up to this point the Cult and its hidden 'gods' have had to control information to manipulate perception to dictate behaviour. Religion has played a

central role in this and now the new religion of Wokeness is coming to the fore with its frenzy of censorship. The censorious 'cancel culture' is vitally important for the Cult as we approach its endgame. What I am describing must be kept from the main public arena or the game could still be thwarted in its finishing straight. Once the AI-brain connection is made even

Figure 316: Step, step, step, tick, tick, tick.

controlling information will no longer be necessary. Human perception and emotional response will come direct from AI with no middleman media required (Fig 316). In those words of Kurzweil: 'As the technology becomes vastly superior to what we are then the small proportion that is still human gets smaller and smaller and smaller until it's just utterly negligible.' Individuality of human perception would be history with a centrally-controlled AI hive-mind taking its place (Fig 317). The AI-brain connection is designed to absorb humanity even deeper into the simulation on the road to absorbing Body-Mind awareness in its entirety into cyberspace. The code-term for this transition is 'immersive technology' which is described as 'technology that attempts to emulate a physical world through the means of a digital or simulated world by

Figure 317: The Hive Mind. Connecting the human brain to AI means that whatever controls – or is – AI controls the perceptions of the entire human race. (Image Neil Hague.)

creating a surrounding sensory feeling, thereby creating a sense of immersion'. It is the Tiptoe to assimilation in steps that include 'augmented reality' which combines the 'physical' world with the digital. It's being very cleverly done unless you are awake in which case it is a pathetically open book.

Simulation within a simulation

'Learning AI' is the level planned to run the 'Smart Grid' control system which is fast being introduced by the Cult and its unseen 'gods'. People are rightly concerned with the mass-surveillance state in which our every move is being tracked, every Internet post, opinion and behaviour, but this is not only for surveillance. All the information about human activity, thought, emotion and reaction gathered digitally worldwide minute by minute is being fed into Learning AI to provide ever-expanding fine-detail knowledge of what makes humans 'tick'. The processing of this information means that AI already knows humanity far better than humanity does. This is being used to further manipulate perception and action. Every time you post personal information on Facebook, Twitter and all the other Cult-controlled platforms it is absorbed by Learning AI to add to its awareness of human thought, emotion and behaviour and the data-gathering includes live microphones embedded in computers and smartphones to track what should be private conversations. For this we can thank those lovely fake New Wokers like Zuckerberg, Brin and Page who always say one thing and do the other while the New Woke army applauds and worships. Learning AI is behind the 'Sentient World Simulation' (SWS) based at the Synthetic Environment for Analysis and Simulations Laboratory at Purdue University in Indiana. The SWS is mass-collecting data to predict (and manipulate) human behaviour and operates under DARPA, one of the world's most sinister organisations (and think of the competition), which I have been exposing for decades. DARPA, or the Defense Advanced Research Projects Agency, is the technology arm of the Pentagon and the force that oversees Silicon Valley corporations and their direction on behalf of the global Cult. It has seed-funded vital Cult

operations such as Google and works in tandem with the CIA
technology venture capital firm In-Q-Tel (also IQT). Both fund the
development of technology and organisations to advance the Cult
technocracy agenda. DARPA claims to have created the Internet which
required military technology to launch and it just so happens that the
Internet is the foundation of the technocracy and the unfolding
technology control grid or 'Smart Grid'. This Cult agency is behind the
Sentient World Simulation ('sentient' = AI) which is constantly
processing information from every man, woman and child on the planet,
scanning behaviour and buying patterns, and producing a 'continuously
running, continually updated mirror model of the real world that can be
used to predict and evaluate future events and courses of action' (Fig
318). The Sentient World
Simulation is a micro-
version of the Time-Loop
simulation which is
impulsing the collective
human mind to follows
its agenda. The defence
against both is
consciousness in
awareness of its true self
that has burst through the
Bubble in which the
simulations operate and
here we have another
reason why the Cult

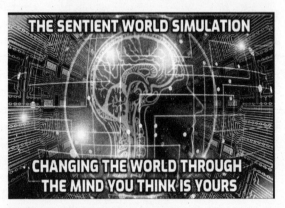

Figure 318: Real-time mirror of human society to
manipulate events in human society.

works so hard to keep the Bubbles intact. The Smart Grid is laying
another simulated information field over the main simulation field
which itself is laid over the Infinite information field beyond that.
Humans were first attuned with the overall simulation and now they are
being connected to the 'smart' information grid to further contract their
perception in deeper myopia and block out with even greater efficiency
any connection to Infinite Self.

The Sentient World Simulation and its data predictions explain why
we are hearing more and more about identifying 'pre-crime' in the way
portrayed in the movie, *Minority Report*, set in the year 2054. Pre-crime
is a version of pre-censorship in which potential posts are
algorithmically blocked before they can appear. People would be
targeted for pre-crime on the basis of Sentient World Simulation
predictions and not necessarily on what they really planned to do. The
motivation for this is not pre-crime but pre-deletion of any people or
groups planning to challenge the AI dystopia and the force behind it.
Cult-controlled Hollywood and other media increasingly portray

dystopian themes which portray the world the Cult seeks to impose and this relates to a psychological manipulation technique known as 'pre-emptive programming'. The Cult's Brave New World is so extreme and beyond anything humans alive today, or in known history, have ever experienced. This scale of change has obvious potential to invoke resistance. You want to do *what??* Pre-emptive programming via Hollywood, television and other sources continually feeds the conscious, and especially subconscious, mind with portrayals of the world that the Cult is planning. The idea is to make people *familiar* with an AI technology-controlled dystopia so that when it happens for real a lot of resistance will be diluted by that induced familiarity. Cult psychologists are well aware that once something is familiar it gets a free ride and ceases to be questioned as it fuses into everybody-knows-that. The programming machine ridiculously called 'education' is rarely questioned as a way of bringing up children because people are familiar with it. Introduce the same system today to replace one based on freedom and respect for children's individuality and there would be an outcry. I have spent 30 years questioning the familiar and accepted realities and when you do they dissolve like ice in a heatwave. Unquestioned familiarity is their only means of survival.

Aligned to pre-emptive programming is the very fact that AI extremists like Kurzweil are openly telling us about an AI connection to the brain. Why would they do that? The endgame has reached the point where this is happening and they can't hide that any longer at a time when they want to actually *do it*. Instead they have to sell it rather than hide it. The sales-pitch is that an AI connection will make us super-human when the plan is to make us sub-human and post-human. Once AI attaches to the brain human thought patterns can be fed into the Sentient World Simulation to produce an even more accurate picture of individual and mass perception and with that their predictions of human behaviour. Another fact crucial to understand is that through an AI connection the World Simulation can send thoughts and emotions *the other way* to defuse those with a challenge to The System in mind. 'I am going to stand up for freedom … Nah, actually, I won't bother it's not worth it.' The development of quantum computers capable of infinitely more than conventional computers is taking the potential for all this to a whole new level as is the roll-out of 5G. In the end human 'thought' would be AI in totality. Professor Oren Etzioni, CEO of the Allen Institute for AI, has said in a paper entitled 'How to know if artificial intelligence is about to destroy civilisation' that humanity must be ready for signs of robotic super-intelligence. He asked: 'Could we wake up one morning dumbstruck that a super-powerful AI has emerged, with disastrous consequences?' Well, given that this is the idea the answer must be 'yes'. Etzioni said one test suggested for this was that 'human-level AI will be achieved when a person can't distinguish conversing with a human from conversing with a computer'. This is a point that we are clearly heading for very, very fast, and Etzioni rightly says that this isn't really a warning sign because it would be confirmation that human-level AI had already arrived. Etzioni then destroys his credibility and grip on reality by saying we are far away from machine super-intelligence and we will have a comfortable amount of time to deploy 'off-switches'. He must have majored in naivety, surely?

'Smart' Grid to make you stupid

Know the outcome and you'll see the journey comes into play again. If I describe the planned outcome for the technological control of humanity you will certainly see the journey over decades to where we are now. Kurzweil's 'cloud' would cover every inch of the planet and every human would be attached through an AI-brain connection. The AI-controlled cloud would then *be* the human mind (Fig 319). It's only a few years ago that I was warning in my books and talks about the then-planned Internet of Things (IoT) in which all aspects of life including domestic appliances, vehicles, heating systems and a stream of surveillance devices would be connected to, and controlled from, the Internet (an expression of

Figure 319: The idea is that attachment to the 'cloud' via AI will block all influence from expanded states of awareness.

the cloud). Today we are already there with more devices added by the day. The Internet of Things is critical for the technocracy to control all aspects of human life and so is 5G and digital control of information via Silicon Valley censorship (Fig 320). The plan is for humanity and all technology to be connected to artificial intelligence via the Internet and Kurzweil's cloud which would give AI (and whatever is behind it) control of everything including human thought and perception. Driverless autonomous vehicles would dictate where you can and cannot go and that's why their introduction is planned to be enforced with each new generation of vehicles adding more AI features on the Tiptoe to total computer control. The University of Glasgow is working with the European Space Agency and UK Space Agency on 'Project DARWIN' which aims to introduce driverless cars in Britain guided

Figure 320: The Internet of Everything is the Internet of Things – plus the human brain. (Image Neil Hague.)

(controlled) by satellites using 5G communication. Passengers would be fried on every journey in other words. We have the British road system being transformed into 'smart motorways' specifically for the use of smart autonomous vehicles and the fact that the changes are making the roads far more dangerous and killing a lot of people is irrelevant to the psychopaths. The agenda is all that matters. There would be nothing in your life that AI would not control – even which doors would open or close – and there would be nothing you do or say that AI wouldn't immediately know about. Look around – it's happening with a gathering pace and it's all been long planned.

We have smart televisions with their cameras and microphones, smart assistants, smartphones, smart doorbells with cameras, smart meters, smart cards, smart cars, smart driving, smart pills, smart patches, smart watches, smart skin, smart borders, smart pavements, smart streets, smart cities, smart communities, smart environments, smart networks, smart growth and smart planet (the Smart Grid). These are only a few of them. Every technology dubbed 'smart' (almost everything these days) and any system called 'smart' are all designed to interconnect to form the global grid or what I have been describing for

Figure 321: The technological sub-reality or Smart Grid isolating human awareness from Infinite Awareness. (Image Neil Hague.)

many years as the technological sub-reality (Fig 321). What a surprise that it was announced in late 2019 that Amazon, Apple and Google will work together to create a new common standard that will make it easier for smart devices to speak to each other. I was so shocked I had to take to my bed. The Zigbee Alliance is part of the group that includes companies such as IKEA, Legrand, NXP Semiconductors, Samsung and Signify. The 'alliance' will connect existing smart assistants such as Google Assistant, Amazon Alexa, Apple's Siri, and others, which in the end all transmit their data and surveillance to the same Cult sources. They claim this will benefit users when it is another step forward for the Smart Grid. The same is true of the Amazon device called Ring with its camera on your doorbell which can be accessed from anywhere by smartphone and allows a conversation between a visitor and a distant resident. This is a great example of how the public is sold technology with a cover story to hide the real reason for its introduction. Amazon promotes Ring for home protection and convenience when it is another Trojan horse to add still further to the Smart surveillance grid. An article at Technocracy.news revealed:

> Ring has over 600 partnerships with law enforcement agencies around the country, and this number is increasing daily. The company has spent the past three years systematically making sure police everywhere know and recognize Ring, quietly building a nationwide surveillance network through police partnerships, and embedding itself into the functions of law enforcement … Behind the scenes, Ring is experimenting with emerging technologies, as well as pursuing a partnership with at least one other private surveillance company.

> The number of Ring partnerships with police grows almost daily, and, to date, there has been limited public debate about whether these partnerships should exist in the first place. Unless lawmakers curb or regulate the expansion of these partnerships, what we are seeing now is just a minuscule version of this company's full potential.

Also connected to the Smart Grid are 'green' lightbulbs that produce crap light compared with incandescent bulbs and emit radiation that can permanently redden the skin if you get too close. LED lights must have killed a lot of people already because they are so dim when used as street lamps. I know from experience how in many streets you can't see people crossing the road until they are in your headlights. All forms of 'green' lighting (or lack of it) have come courtesy of Climate Cult and the climate hoax along with wind turbine farms that have technologised landscapes and seascapes and destroyed their natural beauty. The same people call themselves *environmentalists*. Greens pressed for diesel to be encouraged over petrol until it was found that particulates in diesel were killing large numbers of people who breathed them in. What a gift to humanity and the environment the Climate Cult has been. The speed of the technological takeover is designed to have it installed and in control before most people realise what's happened. To them the Tiptoe has just been an endless series of unrelated new devices and technologies 'the latest thing' and only when the control system is in place will they see that what appeared to be random was really a calculated sequence to impose total control. Or maybe they won't even see it then with AI controlling their minds. AI will tell them not to.

Cutting edge 'new' technology has been there all along

The Cult is not sitting around waiting for essential ever-advancing technologies to be invented. The Archontic force as I call it, manipulating from the unseen, had the know-how for Smart Grid technology – and far ahead of even what we see today – when humanity was supposed to be knocking rocks together and living in caves during another simulation stage of 'history'. Human limitations of knowledge and technology apply only to this tiny band of frequency we experience as the world (the *simulation*). Beyond its firewall lies Infinite Reality and Possibility with even the low-vibrations occupied by the Archontics having far more knowledge than humans in Bubble-mode can access. *Some* of that knowledge is transferred to initiates of the Cult to advance the perceptual control of humanity. The transfer has included technology crucial to the Smart Grid which has been developed in beyond-top secret underground and within-mountain facilities before being introduced to the public arena in a carefully-planned sequence through a list of front men and women and their companies. These Cult agents are used, along with well-crafted cover stories, to explain where the technology came from (geeks in garages is often in the script) and we have a long list of cover-story tellers like Gates, Zuckerberg, Brin, Page, Wojcicki, Bezos and Musk among so many others. The world of high-technology is awash with Cult operatives in among genuine people who have no idea what is really going on around them. Humanity, in turn, has had to be perceptually developed to have enough intellectual (Bubble) awareness to work with and enslave itself with technology while not being wise enough to see that this is what is happening. Developing cleverness without wisdom was the plan and as I said earlier this is the most destructive force on earth. It is clever to make a nuclear weapon, but not wise to do so. The Cult 'education' system is all about cleverness, not wisdom. We have brilliant engineers and others with incredible intellectual abilities who, at the same time, believe that a man was born to a virgin mother and walked on water, or that 'God' parted the Red Sea and men should wear beards because a bloke called Mohammed had one some 1,500 years ago. I have used the following quote from a Central American shaman several times in my books and it captures the theme magnificently. He refers to the Archontic force as 'the predators':

> Think for a moment, and tell me how you would explain the contradictions between the intelligence of man the engineer and the stupidity of his systems of belief, or the stupidity of his contradictory behaviour ...

> ... Sorcerers believe that the predators have given us our systems of beliefs, our ideas of good and evil; our social mores. They are the ones who set up our dreams of success or failure. They have given us covetousness, greed, and cowardice. It is the predator who makes us complacent, routinary, and egomaniacal ...

> ... In order to keep us obedient and meek and weak, the predators engaged themselves in a stupendous manoeuvre – stupendous, of course, from the point of view of a fighting strategist; a horrendous manoeuvre from the point of those who suffer it. They gave us their mind. The predators' mind is baroque, contradictory, morose, filled with the fear of being discovered any minute now.

The shaman is describing from my perspective the impulses delivered by interaction with the Archontic simulation while the direct AI-brain connection is meant to take this to a whole new level of perceptual control. We must be able to build our own AI prison without realising that we are doing so and every day I watch it happening.

Here kitty, kitty ...

Humanity has been brought to the point where many of its number have become technologically savvy enough to build and operate the control grid while the masses have been enticed along the road to an AI mind in the way a donkey might trot forward in pursuit of a carrot always dangling just out of reach inches from the end of its nose (Fig 322). The technology version of this is to constantly bring out new devices each one slightly closer to the endgame of AI-brain connection. As people seek out each latest gadget or 'upgrade' they are unknowingly being seduced down the trail to the end of humanity as we know it (Fig 323). Apple was fined for slowing down older phones that made people more likely to upgrade with new products because, as you

Figure 322: Keep walking – just a bit longer and the carrot will be yours.

Figure 323: This has been the aim of the Cult and its 'gods' since the hijack of humanity began.

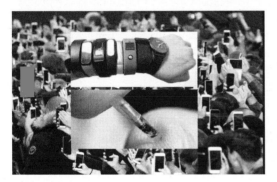

Figure 324: The premeditated sequence ... hold, on, in.

Figure 325: Anyone observing humanity today knows that this is working big-time. (Image Gareth Icke.)

know, Apple is Woke and has 'values'. The cold, calculated sequence planned from the start goes like this: First you get the target population addicted to technology they hold – i.e. smartphones; next you advance to on the body with Apple watches, Bluetooth earphones, fitness wristbands, internet-connected spectacles and an explosion of other devices; finally you get inside the body (your goal all along) with microchips which is already happening as I have been predicting and warning about for nearly 30 years (Fig 324). Today 95 in every 100 Americans have access to cell phones and three out of four adults worldwide as the first stage of 'kitty, kitty' is almost complete and human discourse and relationships have been devastated (Fig 325). When I say microchips I am not referring only to those that we can see and agree, however stupidly, to be implanted. Most sinister of all are the nano-microchips invisible to the human eye known as 'smart dust' and 'neural dust' that are being released into the atmosphere for the population to breathe in. I have exposed this at length in *Everything You Need To Know*.

Crucial to this whole scenario has been to get people addicted to technology so *it* becomes the master and not them. This has clearly been achieved with fantastic numbers of global humanity addicted to phones

Figure 326: Technology is already in control of vast numbers of people.

and especially the young who are the prime target for everything when they will be the adults at the time the Smart Grid is planned to be imposed full-blown (Fig 326). They are manipulating the perceptions of the young to compliantly agree to the AI takeover of their minds and world a few years hence. I will be revealing an immensely important aspect of induced smartphone addiction that no one seems to be talking about and it absolutely *is* addiction. Schools in America who take away phones during the school day found that students were suffering from 'separation anxiety'. Some allowed students to *hold* their phones in pouches when they can't open them during class time. One school principal said they were allowed to 'personalise' the pouches to 'make them as cool as humanly possible for something that's keeping them from their device'. What the hell are we doing standing by while Big Tech psychopaths addict young people worldwide in this way? What I have described with the hold-it-wear-it-insert-it sequence from phone to microchip can be identified in two other Tiptoes involving the progression from 1G to 5G and the progression of the Internet and its dominant corporations. The Cult wants us to believe that 5G is only the next more advanced stage after 1G, 2G, 3G and 4G when in fact 5G is a whole new frequency band called millimetre waves (millimeter in the US) and a whole new ball game. 5G was known about in the inner core of the Cult before 1G was even introduced through cutting edge research and the technology transfer between Cult initiates and their non-human 'gods'. I was sent a study dated 1974 from Soviet era Russia that was detailing research on the effect of millimetre waves now called 5G on viruses and pathogens and adverse effects on reproduction processes. The sequence has been a step-by-step deception to turn our reality into a microwave oven and the same technique has been used with the Internet itself.

Trojan Internet

Cult Pentagon agency DARPA claims credit for the Internet using military technology and whatever DARPA wants is bad for humanity (Fig 327). Stage one was to create the Internet and introduce the World Wide Web. The know-the-outcome-and-you'll-see-the-journey here was to make the Internet the foundation pillar of human society in a way that was irreversible in preparation for the Smart Grid. Technology needed to

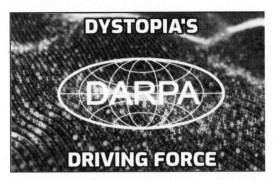

Figure 327: One of the world's most sinister organisations.

do this was once again known to the Cult long before it ever became public. Cult-insider Dr Richard Day was therefore able to describe the coming World Wide Web in his speech to those paediatricians in Pittsburgh in 1969 when it would not be officially 'invented' until 1989 and publicly available until 1991. DARPA and the Cult had to allow the free-flow of information and opinion in the early years to attract a global population to use the Internet. They would not have made the Web the central pillar of society if they had started with the endless wave of censorship we have today. In this period people like me were able to use the Internet to circulate information worldwide that the Cult certainly didn't want people to see. They had to bite the bullet on that in pursuit of longer-term ambitions. Once the Net had become the said central pillar and irreversibly so through functional dependency the kind of Internet planned all along removed the mask from its face. The censorship began and has become more extreme by the month. The Cult had the means which it set out to create of mass surveillance, a vehicle for AI control, and the ability to delete information it didn't want the public to see. The same sequence has been followed by Cult corporations specifically developed to dominate the Internet. The Facebooks, Googles, YouTubes, Twitters, Amazons, etc. also allowed the free circulation of information and opinion in the beginning as they had to do to pave the way for their near-monopolies. Once that had been achieved through securing a situation of 'Where else are you going to go?' their censorship began in earnest and has continued ever since picking off more and more dissenting voices.

These sequences that were planned from the start have been fishing lines thrown out to catch the people and then reel them in for the Hunger Games technocracy. Silicon Valley giants like Facebook and Google (YouTube) have fundamental connections to DARPA and the Pentagon as do Microsoft and Amazon (Fig 328 overleaf). All of them are at the centre of the AI-controlled surveillance society while posing as New Woke and supported by Wokeness mobbery. Regina Dugan, promotor of transhumanism and post-humanism, was DARPA director between 2009 and 2012 before being hired as an executive of Google. She then transferred to Facebook in 2016. That's quite a career CV – heading DARPA, one of the world's most sinister organisations, before moving to

Figure 328: America's real Silicon Valley with Israel emerging fast through Sabbatian-Frankism.

Figure 329: Regina Dugan – strange career unless you know what's going on. This was her job-description at Facebook.

a global search engine and social media platform (Fig 329). When you know the game there is a clear thread of consistency and that is AI control of humanity. Her brief at the secretive Facebook Building 8 operation was to develop 'technologies that fluidly blend physical and digital worlds.' Her *theoretical* 'boss' Mark Zuckerberg has talked of the need for 'a global superstructure to advance humanity'. Post-human advocate Ray Kurzweil is a Google executive and co-founder of the Singularity University in Silicon Valley which seeks to promote the AI human. Not without reason I refer to Silicon Valley as the Devil's Playground. It is a very sick place run by very sick people with a very sick agenda for humanity while posturing its New Wokeness to get the desperately naïve on board.

Behind the Musk

Big names in Silicon Valley are all technocrats driving the world into technocracy including Jeff Bezos at Amazon (an orgasmic company for technocrats); Brin and Page at Google/YouTube and parent company Alphabet; Zuckerberg, the frontman at Facebook; and Elon Musk at Tesla and SpaceX. There are so many others, too. Musk is a mega-fraud Silicon celebrity who comes into the story in many guises. For the Smart Grid to enslave the totality of humanity Kurzweil's 'cloud' has to cover every inch of the planet and that can only be done from space. Enter Mr Showman-Bullshitter Elon Musk (Fig 330). This is the man who said that AI could be the end of humanity (true) and heads a company called Neuralink working to connect the human brain to computers. *The Wall Street Journal* reported that this involves a 'neural lace' or mesh-like system which would 'implant tiny brain electrodes' with a view to uploading and downloading thoughts. Musk is the big name at Tesla

'AI COULD BE THE END OF HUMANITY'
'SO WHAT ARE YOU GOING TO DO ABOUT IT?'

'I'M GOING TO HELP MAKE IT HAPPEN'

Figure 330: Elon Musk, the smirking fraud making possible the Smart Grid of mass and total human control.

cars which is developing 'smart' electric driverless vehicles and in terms of the global cloud he heads the rocket corporation SpaceX which is in the process of delivering thousands of satellites into orbit to fire the Wi-Fi cloud at the entire Earth. Space X received $1billion in funding from Google and Fidelity Investments in 2015 amid the usual incestuous Silicon Valley interconnections. Musk officially requested permission from the Federal Communications Commission (FCC) in late 2016 to launch 4,425 satellites into low orbits at between 715 and 823 miles to provide Wi-Fi worldwide when at the time there were only 1,500 active satellites in orbit. The number planned by Musk is actually far, far higher as we'll see shortly. The UK *Independent* questioned the economics involved without realising that to the Cult agenda money is no object:

> The astronomical cost of the satellites and launch may be the limiting factor. The customers for the service are the very poorest populations in the most remote regions on earth. The initial cost of the satellite network will be difficult to recover.

Covering costs is not the prime goal – covering the Earth with the Wi-Fi cloud and 5G is the goal. Elon Musk is an extraordinarily arrogant man and very dangerous in terms of human freedom and health. He only gets away with his behaviour because what he's doing serves the Cult. He was warned that his Starlink programme to launch *12,000* satellites to, among other things, fire 5G/Wi-Fi at the planet would seriously damage astronomy by blocking out the stars with light. Musk of course didn't give a shit and did it anyway. *Forbes* magazine reported how in November, 2019, Musk's SpaceX launched 'a network of 60 bright, large, reflective and radio-interfering satellites … ruining numerous professional observations'. If 60 are doing that what are 12,000 going to do or the *42,000* that Musk wants? How much skin cancer alone are Musk's satellites going to cause as well as a long list of other health and psychological problems from 5G transmitted from space? Skin and sweat ducts directly interact with 5G. Musk announced a programme to launch 60 new satellites every two weeks to have 1,500 in orbit by the end of 2020 and the *Forbes* headline described the consequences: 'Latest Starlink Plans Unveiled By Elon Musk And SpaceX Could Create An Astronomical Emergency'. The article said: 'With competitors such as Kuiper Systems and OneWeb planning on launching similar networks, and Starlink attempting to procure approval for a total of 42,000 satellites, it's possible that looking through a pair of binoculars in 2030 [that year again] would reveal more satellites than stars.' Facebook is also involved in satellite Wi-Fi cloud-creation through a front company called PointView Tech along with other companies including Boeing. A Musk Space X rocket exploded at Cape Canaveral in 2016 before it was due to launch an Israeli-built communications satellite for Facebook to bathe a large area of sub-Saharan Africa in Wi-Fi. I'm sure as many search for food to survive they are desperate to watch cat videos on YouTube and CNN. Mark Zuckerberg said after the explosion that Facebook was 'committed to our mission of connecting everyone and we will keep working until everyone has the opportunities this satellite would have provided.' Google is also involved in the race to 'get everyone connected' purely from the light of human kindness. Satellite systems can also manipulate Earth weather which can then be blamed on human-caused 'climate change'.

This is what is happening to our world as the technological sub-reality I have for so long warned about is put in to place with no public approval or even knowledge in most cases. More confirmation of Musk's arrogance and fakery came in Germany where his Tesla electric car company fought off a campaign from the public and environmental groups to build a 'Gigafactory' that involved levelling 227 acres of what was described as serene forest in the ironically-named in the circumstances Gruen[Green]heide municipality. Protestors said it would turn the idyllic area into a dirty industrial zone. What does Musk care? Billionaire fake Wokers say one thing and do the opposite. Musk claims that electric cars are the future with 'the advent of sustainable transport and energy production'. First of all electric cars are not sustainable with the devastation caused in Africa alone in making the batteries and what is 'sustainable' and morally sustainable about deleting 227 acres of forest in a community that doesn't want that when you live on the other side of the world? Musk's activities are typical of a technocracy in which technocrats like him do what they like without the global population having any say and working above and beyond the level of elected politicians. Unbelievably self-obsessed people like Musk think they own the world and yet he is seen by many New Wokers as some kind of hero. How did Musk get permission for what he's doing? Cult asset Musk was given approval by the Cult-owned Federal Communications Commission – the usual story. He doesn't hold the positions that he does by accident. How interesting that his Jewish grandfather Joshua Haldeman was head of the Canadian Technocracy Party and campaigned for a technocracy between 1936 and 1941 when the movement was banned for a time by the Canadian government over alleged subversion. Now here we have grandson Elon Musk playing a front-line role in leading the world into technocracy. Aren't coincidences amazing?

Demonising democracy

The world government is planned to be a technocracy as the Cult leads us into a post-democratic society without elected representatives and a psychological campaign has been underway for decades to discredit the concept of democracy in the public mind. This is done by misrepresenting democracy by equating it with corrupt place-people in all parties doing the will of the Cult in the same way that cartelism is sold as the 'free market'. The Bennett Institute for Public Policy, a think tank based at the UK's University of Cambridge, published a survey of 400 million people worldwide conducted between 1973 and 2020 which claimed that nearly 58 percent were 'dissatisfied' with democracy. The highest level on record came in 2019 when violent street protests broke out across the world. The World Economic Forum of the One-percent was quick to highlight the survey results given that dissatisfaction with democracy is the whole idea. The Cult is encouraging contempt for politics and politicians to transform democracy into technocracy and not least by ensuring that so many crooked and clueless people get elected to office. The System isn't working because it is not *meant* to work. Witness the ever-increasing power over global society by the big names of Silicon Valley and how they are usurping and buying the political class. Politicians have already lost control of Silicon Valley technocrats, their Deep State handlers and the technology they oversee. The ground is being prepared for a full-blown technocracy wherever you look. *The Atlantic* magazine, yet another vehicle to promote the elite agenda, praised the technocrat takeover in an article headed: 'It's Jeff Bezos's Planet Now':

> … in an age of political dysfunction … Bezos has begun to subsume the powers of the state. Where the government once funded the ambitious exploration of space, Bezos is leading that project, spending a billion dollars each year to build rockets and rovers. His company, Amazon, is spearheading an experimental effort to fix American health care; it will also spend $700 million to retrain workers in the shadow of automation and displacement.

> Meanwhile, swaths of the federal government have contracted with Amazon to keep data on the company's servers. Bezos is providing the vital infrastructure of state [is absorbing the state]. When Amazon locates its second headquarters on the [Washington DC] Potomac, staring across the

river at the capital, it will provide a perfect geographic encapsulation of the new balance of power.

The article asked, perfectly describing the Cult methodology for destroying elected government: 'Isn't a private government run by Bezos preferable to a public government run by Donald Trump?' How transparent can you get if you know what is going on? Even UK Prime Minister Boris Johnson has warned about what I am calling the Smart Grid. He said in a 2019 speech at the United Nations that 'digital authoritarianism is not, alas, the stuff of dystopian fantasy, but of an emerging reality.' When I said the same decades ago it was called conspiracy nonsense and here was a Prime Minister saying the same at the UN. He called for new technologies to be designed for 'freedom, openness and pluralism, with the right safeguards in place to protect our people'. That ship has already sailed, Mr Johnson, and it's going to be a hell of a job to roll back what is already happening never mind what is becoming more Orwellian by the day (written before the lockdowns). Fake 'populist' Johnson was handed a big parliamentary majority in 2019 which he could have used to defend freedom and put his policy where his mouth is. Instead he has done quite the opposite. Ofcom, the UK media watchdog tyranny, has been given new powers by the Johnson government to censor social media platforms, websites, comments, forums and video-sharing. Content deemed (by the state) 'harmful' would have to be removed by law. This is sold as protection for children when as always the plan is to expand the law and its interpretation to include critics of the official narrative. 'Harmful' is so open to interpretation you can make it apply to anything and that's why that term is used. Platforms would have to remove 'illegal' (state censored) content quickly and 'minimise the risk' of it being posted at all. The latter means using AI pre-post censorship algorithms which Facebook and company have long said they have been developing. Cult-controlled governments tell Cult-owned Internet giants what they must do and they comply to ensure the introduction of Cult-demanded censorship. This is happening with regard to an increasing list of countries. It is also interesting, and I say that ironically, that this UK government law is in line with the World Wide Foundation of 'Web-inventor' Tim Berners-Lee which proclaims to be saving the Internet from 'digital dystopia' with censorship dystopia. Authors of the Berners-Lee plan include … Google, Facebook, Microsoft, and the censorship-obsessed German and French governments. Johnson's regime also employs an absolute Israel *fanatic* policing 'anti-Semitism' (criticism of Israel) in the form of one-time Labour Party MP John Mann with his blue and white tongue on permanent stand-by. Any connection between Johnson and freedom is purely coincidental on his record and he allowed himself to be overridden by 'the scientists' and outrageous 'computer modellers' to lockdown Britain and create economic Armageddon and fascistic control.

(Cyber) Space: the final frontier (for the end of freedom)

The Smart Grid cannot function without communication systems of at least 5G, or 'Fifth Generation', which operates in the millimetre wave band of the electromagnetic spectrum. Cumulatively-lethal 5G is being rolled out across the world and beamed from satellites without any official independent testing for its health and psychological implications. There is a simple reason for this lack of testing: 5G is crucial to the Smart Grid and independent, publicly-circulated, studies of 5G consequences for body and mind would mean it would never be allowed to happen in the face of mass public opposition. China is a world leader in 5G and already talking about 6G using terahertz waves. The authorities and the Cult telecommunications industry know that truly independent publicly-funded testing published in the mainstream would be the death knell of 5G and so they don't have any. If you can't win a debate don't have one. Senator Richard Blumenthal asked US telecommunications industry representatives during a session of the US Senate Commerce, Science and Transportation Committee how much money they had spent on independent research into the effects of 5G. Their answer was *nothing*. Blumenthal said: 'No research ongoing – we're flying blind here so far as health and safety is concerned.' It may appear to be that way from the public perspective, but industry insiders and the Cult are not 'flying blind' at all. They know the cumulative health and psychological consequences for large numbers of people and they don't want you to know. The International Society of Doctors for the Environment, with subsidiaries in 27 countries, joined more than 200 doctors and scientists in urging the 5G roll-out be stopped over concerns that its radio frequency radiation will harm human health. The body and its systems are an electromagnetic field communicating and processing information electrically as does the brain. Any frequency that disrupts this electrical and electromagnetic harmony will cause 'physical' and psychological dis-ease or disruption and the more powerful the frequency the greater the disruption. The Cult doesn't care – that's the effect it *wants* in its war on humanity. Tom Wheeler, then chairman of the US Federal Communications Commission (FCC), told the media that all urban and rural communities would be saturated with 5G to connect to the Internet everything from water supplies to pharmaceutical drugs and domestic appliances. Obama-appointed Wheeler was formerly a venture capitalist and lobbyist for the cable and wireless industry which he then became responsible for 'regulating'. No wonder this disgraceful man said that 5G safety standards simply didn't matter:

We won't wait for the standards to be first developed in the sometimes arduous standards-setting process or in a government-led activity. Instead, we will make ample spectrum available and then rely on a private sector-led process for producing technical standards best suited for those frequencies and use cases.

We'll allow the industry that admits it has done no testing to set the safety standards in line with what they require for the industry (the Cult) to do whatever it wants. The technocracy's need to cover the planet with 5G or higher can be seen in the $9 billion fund announced by the same Federal Communications Commission (now chaired by Ajit Pai) to 'help' the billionaire telecommunication industry to specifically install 5G connection (radiation) across rural America. How kind.

5G coming to your street

5G is designed to add still further to the technological sub-reality disconnecting humanity from Infinite Reality which is being constructed all around us step by step. Its millimetre waves don't pass well through buildings and other dense objects which means that 5G transmitters are needed down every street (Fig 331). Some estimates claim one for every twelve buildings. This will mean having untested 5G transmitted directly outside homes and children's bedrooms. The human cost is going to be

Figure 331: 5G with its destructive frequencies will require transmitters along every street.

considerable over a period and it's meant to be for reasons I will be explaining. In fact 5G is so potentially destructive that the International Commission on Non-Ionizing Radiation Protection (ICNIRP) which is recognised by the Cult-created World Health Organization said it is 100 percent safe. Wow, it must be bad then. The ICNIRP calls itself 'independent' which it is perfectly at liberty to do, but I don't believe it. The inability of 5G to pass through dense objects explains why phenomenal numbers of trees, especially in urban areas, are being cut down. You know those trees we are told are so essential to 'stop global

warming'. A *Sunday Times* investigation using the Freedom of
Information Act found that 110,000 trees had been chopped down in
three years by UK councils including Newcastle (8,414), Edinburgh
(4,435) and Sheffield (3,529). The excuses for doing so were pathetic and
the real reason is 5G and the preparation for autonomous vehicles which
need a clear connection to 5G. Scientists and doctors independent of the
industry and the Cult have spoken out about the multiple dangers
posed by 5G. One is Dr Joel Moskowitz, a public health professor at the
University of California, Berkeley, who says the deployment of 5G is a
mass experiment on the health of all species because millimetre waves
are weaker than microwaves and predominantly absorbed by the skin
which takes the focus of the 'hit'. He says skin contains capillaries and
nerve endings which allow 5G bio-effects to be transmitted through
molecular mechanisms and the nervous system (the skin is actually an
antenna like the skeleton and the body in general). Dr Moskowitz
warned that '5G will use high-band frequencies, or millimetre waves,
that may affect the eyes, the testes [end of procreation agenda], the skin,
the peripheral nervous system, and sweat glands ... Millimetre waves
can also make some pathogens resistant to antibiotics.' Something rarely
mentioned is that 'viruses' and diseases are, like everything, expressions
of specific frequencies and if you broadcast those frequencies powerfully
enough you can spread disease among the population without
chemicals and direct contact and most certainly weaken the immune
system which makes 'viruses' and pathogens more destructive (you'll
see why I am putting 'virus' in quote marks when we get to the
pandemic hoax). Dr Ben-Ishai from the Department of Physics at Israel's
Hebrew University has warned that human sweat ducts 'act like an
array of helical antennas' when exposed to 5G wavelengths and Dr
Devra Davis, an internationally-renowned American epidemiologist,
President of the Environmental Health Trust and director of the Center
for Environmental Oncology at the University of Pittsburgh, said at the
start of the 5G roll-out:

> If you are one of the millions who seek faster downloads of movies, games
> and virtual pornography, a solution is at hand, that is, if you do not mind
> volunteering your living body in a giant uncontrolled experiment on the
> human population. At this moment, residents of the Washington, DC region –
> like those of 100 Chinese cities – are about to be living within a vast
> experimental millimeter wave network to which they have not consented – all
> courtesy of American taxpayers.

> This work shows that the same parts of the human skin that allow us to sweat
> also respond to 5G radiation much like an antenna that can receive signals.
> We need the potential adverse health impacts of 5G to be seriously evaluated

before we blanket our children, ourselves and the environment with this radiation.

Unravelling human biology

Frank Clegg, former President of Microsoft Canada, is another vocal campaigner highlighting the dangers of 5G to health and DNA which is another receiver-transmitter of information waves and immensely vulnerable to being unravelled and mutated by waves of technological radiation. Then there is John Patterson, an Australian telecommunications engineer and radiation expert, who was so concerned about the dangers he identified that he 'borrowed' a former British army tank and demolished six Sydney mobile phone transmitter towers in 2007. He wanted to highlight what he called the devastating risk to human life, nature and the planet all of which are wave and electromagnetic fields and seriously affected by technologically-generated electromagnetic waves. Patterson's protest came even before the roll out of 5G and we should not allow a focus on 5G to obscure the fact that all electromagnetic technology is potentially harmful to humans, 3G, 4G, or whatever label is used. It's only a matter of scale. John Patterson took his drastic action after being fired for producing a report revealing mega-levels of technological radiation and being ignored by every government and telecommunications agency including Standards Australia, Australian Communications Authority, Australian Radiation Protection and Nuclear Safety Agency, Local Government Association, national parliament and the military – all of which will be tools of the telecommunications industry which is a tool of the Cult. The same story can be found throughout the world because the Cult is running the show. Patterson's campaign began when he was very sick himself and this became even worse when two mobile phone base stations were installed close to his place of work. By then he was having regular heart attacks and suffering many health effects that he saw in work colleagues, some of whom died. Patterson said that 'Telecom had a very high number of suicides' and we have suicides soaring among young people deluged with technological waves from smartphones and masts. Electromagnetic wave disruption imbalances the wavefield mind as well as the body while the brain processes information (perception) electrically. Remember, too, that when you make a call the cell tower broadcasts a dedicated radiation connection just for you and you unknowingly irradiate everyone and everything in its path *every time you use the phone*. Patterson offers this advice to mobile phone users: Minimise the use of phones in buses and trains in peak hours; avoid closed rooms with mobile phones; wind all the windows down if you use a mobile phone in the car – ('For a mobile phone signal to go through 3mm of glass it has to double its power'); Tinted glass is less permeable to mobile phone signals so causing the phone to increase power; pregnant women definitely should not use mobile phones given that the foetus absorbs radiation that its mother absorbs; don't send SMS text messages as the mobile phone transmits at maximum power for this. These are some of the mind and body effects described by Cairnsnews.org which Patterson experienced himself and witnessed in others after radiation exposure from nearby phone masts:

- Short-term memory loss
- Long-term memory loss
- Involuntary contraction of muscles and tendons
- Sleeplessness
- Chronic fatigue
- Problems with balance
- Sore neck muscles
- Jaw out of alignment
- Vertebrae in shoulders and bottom four vertebrae out of alignment caused by cramping of muscles
- Reduction in elasticity in body, especially throat, resulting in a 'choking' effect when swallowing
- Thyroid problems [which delete the immune system]
- Heart problems (including heart attacks)
- Stomach valve not opening properly, leading to heartburn and nausea
- Changes to gait
- Numbing of the skin
- Black rings around the iris
- Kidney problems
- Liver problems leading to skin problems, rashes and pimples that don't heal. Patterson says he saw at least a thousand workers with similar skin problems.
- Inappropriate emotional responses

I repeat – this was even before 5G. Patterson points out that overhead powerlines become conductors of mobile phone signals when people make calls close by and while science tests the impact of single phones the public is being exposed to simultaneous sources from multiple phones and masts making the cumulative effect far, far worse. He likens a crowded bus or train with many people using phones to a microwave oven. Now they are making them possible on aircraft. Patterson's overall conclusions are the same as those I have highlighted in my books over decades – technological fields disrupt natural fields and the consequences are cumulatively catastrophic. A major effect is on the polarity spin of body cells. Patterson said:

The body is like a spinning top charged through nature's fields and waves. Synchronicity to these fields creates good health. When we're unsynchronised to the spinning top effect, sickness and disease appear. Continual exposure to the polarisation of mobile phones is diminishing our ability to recognise nature.

Martin Pall is a Professor Emeritus of biochemistry and Basic Medical Sciences at Washington State University and a man I will quote later with regard to 5G and 'coronavirus'. He has published a very long list of articles and papers on the subject of electromagnetic fields and 5G. His findings support the direct experience of John Patterson and he emphasises the effect on the heart for all ages, a 'rapid crash in collective brain function', very early-onset Alzheimer's and both 'a rapid and irreversible crash in human reproduction to close to zero, based mainly but not solely on the impacts on male reproduction' and 'massive deterioration in the human gene pool, caused by the DNA effects in human sperm and possibly also on human eggs'. The latter two relate to the Cult's end-of-procreation and population cull agendas which I will detail in the next chapter. Professor Pall relates how widespread neuropsychiatric effects are produced by low-intensity electromagnetic field exposures, including depression: 'Depression can cause suicide and various neuropsychiatric effects may well lead to abusive behavior.' Here we are with suicide rapidly increasing especially among the young in the 'smart' era with 5G exponentially increasing the impact of technological electromagnetic fields. Pall also said in 2018:

> I predict that many organisms will be much more impacted than we will. This includes insects and other arthropods, birds and small mammals and amphibia. It includes plants including even large trees, because trees have leaves and reproductive organs that are highly exposed. I predict there will be major ecological disasters as a consequence of 5G. This will include vast conflagrations because EMF exposures make plants much more flammable.

Professor Paul said that 'putting in tens of millions of 5G antennae without a single biological test of safety has got to be about the stupidest idea anyone has had in the history of the world'. Stupid if you care about humanity, but perfectly explainable if you don't. Pall's assessment is that '5G presents threats of the sort that we have never seen before – multiple imminent existential threats to our survival.' From the Cult's point of view that's the idea and what better way to hide that reality than behind a fake 'climate emergency' promoted by your puppets in the Climate Cult and claimed to be 'an existential threat' to humanity?

World-changing

Confirmation for Pall's and Patterson's words comes from the devastating impact of technological radiation on the planet's natural frequency state known as Schumann Cavity or Schumann Cavity Resonance which is named after German physicist Winfried Otto

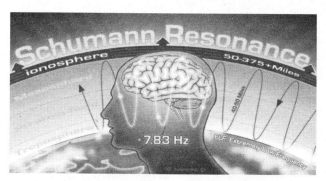

Schumann. This operates in the extremely low frequency or ELF range between 6 and 8 Hertz which is the frequency band of human brain activity and all biological systems (Fig 332). The frequency of 7.83 Hz is said to be where everything can

Figure 332: Schumann Resonance through which life in our reality can connect and interact is being destroyed by the tidal wave of technologically-generated electromagnetic frequencies.

connect and communicate in unity. The Cult is purposely scrambling the frequency connection – *Oneness* – between humans and nature and humans and each other. We are part of a vast universal electrical system and we interact with the Earth's magnetic field which itself is part of the universal field or The Field. Humans have a flow of electromagnetic energy from The Field entering through the top of the head (crown chakra) which is distributed throughout the body by the chi acupuncture network – chi is electricity encoded with information. The dismantling and distorting of this connection by technological radiation (with 5G taking the effect to a level beyond anything we have yet experienced) is having untold consequences for body/mind health and the term 'health' is just another way of saying balance or harmony. This interaction with The Field has a profound impact on the body-field oscillation which is what we call life in this reality. When the oscillation stops the body dies and the weaker the oscillation gets the weaker we get. The same interaction applies to the entire natural world and this is why bees and insects among much else are disappearing. Older people will remember how insects were constantly hitting their windscreen in the summer because they were so abundant; but now? None of this appears to be a problem for the 'Green movement' and its Climate Cult which in many ways sees the technology dystopia as an answer to 'climate disaster'. I described earlier how members of the UK Green Party were denied by its Climate Cult hierarchy a debate on 5G at the 2019 annual conference and one member was threatened with the police

Figure 333: While the 'Greens' are obsessed with the human-caused climate change hoax the real danger to the natural world and humanity is ignored or even supported.

Figure 334: Plant growth with Wi-Fi and no Wi-Fi.

Figure 335: Plant growth with microwaved water and purified water.

while protesting the decision outside the venue (Fig 333). They don't seem at all interested in a 5G technology that threatens the natural world in all its forms with mass disruption from its wave frequency impact on animals, insects, plants, trees, the lot. What does the US Green New Deal call for? The building or upgrading to energy-efficient, distributed, and 'smart' power grids. I saw a headline at the New Woke 'Eco Warrior Princess' website which said: 'Smart Grid Technology in the US: Benefits to Environment and Social Justice.' Many experiments have revealed how Wi-Fi blocks plant growth and 5G has the potential for a serious effect on nature and food production to add to the Green demand to reduce the gas of life or plant oxygen (Figs 334 and 335). Nature is being destroyed from insects to bees to birds by technological frequencies and humans are going the same way. A study in India exposed bees to a cell phone for ten minutes and found that they stopped metabolising sugars, proteins and fats – in *ten minutes*. Now apply this to the staggering increase in human diabetes (flawed metabolising of sugars); heart disease (which is affected by frequency impulses); and cancer (cell growth can be distorted by technological electromagnetic fields). Is it really a coincidence that in the period that all this has happened dementia has soared? We are in a real crisis caused by technological wavefields while the Cult sells the fake crisis of climate change and has hijacked the Green movement to attack those exposing the facts. Whales and dolphins that navigate through a Schumann connection have been beaching themselves in large numbers while birds, bees and insects are being similarly affected through navigational disruption. Physicist and Schumann researcher Wolfgang Ludwig said: 'Measuring Schumann resonance in or around a city has become impossible ... electromagnetic pollution from cell phones has forced us to make measurements at sea.' Professor Rutger Wever from the Max Planck Institute for Behavioural Physiology in Germany built an underground bunker isolated from Schumann resonance to study student volunteers for a month. Isolation from Schumann frequencies caused biological rhythms (circadian rhythms) to be scrambled and they suffered emotional distress (see humanity today) and migraine headaches. These symptoms disappeared after only a short exposure to 7.8 Hz. There are gathering numbers of people worldwide suffering so seriously from what is termed 'electrical sensitivity' that they have to live alone as far from technological radiation as possible, but where can they run with this shit blasted everywhere from satellite thanks to Musk and his masters? They are technology-generated radiation sensitive and the number is bound to soar with 5G. American activist Arthur Firstenberg, author of *Microwaving Our Planet: The Environmental Impact of the Wireless Revolution* and *The Invisible Rainbow: A History of Electricity and Life,* said in 2018:

> At least 20 million people in the world, and I estimate that conservatively, have already been injured by cell phones and their infrastructure so severely that they cannot work. They are driven out of their homes and cities and cannot live in society.

> They are environmental refuges and they are in every country. Many are housebound and cannot venture outside … many of these people are homeless, living in cars and tents, in remote areas, committing suicide and no one comes to their aid.

Firstenberg was speaking even before 5G. The manipulated frequency disconnection between humans and their environment has many benefits for the Cult agenda including that technocracy requires a disconnection from the natural world. A survey by Britain's National Trust in 2020 found that more than 70 percent of children say they rarely or never watch clouds, butterflies and bees and most adults had rarely or never listened to birdsong or smelled wild flowers over the previous year. Never mind they could always watch videos of them on YouTube or download images from Instagram.

Give children smartphones?

Children are far more damaged by radiation and they are sitting in Wi-Fi fields at school all day and then going home to the same Wi-Fi along with the added radiation fields of smart meters, smartphones and Wi-Fi in the street. *No safe level* of wireless radiation has been determined for children or pregnant women and that's likely true for everyone. Brain cancers in children have rapidly increased where they put phones to their ear – adults, too – and tumours of the heart (disrupting the heart on the wavefield level is a prime objective of the Cult). What a grotesque sight it is to see parents allowing babies to play with these devices or toddlers in highchairs for no other reason than to keep them placated (Fig 336). Phone use for just 20 minutes a day can triple the risk of a brain tumour with thinner-skulled children at the greatest risk. The

 *Chicago Tribune* reported in 2019 that eleven smartphone models exceed federal radiation safety levels (already ridiculously high) by *500 percent.* An investigation by the Swiss Tropical and Public Health Institute which

Figure 336: Assimilation now starts early.

replicated an earlier study established memory damage in teenagers who had used a cell phone for a year. This was especially the case with those putting the phone to the same ear with impaired memory in those parts of the brain getting the biggest exposure to phone radiation. A BBC report revealed that most children surveyed in the UK sleep with their phone by the bed, which can be seriously detrimental to both health and sleep, while mobiles are being handed to children at an ever earlier age with most having a phone by age seven. Ownership becomes 'pretty universal' by age eleven. Even against this background of phone and Wi-Fi health consequences Apple is selling 'Airpods' which people stick in their ears to pick up Wi-Fi. Bluetooth does the same. It is cumulative suicide and the *companies don't know that?* How many phone users realise that in the fine print these companies tell you not to put the phone to your ear? This is the get-out clause for the tidal wave of lawsuits they know will eventually come their way. Lloyds of London, one of the world's premier insurance groups, refuses to insure health claims made against 5G and Wi-Fi technologies. What do they know that the public is not being told? *Plenty.* Cancer, heart malfunction, dementia, weakened immune systems, miscarriages, stillbirths, insomnia, extreme nosebleeds, eye problems, depression, suicide, and other conditions and behaviour are all potential effects of 5G. Firefighters in San Francisco have reported memory problems and confusion after 5G was installed outside their stations and they said this only stopped when they moved to non-5G locations. These are the 5G waves impacting on the information processing of the brain and imagine what the situation will be when it is *everywhere* and being fired at us from Musk's satellites. Anyone still surprised at the soaring increase in teenage suicide when electromagnetic frequencies emitted by technology affect information processing by the brain? *The Cult is taking over the human mind* and for this reason laws are being passed to impose 5G on every community and stop anyone opting out. Another effect of technology waves is to break down the blood-brain barrier that keeps toxins out of the brain including nano-chips. Children are being hit with this stuff before their blood-brain barriers are even fully developed. The telecommunications and Silicon Valley corporations promoting all this are controlled by pure psychopathic evil (the extreme absence of love). I hear some say there is no such thing as evil when there *is* by that definition. Indeed there must be the potential for evil and the absence of love within the infinity of All Possibility.

Cauliflower blood

American researcher Lena Pu is the environmental health consultant for the National Association for Children and Safe Technologies and she has the experience of working with military and government agencies. She is a vehement campaigner against 5G and Wi-Fi in schools, but even she was taken aback when she tested the blood of a teacher after a day in a classroom that wasn't even dowsed in maximum Wi-Fi power as many others are. She said the teacher's blood was the worse she had ever seen – 'sticky', coagulating and brown in colour. 'This is the first time that the blood was so thick that I could see the colour on a slide', Pu said. She described it as 'looking like cauliflower'. It took her a few minutes to talk to the teacher because she was in 'pure shock'. What was happening to the blood of the students in the same environment? What is happening to all children at school across the world every day with Wi-Fi transmitted in almost every classroom whether they use it or not? Now 5G is being installed in schools across the world and hospitals. Blood is liquid and the Wi-Fi affect becomes obvious when you think that Wi-Fi operates in the same frequency band as microwave ovens which generate frequencies specifically designed to energise water molecules. What does the holographic human body mostly consist of? *Water.* Microwave ovens dry out food and Wi-Fi dries out (dehydrates) humans. What could possibly go wrong and what a coincidence, eh? I guess it's also a coincidence that driverless cars operate in the waveband that affects water. Consequences for body and mind include depression (see skyrocketing teen suicides again). Apathy is another symptom which is exactly what the Cult wants to provide a free run to its endgame.

Lena Pu found that Wi-Fi and technology transmitters can change their frequency which means that while they are officially transmitting on one frequency they can covertly be delivering other frequencies at the behest of whoever is in control. Pu's research has also shown her how technology frequencies are effecting the very formation and intake of oxygen and this connects with the global population cull I have been warning about for decades. The Smart Grid is the delivery system, but the controllers of the Grid decide at whatever time what is *being* delivered. We are told that this network is for 5G or 4G when that is only the technology to deliver other frequencies far beyond what we are told about. Humanity is not only building its own prison cell. It is watching its own microwave oven being installed step-by-step every day. Pu said something else that I have been pointing out year after year. These 'technology' waves are actually '*alive*' and a form of consciousness. Remember what I said about the most advanced AI being in truth a name for the very force behind human control? The introduction of 5G is going to increase the radiation effect of all of the above by many, many times. Nevertheless the mainstream media takes the side of industry and government, *of course*, with the *New York Times* running headlines such as 'The 5G Health Hazard That Isn't'. This was the same *New York Times* that partnered with Verizon 'to explore how 5G can be used in journalism'. Why the *Times* would want to know about the effect on journalism when it doesn't do any was not explained. A *Times* reporter was accused of violating a truth and accuracy code by the Press Council of Ireland with regard to an article about 5G. Given that the paper is an ultra-Zionist-owned rag that serves the interests of the Cult there is no surprise there then. A 'journalist' called Alex Hern wrote an article in the 'anti-Establishment' deeply-establishment London *Guardian* headed: 'How baseless fears over 5G rollout created a health scare'. Hern licked the arse of the industry and its '5G is perfectly safe' propaganda while basically dismissing any concerns as 'junk science'. What a disgrace to journalism, but oh, so typical of his kind across the media. All these health concerns are believed acceptable for faster Internet speeds that are already fast enough. Endanger your health and you can download your movies quicker – you know it makes sense. Faster speeds are just another 'here kitty, kitty' to the Smart Grid dystopia (Fig 337).

Figure 337: Faster downloads – faster survellience and data collection – and faster and more powerful the impact on human wavefields. (Image by Ben Garrison at Grrrgraphics.com.)

Figure 338: Active Denial weapons millimetre band of 5G. The skin – an antenna – decodes the frequencies into the feeling of intense heat as if the skin is on fire.

5G is a weapon

Ultra-high millimetre frequencies used by the 5G band are in fact employed as a *weapon* by the American, Israeli and other military and law enforcement (same thing) under the name 'Active Denial Technology' (Fig 338). This transmits millimetre band frequencies from military/law enforcement trucks to rapidly disperse protests and crowds. People scatter when their skin (an antenna) decodes the frequencies into the feeling that their skin is on fire and they run to get away from it. A US Department of Defense report said: 'If you are unlucky enough to be standing there when [the beam] hits you, you will feel like your body is on fire.' With such skin-5G interaction how many people will die of skin cancer as a result of its imposition? The disruptive potential is obvious for body and brain of 5G waves everywhere you go and for affecting even the wave oscillation of the body that gives it life. Consider the effect on the whole electromagnetic soup in totality on the wave oscillation of the body. The military potential is fantastic and NATO countries agreed to 'guarantee the security of our communications, including 5G' at their 2019 summit in London. The real reason for the 5G roll out is military and anti-human. The Pentagon-advising Defense Science Board detailed the military potential of 5G in a document called Defense Applications of 5G Network Technology: 'The emergence of 5G technology, now commercially available, offers the Department of Defense the opportunity to take advantage, at minimal cost, of the benefits of this system for its own operational requirements.' Get your Cult 'private' companies and taxpayer money to fund a 5G

network that's really intended for the Cult military. 5G will take war
fighting, mass killing and mass surveillance on to a new level.
Fortunately, public resistance to 5G is growing despite Cult industry
propaganda parroted by the Cult media and Cult social media and the
Cult's YouTube deleting accounts and videos of those exposing the
dangers. Be careful, however, as with all apparent opposition groups,
that some are not fronts for what they claim to oppose. Astroturfing is
everywhere today.

Poison from the sky

One other crucial point about 5G and other forms of technological
radiation is the phenomenon known as 'chemtrails' which started to be
noticed in the 1990s and has subsequently been reported all over the
world. I will be brief because I have detailed this subject at length in
Everything You Need To Know. People are familiar with *con*trails, or
condensation trails, that flow from the back of aircraft and quickly
disappear. *Chem*trails, or chemical trails, do not disappear. They slowly
expand and combine until even a clear blue sky can appear cloudy and
hazy. The content of chemtrails falls to earth to infest people, animals,
water sources, trees, plants, soil, everything (Fig 339). Tests have
revealed that chemtrails contain aluminium, barium, radioactive
thorium, cadmium, chromium, nickel, mould spores, yellow fungal
mycotoxins, polymer fibres, smart dust nano-technology, and so much
more in cumulatively lethal
concentrations for human
health. The aluminium
content is a major source
for the
aluminium/glyphosate
impact on the pineal gland
and aluminium, a brain
toxin, has been rightly
linked to Alzheimer's and
other forms of dementia
which have become an
epidemic affecting younger
and younger people. Why

Figure 339: The chemtrail phenomenon all over the world.

wouldn't that be when aluminium, in effect, short-circuits the brain?
With regard to the technological sub-reality, or 'cloud', chemtrails add to
the conductivity of the atmosphere and turn it into an antenna. It's all
connected to the same end. Chemtrails were dismissed as a 'conspiracy
theory (of course) and then Bill Gates (of course) began officially
promoting and funding them to 'block the sun' to save the world from
'global warming'.

AI world army

The world army enforcing the will of unelected technocrat world government is not ultimately planned to be human and the transition to an AI military is already well underway. We are moving rapidly to artificial intelligence (the Archontic force essentially) making global decisions about life and death through control of weapons that truly are weapons of mass destruction. AI won't only control the Smart Grid and every facet of 'human' life. It will decide if you live or die and that can be done en masse through humanity's AI connection to the Grid. The middle strata of the Hunger Games Society between the elite and the masses is planned to be occupied by an AI world military/police state of constant surveillance with the elimination of all dissenters. If you've seen the *Matrix* movies you'll be aware of the 'Sentinels' or machines in their seek-and-destroy missions against humans operating outside the AI control system. This in theme is the AI world army consisting of AI robots and weapons systems that even military commanders would not in the end control. For autonomous vehicles see autonomous weapons, too, directed by the Archontic force and its Cult operatives. AI control would at some point allow the Cult elite and its technocrats to take refuse from any protesting humanity in mega underground and within mountain cities that I was writing about as long ago as the 1990s. All this has been planned a very long time. Cult arms companies are developing laser weapons controlled by AI – tanks, planes, helicopters and battleships are all being designed and introduced with AI making the decisions. DARPA as you would expect is at the centre of this although itself answers to those much deeper in The Web. This is the same dark and sinister Cult-created DARPA behind the Internet and Silicon Valley corporations like Google and Facebook. Aircraft drones equipped with weapons are being developed with a 'neural microchip' that lets them 'think like a human'. Drone surveillance systems are well advanced and in 2019 Turkey unveiled a fleet of drones equipped with a machine gun and 200-rounds of ammunition. The thought of the military flying AI drones with machine guns would once have been science fiction territory. Even so Turkey is way back from the cutting edge of drone capability compared with the United States, China, Russia and Israel. How about AI controlling laser and other focused energy and beam weapons that can strike anywhere on Earth from satellite? Anyone who dismisses that has not been paying attention to what is actually *happening.* The contempt that the Cult has for the human population was confirmed yet again when the US Department of Defense appointed Eric Schmidt, Trilateral Commission member and former CEO of Google, to chair the Defense Innovation Board established in 2016 to formulate 'ethical standards' in the use of AI in the battlefield in line with the 'best practice' of Silicon Valley. What 'best practice'? Walter Isaacason, another Trilateral Commission member, former President of the One-percent's Aspen Institute, chairman and CEO of CNN and Managing Editor of *Time*, is also on the board. The members are selected by Schmidt in consultation with the Secretary of Defense. The idea that Schmidt is going to propose genuine and enforceable 'ethical standards' on military AI is a joke so sick it is beyond laughable when he fronted for Google as it was transforming the Internet into the censorship-ridden, freedom-deleting, AI-dictated abomination that it has become.

Satellites are being launched all the time without publicity in pursuit of global control and when they are mentioned it is their civilian and commercial uses that are emphasised when many have military applications. Russia's President Vladimir Putin made this point in 2019 when he said that world powers were increasingly weaponising space and Russia had to respond: 'The US political and military leadership openly consider space a war theatre ... Developments demand that we pay increased attention to strengthening our orbital group as well as our rocket and space industries.' Russia's 'orbital group' is reported to have 150 satellites with two-thirds of them having military applications. The United States will be much further ahead than that and then there is China, too. President Trump created the US Space Force, the first new military branch since 1947, when he signed the 2020 National Defense Authorization Act. 'Space is the world's newest warfighting domain', Trump said. 'American superiority in space is absolutely vital.' This was delivering exactly what the ultra-Zionist Project for the New American Century called for in its September, 2000, document demanding that list of regime changes which followed the Sabbatian-Frankist-instigated 9/11. The fact that Trump is owned by Israel is naturally purely coincidental. Space is another 'domain' for the child-like playground bullies to fight. The world is run by a psychopathic playschool. Academics and scientists have warned that killer robots will leave humans defenceless while not appearing to realise that *this is the very idea*. (Fig 340). Even using humans in the military/police state carries with it the possibility of rebellion once they see what the game is. That is avoided with AI and those in the military and police today

Figure 340: The Cult is creating a world military force in which decisions are made by artificial intelligence outside the control of humans.

should realise that they would be in the Hunger Games masses once AI law enforcement took over. The world's first robot officer officially joined the Dubai police in 2017. 'Robocop' can read facial expressions, respond in six languages, and has a built-in tablet that can be used to report crime and pay fines. Brigadier-General Khalid Nasser Al Razzouqi, Director-General of Dubai Police 'Smart Services', said:

> With an aim to assist and help people in the malls or on the streets, the Robocop is the latest smart addition to the force and has been designed to help us fight crime, keep the city safe and improve happiness levels. He can chat and interact, respond to public queries, shake hands and offer a military salute.

Dystopian vision

Authorities in the Dubai fake-royal tyranny want at least a quarter of its police force to be robots by that year again – 2030 – which also turned up in an article by Danish politician and World Economic Forum insider Ida Auken which was posted on the Forum website in 2016. It was headed: 'Welcome to 2030. I own nothing, have no privacy, and life has never been better.' She described her home at that time as 'our city' and was concerned for those who did not want to share the then AI technocratic society. She described them as 'Those who decided that it became too much, all this technology' and 'Those who felt obsolete and useless when robots and AI took over big parts of our jobs.' In Auken's scenario such people lived a different life in 'little self-supplying communities' or 'just stayed in the empty and abandoned houses in small 19th century villages'. She continued in her 2030 prediction:

> Once in a while I get annoyed about the fact that I have no real privacy. Nowhere I can go and not be registered. I know that, somewhere, everything I do, think and dream of is recorded. I just hope that nobody will use it against me.

> All in all, it is a good life. Much better than the path we were on, where it became so clear that we could not continue with the same model of growth. We had all these terrible things happening: lifestyle diseases, climate change, the refugee crisis, environmental degradation, completely congested cities, water pollution, air pollution, social unrest and unemployment. We lost way too many people before we realised that we could do things differently.

She was describing the Problem-Reaction-Solutions and NO-Problem-Reaction-Solutions that led to the technocracy so long planned by the One-percent mentality behind the World Economic Forum except that the 'little self-supplying communities' would not be allowed.

We can see how a very few could control the entirety of humanity through an AI brain connection, a centrally-directed AI global army and a Smart Grid controlling everything. A further aspect of AI in relation to the Hunger Games Society is the absolute carnage which Auken indicated that is coming for jobs and income through the mass-replacement of humans with AI technology which is already happening at a quickening speed (written before the carnage of jobs and income that came with the manipulated lockdowns).

Even news items are being written by artificial intelligence with AI digital news and sport presenters being developed. None of this is by chance. It's by Cult. How few do you need to dominate the world through the global Smart Grid when centrally-controlled AI can decide what happens with everything connected to the Internet, all surveillance, communication systems, transport, economics, food production and distribution, what news items say, and even the digital AI that presents them? All this and so much more is planned to be centrally dictated and I make the strong case in *The Trigger* that this point of control in the Smart Grid is planned eventually to be Israel, the fiefdom of the Sabbatian-Frankist cult, the prime network in the global Cult.

CHAPTER THIRTEEN

What is really behind transgender hysteria?

Tolerance isn't about not having beliefs. It's about how your beliefs lead you to treat people who disagree with you - Timothy Keller

I have indicated a number of times so far that there is a deep and sinister motive behind transgender hysteria that has gripped the mind of New Woke and been tyrannically imposed on the rest of society. Know the outcome and you'll see the journey.

The Cult wants a no-gender synthetic 'biological' human to replace what we have now. The new human body is being designed to better interact with AI and to be able to survive the catastrophic levels of destructive radiation necessary for the Smart Grid to function in its final form which the current human body would struggle to survive. 5G is not the end in terms of the impact of frequency transmissions; it is only the next stage. Synthetic genetics is advancing rapidly in public arena projects and far more so in underground bases where the Archon-to-Cult knowledge transfer takes place. Synthetic biology or 'SynBio' is a fast-emerging area of science that includes everything from genetic and molecular engineering to electrical and computer engineering. The content of the Bill Gates 'virus vaccine' is designed to advance this process as I will be explaining. Definitions of synthetic biology include: 'A multidisciplinary area of research that seeks to create new biological parts, devices, and systems, or to redesign systems that are already found in nature'; 'the use of a mixture of physical engineering and genetic engineering to create new (and, therefore, synthetic) life forms'; and 'an emerging field of research that aims to combine the knowledge and methods of biology, engineering and related disciplines in the design of chemically-synthesized DNA to create organisms with novel or enhanced characteristics and traits'. When translated from the Orwellian this means synthetic post-humans. Transgender hysteria is the Tiptoe on a road that leads to synthetic *everything*. The pressure for vegan diets being pushed to 'save the world' is only a Tiptoe to synthetic food which will be further advanced by manipulated food shortages in the wake of the 'virus' hysteria – if we let them do it. American scientists claimed in 2020 they had developed 'Xenobots' that are 'neither robot nor animal' constructed from living frog cells and described as 'living machines'. Research groups are leading the world to artificial wombs and gestation and these are only projects publicly known, not the cutting edge that we don't see. A lamb was grown in an artificial womb for four weeks and Australian researchers have experimented with lambs and sharks. A 2017 article in the London *Guardian* was headed 'Artificial wombs could soon be a reality. What will this mean for women?' It said:

> We are approaching a biotechnological breakthrough. Ectogenesis, the invention of a complete external womb, could completely change the nature of human reproduction. In April this year, researchers at the Children's Hospital of Philadelphia announced their development of an artificial womb
> ...

> ... Researchers at Cambridge University, meanwhile, have also kept a human embryo alive outside the body for 13 days using a mix of nutrients that mimic conditions in the womb. The embryo survived several days longer than previously observed and research only stopped because they were approaching the 14-day legal limit for the length of time an embryo can be kept in a lab. In other words, our ethics rather than our technology are now the limiting factor.

Reflect on that phrase 'could completely change the nature of human reproduction' in the light of what I have said in this book and much earlier ones about the plan for the end of human procreation described by Aldous Huxley. Many research centres around the world are seeking to develop synthetic skin, organs, blood, even brain tissue. Public experimentation reveals the direction while giving the impression that the development is at a really early stage. Behind the scenes synthetic biology is extremely advanced through Archon-Cult knowledge transfers in the underground facilities hidden far from the public gaze. Genuine research by genuine people provides the cover with an apparent process of development while the finished article is already waiting to be played out in the public arena when the time is right. Synthetic robots are even looking ever more like the humans they mimic and the 'consciousness' of these robots is artificial intelligence (Fig 341). We should not only think of AI with regard to robots and machines, but also with digital virtual people that don't exist except in cyberspace. The plan in the end is to absorb human minds into only cyber reality with no 'physical body' at all and the stepping stones to that are already clear to see. Remember that picture from earlier of very human-looking people that don't exist except as cyber creations. Once you know the game the

Figure 341: This is how far machine humans have come in the public arena and this is far from the cutting edge in the secret projects and underground facilities.

YOU REALLY BELIEVE THAT? YOU'RE NUTS

Figure 342: It goes with the territory once you break free of The Program.

world becomes an open book and Bubble minds confirm that by calling you crazy (Fig 342). Transgender hysteria has come out of nowhere to be suddenly everywhere because the Cult has pressed the button on the preparation for the synthetic human which will have no gender and not be able to procreate. Aldous Huxley who operated in the arena of Cult operatives envisioned just such a society in his prophetic *Brave New World* in 1932:

> Natural reproduction has been done away with and children are created, 'decanted', and raised in 'hatcheries and conditioning centres'. From birth, people are genetically designed to fit into one of five castes, which are further split into 'Plus' and 'Minus' members and designed to fulfil predetermined positions within the social and economic strata of the World State.

Huxley was precisely predicting the Cult agenda the best part of 100 years ago. Understanding how Huxley in 1932, George Orwell in 1948 and Dr Richard Day in 1969 could know what was coming relates to how I have been able to so accurately predict events in my books over the last 30 years. If you have access to the hidden agenda as an insider, as with Day, or penetrate the plan by decades of research, you can comfortably predict what we perceive as the future. It can be done on this basis: If there is an agenda for the world and nothing intervenes to stop that then what is planned will happen and in this way by uncovering the plan you 'predict' the 'future'. The idea from my perspective is to alert enough people so the plan is stopped. It will rightly be asked how Huxley and Orwell could predict events so far ahead which involved technology and drugs that didn't even exist at the time. This included Orwell's Big Brother 'Telescreens' keeping constant surveillance in every home. Today they are known as Smart TVs although there are much more extreme versions in the pipeline. That question of how they could be so accurate about technology that didn't exist can be answered this way: There are two realties in human society working alongside each other with very different levels of knowledge. One is Postage Stamp Society with strictly limited information and the other is Cult reality interacting with Archontic reality through the inner sanctum of secret societies and Satanism. The latter connection especially allows inner-core Cult initiates to know about technological possibility and projected plans even when they are not yet available or happening in human reality. Those that operate in those circles can pick up themes of where the world is being taken and technology that will be possible to take us there even if they are not directly part of the Cult itself. Non-insiders who don't operate in those circles have to work their backsides off to breach the secrecy with both five-sense research and expansions of consciousness that can connect with levels of awareness working to end human enslavement and help people awaken from their perceptual coma.

Confuse gender then fuse gender

The current obsession with transgender and its imposition on children and the young (as always) by schools, universities, media and peer pressure is an intensely malevolent campaign to confuse gender on the way to *deleting* gender with the synthetic technologically-created no-gender human. From this comes an even smaller Bubble of self-identity (Fig 343). Cult insider Dr Richard Day told the paediatricians in 1969 that the plan was to make boys and girls the same and children would be produced without sexual procreation. The Cult is confusing gender on a Totalitarian Tiptoe to *fusing* gender. The largely unnoticed first stage was to dilute the differences between men and women

Figure 343: Non-binary on the road to no-binary as self-idenity goes on being squeezed into smaller and smaller Bubbles.

and increasingly treat them as biologically the same when they have clear differences that should complement each other. Their body information fields process information differently and women have gifts and aptitudes that most men don't have and vice-versa. The idea has been to dilute that uniqueness and most importantly the *perception* of uniqueness with slogans like a woman can do anything a man can do just as well. Actually that's not true in many cases and the same with a man doing anything a woman can do just as well. There are differences and we must not let New Woke insanity kid us otherwise. I am not saying that women should not do whatever they choose and good luck to them. My point is how the manipulation has been operating slowly and then ever-quicker towards the end of gender and the blurring of differences between men and woman was stage one. We have had as a result the feminising of men and masculinisation of women. Recall the progression (Tiptoe) in how first we had 'unisex' clothing for both men and women and now no-gender clothing. Female uniforms are being phased out for a no-gender variety with police forces and military increasingly scrapping traditional men's and women's uniforms for 'gender-neutral' versions and the same with school uniforms. Tiptoe, Tiptoe, Tiptoe.

The deletion of the terms 'ladies and gentlemen' and 'boys and girls' are also calculated to delete the concept of male and female gender from the language and so the psyche. We are well into the next stage today with the number of young people questioning their gender increasing dramatically and kids suddenly bewildered about their gender who would not have been before without the systematic programming. Why does anyone think 'question-your-gender' studies are becoming compulsory in schools? Why do they think gender-confusing drag queens are being invited into schools in country after country to read gender-confusing stories to even very young children? Why are parents and anyone else challenging this calculated and disgraceful manipulation of kids instantly branded 'transphobic' by often viscous transgender New Woke activists and the media? It's the same modus operandi that we have with climate change activists, 'anti-racist' activists, gay activists, political correctness activists and all the other mix-and-match permanently-offended intersectional expressions of New Woke serving the Cult while overwhelmingly in ignorance that there is a Cult. Nothing is more certain to scramble the brain than the virulent up-your-own-arse syndrome that pervades New Wokeness like a roaring epidemic. Maybe we should shut down the global economy and put everyone under house arrest until it passes. The consequences of this tyranny for many children are horrific and life-long. Research by doctors in Australia revealed that those attending gender identity clinics are many times more likely to show signs of autism than the general population. The doctors reported their findings in the *Journal of Autism and Developmental Disorders* and quoted a US study of nearly 300,000 children that suggested those with autism were more than four times more likely to be diagnosed with gender 'dysphoria' compared with those without autism. Stephanie Davies-Arai, founder of the campaign group Transgender Trend, said people with autism spectrum disorder

(ASD) are more likely than others to become fixated on an idea which they can find almost impossible to drop (see Greta Thunberg). She warned: 'We should not just be cheering on this vulnerable group towards life-changing medical interventions.'

Transgender Trend is a group of UK-based parents questioning the trend to diagnose children as transgender which has led to the unprecedented number of teenage girls suddenly self-identifying as 'trans'. The group challenges laws which put transgender rights 'above the right to safety for girls and young women in public toilets and changing rooms along with fairness for girls in sport' (Fig 344). These legitimate questions and concerns are condemned as serious

Figure 344: And it is planned to become ever more a thing of the 'past'. Female is a sex/gender and they are all planned to disappear. Men are the first target, but women are following fast.

transphobia by the ever-scornful face of New Wokeness. I mean how could it possibly be valid to protect young girls and women from a strapping bloke walking into their toilet or changing room with his bollocks dangling claiming to be female; or a big muscular man taking part in the women's weightlifting championship because he goes by the name of 'Vera'? American Fallon Fox is a transgender mixed martial arts fighter who identifies as a woman while walking around in a powerful male body. Her/his self-identification allows her/him to compete against much less physically powerful women and she/he knocks the crap out of them. One woman had her skull broken. Criticism she/he faced for this, however, was purely transphobic and nothing to do with protecting women from life-changing harm. Outsports, a sports news website focusing on LGBT issues in sports, described Fox as the 'bravest athlete in history' to confirm yet

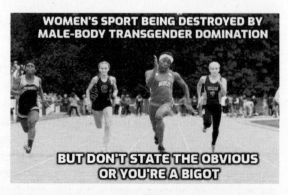

Figure 345: Big powerful male bodies self-identifying as women are destroying women's sport – another way that the female sex/gender is being targeted for eventual elimination.

again that transgender activism is not interested in fairness, balance and inclusivity. It seeks dominance for its view while itself being clueless about how and why it is being used by the Cult. What New Wokers call 'inclusivity' for one minority means exclusion and even a broken skull for another. Where you are in the hierarchy of Wokeness decides who dominates who and transgender is now way above female. Consequently women's sport is being destroyed by those in men's bodies self-identifying as women running away with the prizes and destroying previous female performance records. Why? Their bodies are *not female* (Fig 345). By the way, how come 'women' in male bodies can so out-perform those who are born women if males and females are not biologically different? Transgender extremism is a parody of itself (Fig 346). Transgenderism gets whatever it wants even though Catherine McGregor, a highly-intelligent and perceptive Australian transsexual, said: 'We are a telephone booth minority.' That's correct even with all the propaganda, but the Cult's no-gender human Tiptoe demands what is happening and so it happens. Transgender activist extremism is nothing *whatsoever* to do with support for transgender people. They are only pawns and the excuse just as with the Jewish community and Sabbatian-Frankism. Support for Cult ambitions is what this is all about and as you would expect Sabbatian-Frankist, Cult-owned Hollywood

Figure 346: : Parody is now almost impossible in the face of what is really happening.

has taken up the cause with transgender 'superheroes'.

'Unregulated live experiments on children'

I have detailed in *Everything You Need To Know* the list of ways that gender confusion is being manipulated from indoctrination in schools from the earliest ages to inhuman pressure applied by 'gender' doctors and clinics to push children and adults into gender transition without any evidence that this is necessary or advisable. Gender-changing and puberty-blocking drugs are being handed out at an alarming rate because that's what the Cult wants. So blatant and extreme has this become that 35 psychologists resigned in three years from London's

Gender Identity Development Service (GIDS) at the Tavistock and Portman NHS Foundation Trust. They cited 'over-diagnosis' with too many children put on puberty-blocking drugs when they should not have been diagnosed with so-called gender dysphoria. Whistleblower workers have said children as young as three are having 'unnecessary gender reassignment treatment' after being incorrectly diagnosed with gender dysphoria. Carl Heneghan, director of the Centre of Evidence-based Medicine at Oxford University, described the policy as 'unregulated live experiments on children'. The number of children treated at GIDS is reported to have increased in a decade from 77 to 2,590 – a trend that is happening across the world as the Cult agenda is enforced. Former GIDS staff said they were not able to properly assess people for fear of being dubbed 'transphobic'. New Wokeness is nothing if not predictable and desperately naïve although its inner core knows exactly what it's doing. One psychologist said: 'We are extremely concerned about the consequences for young people ... For those of us who previously worked in the service we fear that we have had front row seats to a medical scandal.' Another said:

> The alarm started ringing for me ... I didn't feel able to voice my concerns, or when I did I was often shut down by other affirmative clinicians. Looking back there are young people who I now wouldn't necessarily put on medication.

Lisa Littman, assistant professor of the practice of behavioural and social sciences at Brown University in Rhode Island, said that many teenage girls are identifying as transgender after seeing a friend do so or after reading transgender material online. Teenagers with no previous history of 'gender dysphoria' suddenly proclaimed themselves to be transgender in the wake of an individual or multiple members of their peer group doing the same. Littman called these 'cluster outbreaks'. A decade ago most 'gender dysphoria' children were biologically male but today they are biologically female. Clearly perceptual programming and group-think is playing a major role here. As you would expect Lisa Littman was subjected to major abuse from transgender activist extremism – so much so that her study was withdrawn and revised. Michelle Cretella, executive director of the American College of Pediatricians, said she has heard from dozens of families about teenagers experiencing 'rapid-onset' gender dysphoria. The majority are girls between 13 and 15 with often a history of depression and no previous signs of gender dysphoria. They suddenly announce they are transgender and should have hormone treatment. Cretella said:

> Human beings are biological creatures heavily shaped by social relationships, especially during adolescence. It is at this most critical stage of development

that our culture now holds out the lie that teens should embrace a mental illness – gender dysphoria – not only as their 'authentic transgender identity' but as the answer to all that ails them mentally and emotionally … [these children are] being needlessly led down a path of irreversible long-term physical and emotional harm.

The programming is incessant today with the BBC as always right up there. It aired on its *children's* channel CBBC the documentary *I Am Leo* about a 13-year-old going through transition treatment at the increasingly infamous Tavistock and Portland clinic. It naturally won an award. I have no problem with those who genuinely believe they are transgender. The problem is confusing children about gender who were not confused before. That's child abuse. Former BBC journalist John Humphrys – far too much of a journalist for today's BBC – recounted his experience of a doctor seriously concerned about what was being done to children in the transgender arena, but she was terrified of the backlash for saying so. Humphrys said the doctor 'was afraid of being viciously attacked on social media and having her reputation destroyed. She is not alone in her fear. Far from it.' He said the doctor was 'desperately worried' over far too many children being treated as victims of 'gender dysphoria' when they were suffering from a more common condition – 'being a confused teenager'. What can you say in the light of all this about the UK Liberal Democrat Party taking money from a puberty-blocking company while peddling an extreme transgender policy that benefits such organisations? *And the kids …?* Graham Linehan, co-creator of the hit TV comedy *Father Ted*, spoke out against both this mistreatment of children and transgender extremism after seeing a feminist beaten up by trans activists. He faced an onslaught of abuse and hate from the anti-hate brigade that hasn't looked in the mirror for years. It wouldn't dare. Work opportunities dried up for Linehan from gutless potential employers. He said: 'I think there's just a stink around me, the stink of bigotry, you know, that has deliberately been created, by radical trans-rights activists. It has had a chilling effect.' Good on him for refusing to back down although with the proviso that Linehan himself had been involved in Woke-style censorship before he realised by experience what a tyranny it is. This chilling effect is now increasingly being written into law and the incessant propaganda led to Swiss voters supporting in a 2020 referendum the plan to make it illegal to 'publicly denigrate, discriminate or stir up hatred based on a person's sexual orientation'. This sounds fair enough, but it's the way this will be applied that is the danger to free speech. Who decides if something is discrimination or a freely held opinion? Who decides if transgender people don't get a job because they are transgender or because the potential employer thought another applicant was better qualified? Well, the state does and that's the Achilles heel of such laws when it comes to the deletion of basic freedoms.

In writing ...

Law website Rollonfriday.com and its reporter Jamie Hamilton revealed documents in 2019 that exposed the covert and highly manipulative nature of transgender activism targeting children. The document advises on campaign tactics and was written by staff at Dentons, described as the world's biggest law firm measured by the number of lawyers, which merged with Sonnenschein Nath & Rosenthal in 2010. The document was produced in conjunction with the Thomson Reuters Foundation and LGBT pressure group IGLYO. A Denton disclaimer states that the content 'does not necessarily reflect the personal views of any of the lawyers, staff or clients of Dentons'. Thomson Reuters Foundation apparently said something similar. Reporter Jamie Hamilton wrote that Mosaic, an LGBT youth group, contributed to the UK portion of the report along with an NGO that 'wished to remain anonymous'. The Denton report, headed 'Only adults? Good practices in legal gender recognition for youth', says in the foreword: 'We hope this report will be a powerful tool for activists and NGOs working to advance the rights of trans youth across Europe and beyond.' It contends that 'every child has an accurate conception of their own gender identity which they should be entitled to affirm in law without impediment'. To anyone still in touch with reality this is a breathtakingly ridiculous statement, but extreme transgender activism is dependent on not staying in touch with sanity let alone reality. We see the ever-recurring theme of deleting parental rights over their children to isolate the kids and hand power to the state and transgender extremists. Reporter Hamilton described the main thrust of the Denton document:

> 'The right to legal gender recognition is crucial for young trans persons to secure all other rights', it states, advising that the UK should 'eliminate the minimum age requirement' at which children can change their legal gender 'on their own volition, without the need for medical diagnoses or court determination'. The document emphasises that there should be 'no eligibility criteria, such as medical or psychological interventions'. And UK authorities should 'take action' against parents 'who are obstructing the free development of a young trans person's identity in refusing to give parental authorization when required.

Could it be any more sinister? Allow children to make life-changing decisions about their gender and 'take action' against any parents who challenge what is being done to their kids. In the words of the document: 'It is recognised that the requirement for parental consent or the consent of a legal guardian can be restrictive and problematic for minors.' Restrictive and problematic for transgender activism and extremism would be a better way of putting it. The Denton document says it is 'crucial' there are 'no limitations' to 'gender confirmation treatment', including 'no requirement to be diagnosed with gender dysphoria'. It deletes all potential barriers and delays on any child 'persuaded' they are living the 'wrong' gender to be set on course to puberty blockers and surgery. Maybe someone could give me a better definition of child abuse because I can't think of one in this moment. Another point is that through epigenetics or passed-on gene sequences the changes in one generation's transgendered hormonal re-write will passed to the next. Rollonfriday.com reporter Hamilton continues:

> The report advises activists to 'de-medicalise' their campaigns 'so that legal gender recognition can be seen in the eyes of the public as distinct from gender confirmation treatments'. It explains that this is because one of the reasons opponents often cite for 'denying such access to minors' is the view that 'young people should not have irreversible surgeries until they are of the age of maturity'.

The document really is a shocker and confirms in writing the experience of parents and wider society of transgender impositions that have become the norm. Such are the sinister extremes demanded by transgender activism that the Denton report warns campaigners to 'avoid excessive press coverage and exposure' because the 'general public is not well informed about trans issues, and therefore misinterpretation can arise'. Translated from the PR-speak this means 'avoid excessive press coverage and exposure' because if the 'general public knew what you really want then horror and fury can arise'. The document describes how activists in Ireland 'have directly lobbied individual politicians and tried to keep press coverage to a minimum in order to avoid this issue'. It says the chances of success are increased if activists 'target youth politicians' who in successful campaigns in Europe 'brought up the issue at every meeting of any sort – even ones which were not directly relevant, to ensure the issue was at the forefront of everyone's minds'. You can see why the transgender 'issue' involving 'a telephone box minority' is everywhere and impinging on everything. Writer James Kirkup featured the Denton document in an article for *The Spectator* in which he summed up the content (and the transgender agenda) in two sentences:

> In short, this is a handbook for lobbying groups that want to remove parental consent over significant aspects of children's lives … A handbook written by

an international law firm and backed by one of the world's biggest charitable foundations.

Transgender lobbyists will always have the system on their side when they have the Cult on their side. Kirkup said the document explained some transgender mysteries such as why bodies like the police – 'not famous social liberals' – were in the vanguard of the transgender transformation of society 'even to the point of checking our pronouns and harassing elderly ladies who say the wrong thing on Twitter'. Kirkup notes the advice given to activists on how to secure pro-trans laws. This includes 'get ahead of the government agenda' which means publishing 'progressive' (New Woke) legislative proposals before governments had time to develop their own and in this way have the proposals of activists simply transferred into official policy. New Woke employs this tactic across all its fronts with the Cult pulling the necessary strings. Kirkup points out that a UK House of Commons select committee report in 2016 'adopted several positions from trans groups' and was followed in 2017 by 'a government plan to adopt self-identification of legal gender'. Another way to scam the public is to 'tie your campaign to more popular reform', the Denton document says. Slip it in alongside something that most people would support. This happens constantly with government and lobby groups to hide otherwise controversial plans behind non-controversial legislation. The document offers an example:

> In Ireland, Denmark and Norway, changes to the law on legal gender recognition were put through at the same time as other more popular reforms such as marriage equality legislation. This provided a veil of protection, particularly in Ireland, where marriage equality was strongly supported, but gender identity remained a more difficult issue to win public support for.

The Denton document stresses that countries where deletion of parental rights over their children's gender decisions have moved with the greatest speed have been those where trans lobby groups have been successful in stopping the wider public learning the extreme nature of the plans and the consequences for kids before they were a fait accompli.

It's about 'discrimination'? Yeah, right

A good way to assess the genuineness of New Woke activism is to observe how they treat members of the community they claim to be representing who don't support the party line. In all aspects of New Wokeness the response to this is the same – attack them, abuse them and do everything you can to silence them. New Woke censorship has taken its blueprint from the 'anti-Semitism' industry Protection Racket specifically created to protect the far right Sabbatian-Frankist-controlled government in Israel from criticism and *not* to protect Jewish people from discrimination. The same approach can be witnessed every day with climate change, 'anti-racism', extreme feminist, gay and transgender activism. You may care about the environment, oppose racism or be a woman, gay or transgender, but that doesn't matter if you don't believe *everything* we tell you. Those who have been through gender transition, regretted that and warned others, are subjected every time to abuse from transgender activists who set out to gag them. I have read books by transitioned people who had their lives destroyed by the decision they were encouraged to take by the 'experts' and they are doing this to *children*. It is absolutely tragic to see how their lives have been devastated. In many cases the reason they initially questioned their gender was being sexually abused as a child that led to a psychological state in which they wanted to be a different gender to the one that was abused. Psychological support and understanding was what they needed. Instead the puberty blockers were handed out and their lives torn apart. One example is Debbie Karemer from Hertfordshire in England who lived as a man for 17 years only to realise after counselling that she was suffering the psychological consequences of sexual abuse. She said other transgender people she knows regret their surgery and are too frightened of the activist backlash to be honest about it. See what I mean – she said they weren't *brave enough* to tell their story. Why do they need to summon such courage? Is it because of the reaction of general public? No – because of the reaction of *transgender activists* who are a tyranny and everything they attack others for being. In fact, they could not qualify for any version of New Woke if they didn't condemn others for what *they* do. That's in the contract.

Transgender activist extremism and its contempt for genuinely transgender people and for freedom of speech and opinion was confirmed in two stories and their aftermath in 2019. Debbie Hayton, a 51-year-old physics teacher in the English Midlands, changed her gender from male to female in 2012, but sent transgender activists into a fury of knicker-twisting (or underpant-twisting) when she wore a t-shirt that said: 'Trans women are men. Get over it.' Well, my goodness, you could hear the sound of gusset tearing from ten miles away. Debbie wore the shirt at an event organised by campaign group Fair Play for Women which has not been the case since transgender storm troopers imposed their will (the Cult's will) over women's rights. Hayton served on the LGBT+ committee of the New Woke-hijacked Trades Union Congress (TUC). This was irrelevant once she became a *blasphemer* and twelve members of the committee complained to TUC General Secretary Frances O'Grady. They said that wearing the shirt had 'gone beyond discourse, and the expression of alternative viewpoints, and is now propagating hate speech against the trans community.' Don't be ridiculous, oh, sorry, you are being. New Woke definition of 'hate speech': 'Any statement that we don't want people to hear.' I love the bit about going beyond discourse and alternative viewpoints – there are no alternative viewpoints about transgenderism that activists don't want to silence. Nicola Williams, founder of Fair Play for Women, summed it up when she said:

> Accusations of transphobia are thrown at women so often for so little that the word has lost all meaning … When even trans people can get called transphobes, I hope people now understand how ludicrous and far-fetched these attacks have always been. The trans movement has been hijacked by gender extremists.

Exactly right and in their extremes of arrogance they are destroying freedom on behalf of the Cult. The British Labour Party, closely-associated with the TUC, has long been licking the arse of the 'anti-Semitism' industry Protection Racket in 24-hour shifts. Now the same is happening with transgender extremists. Getting slaughtered at the polls in 2019 was no Wake-up call for the Labour Party. Woke doesn't do Wake. Would-be Labour leader Rebecca Long-Bailey supported a campaign to label a party women's rights organisation as a 'trans-exclusionist hate group'. The Labour Campaign for Trans Rights published a plan designed to 'rid the Labour Party of transphobia and to stand up for trans people'. The Protection Racket modus operandi is repeated. Well, if it works why not? It got rid of anyone who criticised Israel and now it can be used to delete the membership of anyone that won't concede their own rights to transgender extremism. The Long-Bailey-supported campaign called for 'expulsion from the Labour Party of those who express bigoted, transphobic views'. Keir Starmer, who beat Long-Bailey for the leadership of this excuse-for-an-opposition party, is another New Woker who lives on his knees with his tongue extended pointing to Tel Aviv. The Labour Party was already on a life-support machine and then someone switched it off. The New Woke war on women's rights is constantly gathering pace. The students union at Leicester University in the city where I was born changed International Women's Day into International Womxn's Day in reference to 'transgender women' to include a 'more inclusive spelling of women'. This is the same student body that elected a trans woman called Dan Orr to the position of women's officer. International Women's Day of 2020 also saw Sefton Council in the UK take down two flags at town halls which displayed the dictionary definition of 'woman' as an 'adult human female'. It took a single complaint from a New Woke *man* to have the flags taken down. A bloke posting with the name 'Adrian Harrop' told the council: '… the flag you're flying at the moment is a hostile transphobic dog whistle, recognised as a symbol and brand of one of Britain's most outspoken and visible trans-antagonists, and the leader of a transphobic hate group.' The dictionary definition of woman is now transphobic and offensive. I did mention that male and female sexes are the target of the Cult didn't I?

Promotion and relegation

Figure 347: The illusion of inclusion and equality. Privilege (ironically) is the real goal.

Women were once top of the PC sexual hierarchy in its early days. Now this has entered the next stage of the Totalitarian Tiptoe to the no-gender human they have given way to the transgender movement. Women who challenge the imposition of transgender rights on women's rights have become enemies of the revolution (Fig 347). No-gender people will eventually take over and transgenders will become enemies of the revolution. This is how it works. Women are falling down the PC hierarchy because they are a *gender* and their only remaining role from the Cult's perspective is to diminish the influence of men before themselves being deleted. How about men and women coming together in mutual support? How about that for an idea? Far more important than women to the Cult is mass immigration of other cultures into Western Society and this also puts those cultures and religions above women in the PC hierarchy. New Wokeness says it stands for women's rights while silencing criticism and exposure of religions that treat women like slaves and garbage. Criticism cannot be allowed, nor exposure of the effect of mass immigration of other cultures in transforming communities, oppressing women and reducing work opportunities. That would open the whole mass-immigration strategy to public questioning and any open debate must be stopped. This is the real reason that ultra-Zionist censors say they won't debate with 'anti-Semites' while 'anti-racist' censors often won't debate with 'racists' or 'anti-transphobia' censors with 'transphobes'. They know they will lose on the facts and they make an excuse to avoid that exposure. Women who highlight the effect on rape crisis centres, single-sex hospital wards and women's sport of 'gender self-ID' (decide your gender any time you want) are dismissed as 'TERFs', or 'trans-exclusionary radical feminists' (Fig 348 overleaf). It is an age-old trick for

Figure 348: It's already well underway. (Image Gareth Icke.)

those with extreme positions to paint their reasonable opposition as extremists. This happens right across the New Woke arena and with ultra-Zionists who treat Palestinians like vermin while branding any challenge to that as 'anti-Semitic'. Another example of the transgender war on free speech was that of Maya Forstater, a tax expert at the think tank Center for Global Development, who did not have her contract renewed (she was fired) after posting tweets disagreeing with government plans to let people declare their own gender without any supporting evidence. She demanded her right to refer to people by the gender she felt appropriate and not by how she was told to do so. It's an opinion that she has a right to have in any free society. Not, however, according to employment judge James Tayler who spouted New Woke orthodoxy in his verdict after Forstater appealed against her dismissal to an employment tribunal (she never stood a chance). Mr Woke Tayler said with jaw-dropping irony that her views were 'not worthy of respect in a democratic society'. But, of course, Tayler's *are* because they represent the imposed orthodoxy. To have someone legally judging others who clearly does not grasp the basic tenets of freedom or democracy is both appalling and par for the course in the Brave *New Woke* World. Once you set the perceptual blueprint for what society must believe you co-opt the entire system including academia, government agencies, police and judiciary to enforce that blueprint. Go to court with something the system supports and you will win almost no matter what the evidence. Go to court with something the system does not support and you will invariably lose. This is how society is stitched up all over the world. *Independent judiciary??* You must be joking. Christians have lost cases over the right to express their beliefs, such as wearing a cross, while vegans who avoid buses because flies hit windscreens win cases to protect their beliefs. The question is not about right or wrong; it's whether the Cult via authority wants it or doesn't. How much abuse you get from New Wokers is directly associated with where your subject of criticism stands in the PC hierarchy.

Harry Potty

Maya Forstater made the intelligent response to Judge Woke Tayler that 'framing the question of transgender inclusion as an argument that male people should be allowed into women's spaces discounts women's rights to privacy and is fundamentally illiberal (it is like forcing Jewish people to eat pork)'. Her solicitor Peter Daly said: 'Had our client been successful, she would have established in law protection for people – on any side of this debate – to express their beliefs without fear of being discriminated against.' No wonder she lost. The decision becomes all the more outrageous when you see a picture of the person Forstater refused to call 'They' – local Dundee councillor Gregor Murray who looks exactly like a man including a male haircut and a beard. He was suspended for two months in May, 2019, for calling feminist critics 'scum', 'hateful' and 'vile'. I wonder if that fits Judge Tayler's criteria for being worthy of respect in a democratic society? The controversy of Tayler's ludicrous decision kicked off further when *Harry Potter* author J.K. Rowling posted this:

Dress however you please.
Call yourself whatever you like.
Sleep with any consenting adult who'll have you.
Live your best life in peace and security.
But force women out of their jobs for stating that sex is real?
#IStandWithMaya #ThisIsNotADrill.'

This was the cue for New Woke virtue-signalling to reach still new heights of gusset wringing as 'human rights' organisations including the New Woke Amnesty UK gushed forth in condemnation of Rowling that 'trans rights are human rights'. And, er … *women's* rights? How about the right to free speech and opinion? My god, it's pathetic. The response was ironic in that Rowling often tweets in support of multiple New Woke causes. This is no defence. Your loyalty to Wokeness must be total in every facet and form or you are an enemy of the revolution. *Star Wars* actor Mark Hamill further infuriated the permanently-infuriated New Woke Mafioso by 'liking' the Rowling Tweet and as with so many in the world of spineless celebrity he fell to his knees begging for forgiveness:

Ignorance is no excuse, but I liked the tweet without understanding what the last line or hashtags meant. It was the 1st 4 lines I liked & I didn't realize it had any transphobic connotation.

Put your tongue back in, mate, and consider the 'connotations' of your gutlessness for human freedom.

New Woke Stasi closing in

Former British police officer Harry Miller was contacted by police to 'check his thinking' over a series of tweets about transgender issues that were not 'hateful', but simply his opinion. They admitted he had not broken the law and put him in the Orwellian category of 'crime, no crime', whatever the hell that supposed to mean, and recorded the matter as a 'hate incident'. Miller took the police to the London High Court where fortunately the case was handled by a judge who wasn't Woke-obsessed. Justice Julian Knowles said Miller's tweets were 'lawful' and police actions had a 'substantial chilling effect' on his right to free speech which should not be underestimated. 'To do so would be to undervalue a cardinal democratic freedom' the judge said. 'In this country we have never had a Cheka, a Gestapo or a Stasi. We have never lived in an Orwellian society.' On that, in current circumstances, I would beg to differ. Police across the world are now ignoring real crime to seek out thought-crime like this with 120,000 'non-crime hate incidents' logged since 2014 in the UK on a system that appears in criminal record checks that can stop people being employed. While many officers are appalled and aghast at having to do this their careers depend on compliance as the Cult co-opts foot soldiers of The System against their will. New Woke police are destroying freedom by the hour orchestrated in the UK though the College of

Figure 349: Freedom-destroying New Woke lunacy is being infused into the police and all institutions because it's the Cult agenda.

Policing established in 2012 to infuse New Woke into law enforcement (Fig 349). The College defines a 'hate incident' as 'any non-crime incident which is perceived, by the victim or any other person, to be motivated by a hostility or prejudice against a person who is transgender or perceived to be transgender'. It's a victim's charter as it is meant to be and it takes only a tiny few – sometimes *one* – to complain for a police investigation to be launched or for Silicon Valley and other corporations to ban speech or withdraw products from sale. This would appear to be insane when in fact the agenda needs complainants to justify its imposition and if there is only one that will have to do. Even transsexual women who say *themselves* they are still a biological man have been banned by Twitter. Madness? Yes, calculated madness to serve the Cult agenda. Jon Caldara, the most-read columnist on the *Denver Post*, said he was fired for believing there are only two sexes. He said of his sacking: 'What seemed to be the last straw for my column was my insistence that there are only two sexes and my frustration that to be inclusive of the transgendered (even that word isn't allowed) we must lose our right to free speech.' Caldara said he supported gay marriage, had LGBT friends and didn't care who used what bathroom. Even this was not enough to save him. New Woke demands total obedience or else. Another sinister aspect of the Caldara story is that his article was about the 'style book' of the *Associated Press* which lays out for staff a common grammar and word style. He said the book claims there are more than two sexes and that 'They' is now a word to describe a single individual. 'Illegal alien' was also banned in favour of 'undocumented alien'. This is all agenda-pushing language. There are not more than two sexes. There might be multiple self-decided sexual *identities,* but that's not the same as *biological* sexes, and the idea that 'They' can be seriously used to convey the singular is so grammatically crazy I'll move on. We really are looking tyranny in the eye here. You will have seen the extremes to which children, adults and whole populations are being subjected to transgender manipulation with endless examples every week. Here are just a few headlines at Davidicke.com over a period of only a few months:

Jury rules against dad trying to save his 7-year-old from gender 'transition'; California Adds Iowa to 'Travel Ban' Because of Refusal to Fund Gender Transitions; Ban on harmful gender stereotypes in ads comes into force; UNESCO claims Siri & Alexa promote gender stereotypes; Three-year-old changes gender from boy to girl after being sent to live with foster parents whose own son had just transitioned to become a female aged seven; Transgender lessons for two-year-olds: Girls are skipping school to avoid sharing gender neutral toilets with boys after being left to feel unsafe and ashamed; France seeks to 'desegregate' children's toys in battle against gender stereotypes (to create a new gender stereotype); School locks out protesting pupils outside gates as they rail against new 'pointless' gender neutral uniforms that force girls and boys to look the same; Drag artists read to children as library aims to teach youngsters about gender identity at story time sessions; Swedish Government Grants $175,000 to Fund Drag Queen Shows For Children; Drag Queen Flashes Children During Story Hour; School in Brooklyn Hands Out 'Drag Queen in Training' Stickers to 4-Year-Olds; Drag Queen Teaches Toddlers How to Twerk; Another Drag Queen Story Hour pervert exposed as a sex offender ... why are public schools subjecting our children to these deviants?; Houston Chapter of 'Drag Queen Story Hour' Folds Amid Paedophile Scandal; Child drag queen poses next to almost-naked adult counterpart, but mother says boy not sexualized; Drag queen who teaches toddlers about sexual tolerance posts abusive tweets including one calling former Tory Minister Ann Widdecombe a 'fucking venomous hypocritical bint'; Drag

queens drafted into nursery schools to teach children about sexual
diversity; Drag Queen strips for kids in the King County Library;
Elementary School Invites Convicted Felon Drag Queen to Talk to
Children; Vice News Celebrates Prepubescent Boys Dressed in Drag,
'Next Generation of Drag Queens'; Drag Queen Admits He's 'Grooming
Next Generation' in 'Story Hours'; Furious parents slam primary school
for inviting drag queen who calls herself 'Bristol's Resident Slag' and a
troupe of cross-dressers to read stories about tolerance to the children;
Progressive men literally start cutting off their own balls as gender
insanity reaches new level of dangerous mental illness; Transgender
model claims sanitary brands should be re-designed because using
'pretty and pink' products targeted at women causes him psychological
pain; United Airlines to Introduce 'Non-Binary' Gender Flight Booking;
Northamptonshire Police now issues US-style baseball caps which they
think will somehow encourage transgender recruits.

Story follows story day after day and we have already reached the
point where it is impossible to exaggerate through parody what is really
happening.

Some of those
headlines reflect
the out-of-
nowhere
explosion of
drag queens all
over the world
suddenly
recruited to read
stories to small
children as
young as five or
less in schools
and libraries –
everywhere from
North America

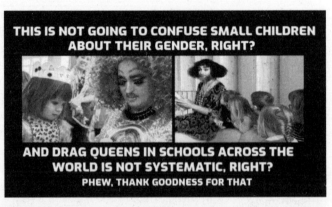

Figure 350: The fact that it's suddenly happening in country after country
is pure coincidence and nothing whatsoever to do with systematically
confusing the gender perceptions of children from the earliest possible
age.

to Scandinavia to Europe and Australia. It's just another coincidence (Fig
350). The idea is to sexualise children and confuse them about gender.
Scottish National Party MP Mhairi Black invited a drag queen called
'Flowjob' who posts explicit images on Twitter to read stories to children
as young as four at a primary school and when parents complained she
dubbed them in typically New Woke fashion as 'homophobic'. An
Internet video shows a drag queen dancing suggestively and crawling
on her/his hands and knees in front a little girl while adults applaud
and cheer. The drag queen then strokes the girl's hair and kisses her. It's

a sickening display and will any of the parents involved be getting a visit from social services like loving parents do? Not a chance. An American drag queen called Kitty Demure posted a video in which he said he was shocked that parents allowed this to happen. He asked: 'Would you want a stripper or a porn star to influence your child?' Demure further questioned why the Woke 'Left' had so much respect for drag queens when they 'put on make-up, jump on the floor and writhe around and do sexual things on stage'. He said this was not an avenue that parents should want their children to explore and he rightly said that many did so because they wanted to appear cool or Woke. 'You can raise your child to be just a normal regular everyday child without including them in gay, sexual things.' Not if the Cult has its way you can't. I have no problem with drag queens. What people do is none of my business among consenting adults. The systematic indoctrination and manipulation of children is *quite another thing* and we should say that loudly and constantly until sanity dawns (Fig 351). It is sobering to ponder that we are still only in the first stage. Imagine what is to come for children if parents don't grow a backbone and get together to stop

Figure 351: Why would schools and The System do this if not to target children and their perceptions of gender? What consenting adults do is none of my businesses. The manipulation of children, however, is ALL of our business.

this. We have even had claims that the murder of transgender people, and especially those of colour, is an 'epidemic' when the figures expose this as still more mendacity. This lie has been repeated by Democratic presidential candidates, the Cult-controlled American Medical Association and New Woke organisations like the US Human Rights Campaign. The 'epidemic' numbered 26 transgender murders in 2018 using Human Rights Campaign figures which means an average of 1.8 per 100,000 transgender people. The murder rate for the general population in 2018 was *4.9* per 100,000 meaning that transgender people are considerably *less* likely to be killed by violence. An *epidemic*? The technique is to fire lies in all directions knowing that almost everyone that hears them will not check the facts and believe the lies to allow the agenda to be advanced.

One conspiracy with many faces

Falling global sperm counts, especially in the West, connects with the plan for the transgender, then no-gender, non-procreating human. Sperm counts are plummeting though gender-bending chemicals in the environment, including food and drink, and radiation constantly generated from smartphones in the pockets of men, Wi-Fi and the 5G roll-out. Confirmation comes with all the fertility clinics now on a scale never seen before. The fertility rate in America fell by nine percent between 2007 and 2011 and in 2016 fell to the lowest since records began. Meanwhile the benefits of staying single are being promoted with Dr Elyakim Kislev, professor at the Hebrew University of Jerusalem, saying that 'being single can be an advantage instead of a source of agony'. This is a theme that turns up in many guises. The lifestyle that people choose is their own business, but when you put all these things together there is a clear theme: The Cult *wants humanity to be infertile*. There will be no need for male and female sexes in a no-procreation world and we are witnessing their systematic elimination. We may be in the relatively early stages but that is the goal and Cult agendas move faster and faster as they get closer to the stage of 'normalisation'. When non-white people celebrate the demise of the white race they should know that they will be next. This is not a war only on white people, but the entire human race and we need to come together and not allow the Cult to drive us apart (written before imposed 'social distancing'). Remember that to children being born today the madness that many older people can see through is their 'normal'. This is another reason why divisions are being manipulated between young and old. By 'normalisation' here I mean the normalising of insanity brilliantly captured in George Orwell's concept of 2 + 2 = 4 versus 2 + 2 = 5. He wrote in *Nineteen Eighty-Four*: 'Freedom is the freedom to say that two plus two make four. If that is granted all else follows.' If the freedom survives to speak facts the official lies can still be challenged. Big Brother knew that and decreed 2 + 2 = 5 and everyone had to believe it – or else. What happens at first is that you know the answer is 4, but eventually it is easier to agree the answer is 5 and finally to protect your own self-respect you *believe* the answer is 5. The transition period we are now experiencing between '4' and '5' is dependent on another Orwell concept – that of 'doublethink' which is defined as holding two contradictory beliefs and accepting both to be true. This way 4 and 5 can coexist until 5 takes over completely. Having open borders *and* enough homes, jobs, school and hospital places, is a potent example of doublethink. Orwell's book and methods of manipulation and control are everywhere you look. He wrote:

In the end the Party would announce that two and two made five, and you would have to believe it. It was inevitable that they should make that claim sooner or later: the logic of their position demanded it. Not merely the validity of experience, but the very existence of external reality, was tacitly denied by their philosophy. The heresy of heresies was common sense.

And what was terrifying was not that they would kill you for thinking otherwise, but that they might be right. For, after all, how do we know that two and two make four? Or that the force of gravity works? Or that the past is unchangeable? If both the past and the external world exist only in the mind, and if the mind itself is controllable – what then?

This is what becomes possible when a few know the truth about reality and keep that from the masses. External world or not the point is that we need to recognise that we are Infinite Awareness *and* an individual unique perception. I am a unique experience called David Icke and *All That Is, Has Been, And Ever Can Be*. New Wokeness is enforcing upon the population a long list of demands that come down to $2 + 2 = 5$. These range from human-caused climate change to political correctness and most certainty to post-biological sexual orthodoxy. Professors of biology are being attacked, abused and 'investigated' for saying that men and women are biologically different. Oxford University professor Selina Todd, a historian who specialises in the lives of women and the working class, was given security guards after threats from transgender activists over her support of women's rights. Dr Allan M. Josephson, a former head of Child and Adolescent Psychiatry and Psychology, was demoted by the University of Louisville for saying children who insist they are transgender should not be instantly believed and Professor Nicholas Meriwether at Shawnee State University in Ohio was rebuked for refusing to refer to a student with a male body using 'female pronouns' when it was against his religious beliefs. Many others have already been outright fired or forced out by mass, even violent, New Woke protests for the mildest of statements based on $2 + 2 = 4$. Such activists insist that society be transformed on the basis that there are no genders except what people choose them to be any time they like … $2 + 2 = 4$ usurped by $2 + 2 = 5$. The Cult plan for the world can only happen if facts and freedom to express them is abandoned. To do that $2 + 2 = 5$ must be the norm and $2 + 2 = 4$ the enemy of the revolution. Facts are replaced by *perceived* facts and once generations born in the $2 + 2 = 4$ era have gone all humans will be born ('decanted' in Huxley's words) into the post-fact world of $2 + 2 = 5$ which is all the population will hear from cradle to grave. This is a quote from Adolf Hitler:

When an opponent says to me, 'I will not come over to your side,' I reply calmly, 'Your child belongs to us already … What are you? You will pass on. Your descendants, however, now stand in the new camp. In a short time they will know nothing but this new community'.

Another 2 + 2 = 5 imposition is the 'pronoun' tyranny in which transgender men and women insist they are called by their preferred pronouns of 'he', 'her' or the utterly bizarre 'They' and 'Them'. I will never call an individual 'They' or 'Them'. I have some respect for language and if you concede to stupid you become stupid. The way around this is real simple. Transgender people in male or female bodies that call themselves by the opposite pronouns should be free to do so and anyone referring to them who doesn't feel comfortable using 'he for a woman's body or 'her' for a male body should be equally free *not* to do so. This is the solution in which freedom is the winner on both sides. It doesn't happen because freedom is the *target* of the Cult and not the desired outcome.

Silence the parents, program the teachers

Many parents who are deeply unhappy with what is happening to their children at school fear the consequences of saying so. Most teachers are programmed to believe in the program and those that can see through the insanity, and even the conspiracy, know that if they challenge the imposed orthodoxy their career will be over. New Woke follows the methods of the Cult as an expression of the Cult by imposing an agenda while intimidating or silencing anyone who can see what is happening. If people concede to that intimidation the world's children are lambs to the perceptual slaughter. We are seeing the Totalitarian Tiptoe to complete state control of children and the end of parental rights which are being constantly eroded to this end. A teacher in Texas personified what is happening when he said that parents should not have the 'final say' in raising their own children. He was responding to complaints by parents about yet another drag queen employed to indoctrinate their children. The adult drag performer (stage-name 'Lynn Adonis') spent the day with the kids at Willis High School and exchanged social media contacts. School Principal Stephanie Hodgins defended the decision and proved she is in the wrong job while clueless English teacher Anthony Lane said parents should submit to the will of the 'community' over the upbringing of their own kids. Here we go – right on message and it's becoming a common theme as the Cult targets parental rights and the family unit itself. 'I believe that raising a child is the responsibility of the community and that parents should not have the final say,' the brain of America gushed forth. 'Let's be honest, some of you don't know what is best for your kids.' Ah, but this expression of academic arrogance does know (I *am right*) and insists that their well-being is best served by advice from 'Lynn Adonis', a man dressing as a woman who dances provocatively while people wave dollar bills as an Internet video revealed.

The Vatican has long been controlled by the Sabbatian-Frankist wing of the Cult (see *The Trigger*) which owns the position of Pope. The current incumbent, Pope Francis, can often be seen promoting the Cult agenda like climate change and subjects relating to education and the upbringing of children. He called for a new 'Global Pact on Education' to create a 'new humanism' under the title 'Reinventing the Global Educational Alliance'. The Pope hosted a conference of people from politics, economics, academia, science and sociology along with celebrities from areas like sport. A 'Global Pact on Education' was signed to 'hand on to younger generations a united and fraternal common home' and 'create a global change of mentality through education' (indoctrinate the young). Orwell would have noted the language that included a quote used by Cult asset Hillary Clinton: 'It takes a village to raise a child.' Pope Francis called for an 'educational village' with an 'educational path involving everyone'. Nowhere did the Francis announcement refer to parents as the central voice in the education of their children because the state is taking over as the Pope well knows and promotes. He has also said it's our 'duty' to 'obey international institutions' like the United Nations and European Union. His call for a 'new humanism' is ironic given the word is defined as 'a rationalist outlook or system of thought attaching prime importance to human rather than divine or supernatural matters'. A rationalist outlook or system of thought in this context means the technocracy which requires the deletion of spirituality in all forms to be replaced by the religion of New Wokeness. The Pope is a 'man of God'? Yep – and I'm a jelly baby.

A major Cult vehicle for the intimidation of parents is the social services Mafia operating in all countries of the West (and elsewhere) through which enormous and ever-increasing numbers of children are stolen by the state from loving parents for ridiculous and patently invented reasons. Paedophile and Satanist rings operating through social services even have children stolen to order. I have exposed this outrage and its consequences for children and parents in other books. Secret 'family' courts

Figure 352: Secret courts in alleged 'free' countries are stealing children from loving parents on an industrial scale while parents are banned from speaking publicly and the media is excluded.

which can include Satanist and paedophile judges, lawyers, social service operatives and police, are used to seize children for the state and the Cult from parents who adore them (Fig 352). 'Family' courts do not have juries so paedophile or satanic judges – or paedophile and satanic rings working through the judges – can control the outcome. The phone call or knock on the door from social services is now one of the biggest fears that parents have and this state-kidnapping is part of the Tiptoe to the end of parenthood and procreation. Teachers, doctors, police and other professions are encouraged and mandated to tell tales on parents to social services and that would be justified if real abuse was evident. In the cases I am talking about (and they are legion) the children are not being abused at all – quite the opposite. Parents are frightened to stand up, challenge and complain about drag queens and transgender indoctrination in schools in fear of reprisals from increasingly authoritarian schools and social services or abuse from New Wokers and even other parents locked away in the land of Cult-induced perceptual coma. The poor kids are left unprotected to have their minds absorbed into the belly of The Beast to become the next and even more extreme generation of New Woke as the family unit is dismantled to be replaced by AI technology and the world state.

I can understand how intimidating it must be to face the potential wrath of the school and social service tyrannies, but if that doesn't happen your kids will be left at the non-existent mercy of the Cult and Cult-owned state every day when they go to school. Parents coming together in groups for mutual support must happen to challenge and expose what is going on so that individuals are not isolated and alone. They are after your kids and even more so with your kid's kids. It's time to draw a line while there is still one to be drawn.

CHAPTER FOURTEEN

What is the New World Symphony?

Control your vibrations to be the master of your own harmony
– Suzy Kassem

The conventional answer to the question posed in the chapter title is that the New World Symphony is a piece of music by the Czech composer Dvorak made most famous in Britain in a television advertisement for Hovis bread. I am talking instead about another version that I shall call the *Brave* New World Symphony.

Dvorak's work is made possible by vibrations emanating from musical instruments while my version is played by vibrations emanating from people via perception. I have focused in the last few chapters on the effect of Cult manipulation in the realm experienced by the five senses or the 'seen', a holographic projection of the wavefield unseen. The foundation of our reality is information encoded in vibrations and waves that express in their frequencies the nature of that information. For example hate is a slow, dense frequency while love, joy, gratitude and forgiveness generate quick, high and expanded frequencies. One represents a vibrational prison cell and the other is the way out of the Matrix. The *Brave* New World Symphony is a low-vibrational information and perceptual construct that disconnects humanity from its expanded self and the True 'I'. If we could hear this 'symphony' of waves it would sound like the backdrop to a horror movie, slow, low, morbid, heavy and dense. It would be akin to the guttural voice of life-long Cult operative Henry Kissinger and the sound transmitted by Saturn which you can hear in YouTube videos. The association between Saturn and what I am calling the wave 'symphony' of the simulation is explained in *Everything You Need To Know*. To build prison walls around ourselves with bricks and bars would be seen as crazy. When humans do that with the frequencies we emanate this is called being 'normal' and living in the 'real world' (Fig 353 overleaf). Those that refuse to comply with their own perceptual/vibrational imprisonment are by contrast 'weird, mad, pseudo-scientists and

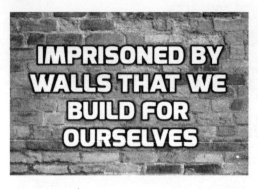

Figure 353: We built the walls – so *WE* can take them down.

conspiracy theorists'. The world is indeed upside down. The sequence is simple: Information = perception = nature of the vibrations and frequencies emitted by people in the form of waves. These waves entangle with like-waves to generate collective networks of the same vibration/frequency which influence the perceptions of all involved (Fig 354). This is the wave equivalent of only hearing one version of something to the extent that you believe what it says in the absence of any alternative. It is a collective version of the Bubble.

Perceptions are not only ingrained by information received by the five senses. They are most powerfully embedded by wave-entanglement with those of like-mind – like-vibration/frequency – a vibe which

Figure 354: Wave-entanglement, perception-entanglement, perfectly symbolised.

solidifies the longer you remain in that perceptual state. The vibration becomes more powerful through unchallenged repetition and the constant confirmational connection with the collective field of like-wave entanglement. In turn, the wave-state impacts upon the formation of brain pathways or neuron networks (also waves in their base form) that dictate how information is processed into perception. When I speak of people not being able to process or compute certain information or concepts I mean that literally. Wavefields emanated by Postage Stamp perceptions and processed through brain pathways reflecting those wavefields cannot decode information outside their perceptual limits any more than a computer can process information when encoded and firewalled not to do so. 'I can't get my head around that' is the phrase you often hear in response to off-stamp information accompanied by the assumption that if they can't understand (process) that possibility then it can't, by definition, have any validity. I can best describe what I mean with the assumption of the mainstream scientific mind that if I can't see, touch,

Figure 355: Bubbles and burst Bubbles speak a different launguage.

taste, smell or hear it then whatever is being claimed can't be true. I am describing here a self-generating vibrational prison cell that I call the 'Bubble' (Fig 355). Limited perceptions and self-identity transmit limited frequencies which can only connect or entangle with like-frequencies. These Bubbles transmitting the same frequency waves (perceptions) entangle with each other and through those connections mutually and collectively confirm *'I am right'*. This is the wavefield basis of the New Woke mentality and why it is so Dalek-like immovable no matter what the evidence – *emergency, emergency, cannot compute, cannot compute.* Try telling Greta Thunberg that CO2 is the gas of life. Internet AI systems such as Google-owned YouTube that continually offer you information that corresponds with your search history are feeding the Bubble with perception-confirming information as is the censorship through Silicon Valley and political correctness of information and opinion at odds with the official Postage Stamp narrative.

Wave awakening

As people's perceptions change so do the frequencies they transmit and what follows is disentanglement from the previous wavefield networks created by former perceptions. In the world of the seen those once close to you, or of like-mind, drift apart as new wave networks are formed

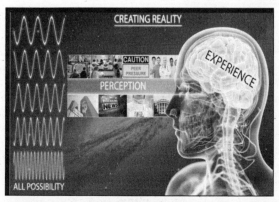

Figure 356: Another version of the Bubble and how they are formed. (Image Gareth Icke.)

with others that match the new perceptions. You are beginning to see what they can't see (Fig 356). In the transition period people can feel alone and isolated as they disconnect from the old before synchronising widely with the new. Stick with it – it'll all work out. The more that we expand our sense of self-identity and

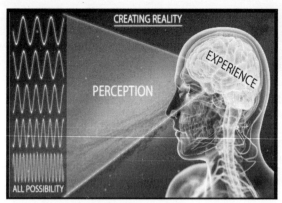

Figure 357: Bursting the Bubble. (Image Gareth Icke.)

Figure 358: Another inversion. When madness calls you mad it is confirmation that you are not. (Image Neil Hague.)

perception of reality the more the frequencies we generate expand and quicken and the more of Infinite Awareness that we can consciously access (Fig 357). This is known as 'waking up', a term that means the opposite to being New Woke. Brain pathways re-form to sync with expanding consciousness and they are able to process information and awareness beyond the Bubble. By this time the Bubble has burst anyway and confirmation that your consciousness is really 'de-Bubbled' comes when you are censored or called crazy, mad and even dangerous. Whenever I am described by Bubble people in those terms I quietly say thank you, much appreciated. There comes a point in this expansion where you breach the firewalls of the simulation and begin to see what human reality really is. You become aware of the illusions, manipulations and smokescreens designed to enslave us in ongoing ignorance and the scale of the perception program begins to dawn. When you first speak out to expose what is happening those still in the Bubble – the ones you are trying to alert – will be your greatest opposition. This is not because they are 'bad' people just as New Wokers are not bad people in and of themselves. They just can't see – *yet* – what you can as your consciousness expands beyond the Matrix. Expanded awareness is perceived as insane by enslaved awareness (Fig 358). We have to understand and be patient or we'll be in a permanent state of frustration and anxiety which feeds the dragon its low-vibrational fix. Almost everyone is in the Bubble to start with and being holier-than-thou is never justified. A scene in the first *Matrix* movie has the Morpheus character giving Neo the facts of life about what I am calling Bubble people:

> The Matrix is a system, Neo. That system is our enemy. But when you're inside, you look around, what do you see? Businessmen, teachers, lawyers, carpenters. The very minds of the people we are trying to save. But until we do, these people are still a part of that system and that makes them our enemy. You have to understand, most of these people are not ready to be unplugged. And many of them are so inured, so hopelessly dependent on the system, that they will fight to protect it.

That's an excellent description of how the program works except for the bits about 'our enemy' and saving people. I don't see anyone as an enemy. We are all *One* even though we may have dramatically different attitudes and patterns of behaviour. Once we refer to 'enemies' we externalise those we are challenging when they are only another aspect of ourselves in a different mental and emotional state. I am challenging and exposing patterns of behaviour as they impact negatively upon others and their freedom. I don't see those involved as enemies. From my perspective they are being perceptually misdirected and enslaved. Nor am I trying to 'save' anyone. People can only emerge from a perceptual straight-jacket through personal choice. I am only offering a different way of looking at life and the world. What people do with that, or don't, is up to them and none of my business except where it impacts on individual and collective freedom. With this proviso we need to find peace with others having different views. Freedom is the freedom to make choices, experience the consequences, and make new choices. It is not to be forced to make someone else's choices. That is called tyranny and New Woke (same thing). If you focus anger, hatred and resentment on those with whom you disagree that very focus creates a wave entanglement with them on the frequency of anger, hatred and resentment *if* that person feels the same about you. This sets up a wave connection through which frequencies of anger, hatred and resentment are mutually exchanged to the emotional and vibrational detriment of both or, in the case of the Cult and its unseen 'gods', you feed them the low-vibrational energy that sustains and empowers them. Are we really going to change anything by making such a frequency wave connection with the Cult through hatred of the Cult? What you hate you become. What you fight you become. Wave entanglement is how that happens. Burst your Bubble and everything changes (Fig 359 overleaf).

Mirror, mirror ...

I have watched so many
people become what
they first set out to
oppose and you see this
in politics all the time.
The Cult wants us to
hate its assets because it
knows that in this state

Figure 359: Bursting the Bubble.

we will be fly-trapped in
its vibrational lair. Martin Luther King said: 'Darkness cannot drive out
darkness; only light can do that. Hate cannot drive out hate; only love
can do that.' Hate empowers the vibration of hate while love empowers
the vibration of love. It really is that simple. In fact once we love in the
totality of *The One* there is no vibration at all – just the still and silent *All
That Is* which is love in its Infinite form and that means *intelligence* in its
Infinite form. We can feed the Cult and its non-human masters with our
low-vibrational focus or we can starve the Cult of its power source by
not transmitting on its frequency. Macho-man fury and hatred may seem
to many to be the way to respond to Cult manipulation when the
opposite is the case. Loving (or at least not hating) perceived 'enemies'
while challenging vociferously what they do are not contradictions. This
is the only way to challenge behaviour while not entangling with its
vibrational state and becoming what you claim to oppose (see New
Woke). What is not transmitting on your frequency cannot connect with
you. You can be affected by the actions of others who *are* on its
frequency, but not you directly. As your consciousness expands and
your frequency quickens you are operating on a completely different
vibe to mainstream society and become less and less affected by its
madness. In that state we stop emitting the waves that can connect with
those that seek to hurt us and if we do that they *can't* hurt us. I am often
asked how come I am still alive while exposing such *apparently* powerful
forces. My answer is that if they can't make a wave connection with me
they cannot affect me in the holographic 'physical' realm which is a
decoded projection of wave information fields. It's at the *wavefield* level
that everything happens and holographic reality is only its projection on
the symbolic movie screen. If you want to change a movie do you
scream at the screen or pull out a banner and protest? No – you change
what is being projected on the screen. Human life is the same. Change
what is happening at the wavefield level and the holographic movie
screen of 'human society' must automatically change to reflect that.
Humanity is constantly seeking change in the wrong place and the Cult
encourages this. Change yourself and you change your life experience.
Change collectively and we change the world. If you want change

without *personal* change – vibrational change – you will be waiting forever. I said that we entangle with people on the frequency of anger, hatred and resentment *if* they feel the same about us. If they don't there can be no wave connection on that frequency when the other person is not transmitting on that frequency. You are then generating frequencies of resentment with nowhere for them to go except to entangle you with others consumed by resentment. For this reason forgiveness does not only benefit the forgiven, but also the forgiver. Here's a way to disentangle destructive relationships and their aftermath *if* you mean it: 'It was just a mutual experience for, in the end, mutual benefit, so let's shake hands and wish each other a great life – all my love to you and see you on the other side when we'll laugh at what we thought was so important.' Isn't that rather better than 'I'll always hate that bastard' (and always be affected myself by that same hatred)? The mutual vibe of hatred and fear is the basis for all conflict and war and when it's gone so have they. As John Lennon wrote: 'War is over if you want it.'

Frequency freedom

From this perspective of how we are vibrationally enslaved and how we can set ourselves free *everything* starts to make sense when it didn't before. Human society has been specifically structured and manipulated to create maximum possible fear, anxiety, hatred, anger, depression, resentment, and all the other low-vibration emotions and their consequences like conflict and war that entrap people within the firewalls of the simulation. Love in its Infinite sense is to the Cult like garlic to a vampire and this explains why authority throughout 'history' has been terrified of anyone saying that love is *The Answer*. Anything that would expand and raise the vibrational state of the population is all the Cult's worst nightmares arriving at once. It knows that once that happens the game is over and the outward arrogance of the Cult masks the constant terror that somehow humanity will awaken and call 'time' on the plot. They need *us* – we don't need them. We are their power source. What appears to be swagger is really whistling in the dark as they desperately pursue the AI-brain connection to block perceptional change and frequency change. Low-vibrational states of Bubble consciousness have been achieved through the rule-book myopia of religion; by playing off cultural, racial and religious groups against each other in wars of control, dominance and acquisition; giving the population constant reasons to fear (especially fear of death) and to be in states of anxiety hatred, envy and resentment; selling a self-identity based purely on human labels and/or servitude to an ever-demanding god; and downloading the Postage Stamp narrative every day that excludes everything that people need to know to see through the camouflage and deception. You will observe many other ways that this is done, too. What a coincidence that New Woke delivers everything on that list including religion because New Woke *is* a religion. The constant sub-division of labels into micro-labels is taking self-identity further and further away from I am an expression of *All That Is* and the expansion of consciousness that follows from that. With each sub-

Figure 360: No, no, no – I am *All That Is, Has Been, And Ever Can Be.*

division into micro-identities we see that identity myopia becomes consciousness myopia. I am LGBTTQQFAGPBDSM? You are Infinite Awareness having a brief experience that you *call* LGBTTQQFAGPBDSM (Fig 360). It's all a trap which particularly the young are being indoctrinated to walk into through Cult control of the 'education' system, mainstream media and all the New Woke activist groups supported by giant Cult-owned corporations and frontmen like Bill Gates, George Soros and Silicon Valley celebrities such as Musk, Zuckerberg, Brin, Page, Wojcicki, Bezos, Kurzweil, and a long, long, list of others.

Once the Cult has captured perception and self-identity everything else follows. Perception dictates the frequency of the waves we transmit and those frequencies dictate how much Infinite Awareness we can access. The extent of Infinite Awareness that we connect with dictates the size of our Bubble and that becomes our perception of everything. This in turn becomes a self-fulfilling prophecy as our perceptions create the Bubble and the Bubble confirms our perceptions in a feedback loop of perceptual enslavement (and therefore every other kind). Who enslaves us? *We do.* We do so by allowing the Cult and all its agencies of state and media to impose our perception of both the world and our very self-identity. This is great news because what we have created we can uncreate. Break that feedback loop and the power of the Cult is no more. How do we do that? Open our minds to all possibility. Open our hearts to the love and wisdom of *The One*. It can't be that simple? Oh, but it *is*. The Cult knows that it is and constantly works to keep minds and hearts closed to the greater reality beyond the simulation which is nothing more than a perceptual feedback loop. The simulation is *in our heads* (Fig 361). It's a perceptual program which can close hearts, but not enter them when the frequency difference is so great. Open your heart and what is released as love, intelligence and wisdom will change your life and collectively transform human reality. The whole foundation of

Figure 361: The simulation is a wavefield interactive information source that humanity decodes into holographic reality in the brain. (Image Neil Hague.)

the Cult agenda is to close hearts and minds to turn Infinite humanity into perception Bubbles which then connect to form a hive mind through wave entanglement. New Woke is a hive mind which is policing everyone who won't conform to the hive. The illusion of diversity allows Bubbles and groups of like-Bubbles to be set at war with each other to divide and rule. We have 'anti-fascists' acting like fascists. The Bubble perceptions of both are basically the same which makes their behaviour the same because their *frequency* is the same. They are convinced they are polarities of each other while being 'opposames'. Beyond the realm of the seen they will be seriously wave entangled by the like-frequency connections between them. Extreme Muslims (or fake Muslims) such as the Saudi Sabbatian-Frankist 'royal family' and their terror groups do the work of the Devil while claiming to serve 'God'. Their hatred and violence wave entangle with all others who express hatred and violence and even those like the extreme right that think they oppose extreme Islam. The way the vibe is expressed may be marginally different, but it's the *same vibe*. Indian author Nitya Prakash said: 'Do you ever notice how much you have in common with the person you hate?' This is true on many levels and one is most certainly the same vibe at war with itself through the illusion of being different.

Digital drugging

The plan is to make humanity in its entirety one centrally-controlled hive mind through the collective connection to artificial intelligence. I have described the Tiptoe to this in the world of the seen, but again the real deal can be found at the wavefield level of reality. The endgame is to connect the human mind to machines and the manipulation of wave entanglement between people and smart technology is happening all around us while at the same time destroying human to human discourse (entanglements). Here is the prime reason for social media which achieves both goals. People are not communicating with each other face to face – human waves to human waves – but via technology in which AI machine waves act as the conduit. In this way machine waves intervene and intercept human wave connection (this has happened on an unprecedented scale during the 'virus' lockdowns). People who used to talk with each other at home, in the street, in restaurants, now stare mesmerised at the screen (Fig 362). I will first discuss the holographic effects of this on a chemical level and then how this plays

Figure 362: The childhood hijack.

out in wavefields to connect humans to machines and AI. High-placed insiders of deeply sick organisations like Facebook have publicly exposed how Zuckerberg and his cohorts set out to addict Facebook users to stay on the site for as long as possible. Sean Parker, the first president of Facebook and now a critic, said the idea was to absorb as much of a Facebook visitors time and attention as possible. Floyd Brown and Todd Cefaratti describe how successful this effort has been in their Silicon Valley exposure, *Big Tech Tyrants*:

> … Facebook is only the tip of the social spear. It's well documented that kids are spending an average of ten to twelve hours a day across all digital media. And adults aren't far behind at almost six hours, up from three hours a day in 2009. This includes all the time spent on cellphones, computers, gaming consoles, and streaming devices. Cellphone use alone has mushroomed from a third of an hour a day in 2008 to 3.3 hours currently.

This is partly explained by techniques to trigger a 'dopamine rush'. *Psychology Today* describes dopamine as 'the feel-good neurotransmitter – a chemical that ferries information between neurons'. Dopamine contributes to 'feelings of pleasure' and acts as a 'reward system' which can very soon become addictive. *Psychology Today* says that 'a person seeking pleasure via drugs or alcohol or food needs higher and higher levels of dopamine … This neurotransmitter enables us not only to see rewards but to take action to move toward them.' It points out that drugs such as cocaine increase levels of dopamine and 'alter behavior accordingly'. Facebook and other disgusting companies abusing mostly the young have exploited the dopamine rush to addict people to their sites. A Facebook 'like' for a post can stimulate a dopamine reaction which becomes addictive and leads to people only posting what they think the majority will like to ensure their dopamine fix. This slowly at first and then more quickly modifies behaviour and opinion to the majority (Cult-induced) view especially when to go against that view is to unleash often systematic abuse. What starts out as a conscious posting of an opinion that may not be genuine just to get maximum 'likes' eventually fuses into the perception of the person – 2 + 2 = 5. Chamath Palihapitiya, an early senior executive at Facebook, said that 'the short-term dopamine-driven feedback loops that we have created are destroying how society works'. But, then – that's the idea. I have seen it called the 'magic of maybe' when people keep looking at the phone to see if 'maybe' they have a communication or 'maybe' they got a 'like'. Studies have shown that when communications or likes appear there can be a 400 percent spike in dopamine which is only slightly less than the effect of cocaine. Part of the addiction is concern about what other people think and how others respond to a post or picture when freedom comes from not giving a damn what anyone thinks of you. Concern with what others think deletes your personal power. You become *them* so they like you. Seek popularity as a goal in itself and it will destroy your uniqueness. Comparing self with others and their often fake lives portrayed on social media leads to depression, loss of self-esteem and feelings of inadequacy. Studies reveal that the more time people spend on social media the more lonely and isolated they become. Phone addiction also hijacks and scatters concentration with the potential to permanently destroy the ability to concentrate. Social media and smartphones are Cult behaviour modification devices and it's all been carefully worked out by psychological specialists in the pay of Silicon Valley psychopaths like Zuckerberg. One observer rightly said that highly addictive drugs are being put into the hands of children before they have any defences against them. Sam Vaknin, a contributor to the Internet documentary *Plugged In* which exposed the effects of social media, said this about the calculated assault on the minds of the young:

> Facebook, Twitter, all these networks are surfing the wave. They know it's a dangerous wave. They know that people are drowning. They read all the statistics, the increased suicide rate, depression, anxiety. They know absolutely everything. They have designed maliciously, malevolently and possibly criminally, they have designed the networks exactly to cater for human pathology in its most extreme form.

Even those who can see some of what is happening tend to explain this calculated manipulation as an effort by Zuckerberg and Chief Operating Officer Sandberg to extend Facebook visits to increase the value of advertising. It's actually far darker and more sinister than that and the real explanation comes with the understanding that these platforms are fronts for the Cult. Their domination of discourse and information exchange allows the Cult to modify and manipulate perception and behavior while censoring to ever-increasing extremes information and opinion that challenges that narrative. Social media is a very foundation of the technocracy. The minds of the young (tomorrow's adult population) are being fucked-with on a monumental scale and New Woke is one of its creations in league with other Cult agencies including the Gates-manipulated 'education' system. Are people so totally lost in Fairyland that they don't see how soaring rates of suicide, depression and anxiety among the young that have taken off in the smartphone/social media era are centrally connected to the emergence of those phones and platforms? In this period there has been a 50 percent increase in suicides in America among girls under 17 and a 30 percent increase in boys. Anxiety in teenagers is reported to have increased by 70 percent in 25 years; children and young people attending accident and emergency units with a psychiatric condition has more than doubled since 2009; teenagers admitted to hospital with eating disorders almost doubled in three years up to 2019. English schools buying in professional mental health support for pupils has nearly doubled in three years from 36 per cent to 66 percent because the National Health Service (NHS) can't cope. Some of this is due to growing up becoming a medical condition and some is the effect of social media and the smartphone culture. Should we be surprised when insiders have described how Silicon Valley technocrats are so deeply sick they boast about how they capture users in 'isolation boxes' and 'filter bubbles' in which they 'inflict torments that anger or sadden the users without them realizing why'? Facebook and other social media companies hire 'attention engineers' using techniques employed by casinos to make their platforms as addictive as possible. People like Zuckerberg are calculated abusers of young generations on a scale that defies belief. Headlines galore tell the story and reveal the consequences of this psychopathy: 'Social Media Use and Perceived Social Isolation Among Young Adults'; 'Facebook's Emotional Consequences: Why Facebook Causes a Decrease In Mood and Why People Still Use It'; 'Facebook Use Predicts Declines in Subjective Well-Being in Young Adults'; Association of Facebook Use With Compromised Well-Being'. The young are being conditioned and broken to be the unquestioning adults that will passively accept the technocracy and AI-brain assimilation. The war on men and 'toxic masculinity' is precisely planned to induce such passivity. Jaron Lanier, an American computer scientist, said:

> Society has been gradually darkened by this scheme in which everyone is under surveillance all the time and everyone is under this mild version of behaviour modification all the time. It's made people jittery and cranky. It's made teens especially depressed which can be quite severe.

He's right although Lanier is considered a founding father in the field of virtual reality and he might ask himself where that is heading when the Cult agenda of augmented reality and immersive technology leading to full-blown assimilation is factored in.

Virtual 'humans'

We have the emergence of virtual humans with body movements, voices and emotional expressions generated by AI that you could not tell from 'real' humans. The Smart Grid is a simulation within a simulation and virtual reality technology is a virtual reality within a virtual reality. Samsung's highly secretive Neon project was reported in early 2020 to have developed artificial intelligence virtual 'avatars' almost indistinguishable from biological humans. Samsung engineer Pranav Mistry said the technology can 'autonomously create new expressions, new movements, new dialogue (even in Hindi), completely different from the original captured data.' Base the original on a human and then have it become its own personality. Facebook has its Codec Avatars project designed to let people create realistic virtual versions of themselves for use in cyberspace. The company claims the avatars would help 'social connections in virtual reality become as natural and common as those in the real world'. The avatars are planned to allow Facebook users to connect with friends and family in a three-dimensional social network. Yaser Sheikh, the director of research at Facebook Reality Labs, said: 'The real promise of augmented reality and virtual reality is that it lets us spend time with whomever we wish and build meaningful relationships no matter where people live.' Excuse me I feel a 'bollocks' coming on. This is really about absorbing humanity and particularly the young into a virtual reality world in which the one we currently experience is lost and even more importantly further disconnect humanity from expanded reality outside the simulation. The human mind is being prepared for assimilation into AI and drawing the young particularly into a virtual world generated by technology is a

vital stage and step in that direction (Fig 363). Young people are already living their own virtual lives presenting a perfect face to the world through social media with the downsides deleted by omission, self-delusion and Photoshop. There is even a term now of 'Snapchat dysmorphia'

Figure 363: Assimilation masquerading as the 'latest thing'.

for young people who have plastic surgery in an effort to make them look like the fake image they have Photoshopped to post on social media. Beyond the facade so many are drowning, desperate and unable to compete with the illusory perfect lives they read about while their true and unique self is lost to them in the deluge of 'this is how you should be'. Envy turns to depression when you cannot be what you have been conditioned to envy. Jamie Chiu, a Hong Kong-based psychotherapist, said growing up in a social-media-obsessed environment damages self-esteem with camera filters in particular 'leading to a dangerous trend where people feel insecure about not being as beautiful as their own filtered selves'. The Cult is creating an illusion within an illusion so that its targets become utterly lost with no grip on *any* reality. With every step along this dark tunnel of manipulated myopia and misdirection the influence of the True 'I' is diluted by fake self-identity. Virtual interaction via AI has diminished the life-skills of personal interaction eye to eye with real live people.

Eyes are more interested in staring at screens than looking into other eyes to see the window on the soul that a Facebook post can never do (Fig 364). Social media has been specifically designed by the Cult to generate psychosis in the population which is defined as 'a severe mental disorder in which thought

Figure 364: You are feeling *sleeeepy.*

and emotions are so impaired that contact is lost with external reality'. The Cult knows that once a sense of reality is lost a new reality can be imposed to fill the void – the technocracy and assimilation into AI. Floyd Brown and Todd Cefaratti write in *Big Tech Tyrants*:

> With everyone carrying a cellphone all the time [not me!]; with teens even sleeping with theirs; with the majority of girls telling researchers they would give up their boyfriend before they would relinquish their cell phone, Facebook had the perfect behavior modification platform designed to detect, examine, react, and provide feedback on the most mundane, or the most intimate, of human activities.

> Users could now be constantly tracked and measured and unknowingly given cues and prompts on a steady drip, all custom-tailored. Users could be hypnotised little by little by technicians [technocrats] they'd never see, for purposes they may or may not approve of. They could be reduced to prompt-

and-respond lab animals … which is exactly what happened.

The authors describe social media platforms as essentially 'a crime scene'. Yes – crimes against humanity and the young. Anyone still think Zuckerberg and company who coldly calculated this are New Woke heroes? Jaron Lanier's point about being under constant surveillance is why the Cult *wants* us to know we are tracked 24/7. This in itself leads to behaviour modification through the fear of whatever you do being seen and recorded. In response people stop doing, even in what used to be called 'privacy', what they think the state might find unacceptable (see China). Cameras everywhere in streets, schools, universities, and other buildings and those constantly checking speed on the road network are designed to make people constantly aware of authority and trigger anxiety about 'breaking the rules' to cumulatively induce acquiescence (see lockdowns). When we at Davidicke.com post news stories about certain subjects on social media we know the sharing numbers and likes will be lower when those opinions can be accessed for example by potential employers. It's time to summon the courage and do it anyway. Not to do so is a dark and dangerous road that ends only one way in total human subjugation (Fig 365).

Figure 365: This is where self-censorship ends with the silencing and subjugation of all humanity. Speak your truth or there will be no truth for anyone to hear.

Who creates the Matrix? We do

Extraordinary mass-addiction to smartphones and social media cannot be explained in total by dopamine. You see people transfixed by smart screens while not on social media in search of 'likes' and approval. I have been saying for years something is coming off those phones to induce such addiction and that something are electromagnetic waves which entangle with the human waves of the user and make the person's energetic field (mind) literally part-human and part-machine. This is crucial to the Tiptoe leading to assimilation of the human mind into AI (Fig 366 overleaf). Influence through entanglement of technology-generated waves explains the multiple electromagnetic effects on the body that change the nature of cells, blood, tissue, bone marrow and brain by impacting upon the wavefield body blueprint to manifest as dementia, cancer, autoimmune diseases and so much more.

Figure 366: Smart technology and Wi-Fi are emitting waves of frequency that are entangling with human wavefields to create addiction and assimilate human frequencies into AI machine frequencies. Those that capitulate become ever more machine-like until they *are* machines. See Neil Hague colour section.

AI smart technology is assimilating the human consciousness field through entanglement ever more profoundly with each screen session for those *un*conscious to this effect. It is a form of possession by machine and AI. People are literally being *possessed by their phones* and other smart technology through wave entanglement. I will come later to how being conscious of the process can lessen or block the connection. You can tell if you are wave-entangled with smart technology by how easy it is for you to stay away from it. Do you feel anxious or that almost *part of you* is missing if you don't have your phone? If so you are wave-entangled with what the phone emits. It is taking you over. Try putting your phone in a drawer and forgetting about it. Can you do that? If not, it's got you. Should you need to use a phone for work and income observe how many times you are scanning the screen when work is not involved. Can you stop? If you can't you are machine wave-entangled – machine *possessed* – and through that connection perceptions can be fed to your subconscious mind. *This is happening all the time.* It's not only about dopamine. Wave connections between machines, AI and humans are feeding people states of perception. If you are not conscious beyond the Matrix then the Matrix is thinking for you. I observed long ago how the Cult agenda was being introduced in country after country, culture after culture, at the same time and this could only be partly explained by the secret society networks of The Web. It is happening in far too much

Figure 367: If humanity can be manipulated to subconsciously believe that the technocratic dystopia is inevitable we will decode it into experienced reality. This is the foundation of all human control – subconscious programming becomes experienced reality. (Image Gareth Icke.)

common detail in far too many communities worldwide for that to be the whole story. The Cult transformation of human society is actually being imposed as a wavefield construct absorbed and decoded by the collective human mind through these hive connections (Fig 367). What I call The Web is in fact a web of *waves* – frequencies – which attach to human wavefields as flies are caught by a spider. The Cult and its secret society inner cores create and surf those waves and seek to lure humanity into their frequency lair.

We decode holographic reality from wavefield information fields and the Cult and its 'gods' are technologically infusing their Brave New World into those fields in the form of information which humanity is decoding into holographic experience. Information waves are encoded by the Cult with its endgame reality for humanity to decode and manifest and this is what I am calling the *Brave* New World Symphony. One of the reasons the speed of change has quickened so dramatically since smart technology appeared is because it gives powerful entanglement access to the human energy field through which that information can be fed. Those in sync with its frequencies will succumb first to the agenda and support its introduction and the idea is to pull everyone into those frequency states to ensure that even those resisting today eventually submit to its oscillation. This does not have to happen. Consciousness in its expanded form is far more powerful than the Cult and its silly games. Consciousness isolated in a perception Bubble is, by contrast, a babe in arms. New Woke once again provides the most potent example. The perception system, the result of life-long programming (frequency programming), cannot process possibilities beyond *I am right* while it is held fast in the vibrational control of the *Brave* New World Symphony. Every time someone censors themselves in fear of the consequences they are being teased further into the 'symphony' and the frequencies through which society is being transformed. Saying what you believe without fear and censoring yourself *because* of fear are quite obviously not the same frequencies. The first cannot be synchronised with endgame information fields while the second certainly can be even if this happens in stages. The process is further empowered by people like Ray Kurzweil and others telling us that the AI endgame is inevitable and unstoppable and through the technique of pre-emptive programming that I highlighted earlier. Both induce the population into the endgame frequency which they can then make manifest.

AI-brain sychronisation - how smart

Another major impact on perception related to what I have described and to smartphone wave addiction is something called entrainment which means that the most powerful frequency in any given situation will 'entrain' other frequencies into its own. It's another example of entanglement. The best example is one I gave earlier of the string vibrations of three violins tuned to the same note causing a fourth violin to vibrate to the same note as the most powerful frequency entrains the other into sychronisation. Technological frequencies that now flood our reality and atmosphere are getting more cumulatively powerful and they are entraining brainwaves and human wavefields to sync with those frequencies. 5G is a massive stepping up of that potential. Once human waves are entrained with technology waves information (perception) can be transferred from AI to the human mind. Even before a direct connection to the brain we have AI assimilating human consciousness through entrainment with waves emitted by smart technology. Disruption of human wave patterns explains why people living or working close to phone and communication towers, electricity pylons or nuclear stations, can suffer depression, anxiety and diseases like cancer to a much greater extent than the average. Mainstream scientists parroting the official line say there is no evidence of such a connection and they cannot explain how it would be possible while ignoring wavefield connections or entanglement. If they did the mist would clear. Entrainment of brain frequencies connects with brain placidity that I described earlier in which the way the brain processes information is changed by the nature and form of that information. The brain has been bombarded by wave and digital information from technology in an extremely short period that it has never had to deal with in all known human history. Study after study has concluded that the human brain is being seriously rewired by digital/electronic stimulus and I say this is a holographic reflection of wavefield rewiring. *Of course* the brain must change in the circumstances I have described. We have yet another way that human perception is being transformed and a further reason for smartphone addiction. The brain is stimulated by digital input, rewires itself to sync with that input, and then goes into cold turkey when you put the smartphone down and the stimulus stops. We see this with people putting down the phone after an already long session and immediately pickling it up again for no particular reason. This is the brain screaming 'Hey, I want my fix'. Once these new body wave and brain wave frequencies and codes are in place they are passed on via epigenetics to the next generation who start out the way their parents had to be manipulated into becoming. With each generation they are more and more machine-wave dominated until they *are* the machines. Frequency-matched communication with DNA can transmute the body into another form in the same way until it is nothing like we see today. Genetic manipulation in laboratories is the Stone Age by comparison.

The human mind is being entrained with AI through all the smart gadgets that are vehicles for AI and another aspect of the assimilation is to manipulate human interaction with AI as if it is human-human interaction. How many people now interact with their smart assistants as if they are human or are induced into perceiving the AI voice on the Sat-Nav as human? Smart assistants are being introduced to vehicles to add to Sat-Navs and make car journeys a constant interaction with AI (Fig 368). Call government agencies and big companies and you will be greeted by an AI voice. Observe the burgeoning number of dolls and other characters for young children that speak with AI voices through Internet connection (Fig 369). All is systematic preparation and conditioning for the fusion of AI with the human mind while human-human interaction is being destroyed equally systematically through smartphones, social media and the technology takeover (more words written before the lockdowns and social distancing). Everywhere direct human discourse is being deleted and this includes supermarkets where check-out staff you could chat with are

Figure 368: What's the best way to deal with these surveillance tools if you already have one? *Smack* - in the bin. Job done.

Figure 369: Perception assimilation before total assimilation.

being replaced by technology to delete human-human contact. Cult technocracy giant Amazon is opening stores that are entirely automated and the plan is for that to be the case everywhere as it is with banks as local branches disappear and people are forced online. Bricks and mortar shops where you interact with human beings are being destroyed by online shopping and faceless, soulless AI. People find it increasingly difficult to buy things away from the Internet as this trend increases apace. Laws are going to come which protect AI machines and eventually they will go above transgender in the New Woke hierarchy. I know that sounds fantastic, but who would have guessed what would happen with transgender in such a ridiculously short time? Who would have believed that Democratic presidential candidate Elizabeth Warren would say that as president she would have her Education Secretary chosen or vetoed by a transgender child? I had to check the speech video to confirm she really said it. She did. If what is happening now with transgender activism had been predicted only a few years ago they would have said that was crazy. It *is*, but it's here anyway. The Cult agenda is protected from all criticism and exposure. How can you criticise AI robots for taking over human society? That's an 'anti-Semitic' trope or transphobic – no, wait, it's transtechnologic, yes, a *transtechnologic* trope and you are *transtechnophobic*. As AI becomes ever more pre-eminent (and it's happening so fast), so a conscious connection with expanded awareness and *The One* is ever further diminished until we are completely isolated. This is the game and a crucial part of *The Answer* is to know that.

Vaccine shit, food shit, drink shit, it's all shit

Vaccinations and toxic food and drink would appear to affect the body on the chemical/biological level and obviously in one sense they do. Chemical/biological, however, pertains to the hologram and that is a decoded projection of wavefield information. Toxicity, whether in the form of vaccinations, food, drink, pesticides, herbicides and poisons of every kind, are in their base state highly distorted wave frequencies. Toxic gunge pouring from a pipe into a river is changing the wavefield nature of the river and this affects the wavefields of the fish and other marine life. Remember the work of Japanese researcher Dr Masaru Emoto and how toxicity distorted the water crystals (wavefields) of water. Toxicity appears to affect the body directly as poison-to-biological when in fact it distorts wavefields of the body which plays through to the hologram as a reflected distortion. If extreme enough this can so damage the body's wavefield oscillation that it stops and the person dies. Vaccinations, toxic food and drink, pharmaceutical drugs, vaccines, technological radiation and ultimately an AI connection to the brain are all weapons in the Cult's anti-human armoury through Body-Mind wavefield distortion. I have detailed in *Everything You Need To Know* the near-unbelievable shite in vaccines, food and drink that you would never think anyone would put into anything destined for the body. When you know that the Cult is specifically targeting Body-Mind it all makes sense. The Cult wants the population addicted to shit food, shit drink, shit drugs, shit smartphone waves, shit everything, and all of that is produced by giant Cult corporations. Shit in these cases means shit frequencies which are absorbed by human frequencies that become shit themselves through entanglement. This entangled shit becomes holographic shit which we experience as mental, emotional and 'physical' dis-ease, dis-harmony. To make this happen the Cult wants control of what enters the body through mouth or injection and the ever-increasing pressure through many and various agencies and stooges to impose mandatory vaccinations is a *key* part of the war on humanity and the young (Fig 370). I wrote those words once again before the 'pandemic' and the subsequent Bill Gates global vaccine agenda.

This is a summary of vaccine ingredients and substances used in manufacture: Aborted foetal tissue; aluminium; mercury-based thimerosal; gelatine; human serum albumin (found in blood plasma);

Figure 370: Welcome to the world where you are a pin cushion for toxic shite. It's only because we care.

sorbitol and other stabilisers; emulsifiers; taste improvers; antibiotics; egg proteins (ovalbumin); yeast proteins; formaldehyde (used to embalm dead bodies); acidity regulators; human cell strains, animal cell strains and genetically-modified organisms (GMOs); recombinant DNA technology; bovine products. Aluminium alone is a brain toxin. Health consequences linked to vaccines and it is far from a full list include: Anaphylactic shock; aseptic meningitis and meningitis; Bell's palsy, facial palsy, isolated cranial nerve palsy; blood disorders; brachial neuritis; cerebrovascular accident (stroke); chronic rheumatoid arthritis; convulsions, seizures, febrile seizure; death; encephalopathy and encephalitis (brain swelling); hearing loss; Guillain-Barré syndrome; immune system disorders; lymphatic system disorders; multiple sclerosis; myocarditis; nervous system disorders; neurological syndromes including autism; paralysis and myelitis including transverse myelitis; peripheral neuropathy; pneumonia and lower respiratory infections; skin and tissue disorders including eczema; sudden infant death syndrome (SIDS); tinnitus (ringing in the ears); vaccine-strain versions of chicken pox, measles, mumps, polio, influenza, meningitis, yellow fever, and pertussis vasculitis (inflammation of blood vessels).

Against this background the number of vaccines and insane combinations, including *six*-in-one, have exploded and we have ever-quickening and expanding moves around the world to impose compulsory vaccination (Fig 371). Why would they do this with so much potential harm? Why would they do this when there can be few better definitions of fascism than telling people what they will and will not by law put into their own bodies and those of their children? One answer is they were preparing for the 'pandemic' hoax and the Bill Gates-fronted vaccine being prepared in response that they want to be compulsory worldwide or at least with people facing major restrictions on movement if they don't agree to have it. I'll have *much* more about that in the next two chapters.

Figure 371: Herd immunity means natural immunity, not shite in vaccine immunity.

Immunity by vaccine? No – immunity from prosecution

Cult-owned pharmaceutical companies or Big Pharma were facing so many lawsuits for life-changing and life-ending vaccine damage that laws were passed in 1986 by Cult-owned Capitol Hill to give them *immunity from prosecution*. No matter what vaccines do to your kids the National Childhood Vaccine Injury Act (NCVIA) protects Big Pharma from any consequences. Instead compensation claims are handled by a federal 'vaccine court' on a no-fault basis without a jury and payments are made by taxpayers for the results of Big Pharma actions. This is the same Big Pharma that makes staggering fortunes every year for killing and damaging extraordinary numbers of children and adults through vaccines and pharmaceutical drugs. One of the biggest causes of death in the United States alongside heart disease and cancer is pharmaceutical-based *treatment* and that's without all the cases never recorded because another cause is given to hide the real one. Add them to the number and it would be by far the biggest cause of human demise. Aldous Huxley said long ago: 'Medical science is making such remarkable progress that soon no-one will be well.' Even with a very high bar to prove your case the US vaccine court had paid out $4.2 *billion* as of October, 2019, for damage by vaccines that the Cult wants to make compulsory worldwide and is already doing so in the United States and elsewhere. Robert F. Kennedy Jr, son of the US attorney general assassinated by the Cult in 1968, is among America's leading opponents of the vaccine narrative. Writer Kristina Kristen described at the Kennedy-connected childrenshealthdefense.org how the number of vaccinations soared after the immunity law was passed and how Big Pharma is actually producing drugs for profit to 'treat' health effects of vaccines:

> Following the passage of NCVIA, the number of vaccines on the childhood schedule mushroomed, creating a gold rush for vaccine makers: the vaccine industry went from a $1 billion industry to a $50 billion industry. But this expansion in the vaccine industry, in fact, is relatively small in comparison to the even greater gold rush for the BIG 4 companies. The drug 'treatment' side of the equation, which is substantially more lucrative than the 'gateway' vaccine side the BIG 4 already monopolized, now also increased substantially.

> The vaccine manufacturers began to capitalize on the known adverse effects of their vaccines, and have since created drugs for the 'treatment' side of the equation as well. The lack of incentive to make safe products, which created the bloated vaccine schedule, became the gateway to the lucrative drug treatment side for these companies. Today, the BIG 4 monopolize vaccines as well as the drug 'treatments' for chronic illnesses known to be induced by vaccines. First, vaccines push kids off the cliff, and then vaccine makers profit from 'rescuing' those they don't kill.

If ever you needed a concise description of Cult psychopathy and empathy deletion then there it is. If evil is the absence of love, which I suggest it is, the Cult can justifiably be described as evil and that same evil is being applied across its entire agenda for humanity. 'They wouldn't do that'? Oh, yes, they would and get sexually high while doing so. Yale University researchers studying records from a health insurance database discovered correlations between specific vaccines and neurological problems in children aged between six and 15. They included obsessive-compulsive disorder and anorexia nervosa which were found more likely to be diagnosed in children three months after vaccination. Influenza vaccine was one highlighted – 'get your flu shot' as the idiot media tell people every year. The study was published in the journal *Frontiers in Psychiatry*. No matter the documented health and psychological dangers to children we are going to make vaccines compulsory. In typical Cult fashion anyone who challenges and exposes the consequences and motivation of vaccines is demonised. Those dubbed 'anti-vaxxers' are attacked by moronic people in the media and by parents who have conceded the right to think and so believe whatever the Cult tells them is true. It brings us back to that quote from Morpheus in *The Matrix:* 'You have to understand, most of these people are not ready to be unplugged and many of them are so inured, so hopelessly dependent on the system, that they will fight to protect it.' Those that refuse to vaccinate their children – 'anti-vaxxers' – and seek to circulate information Big Pharma doesn't want people to know are increasingly censored by Cult-controlled Big Tech including Facebook, Twitter, Google and Amazon. The Cult makes the vaccines, passes laws for immunity from prosecution for the consequences of vaccines, and silences opposition through its Big Tech near-monopolies in league with the Cult-controlled mainstream media. It's simple when you connect the dots. If the population allows the few to dictate events for much longer no one will escape vaccination or be allowed to campaign against it. This is the real reason for attacks on 'anti-vaxxers' (written before the 'virus' scam when those attacks increased dramatically).

Britain is now a totalitarian state and a new Law Commissioner called Penney Lewis announced in 2020 that she was 'considering' making the posting of 'anti-vaccine propaganda' on social media a criminal offence even when people believed the information to be true. 'She' was not considering anything. 'She' is just a place-person to officially make it happen and what a coincidence this happened just before the 'pandemic' hoax along with Bill Gates stepping down from Microsoft to spend more time on his 'charitable' (vaccine) interests. The System (ultimately the Cult) is the force behind this fascistic plan and the same with the pathetic puppet who said in the same period that he was 'looking very seriously' at making vaccinations compulsory in the UK. This was 'Health Secretary' Matt Hancock in temporary *official* charge of health policy that is really driven by the civil servants in his department representing the Permanent Government. It is highly unlikely that either Lewis or Hancock will know their arse from their elbow about how what they are 'considering' is really part of a global agenda emerging out of the shadows. 'Considering' obviously means planning to impose when we think we can get away with it. Attacks on 'anti-vaxxers' get more hysterical by the week. Republican political strategist, media consultant and Deep State insider Rick Wilson said: 'Anti-vaxxers are a scourge and a strong argument for re-education camps, the immediate seizure of their property, and putting their children into protective custody.' Those concerned about their children's safety are a 'scourge' but someone advocating outright extreme fascism/Marxism is not? Such is the lunacy of New Woke. American Medical Association (AMA) delegates want laws to allow minors to 'override refusenik parents on vaccination' (after they've been indoctrinated by the authorities, of course). The direction we are being taken is so clear once eyes are truly wide open and not wide shut. It is all the more grotesque when you think that compulsory vaccinations for those who would not otherwise have them is statistically alone condemning some of those children to vaccine damage, even death, and effects of their psychology. The arrogance and psychopathy of these people is stunning.

Herd immunity is the problem? No it's not

One of the biggest scams to justify compulsory vaccination is the lie about 'herd immunity' which claims that almost everyone has to be vaccinated for a vaccine to work (Fig 372). They need to sell this deceit to both support mandatory jabs and explain why so many vaccinated children get the very diseases they are supposed to be vaccinated against. It's not that the vaccines haven't worked. It's those terrible parents who won't have their kids injected with toxic potions. American neurosurgeon Russell Blaylock put this myth to bed:

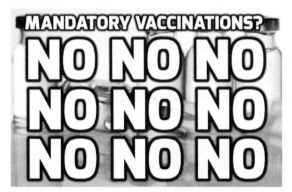

Figure 372: Mandatory vaccinations are only fascism under another name.

> In the original description of herd immunity, the protection to the population at large occurred only if people contracted the infections naturally. The reason for this is that naturally-acquired immunity lasts for a lifetime. The vaccine proponents quickly latched onto this concept and applied it to vaccine-induced immunity.
>
> But, there was one major problem – vaccine-induced immunity lasted for only a relatively short period [if at all] and then this applies only to humoral [body fluids] immunity. This is why they began to suggest boosters for most vaccines, even the common childhood infections such as chickenpox, measles, mumps, and rubella.

The claim is that vaccinations produce antibodies for a disease, but this does not constitute proof of immunity. The following quote is from Learntherisk.org:

> … science has long known that antibodies alone do NOT create real immunity. Some people with high levels of antibodies can be exposed to an illness and still get sick, while others without antibodies can be exposed and not get sick. Dr. Merrill Chase, nicknamed the Grandfather of Immunology for his pioneering work, did clear-cut research on this issue back in the 1950s.
>
> His results are clear: antibody levels don't determine immunity. The immune system is a highly complex system and science is still in its infancy understanding how it functions. In fact, immunology textbooks were completely rewritten recently after a University of Virginia study finally proving the link between the gut and the brain through the lymphatic system. Before this 2014 study, immunology books were adamant there was no link.

The quickest way to understand the world is to invert everything you've been told is real by The System (the Cult). The method is next to foolproof. American children and young people are now given from birth to 18 years between 53 and 70 vaccines depending on how you count them. Many are given in one jab and the childhood schedule has tripled in little more than 30 years which takes us back to the time when Big Pharma secured immunity from prosecution. In this same period children have got sicker with once-rare autism, food allergies, asthma, brain malfunction, autoimmune diseases and cancer in children dramatically increasing. There has been a mega-rise in autoimmune diseases in the vaccine era and especially the mass vaccine era. The immune system attacks its own body by picking up signals indicating a threat from foreign bodies that shouldn't be there and this is known as autoimmune disease or malfunction. Does anyone really believe that injecting or swallowing toxic substances and material that attach to the body does not cause the immune system to attack itself in this way? Still-developing immune-systems of babies are deluged with this toxic crap and the body's natural protection will never be what it would have been after that assault so early. These are the same immune systems targeted by 5G and Wi-Fi. Childhood diseases were just part of life when I was a kid and parents would take their children to those who were sick so they would get the disease. It was seen as kicking in the immune system to protect them for life and give life-long immunity to conditions that can be far worse in adults. Today an outbreak of measles is propagandised into a deadly threat that justifies compulsory vaccinations and vicious attacks on 'anti-vaxxers'. It's all manipulation. New York mayor Bill de Blasio declared an emergency after a measles outbreak and ordered vaccinations on threat of a fine of up to $1,000.

'We cannot allow this dangerous disease to make a comeback here in New York City', he said. This was the 'dangerous disease' that was met in my childhood with 'So and so's got measles' – 'Oh, week off school. then.' It should also be stressed that when we are told there has been an 'outbreak' we are not informed how many vaccinated kids have the disease and how many *un*vaccinated are not affected. That would be bad for the sales-pitch. My two big strapping sons were not vaccinated and they somehow seemed to have survived. I can't think how and maybe someone can explain how their vaccinated mates got diseases they didn't.

Vaccine waves

To understand the deeper agenda of vaccinations and all the other shite I've described we need to return once more to the wavefield level of reality. Here vaccines are disrupters of wavefield harmony which in itself undermines wavefield information codes that are the immune system. At the wave level information can also be encoded with perception patterns and disease patterns. Once you have access to the body field anything becomes possible with the knowledge the Cult is working with. Toxic fast food and processed food and drink have the same effect as do pharmaceutical drugs and technological radiation. Drug 'side-effects' are wavefield disrupting effects (nothing 'side' about them) caused in the same process as the one effect that is claimed to be beneficial to a condition. Even then drugs and alternative treatments can appear to have 'cured' a problem when it has only caused the wavefield flaw to move to somewhere else in the field to manifest as another condition that is not apparently related to the first one that was 'cured'. But it *is*. The 'cure' has only made the symptom disappear and not the flaw. You could think of it as like a bubble in a bottle of water that moves from one place to another as you turn it around. These wavefield flaws are caused overwhelmingly by emotional trauma as imbalanced waves of low-vibrational emotion impact upon Body-Mind fields, but they also result from the toxins swallowed and injected which can lead to diseases many years after they have been consumed and administered. Cause and effect is never identified because of this delay. Only when the flaw is deleted rather than moved is the healing process over and this is mostly done by bringing to the conscious mind the emotional trauma that has manifested the flaw. This can be something that happened in childhood which didn't show itself as a condition in the body for maybe decades. Once the conscious mind acknowledges the cause and effect of the flaw the wavefield is rebalanced. The acknowledgement generates a wave pattern that does the job. For most people the connection remains in the subconscious given that mainstream medicine does not recognise these connections. Disease really is all in the mind, and has to be when the body *is* the mind, and it can be 'cured' (rebalanced) by the mind.

Vaccinating chips

There is still another reason for vaccinations to benefit the Cult. I was told by a CIA scientist in California in the 1990s that nano-microchips far too small to be seen by the human eye were being infused into the population through hypodermic needles in public vaccination programmes. Nano-technology is now commonplace and can be found in an ever-increasing number of foods. When I met the scientist it was not nearly as widely known about as it is today. I cannot emphasise enough that the cutting edge of technological possibility in the secret projects is far in advance of anything we see in the public arena. Nanotechnology is easily small enough to be injected with vaccines and no one would know. It takes a tiny few to add the nano-chips which large numbers of unsuspecting 'medical professionals' then inject. Today these chips are called nanobots, nanorobots, nanoids, nanites, nanomachines, nanomites, neural dust, digital dust and smart dust (Fig 373). Once in the body these micro-machines can according to the literature 'assemble and maintain sophisticated systems and build devices, machines or circuits through molecular manufacturing and produce copies of themselves through self-replication'. They can also connect the body to the Smart Grid and manipulate genetics. What an amazing coincidence with all these crucial benefits to the Cult agenda of vaccinations that we find their most prominent global promotor to be Microsoft billionaire technocrat Bill Gates. His father, William H. Gates Senior, supported the beliefs of infamous eugenicist Thomas Malthus (as did his son 'at one time') and Father Gates headed the Rockefeller-created Planned Parenthood

Figure 373: Nano-technology released in the air, water and food is designed to connect humanity to the Smart Grid.

which was part of the eugenics movement and involved Cult 'prophet' Dr Richard Day who told those paediatricians in 1969 that diseases would be inoculated through vaccinations (very relevant when I come in detail to 'Covid-19' and the Gates vaccine). Austrian doctor, molecular biology researcher, and now dentist, Jaroslav Belsky, pointed out a connection between vaccinations and the 1918 'Spanish flu' which actually began in American military bases in the last year of the First World War before spreading worldwide to affect about 500 million people, or one-third of the world's population. At least 50 million deaths were estimated with about 675,000 in the United States according to reports. Belsky said:

> An orgy of vaccination took place for the soldiers of the war. In 1918 up to 36 vaccinations took place with no rules at all. It happened just before the Spanish Flu appeared in different places at the same time. Medical historians confirm today that it was a vaccination disaster.

Bill Gates made his billions from Microsoft technology essential to the Cult technocracy agenda and funds and promotes a long list of Cult demands including vaccines, surveillance technology, education programming like Common Core, geoengineering of the atmosphere (weather modification and so much more), and genetically-modified food which is designed to genetically-modify *us*. You can read about all this in detail in *Everything You Need To Know*. Gates announced in March, 2020, that he was stepping down from the Microsoft board to spend more time on 'philanthropic activities' which means funding the elite agenda. He said he wanted to focus his efforts on global health and development, education and tackling climate change. Yeah, yeah, mate, we get what you mean. (We did indeed because shortly after I wrote those words Gates immediately launched into promoting 'virus' lockdowns and a vaccine without which life would, in his words, 'never get back to normal'.) What a conman this bloke Gates really is – and worse as we shall see. I should emphasise, too, that vaccines damage and change DNA and the next generation of vaccines specifically *target* DNA – including the Gates 'Covid-19' vaccine. The theme is clear. These new vaccines don't inject a virus to stimulate an immune response but instead inject *synthetic* genes – here we go – which will permanently alter DNA. A *New York Times* article about 'immunoprophylaxis by gene transfer, or I.G.T.' quoted Michael Farzan, an immunologist at America's Scripps Research Institute:

> I.G.T. is altogether different from traditional vaccination. It is instead a form of gene therapy. Scientists isolate the genes that produce powerful antibodies against certain diseases and then synthesize artificial versions. The genes are placed into viruses and injected into human tissue, usually muscle.

> The viruses invade human cells with their DNA payloads, and the synthetic gene is incorporated into the recipient's own DNA. If all goes well, the new

genes instruct the cells to begin manufacturing powerful antibodies.

'The synthetic gene is incorporated into the recipient's own DNA.' Ponder on that in the light of what I have been saying about the synthetic human. Is anyone still naive enough not see what is happening, why vaccines are being made compulsory and what the Gates 'Covid-19' vaccine is really all about?

Vaccine surveillance

Crucial to the imposition of vaccination for *everyone* by law is tracking who has been vaccinated and who hasn't. Is it really another coincidence that the major organisation in the Bill Gates campaign to vaccinate the world is calling for the tracking of people to confirm vaccination? Seth Berkley, CEO of the Gates-funded GAVI, the Vaccine Alliance, says the organisation spends an average of nearly $2 billion a year to vaccinate children in the poorest countries and invests tens of millions in 'innovations to monitor immunisation'. He wants technology to track who has been vaccinated and to give everyone an 'identity'. All this fits with the Cult agenda as he might take time to find out if he doesn't already know. I bet he does. Berkley formerly worked for the Big Pharma-controlled US Centers for Disease Control and Prevention and the Rockefeller Foundation. The Rockefeller family – its inner core is Cult to its DNA – was the family that imposed Big Pharma 'medicine' on the world at the exclusion of other forms of healing that they didn't control. Berkley's desire for everyone to have 'identity' carbon-copies is the goal of the United Nations which aims for all 193 member countries to impose a legal form of identity by the ever-recurring year of 2030. Is it random chance that the Bill and Melinda Gates Foundation is funding the development of a 'tattoo' that will identify those who have and have not been vaccinated? Gates has funded research by scientists at the Massachusetts Institute of Technology (MIT) to create a new ink for an

'invisible quantum tattoo' to be embedded in the skin and read by a smartphone camera app (Fig 374). Sciencealert.com reported:

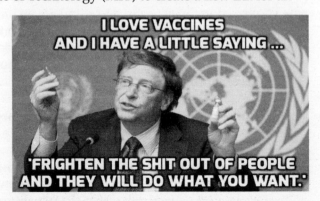

The invisible 'tattoo' accompanying the vaccine is a pattern made up of

Figure 374: This is not only the Gates doctrine – it's the Cult doctrine everywhere you look.

minuscule quantum dots – tiny semiconducting crystals that reflect light – that glows under infrared light. The pattern – and vaccine – gets delivered into the skin using hi-tech dissolvable microneedles made of a mixture of polymers and sugar.

MIT researcher Kevin McHugh described the outcome perfectly while quite probably being firewalled in compartmentalised cluelessness from the real reason behind it: 'In areas where paper vaccination cards are often lost or do not exist at all, and electronic databases are unheard of, this technology could enable the rapid and anonymous detection of patient vaccination history to ensure that every child is vaccinated.' There you have the Cult agenda in a sentence and this will allow authorities – and employers – to know if you have been vaccinated and are therefore 'safe' to roam or be employed. (When the 'virus' hoax was played weeks after I wrote those words Gates was promoting his invisible digital 'tattoo' to track who had been vaccinated with the 'Covid-19' vaccine that *HE* was funding into worldwide use. It's shocking. No wonder I call him the 'Software Psychopath'.) The same tracking system is planned to ensure that everyone is drugged to make them docile. 'Smart systems' already introduced include microchipped 'smart pills' that tell doctors that drugs have been taken in another Tiptoe to this end. The concept was well portrayed in the 2002 movie *Equilibrium* in which the population has all emotion suppressed by a daily injection monitored to ensure compliance. Proposals to add lithium to public water supplies is another Tiptoe. Lithium is used to treat manic depression and its advocates say mass medication of lithium will make people 'happier'. Children and adults are already being mass-drugged with psychology-changing potions on a scale never seen before at the first sign of emotional problems or off-Postage Stamp behaviour. *Brave New World* author and establishment insider Aldous Huxley predicted this in 1961:

> There will be, in the next generation or so, a pharmacological method of making people love their servitude, and producing dictatorship without tears, so to speak, producing a kind of painless concentration camp for entire societies, so that people will in fact have their own liberties taken away from them, but rather enjoy it, because they will be distracted from any desire to rebel by propaganda or brainwashing, or brainwashing enhanced by pharmacological methods. And this seems to be the final revolution.

How did Huxley know this? How did Orwell know what he did? How did Richard Day? How did I? The agenda has been long in the planning and is ultimately sourced from outside this reality which doesn't share the same 'timeline' as the human world. If you are an insider or spend

30 years lifting the stones you can know what is planned.

Micro-everything

The world is being deluged with microplastics that resonate to the frequency of synthetics. Wave entanglement with increasing numbers of synthetic waves will make body wavefields more … *synthetic*. A Reuters report using data from 50 studies on the ingestion of microplastics gave devastating confirmation of how far this has already gone. Microplastics are described as particles under five millimetres. The report, based on the findings of a study by the Worldwide Fund for Nature (WWF), found that people are consuming on average every week some 2,000 tiny pieces of plastic mostly through water but also through marine life and the air. Every year humans are ingesting enough microplastics to fill a heaped dinner plate and in a life time of 79 years it is enough to fill two large waste bins (Fig 375). WWF International director general Marco Lambertini said: 'Not only are plastics polluting our oceans and waterways and killing marine life –

Figure 375: *Mmmm,* yummy.

it's in all of us and we can't escape consuming plastics,' Plastic-wrapped food absorbs the chemicals and I see even fresh food wrapped in plastic labelled 'organic' which by definition it can't be in such circumstances with the content of plastic leaching into the food. American geologists found tiny plastic fibres, beads and shards in rainwater samples collected from the remote slopes of the Rocky Mountain National Park near Denver, Colorado. Their report was headed: 'It is raining plastic.' Microplastics have been found in snow in remote areas and deep in ocean sediment and in plankton. 'Everywhere we look, we find it', one researcher said. Microplastics are also added to foodstuffs with scientists from McGill University in Canada revealing that billions of microplastic particles are released into every cup of tea using plastic tea bags. Who could have forecast that using plastic tea bags would release plastic into the tea? You'd have to be a genius, surely? It's systematic at the inner core of the Cult. Health consequences of plastic infiltration of the body are nothing like fully understood, but the London *Daily Mail* quoted

Rachel Adams, senior lecturer in Biomedical Science at Cardiff Metropolitan University, as saying that among them are internal inflammation (with many knock-on effects) and immune responses to a 'foreign body' (see also vaccine contents and autoimmune disease). She further pointed out that microplastics become carriers of toxins including mercury, pesticides and dioxins (a known cause of cancer and reproductive and developmental problems). These toxins accumulate in the fatty tissues once they enter the body through microplastics. I have described in other books how the body's survival system often will not allow fat to dissolve because it knows that this will release the accumulated poisons – 'No matter what I do I can't lose weight'. A study by Kings College London discovered the astonishing microplastic pollution in the UK capital. Researchers found that 'microplastics in the atmosphere are falling from the skies onto roofs and into human lungs in alarming quantities'. Researcher Stephanie Wright said they found 'a high abundance of microplastics, much higher than what has previously been reported' and the same will be true of all other cities. She repeated the point about unknown consequences: 'The biggest concern is we don't really know much at all. I want to find out if it is safe or not.' Well, clearly it's not safe and what is being missed as always are the consequences at the wavefield level where synthetic vibrations are infiltrating the human energy field which becomes the human hologram. When you are entering your endgame the last thing you want are healthy, strong, psychologically-balanced, sharp-thinking, people. You want the very opposite and you suppress the mind by suppressing the body which together make up Body-Mind. A study by the University of Vermont found that obese children have a thinner region in the brain which relates to decision-making, the ability to plan and control behaviour, and this is where most information is consciously processed.

'Too many people'

I have been warning for decades about a planned mass-cull of the global population and all that I have described makes that possible. When entrainment/entanglement between technology frequencies and the human field is powerfully established one can so disrupt the other that the heart stops beating and the oscillation of bodily life is switched off. If the Cult has the precise frequencies on which a person is transmitting an individual can be isolated and targeted. The Cult is using every excuse to compile DNA databases which provide that information. Many people claim they are already being specifically harassed by Deep State technology and refer to themselves as 'targeted individuals'. They say thoughts and perceptions are delivered to their brain technologically and I have explained how this is possible. I say that in less obvious ways this is being done on a mass scale through information delivered in waves by Wi-Fi, 5G and other technology networks. Taking out people individually and collectively is only a step on from that and based on the same principle. Cult gofers and operatives quoted in other books have long called for a colossal decrease in the global population (and I mean by billions) and now there is the added excuse that too many humans mean more danger from climate change. Climate Cultists are urging a reduction in the population and for people to stop having children at all. Bill Gates is among those very vocal on these subjects and would have talked about this with his father who supported eugenicist Thomas Malthus. The Cult doesn't need anything like as many human slaves any longer with AI taking over everything, male-female procreation due to be replaced by Huxley's World State Hatcheries, and synthetic laboratory babies specifically engineered for life-long slavery. Human bodies have been made toxic through food, drink, pollution and microplastics while electromagnetic frequencies have the potential to enormously increase the effect of that toxicity to fatal levels. The authorities could have wired computer systems in schools and universities and instead imposed Wi-Fi as part of the cumulative cull (remember the teacher's blood) and the same with smart meters (Fig 376). Now you can see why 5G – a military *weapon* – is being rolled-out across the world with no testing. 5G is very much part of the cull agenda. I know that people don't want to face what is happening, but it *is* and we have to deal with it. How could it be any other way with

Figure 376: Another Wi-Fi field planned for every home and business to connect you to the cloud and let the cloud communicate with you.

5G and Wi-Fi when you consider coagulating blood, affecting the molecular structure of oxygen, attacking water molecules, and frequencies that we don't even know about able to be transmitted through a network sold to us for other reasons? What better means do you need for a long-planned mass cull than the ability to absorb enough oxygen as I will come to in the next chapter? 'Humans' in the form we know them are planned to disappear to be replaced by the trans-human, synthetic-human, machine-human, that would not be human at all.

Californian biotech company Epicyte patented the Epicyte gene in 2010 which makes men and women sterile and infertile when ingested. The gene was then genetically-engineered into *corn seeds*. Why the hell would anyone do that if it were not aimed at sterilising people en masse? Cult biotech companies Monsanto and DuPont bought the Epicyte operation to 'commercialise' the sterilisation gene. Rima E. Laibow, Medical Director of the US Natural Solutions Foundation, said that you can't find out if you are consuming the gene because the (Cult-controlled) US Food and Drug Administration (FDA) made it illegal to have that information. Contraceptive drugs are also in the water supply after being peed down the toilet in cumulatively vast quantities while electromagnetic waves are known to influence human reproduction through both male and female systems. We are, of course, drowning in technological waves with now the vastly more destructive 5G. I have already emphasised the falling sperm counts. Professor Olle Johansson from the Department of Neuroscience at Sweden's Karolinska Institute has predicted mass 'irreversible sterility within five generations' due to technological and Wi-Fi radiation and he was speaking before the introduction of 5G. A letter highlighting the serious dangers to male reproduction of the 5G rollout was delivered to UK Prime Minister Boris Johnson in early 2020 along with two petitions. One was signed by 268 doctors and scientists. The letter said:

We are extremely concerned by the vulnerability of our young and very young people to the harmful effects of pulsed RF radiation. Study upon study is showing that this non-ionising radiation is causing oxidative DNA damage in cellular systems and this may be particularly harmful to the reproductive system of young boys, adolescents and young men.

It's all long-planned and the extinction of humanity *as we know it* is the goal. Dr Richard Day told the paediatricians in 1969 about the coming 'demise pill' in which older people would kill themselves when they reached a certain age to make way for the young. The constant efforts to divide young and old is in part related to this plan and so is the Tiptoe to legal euthanasia and 'care pathways' in which doctors stop drugs and nutrition for those they claim are close to death. Many who have been taken off the 'pathway', only thanks to the efforts of loved ones, have lived for years afterwards. The theme continues with increasing numbers of US states, plus the District of Columbia, legalising medical 'assisted suicide'. At the time of writing they are California, Colorado, Hawaii, Maine, New Jersey, Oregon, Vermont and Washington with New York authorities talking about doing the same. People may say it is compassionate to allow everyone to free themselves from 'physical' suffering, but that is not in the top five reasons of those that apply for legalised suicide in Oregon, for example. Among the leading reasons is fear of being a burden on others and fear of losing autonomy. This by definition means mostly the poor and vulnerable which then brings us into the arena of what I will call perceptual eugenics. You convince people they are a burden and then help them kill themselves. Old people have been psychopathically targeted during the 'virus' lockdowns as we shall see. Once you open the door on the basis of 'compassion' the Cult batters it off the hinges and takes the wall down. Humans are just a resource to the Cult and when they cease to be commercially productive the plan is to delete them. Paediatrician Lawrence Dunegan described what Richard Day said in 1969 about the demise pill:

> Medical care would be connected very closely with one's work but also would be made very, very high in cost so that it would simply be unavailable to people beyond a certain age. And unless they had a remarkably rich, supporting family, they would just have to do without care.

> And the idea was that if everybody says 'Enough! What a burden it is on the young to try to maintain the old people' then the young would become agreeable to helping mom and dad along the way, provided this was done humanely and with dignity. And then the example was there could be like a nice farewell party, a real celebration. Mom and dad had done a good job. And after the party's over they take the 'demise pill'.

Day described in 1969 how detailed the Cult agenda really is when he said they would use very pale ink on forms that people had to fill out so that older people would not be able to read them and have to ask younger people for help. He listed other ways that old people would be manipulated into believing they were 'past it' and I quote at length what he said so accurately across a range of subjects in my book, *Phantom Self.* In another reference to the population cull he said that most families would be limited to two children. Where have you seen such a child-limit policy? In *China* – the blueprint for the world. We should also note the emerging pressure for later and later legal abortion.

Ruling the waves

The Answer comes from understanding the problem and that means understanding the foundation nature of waves. The Cult is seeking to impose wave control in every area of life. I have highlighted many times over the years how symbols have been placed throughout global society in the form of the pyramid and all-seeing eye and many others. Why would they bother to do this on such a scale? Symbolism is both the hidden language through which Cult operatives communicate in public and a means of transferring the frequencies of the Cult to the human energy field. The number of times you see the pyramid and all-seeing eye or just the eye is absolutely fantastic and often in animated cartoons and movies for children (Fig 377). Energetically, and in terms of frequency, symbols represent what they symbolise. A symbol representing hate will resonate waves of the frequency of hate and have potential to impact on the human wavefield. You don't even have to consciously acknowledge the symbols for them to have this effect and in fact the Cult doesn't want that. While your conscious mind defences are down through ignorance of what is happening those frequencies are left unchallenged to entangle with the subconscious – the level at which the Cult overwhelmingly operates. The idea is to access human perception at the

Figure 377: The Cult's all-seeing eye symbol in a whole swathe of children's TV *programs* and other sources. It's yet another innocent coincidence, naturally.

subconscious level of waves and have that information filter through to the conscious mind as what people believe to be their own thoughts and perceptions. 'I have not been manipulated to believe what I do; they are my own conclusions.'

Wave connection reveals why the Cult is obsessed with ritual. Energy flows where attention goes and the focus during a ritual on their unseen 'gods' instigates a wave entanglement through which information can be exchanged and initiates possessed. Around the world are ancient and modern sites of ritual to Saturn and Orion and rituals in those places would connect initiates to the frequencies of Saturn and Orion which I say are both crucially important to the simulation and so mega-worshipped by the Cult. Waves are everything in the context of human control both as the cause of enslavement and the knowledge that will set us free.

CHAPTER FIFTEEN

How did they pull off the fake 'pandemic'?

Fear is only as deep as the mind allows – Japanese proverb

Eighty-five percent of this book was written before a 'pandemic' called 'Covid-19' swept through the collective human mind and gave the Cult almost everything that I have said in this and previous books was planned to transform global society. I have been referring to the 'Covid-19 hoax' here and there in earlier chapters and now I'll explain what I mean in detail: *There is no 'Covid-19'*.

This will come as a shock to most people and be immediately dismissed as crazy not only by mainstream society, but by swathes of the 'alternative' media. I know that is true because it already has been. When, however, people have bothered to look at the evidence and background that I will lay out in the next two chapters, instead of instantly dismissing even the possibility and misrepresenting what I am saying, they have seen the sense it makes of what is otherwise a nonsensical and utterly contradictory 'pandemic' narrative. I don't think significant sections of the 'alternative media' have come out of this with much distinction while other parts have been outstanding. We have seen during the events of 2020 a parting of the ways between those 'alternative' voices still willing to accept blatantly flawed official stories and those who are not. I will first summarise the official 'pandemic' narratives, mainstream and otherwise, and then offer a very different explanation thanks to medical professionals who have seen through the bullshit.

The official story(s)

There have been a few official and semi-official versions, but all encode the same theme: There *is* a virus, natural or emerging from a Chinese bio-lab, labelled SARS-CoV-2 and this caused an infectious respiratory disease called 'Covid-19' (I will refer to this alleged virus package as 'Covid-19' from hereon to keep it simple). We were told that this 'coronavirus' and its effects are so dangerous that whole countries had to be put under house arrest to stop it spreading and causing catastrophic loss of life. We will see that none of these claims is supportable by the evidence, but lockdowns based on those lies and flawed assumptions have been used to destroy the independent incomes and livelihoods of potentially billions and made them dependent on their Cult-controlled states and governments in a massive advancement of the Hunger Games Society. The 'outbreak' in China in the closing weeks of 2019 was met with a fierce and draconian lockdown in which what little is left of freedom in China was deleted and vast populations were put under house arrest policed by 'smart' face-recognition surveillance technology and the vicious, brain-dead Chinese law enforcement and military (same thing). The Western media reported the frenzy of activity from the Cult-owned Chinese government which included building whole new hospitals in little more than days to meet the demand from 'teeming numbers of dying people'; but the new hospitals built amid global media hysteria about the 'deadly virus' responsible were closed in a ridiculously short time when compared to the apparent human disaster that we were told was unfolding. As the 'virus' was said to be circulating in the West the Chinese 'epidemic' was already beginning to dramatically recede and while the Western economy went into meltdown China was reopening business and industry, ending the extremes of the lockdown, and travel was restored. The big point to make here is that *what happened in China set the blueprint for how to respond to the 'virus' – mass lockdown, house arrest and keeping the population apart from each other.* This was the plan from the start with Bill Gates saying that 'basically the whole country (America) has to do what was done in the part of China where they had the infections'. The cover-story promoted by the Cult-created-and-controlled, Gates-funded World Health Organization (WHO) was that China had dealt with the 'health disaster' very effectively and so that's how the rest of the world had to respond when it came their way. Cult and Gates puppet WHO Director-General Tedros Adhanom Ghebreyesus said:

> The Chinese government is to be congratulated for the extraordinary measures it has taken to contain the outbreak. China is actually setting a new standard for outbreak response and it is not an exaggeration.

The scene was set. The dye was cast. The Western economy and the lives of billions were about to be devastated.

The opening version of the official story was that the 'outbreak' began in a 'wet market' in Wuhan where bats and other animals are bought and eaten in the most appallingly dirty and unhygienic conditions and when this narrative didn't stand up another theme began which was promoted and advanced by the alternative media. This surrounded the 'BSL-4' laboratory in Wuhan not far from the wet market where lethal agents are studied and manipulated to create bioweapons for military purposes. The Wuhan facility is the only one of its kind in China. BSL-4 refers to biosafety level 4 which is the designation given to laboratories with the highest level of biosafety precautions capable of containing the often instantly fatal agents stored there. Francis Boyle, professor of international law at the University of Illinois College of Law who drafted the US Biological Weapons Anti-Terrorism Act of 1989, went public in February, 2020, to say he was convinced the 'coronavirus' strain said to be involved was an engineered bioweapon released from the Wuhan bio-lab by error or otherwise. He appeared across the alternative media and what he said about the *existence* of offensive biological warfare weapons with genetically-engineered DNA was clearly true. What followed, however, in actual dead people around the world did not in any way support the claim that a lethal bioweapon had been released. Just because a known arsonist lives near the scene of a fire does not mean only by association that he started the blaze, but the person who *did* start it will try to make you think so. No matter – a significant swathe of the alternative media would believe and promote this Wuhan lab scenario and later it would become a mainstream narrative which, of course, focussed attention and fury on China. Some Deep State-connected US politicians like the Israel-owned Tom Cotton suggested the Wuhan laboratory could have been the source and this was more reason for red flags to flutter in the breeze. It was suggested that the 'deadly agent' – by now dubbed a 'virus' – was stolen by the Chinese from a Canadian laboratory in Winnipeg, the country's foremost centre for developing and testing biological warfare weapons, or from a US BSL-4 laboratory of which there are many. Others said the 'virus' could have been sourced to the US military and released under the cover of the 2019 Military World Games held between October 18th and 27th in Wuhan just before the outbreak became public. The Games involved ten thousand military personnel and support staff gathered from more than 100 nations including a team from the United States. Professor Boyle estimated that the US has spent in excess of $100 billion on biological warfare research since 9/11 rising by $5 billion a year. This would sync with the Sabbatian-Frankist Project for the New American Century plan for the development of biological weapons that target specific genotypes. Biowarfare research is going on across the world in the United States, China, Israel, the United Kingdom (the infamous Porton Down), France, Russia, and many other locations. Sabbatian-Frankist-controlled Israel has a major chemical and biological weapons programme (hidden behind 'research' facilities) and as always refuses to sign the Biological Weapons Convention or Nuclear Non-Proliferation Treaty to prevent international inspections because, thanks to the

Sabbatian-Frankist networks, it is a law unto itself. The Israel Institute for Biological Research near Tel Aviv which runs the programme is one of the country's most secretive organisations (and think of the competition). The Globalresearch website said of Israel:

> The greatest secrecy surrounds research on biological weapons, bacteria and viruses that spread among the enemy and can trigger epidemics. Among them, the bacteria of the bubonic plague (the 'Black Death' of the Middle Ages) and the Ebola virus, contagious and lethal, for which no therapy is available.

So do deadly agents exist at laboratories like Wuhan? They definitely do. The question to be asked is was the 'Covid-19' coronavirus one of them? The data from actual *happenings* and not speculation says 'no' and I will elaborate my case for that in fine detail. For sure the first official story that the virus broke out in an animal food market or 'wet market' in Wuhan has not stood up to scrutiny. Bats were blamed to start with which has been done before in similar situations to hide the truth. There were diversions and false 'leads' flying around all over the place and the more of those you can scatter the more confusing the situation becomes and the truth is lost. I observed the scene from the perspective of tracking what was happening and not making what was happening fit a preconceived belief. As the 'virus' expanded into the West the consequences simply did not match in any way what you would expect from a 'deadly bioweapon' in terms of dead people. So what was going on?

The Web

It is worth re-emphasising how the Cult globally manipulates to put the 'pandemic' hoax into another perspective. The first thing to do is forget borders which do not exist in the Cult networks. Picture a transnational corporation with a headquarters in a particular country (in the case of the Cult that headquarters or central control centre – The Spider – is in the shadows). A corporation has subsidiaries in other countries around the world which take their orders and direction from the headquarters. The Cult system operates in the same way. In every country, especially those that most affect the direction of the world, the Cult has subsidiary networks of secret societies, satanic covens and interbreeding Nephilim hybrid families that are tasked with controlling that country's politics, government administration (Deep State), finance and banking, media, medical structure to benefit the Cult's Big Pharma, and so on. By this means the Spider-directed agenda is imposed on 'different' countries at the same time to instigate global change and coordinated happenings. I have already said that China is a major centre for the Cult along with the

United States, Israel, Britain, Italy, France, Germany, and elsewhere. At the Cult level China *is* America *is* Israel *is* Britain *is* Italy *is* France *is* Germany. Through this Cult coordination it is absolutely possible to orchestrate the extraordinary hoax that I am going to describe. Even many researchers in the alternative media do not seem to understand this structure and its manipulative potential judging by their comments during the 'pandemic'.

The structure requires very few people 'in the know' and consciously working for the Cult to dictate events in an entire country and together the entire world. You only have to control the key positions of decision-making and most of these do not even involve politicians. You want the technocrats to have the control and that includes in the case of 'Covid-19' the medical technocrats which have driven 'virus' policy throughout this human catastrophe with elected politicians almost entirely bystanders. We will see as we proceed the coordination of action between China (the Cult) and the West (the Cult). I have already highlighted the connections via the Cult of the Deep State and academia in China and the United States. As the 'Covid-19 virus' was coming to the centre of public attention Harvard University professor Charles Lieber, chair of the Harvard Department of Chemistry and Biology, was charged with lying about his role in a Chinese talent recruitment programme and was ordered to post a $1 million cash bond by a judge at Boston's federal court. Prosecutors said Lieber agreed to conduct research, publish articles and apply for patents on behalf of China's Wuhan University of Technology in exchange for $50,000 per month and some $150,000 in living expenses. Authorities said he was also given $1.5 million to establish a research laboratory at a Wuhan university. I have said that a stream of 'former' Pentagon officials end up working after 'retirement' for China either directly or indirectly. It emerged that the United States had handed $3.7 million to the Wuhan Institute of Virology and Canada had done something similar. The American grant was reported to have been approved by the Bill Gates-connected Anthony Fauci – Trump's advisor on the 'Covid-19' lockdown response. Why would the *United States* and *Canada* give millions to a lab in *China*? It was the American and Canadian 'subsidiaries' of the Cult handing over money to the China 'branch'. This is the borderless world of the Cult through which the pandemic hoax was coordinated. So is the Cult connected to the Wuhan lab? Yes, and this may become significant ongoing; but is it the source of 'Covid-19'? Hardly when 'Covid-19' is a phantom 'virus'. The Wuhan lab story is a diversion from that.

I will be adding the detail, but in summary this is how they pulled it off. The Cult network that controls China triggered global hysteria with an apparent outbreak of a 'deadly virus' which they dealt with through draconian lockdowns and mass house arrest. There was no 'virus' and the numbers of apparent deaths were generated by re-diagnosing people dying of other respiratory disease and pneumonia in the grotesquely toxic air of Wuhan as dying of a non-existent 'virus' dubbed 'Covid-19' which had the same 'flu-like' and respiratory symptoms as a long list of other conditions common in Wuhan thanks to its extreme toxic environment. A 'test' was then introduced that didn't even test for 'Covid-19' and this same test has since been used by the rest of the world to *not* test for 'Covid-19'. The Western media fanned the flames of hysteria by selling the story of mass deaths in China and how its government was hiding the truth about millions of dead. The media and Cult networks in Western and other countries screamed '*Ahhhhh* – it's us next!!' Amazingly the Chinese 'death figures' suddenly began to fall which is easily done when they are based on calculated miss-diagnosis and a fake 'test'. Cult assets controlling the medical hierarchies in other countries ordered doctors and other medical staff to begin diagnosing 'flu-like' symptoms and pneumonia as 'Covid-19' and indeed almost any condition as a 'Covid-19' death with no evidence necessary. If you haven't come across this background before you are going to be shocked when I get into the detail. The narrative was supported by the same fake test and the media screamed some more about hospitals being like 'war-zones' overwhelmed by cases. In fact, hospitals had never been so quiet, but with security staff guarding them, visitors not allowed and the media banned from filming the illusion was perpetuated of a tidal wave of patients with medical staff on their knees. Other operations and treatments were cancelled to ease the burden of 'overworked' medical staff who were largely sitting around with nothing to do. Lockdowns like that in China were instigated to 'protect the people' from a 'virus' that didn't exist urged on by the Cult-owned, Gates-funded World Health Organization which pointed to China's draconian lockdown 'success' as the way to deal with what it declared was a global 'pandemic'. This is the barest framework and the detail is on the way.

Fact-free propaganda

I was quite happy in the early weeks of the hysteria to accept the possibility of a bioweapon of some kind being involved with much *circumstantial* evidence to point in that direction. The word, however, is circumstantial and the only way to assess the validity of that is for real-world events to support the hypothesis. It became clear to me as a few weeks passed that this was not the case at all. Death-rates did not support that scenario, but a good slice of the alternative media still clung to it. The overwhelming majority of those who 'caught the virus' had 'very minor symptoms' or none at all and this number would increase as the weeks passed. You wouldn't know this if you read the daily war-zone headlines and on the basis of this perceptual magic trick the global economy was devastated. Were all the 'journalists' (you're joking) in on the plot? No, of course not. They just repeated unquestioned the official story as they do as a matter of course. As the saying goes and I summarise: 'You cannot bribe or twist the great British journalist; but seeing what they will do unbribed there's no reason to.' What was alleged to be 'Covid-19' was certainly not a lethal bioweapon. One of the first people in Scotland to be diagnosed with 'the virus' after a trip to Italy told BBC radio he had a mild fever and felt shivery like he had 'a bit of flu coming on'. The worst symptoms were aches and pains especially in his legs. He said:

> By the time I went to hospital, I was feeling fine. The mild flu symptoms quickly dissipated, I had no leg pain, no fever, no cough and no shortness of breath … I felt well. My symptoms seemed to have gone within three or four days.

Ahhhhhhhhhhhhhhhh!!!! We're all going to *DIE!!!* Once the hysteria began almost anyone with 'flu-like symptoms' was being diagnosed 'Covid-19' with no supporting proof whatsoever. 'Flu-like' symptoms have a long list of potential causes – *including the bloody flu* which is always around at the same time of year. We will shortly see that even the 'test' for 'Covid-19' is a sick joke that doesn't 'test' for that at all. American journalist Jon Rappoport, who has researched health, drug and related subjects for decades, wrote:

> Before the announcement of the coronavirus epidemic, people who showed up at those hospitals, with flu, flu-like symptoms, lung infections, pneumonia would be placed in the general wards and treated, or even sent home with drugs.

> But now they would, many of them, be called 'presumptive cases' of coronavirus, without any tests at all, or after tests which don't work … By labeling these patients 'contagious coronavirus', the hospital doctors are forced to send them to the [intensive care unit] to 'protect others from the infection'.

The manipulation of 'Covid-19' case and death figures had begun and it would reach utterly shocking proportions. Then came news of an extraordinary posting on the UK government website Gov.uk. A freelance journalist friend saw the relevant page while perusing the site for coronavirus information and found a posting from just *days before* Prime Minister Boris Johnson announced a draconian lockdown of the country because 'the virus is so dangerous'. The post was on the page concerning official government guidance for 'high consequence infectious diseases (HCID)'. It said this about Covid-19:

> As of 19 March 2020, COVID-19 is *no longer considered to be a high consequence infectious diseases (HCID) in the UK* [my emphasis]. The 4 nations public health HCID group made an interim recommendation in January 2020 to classify COVID-19 as an HCID. This was based on consideration of the UK HCID criteria about the virus and the disease with information available during the early stages of the outbreak.
>
> Now that more is known about COVID-19, the public health bodies in the UK have reviewed the most up to date information about COVID-19 against the UK HCID criteria. They have determined that several features have now changed; in particular, more information is available about mortality rates (low overall), and there is now greater clinical awareness and a specific and sensitive laboratory test, the availability of which continues to increase. The Advisory Committee on Dangerous Pathogens (ACDP) is also of the opinion that COVID-19 should no longer be classified as an HCID.

Days after the 'danger' from the 'virus' was downgraded by the government the country was locked down on the excuse that the virus was indeed a 'high consequence infectious disease'. What a scam was being visited upon Britain and the world. Soon after the government had been exposed for downgrading the risk they upgraded it again. The same freelance journalist who alerted me to the downgrade also researched the figures for deaths in the UK from all causes in the 'virus' period of 2020 at that time and compared them with the same weeks in 2019. They were close to the same – 11,661 (2020) and 11,431 (2019). European death rates in general told the same story in the same period. As of April 3rd, 2020, the total number of deaths in England and Wales was actually around six percent *less* than the same period in 2018. American doctor Andrew Kaufman, who will become very relevant shortly, described how he followed the weekly death rates up to the end of April and beyond – months into the 'outbreak' as issued by the US Centers for Disease Control and Prevention (CDC). He found them to be six percent less than the average of the previous three years – 'If there is no increase, and in fact there is a decrease, then what's the evidence that there's a new disease?' Yes indeed. Where were the additional dead people from 'Covid-19'? My journalist friend further compared the figures for people attending hospital emergency departments for the same two years in the same period of weeks and they were virtually identical with 2019 slightly *higher*. Where were all the 'new' cases of 'Covid-19' overwhelming hospitals in need of treatment – the 'war zones' that the media was raving on about? German doctor Wolfgang Wodarg, former chair of the Parliamentary Assembly of the Council of

Europe Health Committee, made the same point: 'You can check the total body count monitoring – people are dying less than during the last years.' He said there were no more 'flu-like' diseases than any other winter. With the 2019-2020 death rate comparison continuing to show into April no significant difference to explain the 'new' deaths from Covid-19 we suddenly had the UK National Statistics Office counting the figures in a way that had not been done before: 'A death can be registered with both Covid-19 and influenza or pneumonia mentioned on the death certificate, therefore a death can be counted in both categories.' The figures would go on to be massively manipulated to make it appear there was a 'Covid-19 pandemic' when there wasn't. Dr Malcolm Kendrick who works for the NHS in England said: 'I do know that other doctors put down Covid-19 on anyone who died from early March onwards.' Shocking and it is happening worldwide.

Empty 'war-zone' hospitals

Next the UK National Health Service announced a change in its publication of data that would no longer include the figures on 'critical care bed capacity and urgent operations cancelled'. They had to do this to hide from the public the glaring fact that 'war-zone' hospitals were near *empty*. Yes, *empty*. This came about for two main reasons: (1) There was no 'Covid-19' war-zone pandemic bringing hospitals to their knees; and (2) almost all non-'Covid-19' treatment, operations and hospital consultations had been cancelled to protect medical staff from being 'overwhelmed'. On that basis how could hospitals be anything except near-empty and the same was happening all over the world. Hospitals were defended and controlled by security staff with the few patients that were in hospital denied visitors 'because of "Covid-19" rules' (because they would see that the war-zone hospitals were near-empty). This meant that children were dying in hospital from other conditions without their mum and dad to emphasise to breathtaking extremes the nature of the psychopaths that we are dealing with. A German journalist managed to gain entry to the 'coronavirus emergency centre' at Charité – Universitätsmedizin in Berlin, one of Europe's largest university hospitals, and found that it was *empty* (Fig 378). It even had two 'emergency tents' outside which were also

Figure 378: Many videos appeared on the Internet of hospitals reported to be 'like war-zones' where nothing out of the normal was happening and often had no one to be seen.

unused and he said that staff were privately very critical of the media for so hyping something that wasn't happening. Medical staff were banned from officially talking about the situation and all information was channelled to the media through a central press office to ensure control of the narrative. The German journalist's video also included a list of doctors and specialists spelling out why the virus scare was an outrageous sleight of hand. The 'journalist's' video also included a list of doctors and specialists spelling out why the virus scare was an outrageous sleight of hand. YouTube deleted the video but we managed to find another version and downloaded that to the no-censorship BitChute video platform which I highly recommend. BitChute hosts the videos deleted by YouTube and anything YouTube bans that challenges the Cult narrative you need to see. Put these words into the search engine at Davidicke.com to watch the video: 'New source for banned YouTube video: German journalist goes to hospital 'teeming with coronavirus patients' – how can doctors cope? – and finds NO ONE

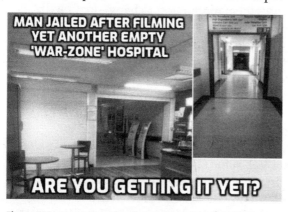

Figure 379: Images and footage of empty hospitals that were supposed to be 'war zones' appeared from all over the world. The British man who took these pictures was jailed to deter others from exposing the truth.

THERE'. Many people began to film at their local hospitals around the world and found them to also be empty with no stampede of 'virus' patients. Meanwhile the media was telling us of the said 'war-zone' conditions. One British man was jailed for three months for walking around a hospital and posting pictures on Facebook showing it to be empty (Fig 379). He was sentenced for visiting the hospital 'with no good reason' and of course showing it to be empty and the authorities to be lying to the British people was never going to be considered a 'good reason'. I met a hospital worker who said: 'You're right about what is happening'. He said the hospitals have 'never been so quiet' with hundreds of empty beds and staff sitting around. A UK whistleblower at Southmead Hospital in Bristol told the media platform Bristol Live that hundreds of hospital staff were laid off. She was a healthcare assistant in accident and emergency who normally worked full-time, but she was now struggling to get one shift a week. She was on a zero-hours contract which means you only get paid when work is available and she had

virtually no income. There were 'easily' more than 200 in the same
situation, including some nurses, where she was located. The
whistleblower said:

> There were hardly any patients when lockdown hit. The hospital closed seven
> wards and 150 beds, including the wards for stroke patients, orthopaedic
> trauma and neurosurgery. The hospital is like a ghost town. You could walk
> through and hear a pin drop. Pretty much the only patients in the hospital
> seem to be coronavirus patients.

Hugh Evans, Bristol Council's director of adult social care, said the
city's hospital bed occupancy was at an 'all-time, unforeseeable low'
while Jacqui Marshall, director of people and transformation at North
Bristol NHS Trust, said without a hint of embarrassment or irony … 'We
have not yet seen the surge in volume of patients that was initially
anticipated due to the Covid-19 pandemic.' You would not have known
any of this reading or watching the national and international media.

Happy clappers

Empty hospitals were a constant theme across the world and yet the UK
government instigated a weekly mass clapping by the unquestioning,
performing-penguin population for health workers who were 'saving us
from the virus' while most were sat strumming their fingers, being laid
off, or making a long stream of dancing videos that appeared on
YouTube featuring doctors and nurses prancing around empty hospitals.
They seemed to have no problem standing inches from each other or
closer despite social distancing rules imposed on everyone else by police
who also universally ignored them. I have emphasised in this book that
the global Cult conspiracy is about manipulating perception and never
has there been a more blatant example than the fake 'pandemic'. To that
end the usual mindless 'celebrities' were wheeled out like Lady Gaga,
Paul McCartney, Mick Jagger, Elton John and a long list of others
performing from home in the One World: Together At Home 'event'
organised jointly by the World Health Organization owned by Bill Gates
and an organisation called Global Citizen owned by Bill Gates. British
singer Rita Ora urged viewers to stay safe and follow WHO
recommendations. Gates would have been most grateful for yet another
clueless celebrity to advance his agenda while having no idea that this is
what she was doing. The 'event' was officially to celebrate health
workers and at least most of them would have had plenty of time to
watch. The psychological undertones however were selling the
perception of 'One World' (the Cult's long-time code for world
government dictatorship) and 'global citizen' (the end of borders and
nationalities). This and the mass clapping for health workers were all

part of the perceptual illusion that hospitals were overwhelmed.

The fact that comparatively few health workers came out to tell the truth of what was happening is something they will have to carry for the rest of their lives as they survey the catastrophic human consequences of the 'pandemic' lie – including for themselves and their kids. The mainstream media which could have easily confirmed and exposed the empty hospitals continued to present the war-zone illusion. The nearest anyone came at the time of writing was London's *Mail Online* report about *private* hospitals taken over by the UK National Health Service (NHS) being empty and unused. The hospitals seconded by the NHS at a cost of hundreds of millions of pounds because of the 'crisis' were described as 'sinfully empty' by senior doctors. They said hundreds of the country's best doctors were left 'twiddling their thumbs' during the 'outbreak' putting other patients at risk through untreated and undiagnosed other illnesses and cancelled operations. Eight thousand beds in private hospitals were seconded by the NHS in March, 2020, when it was claimed that 20,000 fully qualified staff in the hospitals, including 700 doctors, were needed to 'battle Covid-19'. They even appealed for thousands of qualified staff to come out of retirement to help. A London-based consultant orthopaedic surgeon said: 'What we are seeing at the moment is a sinful and shocking mass of empty private hospitals and empty beds.' The surgeon said that only 'emergency' and 'time-critical' operations were being allowed at his hospital: 'I have a waiting list of 25 people who need major operations right now. One with severe arthritis is crying out in pain every night, unable to sleep.' The *Mail* then spoiled it all by saying that NHS wards were 'overrun'. Like hell they were. Another phenomenon that made no sense in relation to the numbers was to build special intensive care facilities like the 'Nightingale' facility built in nine days at East London's ExCeL exhibition centre to provide an extra 4,000 intensive care beds while regular hospitals were operating at immense under capacity. The government then explained why 'Nightingale' was barely used by claiming a 'shortage of nurses' while great numbers sat virtually idle in near-empty hospitals and others made dancing videos in empty wards. The story was the same with other 'Nightingale hospitals' around the country. A massive army field hospital built inside a Seattle convention center by hundreds of troops was dismantled before treating a single patient. Then there were the emergency 'mortuaries' the size of football pitches and articulated trucks at hospitals said by the media and officialdom to be for dead bodies overflowing from normal mortuaries. People who filmed them with phone cameras showed the trucks to be empty. The British Army came to the Isle of Wight where I live to rearrange the local St Mary's Hospital to provide 200 extra beds when staff were telling me the hospital had never been so quiet and this was the location of one of the nurse dancing videos confirming how much 'pressure' they were under. If you think none of this makes sense – and it doesn't in terms of health and the official story– then read on.

How the scam works – a doctor explains

It became clear to me as I observed events that there was no 'Covid-19' and the puzzle pieces started to connect. A crucial contribution was provided by the research of Dr Andrew Kaufman, a practicing forensic psychiatrist in New York State, a Doctor of Medicine and former Medical Instructor of Hematology and Oncology at the Medical School of South Carolina. He also studied at the Massachusetts Institute of Technology (MIT). Kaufman provided a pivotal piece in the puzzle for me as I sought to uncover the way the Covid-19 hoax was manipulated. I was sure by the time I saw his video presentation that Covid-19 didn't exist and said so in Internet videos, but Kaufman revealed some vital detail. You can watch his interviews and presentations at Davidicke.com if you put into the search engine: 'Videos of Dr Andrew Kaufman exposing Covid-19 deceit'. His website is Andrewkaufmanmd.com. Kaufman explains how the Chinese authorities immediately concluded that the cause of an illness that broke out among about 200 initial patients was a 'new virus' and he details how they had no grounds for such a conclusion. They were blaming a 'virus' almost from the start for reasons that would become clear to anyone who has researched the global Cult and how it operates in every country and has no borders. Kaufman said Chinese investigators took unpurified genetic material from the lungs of only a handful of the first patients which can be found in large numbers of people all the time from a variety of sources including their own cells, bacteria, fungus and other microorganisms living in their bodies. This therefore proved nothing at all. *A 'viral disease' that would be called 'Covid-19' was never isolated and identified and other possible causes of the illness were barely considered.* The script was being written that would be repeated around the world. They identified a sequence of RNA (ribonucleic acid) which contains genetic material as DNA does although there are differences in their function. This genetic sequence is *what they have been testing for* – not a fantasy 'viral condition' called 'Covid-19'.

They could have isolated a virus if it existed through filtration because viral particles are much smaller than other material. They didn't. Instead they compared the contaminated, impure, RNA sequence with other RNA sequences and declared that because it was just under 80 percent identical to the SARS-CoV-1 'virus' claimed to be the cause of the SARS (severe acute respiratory syndrome) outbreak in 2003 that they must be related. They called the 'new virus' they had not even identified SARS-CoV-2 and claimed it was the cause of what has been termed 'Covid-19'. Kaufman highlights major problems with this claim. First of all the SARS-CoV-1 'virus' was not purified and isolated either (like all recent 'scare' viruses) and so could not possibly be proven to be responsible for 'SARS'; secondly, the 'just under 80 percent identical' is basically meaningless. Kaufman points out the 96 percent correlation between humans and chimpanzees when 'no one would say our genetic material is part of the chimpanzee family, but yet they are using a sequence identity that has a much lower percentage, under 80 percent compared with 96, and saying it's a coronavirus because of that'. He said, quite rightly, that this is extremely weak science. German physician and bacteriologist Robert Koch produced in 1890 the four criteria for proving that a particular bacteria, or 'virus' in this case, is the cause of a given disease. These criteria have been used ever since by mainstream medicine as the 'gold standard' (but not in the case of 'Covid-19' and other recent 'deadly viruses' they want to use to scare the population shitless). These are the so-called Koch Postulates:

1. The bacteria must be present in every case of the disease and all patients must have the same symptoms. It must also not be present in healthy individuals.
2. The microorganism must be isolated from the host with the disease and grown in pure culture (you must isolate only the 'virus' and no other material which is known as 'purification').
3. The specific disease must be reproduced when a pure culture of the infectious agent is inoculated into a healthy susceptible host (the isolated 'virus' must be proved to cause the disease that you claim and healthy people without the 'disease' must not be found to have any of the 'virus' or material that you say is causing the disease).
4. The bacteria must be recoverable from the experimentally infected host and everyone who comes into contact with the 'virus' or bacteria must get the same disease.

With 'Covid-19' none of these criteria – NONE – were met. Not ONE. The alleged 'Covid-19' has never been isolated or purified and the whole hoax has been perpetrated by diagnosing from symptoms with a long list of potential causes and by testing for genetic material (NOT 'Covid-19') and this genetic material also has a long list of other potential reasons for being there including lung cancer. In fact, the same test has been employed in attempts to identify lung cancer. Kaufman read the scientific papers describing the 'Covid-19' identification process and found them all to have seriously failed the Koch Postulate criteria and even the much less stringent adaptation of the postulates known as 'Rivers criteria' for viruses developed by American bacteriologist and virologist Thomas Milton Rivers, the 'father of modern virology', when he was director of the Rockefeller Institute for Medical Research in 1937. Papers claiming to have identified other more recent 'viruses' also failed both tests and all the papers failed on the most important criteria – isolating the alleged disease-causing agent from other genetic material that would contaminate and skew any testing method. Dr Kaufman's conclusion was that there is no 'Covid-19' virus: 'This entire pandemic is a completely manufactured crisis. In other words there is no evidence of anyone dying from [this] illness.' Many will be astounded at that statement, but you will see that this is confirmed by evidence across multiple subject areas and happenings.

The Chinese (Cult) authorities began to diagnose all people with 'flu-like' symptoms and pneumonia as infected with 'Covid-19', an alleged 'virus' they had not proven to exist and certainly not to be the reason that people were ill. Wuhan, like most Chinese cities, has notoriously toxic air and so widespread lung and respiratory problems – the same with Lombardy at the centre of the 'Covid-19 pandemic' in Italy. From the start Chinese medical staff were diagnosing what would become the infamous 'Covid-19' purely on 'flu-like' and pneumonia symptoms with their long list of other potential causes. The number of cases obviously soared as all respiratory disease was dubbed 'Covid-19' and all deaths diagnosed the same way. Death rates from the non-existent 'Covid-19' were hysterically hyped to build fear in the West that the 'deadly virus' was coming their way, but the 'death rates' were people dying from what they have always died from in toxic Wuhan. Then the Chinese authorities began 'testing' people for their alleged 'virus' which they had not identified. They rolled-out a diagnostic 'test' *before they had proved anything let alone that a new virus was involved.* 'How did they know what the source was of that genetic material?', Andrew Kaufman asked. Well, they didn't. The test is called the RT-PCR test or reverse transcription polymerase chain reaction. It is the 'qualitative rather than quantitative' protocol which can only measure the presence or absence of an RNA code sequence, but not the *amount* of RNA. I emphasise again – the PCR process is being used to 'test for the Covid-19 virus' when in fact it is … *not testing for 'Covid-19'.* It is testing only for a genetic material sequence that is present in large numbers of people for a large number of potential reasons. No wonder so many test positive and no wonder the deeply corrupt World Health Organization says that people are not developing immunity from 'Covid-19'. How can they become 'immune' to something they have never had because it doesn't exist? How can they become immune to a genetic sequence that is part of their own genetic make-up?

Almost everyone has coronavirus present in their bodies and, if measured, it could show up in genetic material. Not 'Covid-19', I stress, but *coronaviruses*, a large 'family' of viruses that include the common cold and other more severe strains that can lie dormant ongoing in the body kept in check by the immune system. A test for coronavirus, and not specifically 'Covid-19', will be positive in enormous numbers of people. The World Health Organization claims that 'Covid-19' is 'an infectious disease caused by a newly discovered coronavirus called Sars-CoV-2'. Kaufman and increasingly others seriously dispute this claim. He said of the PCR test, invented by American biochemist Kary Mullis in the 1980s: 'We can't trust the results of this test at all.' The Quantative PCR, sometimes called digital PCR, can be used to establish degradation of genetic material – which is what the Chinese took from the lungs of people sick at the start of the 'outbreak' – but clearly not the phantom 'Covid-19'. The PCR test involves 'amplification'. This means they take extremely small amounts of a sample and amplify that so they can better identify the content. The trouble is that amplification expands everything else in the sample. This means that what you are looking for becomes ever more contaminated by the other material. The more you amplify the more you find material in the sample that almost everyone has and so the greater the amplification the more people will test 'positive' for other things in the sample and not what you are supposed to be testing for. Amplify genetic material claimed to be 'Covid-19' say 35 times and you will get positives and negatives for content of the genetic material (not the 'virus') in the bodies of those tested; but amplify say 60 times and so much other genetic material comes into the picture that virtually everyone will test positive not for the 'virus', but different elements of what is contained in the 'genetic material'. This means that how many 'positives' you get depends on how many times you amplify the genetic material and if different countries use different amplifications this would be one way to explain *different numbers*. They also often dilute the samples as a way to determine the number of positives/negatives which allows them to do fewer cycles of amplification and takes less time. The authorities can control the number of 'cases' by these methods. If in China, for example, they used high amplifications at the start to terrify people they would get big numbers of 'cases'. If they then used lower amplifications the number of cases would suddenly fall to nothing and they could claim that their draconian lockdowns were responsible – so providing the response blueprint for other countries. The same monumental deceit has been employed in Britain, the United States and elsewhere. When the vaccine is introduced they will manipulate the test (so easy) to make it seem like the vaccine has worked.

The 'deadly virus' is a natural immune system response

Dr Andrew Kaufman introduced a devastating piece of information which relates to something called 'exosomes'. Cells release exosomes all

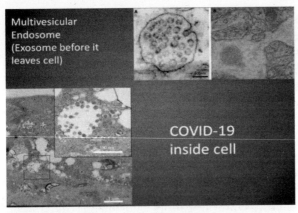

Multivesicular
Endosome
(Exosome before it
leaves cell)

COVID-19
inside cell

Figure 380: American doctor Andrew Kaufman exposed how exosomes, a natural immune system response by poisoned cells, looked the same under the microscope as what is being called 'Covid-19'. Cult operatives had taken a natural immune response and called it a 'deadly virus'.

	Exosomes	COVID-19
Diameter inside cell	500 nm (MVE)	500 nm
Diameter outside cell	100 nm	100 nm
Receptor	ACE-2	ACE-2
Contains	RNA	RNA
Found in	Bronchoalveolar (lung) fluid	Bronchoalveolar (lung) fluid

Figure 381: Andrew Kaufman further showed that in all relevant ways exosomes and the fake 'Covid-19' were the same even down to the cell receptors that both lock into. Exosomes and 'Covid-19' are one and the same. What a scam.

the time but they increase substantially when there are toxins in the tissues. They also communicate a warning about a problem to remote parts of the body and can even remove toxins from the extracellular space. Any form of toxin, whether chemical or electromagnetic, will cause cells to release exosomes as part of the body's system to protect from cell damage and death. Kaufman shows images of exosomes and what is alleged to be 'Covid-19' under the microscope and they are ... *exactly the same* in every relevant way (Fig 380). They both attach to the same cell receptors, contain the same genetic material in the form of RNA or ribonucleic acid, and both are found in lung fluid which is what the Chinese initially took from those first few patients before claiming the cause of their illness was a 'virus' (Fig 381). There is a reason they mirror each other – they are the *same phenomenon*. James Hildreth MD, President and Chief Executive Officer of the Meharry Medical College at Johns Hopkins, a researcher into HIV, said of viruses: 'The virus is fully an exosome in every sense of the word.' Exosomes, a natural mechanism for cells to cleanse themselves and alert other cells, and what is claimed to be 'Covid-19', are the same thing. Cult operatives in China and like-agents throughout the world simply renamed exosomes as 'isolated Covid-19' and developed a 'test' that produced a positive for *RNA of unknown origin* now transformed in the public mind into a non-existent 'virus' dubbed 'Covid-19'. Some of the conditions that trigger the release of exosomes ('Covid-19') include: Toxicity; fear and stress [see 'virus' hysteria and lockdowns]; infection; injury; immune system responses; asthma; disease; and electromagnetic radiation which is getting more powerful by the day. Andrew Kaufman also points out that part of the process of identifying the genetic material involves adding antibiotics which cause the cells to *release exosomes* into the sample. They have re-named a natural immune reaction 'Covid-19' knowing that large numbers of people will test positive for that immune response and content within a genetic material RNA code. When people test positive and then die from other causes doctors are told to put 'Covid-19' on the death certificate as I will show. This is how the number of 'cases' and 'deaths' from the non-existent 'Covid-19' have been scammed into a widespread public perception about a 'deadly virus' that can only be stopped by lockdown, mass global house arrest, destroying the independent livelihood of potentially billions, and a Bill Gates-produced mandatory 'vaccine'.

Can you 'catch' a virus?

Lockdown and 'social distancing' have been justified by the authorities on the grounds of protecting the public from an infectious disease – a 'virus' that has never been shown to exist. Then there is the question of whether even if the 'virus' was real that anyone could catch it from other people when a virus needs host cells to replicate. The *Encyclopedia Britannica* defines a virus as an agent that 'can multiply only in living cells of animals, plants, or bacteria' and says 'they cannot reproduce and carry on metabolic processes without a host cell'. Can 'Covid-19' therefore be 'caught' from work surfaces, door handles, and money and how can it jump between humans or animals and humans when it requires a cellular host inside a body? As the lockdowns continued, Professor Hendrik Streeck, a virologist working on the German response to the 'pandemic', said the 'virus' had not been spread by shopping or going to the hairdresser. His studies in one 'infected' home found it 'did not have any live virus on any surface' including on phones, door knobs or even the pet cat's fur. 'We know it's not a smear infection that is transmitted by touching objects', he said, and he believed it could only be transmitted by very close contact. I would say from what I've read that even that is not correct, or at least unproven. Meanwhile, the public was ordered to keep six-feet from other people, including when standing in the rain waiting to enter a one-in, one-out store, and to stay at home out of the sun while using sanitiser to wash every surface. Streeck's words take us into the territory of Dawn Lester and David Parker in their book widely-quoted by inquiring physicians, *What Really Makes You Ill – Why everything you thought you knew about disease is wrong*. Lester and Parker seriously question that a 'virus' can be transmitted between people or people and animals and they point out there is no provable scientific evidence to show that it can. They are not alone in this assertion either. The book quotes the establishment definition of a 'virus' as 'a minute particle that is capable of replication but only within living cells'. The authors write:

> The definition also claims that viruses are the cause of many diseases, as if this has been definitively proven. But this is not the case; there is no original scientific evidence that definitively demonstrates that any virus is the cause of any disease. The burden of proof for any theory lies with those who proposed it; but none of the existing documents provides 'proof' that supports the claim that 'viruses' are pathogens.

How can a natural immune response – which is what a 'virus' really is – cause or transmit disease? The exosome reaction is a response to a problem (poisoned or otherwise injured cells) and not the problem itself. To say otherwise is to say that firefighters responding to a blaze *are the fire*. The very word 'virus' comes from a Latin word meaning 'poison'. Various manifestations of 'pus', as with smallpox, were once associated with the word 'virus'. Lester and Parker quote Dr Lynn Margulis, acclaimed biologist and member of the National Academy of Sciences, as saying that viruses are not even alive in her definition:

> They are not alive since outside living cells they do nothing, ever. Viruses require the metabolism of the live cell because they lack the requisites to generate their own. Metabolism, the incessant chemistry of self-maintenance, is an essential feature of life. Viruses lack this.

Margulis further said that '… any virus outside the membrane of a live cell is inert' and inert means 'lacking the ability or strength to move'. Wow, 'deadly viruses' suddenly seem a lot less scary, eh? Lester and Parker ask how inert 'virus' particles that cannot move are supposed to somehow be transmitted between people and enter cells to 'infect' them. This poses a similar problem to medical authority as that faced by the inconvenient fact for the Climate Cult that carbon dioxide has to double in volume to affect temperature by any significant degree. This is not going to happen and the climate extremists have had to invent a whole cover story about 'feedback loops' to overcome these facts and claim that CO2 is dangerous. In the same way virus particles outside a living host cannot move and without that they can't be passed on to 'infect' anyone. Hold on a while and I'll work something out. Let me think. Ah, yes, they hitch a ride on particles that can move and then drop off at just the right time to enter a body. Phew – do you think they'll buy that? This is what is claimed to explain the mystery although *how* this is supposed to happen has never been explained. Lester and Parker write:

The transmission of any viral particle attached to saliva or mucous travelling through the air has never been observed; viral particles are only ever observed in a laboratory under an electron microscope. The transmission of viruses in the air is an assumption; as is their ability to travel through the human body.

The authors note that investigations, including those by virologists, have 'failed to unearth any original papers that conclusively prove that any virus is the cause of any disease. Functions attributed to viruses in the cause of disease were based on assumptions and extrapolations from laboratory experiments that had not only failed to prove, but were incapable of proving, that viruses cause disease. 'The inert, non-living particles known as viruses do not possess the ability to perform such functions because they lack the necessary mechanisms.' So what is the point of 'social distancing', masks and lockdown? There is none. What divides people more than wearing masks hiding facial expressions and yet they were seen everywhere as people once again unquestioningly believed they would offer protection from the virus that didn't exist. Pores in the masks are far bigger than viral particles and Dr Kaufman described this as like putting up a chain-link fence to stop mosquitoes. He also warned that masks restrict breathing which can be 'problematic' with healthy people never mind those with asthma or lung and airway disease. For them it could be devastating. Masks, social distancing – none of this is about health. It's about control and economic destruction. By the way, newspapers were quick to claim that the 'virus' could be caught from handling money (wrong), but they emphasised that it cannot be caught from handling newspapers. How come it can be 'passed on' through paper money, but not paper newspapers? The newspapers are selling newspapers and not money. My god, it's pathetic.

The propaganda has been so incessant that to suggest there is no evidence of a 'Covid-19' is to be crazy by definition to most people. They wouldn't lie that much, surely? Oh, they *would*. Absolute super-massive whoppers are their calling card – the bigger the lie the more will believe it. The response by Cult-controlled Silicon Valley to two videos within days of each other was very significant with regard to this. The first was an interview I did with Brian Rose at London Real that was live-streamed and attracted the second-biggest live-stream audience in the world that day on YouTube. Within minutes of completion and with more than 300,000 already watching the recording YouTube deleted the video followed quickly by Vimeo and Facebook. The latter version had been watched a million times before Facebook pulled the plug. The mainstream media and sadly much of the alternative focussed on what I said about a 5G angle to current events which was only a relatively small part of the interview. The whole thrust of what I said was to question the existence of 'Covid-19'. A few days later my son, Jaymie, interviewed Andrew Kaufman for Davidicke.com in a video that did not even mention 5G, but it was deleted by YouTube after passing 300,000 views. The common denominator of both deleted videos was not 5G – it was to question the existence of 'Covid-19' which, when widely known, would bring down the house of cards. The unthinkable needs to be thought when the evidence points in that direction. I have been constantly misquoted as saying that 5G is causing the 'virus' which is rather difficult to sustain when I am saying there *is no* 'Covid-19' virus. My point has been that 5G can trigger *symptoms* that have been *called* 'Covid-19' which is very different from 5G 'causing the virus'.

How the scam works – a scientist explains

In late March, 2020, I received an email from Sir Julian Rose, a writer, researcher, and known in the UK for his promotion of organic farming. He sent me an explanation of the coronavirus hoax sent to him by an American scientist friend who works in the healthcare field. It is a superb breakdown of the systematic deceit and absolutely supports many of the findings of Dr Andrew Kaufman. The scientist said they were not testing people specifically for 'Covid-19', but for *any* strain of a coronavirus of which there are a long list. 'There are no reliable tests for a specific Covid-19 virus', he said. Nor were there any reliable agencies or media outlets for reporting numbers of actual Covid-19 virus cases. 'Every action and reaction to Covid-19 is based on totally flawed data and we simply cannot make accurate assessments.' He said this was why most people diagnosed with 'Covid-19' were showing nothing more than cold/flu like symptoms. 'That's because most Coronavirus strains are nothing more than cold/flu like symptoms.' An 84-year-old German man tested positive for 'Covid-19', his entire nursing home was quarantined, and then he was found to have only a common cold. The Tanzania government sent samples from a pawpaw and a goat to the WHO for testing (to expose the scam) and both came back *positive* for 'Covid-19'. The PCR test used to detect 'Covid-19' does not do that, the scientist said, but instead 'basically takes a sample of your cells and amplifies any [RNA] to look for "viral sequences", i.e. bits of non-human [RNA] that seem to match parts of a known viral genome'. The problem he said was that … *the test is known not to work*:

> It uses 'amplification' which means taking a very, very tiny amount of [RNA] and growing it exponentially until it can be analyzed. Obviously any minute contaminations in the sample will also be amplified leading to potentially gross errors of discovery. Additionally, it's only looking for partial viral sequences, not whole genomes, so identifying a single pathogen is next to

impossible even if you ignore the other issues.

He said what he called the 'Mickey Mouse test kits' that were being sent out to hospitals told analysts – 'at best' – that you have some viral (RNA) in your cells. This was irrelevant because most people had coronavirus (RNA) most of the time:

> It may tell you the viral sequence is related to a specific type of virus – say the huge family of coronavirus. But that's all. The idea these kits can isolate a specific virus like Covid-19 is nonsense.

He said the other issue was 'viral load'. The PCR 'Covid-19' test (that isn't) works by amplifying minute amounts of RNA. It was therefore useless at telling you how *much* virus you may have – the only question that really matters when it comes to diagnosing illness:

> Everyone will have a few viruses kicking round in their system at any time, and most will not cause illness because their quantities are too small. For a virus to sicken you – you need a lot of it, a massive amount of it.

> But PCR does not test viral load [They use qualitative rather than quantitative PCR] and therefore can't determine if [a virus] is present in sufficient quantities to sicken you. If you feel sick and get a PCR test any random virus [RNA] might be identified even if they aren't at all involved in your sickness which leads to false diagnosis.

What is said here is supported by Kary Mullis who won the Nobel Prize in Science for *inventing* the PCR in the 1980s. Yes, the inventor of the PCR test said that it *cannot accurately test for infectious diseases* and yet this is what the test is being used for with regard to 'Covid-19'. Mullis said: 'Quantitative PCR is an oxymoron.' He said that PCR is intended to identify substances *qualitatively*, but by its very nature the test is unsuited for quantity. Mullis said there was a common misimpression that the viral load tests count the number of viruses in the blood, but the test *could not detect free, infectious viruses at all*. The test could detect genetic sequences of viruses, but not viruses themselves. You can see from all this that the numbers of cases and therefore deaths from 'Covid-19' are utterly unsupportable. The scientist said coronavirus is incredibly common. 'A large percentage of the world human population will have covi … in them in small quantities even if they are perfectly well or sick with some other pathogen.' He asked: 'Do you see where this is going yet?' All this meant that 'if you want to create a totally false panic about a totally false pandemic – pick a coronavirus':

They are incredibly common and there's tons of them. A very high percentage of people who have become sick by other means (flu, bacterial pneumonia, anything) will have a positive PCR test for covi even if you're doing them properly and ruling out contamination, simply because coronaviruses are so common. There are hundreds of thousands of flu and pneumonia victims in hospitals throughout the world at any one time.

He said all you needed to do was select the sickest of these people in a single location – 'say Wuhan' – and administer PCR tests to them. You then claim that anyone showing viral sequences similar to a coronavirus 'which will inevitably be quite a few' is suffering from a 'new' disease:

Since you already selected the sickest flu cases a fairly high proportion of your sample will go on to die. You can then say this 'new' virus has a CFR [case fatality rate] higher than the flu and use this to infuse more concern and do more tests which will of course produce more 'cases', which expands the testing, which produces yet more 'cases' and so on and so on.

Before long you have your 'pandemic', and all you have done is use a simple test kit trick to convert the worst flu and pneumonia cases into something new that *doesn't actually exist* [my emphasis].

The scientist said you then 'just run the same scam in other countries' and make sure to keep the fear message running high 'so that people will feel panicky and less able to think critically'. The only problem to overcome was the fact *there is no* actual new deadly pathogen but just regular sick people. This meant that deaths from the 'new deadly pathogen' are going to be way too low for a real new deadly virus pandemic, but he said this could be overcome in the following ways – all of which would go on to happen:

1. You can claim this is just the beginning and more deaths are imminent [you underpin this with fake 'computer projections']. Use this as an excuse to quarantine everyone and then claim the quarantine prevented the expected millions of dead.
2. You can tell people that 'minimizing' the dangers is irresponsible and bully them into not talking about numbers.
3. You can talk crap about made up numbers hoping to blind people with pseudoscience.
4. You can start testing well people (who, of course, will also likely have shreds of coronavirus [RNA] in them) and thus inflate your 'case figures' with 'asymptomatic carriers' (you will of course have to spin that to sound deadly even though any virologist knows the more symptom-less cases you have the less deadly is your pathogen.

He said that if you take these simple steps 'you can have your own entirely manufactured pandemic up and running in weeks'. In short the authorities cannot 'confirm' something for which there is no accurate test and they certainly cannot produce a vaccine as Cult asset Bill Gates (*a lot* more to come) soon began to peddle on the back of the 'crisis'. What the scientist and Andrew Kaufman had said would be supported by an ever-increasing body of evidence. My son Gareth and I live hours apart but we both had exactly the symptoms of 'Covid-19' in the run-up to Christmas, 2019, before the scare began. I was later to learn that others did, too. I am very rarely ill because I am blessed with a strong immune system which I constantly boost with the daily supplements missing from the modern diet and Gaz almost never gets ill for the same reason with his immune system on fire because it wasn't undermined by childhood vaccination. Gaz and myself both had a highly unusual experience of illness when we went down at the same time with what would now be called 'Covid-19 symptoms' – every one of them. It wasn't pleasant for a few days with coughing, aches and a mild fever, but we both carried on working and I wrote some of this book in that period. The immune system did its job without doctor involvement. The point is that if we had those same symptoms a few weeks later we would have been dubbed 'Covid-19 victims'. Tens of thousands of people die in the United States alone every winter from flu (many with pneumonia complications) with Centers for Disease Control (CDC) figures recording that 45 *million* Americans were diagnosed with flu in 2017-2018 of which 61,000 died. Some reports said 80,000. Anyone remember the same hysteria that we have seen with 'Covid-19'? Around 250,000 Americans are admitted to hospital with pneumonia every year and about 50,000 die. With the manipulation of death certificates those people are all potential 'Covid-19' fake statistics and then add the fact that 65 million people suffer from respiratory disease every year with three million deaths which makes it the third biggest cause of death worldwide.

Where did the numbers and 'projections' come from?

The serious lack of enough dead people to justify the 'deadly virus' fear-fest was dealt with as the scientist said it would be. They said that although people were not dying in big numbers *yet* that was going to happen ('you can claim this is just the beginning and more deaths are imminent') and when the numbers didn't materialise they said it was because of the lockdown ('then claim the quarantine prevented the expected millions of dead'). The death projections were never going to happen and their purveyors knew that. They were simply falsely created to secure the lockdowns for purposes of economic catastrophe and control over billions. The experience of Japan which avoided draconian lockdowns exposes the mendacity that lockdowns affected events except to crash the world economy for very sinister motives. With the figures being fixed through tests and death certificates what difference would either lockdown or no lockdown have made? It is worth remembering this at all times: Statistics don't speak for themselves – they speak for those that compiled them. If you take the example of the UK – the same happened globally – the outrageously exaggerated projections of deaths (to justify house arrest for billions) came from … *computer models*. You know, the same technique used with the ludicrous exaggerations of climate change *computer models* which have proved so laughably inaccurate, but so useful to sell the climate lie. It is so easy to get the projection you want when all you need to do is upload shite to download shite. Andrew Kaufman has worked in computer modelling and explained how easy it is to fix the outcome. Computer 'projections' depend on the nature of the data input from which the 'projections' are produced. The 'Covid-19' projection insanity was that up to *'500,000 people will die in the UK if we don't have lockdown'*. I'll repeat that just to let the lunacy of this sink in: '500,000 people will die in the UK if we don't have lockdown'. This was the work of Neil Ferguson, Professor of Mathematical Biology and head of the MRC Center for Global Infectious Disease Analysis (funded by Bill Gates and his vaccinate-the-world fronts Gavi and the Global Fund). *Business Insider* said of the Ferguson operation:

> It gets tens of millions of dollars in annual funding from the Bill & Melinda Gates Foundation, and works with the UK National Health Service, the US Centres for Disease Prevention and Control (CDC), and is tasked with supplying the World Health Organization with 'rapid analysis of urgent infectious disease problems'.

The biggest funder of Gates's Gavi is … *the British government* which took its lockdown advice from Gavi-funded, Gates-owned Ferguson and London's Imperial College. During the 'pandemic' the UK government pledged £330 million a year of taxpayers money to Gavi for at least five years through the Department for International Development. Gavi in turn connects into the Gates-controlled World Health Organization (WHO), the United Nations and the World Bank. The WHO is part of the Cult-created-and-controlled UN, the stalking horse for world government. Ferguson is a wholly-owned subsidiary of Gates who is a wholly-owned subsidiary of the Cult and what a surprise that Ferguson produced the 'computer models' that terrified governments to impose the human-catastrophe of lockdown. It was also reported that the code being used by Imperial College for their 'models' was 'tidied up' by

Figure 382: Neil Ferguson – UK Prime Minister Boris Johnson and other politicians believed Ferguson's ludicrous computer 'projections' and utter disaster followed in destroyed lives and livelihoods. (Image by Gareth Icke.)

Gates's Microsoft. Ferguson advised governments and the Gates World Health Organization while based at the Gates-funded, Freemason-connected Imperial College. The college has received the best part of $200 million in Gates funding so far. Gates is everywhere in the fake 'pandemic' story and he and Ferguson should be in jail for the rest their lives in my view for what they have done to human society. Ferguson's fantasy 'projections' which were never going to happen caused an until-then reluctant Prime Minister Boris Johnson to turn Britain into a fascistic police/military state (see Hunger Games Society). Johnson was resisting full-blown lockdown, but faced with such a projection for which he was told he would take responsibility the technocrats broke him and took complete control of policy from then on (Fig 382). They included SAGE, the Science Advisory Group for Emergencies, which is part of the UK government's 'emergency response structure' and a subcommittee of the appropriately dubbed COBRA which 'coordinates the actions of government bodies in response to national or regional crisis'. SAGE is headed by Patrick Vallance, UK chief scientific advisor, and former head of drug discovery, medicines discovery and research and development at British-based Big Pharma giant, GlaxoSmithKline (GSK), which has absolutely enormous funding and business connections to Bill Gates. The UK government's Vaccine Network, a group of academics and Big Pharma 'experts' advising on vaccination policy, has a membership that has almost in its entirety taken hundreds of millions (*at least*) in donations from the Gates Foundation and includes employees of GSK which is involved in a 'Covid-19' testing campaign and the 'search' for a vaccine. GSK and Gates stand to make an extraordinary fortune from the fake 'pandemic'. Former GlaxoSmithKline chief executive Sir Andrew Witty has taken a leave of absence from his current day job to lead the push to develop vaccines for Covid-19 at the World Health Organization. Gates has bought and controlled everyone and everything needed to dictate the 'pandemic' narrative and press for the mass vaccination of the whole of humanity for a 'virus' never shown to exist. UK chief scientific advisor Patrick Vallance, a GSK executive, announced in April, 2020, that the SAGE 'advice' to the UK government would not be made public until after the 'pandemic' was over (and the irreversible transformation of human society achieved). Allyson Pollock, director of the Institute of Health and Society at the UK's Newcastle University, was among dozens of experts who signed a letter in The *Lancet* medical journal demanding government advisors should be more transparent (no chance). She said:

> We ought to know who is advising the government [Bill Gates] … What is the government hiding [Bill Gates] and who is it protecting? Government employees and publicly funded university scientists – likely to make up a large number of SAGE members – are accountable to the taxpayer.

No, no, Allyson. They are accountable to Bill Gates who is accountable to the Cult. Boris Johnson's own 'infection with Covid-19' (illness from something, not 'Covid-19') took him out of the loop for a significant period very conveniently. With British people in lockdown, under house arrest and living in a police state justified by these 'projections' Ferguson dramatically reeled back his figures and said in late March that the death toll was likely to be '20,000 or fewer'. Even this was an exaggeration when deaths attributed to 'Covid-19' are an administrative, death-certificate, mathematical trick supported by an irrelevant 'test'. Ferguson and his cohorts at Imperial College sold the fascistic lockdowns by the usual method – fear and lies. Their report to Boris Johnson said:

> Perhaps our most significant conclusion is that mitigation is unlikely to be feasible without emergency surge capacity limits of the UK and US healthcare systems being exceeded many times over. In the most effective mitigation strategy examined, which leads to a single, relatively short epidemic (case isolation, household quarantine and social distancing of the elderly), the surge limits for both general ward and ICU beds would be exceeded by at least 8-fold under the more optimistic scenario for critical care requirements that we examined.

Deborah Birx, coronavirus response coordinator to the Trump administration, told journalists that the Imperial paper – Ferguson's computer projection of more than two million deaths in America – had prompted new advice 'to work from home and avoid gatherings of 10 or more'. Ferguson's message was the Gates message because Gates owns him and we had the recurring theme of establishing the draconian lockdowns in China as the blueprint for the West to follow in pursuit of the Cult's agenda to mass-destroy independent livelihoods and install the Hunger Games Society. Ferguson said:

> One has to adopt the kind of community measures which have been adopted in places like Wuhan and China where you try to reduce contacts between people in the community, so the sorts of measures which are important are

first of all anyone who has any sort of respiratory disease, a cold, they should stay at home until those symptoms are fully resolved.

What followed was the mass cancellation of other hospital activities like operations and consultations while at the same time the Ferguson Imperial College predictions of hospitals being overwhelmed by 'Covid-19' cases could hardly have been more wrong. So much so that the UK authorities stopped publishing figures about intensive care bed use to hide the fact that intensive care units were not overwhelmed and whole major hospitals across the locked-down world had hundreds and hundreds of empty beds. News organisations had no footage of the 'war-zone' hospitals they were describing and so devoid were they of proof that CBS was caught using footage of an Italian intensive care ward while claiming it was in New York. The UK's Channel 4 News showed pictures of a *dummy* being worked on in a training centre while presenting it as a live human. Yet as late as March 26th, 2020, the calculated lunatics at Imperial College were warning that 'Covid-19' could kill 30 million around the world and lives could only be saved if countries acted quickly (that is put their populations under house arrest). Imperial College was not responding to a health crisis. It was following a script and justifying Cult agenda demands with blatantly and vastly exaggerated computer 'projections'. They must face the consequences for their actions with an independent open and public inquiry to expose what happened and how it was clearly orchestrated. Ferguson and Imperial College produced 'projections' for other governments including a Ferguson claim that up to 2.2 million people could die in America without a lockdown. This is the very lockdown that Bill Gates wanted for his Cult economic and vaccine agenda and for which Gates-funded Imperial College provided the projected excuse. Key advisors around Johnson, Trump and other leaders were also financial beneficiaries of Gates largesse and this is the same Bill Gates who in effect owns the Cult-created World Health Organization (WHO) as its second biggest funder behind only the government of the United States. He might even be the biggest by the time you read this. The Gates-controlled WHO has been driving the 'Covid-19' response worldwide and promoting in the West the lockdown policy of China because 'it was so effective'. Are you getting it? In the United States the Cult-controlled Johns Hopkins Coronavirus Resource Center was counting the numbers and 'briefing' the media. You will see the significance of that in the next chapter. Another organisation producing projections for 'Covid-19' deaths has been the Institute for Health Metrics and Evaluation (IHME) funded – like Imperial College and Neil Ferguson – by Bill Gates.

Comedy of 'errors'

Imperial College promotes every aspect of Agenda 21/2030 and has
been heavily involved in 'climate change' computer model 'projections'.
The Climate Cult demands a whole new economic system – one of the
prime reasons for the 'Covid-19' hysteria and its extreme economic fall-
out. Ferguson and his manufactured 'models' predicted that up to
150,000 people could die from BSE, or 'mad cow disease', and its
equivalent in sheep if it made the leap in humans. Fewer than 200 deaths
from the human form of BSE followed. BSE was shown to be due to an
organophosphate pesticide used to treat a pest on the cows. Ferguson
and the goons (oops, I repeat myself) with their computer models at
Imperial College triggered the unnecessary mass 'pre-emptive' cull of
millions of pigs, cattle and sheep during a foot and mouth outbreak in
2001 that destroyed the livelihoods of untold numbers of farmers and
their families. Imperial College and Neil Ferguson seem to be good at
that. The culled animals had no contact with the disease let alone had it.
Remind you of anything? The government was also advised to do this
by Professor Roy Anderson, a computer modeller at Imperial College
specialising in the epidemiology of human diseases (God help us), but
without any experience in veterinary matters. Anderson serves both on
the Bill and Melinda Gates Grand Challenges in Global Health advisory
board and chairs another organisation funded by the Gates Foundation.
Imperial College has received grants worth tens of millions from Gates
aimed at influencing global 'health' and vaccine policy including one of
$14.5 million 'to improve methods to detect circulating polioviruses
through environmental surveillance'. At the same time President Trump
was being 'advised' by people like 'Dr' Anthony Fauci in his
'coronavirus taskforce'. Fauci is director of the National Institute of
Allergy and Infectious Diseases (NIAID) which has received major
funding from the Gates Foundation. He also was named on the
'Leadership Council' of the Decade of Vaccines Collaboration funded by
the Bill and Melinda Gates Foundation. A headline on the Gates-created
Gavi website in 2012 proclaimed: 'Fauci: forging closer ties with Gavi'.
The same Gates connections apply to 'Dr' Deborah Birx who was
appointed White House Coronavirus Response Coordinator in February,
2020. An article at Nationalfile.com said:

> Gates has a lot of pull in the medical world, he has a multi-million dollar
> relationship with Dr. Fauci, and Fauci originally took the Gates line supporting
> vaccines and casting doubt on [the drug hydroxychloroquine]. Coronavirus
> response team member Dr. Deborah Birx, appointed by former president
> Obama to serve as United States Global AIDS Coordinator, also sits on the
> board of a group that has received billions from Gates' foundation, and Birx
> reportedly used a disputed Bill Gates-funded model for the White House's

Coronavirus effort. Gates is a big proponent for a population lockdown scenario for the Coronavirus outbreak.

Yes he is because that is the reason the Cult launched the 'Covid-19' hoax to destroy independent livelihoods and impose a vaccine to 'end' the lockdowns. The world is waking up to Bill Gates and it is not waking up from a nightmare, but *to* one. This deeply sinister man was at the centre of the 'Covid-19' hijacking of human society pulling the strings of Gates-funded Neil Ferguson and his computer models behind the lockdowns in many countries including the United States where Ferguson was cheer-led by Fauci and Birx. American researcher Daniel Horowitz highlighted the impact of Imperial College 'Covid-19' 'projections' on the lockdown policy in the United States:

> What led our government and the governments of many other countries into panic was a single Imperial College of UK study, funded by global warming activists, that predicted 2.2 million deaths if we didn't lock down the country. In addition, the reported 8-9% death rate in Italy scared us into thinking there was some other mutation of this virus that they got, which might have come here.

> Together with the fact that we were finally testing and had the ability to actually report new cases, we thought we were headed for a death spiral. But again … we can't flatten a curve if we don't know when the curve started.

The lockdowns were claimed to be 'protecting the people' while 'the people' die all the time in enormously greater numbers from other conditions, including cancer and heart disease. I'll tell you how much the Cult and its political and Deep State psychopaths care about humanity. Ultra-Zionist Dr Richard Day, professor of paediatrics at Mount Sinai Hospital in New York and executive of the Rockefeller-created Planned Parenthood, told those paediatricians in Pittsburgh, Pennsylvania, in *1969* that they already had the cure for cancer but were keeping it secret: 'We can cure almost every cancer right now. Information is on file in the Rockefeller Institute [now the Rockefeller University], if it's ever decided that it should be released.' Day said that the plan was to control and cull the population through medicine, food, *new laboratory-made diseases* and the suppression of a cure for cancer. He said that letting people die of cancer would slow down population growth: 'You may as well die of cancer as something else.' Pause for a ponder on the level of empathy-deleted psychopathy that we are dealing with from a Cult that claims it has devastated human society to 'protect the people' it absolutely despises.

The Gates of Hell

Neil Ferguson and his fellow 'modellers' at Imperial College are nothing if not utterly without self-awareness and they continued to promote an indefinite lockdown *until a vaccine is available* in perfect sync with the demands of Bill Gates and his masters. This is what you would expect from Gates-puppet Ferguson given that he heads up the Vaccine Impact Modelling Consortium out of Imperial College which 'coordinates the work of several research groups modelling the impact of vaccination programmes worldwide'. The Ferguson 'consortium' is a global vaccine promotion operation funded by the Bill Gates-created Gavi, the 'vaccine alliance', and the Bill and Melinda Gates Foundation. Ferguson's conflict of interest is extraordinary, but no one in government (Cult-owned governments) seems to care. Why would they when there is a global agenda to impose? If you are under some level of lockdown for months and the only way out is to have the eventual vaccine do you think people are more likely to have it despite their reservations? These unelected technocrats are 'advising' governments, less we forget, made up of politicians who treat them with the reverence and certainty they don't even begin to deserve. Ferguson, who was diagnosed with 'coronavirus' and somehow managed to survive, has sold his nonsense to the UK government that led to lockdown while an associate of his, Christopher Whitty (another virus 'survivor'), has been Chief Medical Officer to the UK Government on coronavirus policy and a member of the UK government SAGE 'science advisory' body headed by Patrick Vallance. Whitty was described by the BBC as 'the official who will probably have the greatest impact on our everyday lives of any individual policymaker in modern times'. Not a politician you will note – a technocrat. Whitty was handed a $40 million grant by the Bill and Melinda Gates Foundation for malaria research in Africa. Ferguson and Whitty wrote a paper together entitled 'Infectious disease: Tough choices to reduce Ebola transmission'. This was another exaggerated health scare in which both were involved.

Ferguson supported closing schools 'for prolonged periods' over the swine flu 'pandemic in 2009. He said the swine flu virus would infect a third of the world's population if it continued to spread at the current rate and he and other 'researchers' at Imperial College London predicted the virus was likely to cause an epidemic in the northern hemisphere. A news report said: 'One of the authors, the epidemiologist and disease modeller Neil Ferguson, who sits on the World Health Organisation's emergency committee for the outbreak, said the virus had "full pandemic potential".' He supplied 'computer models' to then chief medical officer, Professor Sir Liam Donaldson, which said in the worst case scenario 30 percent of the UK population could be infected by the H1N1 'swine flu' virus, with 65,000 killed. The number who officially died by the end of the year: 392. This was more Ferguson 'modelling' that could hardly have been more inaccurate. Oh yes, and no-one caught Ebola from someone else in the UK let alone died from it. Never mind, without self-awareness (or with an agenda) you just carry on pontificating your 'expertise' regardless. A newspaper quoted 'scientists from Imperial College' in an article headlined 'UK lockdown could be indefinite until a vaccine is found, warn scientists advising government'. They said countries would have to go through repeated cycles of restrictions being lifted and re-imposed (exactly in line with the Cult agenda). Ferguson said the UK government had wrestled with the idea of adopting strict measures and then going back to normal, but 'we don't think that's now possible'. So who is this *'we'*? The 'we' is Bill Gates and the bigger 'we' is the Cult that owns him.

People only die from 'Covid-19'

The biggest problem the figure-manipulators faced was producing enough dead people from a 'dangerous disease' that doesn't exist, or a 'bioweapon' depending on which version of deceit that people chose to believe. The Cult subsidiary networks in each country solved this (at least at first) through their top-down control of the medical pyramids. You need very few people to dictate policy to tens of thousands in national 'health' systems – you just need to control the key positions that dictate what the lower-ranks must do. As with China the first diagnosis of 'Covid-19' in the West and wider world came purely from symptoms. Doctors and other medical staff were told that pretty much anyone with 'flu-like symptoms' or pneumonia had to be diagnosed 'Covid-19' and given that so many have those symptoms and develop pneumonia from a host of causes the numbers began to climb solely from this top-down demand for diagnosis. When the PCR test (not testing for 'Covid-19') came into play the potential was almost limitless to fix the figures of not only cases, but deaths. Medical staff were told that everyone that came to hospital or was treated anywhere had to be tested for 'Covid-19'. Many tested positive as the Cult knew they would because the test is for a genetic material that large numbers of people have in their bodies as a matter of course. Staff were then told that anyone who died (of other conditions) who had tested positive must have 'Covid-19' declared on the death certificate as the cause of their demise. People who have died in road accidents have had 'Covid-19' given as the cause of death. None of this is speculation. Many medical staff have had the courage to speak out and expose that this is happening. The overwhelming majority have not, however, and they will have to live with that for the rest of their lives as the consequences for global humanity become ever clearer. The UK's National Health Service (NHS) told doctors that they could put 'Covid-19' on a death certificate without any evidence whatsoever:

If before death the patient had symptoms typical of COVID-19 infection, but the test result has not been received, it would be satisfactory to give 'COVID-19' as the cause of death, and then share the test result when it becomes available. In the circumstances of there being no swab, *it is satisfactory to apply clinical judgement* [My emphasis].

The UK Chief Coroner said in a note of guidance that the 'emergency' Coronavirus Bill means that 'Covid-19' deaths *don't have to be referred to a coroner at all* and the same is happening in many countries and US states including a directive to this effect in New Jersey. Medical practitioners can sign off a cause of death as Covid-19 for someone they have never even seen without any cause-of-death oversight by a coroner or autopsy because an autopsy would reveal the *real* cause of death – not 'Covid-19'. The UK Chief Coroner directive said:

Any registered medical practitioner can sign an MCCD [Medical Certificate for Cause of Death], even if the deceased was not attended during their last illness and not seen after death, provided that they are able to state the cause of death to the best of their knowledge and belief.

Deaths 'in the community' can also be listed as Covid-19 deaths without being tested for the disease, or even seen by a doctor. The Crown Office took such actions under emergency powers in the fascist-charter Coronavirus Act of 2020 'to ease the burden faced by the NHS as the UK moves towards predicted peak levels of infection and death'. This was the burden faced in near-empty hospitals where medical staff were making YouTube dancing videos to ease the boredom of inactivity. Scotland's Cult-controlled government via the Scottish National Party declared that anyone who died within 28 days of a 'laboratory confirmed' (fake test) diagnosing 'Covid-19' must have that recorded as the cause of death. Remember that the overwhelming majority of those who test positive for the fake test have 'mild symptoms' or mostly none at all. Let that sink in with regard to the Scottish death record policy and you will see the size of the deceit in that small country alone to fix the figures. This is the same Scottish government that dropped the requirement for post-mortems to be carried out on alleged 'Covid-19' victims so the real cause of death could not be established and 'Covid-19' could go on the death certificate and the cumulative figures. A newspaper report said: 'Normally, patients who die in hospital have a post-mortem to establish beyond doubt the cause of death.' Finding out what people really died of was is not the idea – it's to get the non-existent 'Covid-19' on as many death certificates as possible to increase the perception of a deadly 'pandemic. Scotland is a lovely place, but its control networks are literally satanic. Northern Ireland's Public Health Agency mirrors Scotland and other countries by defining a 'Covid-19' death as 'individuals who have died within 28 days of first positive result, whether or not COVID-19 was the cause of death.' England's NHS Office of National Statistics (ONS) tweaked the death figure deception even more by changing the way they counted the numbers. Before the 'Covid-19' fraud they had counted deaths each week by the number of death certificates. Now they would include 'provisional' death figures from the fake 'virus' before a death certificate had been registered and this would be 'included in the dataset in subsequent weeks'. This means a death could be counted 'provisionally' one week and 'officially' the next leading to the same death being counted twice. The ONS also announced the inclusion of 'Covid-19' deaths in the community 'to include those not even tested for the virus [irrelevant as that would be] and those suspected to have Covid-19' or that presumed to be a 'contributory factor'.

'It's Covid, stupid – *always* Covid'

The fixing of the case and death figures, which were compiled for the media worldwide by the Cult-owned, Gates-controlled, Johns Hopkins University operation in America (more later), was happening in virtually every country using the same top-down technique of ordering 'Covid-19' to be designated the cause of death almost no matter. The Cult-owned US Centers for Disease Control and Prevention (CDC) – really an agency of the Gates-controlled World Health Organisation and Big Pharma – issued 'guidance' to doctors and medical staff telling them to list 'Covid-19' as a cause of death regardless of any confirmation. No – not even the fake test. If 'Covid-19' was 'assumed to have caused or contributed to death' it could be listed as the primary cause. The authorities further underpinned this manipulation with the payments policy to hospitals (with some going to doctors) through the US Medicare system. This was exposed by Dr Scott Jensen, a Minnesota state senator, in an interview with Fox News. He said that if a hospital diagnosed someone with 'simple non-Covid pneumonia' they would be paid $4,600 by the Medicare system. If they diagnosed the patient with 'Covid-19' pneumonia they would be paid *$13,000* and if they put the 'Covid-19' diagnosed patient on a ventilator the payment leaped to *$39,000*. Could the game be any more obvious? Hospitals which in many cases were headed for bankruptcy due to a lack of patients were able to make big money (or stay in business) through Medicare payments by diagnosing patients with 'Covid-19' with no symptoms (ka-ching) and moving them out for the next one to come in or putting them briefly on a ventilator they did not need (even bigger ka-ching). They even changed their procedures to skip ahead directly to a ventilator without the usual intermediary steps, including a venturi mask, non-re-breather mask, and positive airway pressure machines. All they need to do is diagnose the non-existent 'Covid-19' to fit the Cult agenda and the tills are ringing. People should get the idea out of their mind that all medical staff are angels of mercy. Some absolutely are, but they also include liars, deceivers and psychopaths, too, and anyone who takes advantage of this clearly targeted diagnosis payment system by putting people on ventilators for no medical reason is a psychopath. Illinois Public Health Director Dr Ngozi Ezike was open about the way 'Covid-19' death figures were being compiled. She told a news conference while her superiors clenched their teeth:

> If you were in a hospice and given a few weeks to live and you were then found to have Covid that would be counted as a Covid death. [There might be] a clear alternate cause, but it is still listed as a Covid death. So everyone listed as a Covid death doesn't mean that was the cause of the death, but that they had Covid at the time of death.

Or, rather, had tested positive in a test not testing for 'Covid-19'. UK chief scientific advisor Patrick Vallance bizarrely said the same as Ezike – *Covid on the death certificate doesn't mean Covid was the cause of death*.The apparent death rate from 'Covid-19' can be seen in an entirely new light from this perspective of its mass diagnosis for those dying from other conditions. The centre of the Italian 'epidemic' in the Lombardy region is globally notorious, like Wuhan, for its filthy toxic air that produces widespread lung disease especially in old people who have been breathing in that crap all their lives. This presented phenomenal potential to re-designate people dying of pneumonia and other respiratory problems as dying of 'Covid-19' when they were not. To highlight the extreme nature of Lombardy mortality – 99,542 people died from all causes in Lombardy in 2018 while Lazio, the second region in terms of death-rates, had a figure of 57,289. Italian authorities revealed that 99 percent of those who have 'died from Covid-19' in Italy have had one, two, three or more 'other morbidities' or illnesses and health problems that could have ended their life. Are we getting it yet? Seventy percent were men and less than one percent of those said to have 'died from Covid-19' had no known other life-threatening conditions. The Italian National Health Institute revealed that the average age of the positively-'Covid'-tested deceased in Italy is about 81. Ten percent of the deceased are over 90 with 90 percent over 70 and 80 percent had two or more chronic diseases. Half had three or more. These included cardiovascular problems, diabetes, respiratory problems and cancer. Re-designate these people as 'death by Covid-19' and you instantly have your 'devastating health crisis' in Italy which locked down the country and was used to terrify the rest of the West that this could be coming their way. A list of doctors who 'died from Covid-19' were published in Italy who turned out to be of the advanced age when you would expect people to die – most retired – and with no evidence that the cause of death was the dreaded 'virus'. Once the 'Italian disaster' propaganda had been sold by the worldwide Cult-owned media we had Professor Walter Ricciardi, scientific advisor to the Italian minister of health, saying the country's apparent 'Covid' death rates were due to Italy having the second oldest population in the world and … *the manner in which hospitals record deaths*:

> The way in which we code deaths in our country is very generous in the sense that all the people who die in hospitals with the coronavirus are deemed to be dying of the coronavirus. On re-evaluation by the National Institute of Health, only 12 per cent of death certificates have shown a direct causality from coronavirus, while 88 per cent of patients who have died have at least one pre-morbidity – many had two or three.

That's how it's been done and even the twelve percent is not true when you can't die of a 'Covid-19' that doesn't exist or be diagnosed with a 'virus' you can't even test for. Two-thirds of alleged 'Covid-19' fatalities in New York have been over 70; more than 95 percent were over 50; and some 90 percent of all fatal cases had another underlying illness making the diagnosis switch so easy. Scott Atlas, former chief of neuroradiology at Stanford University, said that more than 99 percent of those who have died in New York had an underlying condition and the rate of death for all people aged between 18 and 45 was 0.01 percent. Think about it. The reason children and younger people below old age have not been dying from the fake 'virus' is because they are infinitely more likely not to have 'other morbidities' that can be blamed on 'Covid-19'. The same deceit is being perpetrated in other countries under the overall control of the Cult. The President of Germany's Robert Koch Institute said that Germany counts any deceased person who is infected with coronavirus as a Covid-19 death, whether or not it actually caused the death. German virologist Dr Hendrik Streeck said: 'In Heinsberg, for example, a 78-year-old man with previous illnesses died of heart failure, and that was without SARS-2 lung involvement. Since he was infected, he naturally appears in the Covid-19 statistics.'

Doctors and experts speak out

Stories from doctors, medical staff and families began to emerge and grow telling how patients and loved ones who died of cancer, heart disease and other fatalities were designated 'Covid-19' on the death certificate. This diagnosis fraud came by order of the authorities – Cult agents within the authorities – who demanded that every patient no matter what their ailment must be fake-tested for 'Covid-19' and if they are positive for the widespread genetic material they should have 'Covid-19' on their death certificate to bloat the figures. Hospital staff from many locations confirmed to us over weeks at Davidicke.com that this was happening worldwide. Eddie Large, a one-time famous comedian in Britain, went into hospital with heart failure amid long-standing heart problems, tested 'positive' for 'Covid-19' (the genetic material) and that was designated his cause of death. In fact, the media's wording in reports of Eddie's demise was repeated over and over to such an extent that it would not have been coincidental. They don't say this or that person died *from* 'Covid-19', but that they died *after testing positive* for 'Covid-19'. The two statements are clearly not the same and similar wording spewed from the mouths of officialdom. However, once that death has been added to the Covid-19 hoaxed figures they are morphed into *this number of people have died* from 'Covid-19' courtesy of the Johns Hopkins and other official compilations. Most doctors and medical staff have outrageously stayed silent about the deceit, but others have had a commitment to truth and their patients' welfare and called out the conspiracy to defraud the entire human race. Their numbers have grown the longer the lockdowns and their horrific effects continued.

Dr Annie Bukacek, a board certified internal medicine physician in Kalispell, Montana, and council member and a fellow of the American College of Physicians Montana chapter, was one who exposed the magic trick. She said she questioned the official story immediately after seeing previous 'we're all going to die' hypes over H1N1, Ebola, Zika, SARS and MERS come to nothing except for new vaccines tested on innocent children in Africa or the Caribbean – a speciality of Bill Gates programmes. He's a lovely man. Bukacek described how the 'Covid-19' figures were being inflated by death certificate manipulation and how other patients were suffering and dying from being denied treatment, operations and consultations by a system only interested in 'Covid-19'. Dr Scott Jensen, who exposed the Medicare incentives to diagnose for 'Covid-19', said in a TV interview that he had received a seven-page document by email from the US Department of Health 'coaching' him on how to fill out death certificates which had never happened before. He said the document told him that he didn't need to have a laboratory test for 'Covid-19' to put that on the death certificate. Jensen was shocked because death certificates are supposed to deal in facts. Another doctor had his video deleted by YouTube for exposing the death figures manipulation and how numbers for other causes of death were going down in line with the Covid-19 numbers going up through re-designation. Dr Rashid Buttar, an American osteopathic physician from

Charlotte, North Carolina, furiously railed against the manipulation and the doctors and medical staff staying quiet about what they knew was happening. He confirmed the death certificate charade and said that even death certificates previously written were being changed to include 'Covid-19'.

Two California doctors, Dan Erickson and Artin Massihi, at Accelerated Urgent Care in Bakersfield, held a news conference in late April calling for their county to 'reopen'. They explained what was really happening behind the hysterical headlines. Intensive care units in California were 'empty, essentially', with hospitals shutting floors, not treating patients and laying off doctors. The California health system was working at minimum capacity 'getting rid of doctors because we just don't have the volume'. They said that people with conditions such as heart disease and cancer were not coming to hospital out of fear of 'Covid-19'. Everything they had ever learned about quarantine involved quarantining the *sick*. They had never seen before the quarantine of the healthy 'where you take people without disease and without symptoms and lock them in their home'. Projection models of millions of deaths had been 'woefully inaccurate', they said. Dr Erickson detailed figures to show that Californians have a 0.03 chance of dying from 'Covid' based on the number of people who have tested positive. But hold on. They are (a) testing positive for a widespread genetic material and not 'Covid-19, and (b) alleged deaths have been re-diagnosis of other conditions with similar symptoms (or none) to the 'virus'. Erickson said the figures revealed there was a 0.1 percent chance of dying from 'Covid' in the *state*, not just the city, of New York, and a 0.05 percent chance in Spain, a centre of 'Covid-19' hysteria at one stage. 'Covid' [even if you believe the lies] was less dangerous than the flu. There was no justification for the lockdowns and economic devastation, the doctors said. Their figures were supported by a Stanford University study that put the fatality rate at between 0.1 to 0.2 percent. Take away the diagnosis deception from those figures and you are left with zero. Death estimates of the Cult-owned, Gates-run, World Health Organization were 20 to 30 times higher than the Stanford numbers simply to secure widespread lockdowns. Everyone involved must go to jail for crimes against humanity. Dr Erickson also pointed to a list of consequences of the lockdowns in increased child abuse, partner abuse, alcoholism, depression, suicide and other impacts they were seeing every day. Erickson described how immune systems become weaker and weaker the more people are locked away in homes amid hygiene obsession in which immune responses are not being developed by coming into contact with agents they need to experience to build defences and immunity. 'The immune system needs this interaction ... sheltering in place reduces your immune system and when you come out what do you think is going to happen? Disease is going to spike.' He said that when disease spiked in this way the hospitals were not going to cope with laid off doctors and nurses. Erickson then turned to the pressure being applied to doctors to put 'Covid-19' on the death certificate. 'Why are we being pressured to add Covid? To increase the numbers and make it look worse than it is? I think so.' He said he was hearing this from physicians everywhere. The doctors' video passed five million views in days, but never appeared on YouTube trending lists and then was deleted for 'violating YouTube's terms of service'. What a disgusting and fascistic organisation Google-owned YouTube has proved itself time after time to be and it comes from the top – Susan Wojcicki and those who own her. Wojcicki is clearly a Cult asset like Gates, Brin, Page, Zuckerberg and the rest of them and they must all now face the consequences in ongoing public exposure of their anti-freedom, indeed anti-human, agenda at every opportunity. How more blatant and low can you get than to delete doctors who are questioning medical policy on the basis of personal experience just to serve the interests of a global Cult with an horrific genocidal plan for humanity? *Well, Wojcicki?*

A hospital respiratory operative took to the Internet to expose the lies. He said there was no ventilator shortage as the hysteria-hype claimed and they were running fewer ventilators than they normally would. Any patient that came to his hospital with a respiratory problem was labelled 'Covid-19' and he said it didn't matter if they were suffering from late stage lung cancer, heart disease or anything else. 'You come in with breathing problems and you are labelled a Covid patient' … 'then they would die of Covid and not stage four lung cancer.' He said they had only one person qualified to administer the test and so most patients 'under investigation for Covid' were never tested (which would have been irrelevant anyway). '… Every patient [who] is under Covid investigation and dies … [becomes] a Covid death and they are showing the numbers like a football game to scare you.' He said the public was being shown bodies loaded on to a tractor trailer simply to scare people and he had never in his entire career seen bodies loaded on anything like that. He said 'it just doesn't happen' and he wondered if they were even bodies – 'all of this stuff is fake'. Behind him in the video made in his hospital were machines that helped patients breathe with a mask rather than putting them on a full-blown ventilator. He said that since the 'Covid-19' scare began they had been banned from using those machines and people had to be allowed to 'crash' and go straight to a ventilator. 'That is not the traditional way we use to treat a patient – everything that we would traditionally do we are not allowed to do.'

New York intensive care doctor Cameron Kyle-Sidell said in his own video that people were being put on ventilators when their lungs were not strong enough and they were dying. Another whistleblower video communicating the experience of a New York intensive care nurse said the same. 'People are being murdered and no-one cares' was one line from the video and with no family allowed at the hospitals the patients were at the mercy of staff and left to rot. A second New York nurse took to the Internet in tears to describe exactly the same situation: 'I am literally coming here every day and watching them kill them.' She listed a catalogue of examples of how patients were either just allowed to die or directly killed by the wrong treatment or no treatment through 'gross negligence and medical mismanagement ... nobody has listened to anyone's lungs the whole time I've been here.' 'Covid-19' obviously went on the death certificate. She said she tried talking to management and nursing administration, but they didn't want to know and moved her away from patients and departments that she was complaining about. It's murder, no other word for it, to kill people knowing you are killing them, but good for the 'Covid-19' figures. The nurse said: 'It's like going to the fucking Twilight Zone – everyone here is okay with this.' She rightly asked: 'Am I the only one who is not a sociopath?' The respiratory medic confirmed that they were 'not testing for a virus' – 'there's not one test that tests for a virus'. They were testing for a genetic 'RNA sequence' and anyone with even microscopic content from that sequence would test positive when it could come from lung cancer and many other things. 'If this is as infectious as they are telling us ... everybody would be dying and that's not what we're seeing – this is unbelievable, every bit of this has been created.' He said they were not seeing lots of health workers getting sick even though they were in close contact with people who had tested positive. He was not convinced there even was a virus and 'I've been doing this a long time'. Doctors were believing the lies as much as the public, but doctors were not looking at the real information. 'They're told something and ... they got lives, they got jobs ... they're not going to look up what this test is and why they weren't getting the infection rates – they just look up the things they're told to look up like anyone else.' He then said something centrally relevant to what has happened:

For the Trump supporters out there I want to ask you something. Think about this for a minute. We're doing the same thing they're doing in France ... Italy ... the UK. So does that mean Trump's in charge of this whole thing because I really don't think he is. I think he's being told to do what he's doing ... this is Deep State, Illuminati stuff ... they are shutting the world down.

Exactly. This video by someone specialising in respiratory care and revealing how his direct experience in a hospital was at odds with the official narrative and so was deleted a number of times by YouTube for breaching their 'community guidelines'. What more can be said about this Cult censorship operation fronted by Susan Wojcicki? Her contempt for freedom and the most basic human rights is unimaginable. John Lee, a recently retired professor of pathology and a former consultant pathologist with the UK National Health Service (NHS), highlighted in an article for *The Spectator* exactly the point I have made about the careful wording of media and medical reports. They were saying that people had died 'after testing positive *for* coronavirus' and not that they had died *from* coronavirus:

> Many UK health spokespersons have been careful to repeatedly say that the numbers quoted in the UK indicate death *with the virus*, not death *due to the virus* – this matters [My emphasis]. When giving evidence in parliament a few days ago, Prof. Neil Ferguson of Imperial College London said that he now expects fewer than 20,000 Covid-19 deaths in the UK but, importantly, two-thirds of these people would have died anyway. In other words, he suggests that the crude figure for 'Covid deaths' is three times higher than the number who have actually been killed by Covid-19. (Even the two-thirds figure is an estimate – it would not surprise me if the real proportion is higher.)
> …
> … Unfortunately nuance tends to be lost in the numbers quoted from the database being used to track Covid-19: the Johns Hopkins Coronavirus Resource Center. It has compiled a huge database, with Covid-19 data from all over the world, updated daily – and its figures are used, world over, to track the virus. This data is not standardised and so probably not comparable, yet this important caveat is seldom expressed by the (many) graphs we see. It risks exaggerating the quality of data that we have.

Yes – on purpose. Professor Lee added that 'Covid19' was not a disease with unique or rare symptoms and the range of severity matched dozens of extremely common respiratory infections. He said that you cannot diagnose 'fever' and 'cough' and then diagnose 'probable Covid-19' with the slightest chance of accuracy. As the Off-guardian.org website said:

> Italy, Germany, the United States, Northern Ireland and England. That's five different governments, across four countries, all essentially saying it's OK to just assume a patient died of Covid19, and then add that to the official statistics. Is that really responsible practice during a potential pandemic? Are any other countries doing the same? To what extent can we trust any official death statistics at all, at this point?

Try zero. Off-guardian, which has done great work exposing the figures, highlighted another outrageous manipulation in which the UK government's 'daily death toll' numbers were not from a single day at all. The 'daily' figures include alleged deaths from other days going back *six weeks* or more. The website gave the example of April 10th which was described as the UK's 'deadliest Covid19 day'. Media headlines included: 'UK death toll jumps 980 in 24 hours in biggest rise yet'; 'Britain records Europe's highest single-day death toll: Number of victims jumps by 980'; and '980 tops Spain and Italy's highest daily number of deaths'. In fact, the deaths attributed (wrongly) to Covid-19 on that single day were 117 for England and another 90 for other UK countries bringing the total to 204 and *not* 980. Off-guardian reported that the other 776 people included in the report had died 'at seemingly random points *between March 5th and April 8th'*. The website said the same was true with all 'daily' death figures. It is also clear that the numbers have been boosted by yet another ruse – counting the same deaths more than once. The mass of the media never acknowledged these facts and instead daily fuelled the hysteria that led people to support the lockdowns through false perceptions of what was really happening. The media claimed on March 24th that an 18-year-old in Coventry, England, was the youngest person to die from the 'virus' and continued to say so even after the hospital said this was not true. The youngster had died from a 'significant' health problem not connected to 'Covid-19'. It didn't matter – don't let the facts spoil a good hoax. Other young people said to have died from the 'virus' turned out to have died from other causes. The death and case figures have been a complete stitch-up and you only fix the figures to deceive. When Neil Ferguson's ridiculous 'computer model' figures turned out to be fantastic overestimates he and the authorities claimed that this was because of the lockdowns and house arrest that the fantastic figures 'justified'. It was the very scenario that had been predicted they would go for by the US medical scientist I quoted earlier. Data as of April 6th in Figure 383 showed the China lockdown blueprint was not as black

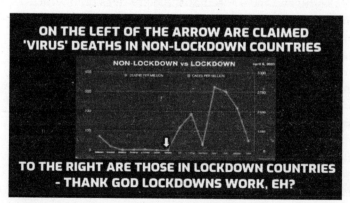

Figure 383: A graph from April 6th, 2020, which showed that lockdown was not the only possible response. Cases counted from a test not testing for 'Covid-19' and deaths monumentally manipulated by fixing death certificates was the real decider of how many were claimed to be 'infected' or 'killed' according to the official figures – not lockdown or otherwise.

and white as claimed and with cases and death figures dependent on a fake test and fake cause of death what difference would lockdown or no-lockdown have made to numbers anyway?

Killing old people

The death figures from all causes in Britain and Europe remained about the same as the previous year for many weeks of the alleged global 'crisis' and as more people were recorded to have died from 'Covid-19' so miraculously death from other causes went down. There was always coming a time, however, when death figures would increase in 2020 because of all those who were sure to die from the consequences of lockdowns and cancellation of operations and consultations for almost all other illnesses and conditions. People were sitting at home in pain and in need of urgent diagnosis and treatment for a range of life-threatening problems, but they could not get to see a doctor while being discouraged to go to hospital accident and emergency because they were 'war-zones' over 'Covid-19'. The truth was that the hospitals that could have treated them were near empty with hundreds of beds at major ones not being used and operating theatres like the Mary Celeste. The biggest victims of this psychopathic policy – as the Cult intended – were old people. The lockdowns to a large extent were justified by 'protecting old people and the vulnerable' and to 'protect the hospitals from being overrun' (see empty). Yet at the same time old people were being systematically killed in line with the Cult agenda I outlined earlier and in the words of one nursing home nurse they were being 'murdered' through denial of treatment. Almost every one of them that died because of this would have had 'Covid-19' on the death certificate. Old people were told to stay at home and have essential supplies delivered which would have led to a range of other potentially fatal conditions and the Cult knew that. How many were literally left alone with their partners already diseased and families living far away? The overwhelming majority of those said to have died from 'Covid-19' were old people merely because they are most likely to be ill and so most available to re-designate 'Covid-19' instead of what they really died from. One UK nursing home nurse who contacted Davidicke.com said:

> I'm seeing first-hand now what's going on at the nursing homes including mine. It's murder, mate. I am not saying it lightly. I'm willing once this is done to go on record with the bastards. If there is any information I can give you I will help.

> Well, I've seen first-hand now the community matrons and doctors following orders basically just denying treatments to residents on the account they have Covid. No test, no nothing. Doctors are now not coming into my home to

examine anyone. I've had absolute murder with people begging to be placed on antibiotics.

In a few weeks you gonna see fucking dead old people all over the place. I'm done me, mate, to be honest, once this is over. This is not what I became a nurse for.

The media would naturally spin this phenomenon another way. Alex Thomson, 'Chief Correspondent' at Britain's Channel 4 News, posted an article headed: 'Coronavirus causing "devastation" in care homes as pressure grows to release full death numbers.' He said that 'one in five of all deaths in England and Wales in the week ending April 3rd are linked to coronavirus – with the overall death rate pushed to a record high'. Why do you think that is you excuse for a 'journalist'? Old people were being designated positive for 'Covid-19' and when they died of other causes, not least from the effect of the lockdowns and denial of treatments, they were added to the death figures for 'Covid-19'. Any idiot with an hour's research could have worked out what was really happening, but not, it seems, Thomson and his fellow mainstream media. The problem was made worse by UK government-directed NHS hospitals 'clearing out' patients to free up 15,000 beds in a week with many moved to a 'suitable rehabilitation bed or care home'. The Gates-owned World Health Organization stated in late-April, 2020, that half the 'coronavirus-related deaths' in Europe could be in long-term care homes. It might have added: 'So the plan is working.' Shortly after the WHO statement HC One, the UK's biggest care home provider, was reporting a rise in deaths among old people at its centres that have nothing to do with coronavirus as hospitals failed to take in residents as patients. Israeli doctor Gai Peleg working in Parma, Italy, said that from what he saw and heard the instructions were not to offer access to respirator machines for patients over 60 in a who-lives-and-dies-decision. This became another common theme. These were the same old people that were being used as an excuse to lockdown the world to 'protect them'.

They want rid of old people so the young, programmed through the new and extreme 'education' system all their lives, will be left at the perceptual mercy of the Cult. One legacy will be some young people turning on the old as the ones to blame for the economic disaster triggered by the reaction to the 'crisis'. 'This would not have happened if we didn't have to protect old people – you know the ones responsible for climate change and Brexit.' Some schoolchildren and others dubbed the virus the 'boomer remover' referring to the 'baby boomer' generation born approximately between 1946 and 1964 which includes me. Don't worry, though, I have somehow fought off the impulse to be offended. How ironic that the baby boomers were the 'flower power', 'counter-culture', 'anti-establishment' generation now perceived by many young people as the old and 'past-it' Earth-destroying establishment that must be usurped. Messages by some medical staff and emails from loved ones to Davidicke.com revealed a widespread theme along with social media posts of old people being pressured to sign do not resuscitate (DNR) agreements so they could be allowed to die (and 'Covid-19' falsely put on the death certificate). The daughter of an 83-year-old mother said she could 'categorically confirm that DNR notices are being placed on elderly patients, including those who are healthy and for whom there is no existing health condition to justify it'. She said this was happening to everyone including people with no 'virus' or underlying health conditions that threatened their life: 'This is being done on age alone.' She described how a ward consultant tried to coerce her mother into signing a DNR form when she was only in hospital for an *orthopaedic* problem:

> A few days later, earlier this week, the ward matron told her that she had not been singled out, and that everybody was being treated in the same way – all the elderly patients were being required to sign these forms. And that it is a 'rule', something that has come down from on high, that has to be done, and has to cover all the older patients, 'because the government says so'.

The elderly were ordered to 'self-isolate' – cut themselves off from society – for months for their own protection by a global state in all its expressions that clearly doesn't give a *shit* about them and wants them dead. These are the same authorities that ensure that great swathes of the elderly live out their lives in poverty choosing between warmth and food as they exist on a pathetic, derisory state pension (where there is one) after paying taxes all their long years. The effect of this is to devastate their immune systems through lack of nutrients they cannot afford (or mainstream information that they need them) while consuming the cheapest, toxin-ridden excuse for 'food' together with toxic water and other drinks, breathing toxic air and living in a toxic irradiated atmosphere. All of these things, together with immune system-demolishing vaccines and a deluge of immune system-weakening sugar, have been allowed or instigated by the very authorities that tell us how much they care about our health and survival when a disease strikes. The starting point to see through the 'state cares' illusion is to realise that they don't give a damn about you. From this all other understanding will come. With the most head-shaking predictability the UK Department of Health began adding deaths in care homes to the 'Covid-19' fatality figures by fraudulently designating cause of death from a long list of other conditions as 'Covid-

19'. Fascism is nothing if not predicable.

Intelligent doctors and specialists agree: You've been had people

A stream of medical professionals ignored by the mainstream media spoke out through alternative sources about the blatant manipulation they could see of the figures for cases and deaths and the claim that 'Covid-19' was some kind of new and deadly virus. Professor Dr Sucharit Bhakdi, a highly-acclaimed infectious medicine specialist in Germany, said of virus lockdowns: 'They are grotesque, absurd and very dangerous … All these measures are leading to self-destruction and collective suicide because of nothing but a spook.' The theme that 'Covid-19' was indeed a 'spook' was common outside the mainstream media. Doctors and specialists said there was not a medical crisis, but a political one and this included doctors in Italy as you can see in the German journalist's video that I mentioned earlier. One Italian doctor said: 'No one in Italy died of corona – it's an ugly influenza.' German doctor Wolfgang Wodarg said that without the new 'test' no one would notice anything different. 'If you change the definition of pandemic you can create it', he said, 'If you talk about a virus spreading around the world you have a permanent pandemic.' Dr Claus Kohnlein, another German physician, agreed. He said that without the new test there would be no 'pandemic': 'I don't believe it's a new virus. It's just a new test.' Hamburg doctor Marc Fiddike said you can turn any pneumonia into a corona case and 'you could turn a man falling down the stairs into a virus victim'. Confirming the view of other doctors he said: 'It's a kind of magic.' He made the same point as the American scientist I quoted in that just because someone is sick and tests for coronavirus [there are many in that 'family' of viruses] doesn't mean the virus is responsible for their sickness. John Ioannidis, a Professor of Medicine, Health Research and Policy and Biomedical Data Science, at Stanford University School of Medicine, described the coronavirus scare as possibly 'a one-in a century evidence fiasco' in response to the insane claim that the 'virus' was a once in a century pandemic. He said the data was not there to support the numbers of deaths and cases that were being circulated. Dr Yoram Lass, an Israeli physician and former member of the Knesset for the Israel Labor Party, pointed out that according to World Health Organization figures between 250,000 and 500,000 people died every year worldwide from seasonal flu, but this didn't cause a meltdown of the global economy due to government reaction: 'It is absolutely insane to have this Biblical crisis.' He said this was the first 'Zuckerberg epidemic' in which social media could transmit fear all over the world at the same time.

Jaroslav Belsky, an Austrian doctor and dentist who studied for two years in a molecular biology laboratory, said that between 1,600 and

2,000 people died every day in Italy before the corona scare and this could rise to 3,000 in autumn and spring. The authorities had simply used a 'technical trick' to blame corona 'in order to close the economy and ban people from moving'. He also pointed to the fact that 99 percent of people said to have 'died from coronavirus' in Italy had other health problems with half the fatalities having three or four. What's more it was well known that at the end of their lives in hospital people did tend to die of an infection. Belsky said the real cause was never investigated when in fact people with influenza would test for all kinds of virus, even bacteria. 'Only after discovering the viral load can I assume that is what sickened them.' This is not being done with the 'Covid-19' hysteria – the 'test' doesn't measure viral load – and so the data does not exist to justify extreme government action. 'If you demand the data you are stamped a conspiracist,' Belsky said. He also pointed out that staging fake epidemics was not new with avian or 'bird' flu projected to cost 30,000 lives per year and ending up being officially responsible for very few. He said he had heard from Italy that they were 'testing dead people and even cancer and accident victims'. Belsky described how friends in the medical profession had sent him pictures of normal conditions in their critical care units. He also made an important point about why Germany's death-rate ratio was so small compared with Italy. Belsky said this was because the Italian testing company was only focusing on seriously ill people while in Germany tests were done even on people with a minor cold. 'It's playing with numbers and emotions.' You see how easy it is to manipulate perception by manipulating figures. Doctors and specialists also pointed out the effect of fear in making people ill in a world in terror about 'the virus'. How many developed psychosomatic 'symptoms' as the 'virus' symptoms were pounded out in all directions by the Cult-owned media? Belsky put the hysteria into perspective when he said 'there are up to 20,000 deaths in Germany from hospital bugs every year – even more in Italy'. None of these doctors and scientists appeared in the mainstream media which instead gave all the air-time to establishment mouthpieces like Neil deGrasse Tyson in the United States who told the 'satirical' (mainstream establishment) TV host Stephen Colbert: 'I think we're in the middle of a massive experiment worldwide – the experiment is: Will people listen to scientists?' Not if you're one of them, mate.

Systematically weakening natural defence

Dr Shiva Ayyadurai, an Indian-born American scientist and biological engineer at the Massachusetts Institute of Technology (MIT), spoke out against the coronavirus narrative and what he called the 'overreaction'. There was an 'overreaction'? Oh, just a little bit. Ayyadurai's main thrust was right on the button. Cause of death is not 'from a virus' but dismantled immune systems. Anyone with an immune system in some kind of order had only 'very mild flu-like symptoms' or even none at all. The alleged symptoms of 'Covid-19' (with a long list of potential causes) are manifestations in part of the immune system at work. Fever is the immune system using heat to kill a predator while coughing up mucus is the immune system ejecting toxins the body needs to get rid of. Vomiting in other circumstances is also the immune system removing threats to health before serious damage can be done. Medical website webmd.com said: '… higher body temperatures make it harder for bacteria and viruses to thrive in the body.' Many symptoms which Big Pharma medicine 'treats' are the immune system doing its job and to suppress those actions is to potentially do great damage to health. The key to who dies from what is the state of the immune system and those with the weakest are older people and those with other medical conditions already putting pressure on immune system resources. This doesn't have to be the case if immune systems are supported in their nutrient needs with vitamins like A, D3 and C. Some New York and other hospitals eventually began to treat 'virus' patients with 'massive doses' of vitamin C while at the same time social media platforms like Facebook and their system-serving 'fact-checkers' were dubbing posts about the benefits of vitamin C as 'fake news' and 'false information'. Dr Ayyadurai also recommended such key vitamins to enhance immune response. Where have you seen the Mainstream Everything talk about boosting the immune system? Why would Big Pharma and the Cult want strong immune systems when the agenda of both demands sick and weak people? Dismantling immune systems is necessary to keep Big Pharma's mega-profits rolling for a start with strong immune systems meaning less illness. Dr Ayyadurai pointed out that we have fantastic numbers of 'viruses' in our bodies and we are not even aware of them because the immune system keeps them in check. 'Viruses don't kill or harm us', he said. If viruses did kill us then we would all clearly be long dead. He said the danger is more the immune system response to threats. Different levels of the immune system kicked in to play different roles when a threat is identified and in the overwhelming number of cases any danger was quickly snuffed out. The problem comes when the immediate immune reaction is too weak to deal with the threat and in effect the system panics and unleashes what is called a 'cytokine storm'. Cytokines are defined as 'a small protein released by cells that has a specific effect on the interactions between cells, on communications between cells or on the behavior of cells … [They] trigger inflammation and respond to infections'. This response is the key. If other levels of a weakened immune system don't deal with a threat it unleashes in its desperation a 'storm' of cytokines which can be symbolised as a crazed person firing a machine gun in all directions. You can symbolise this as an intruder breaking into a house and the homeowner struggling to resist and throw them out. In the panic to survive the homeowner grabs a gun and instead of just firing at the intruder he also turns the gun on himself. The cytokine storm attacks its own body, often fatally. Sciencedaily.com puts it this way:

> A cytokine storm is an overproduction of immune cells and their activating compounds (cytokines), which, in a flu infection, is often associated with a surge of activated immune cells into the lungs. The resulting lung inflammation and fluid build-up can lead to respiratory distress and can be contaminated by a secondary bacterial pneumonia – often enhancing the mortality in patients.

Death by 'respiratory distress' is a cytokine storm immune response that attacks the lungs and can open the way to pneumonia. If your immune system is properly operational this does not happen. Why isn't the Mainstream Everything telling you this? For the same reason that Ayyadurai called for the arrest of three-quarters of the academics in the United States 'who are pilfering money from our tax-dollars ... by doing bogus research and research based on political leanings'.

What about 5G?

It never ceases to amaze me that billions of people believe that even though we now live in a technologically-generated electromagnetic 'soup' or sea, which is 200 million times the radio frequency energy naturally produced by the Earth, that somehow this will not have any, let alone profound, effects on human beings, animals, insects and the rest of the natural world. I find that to be a form of insanity and certainly a most extreme example of denial. There is an obvious relevance of some kind between current events and the roll-out in 2019 and 2020 of 5G around the world because this was made clear by the actions of Cult Internet platforms and government agencies in banning mention and debate about that connection. I have already pointed out that the common theme between the systematic deletion by Cult-owned Silicon Valley of my London Real interview and one a few days later between Dr Andrew Kaufman and my son, Jaymie, was questioning the existence of 'Covid-19' and not 5G which the Kaufman interview did not mention. However, there is clearly a connection of some kind confirmed by the extremes of enforced censorship. The UK government Office of Communications, or Ofcom, is the 'regulator' (censor) of the broadcast media and threatened any broadcaster with severe sanctions if they even engaged in discussion about a link between 5G and the 'virus'. Ofcom is so obsessed with 5G censorship that a small community radio station was threatened by the broadcasting Stasi for having a single person on a single programme discussing a connection between 5G and 'Covid-19'. Ofcom was created by war criminal Tony Blair so you can appreciate how bad it must be. Somehow these ridiculous people manage to equate 'false health advice' with 'baseless conspiracy theories that the pandemic is linked to the rollout of 5G phone networks'. The all-knowing system-worshipping Ofcom knew they were baseless because they were 'not aware of any reputable scientific evidence to corroborate such a contentious claim which runs contrary to all official advice, both in the UK and internationally, about coronavirus' (in other words the 5G claim was at odds with official propaganda). Ofcom's censors and designated media protectors of the Cult narrative said they were 'actively monitoring television and radio stations that might be broadcasting potentially harmful views about the causes and origins of Covid-19 that have the potential to undermine people's trust in the advice of mainstream sources of information during the crisis' – (which have the potential to demolish the official Cult narrative). This is exactly what you would expect to hear in a fascist/communist dictatorship.

For the record and reference the chief executive of Ofcom in this period of fascistic censorship has been Melanie Dawes, a career government bureaucrat formerly with the Ministry of Housing, Communities and Local Government, the Treasury, HM Revenue and Customs, and the Cabinet Office. The establishment runs through her bloodstream. Ofcom is chaired by Terence Burns, a British economist, who was former Chief Economic Advisor and Permanent Secretary to the UK Treasury and now a senior advisor to the bank Santander UK. These are the people overseeing the censorship of the British media and blocking any discussion of a connection between 'Covid-19' and 5G while the UK Health Secretary Matt Hancock, a clueless but willing prisoner of his civil servants and advisors, called for social media to ban '5G virus conspiracy theories'. The man is so bewildered and self-deceiving that he will say he believes in 'democracy and freedom'. YouTube, Vimeo and Facebook all deleted the video interview that I did with Brian Rose at London Real in which I mentioned the possible involvement of 5G. I did not say that it caused the 'virus' only that 5G had major negative effects on human health and psychology which had to be taken in account and that 5G can generate the symptoms that are being called 'Covid-19'. Ofcom, is major promotor and facilitator of the 5G roll-out and "regulates' the UK telecommunications industry (do what you like). This is a shocking conflict of interest when the promoter and facilitator of 5G and the censor of debate over 5G are the *same people*. They were of course on my case immediately with the pathetic mainstream media cheering in support. So there *is* a connection to 5G as confirmed by the vehement censorship of even discussion by Ofcom and Silicon Valley. The question is what? And is the censorship over what is happening now or what is to come? I will summarise here some of the possibilities and impacts.

Arthur Firstenberg, scientist, journalist, and author of *The Invisible Rainbow: A History of Electricity and Life*, said in 2018 before 'Covid-19' or 5G: 'Every time we have dramatically changed the properties of the Earth's magnetic field, which is called the magnetosphere, it had dramatic effects on health down here on Earth.' Firstenberg writes that every 'influenza' epidemic since electricity was introduced has coincided with a new and more powerful level of electromagnetic radiation. He says that one example was 'Spanish flu' (which started in the United States) and is said to have infected an estimated 500 million people worldwide in 1918 with tens of millions killed. Some estimates were as high as 100 million. These are officially compiled figures and so must not be taken as accurate, but it's safe to say a lot of people were affected and killed. By *what* is quite another question. I have pointed already to a mass-vaccine relationship to the outbreak. Here we have another possible electromagnetic field angle happening at the same time along with, it should also be added, the appalling living conditions in the wake of the First World War when immune systems would have been on their knees. Firstenberg explains that 'Spanish flu' began at military naval bases in America and Europe which were the first to install high-intensity radar with an initial 400 cases at the Naval Radio School of Cambridge, Massachusetts. Even though dubbed 'flu' a common symptom was nosebleeds (also reported with 5G) and a third of those who died did so through internal bleeding in the brain and lungs. These effects and others related to impaired blood coagulation were not at all symptoms of 'flu', but rather a potential effect of electromagnetic fields. Doctors were quoted as saying: 'We have yet to receive a report of a case in which the time of coagulation was not prolonged.' Remember the effect on the blood that was found in the teacher after a day in a classroom bathed in Wi-Fi. Another blatant red flag was that as radar was introduced worldwide 'Spanish' flu outbreaks followed in the same locations without contact with other sufferers at a time when there was minimal world travel compared with recent times.

Firstenberg says that by 1956/57, with the entire earth now subjected to new and powerful radar waves never before experienced, we had the outbreak of 'Asian flu' which is said to have started in East Asia and spread worldwide. Months after the first radiation-emitting satellite system became operational 'Hong Kong' flu swept across the world in 1968. Once again people were dying from internal haemorrhage. In the same way 5G began to be rolled out before the 'Covid-19' scare began and 5G has been rapidly expanded during the lockdowns in city after city and town after town in country after country. When large numbers of children and students return to school, college and university they will find that 5G has been installed while they were away – as will those visiting *hospitals*. Most businesses and employment activity was banned and yet installing 5G towers and satellites was considered 'essential work'. This has both dramatically increased the reach and impact of 5G and prevented protests that would otherwise have happened. 'Flu-like' symptoms are known to be caused by exposure to intense electrical fields (EMF) – a fact that came to light as early as 1779 – and EMF is one of the triggers for cells to release exosomes, the natural immune response dubbed 'Covid-19'. This 'new disease' is said to have begun in Wuhan, capital of Hubei province, which was China's first 5G 'smart city' with tremendous numbers of 5G antennae installed in October, 2019, and expanded with great rapidity. Vodafone Italy made Milan in the 'virus' centre of Lombardy an 'extensive 5G testbed' working with country's Ministry of Economic Development. There were also big vaccine programmes in Wuhan and Lombardy before the 'pandemic' kicked off.

Spanish biologist Bartomeu Payeras i Cifre, who has specialised in microbiology at the University of Barcelona and researched smallpox bacteria and viruses at the Hubber pharmaceutical laboratories, produced a preliminary study in April, 2020, of the connection between the main locations of 'Covid-19' and 5G activity. You can see it at Davidicke.com with the search words: 'Study Shows Direct Correlation between 5G Networks and "Coronavirus" Outbreaks'. The study did not attempt to show a cause and effect between 5G and the alleged 'Covid-19' only that the major countries and regions where the 'virus' was reported to be most prevalent corresponded with 5G locations. The conclusion was that the results 'demonstrate a clear and close relationship between the rate of coronavirus infections and 5G antenna location'. Another study focusing on American states by Dr Magda Havas, Associate Professor of Environmental and Resource Studies at Trent University in Ontario, Canada, reached similar conclusions. Border divisions in the Spanish study were said to be significant in the difference between countries with and without 5G that have a common border. The study notes the distinct case differences between the United States and Mexico and Spain and Portugal and particularly highlights the case of San Marino, the tiny republic within the land mass of Italy. San Marino became the first European country with a 5G network after being chosen as 'an outdoor laboratory used to test the performance of network equipment and applications' in the words of one media report. Is it just a fluke of chance that San Marino would become one of the top five countries in terms of population ratio for 'Covid-19' cases? The Spanish study author said that 'a failure to act in the face of the findings of this study could be considered negligent at the very least and very possibly criminal'. Given that 5G and the 'pandemic' have been orchestrated by criminals no action will surely follow.

The widespread manipulation of death figures confirm that 5G cannot be blamed for the whole 'virus' phenomenon or there would be no need to fix the numbers on such a fundamental scale; but it is connected to the story with the most profound effects still to come. 5G and less powerful electrometric fields can seriously increase the power and consequences of toxins in the body as well as profoundly undermining the *immune system* – just like vaccines. Cells poisoned by 5G and other electromagnetic fields that then release exosomes (fake 'Covid-19') must also be taken into account and the ability of 5G to generate symptoms like those blamed on 'Covid-19'. I have described in other books how electromagnetic fields can vastly increase the potency of toxins in the body to beyond what the immune system can cope with and especially when that system itself is being weakened by the same source. I said earlier that Wi-Fi and 5G networks are a delivery system for frequencies, but the nature of those frequencies can be altered. It is quite possible to zap one area with frequencies that devastate the immune system and poison cells with radiation which then excrete the exosome response that has been dubbed 'Covid-19'. One other point is that 5G causes 'accelerated degradation of genetic material' which is what the fake 'virus test' identifies. With a satellite system in place already capable of targeting 5G at different locations it becomes possible to affect some areas more than others without even 5G antennas on the ground. 5G operates with narrow easily-targeted beams. Martin Pall, a former Professor Emeritus of Biochemistry and Basic Medical Sciences at Washington State University, described the effect of technological radiation and 5G on calcium channels in the cells known as the voltage-gated calcium channel (VGCC). These calcium channels regulate the entry into cells of calcium ions and an imbalance can affect many body systems including heart, brain and muscle contraction. Pall said that the predominant cause of death from 'Covid-19' was pneumonia which can be 'greatly exacerbated by each of those five downstream effects of VGCC activation, excessive intracellular calcium, oxidative stress … inflammation and apoptosis [a form of cell death]'. UK microwave expert Barrie Trower says he trained at the Government's Microwave Warfare Establishment in the 1960's, worked for the Royal Navy and British Secret Service as an expert in microwave weapons, helped de-brief spies trained in microwave warfare in the 1970s, and worked in the underwater bomb disposal unit which used microwaves. His degree in physics specialised in microwaves. He said before the 'pandemic':

> All microwaves of all 'G's … they all reduce immune systems of all living
> things except for three things. One of those is bacteria and viruses. They thrive
> and multiply when they are microwaved. So you have a situation … where all

living things are losing their immune systems but the bacterium and viruses are strengthening theirs, and 5G will only exacerbate the situation.

These are some of the effects of electromagnetic fields and the super-impact of 5G needs to be added to the mix of possibilities.

5G and oxygen

A crucial point is that at the 60 gigahertz frequency 5G interacts with oxygen molecules as the telecommunications industry freely admits. This where a connection is possible between 5G and a few extreme cases of lung malfunction wrongly attributed to 'Covis-19' and its relevance could become more profound ongoing. The industry is keen to transmit at 60 GHz because the way 5G interacts with oxygen allows 'very dense deployment' of the same frequency in the same very localised area without interference between users. It also allows for a beam of 5G at the 60 GHz frequency to target a small area or even an individual. Hold that thought with regard to what will follow. 5G interacts with oxygen molecules at 60 GHz in a way that prevents the body and blood absorbing oxygen in the volume that it should. This can lead to *respiratory problems*, strokes, heart attacks and many other potentially fatal conditions. Here is an explanation of the potential consequences described by those challenging 5G:

… Two atoms form the oxygen molecule and share some electrons. 60 GHz causes electrons surrounding oxygen molecules to spin, akin to how high-powered microwaves running on 2.4 impact molecules in food such as water. They're heating, in part, by impacting those molecules to rotate or oscillate with each wave. The movement energy from the rotation of these super tiny water molecules helps heat the rest of the food.

In a similar way that 2.4 causes H20 to oscillate, 5G/60 GHz even at low power causes electrons on oxygen molecules to spin; changes to the spin frequencies on oxygen electrons impact human biology. When you breathe air into your lungs it gets oxygen into your blood, brain, tissues etc. and oxygen entering your lungs gets picked up by a very important iron containing protein called haemoglobin in your blood.

The impact of oxygen molecules spinning the electrons is that it makes the haemoglobin unable to uptake the oxygen and get it to the rest of your body. Isn't the fact that the telecom companies are admitting that 60 GHz is absorbed by oxygen just stunning information, and shouldn't the fact that 60 GHz even fundamentally interacts with oxygen, the most abundant and arguably most important element to all of biological life, be headline news that stops everything until we deeply test the implications of that?

The potential of this for a mass human cull is obvious. American environmental science researcher, Lena Pu, has studied the effects of 5G technology since it was publicly revealed in 2016 by the Cult-controlled Federal Communications Commission (FCC) which announced its deployment for a few years later. Pu has been environmental health consultant for the National Association for Children and Safe Technologies and has worked with military and government agencies. She points out that the entire electromagnetic microwave frequency or 'EMF' range triggers hundreds of biological effects. She says they are limitless because the waves of varying lengths impact on all parts of the body. Each new generation or 'G' increased that effect leading to the arrival of 5G which operates within the millimetre wave (MMW) range that includes 60 GHz, the resonant frequency for oxygen, and is 'fully absorbed by the oxygen molecule'. Pu said that even at what is considered low power within FCC (fake) safety standards the 60 GHz frequency is going to affect the molecular structure of oxygen and stop it binding properly with the blood's iron-containing protein, haemoglobin. She said that these issues include: (1) Shared electrons between the two oxygen atoms will spin at a rate that is not conducive to human uptake; (2) the orbit angle and distance of the electrons from the atomic nucleus is altered; (3) the possibility that some or all of the molecule itself is changed from O2 (oxygen) to form O3 (ozone). Dr Andrew Kaufman said he read a CIA document from 1977 which described how the frequency of 60 GHz suppressed bone marrow in mice. White blood cells produced in bone marrow are the foundation of the immune system. The document also said that oxygen take-up by mitochondria – the 'powerhouse of the cell' – was adversely affected by 60 GHz frequencies which can lead to devastating organ failure. The consequences can be appreciated from this explanation by the UK Medical Research Council Mitochondrial Biology Unit:

> Mitochondria are organelles found in the cells of every complex organism. They produce about 90% of the chemical energy that cells need to survive. No energy; no life! So it's easy to see why when mitochondria go wrong, serious diseases are the result, and why it is important we understand how mitochondria work.

That must surely include how 5G at 60 GHz affects mitochondria.

A case study

While researching 5G and 60 GHz Lena Pu said she came across 'a clandestine event' between 2016 and 2017 at a Texas junior high school. After a few months of research into what was happening, which included reading declassified reports, she realised that 5G exposures are 'very bad news': 'I discovered that [5G] is 25-100 times more biologically active than the frequencies that are currently being used in everything from cell phones to cell towers.' Other 'Gs' were bad, but 5G was much worse. This background allowed her to quickly realise what was going on at the school where students and teaching staff had fallen ill with a 'mystery illness'. It was obvious this was related to inside the school because they all felt better once they left the building and teachers began to hold classes outside. Pu made contact with a mother extremely alarmed at the behaviour of school administrators and established that the school was part of a pre-roll-out 'pilot' scheme for 5G. This was in 2017. She had found the 'smoking gun' to explain the mass illness. Her instincts were that Wi-Fi systems at the school must have been upgraded to include a new chip to add to the two in use up to this point communicating at 2.45 GHz and between 5 and 5.8 GHz. She went to the school's Facebook page to look through pictures taken inside the building and saw a strange Wi-Fi router that she believed would be necessary for the delivery of 5G:

I looked through the school's Facebook page for router images to give a clue as to the shape, style or make of the Wi-Fi routers, also known as wireless access points, and I found one that resembled a certain style … with a larger grill pattern for heat dissipation. [5G] generates a lot more heat just by the nature of the frequency and power levels.

Fortunately she took a screenshot because the following day all the images were deleted from the School Facebook page. Next she tracked down the new third chip at the Samsung annual expo – a 60 GHz chip called 'WiGig'. She said this was her second smoking gun and she found to her horror as she researched the chip the impact on the oxygen molecule. 'I instantly knew what I was looking at and the implications … the moment I saw the government charts laying out the peak absorptive levels of oxygen and which frequency attenuates [weakens, diminishes] it – I have never discovered anything more shocking.' 5G at 60 GHz that can prevent the uptake of oxygen is being installed in hospitals? What could possibly go wrong? Much of this technology comes from the East and that includes Huawei in China. Leon Pu said the 60 GHz frequency is for use in routers, Wi-Fi, cellphones, and other small devices kept close to the body. This means the skin and sweat ducts which are antennae for 5G and used by the military in this way as a weapon.

Lung effects not caused by any 'virus'

This 5G/oxygen connection has to be even more deeply considered in the light of some intensive care doctors pointing out that the worst cases of respiratory breakdown since the 'virus' scare and the roll-out of 5G are not caused by an 'infectious disease' but by lungs showing symptoms of oxygen starvation. New York intensive care doctor Cameron Kyle-Sidell took to YouTube in his desperation to make people aware of what was happening. YouTube continually deleted uploads of the video and he was reported to have been removed from intensive care. Kyle-Sidell said they were told to prepare to treat an infectious disease called 'Covid-19' but that is not what they are dealing with. Instead he was seeing people with lung conditions he had never seen before and what you would expect to see with people suffering cabin depressurisation in a plane at 30,000 feet or someone dropped on the top of Everest without acclimatisation or by definition an oxygen supply. Kyle-Sidell said that 'Covid-19 is not this disease and we are operating under a medical paradigm that is untrue'. He said that, in short, he believed they were treating the wrong disease. 'These people are being slowly starved of oxygen', he said. Patients would take off their oxygen masks in a state of fear and stress and while they were blue in the face on the brink of death they did not look like patients dying of pneumonia. In these rare cases something different is certainly going on and it's not 'Covid-19'. So what is it? The effect of 5G on oxygen intake must surely be added to the list of possibilities. It should be further noted that nearly *half* the 'deaths' attributed to Covid-19 in the United States have happened in just two places – New York and the neighbouring New Jersey which have 5G and both are awash with cellphone towers. Should this 'virus' spread with 5G expansion people should take serious notice and realise, too, that the impact of 5G will increase with the number of 5G devices and the wave connections they generate. Two other points to make are that some doctors have reported 'Covid-19' patients to have 'mysterious and potentially lethal blood clots' which are not dissolved by blood-thinning agents, and some patients have complained of a tingling or 'fizzing' sensation on or under the skin – 'like being struck by lightning, like pins and needles all over my body', as one woman said. Electromagnetic fields affect the blood and skin, even more so with 5G. Now think that 6G and 7G are in the pipeline if humanity does not get off its arse fast.

I have already mentioned the psychological effects of 5G and Professor Martin Pall notes that malfunctioning calcium cell-gate activity caused by technological radiation produces fear in animals and in humans. It triggers large increases in the release of 'norepinephrine' which is the fight or flight hormone that activates the survival response that we have seen with panic buying, support for draconian measures to 'save us from the virus' and other expressions of fear and distress. Electromagnetic fields at far less than 5G, but at the right frequency, can entrain with brain processing and implant thoughts and emotions to dictate behaviour. This has been known for decades and more and it takes very low energy to instigate – it's the frequency entrainment that allows it to happen. By bouncing frequencies off the ionosphere (between about 37 and 620 miles above the Earth) whole regions of people can be affected. This has been happening for a long time through ionospheric heaters, the best known being the Pentagon/DARPA-driven HAARP in Alaska, the High Frequency Active Auroral Research Program. Ionospheric heaters fire high-power radio waves at the ionosphere which begins to vibrate and divert them back to Earth at far greater power. See *Everything You Need To Know* for the detailed background. 5G is being installed in schools worldwide to destroy the immunity of children and Professor Pall notes that this applies to the immune systems of *all* things – including plants and vegetation which becomes food. During the lockdowns and hysteria the BT-owned mobile operator EE switched on its 5G network in a further 21 British towns and cities, Israel was imposing the same on its citizens and the deeply-sinister Elon Musk was launching still more SpaceX satellites in low altitude to fire 5G at the earth. The telecommunications industry was expressing delight that 'social-distancing' and working from home due to virus laws was increasing demand for more 5G roll-out. The Cult-owned US Federal Communications Commission (FCC) authorised the Cult-owned SpaceX amid the global lockdown to install up to a million ground antenna to connect users to its Starlink satellite internet network and what has been going on in terms of 5G roll-out and other structural changes while people were locked away at home? The ever-increasing 5G explosion will continually diminish immune systems to make them vulnerable to more and more health effects which the Cult will blame on something else. Here we have the road to mass genocide that I described earlier. People like Elon Musk, those running telecommunication companies and politicians and government officials allowing this 5G torture chamber to be created, should be jailed for life for genocidal crimes against humanity. Sitting around watching this unfold and letting Cult psychopaths destroy humanity and take over the world is hardly an option. Professor Pall warns:

> And let me repeat that any effects seen with the initial 'rollout' of 5G radiation will be a tiny fraction of those predicted by a mature 5G system interacting with the 'internet of things' because any initial 5G system has very little to communicate with on initial rollout and therefore will produce only a tiny fraction of highly pulsed EMF effects of such a mature system.

If human life as we know it is going to survive – *5G must go*. The global expansion of the 5G network, its increase in power and impact as more devices are connected to its frequency band, and the oxygen-changing 60 GHz have the potential to inflict enormous amounts of illness that would be blamed on other causes, including further, perhaps more extreme, waves of the illusory 'Covid-19'. It is such a testament to the scale of child-like human perceptual programming that billions could have bought what is an obvious 'pandemic' Big Lie when you take the trouble to think for yourself and make the official narrative justify its claims. Balanced observations don't register with people once the Cult has activated human survival responses channelled through the reptilian brain which is constantly scanning the world for threats to survival of all kinds – life, job, relationships, all of them. The reptilian brain doesn't think, it reacts, and will panic-buy in a frenzy of 'I must survive even at the expense of you'. This is the reaction mechanism that will accept any level of tyrannical imposition if it believes its chances of survival will be increased in any way and the same survival response will demonise anyone questioning, challenging and refusing to cooperate with the said imposition of tyranny.

It is vital to stay calm in these situations to stop survival mechanisms overwhelming you. Unless you are in a situation of immediate danger in which immediate reaction is required nothing good ever comes from the reptilian brain and associated survival responses taking over perception. The first casualty is always thinking straight and my god that has happened to untold numbers since the 'pandemic' frenzy began.

* The Gates-owned Professor Neil Ferguson who produced the computer models that led to the Gates-demanded lockdown, and the man who said (like Gates) that lockdowns must continue until a (Gates) vaccine was ready, fell from his perch with the exposure of extraordinary hypocrisy. Ferguson was forced to resign as a government advisor in the first week of May, 2020, when he was outed by a newspaper for meeting with his married lover against his own lockdown rules.

At a time that he was telling everyone to stay at home and not have anyone visit who didn't live in the same house he enjoyed sexual trysts with his lover at his own home while she was living elsewhere with her husband and children. The girlfriend, Antonia Staats, is a climate change activist and senior campaigner at Avaaz, the global online 'activist' network connected to George Soros which I highlighted earlier.

Even more of a head-shaker was that Ferguson claimed to have the 'virus' in the same period and Staats was telling friends she suspected that her husband had 'virus' symptoms. This is the man who locked down countries with ludicrous 'models' that justified the Gates lockdown agenda and destroyed the lives and livelihoods of at least hundreds of millions of people – exactly what Gates and his Cult masters planned from the start.

CHAPTER SIXTEEN

Why is Bill Gates a psychopath?

Unthinking respect for authority is the greatest enemy of truth
– Albert Einstein

Technocrat mega-billionaire Bill Gates is everywhere in the 'pandemic' hoax and there is no way he doesn't know what he's doing. This is not a man who has been manipulated into funding and fronting the 'pandemic' narrative and response including the punch-line 'vaccine'. Gates is a Cult operative who has bought the global 'health' industry willingly and enthusiastically doing whatever the Cult tells him. I look at his eyes, which never smile, and I see no one home. No life, no vibrance, no emotion. I am reminded every time of biological AI as I am with Zuckerberg, Bezos, Soros, and the rest of their Cult-serving ilk.

I should first explain the background to technocracy AI front-people like Gates (Microsoft), Zuckerberg (Facebook), Brin and Page (Google), Wojcicki (YouTube), Bezos (Amazon), Musk (SpaceX, Tesla, Neuralink), and Soros (Open Society Foundations). There are many others and their role in the structure is basically the same. They are gofers for the Cult that become very rich for being so with some strict provisos on what they do with 'their' (joke) companies and large swathes of their ensuing billions. The Cult is constructing the 'Smart Grid' technological sub-reality technocratic tyranny and they need a host of cover-stories and cover-people to hide the fact that it is all coordinated and being rolled out from underground bases and other secret projects. Notice there are no barren periods while the Cult waits for its next level of technological control to be 'invented'. One stage seamlessly follows the next with no gaps in between. This is because the technology is developed long before we ever see it in the public arena and to hide that fact they need made-up narratives for public consumption and operatives to front-up those narratives. This is where the gofers come in to explain how technology vital to the Cult agenda came to be 'invented' and circulated by unconnected 'individuals'. They become immensely rich, but there are serious strings attached. Enormous swathes of the money secured through Cult operations must be spent on advancing the Cult agenda through 'foundations' of fake philanthropy. They have the added benefit of securing colossal tax-exemptions. Each operative is given an area of specialisation. Soros is deployed funding the Open Society Foundations to secure fake 'people's revolutions', mass migration and the emergence of the New Woke tyranny; Zuckerberg, Brin, Page and Wojcicki have been given the role of global censors protecting Cult narratives and actions from exposure; Bezos is fronting up the takeover of global commerce by the Cult's Amazon, which has benefited fantastically from the 'pandemic' and the demise of *at least* tens of millions of potential competitors, while increasing his wealth by tens of billions during lockdowns which his newspaper, the *Washington Post*, said 'must continue'; Bill Gates has been handed a series of roles which is why he has appeared so many times in the book in relation to many aspects of the Cult agenda that he is funding. His biggest specialisation is the field of Big Pharma 'health' and vaccinating the world.

The Gates vehicle for this Cult 'philanthropy' (it actually makes him an even bigger fortune) is the Bill and Melinda Gates Foundation which he based on the infamous Rockefeller Foundation – a family with which he is extremely close. I have seen ancestry research that says if you go back far enough Gates is from the Rockefeller bloodline. Through this Cult-front 'foundation' Gates created Gavi, the 'vaccine alliance', in 1999 with an initial donation of $750 million and we have already seen his financial connections (many through Gavi) to all the major agenda-drivers of the 'pandemic' including Imperial College, Neil Ferguson, Chris Whitty, Anthony Fauci and Deborah Birx. The web that goes out from the Gates Foundation is extraordinary and includes his control of the Rockefeller-created World Health Organization (WHO) through being its second biggest funder behind only the government of the United States. If Trump carries out his threat to cut WHO funding Gates will be number one. Whatever comes out of the mouth of WHO Director-General Tedros Adhanom Ghebreyesus is Gates speaking and the WHO has been the force dictating the global response to the fake 'virus'. Before being named Director-General Tedros was chair of the Gates-founded Global Fund to 'fight against AIDS, tuberculosis and malaria' and a board member of the Gates-funded Gavi and another Gates-funded organisation. Gates owns him. At the same time Cult fronts like Facebook, YouTube and Google have introduced a policy of censoring or downgrading any information at odds with the World Health Organization version of events (which is why I was deleted from Facebook and YouTube).

You can see how the Web works and these Cult operatives and gofers working as one unit need to face the consequences of their actions and crimes against humanity in life sentences with their money distributed to those whose livelihoods they have mercilessly destroyed. This lack of mercy and empathy for the global population makes them all for me not only psychopaths, but super-psychopaths. But, then, if they work at any in-the-know level of the Cult they would have to be by definition. It's compulsory. Another head-shaker for anyone who knows the game was when Gates's missus, Melinda, who will be well aware of what is going on, announced on CNN that 'soon Africa will have bodies out in the streets'. Africa up to this point was only marginally affected compared with the size of the continent, but Mrs Gates knew better. She said the reason the numbers were low was the lack of testing (for genetic material found in many people) and when the testing expanded so would the number of cases (exactly, that's the whole deceit of the test). In the wake of her African prophecy the Gates-owned World Health Organization and Cult-owned United Nations declared that Africa could see up to 3.3 million deaths from 'Covid-19' and could become the 'epicentre' of the 'pandemic' that had been declared in the first place by the Gates-owned WHO. Was there any way to stop this, pray? Oh yes – lockdown and social distancing. The same hoax that had been perpetrated in the West was now being dumped on Africa where Gates 'vaccine programs' exploit poor children for their 'trials'.

Who's WHO? Er ... *Bill Gates*

The World Health Organization is extraordinarily corrupt and has been since it was created by the Rockefellers and Rothschilds after World War Two. The WHO declared 'Covid-19' a 'global pandemic' in March, 2020, as it was always going to do from day one. Gates hands over hundreds of millions dollars to buy control as he has poured millions into the US Centers for Disease Control and Prevention (CDC) which has directed 'virus' policy in the United States and told doctors to diagnose anyone that moves – or doesn't – as 'Covid-19' without any evidence. The CDC is funded by Big Pharma, medical insurance companies and other medical-related industries while WHO funding also massively comes from the world's major Big Pharma drug companies. Together they and Gates run the WHO on behalf of the Cult agenda and not the world population. As a result this Microsoft technocrat, son of a supporter of eugenics, has been called 'the world's most powerful doctor' and refers to himself as a 'health expert'. Gates doesn't actually strike me as very bright at all, but you don't need to be when you're just a front man. The WHO is based in Geneva, Switzerland, home to so many Cult operations, including the World Trade Organization. Geneva is reported to have a moratorium on 5G. The WHO is another agency of the United Nations and currently headed by Tedros Adhanom Ghebreyesus, a politburo member of the tyrannical Tigray People's Liberation Front

(TPLF) which has been part of the repressive Marxist government of Ethiopia for decades. It has been widely condemned by human rights organisations for its abuse of citizens. Out of this came Tedros, amid many allegations of corruption and misappropriation of funds, to head the Cult's World Health Organization which provides the official 'virus' narrative. Tedros was exposed three times for covering up cholera epidemics while health minister in Ethiopia and when he took office in Geneva he had the mass-murdering Zimbabwe dictator Robert Mugabe appointed as a WHO goodwill ambassador for public health although, naturally, not for the health of all those he had killed to stay in power. The appointment was so outrageous that Tedros was quickly forced to retract.

Tedros is one of the last people who should be WHO Director-General, but then he's not there to serve the human population. He's there to serve the interests of those who secured his appointment and created the World Health Organization – the Cult. Anyone think that the appointment of Tedros was made without the approval of Bill Gates? Tedros is close to China and he worked to make lockdown and social distancing the blueprint for response in the West by praising its effectiveness in China. I guess we should also expect that when the Chinese Communist Party and Tedros share the same politics. Nothing is uttered by the WHO hierarchy or emerges from the mouth of Tedros that is not the Gates agenda and the software psychopath also came out in praise of China just to emphasise the point: 'China did a lot of things right at the beginning.' Yes, they had a draconian lockdown which was planned from the start to be transferred to the West. Gates described his WHO fiefdom as 'phenomenal' when the operation is a Cult-owned farce in relation to human health. We should include in that the same bracket the controlling hierarchy of the Centers for Disease Control (CDC) in the United States which, like the World Health Organization, is owned by Gates, Big Pharma and the wider Cult.

Gates and the 'Davos' mob – the 'prophecy'

Melinda Gates said on BBC radio (Gates has given millions to the BBC) that her husband had 'prepared for years' for a coronavirus pandemic. Oh, I bet he had. Gates predicted a coming global pandemic that would kill many people and devastate the world economy in a TED talk in 2015. The man is a modern-day Isaiah. Then six weeks before the 'outbreak' in China came to public attention a 'simulation' of a *coronavirus* pandemic was run by the One-percent 'Davos' World Economic Forum (WEF), the Bill and Melinda Gates Foundation and the Johns Hopkins Center for Health Security (Fig 384). This was called Event 201 and included major banks, the UN, Johnson & Johnson, and officials from China and the Centers for Disease Control in the United

Figure 384: The prophets of the Bill Gates One-percent at Event 201 simulating a 'coronavirus pandemic' six weeks before the fake 'pandemic' came to public attention.

States. Remember what the American scientist I quoted said: 'If you want to create a totally false panic about a totally false pandemic – pick a coronavirus'. Johns Hopkins Center for Health Security ran its own 'pandemic' simulation in Washington called 'Clade X' in 2018. Since the fake 'pandemic' began the same Johns Hopkins operation has compiled all the fraudulent figures for 'Covid-19' cases and deaths repeated incessantly and unquestioningly by the media worldwide. The Johns Hopkins network of fronts has received absolutely massive funding from … Bill Gates and Big Pharma. News reports were inserted into the Gates simulation and discussions included censorship of those questioning the official line of what the public were told – all of which would be happening within weeks when the fake 'coronavirus outbreak' hit the news. We had headlines appearing such as 'anti-vaccination movement could derail fight against coronavirus, experts warn'. That headline was in the UK *'Independent'* (of course). Cult-owned Mark Zuckerberg announced in March, 2020, that Facebook would give the Gates World Health Organization free advertisements and remove 'false claims and conspiracy theories' in a battle against coronavirus 'misinformation' (anything that challenged or questioned the official Cult narrative). Users looking for coronavirus information on Cult-controlled Facebook would see a pop-up at the top of search results directing them to the official narrative. 'We're focused on making sure everyone can access credible and accurate information', said the little boy in short trousers and a t-shirt. He was equating, as always, 'credible and accurate' with the official story. He would later announce that Facebook would warn users even if they 'liked, reacted or commented' on Covid-19 'misinformation' that the company has removed. This extraordinary fraud had earlier said that Facebook systematically sets out to marginalise those who question vaccine safety. Zuckerberg should absolutely be in jail because he knows what he's doing and it was all in line with the Gates 'simulation' Event 201. Cult-controlled Google, Twitter and Apple naturally engaged in similar coronavirus censorship with Google-owned YouTube announcing:

> With few people to review content, our automated systems will be stepping in to keep YouTube safe. More videos will be removed than normal during this

time including content that does not violate community guidelines.

Passed through my Orwellian Translation Unit this meant that we are coding the AI algorithms to target all information that we can which challenges the official version of the Cult virus narrative. Where this is leading – the West becoming China – was promoted in an article in the elite-owned *Atlantic* magazine by two academics, Harvard Law School professor Jack Goldsmith and Andrew Keane Woods, a professor at the University of Arizona. The heading said it all: 'Internet Speech Will Never Go Back to Normal – in the debate over freedom versus control of the global network, China was largely correct, and the U.S. was wrong.' *Classic.* You Tube, Vimeo and Facebook all deleted my interview with London Real which exposed the zero evidence that 'Covid-19' existed. YouTube gofer Susan Wojcicki then demonetised all my YouTube videos on any subject (followed by complete deletion) and Vimeo deleted some 700 videos on the Ickonic media platform because, among other pathetic excuses, some of them questioned vaccine safety. Ickonic was restored with our own playing system within days and the banned interview has been ginormously circulated by the public outside these digital kindergartens and been translated into many languages including Spanish and Italian. This is what is possible when you don't give up and play the victim. By the way, YouTube and Wojcicki said my interview had been banned as part of a newly-introduced rule whereby …

> … Any content that disputes the existence or transmission of Covid-19, as described by the WHO and local health authorities is in violation of YouTube policies. This includes conspiracy theories which claim that the symptoms are caused by 5G.

Take that in for a moment and smell the fascism. The WHO narrative is the Gates narrative is the Cult narrative protected from challenge by the Cult's YouTube. Golden rule: If YouTube are promoting something or someone then the Cult wants them promoted and if they are deleting them the Cult wants them deleted. We were banned for a time from Twitter for posting another 'Covid-19' video made by an external source and think what the censorship will be like should ultra-Zionist billionaire Paul Singer get control of that company. Add to all this the admission by General Sir Nick Carter, the UK's Chief of the Defence Staff, that the clandestine 77th Brigade of the British Army is involved in 'countering coronavirus misinformation online'. The unit was created in 2015 to specialise 'non-lethal' forms of *psychological warfare* and use social media to 'fight in the information age'. Carter said the 77th Brigade had been tackling 'false information' about the pandemic on the Internet. A unit of the British Army, 2,000 strong, is seeking to manipulate the perceptions of British people by trashing opinions at odds with the state narrative and that of the Gates-owned World Health Organization. That is how the fast-emerging fascism works. The fake 'pandemic' is indeed global psychological warfare on the collective human psyche. Conversations in the Gates-World Economic Forum Event 201 'simulation' were a precursor to what was about to happen for real and anyone who thinks that is a coincidence needs a massive download of reality. Bill Gates's father, William Henry Gates Sr, was head of the Rockefeller-created Planned Parenthood (connected to insider 'prophet' Dr Richard Day) which began life in the eugenics movement. Boy Gates admits he was a 'one-time' believer in the eugenics theory of 18th/19th century cleric Thomas Malthus. The Gates Foundation pledged $100 million to 'fight the virus' and the *Seattle Times* reported as the 'coronavirus' hit America that a project funded by the Gates Foundation was producing home-testing kits for the disease. Gates staff said that positive results would be shared with 'health authorities' who would then track people's movements. The test would involve taking a DNA sample and provide another addition to the DNA database (which all the 'tests' are doing). Gates is also funding the 'vaccine' which I will come to shortly. Billy Boy stepped down from the board of Microsoft, which he co-founded, in mid-March 2020 to 'spend more time on philanthropic activities' and focus on 'global health and development, education and tackling climate change' – all Cult endeavours. The timing of this was, shall we say, telling.

The Rockefeller prophecy

I was further alerted to a document by the Rockefeller Foundation from 2010 headed 'Scenarios for the Future of Technology and International Development' which included responses to an imaginary pandemic of an extremely virulent and deadly influenza strain that infected 20 percent of the world population and killed eight million in seven months. The scenario envisaged by the infamous and One-percent Rockefeller Foundation, the inspiration for the Gates Foundation, had a 'deadly effect' on economies with empty shops and offices devoid of both employers and customers for months on end. The document described how totalitarianism was introduced in countries of the West to 'protect citizens from risk and exposure':

> During the pandemic, national leaders around the world flexed their authority and imposed airtight rules and restrictions, from the mandatory wearing of face masks to body-temperature checks at the entries to communal spaces like train stations and supermarkets. Even after the pandemic faded, this more authoritarian control and oversight of citizens and their activities stuck and even intensified. In order to protect themselves from the spread of increasingly

global problems – from pandemics and transnational terrorism to environmental crises and rising poverty – leaders around the world took a firmer grip on power.

At first, the notion of a more controlled world gained wide acceptance and approval. Citizens willingly gave up some of their sovereignty – and their privacy – to more paternalistic states in exchange for greater safety and stability. Citizens were more tolerant, and even eager, for top-down direction and oversight, and national leaders had more latitude to impose order in the ways they saw fit.

In developed countries, this heightened oversight took many forms: biometric IDs for all citizens, for example, and tighter regulation of key industries whose stability was deemed vital to national interests. In many developed countries, enforced cooperation with a suite of new regulations and agreements slowly but steadily restored both order and, importantly, economic growth.

By mid-March, 2020, the numbers of new cases in China were reported to be falling just as they were increasing in the rest of the world and as the Rockefeller Foundation 'scenario' document had 'prophesised' China began to be praised for its authoritarian response made possible by its authoritarian non-democratic system. A *Forbes* magazine headline said: 'For the US, Coronavirus lessons to be learned from China and South Korea'. This was the pre-planned perceptual preparation for the Chinese lockdown to be seen as the blueprint response when in fact the fake test and cause of death registrations would decide the number of cases and fatalities that would follow. The whole thing was a set-up orchestrated between Cult-controlled China and Cult networks in other countries. The Rockefeller 'prophecy' document of 2010 had said:

> However, a few countries did fare better – China in particular. The Chinese government's quick imposition and enforcement of mandatory quarantine for all citizens, as well as its instant and near-hermetic sealing off of all borders, saved millions of lives, stopping the spread of the virus far earlier than in other countries and enabling a swifter post-pandemic recovery.

The *Forbes* magazine article in 2020 said of China's response '… those measures protected untold millions from getting the disease'. The 2011 movie *Contagion* also pre-empted the events that followed the 'Covid-19 outbreak' in another amazing Hollywood prophecy. This is a summary of the storyline in which bats were blamed to begin with:

> Soon after her return from a business trip to Hong Kong [China], Beth Emhoff

dies from what is a flu or some other type of infection. Her young son dies later the same day. Her husband Mitch however seems immune. Thus begins the spread of a deadly infection. For doctors and administrators at the US Centers for Disease Control, several days pass before anyone realizes the extent or gravity of this new infection.

They must first identify the type of virus in question and then find a means of combating it, a process that will likely take several months. As the contagion spreads to millions of people worldwide, societal order begins to break down as people panic.

Another description of the film says:

In a flashback, days before Beth is infected in China, a bulldozer knocks down a tree, disturbing some bats. One flies over a sty and drops a piece of banana, which is eaten by a pig. The pigs are slaughtered and prepared by a chef who shakes hands with Beth in the casino, transferring the virus to her and making her Patient Zero.

What saves the day? Well, well, a *vaccine* and the US Centers for Disease Control chose who had the vaccine by birthdate. Oh, yes, and 'conspiracy theorists' were demonised. Here we have yet another Hollywood pre-emptive program and two representations of the One-percent describing a pandemic sequence with Event 201 happening with relation to an 'imaginary' coronavirus just before the real imaginary coronavirus 'broke out'.

The Gates vaccine

Bill Gates wasn't even subtle about the No-Problem-Reaction-Solution punchline of the 'pandemic' hoax and I guess he didn't need to be for the billions who have bought the official story without question and have no idea about the big picture of how they are being lassoed and branded. For those of us who have tracked him and the Cult for decades he was an open book. Just as the Chinese did not consider other possible causes for the illness in Wuhan except a 'virus' so Gates would not have any other responses considered except lockdown, isolation and a vaccine. He talked immediately about the need for a vaccine and pledged hundreds of millions to 'find one' through a multitude of his funded sources. I said from the start that the vaccine Gates wanted to inject into the entirety of humanity already existed before the fake 'pandemic' had even started. All this funding and working to develop a vaccine to 'save humanity' is more psychological bullshit to have people on their knees begging to be inoculated by the time it was 'ready' in the wake of 'new waves' of the 'virus just before vaccination was planned to begin. We were told that the vaccine could be ready in months when the normal development sequence and trials takes years. How was this possible? It already existed. They couldn't 'discover' the vaccine and start mass immunisation too quickly or even the non-sceptical might ask how this could be done so quickly. They had to have some delay but they would seek to make that as short as possible. Tucker Carlson, the only US TV anchor with the intelligence and courage to ask relevant questions, made a very potent point about 'coronavirus' vaccines:

> Scientists have never produced a single approved vaccine or anti-viral drug for any coronavirus ... We spent millions of dollars and more than a decade trying to find a vaccine for the SARS virus. Scientists never developed one.

Ah, but if there is no 'Covid-19' virus and you are only creating the illusion of one by fixing the figures through fake diagnosis and death certificates then the vaccine, whatever the content, can appear to have worked if you change the policy on fake diagnosis and death certificates once the vaccine is introduced. Gates, the software-peddling psychopath, had placed himself above elected governments in true technocratic style to dictate vaccination policy for the whole world. He made it clear that 'for the world at large normalcy only returns when we have vaccinated the entire global population.' Can you imagine the scale of arrogance that it takes for the software-peddler to make that statement? It's just a glimpse of the arrogant, narcissistic psychopathy that pervades the global Cult and its operatives. The Cult-Gates plan is to make the vaccination compulsory and failing that to stop people returning to anything like their previous lifestyle unless they agree to be vaccinated. You want to come out of lockdown? Then you have the vaccination or stay as you are. This is why they are so desperate to keep the lockdowns going in some form until the vaccine is produced. These people are undiluted evil – the absence of love. I see also the comments of some 'experts' that because 'older people tend to have weaker immune responses to vaccines' the elderly 'might need two doses of the jab'. Gates further demands that people who have been vaccinated must be marked so that technology can pick up the signal to confirm your branding. Now we see the real reason for the Gates/Gavi 'quantum tattoo' that I highlighted earlier. I described how the Gates Foundation is funding the development of an 'tattoo' that will identify those who have and have not been vaccinated. The excuse was to identify vaccinated children in the developing world, but it is clear what the 'tattoo' was really for – giving the entirety of humanity the 'Mark of the Beast'. Gates has funded research at the Massachusetts Institute of Technology (MIT) to create an 'invisible quantum tattoo' to be embedded in the skin and read by a smartphone camera app. Sciencealert.com reported:

The invisible 'tattoo' accompanying the vaccine is a pattern made up of minuscule quantum dots – tiny semiconducting crystals that reflect light – that glows under infrared light. The pattern – and vaccine – gets delivered into the skin using hi-tech dissolvable microneedles made of a mixture of polymers and sugar.

Yet again Gates's timing was perfect to sync with the 'pandemic' that he predicted. The Gates 'tattoo' is connected to the ID2020 'alliance' seeking to impose a digital identity on everyone. This alliance consists of those legendary lovers of humanity Microsoft, Gavi, the Rockefeller Foundation, Accenture and IDEO.org. Add to this the technology 'being developed' (already developed) by facial recognition camera producers to track heartbeats, temperature and social distancing. This is one description:

Photon-X object recognition and analytics combined with VSBLTY facial recognition will provide an advanced screening tool for facilities to identify and validate that someone with a high temperature is about to enter a building. Fever, cough and difficulty breathing are some of the common symptoms of COVID-19.

The Gates vaccine or vaccines will contain other diseases for further waves of lockdown, a sterilisation agent, and possibly something to 'target specific genotypes' in the words of the Project for The New American Century. Crucially there will be nano-technology microchips or 'smart dust' to connect the human race to the Smart Grid and mutate human DNA and genetics into synthetic biological machines which I say that people like Gates and the rest of the Cult inner core already are – biological AI. Rockefeller insider Dr Richard Day told the Pittsburgh paediatricians in 1969 about plans to inoculate diseases in vaccination programmes and that's being going on for a long time which is one reason why so many children are getting sicker. I described the nanotechnology I believed would be in the 'Covid-19' vaccine in my first interview with London Real on these subjects before the lockdowns got into full swing and Gates came rapidly to the fore about his vaccine. Weeks later I watched a video interview with Celeste Solum, a former employee of FEMA, the Federal Emergency Management Agency, which has been widely exposed in my books since the mid-1990s. FEMA is a 100 percent front for the Cult and is given extraordinary powers over American society once a state of national emergency has been declared and that is what Donald Trump did on March 13th, 2020. Celeste Solum, who worked in a number of roles for FEMA including planning for pandemics, said in her interview that the fake pandemic was designed to enforce vaccinations that would include nanochips or sensors. Everyone in the world would have to be tested for 'Covid-19' and vast numbers will test positive for reasons I have explained. Solum said that the real reason for this was a 'big DNA harvesting' – 'They want all our DNA in the big giant supercomputers.' A series of vaccinations was planned – not only one – which will contain aborted foetal tissue and what she calls 'the DARPA hydro-gel sensor' which had been in development for ten years. This consists of nano-particles in a 'gelatine form' which once injected 'begin to assemble'. Solum is describing what I detailed earlier about smart dust which can replicate inside the body and assemble systems to transform the nature of the body from human to a form of machine. She said the nano-particles fuse with tissue and becomes one with the body. 'You become one with artificial intelligence and the Internet of Things', Solum said. 'You become your own computer interface ... and you are one with the hive, the system, whatever you want to say.' This is precisely what I have been warning about in the books for so long.

Solum said that people would be forced to have this 'sensor' vaccination on the grounds that it will alert the authorities that you are sick before even you know you are sick. This is the real reason for the Gates vaccination and he well knows that which is why he is a super-psychopath who should be in jail for the rest of his life. More confirmation came when he said in a television interview that 700,000 people could be damaged by a global 'Covid-19' vaccination (and the rest) and so governments would have to agree to indemnify vaccine producers from responsibility. In that one sentence Bill Gates personified himself (Fig 385). Another crucial aspect of a Gates vaccine is the emerging new vaccination technique that the Cult is desperate to introduce called DNA or genetic immunisation. This has been described as 'hacking your DNA'. It fits like a glove and it is vital to keep our eyes firmly on this. DNA vaccines are used in animals, but not yet humans. They inject a 'plasmid' which is defined as 'small circular pieces of DNA mainly found in bacteria that replicate independently from the host's chromosomal DNA'. Note that once in the body they *replicate independently*. Plasmids used in vaccines would be genetically-engineered and hence the term 'synthetic DNA vaccines'. They are described as 'mimicking' a 'viral infection'.

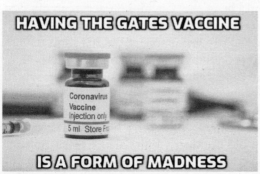

Figure 385: Exactly what it is.

The Gates vaccine horror story by Robert F. Kennedy Jr

I mentioned earlier that Robert F. Kennedy Jr, son of the assassinated US Attorney General Robert F. Kennedy and nephew of former US President John F. Kennedy, has spoken out often and vociferously against the health effects of vaccinations. His father and JFK were murdered in the 1960s by assets of the same Cult behind the fake 'pandemic'. Gates said that Trump told him in 2017 that he was considering 'somebody, I think his name was Robert Kennedy Jr' (the arrogance of it) to head an inquiry into the safety of vaccines. The software psychopath said he told Trump: 'No, that would be a dead end, that would be a bad thing, don't do that.' Robert Kennedy Jr did not mince words amid the demands by Bill Gates for a 'Covid-19' vaccine that everyone must have worldwide. Kennedy said:

> Vaccines, for Bill Gates, are a strategic philanthropy that feeds his many vaccine-related businesses (including Microsoft's ambition to control a global vac ID enterprise) and gives him dictatorial control over global health policy – the spear tip of corporate neo-imperialism.

Kennedy went on to highlight the disastrous effects for hundreds of thousands of children of Gates vaccine programmes. He said Gates polio vaccination campaigns had paralysed 496,000 children in India between 2000 and 2017 while other Gates catastrophes included autoimmune and fertility disorders suffered by 1,200 girls with seven of them dying. He said they were among 23,000 girls from remote Indian villages vaccinated by Gates programmes in league with Glaxo Smith Kline (GSK) and Merck. This is the same shameless Gates that said 'people who engage in anti-vaccine efforts kill children'. Kennedy accused the Gates organisation of using unethical practices to pressure girls to participate in the trial, intimidating parents, falsifying consent forms, and denying medical care to the affected. He was quoting from a case before the Indian Supreme Court. Polio, also known as poliomyelitis and infantile paralysis, is a perfect example of vaccine deceit. Polio paralysis began when lead arsenate started to be widely sprayed as an insecticide and the produce consumed. Lead arsenate spraying began in 1892 and the first US polio 'epidemic' came in Vermont in 1894, but the Big Pharma cartel (created by the Rockefeller family) decreed that polio is caused by … the *poliovirus* which 'spreads from person to person and can infect a person's spinal cord'. Polio continued with the introduction of DDT, another devastating poison, particularly after the Second World War until its virtual worldwide ban in the 1970s and 80s. Lead arsenate and DDT both poison the brain and nervous system which is the cause of polio paralysis and as you would expect cases of polio plummeted when DDT was reduced in use and then banned. In the meantime Big

Pharma introduced a polio vaccine which was then given the credit for the reduction. 'Vaccine-eradicated' diseases were in decline before vaccines were introduced and diseases like scarlet fever for which there was not a vaccine declined in the same way. Dr Andrew Kaufman said: 'If you actually go back and look for the evidence that vaccines have prevented disease you're not going to find it.' Today polio is caused overwhelmingly by *vaccinations for polio* so beloved of Gates. Robert Kennedy Jr wrote:

> In 2017, the World Health Organization (WHO) reluctantly admitted that the global explosion in polio is predominantly vaccine strain. The most frightening epidemics in Congo, Afghanistan, and the Philippines, are all linked to vaccines. In fact, by 2018, 70% of global polio cases were vaccine strain.

The World Health Organisation was accused in 2014 of sterilising millions of women in Kenya by using deception and the evidence was confirmed by the content of the vaccines involved. The WHO admitted its involvement for more than 10 years with the vaccine programme and similar charges were lodged by other countries including Tanzania, Nicaragua, Mexico, and the Philippines. This is the organization controlled by Gates that is not only declaring and driving the 'pandemic', but being protected from exposure by Zuckerberg's Facebook, Wojcicki's YouTube and Silicon Valley and the mainstream media in general. The Gates Foundation is connected through funding and mutual agendas to 20 pharmaceutical giants and laboratories and he is accused of directing the policy of United Nations Children's Fund (UNICEF), Gavi, and other groupings, and using them to both advance the vaccine agenda and silence those opposing the policy. Robert Kennedy Jr also turned his fire on the Gates-connected Trump 'pandemic advisor' Dr Anthony Fauci who he said had 'poisoned an entire generation of Americans'. He accused Fauci of 'an extensive legacy of fraud and cover-ups in his decades-long career with the federal government during which he 'operated as a workplace tyrant and ruined the careers of countless physicians and researchers' who had worked with integrity. Kennedy said that in at least one instance Fauci targeted a whistleblower trying to expose how the American blood supply has been infected with deadly disease strains. He said Fauci ruined the career of this physician and covered up the evidence. Kennedy claimed Fauci was using his position to secure lucrative vaccine patents. Doctors and researchers below him in the hierarchy would develop breakthrough technologies and then be dismissed to allow Fauci to seize ownership of their work. Kennedy said Fauci owned 'many, many vaccine patents' including one for a special protein sheet to circulate vaccine material throughout the body. He said Fauci didn't develop this, but stole it from someone else who was fired after creating it:

> Tony Fauci fired [this person] and he somehow ended up owning that patent, and that patent is now being used ... to make vaccines for the coronavirus ... that company has a 50/50 split with Tony Fauci's agency ... so Fauci's agency will collect half the royalties on that vaccine and there's no limit for how much the agency can collect.

Kennedy said that Fauci's National Institute of Allergy and Infectious Diseases (NIAID) and the Centers for Disease Control and Prevention (CDC) were really subsidiaries of Big Pharma and these so-called federal agencies were corporations in disguise working with Big Pharma to generate enormous profits on the backs of sick and dying people.

The biggest cause of death – lockdown

While we are told to surrender our most basic rights in the name of protection from the 'virus' the death toll from the lockdown, cancelled operations and diagnosis is going to be both monumental and ongoing. Lockdown deaths are sure to be way higher than even the manipulated figures falsely attributed to 'Covid-19'. I have described how old people are denied treatment and pressured to sign do not resuscitate forms, but it's not just old people that are being fatally affected. Others would die from a long list of causes, including cancer and heart disease, by not being diagnosed or treated while hospitals had hundreds of empty beds and doctors and medical staff had next to nothing to do. Here's an example relating to cancer in Britain. Multiply the same situation across the world and the figures for cancer alone will be breathtaking even without all the other causes of death from the same lack of diagnoses and treatment. Cancer specialists were warning before the end of April that thousands in the UK were missing out on cancer diagnosis with the charity Cancer Research UK reporting a decline in screening and referrals of some 2,700 fewer people every week. Richard Sullivan, professor of cancer and global health at King's College London, said there was more fear of Covid-19 than of having cancer. What a testament that is to the power of perceptual programming. 'A lot of services have had to scale back – we've seen a dramatic decrease in the amount of elective cancer surgery', Sullivan said. 'Years of lost life will be quite dramatic', he continued, and there would be 'a huge amount of avoidable mortality.' Sarah Woolnough, executive director for policy at Cancer Research UK, said there had been a 75 percent drop in urgent referrals to hospitals by family doctors of people with suspected cancer. To think that the UK 'Health' Secretary, Matt Hancock, who knows nothing about 'health', said it was not advisable for some cancer treatments to go ahead during an epidemic because of the risks of exposure to the 'virus'.

Professor Sullivan pointed out another consequence of the lockdown – a huge wave of people and health problems that would overwhelm hospitals when they were fully open again. This is the very situation that the lockdowns were supposed to avoid as they 'protected' (empty) hospitals from being overrun. Inversion, inversion, wherever you look – including keeping people out of the sun while saying that sunlight 'kills viruses'. Sullivan said it could take up to a year to return the health service to normal even if the lockdowns stopped then in the last week of April. These were only the consequences for cancer patients. Add all the other untreated conditions and the hospital backlog worldwide was bound to be extraordinary in scale. Another clearly predictable consequence was the psychological effect of locking people away in their homes, often tiny, for weeks on end knowing that their employment or business was gone and money was running out. Despair and desperation were certain to unravel mental and bodily health and increase suicide through lack of hope and a sense of pointlessness. This was already becoming clear in the psychological trauma experienced by many Italians in their longest of lockdowns. I asked staff at food stores if they had noticed any difference in the demeanour of people since the lockdowns. They certainly had. 'People look like they're going to their own funeral', one told me. The ongoing effects of this will have multiple expressions and consequences – as the Cult knew they would. Meanwhile the elite themselves ignored lockdown laws with former US President Barack Obama driven 40 miles by a government chauffeur to play golf on an empty course while his wife Michelle was voicing over a video telling the public to stay at home. Boris Johnson's advisor (handler) Dominic Cummings flouted lockdown laws as did Professor Neil Ferguson.

Hunger Games bonanza

The vaccine is only one aspect – albeit crucial – of why the fake 'pandemic' has been orchestrated. Given what I had written in the book before we reached this stage some of the other central reasons should now be obvious given the impact of the lockdowns on human life with billions in effect under house arrest. Box after box of the long-time Cult agenda are being ticked (Fig 386). I have been writing since the Cult-driven economic crash of 2008 that another even more extreme financial collapse was planned to deliver still greater swathes of people into the Hunger Games Society and here we are – big time (Fig 387). This was the certain outcome of the lockdowns from day one and all was coldly-planned to ensure that untold numbers of businesses would never

Figure 386: Everything I have been warning about for 30 years was potentially delivered by one virus. Pure chance? Yes, of course it was.

Figure 387: The Hunger Games Society agenda that I have been exposing for decades has advanced with incredible speed during the fake 'pandemic' - which is why the Cult hoaxed the 'pandemic'. (Image Neil Hague.)

reopen again throwing both owners and employees out of work. Trillions of dollars were unleashed in 'stimulus packages' which as always benefited the super-rich far more than those truly in need. The richest of universities with billions in the bank were recipients of public money while even the Anti-Defamation League (ADL), the hugely-funded Israel-serving censorship operation, demanded bail-out dosh while the masses went under. Countries were heading for bankruptcy if this continued, but no matter – the lockdowns continued in an exercise in economic suicide that would open the way for the 'new system' that the Cult has for so long pursued. Stock markets nose-dived along with oil prices as the 'virus' officially expanded out of China. As stock prices dropped the Cult was buying up businesses and resources at cents on the dollar to secure even more control. Ultra-Zionist billionaire Bill Ackman told CNBC that the United States was in serious jeopardy – 'Hell is coming' – unless the White House closed the country. He then made a $2.6 billion profit on market bets related to closing down the country. Amazon CEO Jeff Bezos, the world's first 'centibillionaire', a man who vies with Bill Gates for the title of the planet's richest individual, asked for public donations to provide basic support to his

800,000 employees who were suffering in poverty in the wake of the Covid-19 pandemic. These people have no shame.

The restaurant industry was America's biggest private sector employer with 15.6 million jobs before the 'virus' shutdown and that is not including all the food and other suppliers which depend on that industry. All was banned by the Gates (Cult) front-people. Global chains and other Cult corporations circled like vultures to pick up the scraps for a pittance and further increase their monopoly. The James Beard Foundation, a New York-based culinary organisation, reported near the end of April that independent restaurants had laid off 91 percent of their hourly employees and nearly 70 percent of salaried employees as of April 13th. The Beard survey of 1,400 small and independent restaurants found that 28 percent said they didn't believe they could survive another month of closure. Even if they did – and the same with all businesses – where was the money coming from to regenerate custom amid such colossal unemployment? Hotels, pubs, bars, restaurants, entertainment and sport were devastated and everything that in any way gathered people together. More places of potential human gathering, discourse and interaction have been lost – exactly what the Cult wants and this was emphasised by health-irrelevant 'social distancing'. It is literal divide and rule by government diktat. UK government advisor Robert Dingwall from the New and Emerging Respiratory Virus Threats Advisory Group revealed in a radio interview that the two-metre social distancing rule was 'conjured up out of nowhere' and was not based on science. No, it was based on control and division and it didn't come 'out of nowhere', but from the Cult. This is why it was imposed all over the world at the same time and people did what they were told because that's all they have ever learned to do. We had, for example, the 1.3 million people in the US state of Maine kept under lock and key on the say-so of the notoriously arrogant and stupid Governor Janet Mills at a time when just 15 people had died in Maine 'from the virus' even with the fake diagnosis and death certificate scam. The Maine economy was devastated and unemployment soared while Mills continued to take her money as normal. US state governors became one-person dictators imposing the will of the Cult. California governor Gavin Newsom closed 43 miles of Orange County beaches at a time when Will O'Neil, the mayor of Newport Beach, was pointing out the following:

> Orange County has 3.2 million people who live here. It's bigger than 22 states ... and of all of those people we have lost 50 people to this virus. That's 0.001 percent of our population. In our local hospital we have 475 beds. They have never treated more than 25 people at any given time and yesterday they had nine people that they were treating and only one percent of their ventilators

were being used.

Newson is the man who won't enforce American immigration law, but closes 43 miles of beaches in the circumstances the mayor described. These governors serving the Cult agenda and dictatorship must all be removed at the earliest possible moment. To confirm the contempt of the Cult-controlled establishment Trump's Gates-connected 'virus' advisor Anthony Fauci said shaking hands might have to become a thing of the past, but having sex with a stranger you met on the Internet was okay. These people are laughing at you.

The International Labour Organization estimated that some 1.6 *billion* people – nearly half the global workforce – could see their livelihoods destroyed. What does that mean? Dependency and control which is what all this is really about along with the contents of the Gates vaccine. The shutdown consequences have been especially lethal for smaller businesses which the Cult wants to delete to open the way for its corporations to control all commerce, trade and production (see Amazon which thrived during the lockdowns). Ponder the consequences when figures I saw claimed that companies with fewer than 20 staff employ about 90 percent of Americans. Rural areas not affected by even the fake version of the 'virus' were shutdown anyway to advance the plan for rural depopulation and enslavement in smart cities. By the closing days of April *Fortune* magazine was reporting that a staggering 26.5 million American workers were made unemployed by the lockdowns with the numbers rising by millions per week. *Fortune* said that when added to the seven million already jobless before the shutdown it would equal more than 33 million unemployed – 'a real unemployment rate of 20.6% – which would be the highest level since 1934'. Similar surges in job losses have been happening in the UK and across the locked-down world. Of course that was going to happen. It was a prime *reason* for the lockdowns. To secure control of the masses in the Hunger Games Society the Cult needs to destroy independent livelihoods and the 'pandemic' hoax meant they could secure in weeks what would otherwise have taken years and decades. Take away access to independent businesses, employment and income and what are you left with – dependency on the state (Cult) and the Hunger Games Society that I described earlier in this book, and in previous ones, before the 'pandemic' deception was even played.

The New System

I have warned for decades that the plan was to impose a whole new centralised economic system for total global control. This has been pursued through the climate change hoax which demands just such a system to 'save the world' and the economic effects of the fake pandemic provided unlimited potential for economic catastrophe – Problem-Reaction-Solution or, in the case of the 'virus' and 'climate change', NO-Problem-Reaction-Solution. Lower-paid people – the 'serfs' to the Cult – would lose their jobs and their homes through their inability to pay the rent and so would people who considered themselves well-paid and in safe employment until weeks before. The Cult's vulture banks were poised for a frenzy of home repossession that would exceed by many magnitudes the fall-out of 2008 and advance the goal of deleting privately-owned property that I described earlier. Even those that are able to hang on to property have seen the value drop to below what they paid for it so cementing them in to their current abode unable to move due to negative equity. How many more people would fall into the lower reaches of the Hunger Games pyramid as a result of their business or job disappearing in the wake of government response to the 'virus'? Potentially – *billions*. Economic meltdown was not caused by a 'virus', but by the calculated Deep State response to a fake 'virus' and this prompted predictable calls for another Cult ambition – a basic (miserly) guaranteed income with all the consequences for freedom that I laid out earlier. The Cult has controlled the position of Pope for centuries and when a genuine man somehow slips through like Pope John Paul I (Albino Luciani) in 1978 he was murdered through poisoning after the Freemasonically-significant 33 days in office while he was planning to purge the Vatican of Cult influences. He has been followed by the exceedingly ungenuine Pope John Paul II, Benedict and now Francis who predictably called for a guaranteed income as the lockdown consequences struck home just as he has called for world government and a transformation of global society to meet the 'challenge of climate change'. If Pope Francis wants it, the Cult wants it, because the Cult owns him. Italy has been particularly hit by the pandemic hoax with the longest lockdown of all and remember what the Sabbatian-Frankist extremists and 'rabbis' said about the need to destroy 'Edom' – Rome, Italy and Christianity – before their 'Messiah' could arrive. The Cult-owned Pope Francis said of a guaranteed income:

> This may be the time to consider a universal basic wage which would acknowledge and dignify the noble, essential tasks you carry out. It would ensure and concretely achieve the ideal, at once so human and so Christian, of no worker without rights.

You don't give a damn about them Francis, you bloody fraud. The barely survivable 'guaranteed income' (so long as you do what the government tells you) is part of a long-planned new economic, cashless, digital system of total centralised control that I have been warning about for decades. Cash has been systematically demonised during the fake 'pandemic' hysteria on the grounds that handling money can pass on the 'disease' (see insanity). The Cult-owned, Gates-controlled, World Health Organization advised everyone to use contactless digital technology instead of cash to protect themselves from the 'virus'. Better have a cashless society, then, eh? It's so bloody transparent. John Howells, chief executive of Link, which runs Britain's 70,000 cashpoints, said the 'virus' has dramatically sped up the switch from cash to card and online payments and that cash could be almost killed off by the end of the summer as shoppers switch to using cards and never go back. Bill Gates's Microsoft owns the patent for a 'cryptocurrency system using body activity data'. The patent states: 'Instead of massive computation work required by some conventional cryptocurrency systems, data generated [is] based on the body activity of the user ...' A cryptocurrency is 'a digital currency in which encryption techniques are used to regulate the generation of units of currency and verify the transfer of funds, operating independently of a central bank'. Many in the alternative media believed that cryptocurrency was the key to bringing down the elite system when in fact the Cult has been behind it all along. China, the blueprint for the world, responded to the 'pandemic' by launching a digital currency and 'blockchain' (transaction record) system for 'trials'. Cult and Rockefeller insider Dr Richard Day told those paediatricians in *1969* that this very economic system was coming. He is quoted here by paediatrician Lawrence Dunegan:

> The bringing in of the new system he said probably would occur on a weekend in the winter. Everything would shut down on Friday evening and Monday morning when everybody wakened there would be an announcement that the New System was in place. During the process in getting the United States ready for these changes everybody would be busier with less leisure time and less opportunity to really look about and see what was going on around them.

Ticking all the boxes

The Climate Cult and New Wokeness, manipulated by the same force behind the pandemic, disgustingly exploited the 'virus' economic crash to impose the Green New Deal, racism and migrant agendas with the utterly ludicrous Nancy Pelosi-led Democrats insisting that any government financial support must be dependent on companies employing diversity officers and accepting carbon emission targets. New Woke New York Mayor Bill de Blasio linked the 'pandemic' to 'structural racism'. We are truly dealing with heartless psychopathy here and you watch the Climate Cult use the economic fall-out of the 'virus' response to push for deindustrialisation and the Cult's new economic system. The Gate-Davos World Economic Forum published the most pathetically predictable article headed: 'How COVID-19 might help us win the fight against climate change'. You don't say. The author was Victoria Crawford, Project Lead, Environmental Resilience, at the World Economic Forum Geneva. She said:

> While we are reeling in the shock of what is happening around us and coming to terms with our new reality, we could seize this moment as a unique window of opportunity to re-build our society and economy as we want it. With scientists warning we have 10 years left to avoid the worst consequences of climate change, this could offer an opportunity to fix the climate crisis before it's too late. A number of shifts brought on by the COVID-19 emergency lay the groundwork for the transformation required.

Which is, of course, one reason why the virus hoax was perpetrated. Calls soon began for the Marxist, technocratic, 'Green New Deal' to be the foundation of any economic recovery and the almost permanently scowling puppet-child that is Greta Thunberg pronounced: 'Whether we like it or not the world has changed, it looks completely different from how it did a few months ago, and it will probably not look the same again, and we are going to have to choose a new way forward.' Oh, and what way would that be, Greta? *Ahh*, your way – or rather the way of the adults that control you from the shadows. 'If one single virus can destroy economies in a matter of weeks, it shows we are not thinking long term and we are not taking these risks into account', said the saviour of the world. Shakes head, moves on. New York congresswoman Alexandria Ocasio-Cortez, a face of the Green New Deal, surveyed the economic devastation faced by Americans and said of the oil price collapse: 'You absolutely love to see it. This along with record low interest rates means it's the right time for a worker-led mass investment in green infrastructure to save our planet.' The narcissism and lack of self-awareness is breathtaking. Brian May, guitarist with the band Queen, cited eating meat as the cause of the 'virus' as he promoted veganism. May said he had gone into protective isolation early because he 'saw it coming'. I wonder how many have seen him coming? New Woke Germany closed its border to visitors from Europe, but migrants claiming asylum from the Middle East and Africa were still allowed to enter. Something similar was naturally happening in Sweden. Efforts to stop migrants continuing to enter the United States to take well-paid jobs until Americans recovered from the economic hurricane were blocked – of course they were. One Cult agenda could not be allowed to get in the way of another and every opportunity was taken to cash-in on the manipulated panic. George Soros demanded that prisoners be released from jail because of the 'pandemic' to advance his efforts to create the 'jungle environment' described in Cult documents and thousands in jail for serious crime were set free. Typical of the New Woke mentality planned to be unleashed in the wake of the 'pandemic' is British actor Idris Elba who told TV host Oprah Winfrey that the Earth had created the virus to, in effect, punish humanity:

> We've damaged our world. And, you know, it's no surprise that our world is reacting to the human race. It's no surprise that a virus has been created that is going to slow us down and ultimately make us think differently about our world and ourselves … For me, that's a standout thing that's very obvious. This is almost the world's cry out to say 'Hey! You're kicking me! What you're doing is not good. So I'll get rid of you!'

Get the message – humans are *dangerous* and so much so the government says you need to stay six feet away from any of them. Humans are to be feared. They are *horrible*. The ridiculous Elba also told Winfrey that he had tested positive with coronavirus and was 'recovering well' without developing any symptoms. The rather obvious contradiction between the Earth getting rid of humans with a virus from which he was 'recovering well' with no symptoms seemed to pass him by, but then the New Woke mind is good at that. Maybe the Earth is just crap at mass human genocide and leaves it to the Cult. Another ticked box has been the Cult assault on religion (any community group working in mutual support) with churches closed by law – some never to reopen again. This drove a juggernaut through the freedoms enshrined in the American Constitution and the Bill of Rights which were shredded by the Cult and its fascistic operatives and in doing their political goons were acting illegally.

The sequence

The major Cult centre of China came out of the 'pandemic' better than anyone even though the 'virus' is supposed to have started there. Look at the sequence of events and you can make that *because* it started there. It was vital for the pandemic scam to work for the lockdown response blueprint to be secured from the beginning as described in the Rockefeller Foundation pandemic scenario document of 2010. The frenzy about a deadly virus circulating in Wuhan was met with dramatic fascistic lockdowns by the Cult-controlled Chinese authorities with people locked in their homes to die of starvation and others pulled off the streets or from their homes who ended up who knows where? The cases and deaths reported by the Chinese from the 'new virus' suddenly and miraculously started to recede down to a reported *nothing*. This is what can happen when your 'pandemic' is the result of fake diagnosis in a city notorious for respiratory disease because of its profoundly toxic air. Add to this that Wuhan was the first 5G 'smart city' and the potential to fake a health crisis is limitless. I stress that I am not talking about fake as in no one died, but as in what they died *from* and what was causing their symptoms – potentially everything from long exposure to toxic air to particular 5G frequencies. The key was to set in place the perception of the most effective way to respond to the 'virus' when it was said to have spread to the West and Tedros, the Gates-stooge at the World Health Organization, was immediately on-message praising China for its actions and pointing to the Chinese response as how the West should act when the 'deadly virus' arrived. For the Cult deception to succeed this had to be severe lockdowns and the closure of businesses that would collapse the world economy and independent livelihoods. Just as this was being imposed in the West China began its economic recovery to secure more control and power over the ailing Western world. Locked-down Wuhan became locked-down target West (Figs 388 and 389).

Italy was the next media focus of attention to terrify the population in the West, and their out-of-the-loop politicians, with what could be coming to every country. This terror was underpinned by the outrageous death projections pouring off the computers at Imperial College. What they didn't tell you is that the centre of the Italian 'epidemic' of 'Covid-19' was a mirror of Wuhan in terms of infamously toxic air, the subsequent respiratory disease, and exceedingly high death rates. This was a region also recently introduced to 5G. The Italian government locked down the entire country from March 9th, 2020, as cases and deaths increased through fraudulent diagnosis of lung disease by other causes as 'Covid-19'. Public gatherings of every kind were banned including sporting events and all except essential and approved travel. People had to show forms at checkpoints explaining why they were travelling and there were fines of $200 for

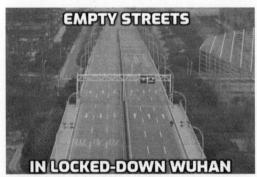

Figure 388: What happened in China would be repeated in other countries – exactly as planned once the blueprint response was created.

Figure 389: Teeming tourists in Venice.

Figure 390: 'Social distancing'.

Figure 391: This is how it works and the 'pandemic' is a classic example.

being outside 'for no reason'. There were threats of long jail sentences for anyone who knowingly had the 'virus' (tested positive for genetic material, not the virus) failing to isolate and 'infecting' others who subsequently died. Law enforcement roamed the empty streets with surveillance drones ensuring compliance with house arrest (Fig 390). It was like a scene – appropriately – from a Hollywood dystopian sci-fi movie and the same sequence followed in other lockdown countries with fines or jail for those leaving their homes without authorisation. What

happened in Italy further embedded the belief that lockdowns were imperative to 'save us' and other countries followed one by one like dominoes falling as they followed the same centrally-dictated Cult script. It's all a mind game. It is amazing how few people and key positions you need to control to dictate policy throughout an entire pyramidal system, be that in terms of government policy or top-down instructions to doctors and medical staff. This is done through a combination of Cult psychopaths (the very few) and clueless people who carry out the policy without question or challenge (Fig 391).

Follow the money – *dependency*

Economies were affected even more seriously by so much global production and supply being handed to China decade after decade by major Cult corporations to take advantage of slave labour while jobs were deleted at home. There is, irony of ironies, an almost total dependence on China for American drugs including antibiotics – a reported 96 percent of which are sourced to China. Similar dependency will be found in other countries. ABC News reported that around *90 percent* of the active ingredients used by American companies in drug manufacturing come from China and some say more. The government-controlled (everything is) official Chinese news service published an article as the 'virus' expanded gloating at the country's control over drug supplies to the United States and speculated on what would happen to Americans if China cut off those supplies. Why would America be so stupid as to become dependent for drugs and other basic products on a country we are told is the 'enemy'? It's not American stupidity in terms of the public, but Cult design through its Big Pharma cartel and compliant politicians while the Cult-controlled media provide cover for the Chinese dictators. The New Woke American media and other extremists said that to call the outbreak the 'Chinese virus' or 'Wuhan virus' was 'racism'. Presidential candidate Joe Biden said referring to the coronavirus as a 'foreign virus' was 'xenophobia'. Criticism of China is racist when the Chinese system is incredibly racist. Observe the New Woke/media theme of protecting the Chinese technocracy whether the subject is the fake 'virus' or 'climate change'. Similar US and global dependency is being manipulated by the hour on Israeli smart and cyber technology with dependency on both China and Israel connected to the same planned outcome. In the end *China* is supposed to win this economic and possible even full-blown 'war', not the United States, with Sabbatian-Frankists out of Israel systematically destroying America to ensure a global society based on the Chinese model. I say 'China' is supposed to win, but I don't mean the country or its people. The Chinese *model* is planned to globally win with the Cult out of Israel at the helm, not the current Chinese dictatorship which answers to the Cult anyway. Look how much stronger China is now in relation to the West than it was before the 'virus' began in China. Claims about a bioweapon released from the Wuhan lab further fuels the fire for conflict with China which is the Cult plan. This does not mean that a bioweapon release (or the *appearance* of one using 60 GHz 5G) is not part of the Cult plan at some point. When the 'prophet' Bill Gates says that a bioweapon could be his 'pandemic 2' to follow what he calls 'pandemic 1' it's important to take note.

Survival response triggered? Yep – now we can do anything

The pandemic scenario is more psychological manipulation playing off the public's fear of death and the unknown to elicit the desired reaction and support for tyranny. An added bonus is that humanity's innate fear of death and the unknown means that large swathes of the population have no problem with the most authoritarian response so long as they believe it will protect them from death and disease. Once the 'virus' hysteria was unleashed what followed was easily predictable as events and actions took on a life and momentum of their own with extreme authoritarian action taken to 'protect the people' amid public fear and panic. Israel, for example, changed the law to allow phones of coronavirus cases to be legally tracked and Google, Apple and other Cult fronts announced they were sharing user location data with governments to track the movements of citizens, detect gatherings and enforce social distancing compliance. France was among the first governments to demand this and others followed. In Britain, Europe, North America and across the world the population was faced with the full imposition of the state (the Cult global state in fact) through police and military – the combination planned for the Hunger Games global society. India began giving indelible hand stamps to people suspected of having the virus. Reuters reported that the Trump White House ordered federal health officials to treat top-level coronavirus meetings as classified which Reuters described as 'an unusual step that has restricted information and hampered the US government's response to the contagion, according to four Trump administration officials'. The classification was apparently ordered in mid-January, 2020, by the National Security Council (NSC) and government officials speaking anonymously were quoted as saying that this prevented experts in the field from taking part in meetings. Other reports have made it clear when dots are connected that the NSC was directing the response to the 'virus' along with the Pentagon and intelligence community which together with government administrators and law enforcement form the fascistic Deep State (owned by the Cult). This should have red flags flying from every pole. Every opportunity was taken to advance all aspects of the Cult agenda I have been exposing for decades. This included restrictions on legally buying guns in the United States with many gun stores forcibly shut down and the ultra-Zionist-owned *New York Times* somehow managing to blame Christians for the 'outbreak'. Clueless politicians just trotted along behind Cult agents and agencies doing whatever they were told.

Divide and rule made literal

Nothing divides a community faster than the fear that others may be carriers of a disease and could give it to you. People have been driven further apart and into further mistrust through what has been dubbed 'social distancing' which is defined as 'reducing the contact people have with each other' to include 'reducing socialising in public places such as entertainment or sports events, reducing our use of non-essential public transport or recommending more home working.' Populations were ordered to stay six feet from each other and not gather in a group of more than two unless they lived in the same home. A quick-step version of the Totalitarian Tiptoe was evident as they swiftly moved through ever more authoritarian measures which had not been considered necessary only days before. I call it the push-the-gate technique. You push the first gate and if there is no resistance you move on to the next one and push that. If there is no resistance you go on to the next, and so on. People were standing in line into the distance outside supermarkets on a one-in, one-out, basis no matter if the sun was shining or it was pouring with rain and blowing a gale (great for health). People just complied without question or challenge. The brainless controlled by the heartless just announced the next stage of the tyranny and like laboratory animals the great majority did whatever they were told. They may be the brainless controlled by the heartless but they are in positions of *authority* and so we must do what they say. Thus, in a sentence, you have the foundation of human control since humans came into existence. A predictable public response followed as panic buying (the survival response) emptied shops of food and other products (Fig 392). I went to a local supermarket which had been normal two days earlier and as I

Figure 392: News report on panic buying. What happens when the reptilian brain survival instinct kicks-in. Never mind the rest of you it's all about ME..

went to walk in a guy on the door who wasn't usually there said that I had to go to the back of the queue. There was so much space between people that I didn't even notice a queue. What queue? I asked. He pointed and there rolling back as far as I could see was this line of people all six feet apart – and this was in a quiet time in the middle of the day. Goodness knows what it was like in the busy periods. I never went back again to find out. Why was this suddenly necessary when it had not been considered to be so throughout the 'virus' hysteria right up to that day? No one seemed to be asking. How easy it is to impose anything in the face of unquestioning compliance (Fig 393).

The police-military state

Draconian laws enforcing these impositions that suspended freedom and democracy were predicted to go on for months, even more than a year, and drive people apart in exactly the way the Cult requires to connect them ever more powerfully in wave-connection relationship with AI technology through which human interaction is conducted during 'social distancing'. The psychology is again that humans are *dangerous* (see 'global warming') and AI technology is *safe*. We should not forget either that while billions can clearly be locked away under house arrest on a global scale their only other means of communication – the Internet – is controlled by Cult agencies and can be switched off any time they choose. *And a few people can't control the world??* Have no illusions that this is part of the plan at some point if we go on acting like rabbits frozen by the headlights of an oncoming truck. Democracy suspended, freedom deleted, but, hey, what's the problem? We have

Figure 393: Freedom deleted – it is so easy. (Image by Neil Hague.)

surely learned from the experience what some of us have been pointing out all along: The police and military are not there to protect human rights and freedom. They are there to impose the will of the state (the few) on the rest of humanity. There are genuine people in the police and military and I most certainly acknowledge that, but alongside them are idiots and psychopaths who have been orgasmic in the new era of unchecked power. To think that some of the moronic people in uniform that have been caught on phone cameras have actually been given power over people's lives. Police (and military in some countries) set up roadblocks to question people on where they were going and why. It was straight from the Nazi/communist playbook for good reason – it *was* fascism/communism or more accurately the fast-emerging police/military state of the Hunger Games Society technocracy.

Streets were tracked by drones straight out of dystopian (pre-emptive programming) movies with some used to bark orders from the air at the public below. Police extremists like those in Derbyshire, England, New York and elsewhere even used drones to track individuals walking in the countryside far from any other human being. In the case of New York and other American states the drones were gifted by *China* which would have access to the data. The UK's Derbyshire police, led by Chief Constable, Peter Goodman, were clearly overcome with excitement at the near-unlimited powers they were given by 'emergency laws'. Goodman's legendary New Woke intellect includes removing Derbyshire Constabulary's male voice choir from any association with his force because they refused to accept women members. It's a *male*-voice choir with a particular sound, but don't waste your breath telling Goodman as he continues to seek help in working that out. Goodman's Derbyshire officers even poured black dye in a beauty spot called the Blue Lagoon to 'deter visitors' from going there and stopped and warned my son, Jaymie, for walking his dog miles away from the next nearest person. They insisted that he walked the dog in his village where there were a lot more people. This made no sense, but it wasn't meant to. Endless and constant examples of such imbecility were imposed to get people used to unquestioned compliance like training a dog not to shit in the house. We even had Nick Adderley, Chief Constable of Northamptonshire in the English Midlands, threatening to have his officers check supermarket trolleys to see if people were buying 'non-essential' items. The level of fascistic idiocy required to make such a statement defies my imagination and at least he was quickly slapped back by political and public reaction. Manchester police connected 'dangerous people' with anyone posting 'conspiracy theories' online. The UK government decreed that people could only leave their homes as little as possible to buy food and to exercise once a day. How could exercising outside 10 times a day be any more 'dangerous' than going out once if you don't go near anyone else? Of course it isn't and how much brain power is required to see that? People were told not to go out in their cars for 'non-essential' travel when the idea that driving alone in a car could possible pass on a 'virus' to anyone is sheer lunacy. The whole nonsensical charade was only to program compliance. I have been out whenever I choose and I have asked for a uniform or dark suit to explain to me how doing that while not going within six feet of anyone can be any more danger than doing so once. I have said I will stop doing that if they can give me a rational, intelligent, credible explanation for why there are added dangers. I am still waiting. Police in 'free Germany' arrested a medical lawyer Beate Bahner, in the southern state of Baden-Württemberg for launching a legal challenge to the lockdown with their version of the Supreme Court and she was held in a mental facility. The Nazis never went away. They just changed their disguise – until now.

This is what happens when you put power-crazed psychopaths and idiots in uniform. The Cult knows that when you give fascist power to the power-crazy they will exploit that and take it to extremes. Psychopaths are naturally attracted to positions of power over others and while there are many decent, genuine police officers there are a very large number of psychopaths in uniform worldwide and this has become obvious in the lockdowns. The authorities and their police enforcers went further by setting up networks for the public to report anyone 'violating lockdown laws' just like the infamous Stasi in Communist East Germany. This was instigated everywhere. Eric Garcetti, the ridiculous and fascistic mayor of Los Angeles, urged the public to 'snitch' on those that 'violated' stay-at-home laws and promised that those that did would be rewarded. He talked about 'hunting down' those that did not comply with his Nazi-like dictates. None of this must be forgotten and enemies of freedom like Garcetti,

Goodman, Adderley, and the long, long list of politicians, officials and law enforcement personnel who have deleted not only human rights, but independent livelihoods, must be held to account and removed from office. They have all shown they cannot be trusted with the most basic freedoms and rights. With so much of the human race little more than software programs responding to 'enter' extraordinary numbers of people were insisting on the deletion of their own freedom and quite willing to report neighbours and others for violating even the fine detail of the fascism. Some even reported neighbours for going into their own garden more than once. You have to be utterly and *totally* unconscious to do that, but you see how tenuous freedom really is when even those who should be demanding it are willing to aid its destruction. Cue Morpheus:

> The Matrix is a system, Neo. That system is our enemy. But when you're inside, you look around, what do you see? Businessmen, teachers, lawyers, carpenters. The very minds of the people we are trying to save. But until we do, these people are still a part of that system and that makes them our enemy. You have to understand, most of these people are not ready to be unplugged. And many of them are so inured, so hopelessly dependent on the system, that they will fight to protect it.

How right that has been shown to be during current events. One woman told the media how she was 'named and shamed' by neighbours on Facebook for not joining in the weekly mass clapping for health workers, most of whom were working hard every day trying to find things to do in near-empty hospitals. She said she missed the (concocted) clapping after a 'rough night with my son' and was told she 'didn't deserve to use the NHS if I or my family get ill'. What a bunch of utter numbskulls. Tell them anything and they will believe it so long as you have a position of authority. All that consciousness always available and yet so little accessed.

The media makes fascism possible (as it did in Germany)

Another group that must be held to account are the mainstream media without which the scam could not have succeeded. Fear and chaos are the Cult's currency of control and the 'virus' propaganda triggered that in unlimited abundance. What people *believe* about a 'danger' is all that matters and the media was deployed as always to terrify the population. I say 'deployed', but most didn't need 'deploying' when their unresearched ignorance did the job without any encouragement. One guy I heard typified the media approach in general worldwide. I switched on the car radio just twice during the hysteria to a show on the UK's TalkRadio station presented by a bloke called Mike Graham who refers to his slot as the *Independent Republic of Mike Graham*. I wonder how 'independent', as in 'not of the system', that the following could be considered. Within seconds of turning on the first time Mr Graham announced that 'Covid-19' was 'the greatest health crisis the world has ever seen'. That would include the Black Death would it, Mr Graham, which wiped out up to 60 per cent of Europe's entire population? What utter garbage. The second time I heard him Graham was immediately into a rant about people whinging over the loss of freedom and talk of troops imposing a lockdown. If that was what the government said must happen we should just accept it, pronounced the 'independent' Mr Graham (Fig 394). This is the same chap who I heard a few months earlier saying that not allowing unvaccinated children to go to school was 'fair enough'. Former CNN host Piers Morgan, a legend in his own mind, screamed (he always screams) that Britain must go into lockdown to 'save lives' because that is what the experts say. Who are these experts, Mr Morgan? What is their background? Do they have an agenda? Who are they connected to? Does what they say about the 'virus' actually make sense in the world of fact rather than unthinking emotion? Such questions would not have breached his *'I am right'* narcissism, but the consequences for the population, in terms of livelihoods and freedom, have been utterly catastrophic. Morgan and Graham were fine, though, because they were designated by the government to be doing 'essential work' which I define in this case as propaganda. The Morgans and Grahams live in the permanent illusion (like most of their profession) that they are 'journalists' and we had best leave them to their self-delusion and move on. Press-enter people should not be journalists because press-enter people cannot *be* journalists. Proper journalists

Figure 394: How the few control the many and the global media.

don't press enter – they question everything. Instead we have fake 'journalists' helping to perceptually program great swathes of the global population that also question nothing.

Even more sinister than the merchants of repeated government propaganda are those in the media who have actively worked to undermine and censor those outside the mainstream who are willing to engage in real journalism. The BBC has been among the worst which will shock very few and none with a mind of their own. The Corporation is funded by a compulsory annual 'licence fee' so the public can be forced to provide the funds for this department of government to program the same public with the official version of everything. Licence-fee payers are funding their own perceptional programming and they may consider that it's time to stop. First of all you simply cannot be a journalist by any proper definition and work for the BBC and the mainstream in general, but especially with organisations like the BBC. A proper journalist looks at all claims and information and then investigates to see if they stand up to scrutiny. Those findings are then communicated without any spin or censorship. By contrast the BBC does not employ journalists. They employ parrots of the government narrative. BBC and other mainstream 'journalists' must operate within clearly defined parameters which means there is a huge array of possibility that they cannot investigate, pursue or communicate. To do so would see the information blocked before ever going to air or getting in a newspaper. If something did slip through in a live situation it would be career suicide. I should also define what I mean by 'official' and 'government' narrative. The BBC often claims to be accused of bias by both Left and Right and so accusations of systematic bias to one side cannot be justified. Oh, but it *can*. I am not saying the BBC is institutionally biased to a *political* government, but to the *permanent* government or Cult government. Often the Cult narrative will coincide with the political government of the day, as with the unquestioning repetition of the official 'pandemic' story; but at other times the BBC will be at odds with the political government like it was with the Boris Johnson government over Brexit and is with any government that does not slavishly sing from the climate change song sheet. I cannot think of a single aspect of the Cult agenda – orchestrated through the permanent government – that the BBC has not promoted while censoring or marginalising alterative views.

All these strands came together in a report by a BBC 'journalist' called Leo Kelion about YouTube deleting my interview with London Real during the 'virus' hysteria. First of all he took the 5G angle which was only a relatively small part of the conversation and tried to link what I said with people who were claimed to have damaged 5G masts in a protest against the affects. Kelion then said that I 'falsely claimed' there is a link between 5G and the 'health crisis'. This was the 'crisis' happening amid empty hospitals that he would not have dared to acknowledge. He had no idea if it was 'false' or not and he merely entrained his 'mind' as always with establishment sources. If Kelion ever did research the subject properly and see through his own 'fake news' he would never be allowed to say so on the BBC and if he tried he would be out the door. He knows that and behaves like a good little boy with an eye on the mortgage. Meanwhile, Ofcom, the government broadcast regulator, had threatened any outlet that allowed even discussion of the possible link between 5G and the 'virus'. Why? Because there *is* one, that's why. Kelion and his like would not dream of rising from their knees and ceasing to worship and pay homage to the government appointed Ofcom chief, the patron saint of censorship and freedom deletion, Melanie Dawes. He's a good lad, a perfect BBC asset – he does what he's told and knows his place. Most sinister, however, was the way he described how YouTube 'changed its rules after the BBC questioned why the video was permitted'. He questioned 'why the video was *permitted*'??An excuse-for-a-journalist working for a publicly-funded broadcaster played a part in the censorship of freedom of speech?? Extraordinary. No one who seeks to censor freedom of expression or asks why it was not done can even come close to being a journalist. Real journalists are in the frontline of demanding freedom for everyone – including those they don't agree with. The BBC 'competitor' known as ITV (*Independent* Television, I kid you not) did something similar. It said that 'shortly after ITV News contacted Facebook, the video was removed for breaking misinformation rules'. I guess that was just a coincidence was it? Fake journalists help to get real journalism silenced. ITV mirrored the BBC line with 'Facebook has followed YouTube in removing a video of conspiracy theorist David Icke falsely linking coronavirus and 5G'. What research had the writer done on the subject? *None.* How did ITV or Facebook know what was 'misinformation? Facebook had the answer: 'The World Health Organization (WHO) are providing us with clear guidance on what misinformation in relation to Covid-19 could lead to real-world harm.' What can you do except laugh? Newspapers covered the story in much the same way including a 'journalist' on the London *Sun*, Charlotte Edwards. The *Sun* is owned by Rupert Murdoch (as is Mike Graham's TalkRadio) and Murdoch newspapers in Australia played a major role in getting me banned from the country by an Immigration Minister, David Coleman, who admitted in 'his' judgement that I had done nothing wrong on any of my previous long list of speaking tours. Edwards said that I made 'the false claim that a coronavirus vaccine will include nanotechnology microchips'. Ms Edwards does not have a clue if the statement is false or not. I have been researching the subject for 30 years – she has not been researching it for 30 seconds. This is still more confirmation that the mainstream media does not employ real journalists and they most certainly will never be employed by anything to do with Murdoch. Then the (Gates-connected) Comcast, NBCUniversal-owned CNBC in the United States bragged that its intervention had led to Spotify deleting one of my 'virus' interviews. All this effort by the 'all-mighty Elite' just to stop 'little me'. Actually, to go to these lengths over one man shows that they are not 'mighty' at all as they desperately sought to remove all trace of me while at every stage they were giving me more credibility and gathering ever more support for my work. No amount of evil can prevail over one open heart.

Banned by YouTube and Facebook – the sequence

The classic 'coming out' of a 'journalist' censor was an Israel-obsessed bloke called Nick Cohen on the London *Guardian* website who writes a column for its sister paper, the *Observer*. These are the most New Woke of UK papers along with the hilariously-named *Independent*. The *Guardian* and *Observer* take every *permanent* government narrative and repeat it as Gospel truth while promoting themselves as 'radical' and 'of the Left'. Among the funders of the *Guardian* group is Bill Gates who also gives money to the BBC, ABC and National Public Radio in the United States, and a list of other media. This Nick Cohen chap said with no evidence whatsoever that I was a danger to public health and that I should be banned from YouTube and social media and then went on to repeat the permanent government narrative in archetypal *Guardian/Observer* fashion. He's entitled to his opinion – he just doesn't think that others should be given the same freedom. I support his right to free speech while he wants to delete mine. Which of us is an agent of tyranny, one could legitimately ask? Cohen described what I say as 'toxic lies' and called for government censor Ofcom to be given the power to censor YouTube content in the same way that it does with UK broadcasters. He also lamented the fact that a video of mine entitled 'Is there a virus?' was still allowed to be seen by the public. The man writing this is under the bizarre impression that he is a 'journalist'. Anyone buying the *Guardian* or *Observer* is not taking themselves seriously and the reason newspapers are now struggling to survive is that ever-larger swathes of the public have both sussed the real role of mainstream newspapers and media and gone beyond them in terms of understanding the world. Their days are over and they have been their own executioner. Suicide I think they call it. One other point relates to Cult-asset Wikipedia and the relentless recorded visits to my page during the 'pandemic' by the 'notorious' Wikipedia 'editor' known as 'Philip Andrew Cross'. Don't fall for the 'people's encyclopaedia' crap – Wikipedia is controlled by very few people. One Internet article described 'Cross' in this way:

> He's the obsessive, at it night-and-day, 365-days a year Wikipedia editor and online stalker whose account is used to pursue personal and political vendettas, but who, despite great publicity in the spring of 2018 about his activities, which included articles in many media outlets and a BBC World Service radio documentary, is still persecuting people – (or allowing people to be persecuted from his account), on a daily basis.

At the time of writing the Philip Cross account had made a staggering 159,607 Wikipedia edits in a fifteen-year period. Incredibly the Cross account did not take a single day off from editing Wikipedia from 29th August 2013 to 14th May 2018. Not even on five consecutive Christmas Days …

Well, old 'Cross'(clearly more than one person) seemed to be obsessed with my page when I began to challenge the 'virus' narrative and to give you an example 'he' took just 19 minutes after Nick Cohen tweeted his 'ban Icke' article for it to be added to my Wikipedia page. They think they are so clever when they're really hilarious. I just laugh and hope that one day, through trial and error, they might get a life. Cohen headed his tweet with archetypal New Woke self-delusion and inversion: 'The *liberal* case for banning David Icke' (my emphasis). You see what I mean about hilarious. When you have been researching the global conspiracy as long as I have, you recognise recurring patterns and sequences. Cohen's article felt to me like the start of something aimed at getting me deleted from mainstream platforms. He is an ultra-Zionist who sees 'anti-Semitism' everywhere and has attacked Jewish people with a mind of their own about Israel. The Canary website dubbed Cohen a 'rancid hate-goblin' for doing so. The label 'anti-Semite' is constantly used to silence those exposing getting too close to the truth and it is the calling card of the Jew-hating Sabbatian-Frankist network of the Cult. I am not saying that people like Cohen know they are serving the interests of the Sabbatian-Frankists – I would certainly not credit him with the intelligence or awareness to know that; but in his obsession with labelling critics of the Sabbatian-Frankist government of Israel as 'anti-Semites' this is what he is doing and there is a whole vast network doing the same in various levels of knowledge of the agenda they are serving from zero to totally in the loop.

Pretty much immediately after Cohen's demand that I be deleted from YouTube and social media platforms came the 'campaign' to secure the same end by a strange group called The Center for Countering Digital Hate (CCDH). This is a man and a dog organisation registered as a private limited British company while using the American spelling of 'Center' in its title. The CCDH is funded by the ultra-Zionist Pears Foundation which is a big red flag to me and its patron is a D-list UK 'celebrity', another ultra-Zionist sees-anti-Semitism-everywhere character called Rachael Riley. The Pears Foundation established the Pears Institute for the Study of Antisemitism in 2010 and has a funding partnership with the ultra-Zionist Charles and Lynn Schusterman Foundation. Lynn Schusterman was born a Rothschild. Another funder of this bunch of prats at 'Digital Hate' is Unbound Philanthropy which has links to George Soros and his Open Society Foundations. Unbound

Philanthropy is described as a 'New York City-based left-wing [New Woke] donor affinity group that primarily funds groups that support left of centre liberal expansionist immigration policies'. I guess after reading the book this far you won't be shocked. The serious American connections to the Center for Countering Digital Hate would explain the spelling of 'Center' in the name of a 'UK' company. Taryn Higashi, Executive Director of Unbound Philanthropy, sits on a Soros Open Society Foundations advisory board and specialises in promoting immigration and 'refugee issues'. Yet another use-'anti-Semitism'-to-silence-your-targets operation in the UK is Hope not Hate, which I say should be more accurately called 'Hate not Hope'. They have sought to have me censored by ironically hurling hate in my direction and they are vocal supporters of the Center for Countering Digital Hate. Purely by coincidence you understand Hate Not Hope has been funded by … Unbound Philanthropy. Further Digital Hate funders include the Barrow Cadbury Trust, Joseph Rowntree Charitable Trust and the Laura Kinsella Foundation.

Soon after Nick Cohen's *Observer* article Digital Hate produced a 'report' on how many people had seen my information on YouTube and social media about the 'pandemic' and demanded that I be deleted. They estimated '30 million', but they were way too low in their numbers. The 'report' was outrageous in its inaccuracies and manipulation of information. Among those acknowledged for their input were Dr Daniel Allington of Kings College London; Dr Rob Ford, University of Manchester, Jonathan Sebire from something called 'Signify', and Dr Siobhain McAndrew, University of Bristol, who is a director of the Center for Countering Digital Hate. Signify is an 'ethical science data company' that clearly believes that 'ethics' should include silencing people they don't agree with and it apparently wants 'to show the world that AI and big data can build social empathy and inspire better products and policies'. Meanwhile Sebire, who appeared to be obsessed with people staying at home, was showing the world he doesn't give a damn about freedom of speech and opinion. The Digital Hate rabble announced they would now seek to have me banned from all mainstream Internet using the hashtag #DeplatformIcke. They claim to be an 'anti-hate' organisation and yet targeted me for what I was saying about the pandemic hoax. Ugh? Why? To serve their masters, of course, who just want me silenced by any means or excuse. Almost immediately afterwards while Digital Hate was crowing pathetically that they had '800 signatures' on a petition (wow!) Facebook pulled my page with three quarters of a million followers (despite the seriously extreme shadow banning and suppression of numbers that went on for five years) and YouTube deleted my channel and all my videos. In doing so they denied nearly a million subscribers from seeing them. The 'petition' was signed by such intellectual giants as MP Damian Collins, as well as 'celebrity' TV medics Dr Christian Jessen, Dr Dawn Harper and Dr Pixie McKenna who all appear in a television series called *Embarrassing Bodies*. It ought to be called simply *Embarrassing* surely? This is the same Christian Jessen who said in a media report on March 13th, 2020, that Italian people were using the coronavirus outbreak as an excuse to have a 'long siesta'. He said of the 'virus': 'I think it's an epidemic lived out more in the press than in reality … I mean if you think about flu right, without getting too heavy, flu kills thousands every single year.' He added: 'This is like a bad cold really, let's be honest.' He then signs a petition to have me banned for underplaying the danger of the 'virus'. Yes, words fail me, too. D-list TV 'celebrity' Rachael Riley, patron of the Digital Hate group, tweeted on news of my ban:

> The hate preacher was banned from Australia. Big arenas have rejected him, yet social media orgs allow him a megaphone (& pocket the profits). Facebook have finally deleted him today!!

She's a lovely lady, so kind, so supportive of human rights, and believes passionately in freedom – for herself. She didn't mention of course that the other bans she refers to were the result of the same lies and disinformation by the same global network. I have seen the pattern so many times of man and a dog organisations being set up to demand something and then getting what they demand. YouTube of the fascism-facilitating Susan Wojcicki said they deleted decades of my videos because they had received a 'complaint'. Oh, you mean the one you knew was coming, Ms Wojcicki? Facebook said that I had breached its 'community standards' (delete anyone challenging the narrative of the deeply corrupt Gates WHO) by posting 'health misinformation that could cause physical harm'. It was straight out of the Event 201 'simulation' run by the Gates Foundation six weeks before the 'virus pandemic' began.

The 'Digital Hate' silence-Icke network

People who support my work worldwide in the now hundreds of millions at least were naturally furious and the Center for Countering Digital Hate Twitter page was inundated. A supporter began to investigate the organisation, nominally headed by 'chief executive' Imran Ahmed. Their website included an 'Our People' section that consisted only of images of Ahmed with one of Rachel Riley taking a selfie with him. The organisation has many connections and the citizen journalist uncovered that two of its directors (they keep changing) – plus CEO Ahmed – were people with extremely close connections to the UK Labour Party of 'leader' Keir Starmer, who I said earlier lives on his knees with his tongue extended pointing to Tel Aviv. One of the Digital Hate directors named by the group is Morgan McSweeney – *campaign manager to Starmer* in his bid for the leadership. McSweeney is a central player in Labour Together Ltd, 'a group of committed Labour members, supporters and politicians', based at the same address as the Center for Countering Digital Hate – Langley House, Park Road, East Finchley, London. The Labour Party was hijacked by ultra-Zionism and Sabbatian-Frankists during the spineless lack of leadership of the previous incumbent, Jeremy backbone-deleted Corbyn. Labour Together's leading light and director is the ultra-Zionist Trevor Chinn, funder of ultra-Zionist arse-licker Labour figures like Tony Blair, Ruth Smeeth, Liz Kendall, Tom Watson and Keir Starmer. The Labour Party is further controlled by a group called Momentum which is the work of Zionists Jon Lansman, James Schneider and Adam Klug. Momentum has also campaigned to have me silenced and produced a video claiming that criticism and exposure of the House of Rothschild is 'anti-Semitism'. Exposure of a global elite banking family is a no-go area to a group that supposed to represent the working class? But you get what is really going on. I say 'group'. In fact all these 'groups' that I've mentioned, including 'Digital Hate', are private limited companies.

Another Digital Hate director is Kirsty McNeil who was a Senior Advisor at 10 Downing Street for three years and a speechwriter for Labour Party Prime Minister Gordon Brown. Having unfortunately heard some of his speeches she obviously wasn't very good. She is now Executive Director of Policy, Advocacy and Campaign at Save the Children UK and a director of the Holocaust Educational Trust. It turns out that 'Chief Executive' Imran Ahmed has 'worked as a political advisor to senior Labour politicians from across Labour's political spectrum for eight years, including in three elections and two referendums'. He wrote a book with Labour MP for Wallasey, Angela Eagle, called *The New Serfdom* which I guess must include censoring those that challenge The System. The emergence of the Center for Countering Digital Hate involved a further recurring pattern. The first mention appears to have come predictably in the *Guardian* on September 18th, 2019, in an article headlined: 'The Best Way to Deal With Online Trolls, Do Like Rachel Riley and Starve Them of Oxygen'. Another appeared on the BBC website – equally predictably. One commentator said: 'It certainly is remarkable that major news outlets would be interested in the launch of a brand new NGO with no track record, which means that the CCDH is clearly very well connected.' Oh, just a little bit. It is part of a vast worldwide web of censorship – see Postscript for more on this.

The BBC and others allowed this rabble to attack me without ever asking for a reply or setting up a debate with me. The same is true of the entire mainstream media even throughout the furore about what I was saying and the multiple bans that were happening. I could be attacked and demonised at will without even a right of reply. What gutless and compromised people they are who masquerade as 'journalists'. The Brain of Britain that is TalkRadio's 'independent' Mike Graham attacked me for 'scaremongering' over what I was saying about the pandemic scam and its goal of global control. Naturally he never had me on to debate with him. Rupert Murdoch and Ofcom's Melanie Dawes would have smacked his bum. To show just how out of touch and meaningless the mainstream media has become with its falling audiences a third interview I did with London Real about the 'virus' and the reason it was being hoaxed got a massive audience worldwide – said to be more than a million – when streamed through non-YouTube sources. Ironically the interview was also streamed live on YouTube and apparently attracted the biggest live-stream audience in the world on the platform that day before Susan Wojcicki adjusted her spinning knicker gussets, screamed very loudly, and had it pulled. Next the ultra-Zionist and Labour Party-dominated Center for Countering Digital Hate produced another 'report' demanding that London Real and others who have even *interviewed* me should be deleted in the same way and all videos with me on any other YouTube channel be taken down. Fascism, anyone? This is the road to Orwell's 'unperson' – someone whose existence was erased from all records. This is how terrified the Cult is of me and with good reason. I am their worst nightmare and every day they confirm that with their desperation to silence me.

Neocon NewsGuard

The Digital Hate group didn't manage to get Twitter to pull my account and so along came another elite censorship front called 'NewsGuard'. I received this email from a Kendrick McDonald, NewsGuard's 'Deputy Editor of Rapid Response'. When I had finished laughing at such a ludicrous title I got round to read what it said:

> My name is Kendrick and I'm a reporter with NewsGuard, a service that reviews the credibility and transparency of websites. I'm reaching out because we are publishing a report highlighting Twitter accounts with high follower counts who have shared what we have found to be COVID-19 misinformation to their large audiences.

> We are including David Icke's Twitter account based on posts reviewed by NewsGuard that have falsely connected 5G technology to the spread of coronavirus.

> If David Icke has an on-the-record comment in response, or if you have one

on his behalf, please let me know as soon as possible. We intend to publish our report the morning of Thursday, May 7 (EST).

I pointed out that being a 'reporter' or 'journalist' and working for NewsGuard was a contradiction in terms and it was simply not possible to do both. I asked him to send me the 'evidence' he had – with sources – that what I posted on Twitter was disinformation and I would not accept as a 'source' that 'the authorities said'. As the book goes to print nearly two months later I am still waiting. Americans Gordon Crovitz and Steven Brill co-founded NewsGuard. Crovitz is former publisher of *The Wall Street Journal* and Executive Vice President of Dow Jones, current member of the Council on Foreign Relations (CFR), and on the board of the American Association of Rhodes Scholars. I mentioned the CFR earlier in the book as a Cult front within the London-based Round Table secret society network and Rhodes Scholars are named after Cecil Rhodes, the Rothschild agent who was the first head of the Round Table and plundered southern Africa for the Rothschilds. Rhodes Scholarships to Oxford University are awarded to those handpicked to serve the elite as adults. Bill Clinton has been among them. Gordon Crovitz has connections to the Neocon American Enterprise Institute with its close associations in mutual ideology and personnel with the 9/11 and 'war on terror' Project for the New American Century. Steven Brill is a Zionist lawyer, journalist, and 'entrepreneur'. He and Crovitz say they created NewsGuard to stop 'fake news' when the real reason is to protect the real fake news by downgrading and demonising websites that expose the real fake news spewing from the official narratives by the minute. Hence NewsGuard squeezed out from under its stone to target me. The following day after the NewsGuard contact a fulfilment company called James and James in Northampton, England, which had been delivering my books to customers for five years with not a problem suddenly told us they were cancelling the contract. They sent us an email out of nowhere that was not even addressed 'Dear Jaymie' when my son had worked directly with them the whole five years. The email was from 'CEO' James Hyde, co-owner with another bloke called James Strachan. It said:

Dear Sir/Madam,

Whilst we appreciate the rights of free speech within the UK, our business does not support the views held by David Icke and does not wish to be associated with those points of view, or David Icke Books in general.

I wonder how many customers would want to work with a company that would deliver their product – in this case books – for five years and then tell them out of the blue that they are no longer going to do so because 'our business does not support the views held by you and does not wish to be associated with those points of view, or you in general'. So why did they not think this for five years and only in the middle of a war to silence me and my work coming from all angles? Well, obviously the question answers itself and it is the very spinelessness and lack of integrity displayed by this pair that allows the few to control the many. *The Answer* was not published and they had no idea what the content was anyway and so they were 'not supporting' views in books they had actually been delivering for *five years*. Pressure had been put on them and they dissolved like a snowball in the sunshine out of pure self-interest – end of story. They couldn't even be honest about it. Only a few weeks earlier James and James had secured investment of £11 million from a company called LDC, part of Lloyds Banking Group. The chairman of Lloyds Banking Group is Conservative Party politician Lord Norman Blackwell who serves on the board of *Ofcom* that has sought through its CEO Melanie Dawes to silence me and exposure of 5G which it enthusiastically promotes in an extraordinary conflict of interest. Are these two James chaps really saying that their company will only fulfil orders for books and other products with which they personally agree? Maybe other potential customers might ask if that is the attitude they want to be associated with. I wish I had a pound for every time I have seen the words 'whilst we appreciate the rights of free speech' being followed by support for destroying them. They will have to live with that decision now for the rest of their lives. I wish them well because I couldn't.

In the same period that I was being banned and deleted in all directions by Cult diktat the super intelligence that is Polly Boiko of Russian station RT re-emerged seven months after she interviewed me for a broadcast 'in a few days' which had never seen the light of day. She wrote an article on the RT website giving an account of our meeting all those months earlier, but still without using the interview. She couldn't believe that the establishment was really frightened of me while at the same time somehow ignoring the fact that the establishment was engaged in a frenzy of deletion of my work. Boiko's most memorable line in her patronising garbage was this: '…from the secret web controlling our every move to the perils of vaccines (there aren't any perils, by the way).' Those words were actually written by a 'journalist' while the Vaccine Court in the United States alone had already paid out $4.2 billion in vaccine injury and death compensation against a ridiculously high bar to prove your case. These are the people telling you what is going on in the world, ladies and gentlemen. Yeah, I weep, too.

By contrast one mainstream television station called London Live did run an interview that I did with London Real at the start of the 'pandemic' scare in Britain which YouTube had not then deleted. Well, their fellow 'journalists' in the mainstream and the regulator Ofcom, so beloved of Nick Cohen, simply could not move for severely twisted knickers and running in all directions at the same time while shouting 'fire'. Ofcom 'imposed a sanction' on the London Live station for broadcasting 'potentially harmful content about the coronavirus pandemic' by which they meant that my interview actually broadcast potentially harmful content about the mendacious official story – which Ofcom exists to defend and clearly Nick Cohen, too. The government censor said: 'While Ofcom acknowledges that Icke has a right to hold and express these views [it doesn't], they risked causing significant harm to viewers who may have been particularly vulnerable at the time of broadcast.' What harm would that be, oh Goddess of Censorship, Melanie Dawes? She doesn't say. Ofcom said that it was 'particularly concerned' by my comments 'casting doubt on the motives behind official health advice to protect the public from the virus' – a line that 'journalist' Cohen also emphasised. No one must ever cast doubt on the motives of officialdom even though their actions have destroyed the lives and livelihoods of billions and their lie after lie that a child could take apart. In that one sentence Ms Dawes and Ofcom you have revealed all we need to know about you and what your job really is. The same goes for Gates, Zuckerberg, Brin, Page, Wojcicki, Levinson and Cook at Apple, Musk, Soros, Bezos, the bloody lot of them. One other thing to mention is the role of clickbait sites claimed to be part of the 'alternative' media which make up stories using made up 'writers' quoting made up people and are easily discredited by elite-serving 'fact-checkers'. In doing so, they discredit in the eyes of many the genuine alternative media. Two of the worst are Los Angeles-based Yournewswire.com and NewsPunch.com (owned by the same people) which turn out knowingly fake stories credited to a 'writer' called 'Baxter Dmitry' who doesn't exist. To think that those that own those sites would do this given what humanity is facing is beyond my comprehension.

What next?

The question of where we go from here unless people wake up fast was laid out earlier in the book even before the 'pandemic' hoax broke cover in China and I will focus here on the 'what next?' in relation to the 'virus' deceit. Having secured so much of its global Orwellian nightmare since the turn of 2020 the Cult will want to retain as much of its new police-military state as possible even when public pressure, defiance of the lockdown, and ever-gathering revelations about the nature of the hoax, force some respite from the worst extremes. They will certainly seek to limit gatherings to avoid mass protest with YouTube and Silicon

Valley censoring footage of any protests on the grounds of 'encouraging illegal activity'. The Cult makes the laws and then bans challenge to them or even videos recording any challenge. 'New waves' of the 'virus' will follow and especially just before the Gates vaccine is ready to be imposed globally. These may even appear again to come out of China. 'Researchers' in Cult-owned China said the 'virus' they have never isolated would keep 'returning in waves every year just like the flu'. We'd better have permanent lockdown then, right? Watch for protesters against the lockdowns being blamed for subsequent 'waves'. You will hear claims about the 'virus' mutating into other strains and that 'recovering' from the 'virus' does not infer immunity so making the case that everyone must be vaccinated even those who have 'had the disease'. People do not have 'immunity' to 'Covid-19' because there is no 'Covid-19' and how can they not keep testing positive when the test is for a genetic code in their body and not a 'disease'? How do you develop immunity to a genetic code that is not a 'disease'? See how much control you have of a situation when you invent a 'virus' that doesn't exist. Gates has already revealed the Cult strategy with his arrogant pronouncement that nothing can go back to 'normal' until the entire human population has been injected with the long-planned, carefully-prepared and Gates-funded toxic shite and nanochips. He has been supported in this no-normal-till-a-vaccine by ultra-Zionist Ezekiel Emanuel, Vice Provost for Global Initiatives at the University of Pennsylvania and hilariously chair of the Department of Medical Ethics and Health Policy. Emanuel's father was a member of the terrorist group Irgun which bombed and terrorised Israel into existence in 1948 and he's the brother of former Chicago mayor Rahm Emanuel, long-time Svengali ('a person who exercises a controlling influence on another, especially for a sinister purpose') to President Barack Obama. Ezekiel Emanuel also seems to have a problem with old people living for as long as possible. He said the lockdowns had to continue until a vaccine was found: 'The truth is we have no choice.' US TV host Tucker Carlson delivered a brilliant reply:

> When a political operative like Zeke Emanuel, someone with a long history of lying, begins a sentence with 'the truth is' you should probably be on guard. When he ends that sentence with 'we have no choice' you should be terrified.

Just as the pressure was mounting to end the lockdowns the Gates-funded Professor Neil Ferguson and Imperial College, who prompted the lockdowns with shockingly inaccurate computer model projections, produced more 'models' in an effort to stop the lockdowns being rolled back. Ferguson said at the end of April before being forced to resign over his lover's visits that at least 100,000 could die in the UK by the end of the year if a gradual lockdown was implemented only to shield the elderly. He said it was impossible to send the young and healthy back to work while keeping the vulnerable in lockdown without seeing a huge increase in deaths. 'Professor Ferguson said some degree of social isolation will continue to be required until a vaccine to the killer bug is released', *Mail Online* reported. This man's doom-laden interventions at just the right time to secure the lockdowns and then his attempts to stop a roll-back surely cannot be explained away purely by idiocy and he must be subject to an open and independent public inquiry for the absolute catastrophic mayhem and human devastation that his 'models' have created. The same goes for the Cult-controlled Johns Hopkins operation in the United States that took part in the Gates 'simulation' Event 201, ran its own one called Clade X and has circulated the blatantly and shockingly false death figures to media and public worldwide. The Gates crowd are pressing for a vaccine to 'save us' from a 'virus' never proved to exist and even if you do accept its existence one which has remarkably low death rates only made possible by fixing the death certificates and numbers. For the Cult mass vaccine plan to succeed, played out through Gates, this information must be kept from the great majority of the global population through ever-more severe censorship by Cult media organisations. My banned videos which are now estimated to have been seen by tens of millions worldwide thanks to circulation by 'The People' have helped to throw a spanner in that works and this book will contribute still further. Please circulate news of the videos and this book to as many as you can.

Food control

Another crucial aspect of the Cult plan for total control is to manipulate a global food shortage to allow them to dictate all food distribution and who gets to eat. This will be decided by the level of unquestioning compliance. So how comforting it is that the Gates Foundation is 'partnering' (funding) the UK Department for International Development in work on 'food security'. Phew. The groundwork for food shortages is already well underway and includes driving independent farmers out of business and off the land – something that the 'pandemic' lockdowns will do in great numbers. Farmers have lost their markets by the closure of restaurants and hotels while other supply chains and markets have not replaced them. At the same time there are enormous and ever-growing numbers of hungry people. Ten thousand cars lined up overnight on one occasion alone in San Antonio, Texas, hoping to get something to eat from a food bank which was already unable to cope with demand as with others across the world. Produce rots on the trees and in the ground as farmers go under and the population goes hungry. One farmer said: 'We are being forced to

plough under vegetable crops from coast to coast.' It's all coldly
calculated to create mass dependence and control through hunger even
famine. Eventually 'food' is planned to be only synthetic and strictly
rationed as the new synthetic human emerges thanks to nano-chips from
the vaccine and other sources fusing the human body with technology
and AI. Guess who is partnering with Cult 'food' giant Tyson Foods to
promote laboratory-produced synthetic 'meat'? Yes, *Bill Gates*. The
focussed and concerted attack on restaurants, cafes and other
independent food outlets are part of this attempt to control and
transform 'food'.

Then there is 5G. The power of 5G transmissions will increase
exponentially the more it is expanded and 5G devices are in use. The
effect on human health and psychology will expand at the same rate.
These effects, which can be made to be severe, will be dubbed 'the virus'
– 'Covid-19' or others – and be used to justify further lockdowns. I still
have in mind those, on the face of it, crazy increases in hospital bed
capacity and mega-mortuaries when the 'virus' does not begin to justify
that. Maybe it's all just to ramp up the fear; or maybe it's not. 5G at
particular frequencies like 60 GHz has the potential to run riot with
human health and psychology. People must demand that 5G is switched
off and not take no for an answer. Pandemics are not the only dice that
the Cult is going to throw – there will be shocks and challenges and
reasons to fear of all kinds as they seek to sprint for their finishing line of
total control; but we can be bigger and more powerful than they are. We
simply have to make that choice.

A peaceful revolution of mass non-cooperation with our own
enslavement is urgently required to state the very obvious. Indeed
'urgent' understates speed at which we must respond. As I write protest
and defiance of lockdown is beginning to mount, but we have to
demand and accept nothing less than truly independent inquiries into
what has happened and all those involved brought to book and sent to
jail for the rest of their 'human' lives. Ultra-Zionist Democrat Adam
Schiff has already made moves to hijack any inquiry in the United States
in the way that happened after 9/11 when those involved in those
attacks also oversaw the 'inquiry' into them (see *The Trigger*). Schiff
needs to be told this is not happening this time around and he can fuck
off. Gates should not only be jailed, but have his mega-billions
confiscated and shared out among those whose lives and livelihoods he
and those he represents have destroyed. It is not only time for The
People just 'to sing' as in *Les Misérables*, but to *roar*. Peacefully, yes, but
ROAR in non-cooperation with our own enslavement. Nothing less will
do.

* See Postscript for 'virus' updates and this is best read before the
final chapter.

CHAPTER SEVENTEEN

What is *The Answer*?

Yesterday I was clever, so I wanted to change the world.
Today I am wise, so I am changing myself – Rumi

The Answer has multiple strands, but one central core. Change what is happening at the core and everything else must change. This cause and effect is so simple that it will be dismissed by many in the belief that *The Answer* to the apparent complexity of human control must be equally complex. No, no, no. That's what the Cult wants us to think.

The control system itself is not really complex, anyway, when you break it down to fundamentals. Its foundation is the manipulation of human perception and emotion into low-vibrational states and the entanglement of the waves emitted by those states with the frequency band controlled by the Cult. Through this connection the Cult further impacts on human perception and emotion in an ongoing feedback loop. *Gotcha* (Fig 395). That's it really. All the perceived complexities are spin offs from that connection through entanglement. These include everything from psychopathy, conflict and division to depression, anxiety and addiction. All result from the Cult mentality (psychopathy), the consequences for the population (depression/anxiety), and the desperation to escape from the effect (addiction). There are two ways to deal with a problem. You can seek a solution or remove the cause. Search for solutions and you will see complexity. Identify the cause and you will see simplicity. While we are in a low-vibrational state of perception and consciousness we remain enslaved in the low-vibrational Archontic simulation. When we expand into higher-vibrational states we reconnect with levels of awareness

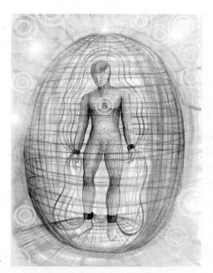

Figure 395: Locked away in the human eggshell of solidified perception. (Image by Neil Hague.)

outside the simulation which then stops dictating all our perceptions and the world as it really is – and *we* really are – comes into focus. Many 'gurus' and 'spiritual teachers' will tell you (often for their own benefit) that the way to achieve such expansion of consciousness is also complex. We must embark on quests, fasting, meditation, yoga, and lots of communal rituals, endless 'workshops', and green tea. I beg to differ. All those things are fine if people choose to go that way and I'm sure they can be helpful to many; but expanding your consciousness to breach the firewalls of the Cult is far simpler and requires just *one* change – your self-identity.

What you *think* you are makes you *what* you are in terms of life experience, behaviour, perception, emotion and the nature of the waves that you emit as frequency projections of what you *think* you are. Self-identity is the Cult's Holy Grail because it knows that everything else comes from that. For centuries it has used religion to sell a self-identity of powerless subordinates to a demanding 'god' (the Cult and its unseen masters). Do what your 'god' wants or face the fires of hell and our agents (most unknowingly) in long frocks will tell you what 'god' wants, or rather what *we* want. Many versions of what I call the 'God Program' have been created and subdivided. This again presents the illusion of complexity when the God Program is deadly simple whatever name may appear on the temple door or 'holy book'. Observe any religion and it's the same blueprint: A version of 'god' or the 'gods' is invented through a holy book, text or legend, and men in frocks, now sometimes women, tell you what 'god' or the 'gods' demand and the consequences of disobedience. Christianity, Islam, Judaism, and Hinduism are all the same in their foundation structure and method of operation. Jewish influence on society and self-identity is way beyond its 0.2 percent of the world population and a key reason is the perceptual influence of its religion, especially on Christianity. Fear is the currency of control and religions are vehicles to frighten the population into compliance through fear of the consequences of not acquiescing to what your 'God' (the Cult) demands you must be and do.

When many began to reject religion other self-identities were employed to ensnare perception and dictate low-frequency wave transmissions. The Cult unleashed mainstream 'science' to tell us that we are a cosmic accident of 'evolution' and we don't exist before conception or after death. There is no other 'you' except the one that you see in the mirror and identify with through a series of labels given and learned during an apparently meaningless lifetime of minutes or decades in which you make the journey from cradle to grave. Er, that's it. If you accept this ridiculous concept you are accepting the narrowest band of self-identity that will hold you fast within the firewalls of the simulation. Today even those self-identities and labels are being subdivided and sub-sub-subdivided into ever greater myopia as New Woke drowns in the five-sense illusion of pansexual, polysexual, monosexual, allosexual, androsexual, gynosexual, asexual, emisexual, grey asexual, perioriented, varioriented, heteronormative, cishet, polyamorous, monoamorous and queer to sadly name only a few. With each new sub-identity the Bubble gets ever smaller and the vibrational disconnect with the True 'I' ever more profound. The Cult knows how we interact with reality while the target population in general does not and it mercilessly exploits this perceptual superiority. All human self-identity prisons are dependent on the flies in The Web not questioning their current sense of reality. The illusions are peddled by Cult advocates and unknowing promotors seeking to impose their reality on others through techniques of overt or covert compulsion. It's not enough for me to believe what I do – *you* must believe it, too, because *I am right!* You'll see this recurring mentality and technique throughout history in almost every culture and setting. Silicon Valley censorship is doing the same today in the latest incarnation. Nazi book-burning has become the digital book-burning of Cult-owned Big Tech. The Cult manipulates minds into smaller and smaller self-identities and many of those that succumb make it their life's work to impose them on everyone else.

Limits of mind are only limits of perception

The consequences of the self-identity label illusion are catastrophic for human and spiritual freedom for another reason. Your sense of self dictates the scale of consciousness, or True Self, that you can access. Perceptual myopia becomes awareness myopia in another feedback loop of ongoing ignorance (Fig 396). Believe that you are only your labels and the scale of accessed consciousness reflects that sense of limitation. Your scale of accessed consciousness feeds-back this sense of limitation to confirm that *you* are only your labels. Round and round the garden it goes often for an entire human lifetime. The Cult, working for its 'gods',

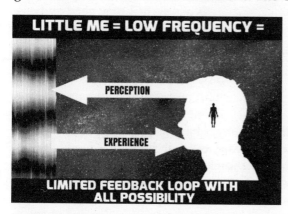

has structured society to achieve this end. There is, you will be delighted to know, a way to break this cycle: *Change your self-identity.* Ask most people who they are and they will give you a list of labels – gender, race, job, age, birthplace, life history; but the labels are not who we are. People define themselves by the

Figure 396: What you believe you will experience.

job they do when it doesn't matter if you are sweeping the streets (vital work by the way) or a movie star (less than vital work). You are the

Figure 397: Ditch the labels – they are not YOU. They are only brief happenings that YOU are experiencing.

same *All That Is* having different experiences. It's just a job – it's not *YOU*! Labels are only a series of *experiences* happening in little more than a blink of an eye (Fig 397). I am heading into my 70s and a human life flies by so fast. It seems only yesterday that I was in love with Janice in class 3A and dreaming of being a footballer. When you compare that with the infinity of no-time forever a human life as it is perceived hardly exists. Yet within this fragment of illusory 'time' our identity with labels directs and dictates everything. I-am-a this. I-am-a that. To re-word a song of the 1960s: I-am-a in the morning, I-am-a in the evening ... all over this land. I-am-a is the human perceptual Bubble that manifests as a vibrational Bubble. We are not an 'I-am-a' anything. We just are. *The One* is always speaking to you. Burst the Bubble and you will hear (Fig 398).

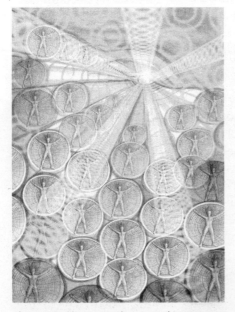

Figure 398: *The One* is always speaking to you. Burst the Bubble and you will hear.

If people feel they need an I-am-a then how about *I-am-a All That Is, Has Been and Ever Can Be*? Even that is a name and so can only partially describe the force with no name and all names. How about a self-identity that says I am a point of attention within *Infinite Forever* having a brief experience as something called 'human' in the awareness that 'human' is merely the filtering and processing of information into a particular sense of reality? How about the size of my point of attention, whether myopic or infinite, is down to me and how much of my mind I am prepared to open? *Now we're bloody talking*. Shift your self-identity from I am my labels to I am an expression of the *Infinite One* and everything starts to change. I can say this with confidence because that is what happened to me. Everything I have done since I consciously began to awaken from the human coma in 1990 has come from that transformation of self-identity. No questing, fasting, meditation, yoga, communal rituals, endless 'workshops', or green tea opened my mind to expanded awareness. I remembered step-by-step who I really am and who we all really are and that transformation of self-identity transformed everything. *Anyone* can start the process anytime by ditching the identification with labels and seeing them as transitory experiences of the True Self. *The One* in awareness of itself talks to us in the silence beyond words and the synchronicity or language of life. We only have to listen.

The transformation of perceived self from Little Me to Infinite Me immediately starts to unravel the firewalls of self-identity perception that have been holding the Bubble together. You realise there never has been a Little Me only a programmed perception of one (Fig 399). Your consciousness begins to move and stir from its density – its perceptual stagnation. You can't create a Bubble unless you believe you *are* a

Figure 399: Little Me only exists in a programmed mind.

Figure 400: All 'awakening' really is.

Bubble. You can't be entrapped in limitation unless you believe you are limited. *You are not.* You are All-Possibility, All-Potential, which the Cult is desperate for you to forget. 'Waking up' is only remembering what you've always known on the other side of the firewall (Fig 400). Now with your entrapped awareness freeing itself from the Bubble-wrap of label self-identity your perceptions expand as your consciousness expands. In fact, it is not even your consciousness expanding. It is your point of attention expanding into ever greater swathes of Infinite Awareness (Fig 401 overleaf). Little Me is expanding into Big Me and ultimately Infinite Me. I am not saying that changing your sense of

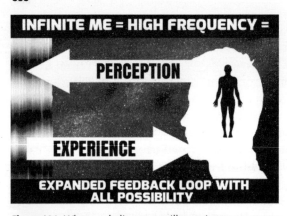

INFINITE ME = HIGH FREQUENCY =

PERCEPTION

EXPERIENCE

EXPANDED FEEDBACK LOOP WITH ALL POSSIBILITY

Figure 401: What you believe you will experience.

self will bring immediate 'enlightenment'. Self-identity with *All That Is* has to be a being and not just an intellectual concept. Many people are convinced of their own awakeness and enlightenment when they are prisoners of an *intellectual* sense of infinite identity. It's not *them*; it's still an intellectual concept external to them. You can observe this in the New Age movement and pseudo-spiritual movements where the mind convinces itself that it is something it's not. Intellectual 'awakeness' does not match its words with its actions and New Wokeness is the prime example. A New Ager once told me that she had given herself 'permission' to see more of her young relatives. *Permission?* Who is giving *who* 'permission' or what is giving what? Expanded consciousness does not give itself permission to do anything. It just *does it*.

Consciousness in awareness of the True 'I', as opposed to having a concept of the True 'I', is an integration or wholeness that you might call *Isness*. Even that is a label too far, but you get my point. It just is and doesn't require labels to identify itself *to* itself. It moves as one 'unit' rather than different parts that require 'permission' from each other. The intellect *thinks* while Isness *knows* as a conscious expression of that which *does know*. By knowing I don't mean in the form of names and dates, or touch it, taste it, see it, smell it, hear it, 'proof'. Isness knowing comes without words, for it exists beyond the human firewall where words are not necessary. Words are concepts of the simulation that are used to overcome induced limits of awareness that deny direct communication through consciousness. Words draw people into the five senses while *knowing* beyond words takes us home. Is it really a coincidence that near-death experiencers, and those that claim extraterrestrial interaction, say that communication was not by word, but by knowing? Again and again we have the theme of 'he communicated to me without words – I just *knew* what he was saying to me.' Even such examples of telepathy are only a low level of knowing without words and not the full-blown *Isness* that I am describing. We refer to knowing in the human experience as 'intuition' and this is predictably dismissed by Cult-controlled mainstream science which polices the realm of the intellect to keep expanded consciousness at bay while mostly having no idea that it's doing so. Why should we consider nonsense like expanded awareness outside the intellectual brain when my intellect is convinced that *I am right?*

Unravelling the fake self

The first stage of *The Answer* is to change self-identity from 'I am my labels' to 'I am a unique point of attention within *All That Is*' (Fig 402). This stage is itself often done in smaller stages as the Bubble is picked away little by little although it can just go *bang* as it did for me on that hill in Peru in 1991. I know from the experience how challenging that can be when your sense of reality transforms in a comparative instant. Most people do it in steps and that is far easier although awakening needs to pick up its pace in the light of events. Expanded self-identity translates into expanded awareness as we access more and more of

Infinite Awareness (intuitive knowing, insight, wisdom and love in its true sense) and our perceptions of reality consequently expand. It may begin with a feeling that the world is not as it seems to be in the sense that events are not happening for the reasons we hear on the news. At this point you might be considered a 'conspiracy theorist'

Figure 402: 'Human' is only a point of attention – state of focus – but it does not have to be myopic. You can be 'in' this world but not *of* it. (Image by Neil Hague.)

and this is where expansion ends for many. To see that daily happenings have other sinister explanations can still be achieved by consciousness confined in a Bubble – albeit a bigger one – within the simulation. The consciousness shift involved will change the waves that such people transmit and they entangle with like-waves in what is called the alternative or independent media. They will also entangle with that they wish to investigate and uncover which leads to synchronistic 'coincidences' in which information drops in your lap or arrives by 'amazing chance'. Energy flows where attention goes and when you focus your attention on something this is what happens – you connect with it. If this is the limit of a perceptual shift then consciousness expansion will not reach a state of 'I am Infinity'. It will be more like: 'I am more aware of what is going on than the rest of the public who I shall refer to as "Sheeple".' This level of awakening will likely still relate predominantly to the realm of the five senses and even follow a religion or seek understanding through only mainstream science. They will see people like me as strange, weird and 'nutters' in the same way that the mainstream media does. For those who continue the process and expand ever closer to 'I am *All That Is*' – as a being and not just a concept – the

Figure 403: The True 'I'. Everything else is illusion.

firewalls of the simulation are eventually breached and amazing changes happen in their wavefield. Perception of self and reality is consequently transformed to one of *Isness*. I am not a body. I am awareness, a state of being aware. Everything else is only the experience of that awareness. All the life history, dramas, upsets, challenges, good times and bad, are only brief and transitory experiences of the True 'I' – a state of being aware (Fig 403). The 'I' is and it isn't. It exists and it is non-existent. It is All-Possibility and No-Possibility. What it is for you is your choice. As you expand into self-awareness the simulation is not the only source of perception and reality. You are now connecting with consciousness beyond the firewalls and increasingly as the process continues you are in the world in terms of your five senses, but not *of* the world in terms of your perception of everything. This is why those who begin to awaken from the Bubble suddenly find their lives are peppered with 'coincidences', synchronicity and 'bits of luck'. These are only detailed possibilities that were denied before by the perceptual self-identity limitations of Label Me. The most powerful interaction with The Field is when we *know* rather than think or hope. Don't think it – *know* it. Don't hope it – *know* it. Hope is a complete waste of space. Hope projects you into a 'future' that doesn't exist like kicking a can down the street instead of picking it up. *Knowing* operates in the NOW which is the only 'moment' in which anything can happen. The Cult is quite happy for you to have 'hope'. It knows that can never manifest when 'hope' is attached to the non-existent 'future'. We must have hope? We must *know* and knowing comes from the heart. As you expand to breach the simulation myopia of random events, or 'dots', you begin to see the patterns and connections. The staggering scale and nature of human control becomes ever clearer. You see that manipulated wars which much of the alternative media believes to be about oil are actually part of a fantastic beyond-Orwellian conspiracy which has its origins not only off-planet, but in unseen bands of frequency.

When you reach this stage and share your views you will likely be seen as crazy and a sandwich short of a picnic. Your perceptions that come from outside the simulation are being judged by those still entranced by illusions within the simulation. If you are a public figure you will be mercilessly ridiculed and attacked by the media, including much of the 'alternative', and otherwise it will be friends, workmates and even family. If you have truly expanded your awareness to this extent you *won't care* what anyone says about you. Expanded awareness knows that whatever is thrown at you is only another temporary experience that doesn't matter in the great scheme of Infinite Forever. You will also understand why you are being treated this way. People have been through a lifetime of perceptual programming that ingrains a myopic view of self and reality. When you question that programming don't expect a round of applause. I have been asked if I knew what ridicule and abuse would follow when I went public with my views about the world and of course I did. I had worked in the media and seen what happens to those in the public eye who step off the Postage Stamp. I was sprinting away from it and so yes I knew what the reaction would be. I just *didn't care*. I am not the David Icke that they abuse and ridicule. I am the consciousness having the experience called David Icke. 'I' am that which is also observing the experience. Only when I *become* the experience and self-identify with that do the 'slings and arrows of outrageous fortune' kick in and trigger emotional response. Negative reaction is something that cannot be avoided when you are challenging the very core of perceived human reality. It goes with the territory and we either want to address the domination of the Cult or we don't. If we do there are challenges to face and if your consciousness is expanded enough into 'I am *All That Is*' you will say 'bring it on'. While low-vibrational responses will be hurled our way we don't have to entangle with them and experience their effect. This happens when we react with low-vibrational emotion to low-vibration emotional attacks. There is wave synchronicity and a feedback loop is secured. The perception of being consciousness having a human experience disconnects you from press-enter human responses. You don't see reality like the majority do and you don't behave in the predictable way. Human programming and ingrained insecurity fears the reaction of others. Expanded awareness doesn't give a fuck. Its focus is on doing what it believes to be right and not winning a popularity contest or being feted by the Mainstream Everything. Attacks by the system created and controlled by the Cult are confirmation you are on the right track. It is to be celebrated, not feared, and you can observe the madness from your own point of *One*-connected peace (Fig 404 overleaf).

Expanded awareness understands that it is not what is done to us

Figure 404: With a connection to *The One* you can observe the insanity and not be affected. (Image by Gareth Icke.)

which impacts upon our lives so much as how we respond – or don't. If someone directs abuse at you and you become upset and offended the abuser has impacted on your life only because of your reaction which *you* have the power to dictate and control. It wasn't what was said that hurt you. It was *you* allowing yourself to be hurt by caring about what was said. If the same abuse was directed at me and I couldn't care less – let alone be upset and offended – the abuser has not affected my life or emotional state in any way except perhaps to feel sad for anyone that gets off on trying to hurt others. Kids are committing suicide over what others posted on social media. They have been so dismantled by insecurity they feel they can't go on in the face of abuse from idiots, sociopaths and psychopaths. This is what the Cult and its Silicon Valley gangsters are doing to the young. If the system really cared about young people (it doesn't) the emphasis would not be on censoring opinions and views. It would be encouraging and helping people *not* to be upset and offended by the words of others. 'I think you are useless, ugly and horrible!!' *And* – your point is? I am supposed to be hurt by the opinion of someone who is so imbalanced and mentally disturbed that they glory in hurting others? I think not, mate, now you have a nice day and I hope that at some point you'll get a life. Bye. Not being offended and hurt breaks the feedback loop that abusers seek with abuse leading to upset leading to more abuse. The abuser is actually vampiring the energy of the abused and this can happen when the abused makes a wave entanglement through the resulting upset and offence. No response breaks the wavefield circuit. Abuse is not the problem, it's the *reaction*, and the more people are upset the more it encourages the abusers to further abuse. The Cult wants people to be upset and offended to justify censorship of alternative information and opinion which is still another way New Woke serves the agenda of human control. The Cult seeks to break the human spirit and then censor hysterically to 'protect' those it has broken from being upset and offended. I did say they were psychopaths, right?

Fear *is* the control system

Fear is a very a low-frequency state that acts as an anchor to consciousness expansion. We talk about being 'frozen with fear' and while on the surface there are fight-or-flight biological reasons for that it is a reflection of how fear slows the oscillation rate of the wavefield self and pulls us into density. The Cult seeks to spread fear everywhere – fear of death, fear of the unknown, fear of the 'future', and fear of the consequences of not conforming to its demands (see mass lockdown house arrest). It is confirmation of global programming and biological (wavefield) press-enter encoding that people in almost every culture tend to react in the same way in similar circumstances – witness all the cultures and religions that all succumbed as one to lockdown house arrest all over the world. You see there is nothing to fear when your consciousness expands into awareness outside the simulation and your true nature comes into view. Death? Well, that's coming for the body at some point anyway. Do we really want to stay in this micro-band of frequency forever? Blimey, perish the thought. Expanded awareness does not fear death which it knows is simply a transfer of *attention*. Oh, no, I'm terrified!! Save me doctor!! We actually don't 'come' here and then 'go' somewhere else. We withdraw our *attention* from the focus of

Figure 405: 'Death' which is so frightening to humans is only a shift in your point of attention.

the five senses and with that we are *where we have always have been*. 'Death' is like removing a virtual reality headset and the Cult's game is to control the nature of that virtual *attention* we call a human life (Fig 405). I have no wish to ditch the headset before I have done all that I can. Once that point is reached I'll welcome it and be joyous in the freedom from limitation that follows. Fear of the future? What – fear of something that *doesn't exist??* How crazy is that? We live in the Infinite NOW and our experiences are created and visually strung together by our state of perception. Little Me will have a very different 'future' to Infinite Me purely by different perceptions leading to different wave frequencies entangling with different wavefields that are people, places, experiences and ways of life. We control our 'future' if only we realised that. Okay, what about fear of the consequences of not conforming? What is the opposite of not conforming? It's *conforming* and that's how we got into this mess by conforming to religious dogma, 'science' dogma, Postage Stamp dogma. How perfectly the definition of 'dogma' describes them all: 'A fixed, especially religious, belief or set of beliefs that people are expected to accept without any doubts.' If we go on doing that there will be far more to instigate fear as the Cult surges to its endgame than if we face this up now. Our own perceptual and wavefield state will dictate any 'consequences' anyway and one thing is for sure: If people fall into the frequency of fear they will entangle with the vibrations of the Cult that uses fear as a weapon. What you fear you make a frequency connection with and attract what you fear. *Know* that *you* are in control of your life and not the Cult or random chance. This is the revelation they want to keep from you.

The process of consciousness expansion is not about 'seeking enlightenment'. We are already 'enlightened' in the sense that we are and have always been *All That Is*. Expansion of awareness means to delete the *perceptual programs* that form the firewalls which block the influence of our greater awareness on five-sense-focused Body-Mind. 'Awakening' is not to become something new; it is to remove the barriers to what we already are. Perceptual programs are like low-vibrational onion skins entrapping our 'human self' in the Bubble. Perceptual programs *are* the Bubble. Persian mystic Rumi said: 'Your task is not to seek for love, but merely to seek and find all the barriers within yourself that you have built against it.' Expansion of awareness can only happen when the mind opens and to do that all current beliefs and preconceived ideas have to be set aside. Imagine you have cleared your home of all extraneous clutter or started with a blank sheet of paper. Nothing is ruled in and nothing ruled out. Using a computer analogy you prepare to reboot or 'shut down and restart' and enter the realm of anything is possible. This is as it should be when you are *All-Possibility*. What you allow on to that piece of paper – your revised sense of reality – is now decided by what you intuitively know to be right and what can be supported by the facts as they appear to be. This is no longer decided by repetition of the same information or by what some system-appointed, system-programmed, academic or scientist tells you; nor by some newsreader or excuse for a journalist. Expanding consciousness remains light on its feet and constantly ready to move. It does not allow new perceptions to solidify in the way of the old. It is aware that what we perceive in any moment is only what we perceive in that moment and certainly not all there is to know. Once you believe you've 'got it' in totality you are confirming that you don't. At any point we only know *some* of what there is to know until consciousness is fully expanded to perceive all consciousness and that requires the full-blown awareness of *The One*. Awareness expands with the understanding voiced by Greek philosopher Socrates when he said that wisdom is knowing how little we know. The full quote says: 'The only true wisdom is in knowing you know nothing.' Awareness of that keeps the mind constantly open to other possibilities and wise enough to see that within Infinite Forever the possibilities are by definition Infinite.

One step, two step

Opening minds cease to be slaves to the program the more their consciousness expands and awakening people don't see the world and reality as the majority do. We can observe this theme throughout perceived human history with open minds standing out from mass conformity and targeted by the Cult enforcing that conformity. The difference today is that the number of minds awakening from the coma is heading towards potentially world-changing proportions although you won't know that if you watch the mainstream news. They'll be the last to see it. What I am saying here can be broken down into fundamentals. You don't have to know all the facts and details to awaken from the Big Sleep. Remember those song lyrics at the start of the book about not knowing all the answers but being set free by asking the questions. There are only two things to remember above all others:

(1): Your perceptions transmit frequencies reflecting those perceptions and they will entangle with wavefields of like-frequency. In this way we create our own reality and this is the wave-basis of what is referred to as 'karma' – 'the totality of a person's actions in any one of the successive states of that person's existence, thought of as determining the fate of the next stage'. My own definition of wave entanglement 'karma' would be: What you believe you perceive and what you perceive you experience. Take control of your perceptions and you take control of your life.

(2): Open your heart and you open to *The One* – a move that will expand your awareness faster than any other action. I'll have more on this shortly.

Those two things alone will change your life and collectively change human reality which is only a holographic manifestation of humanity's *perception* of reality. By perception I mean conscious *and* subconscious perception. Both generate the wavefields that entangle with perceptually-connected frequencies and I'll come to the subconscious in a second. If you give your power away you won't only entangle with others willing to give their power away to form the human herd mentality. You will also entangle with those that want to *seize* that power – the Cult. Willing to give away and wanting to take that power generates a compatible and symbiotic frequency alignment. Reflect on other symbiotic alignments that appear on the surface to be opposites and you'll see how we attract what we transmit. Fear of being violently attacked has a symbiotic wavefield relationship (conscious and subconscious) with those that wish to violently attack. In this way one person will be attacked the first time they walk through a park at night while others will make the same journey night after night and never be

attacked. Before New Woke presses the fury button I am not blaming the
'victim'. It is nothing to do with blame. I am explaining the unseen
wavefield relationships that lead to events in the world of the seen.
Blaming self and others for what happens to us is a mug's game. Self-
blame drives us deeper into self-loathing and low-frequency states while
making no difference to what we blame ourselves for. Acknowledging
behaviour and changing is how you take a negative and transform that
into a positive. But, then, is it really always a negative? Or is it an
experience that allowed us to see something that otherwise we would
not have seen and presented the chance to learn, change, and see
through the illusions that we believe to be real? Life often gives us (we
give ourselves through wave entanglement) our greatest gifts brilliantly
disguised as our worst nightmare. Blaming others for our fate is equally
destructive and there is no more profound way to concede our power to
others. When we say he or she is responsible for what happened to us
we are saying they have power over our lives and we don't. What
happened was the result of wave entanglement and that takes two to
tango.

I am not saying for a second that people don't act badly towards
others and they should take the consequences for those actions that can
include wave entanglement with a prison cell. I am making the point
that if we leave it there the experience can go on being repeated. If our
wavefield frequencies (perceptions) don't change then the same old
entanglements must go on generating the same old experiences. I
reported for the BBC decades ago on what were then dubbed 'battered
wives hostels' where women were given protection from violent
partners. Some of the women had been through two, three, even four,
partners who were violent. The men should be dealt with who do that,
but why did those women keep attracting the same type of violent
people? That question has to be addressed to stop it happening and in
this case lack of self-esteem will be at the core of it. Lack of self-esteem
has a symbiotic frequency relationship with a desire for power over
others and crushing self-esteem. See the humanity-Cult relationship.
Notice how many women who have the living shit kicked out of them
by violent men blame *themselves* (lack of self-esteem) for what happened.
When we take responsibility for attracting what we experience we stop
giving our power away – it's all *their* fault – and we take it back. We are
saying that we are in control of our experience and not someone else. *We*
can change the road we travel and who with and not go on repeating the
same wave-patterns of behaviour and experience. To do this we need to
realise that we *can* control our perceptions which control our wavefields
which attract our experience. I have highlighted in detail in my books
including this one, how the Cult manipulates humanity, but it is
humanity that allows that manipulation to prevail. It's no good focusing

everything on the Cult and ignoring the essential role played in human enslavement by humans themselves. A key to *The Answer* is for humanity to take responsibility for that and change direction.

Subconscious perception

The Cult is programming the subconscious mind individually and collectively in the knowledge that corresponding experience will follow. Manipulate the population to fear something and a symbiotic frequency connection will be secured to make what is feared more likely to manifest. Who will manifest it? *The targets will.* The point about the *sub*conscious is vital to understand. Our conscious mind is only a fraction of Body-Mind which mostly operates in what is *un*conscious to the conscious if you get what I mean. It is unconscious to the human conscious although itself very much conscious in its own realm of operation. Here's a quote from earlier:

> Every second, 11 million sensations crackle along these [brain] pathways … The brain is confronted with an alarming array of images, sounds and smells which it rigorously filters down until it is left with a manageable list of around 40. Thus 40 sensations per second make up what we perceive as reality.

When you think that 40 sensations a second form the perception of the conscious mind and the other 10,999,960 are absorbed by the subconscious it is clear why the subconscious is central to dictating our perceptions, wavefield state and entanglements. Experiences, traumas and other happenings long forgotten by the conscious mind go on affecting subconscious wavefields and generating anything but random events that happen to us. I mentioned earlier how important it is to consciously acknowledge why we attract certain people and experiences or why we have certain fears or health problems. They will invariably be connected to subconscious emotional patterns vibrating away in our wavefields that the conscious mind no longer even thinks about. Maybe a boy or girl you had a crush on at primary school suddenly dumped you out of nowhere and decades later you are married with kids and can't understand why you have a constant fear of your partner walking out on you at any time when there is no conscious reason to believe that will happen. The possibilities are endless. When you make the *conscious* connection between an experience, fear or health affect, and the *source* of them in the subconscious, the emotional field is balanced, the wavefield changes, and the experience ceases to repeat along with the fear and health effect. Explore the patterns and see if you can identify the trigger. Some people have eye problems because there is something they don't – or once did not – want to see. Others have health affects in the throat through a subconscious fear of speaking their truth. I have seen many examples of such patterns over the years and how they were deleted by conscious acknowledgement of the source and cause and effect.

Subconscious connection to both perception and experience is why the Cult focuses so much of its manipulation on subconscious or subliminal programming which includes placing its symbols everywhere as I have already mentioned. Subliminal means 'below-threshold' – below the threshold of the conscious mind – and that allows images and information to by-pass the conscious to be absorbed by the subconscious. Advertisements are awash with them for this reason. Conscious awareness that subliminal manipulation is all around us blocks its effect and the principle is the same as being unconsciously manipulated by people around you which can only be stopped when you become *consciously* aware of it. The subconscious is the stadium in which the Cult game is played. There is a subliminal message in Figure 406 which apparently only about five percent of people see first time. Once you become aware of the subliminal insert that's the first thing you see whenever you look at the image again because the conscious mind has been made aware of what is there. This is the power of conscious awareness to override subconscious programs (the subliminal in the image is the word 'sex'). The principle applies to smartphone and 5G frequencies. If you are not aware of their wave affects you are open to have your subconscious accessed by their wavefields and it's the

Figure 406: A subliminal message that most cannot see at first becomes crystal clear every time once awareness is transferred from the subconscious to the conscious.

same if you *do* know about the dangers and fear them. A combination of acknowledging that those waves exist and what they are designed to do, plus the conscious *knowing* that you are more powerful than they are, is the best defence – as it is against all wavefields, technological or otherwise, including people, food, drink, pollution, disease, whatever. The body is an expression of the *mind*.

My almost constant daydreaming is the exploration of deeper levels of unconscious awareness and making them conscious. Bringing reality into a conscious state is vital when keeping us unconscious is the Cult means of manipulation. I don't mean to see everything through the five senses (which are mostly expressing patterns of unconsciousness). The five senses are irrelevant to this. I simply mean to become *conscious* of information and patterns of programming that are normally unconscious to humanity in general. Expanding awareness can lead to people healing themselves through the mind as they understand the connections. All illness is a wavefield distortion and the mind is constantly transmitting perceptual frequencies that impact on that field. What you believe you perceive and what you perceive you experience applies just as powerfully with health. If you believe a drug or treatment will heal you the mind transmits that perceptual frequency into the wavefield and balances the imbalance that is causing the problem. The treatment itself may not have had this effect at all. If you believe powerfully enough that it will cure you then *belief* in the treatment will heal you when the treatment alone would not. This is the 'placebo' effect and it can lead to spontaneous healing which baffles mainstream medicine that doesn't understand what the body is or how it works as an extension of the mind. In reverse we can think ourselves dead if we believe the words of a doctor who tells us we have a certain amount of time to live. Most people do die within that time and not because the doctor's prediction was necessarily accurate. Some have died within the doctor's prognosis only for an autopsy to reveal they did not have what the doctor told them was going to kill them 'within six months'. We all have to go some time or we would be here forever (nightmare), but we have far more power over when that is than most people even begin to believe. This can extend to deciding when we will leave even before we get here by encoding the body oscillation with an end point. We may see this as someone just 'dropping dead out of nowhere'. I mean he was always so fit and healthy. There is more to 'Heaven and Earth' than ever we are allowed to know – unless we *choose* to know and make it our business to know.

Truth Vibrations

It is important to be aware that other sources of consciousness and awareness well beyond the energetic density and limitation of the Cult are at work in a quest to tease humanity out of its perceptual coma. There are people in the 'world' representing that awareness – symbolically sons and daughters of *The One* – just as Cult operatives represent their non-human 'gods'. In the early months of my own awakening in 1990, which went 'nuclear' on the hill in Peru in 1991, I met synchronistically a series of professional psychics. I made a conscious decision to meet only one of them, Betty Shine, while the others passed through my life 'coincidentally' one after the other. The common theme they said they were asked to pass on to me was that a 'vibrational change' was coming that is also called 'The Rebalancing'. This energetic change would (1) begin to wake up humanity from what I would call today the illusion; and (2) would bring to the surface 'all that had been hidden'. I called the first book that I wrote after my awakening began *Truth Vibrations* to describe the effect of this awakening frequency. I didn't just take what the psychics said and believe it without question although the common theme was compelling. It certainly felt right, but I waited and observed. Not much seemed to be happening for years and then it began. Today incredible and ever-increasing numbers of people are questioning reality and the nature of world events like never before. It won't seem like that if you only watch the mainstream media. I have been travelling the world year after year outside the Mainstream Everything and I can tell you that while it is still far from the majority human perception is stirring across all walks of life and the 'pandemic' lockdowns have caused vast numbers of new people to question the world and what is happening who never did before. It is happening on many levels and, of course, not always as full-blown awakening. The questioning, however, is now so fast gathering pace and people are opening their minds to possibilities they would never have considered before. I meet them all the time when I go out and when I'm travelling and as someone who remembers what it was like 30 years ago I can see the scale of change that is happening. Even what I would term 'System People' are looking afresh at themselves and reality. The part about bringing to the surface all that had been hidden is spectacularly happening. Consider what we know now about the manipulation of the world and the forces behind that compared with when I was told in 1990 about the Truth Vibrations and what they would do. The frenzy of censorship by Silicon Valley and other Cult sources is to a large extent a desperate attempt to thwart this awakening and so is the AI-brain connection and Smart Grid. Unfortunately for the Cult they are dealing with levels of awareness far more powerful than it and its masters will ever be in their current state of perception and thus frequency. An understanding of the wave nature of reality and wave entanglement explains how the Truth Vibrations impact on human awareness (Fig 407). They are a high-frequency information field that change the wavefield oscillation of those they connect with. I was told that the first people to be affected would be the most awake (or least asleep) and eventually even those solid-gold asleep at the time would feel the effect. This does not mean that we can

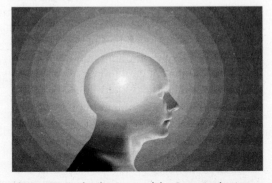

Figure 407: Truth Vibrations and the Great Awakening.

just sit back and wait for these frequencies to transform everything for better. They are a frequency band and we have to sync with it to be maximally impacted. How do we do that? We open our *hearts*.

With all *One's* heart

I talked earlier about the heart as the most potent connection to *The One* way beyond the frequency band of the simulation. The more our heart vortex opens the greater the energetic gateway through which we access love in its prime sense, wisdom, knowing, intelligence, and potentially Infinite Awareness in totality (Fig 408). We feel intuition and love in the centre of the chest for this reason and near-death survivors have

Figure 408: *The Answer.*

described how when out-of-body they experience the same love (although much more intensely) that we can feel *in* the body through the heart. One said:

There was all this light and love and rejuvenation … I felt myself expand within this light like there were no borders and I was just in this light and part of the light … I felt like I was home. I felt … weightless … you don't realise how much you carry in this world [low-vibrational emotional density] and you don't realise until it's gone how light and weightless and free [we are] and expansive and part of something large, huge. It's home and you know it is … It felt like we are all part of one thing.

Our heart vortex is our connection to *The One* and that's why such love is felt through an open heart (Fig 409). The Cult works so hard to close

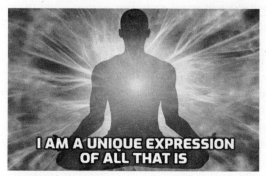

Figure 409: *The Answer.*

the heart for its own ends by generating fear, anxiety, depression, hatred, resentment, guilt and other low-vibration emotions that lead to the phrase 'my heart aches'. These emotions move the focus of attention and perception from the heart to the gut and create a feedback loop between the belly's low-vibrational emotion centre and the head/brain. This oscillation generates perception that is overwhelmingly emotion-dominated and New Woke is a collective example of that. The belly vortex centre should be a phenomenal source of energetic power when in a state of balance and that potential creative power is also diminished by the chaotic impact of low-vibrational emotion. The Cult knows exactly what it's doing, that's for sure. Emotional reaction is constantly mistaken for a heart response thanks to the manipulated misunderstanding of what love really is. Attraction by itself is not love and neither is virtue-signalled emotion. Love in the sense that I am describing is balance – the balance of all forces into wholeness when all constituent parts become *One* and none dominates the other. Each contributes to the whole and none seeks to usurp it. Compassion and empathy only for some people is not love in its Infinite sense. Compassion and empathy for *all*, not a few, is what I mean by *The One*. Nor is this love *only* about compassion and empathy. It is wisdom, fairness, justice and Infinite Intelligence. In its dot-connected wholeness love comes from a perspective of dot-connected awareness. Love is therefore *streetwise* and sees everything from *all* angles.

The head can process information into a perception that is emotionally influenced by the gut and this can trigger a form of compassion and empathy with the planet, migrants, those that identify as LGBTTQQFAGPBDSM, or those offended by what someone has said. This is only one aspect of Infinite Love and if that's the only level that people access, even if it is to an extent heart-centred, they are babes in arms to the Cult. There is nothing more manipulatable than genuineness that isn't streetwise and this is how New Wokeness becomes a puppet on the strings of the Cult. Firstly much of New Woke is emotion-based, not heart-based, and where the heart is involved only the aspects of *perceived* love that suit the Wokeness become part of the perceptual process. For example: 'I "love" and have compassion and empathy for those of colour and transgender people, but I absolutely *hate* white men.' This is not the love of *The One* and neither is it compassion and empathy in its purest definition. *The One* love will have empathy with people of colour, transgender, *and* white men. The circumstances they face illicit the empathy, not the colour or sexuality. Love sees things as they are and does not seek to portray what they are in other terms to serve some personal or collective agenda. Love will have empathy for migrants fleeing war while challenging those migrants running child trafficking gangs. It will have empathy with the kids. I observe the behaviour and responses of New Wokeness and ultra-Zionism and I see hate, not love, while they ironically rail against the perceived 'hate' of others. That's head-gut, not heart, and it's also projection – 'an unconscious self-defence mechanism characterised by a person unconsciously attributing their own issues onto someone or something else as a form of delusion and denial' and 'a way to blame others for your own negative thoughts by repressing them and attributing them to someone else'.

Heart love is not human love

When the heart opens to the point where we connect with *The One* the very idea of judging people by their illusory human labels or self-identifying with them becomes ridiculous and that includes even the term 'human'. We are not 'human'. That's just a brief experience. We are a point of attention within Infinite Awareness and when we delete our Cult-induced perceptual programs we can live that level of self. I don't mean that we merge our uniqueness into a collective 'blob'. We should glory in our uniqueness and sense of personal sovereignty while knowing that we are more than that. We are a unique point of attention *and* we are *All That Is, Has Been And Ever Can Be*. We should celebrate both, but the idea that Infinite Awareness would self-identity the True 'I' with being human, or even worse with the ever-increasing sub-divisions of 'human', seems insane to a genuinely open heart. The heart understands why people do become their labels amid whole lifetimes of perceptual indoctrination. To understand, however, is not to meekly accept in the face of knock-on consequences for all. Empathy is not always about saying what others would like to hear and often it is the opposite. Protecting children from all challenge which later leaves them at the mercy of the adult world is not empathy or love in its widest sense. How can children and young people – or anyone else – learn and grow from the consequences of their actions if they never face the consequences? This creates emotionally weak people that the Cult has for breakfast, dinner and tea. Empathy and love is not handing children a smartphone on demand out of illusory 'kindness' when the consequences for the child long-term can be disastrous. Love will tell people what they *don't* want to hear even when it knows the reaction will be negative or abusive. Love does what it believes to be right and does not seek or need the emotional sustenance of praise or a dopamine rush. What I have said about New Wokeness, climate change, mass migration, political correctness, transgender/vegan activists and the 'virus' hoax will be met with much hostility. I know that, but I don't care. What I care about is ensuring the people who attack me don't live the rest of their lives in a global dystopia. Is that love? Or is love telling them what they want to hear to gather more Facebook likes? There are many levels of heart awakening and it's an ongoing process with Cult frequencies pulling the other way until the line is crossed when the influence of the Cult is no more. By then your self-identity has transformed from Label Self to Infinite Self and with that you disentangle your wavefield from The Program and its influence on your perceptions (Fig 410).

You no longer fear speaking your truth and no scale of intimidation will silence you or impact on the way you live your life. You no longer fear death or see a human experience as who you are. You no longer fear *anything* except perhaps as a brief biological reaction until expanded awareness

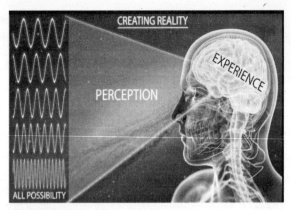

Figure 410: *The Answer.*

kicks back with the perspective of *The One*. The perceptual feedback loop moves from gut-brain to heart-brain and the way you see the world, people and events comes from a dramatically different point of attention. You are *The One* observing through human eyes and you see Oneness, not apartness, unity, not division. You know that labels are the illusions of a deeply manipulated world. From this perspective comes compassion for people who are still where you once were and even those that are nasty to you and wish you harm. Forgive them for they *literally* know not what they do.

Heart knows 'The System' is a basket case

You are not long underway in the process of opening heart and mind before all the perceptual pillars of human reality are crumbling. The idea that it matters what religion someone follows or the colour of their skin becomes laughable. How that affects their *behaviour* towards themselves and others may rightly need to be challenged for its negative impact, but the religious or racial background *in itself* is of no relevance to an awakening heart. When all is said and done and the veil is lifted I am you; you are me; I am everything; and everything is me – and *you*. Following the rules, regulations and imposed beliefs of *any* religion is a head-shaker to an opening heart. How can I confine myself to the limits of a 'holy book' often written by who knows who, who knows when, and in who knows what circumstances, when I am *All That Is* and my home is the limitless realm of Infinite Possibility and Infinite Forever? *What?* I mean – *what?* Infinite Forever, *All That Is*, should allow its perceptions and experiences to be dictated by a priest, bishop, pope, rabbi or imam?? *EXCUSE ME?* These are not representatives of 'God'. They are largely men appointed by men within man-made structures of earthly power and control. Change men to women with the same view of reality and it would be just the same. Religions are earthly structures created for earthy reasons and nothing whatsoever to do with reality as it is or awareness that we are. Do what we tell you or the 'God' that we claim to represent will condemn you forever. Give us your mind and power. We have been appointed by 'God' to rule over you, tell you what to think and play you off against those of other religions run by people just like us with a different (often only slightly) set of rules and limitations. You believe you *are* 'God', an expression of *All That Is*? *BLASPHEMER!* We are told to accept that within the microscopic perceptual confines of visible light, a smear of 0.005 percent of the Universe, all we need to know to understand self and reality is written, with laughable levels of contradiction, between the covers of a single book or set of books. On the say-so of those books, emerging from the mists of 'history', relating to eras long gone and mistranslated over centuries or thousands of years, our lives and interactions with others must be dictated. On the say-so of some religious icon that often little or nothing is known about we must fall to our knees, face Mecca, wail at a wall, worship a bloke in a frock, or dip in the Ganges. I read this description of a Ganges Hindu ritual:

> This impressive religious ritual is held in India every twelve years for 55 days where up to 100 million pilgrims attend for the world's largest religious gathering. The Ganges is the most sacred site for the majority of Hindus, and is a primary destination for kamya. Hindus believe the goddess Ganga lived in the river.
>
> Some Hindus believe that during a battle between demons and gods, the kumbh, or pot that contained sacred nectar, spilled four drops of water onto Earth, blessing four cities. The Ganges River flows through these locations. Hindus who bathe in the river or drink from the waters believe they garner good luck. They also believe the river can wash sins away for those who bathe in it. If Hindus spread the ashes of a deceased person on the river, they believe it improves that person's karma, allowing them to achieve salvation faster.

Why do Hindus believe the goddess Ganga lived in the river? Why do they believe that a pot that contained sacred nectar spilled four drops of water onto Earth, blessing four cities? Why do they believe the river can wash sins away or allow the dead to achieve salvation faster? For no other reason than this is what they have been indoctrinated to believe since they were children with serious pressure and consequences for not believing or believing something else. Young people are told who they will marry and the caste system of discrimination dictated by birth all come from this through rules decided thousands of years ago. You find this recurring theme in all major religions. Why do Christians believe

what they do about 'Jesus'? *Same*. Why do Muslims believe they must
submit their will to 'Allah' and obey the dictates of Muhammad? *Same*.
Why do Jews believe they are the Chosen People and a Jewish King will
come and gather all Jews to live in Israel? *Same*. If Christians were born
into a Jewish family, or a Jew into Islam, or a Muslim into Christianity,
they would believe something different just as vehemently as they
believe what they do today. How many people born into Islam convert
to the Jewish religion, or vice-versa? How many Christians, Jews or
Hindus become Muslims or one of the others? They overwhelmingly
follow the religion they were born into because religion is perceptual
indoctrination policed by fear and guilt and by threatened or actual
consequences. How well this definition of Islam and Muslim, a word
meaning 'one who submits', captures the whole nature of religion:

> Islam is a complete, holistic way of living that covers every aspect of life.
> Islam leaves no stone unturned as it teaches mankind on how to behave in
> every area of life: individual, social, material, moral, ethical, legal, cultural,
> political, economical, and global.

Think about that and all religions are pretty much the same. Religion
tells you, a point of attention within *All That Is*, how to behave 'in every
area of life: individual, social, material, moral, ethical, legal, cultural,
political, economic, and global'. Forget the 'teaches' bit. They are talking
about imposition and indoctrination either directly or psychologically.
The Cult loves religion for all these reasons and created them as a
perceptual and behavioural Alcatraz. You can't make your own direct
connection with *All That Is*. You have to do so through an earthly figure
representing earthly interests to maintain your perceptions in the earthly
realm. Here is my definition of religion: 'Intergenerational illusion
indoctrinated into subsequent generations by those who had it
indoctrinated into them.' Religion is yet another perceptual motion
machine.

The same religious-control blueprint can be seen with Scientism, New
Wokeness, the Climate Cult and Gaia or Earth worship. The theology is
decided and then indoctrinated and imposed by repetition and the
exclusion, demonisation, and censorship of other possibilities. In that
sentence I have described every expression of the God Program from
ancient faiths to the Climate Cult and all have their own heroes to focus
the attention of the congregation – Jesus, Abraham, Moses, Muhammad,
Krishna, Shiva, and Greta Thunberg. Opening hearts can see through the
God Program and part of *The Answer* – a big part – is the rejection of
myopic religion which hijacks perception and parks it in a cul-de-sac for
entire lifetimes. Heart is our connection to the love that is All Possibility
and will never concede its Infinity to programmed myopia. It demands

the right and the self-respect to explore its own truth within the infinity of the possible and will not be imprisoned by the beliefs of others no matter what the level of intimidation. I say up yours to all versions of the God Program that seek to impose perception including the theological dogma of 'science' and New Wokeness. They are all firewalls to Infinite Forever. Those words 'that seek to impose perception' are important. What people choose to believe is none of my business and like all of us people take the consequences, nice and not so nice, of wave entanglements those beliefs attract. I am challenging the *imposition* of those beliefs on others in all the ways I have described. Humanity cannot be free until this imposition is stopped and people awakened by the power of the heart reject perceptual tyranny. If you could see the wavefields of all those who unquestionably follow the dogma of the God Program, in its obvious and less obvious religious forms, they would all be oscillating to the same rhythm. The names on the door may be different, but they are the same perceptual/vibrational state. Freedom by dramatic contrast beats to a different drum.

In search of certainty amid Infinite Uncertainty

The foundation of the God Program oscillation is a need for certainty and a need to worship an external force in pursuit of certainty. Both are the offspring of insecurity. You cannot have certainty within All Possibility. We need to come to terms with this. The consequences of not doing so are extremely destructive. Most of human life is spent trying to eliminate uncertainty to placate insecurity and fear of the unknown. People cling to religious belief 'certainty' and delete any other possibility that would mean a state of uncertainty. Religions of New Woke and the controlling core of mainstream science seek the security of certainty and reject other possibilities. Ignorance can bring a sense of certainty and hence: 'Shut up, I don't want to hear it.' What you don't know, or refuse to know, will not impinge on your self-assembled sense of certainty. Many vehemently reject without a glance information exposing events as they are when their sense of security-promoting certainty is dependent on not knowing. Reality must eventually dawn, of course, and by then we are so far along the road to tyranny, and people so mentally and emotionally ill-equipped to respond, that it's game over. Children and young people are being specifically programmed by schools, universities and society in general to fear uncertainty and not to take risks of any kind. This is the real reason why playground games and childhood pleasures – throwing snowballs, climbing trees, leapfrog, marbles, tag and even skipping – are being increasingly banned by the Thought and Behaviour Police under terms such as 'Health and Safety'. When I was young, hardly in ancient times, these activities and so many more since banned were part of growing up. If you fell over you learned

The Answer

not to do again what caused you to fall over. You learned from experience and what happens when the experience is taken away? You *don't*. These activities that were enjoyed outside under the sky in child-to-child interaction have been replaced on purpose by faceless, isolating and behaviour-modifying videogames and social media. Parents are frightened into stopping their kids from going outside alone or with friends. This drives the process of isolation and fearing uncertainty by eliminating every minuscule risk. Fear of uncertainty and risk is squeezing the options and creativity of the young and hands protection from uncertainty to the World State. Those in fear of uncertainty look to the authorities to give them perceived certainty by taking away their freedoms and those of the entire population to secure certainty through automaton predictability. What are lockdowns and social distancing except the manipulation of certainty? The more that violence and chaos can be infused into society the more solidified becomes this perceptual state. The obsession with uncertainty has even infested professional football with a technology called 'VAR' which assesses every goal in such fine detail that they have been disallowed, often after a long wait, by the position of a player's armpit. Replace human decision-making uncertainty with the certainty (it's not) of technology. Welcome to the technocracy.

Love yourself and you'll love the world

How many who talk of the need for love, compassion and empathy for others have love, compassion and empathy for themselves? They are invariably the one left out. How can I love myself – that's narcissism isn't it? Quite the opposite is true. *Not* loving and having respect for yourself is what leads to narcissism which is a face people put to the world to hide from themselves and others the lack of self-love, self-security and self-respect. Those with open hearts aware that all is *One* don't need to present a fake face to the world. Why would they want to influence another's view of them? What would be the point to a heart that knows its true identity is *All That Is*? Some other questions: Why would the heart desire others to be impressed by a false image of itself? Why would it measure self-worth in Facebook likes and emojis? Who is there to impress when you are already *everything*? Why would you even want to impress? The intent or desire to impress means that you are changing your real self to meet the perceptual requirements of others. Seek popularity as a goal in itself and it will destroy your uniqueness. You are *you* – not them. So *be* you and not them. You are a *unique* expression of *The One*. It doesn't matter what face you present – real or fake – some people won't like it and often through their own lack of worth. I feel unworthy and I am going to attack you so you feel the same. Are we going to let our sense of worth be defined by others or ourselves? I say to young people devastated by social media abuse: Don't let anyone define you except *yourself*. You are a unique expression of *All That Is* – unique – and why would you want to be like anyone else? I don't look right, wear the right clothes, have the right trainers, or say the right things? Who gives a shit? *It doesn't matter.* You only make it appear to matter if you give a shit. *Don't.* You are *you* and no one else. Some don't like that? Well, tough. They should be what they choose to be and you should extend to yourself that same right and self-respect.

The more you allow yourself to be intimidated by others the more you wave-entangle with them and have them disrupt even further your well-being. I was subjected to mass public ridicule and abuse for decades by people who now read my books, watch my videos and stop me in the street to talk about my information. Walk your own truth, speak your own truth, worship nothing and no one, and if your truth has validity the world will eventually come to you and not the other way round. The herd mentality created the society we live in today and walking away from the herd will set us free. Cooperation and respect for each other does not require perceptual cloning. Is the real nature of respect to 'respect' only those that agree with you? Or is it to respect another's right to a different opinion and lifestyle? The question answers itself. Oh, but what about if people are *wrong?* The freedom to be wrong (overwhelmingly subjective) is fundamental to all freedom. Once you lose the freedom to be wrong it means that some force is deciding what is right or wrong. We see where that leads with the mass-censorship of 'fake news' that is often not fake at all and only what the authorities don't want people to see. If someone is factually incorrect in what they say about us, and that misrepresentation impacts upon our lives, it is right that we refute that if we believe it is necessary (it usually isn't); but responding to all criticism, ridicule and abuse gives it a power it does not deserve and reveals extremes of insecurity. I see this in mega-tweeter Donald Trump who presents to the world the face of a narcissist full of bravado and confidence. I see a frightened little boy using narcissism and extreme levels of bravado and apparent confidence to hide that frightened little boy from himself and others. See how quickly and vehemently he responds to irrelevant criticism. This is the opposite of real security which I define as not caring what people say about you. I don't mean not to care about *anything* and we should listen to all views to see if they have validity. I mean not to care what the world thinks of you. That is a freedom and security that has no need for external confirmation of itself. It does not relate its identity to human labels or seek to impose them or compete for superiority with the labels of others. It is the freedom that *knows itself.*

Intimidate the heart? No chance

Heart awareness is *The Answer* and from that all else comes both the
perceptual and the practical. The heart in its true power is not subject to
the debilitating petrification of fear and all the limitations that go with
that. 'Debilitate' comes from the Latin 'debilis' which means 'weak' and
that's what fear does. It makes us weak and this is why Cult control is
based on fear. It can freeze the human wavefield into density and close
the heart vortex that connects us to *The One*. Fear is the currency of the
Cult and its unseen 'gods' while open hearts without fear are the
currency of freedom. They cannot control without fear and they don't
understand anyone who is not in fear. It bewilders them because they
are themselves consumed by it. With their hearts closed to love, and
without the influence of *The One*, the Cult and its 'gods' are terrified
little playground bullies. They are all mouth and full of it until someone
without fear stands up and waits for them to blink. Then their backbone
starts to shiver for they know that they need humanity more than we
need them. We actually don't need them at all while they are dependent
on us for our creativity and as a power source of low-vibrational energy.
The Cult even more than humans wants to control everything and
eliminate all chance – all *uncertainty*. No one is more terrified of the
unknown, the unpredictable, than the Cult and its 'gods'. When
humanity wakes up it's over for the Cult and it knows that.

This is evident in its desperation to censor all opposition no matter
how small. To the Cult with its staggering levels of insecurity and fear a
kid in his bedroom posting conspiracy information becomes a
potentially lethal enemy that must be eliminated. Get Zuckerberg on the
phone – *fast!* The extremes to which Israel and its ultra-Zionist
apologists go to stop all criticism and exposure are displaying the
extremes of their insecurity and fear of uncertainty. They wake up with
that fear in their belly and go to bed in the same state while spending the
time in between trying to convince themselves they are untouchable and
humanity will never see what is going on. They know they're not
untouchable and they constantly zip around with a fire hose in search of
informational danger. Get Brin, Page and Wojcicki on the phone – *fast!*
Then I want Bezos and Gates. The Cult's technocracy with control of
everything by AI and technology is as much about eliminating
uncertainty and the unknown as it is for control for its own sake. We are
supposed to fear these people and think them so powerful when they
are pathetic really. I prefer to smile in their face and laugh at their
ludicrousness. To say I don't fear them is to understate the case a
thousand fold and then some. The heart knows that Cult power is the
perception of Cult power. If it was truly powerful it would not have to
work 24/7 to diminish the power of others to secure its will. I feel sad
for them, lost in their illusions that only survive by enslaving humanity

in even smaller illusions. The heart breaks through those illusions and does not succumb to fear. On both counts the heart and the love it connects us with are *The Answer.*

We are awareness, indestructible eternal awareness. What is there to fear? Whatever happens in a human experience we are and will always be indestructible eternal awareness. Today is the first day of the rest of our Forever just like 'yesterday' and the day before (Fig 411). Everything changes when you open your heart and your heart opens your mind. Old entanglements disperse, including with addictions, and new connections take their place at a higher frequency. Your life starts to change to mirror that (Fig 412). The heart in its wisdom observes how the control system works and refuses to cooperate with what allows it to function. It knows that divide and rule is the foundation of mass control and will not embark on conflict with those of another view. It will make its points; communicate its information and opinions, without falling into low-vibrational hatred and a desire to censor. The heart sees that among the pillars of control are smartphones and 5G. Heart wisdom then finds a bin to dump the smartphone and starts or joins mass movements highlighting the real consequences of 5G. It will do everything necessary short of violence against people to ensure the 5G grid cannot function. Instead of venerating Silicon Valley players like Bill Gates, Elon Musk, Mark Zuckerberg, Larry Page, Sergey Brin, Susan Wojcicki and Jeff Bezos it will challenge them and expose them for crimes against humanity and the deletion of freedom. Heart wisdom will absolutely not agree to be connected to AI and will communicate at every opportunity what AI is really about. It will ditch the Bluetooth, Apple watches and all AI wireless-connected gadgets on the body. It will certainly refuse vaccines, microchipping and anything to do with the Smart Grid including smart meters,

Figure 411: *The Answer.*

Figure 412: You are not the eyes of the body unless the program has you. You are the eyes of Infinitity. The eyes of *The One.*

autonomous vehicles and appliances wherever possible wirelessly connected to the Internet. Computers can serve humanity if not linked to the AI control grid and the Internet of Things which also has to go to secure human freedom. Hearts will challenge every 5G transmitter outside every home either as a whole or where directly affected. Heart wisdom won't buy any device that allows surveillance and behaviour modification. In an open heart society personal assistants like Echo would disappear through lack of sales as would 'Ring' and cameras in the home that allow real-time surveillance of everything you do. Heart-open parents would refuse en masse to send their children to school until the Wi-Fi was switched off and where possible refuse to send them to school at all where they are perceptually programmed every day. If they go to school because of family circumstances open-heart parents would be balancing the programming at home with other information and questioning. I used to tell my kids – 'Remember that just because a teacher tells you something doesn't mean it's true. Question everything.'

Heart is the maverick

Heart wisdom will not allow others to dictate its perception or impose their will. The heart is the maverick that goes its own way while never seeking to force its way on others. Heart wisdom truly celebrates diversity in the knowledge that *Oneness* is All Possibility to be explored and experienced. The heart never wants to censor others which it knows are expressions of itself and it is well aware that limits of free expression always lead to heart-closing tyranny. Limits of free expression are the very antithesis of heart consciousness. The heart *is* freedom. Nor is the heart offended by whatever people say. It knows that it doesn't matter unless *we* make it matter by the act of being offended. You are *All That Is, Has Been And Ever Can Be* and you are upset at being called names by another part of yourself? How daft is that? To be offended is to give your power away, reveal your insecurity and provide the excuse for freedom to be deleted. Heart in awareness of itself doesn't do insecurity. It has the ultimate security in self-realisation of its infinite nature. Call me what you like and I will carry on as if nothing has happened. We are going to be hurt by the words of others when those words are a statement about *them* not us? Whatever we say is a statement about ourselves and that's something abusers cannot grasp. Smile in the face of abuse and you immediately dismantle its power and intent. To be offended is to give power to that you have allowed to offend you. The heart has compassion and empathy for those that peddle in abuse and intimidation. It knows that by definition they are disconnected from True 'I'. The Cult deserves our compassion and empathy while we vehemently refuse to play its game. How about waking up every morning in the empathy-deleted, compassion-deleted state of permanent hatred (for self and others) that is necessary to serve the Cult? Imagine being its non-human controllers – what a thought. The heart doesn't hate the Cult for the heart cannot hate and anyway the Cult is drowning in hate and the last thing it needs is any more. Heart seeks cooperation, not competition, on all the fundamentals of freedom, justice and fairness, and does not desire power over others. It wants everyone in their *own* power and not subjugated by the imposed power of others. Without fear the heart always does and says what it believes to be right and will not self-censor through fear of consequences. It will

Figure 413: *The Answer.*

consider the best way to achieve that without walking into traps, but it will never allow fear of consequences to silence itself or stand by disinterested or trembling while freedom is eliminated. The heart also *laughs* – this is crucial – and has the self-security to be able to laugh at itself. You can't truly laugh and feel fear at the same moment and the world is so outrageously crazy that laughter is the antidote to taking everything too seriously. We are *All That Is, Has Been And Ever Can Be* who think we are Bill the baker and Kate at the call centre. That alone is hysterical (Fig 413).

Opening the heart and *being* the heart

How do we open our hearts? We *become* them. We *self-identify* with them. 'What do you mean?' may come the reply, 'What do you mean by the heart?' It is *The One*. 'What is *The One*?' *It is All That Is, Has Been and Ever Can Be, All Possibility, All Potential, All Knowing.* 'Where do I find that?' In your heart – they are the same. *The One* –True 'I' – has always been there while the head and the gut have been driving perception, reaction and self-identity. It is there now with its arms open for everyone, 'saint' and 'sinner' alike. There is no Day of Judgement. What we are we attract until we change what we are and attract something else. The heart is the circuit-breaker of human feedback loops. Self-identify with your heart and you will feel its gathering influence. When you feel low-vibrational emotions shift your attention to the heart before you react and it will pass. Your heart will tell you what matters and what doesn't. Your very focus of attention on the energetic heart will make you aware of a strengthening vibration in the centre of the chest which gets stronger and stronger as you delete perceptual programs. You are transferring your point of attention (identity) from the head to the heart. Eventually you become the heart and it becomes you. I mentioned earlier how the therapist asked people to describe their problems from the head and then the heart and how in her words it was like talking to two different people (Fig 414). This is what happens when we become the heart. We become different people and expand beyond the self-identity as a 'person' (persona – the actor's mask). We realise we have been living a fake identity in a world of illusion and the power of the Cult depends entirely on that fake identity and world of illusion. This is why the heart is *The Answer* and it will transform human interaction (Figs 415 and 416). Alice says in Wonderland: 'I can't go back to yesterday because I was a different person then.' Once your heart opens the message is the same.

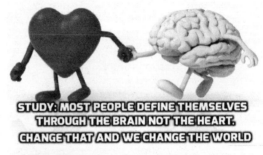

Figure 414: *The Answer.*

Questions worth asking in our daily experience as we journey into the heart awareness are 'what would *The One* do?' and 'what does my heart say?' Never mind what the human mind would do in the given situation. What would *The One* do speaking through my heart? It would respond with compassion, empathy, love and wisdom for all concerned. This does not mean lying down and letting others walk all over you. It means that sometimes people need to

Figure 415: The Problem.

Figure 416: *The Answer.*

be challenged for them to attract the experiences that will set them free. It means that we need that, too, which is why we find that our greatest gifts often emerging from our worst nightmares. When you come from the heart challenges to what you see as unfairness and injustice are not delivered with hatred and desire to hurt; but neither will you blink when you look them in the eye. To challenge and expose is not to hate and wish harm. Or it doesn't have to be. Another reality filter is what I call deathbed perception. You are lying on your deathbed with ten minutes to live. What matters to you now? Think of all the upsets, fear, emotional trauma, hatred, anger, resentment, anxiety and conflict in your life that mattered so deeply to you at the time. Does it matter now in the departure lounge of a human life? Does it matter that you worshipped a different deity or 'god' to somebody else? Or that others had different opinions to you and voted for a politician you didn't agree with? Or that your children went their own way instead of doing what you demanded? Or that your children spilt their dinner on the floor or failed to do exactly what you said? Or that someone was late for a meeting when they were stuck in traffic? What about the colour of your skin and your sexuality in relation to others? Does that matter now? Does it matter what labels you gave yourself and insisted on giving to others? How about the hostility you had for fellow expressions of *All That Is* for supporting a different soccer team? What about how vehemently you competed with others and resented how they reached a few notches higher on the greasy pole of eternal irrelevance? Does it matter that you 'won' and made lots of money to which you are about to wave goodbye? The answer to all these questions for the overwhelming majority will be 'no'. None of it matters. They were all illusions. What *does* matter to deathbed perception? How much you loved and were loved. How much joy you had and how often you laughed. How much joy you gave to others and how you worked together in harmony and mutual support.

Knowing what matters

Many people in retirement go through these reflections. What was it all about? They worked all their life to be a 'winner'. They worked long hours and missed their kids growing up. They sent them to the best residential schools to be winners like them so they could also ask in their retirement: 'What was it all about?' Oh, but they had to compete and cuss and spit and kick their way to 'success'. Life is about dog eats dog, right? Well, only if you choose it to be. There are other choices – within *All Possibility* there always are. They might not be the choice the Cult would like you to make, but they are there for the making. You are not dependent on The System. You are dependent on your wavefield state that will engage you with frequency reflections of itself. If you think you

have to serve The System you will entangle with The System to manifest
the illusion that you have to serve The System. Go your own way
knowing you will attract all you need and you will entangle with all that
you need without serving The System. Go your own way while fearing
the consequences and you will entangle with the consequences. The
perspective of deathbed perception is to see at any point in your life
what matters long before you are lying there waiting for 'God'. Look
through those same eyes, perceive through that same heart, and see
what really matters behind the smokescreens and diversions of human
labels and perceptions of 'success'. It is to love and be loved. It is love for
self and all other expressions of *The One* which is love. Symbols of
human 'success' are merely what we are told they are – big money, big
houses, big cars, big fame. I have met many people with all of those
things and none have been happy, joyful and at peace with themselves. I
know a guy who has spent his life screwing other people for their
money and property. He then contracted cancer, had his bowel removed,
and when he recovered went back to screwing people for their money
and property. The more we don't get it the more extreme the experiences
we attract until we do. He has no bowel and has had at least one heart
attack and still considers himself a 'winner' like all psychopaths and
criminals do by the fact that he has parted lots of people from their
money and property. It is perceptual insanity and often the truth comes
from the mouths of the very young before perception programs and
cynicism have kicked in. An Internet video of a six-year-old recorded
her advice to her mother after conflict with her father. She said she only
wanted people to love each other. If we didn't there would only be
'monsters':

> I just want everyone to be friends. And if I can be nice, I think all of us can be
> nice, too. I want you, my dad, everyone to be friends. I want everyone to be
> smiling … My heart, it's something. Everyone else's heart is something, too.
> And if we live in a world where everyone's being mean everyone's going to be
> a monster in their future … I just want everything to be settled down. Nothing
> else. I want everything to be as good as possible.

At the time of writing that video has been watched by 40 million
people. You know why? We *all* want that, too. The world is full of people
who behind their upsets, traumas, competition, resentment, hatred and
psychopathy just want to be loved. What is 'evil' except the absence of
love? The Cult has sucked so much love from the world and we need to
put it back – *that* is The Answer. We still see an abundance of love in so
many guises despite the Cult's best efforts and we can all open our
hearts to limitless love whenever we make that choice (Fig 417). The
Cult's endgame is to entangle humanity with machines and AI so

completely that all love is extinguished and with that any powerful connection to *The One* and True 'I'. It seeks to isolate mind and perception so that ET can't phone home. It is working to create a new post-human through AI, drugs, the Smart Grid, 5G and 6G, synthetic biology and digital 'avatars' in which heart centres are closed and minds no more than computer software. We are staring this reality in the face and we have to deal with it as the number one priority without delay. How do we prevent the post-human end of humanity? We go *beyond* human (Fig 418). We remember who we are and what we are and live

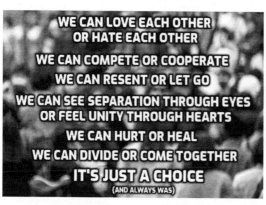

Figure 417: The question.

our lives with that self-identity. Do that and everything follows. We change ourselves and we change our lives. If enough of us do that we together change 'the world'. Things don't change until *we* change them. Or, rather, change ourselves. Rumi, the Persian poet and mystic, could see beyond The Program in the 13th century as his open heart connected him with *The One*. He described himself in these terms:

Not Christian or Jew or Muslim, not Hindu, Buddhist, Sufi, or Zen. Not any religion or cultural system. I am not from the east or the west, not out of the ocean or up from the ground, not natural or ethereal, not composed of elements at all. I do not exist, am not an entity in this world or the next, did not descend from Adam and Eve or any origin story. My place is the placeless, a trace of the traceless ... neither body or soul.

Figure 418: *The Answer.* (Image Neil Hague.)

Rumi was speaking in the 13th century and 800 years later in our

Figure 419: *The Answer.*

illusion of 'time' I am saying exactly the same in my own way. For it is not about 'time' and 'evolution' through 'time'. It is only the scale of awareness that we choose to connect with. That awareness was there when Rumi was 'here' and it is there now. It is always there for anyone who opens their heart to communicate with its wisdom (Fig 419). Rumi was not ahead of his 'time'. How could he be when there is no time? True 'I' is *beyond* 'time' and all its illusions. He put it like this:

> The very center of your heart is where life begins – the most beautiful place on earth; Love is the bridge between you and everything.

He knew with that connection that 'goodbyes are only for those who love with their eyes because for those who love with heart and soul there is no such thing as separation'. He knew that freedom is not freeing others or being freed by others. It is freeing *yourself*: 'I want to sing like the birds sing, not worrying about who hears or what they think.' What Rumi tapped into anyone can and it lies in the silence where all is *One* – 'There is a voice that doesn't use words. Listen.'

Open your heart to The Silence. *The Answer* is waiting there.

Postscript

The desperation of The System to silence my exposure of the 'pandemic' hoax reached still new levels of extremism just before this book went to print when British Member of Parliament Damian Collins demanded that it be made *illegal* for me to challenge the official story. As definitions of fascism go, I think that's pretty good.

Conservative MP Collins, a former chairman of the House of Commons Digital, Culture, Media and Sport Committee, is clearly obsessed with silencing me and any questioning of the official Gates/Cult-controlled World Health Organization narrative being repeated like parrots by governments and technocrat dark suits across the world. Why is Damian Collins so obsessively knicker-twisted with *one man* having a different opinion of the 'pandemic' to the entirety of the global governmental system, entirety of the global mainstream media and entirety of Cult-owned Silicon Valley? *One man!* Well, how about because I am telling the *truth* and that's what they fear more than anything in all existence? Collins could debate me, which is what the 'free world' is supposed to be all about, but he won't because he hasn't got the guts (Fig 1). He just wants to silence me and impose his will on the enormous numbers of people worldwide that want to hear what I have to say. What Collins appears to be terrified of is another person's *right to an opinion*. Why could that be do you think? He called for a new 'requirements in law' to

Figure 1: The silence-Icke-obsessed Damian Collins MP.

stop people like me 'persistently spreading disinformation online' which means that, by definition, the authorities would decree what is 'disinformation'. I think I read that somewhere in *Nineteen Eighty-Four*. 'If there is a certain channel, group or individual that is persistently pushing this information out then that sort of malicious abuse of social media in a public health emergency should be an offence', said a man so breathtakingly arrogant that he believes he should be the arbiter of what you see and don't see. Even before he called for my view on the 'pandemic' to be against the law – mirroring what happened in Nazi Germany and happens in the tyranny that is China – he had already launched a 'fact-checking service' (excuse me, my belly hurts) called Infotagion on March 30th, 2020, 'to combat falsehoods during the pandemic'. No – to target information that questions the official story and here we have a man utterly consumed by having the public hear only the already thoroughly-discredited World Health Organization (Gates) bullshit. This is an example of Collins/Infotagion 'fact-checking':

> Claim: Healthy food and exercise can build natural immunity to COVID-19. Answer: False. Avoiding contact with carriers of the illness is the only way to prevent infection.

The idea that boosting the immune system cannot be a defence against *all* illness is obviously bordering on the insane given that the immune system exists to protect us from illness. The only possible reason such a suggestion can be claimed to be false is because the official story wants you to believe that only by lockdown and social distancing can you prevent infection. Collins therefore, in this example alone, does not run Infotagion to stop 'misinformation', but to spread it in defence of the official Gates-WHO-government line. This is confirmed by the Collins government-supported Infotagion website which declares first that it is 'independent' and then that its information is 'sourced from WHO, UK and other official government advice'. I love it – 'independent' *and* just repeating the official version of everything. Infotagion was created 'in partnership' with marketing company Iconic Labs which urges clients to respond to the fact that 'LGBT+ consumers are more prominent than ever – with up to half of 18 to 25-year-olds saying they are not totally heterosexual'. Iconic Labs was created by Liam Harrington, John Quinlan and Sam Asante. Enemy of Freedom Collins said: 'Disinformation can kill people.' Yes it can – look at how many have already died and the legions that will die from the disinformation which led to the lockdowns that Collins is so determined to protect from exposure. What can be more obvious disinformation than to claim that boosting the immune system is not a protection against disease?? Collins said he was introduced to Iconic Labs to launch Infotagion by David Sefton who resigned as Iconic Labs chairman over 'rumour and market speculation' about his role in Anglo African Oil & Gas from which he resigned in July, 2019. Journalist Tom Winnifrith wrote in early 2020:

… David Sefton was forced to quit Anglo African Oil & Gas (AAOG) after revelations on this website about horrific undeclared conflicts of interest, obscene expenses and other matters. Here we are on January 30th [2020] and after massive pressure about misleading RNS statements, related party deals and other matters I get to claim his scalp again, this time at insolvent Iconic (ICON).

Iconic is holding its AGM today in Sheffield, something guaranteed to ensure no-one turns up to ask awkward questions. Sefton was up for re-election but has decided over Christmas that he will be leaving the company with immediate effect after the GM. It now has no independent directors but since it also has no cash and no future that is not really an issue.

Damian Collins was one of the signatories to the demand by the ultra-Zionist-funded, Labour Party-dominated Center for Countering Digital Hate for me to be banned by Facebook and YouTube. The Labour Party and the Collins Conservative Party of Boris Johnson are supposed to be political 'enemies', but on all the Cult objectives – not least draconian censorship – they seem be in total agreement. Dr Daniel Allington, a senior lecturer in social and cultural artificial intelligence at King's College London, was also quoted in the same media article about Collins demanding my work be made illegal. Allington was acknowledged by the Center for Countering Digital Hate for his help in the 'report' that had me deleted from Facebook and YouTube. He said he had undertaken 'research' and found that people who believe 'coronavirus conspiracy theories' are more likely to flout lockdown rules. He undertook 'research'?? Anyone with a brain cell could have told him that and saved him the trouble. Allington was focused on me getting silenced rather than 'celebrities'. It was pointed out that some celebrities have posted views about the 'pandemic' that questioned the official story, including British boxer Amir Khan, but Allington wasn't too bothered about them:

> I am not sure I want to regulate what someone like Amir Khan says, but then you have someone like David Icke, or (conspiracy theory site) London Real, and their business is creating content which goes online, which they are able to monetise.

Well, actually, Allington, I don't get money for the videos we post on public platforms and maybe you should fact-check yourself. Why is Damian Collins obsessed with silencing my information about the 'pandemic' which you have read at length in this book? Who is this man and who is he connected with? These are legitimate questions given that he is a member of the UK Parliament who is supposed to be defending

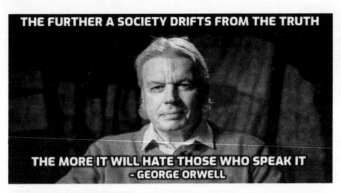

THE FURTHER A SOCIETY DRIFTS FROM THE TRUTH

THE MORE IT WILL HATE THOSE WHO SPEAK IT
- GEORGE ORWELL

Figure 2: An Orwell quote that perfectly describes the censorship war against me and my work.

freedom and democracy, but clearly has contempt for both (Fig 2). I hope voters in his Folkestone and Hythe constituency have the self-respect and the respect for their own freedom to note his shocking behaviour at the next election and that the public call out this blatant enemy of freedom at every opportunity. Collins worked for seven years for M&C Saatchi, 'an international advertising agency', or more accurately a spin machine operation that was created in 1995 as a rival to Saatchi and Saatchi which ran spin campaigns for Prime Minister Margaret Thatcher and the Conservative Party. The CEO and co-founder of M&C Saatchi is David Kershaw, an ultra-Zionist board member of the vehemently and long-time anti-Icke *Jewish Chronicle* with its laughable editor Stephen Pollard which went into voluntary liquidation in April, 2020, before being bought by a consortium of investors. Damian Collins and his 'Infotagion' has 'partnered' with Kershaw's M&C Saatchi and Iconic Labs to target 'misinformation' about the 'virus pandemic' which as always means any information that counters the Cult narrative peddled through the Gates World Health Organization. You will have noticed how many times the ultra-Zionist neoconservative or 'Neocon' network in the United States has appeared in this book and I have exposed this at far greater length in some of my others, most notably *The Trigger*. The Sabbatian-Frankist Neocon web spawned the Project for the New American Century and its closely-aligned American Enterprise Institute. Damian Collins is on the board of British Neocon arm, the Israel-worshipping Henry Jackson Society, and signed its Statement of Principles. Fellow board members include UK government minister Michael Gove and ultra-Zionists Adam Levin and Alan Mendoza. Levin is a trustee of UK Lawyers for Israel, the 'lawfare' operation that targets Palestinian supporters promoting the Boycott Divestment and Sanctions (BDS) movement by lodging complaints with regulatory bodies and threats of legal action. Collins clearly has some lovely friends. Among the international patrons of the Henry Jackson Society are ultra-Zionist Project for the New American Century stalwarts William Kristol, a co-founder, Richard Perle and former CIA Director James Woolsey. I don't know about you, but I kind of get the picture of the circles in which Damian Collins operates and his targeting of me and my information should therefore hardly come as any surprise.

The 'Hate' censorship network

A citizen journalist and visitor to DavidIcke.com began investigating the Collins-supported Center for Countering Digital Hate (CCDH) after it claimed credit for having me banned from Facebook and YouTube (I'm sure they were both kicking and screaming before agreeing to do so). Well, what a web he opened up both sides of the Atlantic with funders, supporters and associations. Among the CCDH directors listed is Simon Clark from the Center for American Progress, a One-percent New Woke front that centrally influences the US Democratic Party. It's founder, first president and CEO was the infamous political manipulator John Podesta who was White House Chief of Staff to President Bill Clinton and chairman of the 2016 presidential campaign of Hillary Clinton. What's that they say about knowing someone by the company they keep? Major funders of the Center for American Progress include George Soros and fellow Zionists Peter Lewis, Steve Bing and Herbert Sandler. Center for American Progress senior fellow Simon Clark is a board member of the Icke-targeting Hope not Hate (Hate not Hope) which supported Digital Hate (so much hate) in its efforts to have me banned in the same way that Damian Collins works so hard to do. His wife, Diana Shaw Clark, is Chair of National Finance Committee for J Street, the Israel lobby group and funder of American politicians. Digital Hate director Simon Clark is an advisor to the Scowcroft Group, the 'international business advisory firm' of Brent Scowcroft who was US National Security Advisor to far-right Presidents Gerald Ford and 'Father' George Bush. How compliant and on message must Scowcroft have been to have served the hate-filled psychopaths Ford and Bush? Scowcroft appeared in many of my earlier books and he was vice-chairman of the absolutely notorious Kissinger Associates of ultra-Zionist Neocon Henry Kissinger, a front man for the Cult virtually his entire adult life and a war criminal on a breathtaking scale. Is it only me that thinks it strange that Simon Clark would be rubbing shoulders with such people while having close connections to self-styled 'left-wing', 'progressive' organisations like the Center for American Progress and Center for Countering Digital Hate? This is even more relevant with Clark's LinkedIn profile claiming that he 'started the Center for American Progress's work on combating far right extremism'. So why the close association with a company headed by Brent Scowcroft given his role with right wing mega-terrorists like Father Bush and Henry Kissinger who are responsible for death and destruction – terrorism – on a gargantuan scale overwhelmingly in non-white countries?

I might ask a similar question of other central characters in Digital

Hate. I said in the body of the book that the group (a limited company) involved Labour Party 'left-wing' (joke) figures such as Imran Ahmed, Kirsty McNeil and Morgan McSweeney, plus academics obsessed with censorship; but clearly these Labour activists are in full agreement in the one-party state with right-wing Conservative Neocon MP Damian Collins when it comes to silencing me. Collins demands that my information and my right to express it be made illegal while Digital Hate has sought not only to have me deleted from all Internet platforms, but also all the interviews with me from any other source with those who interviewed me also banned. Well-known people like singer Robbie Williams who speak out in any way in support of me are targeted for abuse by Internet purveyors of hate. System-servers are terrified of me because they are terrified of the truth and thus their gussets spin like aircraft propellers at the thought of anyone hearing what I have to say. So again *why*? So again comes back the same answer as with Collins – they fear one man's opinion despite all their 'powerful' connections because the official story of the 'virus' is so full of holes and contradictions that only the fiercest of censorship can defend it from being demolished. Digital Hate director Kirsty McNeil, who has been so keen to censor me, sits on the board of a Gates-funded organisation called Coalition for Global Prosperity alongside Carolyn Esser from the Gates Foundation. Esser is 'responsible for designing and executing the communications strategy for the Bill & Melinda Gates Foundation in Europe and the Middle East'. Coalition for Global Prosperity pushes for mass vaccination and the silencing of 'anti-vaxxers' on social media. I can't imagine, then, why Gates would fund the organisation or why Kirsty McNeil would want people like me censored. McNeil is a member of the European Council on Foreign Relations whose main funder is the Open Society Foundations of George Soros. She is also on the board of the Holocaust Educational Trust. Other Digital Hate directors are Bristol University academic Dr Siobhan McAndrew, Lord Jonny Oates, a Chief of Staff to former UK Deputy Prime Minister and now Facebook head of global affairs and communications, Nick Clegg, and Ayesha Saran, Migration Programme Manager at Digital Hate funders, the Barrow Cadbury Trust. Saran is also a trustee of the Barrow Cadbury-funded British Future, a think tank focusing on 'identity and integration, migration and opportunity'. British Future receives funding or 'in-kind' support from the Soros Open Society Foundations, Facebook, BBC, European Commission and Digital Hate funders Unbound Philanthropy. Digital Hate also connects with the ultra-Zionist Community Security Trust (CST), 'a charity that protects British Jews from antisemitism and related threats', constantly inflates those threats and targets Jews who criticise Israel and Zionism. The cross-referencing of people and funders is a massive maze. Digital Hate is funded by the ultra-Zionist Pears Foundation and the aforementioned New York-based Unbound Philanthropy with its connections to George Soros. Unbound's UK Program Director is Will Somerville who is also a Senior Policy Analyst for the Migration Policy Institute (MPI), a think tank based in Washington DC, and a Visiting Professor at the University of Sheffield. He is another connected to British Future. Somerville has worked at the Commission for Racial Equality, the UK Prime Minister's Strategy Unit, Cabinet Office, and the Institute for Public Policy Research. Well connected I think is the phrase and more about the Cabinet Office shortly. Digital Hate is closely linked with the allegedly Labour Party-supporting limited company called Labour Together with its ultra-Zionist businessman director Trevor Chinn who I am sure has a heart that bleeds for the poverty-stricken and downtrodden. Chinn sits on the Executive Committee of the Britain Israel Communications and Research Centre (BICOM), a UK propaganda arm of the Israeli government. Digital Hate founding director Morgan McSweeney, the campaign manager and chief of staff for Labour Party leader, the Israel-centric Keir Starmer, is the secretary of Labour Together which is located in the same East Finchley, London, building as Digital Hate. Genuine Labour members should realise that this is the hijacked 'party' their subscriptions are funding. The D-list 'TV celebrity' patron of Digital Hate is Rachael Riley who constantly employs the slur of 'anti-Semitism' to demonise and silence people. Together they targeted my information and free speech believing they were damaging me when all they did was dramatically increase the number of new people looking at my work in the light of me being so vehemently targeted for censorship after I was dismissed as a 'nutter' for decades (Fig 3). The attacks further increased with attempts by hackers to bring down Davidicke.com and Ickonic.com in the same period followed by PayPal with its ultra-Zionist president and CEO Daniel H. Schulman cancelling our account. This is the same PayPal that bans Palestinians in Gaza and the West Bank from using its services, but

Figure 3: From left to right: Morgan McSweeney (Digital Hate and Labour Party); Imran Ahmed (Digital Hate and Labour Party); Damian Collins (Infotagion, Henry Jackson Society and Conservative Party); Kirsty McNeil (Digital Hate, Labour Party, Save the Children, Coalition for Global Prosperity); Rachael 'you're an anti-Semite' Riley (Digital Hate).

allows Jewish people in the illegally-occupied West Bank to do so. It's
not racist or anything. Attacks came from all angles and will continue to
do so – that's what happens when you speak truth to tyranny. One good
thing while all this was going on came when someone edited the
Wikipedia page for Digital Hate and actually told the truth amazingly. I
recommend a read if it has survived in that form this far. Digital Hate
was perfectly described:

> The organisation campaigns for internet censorship to be enacted against rival
> political actors, lobbying American 'big tech' firms such as YouTube,
> Facebook, Amazon, Twitter, Instagram and Apple to 'deplatform' individuals
> so that they cannot present their views to the general public.

That's correct, but 'rival political actors' doesn't mean rival political
party 'actors'. It means rival versions of world events with Neocon
Conservative Damian Collins and 'left-wing' (joke again) members of
the Labour Party all forming the same playground bully gang against
me. The recurring background can be seen with professional censors
NewsGuard which produced an 'Icke-must-be-deleted' report to Twitter.
NewsGuard was co-founded by ultra-Zionist Neocon Americans
Gordon Crovitz and Steven Brill with the same intention as Digital Hate
and the Infotagion of Damian Collins – to silence those who challenge
the official narrative they all represent and are desperate to protect. Add
the fact that the UK Government's full-time 'advisor' on 'anti-Semitism'
(using the slur of anti-Semitism to censor and demonise critics of Israel's
Sabbatian-Frankist regime) is former Labour Party MP John Mann who
is an ultra-Zionist to his DNA. There must be a common theme and
pattern in these people and organisations, but I'm damned if I can see it.
I'm sure you can, though. There is no way all these characters and
organisations do not lock into this same enormous network which
includes many 'charities' operating as front operations. Imran Ahmed
from the Center for Countering Digital Hate was appointed to the
Steering Committee of the UK Government's Commission on
Countering Extremism Task Force headed by a Sara Khan (Ahmed
seems to do a lot of 'countering'). It calls itself 'independent' which, of
course is the usual garbage and it is really there to impose censorship by
hurling hate at its targets while claiming to be 'anti-hate'. See the hate-
filled comments about me by Digital Hate and company, plus Damian
Collins. While this rabble was seeking to silence all challenge to the
official narrative doctors and funeral directors continued to report that
death certificates were being faked with 'Covid-19' as the cause when it
played no part. Project Veritas, with a long record of exposing official
lies, spoke with funeral directors who confirmed this. One in Williston
Park, New York, said: 'Basically, every death certificate that comes across

our desk now has Covid on it.' Every director contacted said 'Covid-19' deaths are being inflated and every death in New York was being recorded as a Covid death with or without testing to confirm (not that this would be any use). Joseph Antioco of Schafer Funeral Home said: 'They are putting Covid on a lot of death certificates [for] people who are going to their hospital with any kind of respiratory distress, respiratory problems, pneumonia, the flu …' Yes, exactly, and the web of censorship I am exposing here is working to stop the world knowing that. What does that say about them?

UK government's worldwide Psyop 'team'

The UK Cabinet Office is a department of the British Government that 'supports the Prime Minister and Cabinet of the United Kingdom' and has 2,000 staff 'coordinating the delivery of government objectives via other departments'. Okay, so one of the objectives must be to manipulate the behaviour of the British public and those in a long list of countries worldwide because the Cabinet Office is part-owner, with 'innovation charity' Nesta, of the Behavioural Insights Team (BIT). This is also known as the 'nudge unit', a term that comes from a 2009 book by ultra-Zionists Cass Sunstein, an advisor to President Obama, and Richard Thaler called *Nudge: Improving Decisions About Health, Wealth, and Happiness.* Thaler, a proponent of something called 'behavioral economics', is an 'academic affiliate' of the Cabinet Office Behavioural Insights Team whose role is to 'nudge' (manipulate the behaviour) of its targets and has played a prime role in doing just that with regard to the 'pandemic' hoax. Other leading names in the development of behavioural economics are ultra-Zionists Daniel Kahneman and Robert J. Shiller – all three are recipients of the Nobel Memorial Prize in Economic Sciences for their work on behavioural economics which is defined as the study of 'the effects of psychological, cognitive, emotional, cultural and social factors on the decisions of individuals and institutions'. Cut all the bullshit and it means studying the psychological factors to manipulate or 'nudge' behaviour. The Behavioural Insights Team, *a limited company* at the heart of government, was established in 2010 and operates worldwide with several universities, including Harvard, Oxford, Cambridge, University College London (UCL) and Pennsylvania. It brags how it has 'trained' 20,000 civil servants and practitioners worldwide in 'behavioural insights'; how it has 'run more than 750 projects to date, including 400 randomised controlled trials in dozens of countries'; and how its work 'spanned 31 countries in the last year alone'. BIT has an office in New York and has been 'working with cities and their agencies, as well as other partners, across the United States and Canada, running over 25 randomized controlled trials in the first year of operation'. This 'work' involves manipulating human behaviour and it has been at the core of doing just that during the 'pandemic'. The Behavioural Insights Team inflicts 'Psyops' on target populations. Psyops are 'military actions designed to influence the perceptions and attitudes of individuals, groups, and foreign governments'.

How very appropriate then that in March, 2020, with the 'virus' scam going into overdrive, that Rachel Coyle with her six years' experience at the Ministry of Defence should be named the new BIT Director for Europe, the Middle East and Africa to help develop pandemic strategy. The British military cyber Psyop unit 77th Brigade would have no doubt been ecstatic to have one of its own in such a key position given that the aims of both are the same – getting the public to behave as required by everything from 'nudging' to extreme censorship. Coyle is a senior figure from the world of intelligence and defence who specialised in China and cyber warfare – a term which includes deleting me from the Internet for the crime of challenging this web of deceit. The Behaviour Insight Team is headed by psychologist David Solomon Halpern, a visiting professor at King's College London, who has been 'overseeing the UK government's response to the Covid-19 pandemic in the United Kingdom as part of the Scientific Advisory Group for Emergencies, focusing on behavioural changes ...' I bet he has. The central player in the behavioural manipulation network is UK Cabinet Secretary Mark Sedwill who is also the National Security Advisor and sits atop of pyramid of related organisations. Internet site UKColumn has done some excellent work on this in its three-times weekly broadcasts and has connected Sedwill and his Behavioural Insight Team Psyop to the Foreign Office, National Security Council, the government communications headquarters (GCHQ), MI5, MI6, the 77th Brigade and Rapid Response Unit which 'monitors digital trends to spot emerging issues, including misinformation and disinformation, and identifies the best way to respond' – censor and lie. This 'supports the work' of the again *Cabinet Office*-based Media Monitoring Unit. The web includes the military operation jHub, the 'innovation centre' for the Ministry of Defence and Strategic Command, *which is involved in 'symptom tracing' for the National Health Service*. The military is ultimately driving what is happening through the so-called 'Fusion Doctrine' – the fusion of military and civilian law enforcement and government agencies in accordance with the 'Hunger Games' plan I described earlier. The UK government's broadcast censor Ofcom and the BBC will be connected to this network, too, with censorship crucial to the control of information that the public is allowed to see and they are desperate to expand Ofcom's censorship powers to the Internet. Are we really expected to believe that Imperial College in London which produced the Armageddon-like 'computer models' at just the right time to justify the lockdowns are not connected to this same network? The Chinese government, by the way, was not phased by the Imperial College 'modelling' disaster and during the lockdown the college signed a five-year collaboration deal with China tech giant Huawei that will see 'Huawei's indoor 5G network equipment and "AI cloud platform" installed at the college's West London tech campus, as well sponsorship by the Chinese firm of Imperial's Venture Catalyst entrepreneurship competition'. The information control and behaviour manipulation web out of Downing Street through the Cabinet Office is fantastic and every major country will be the same. The United States established a Social and Behavioral Sciences Team in 2015 through an executive order by President Fraud Obama.

Then there is a new UK *Cabinet Office*-connected Joint Biosecurity Centre (JBC) to provide 'expert advice on pandemics' and its role is described officially as: Independent (the jokes go on) analytical function to provide real-time analysis about infection outbreaks to identify and respond to outbreaks of Covid-19; and to advise the government on response to spikes in infections – 'for example by closing schools or workplaces in local areas where infection levels have risen'. It is reported to be based at the Joint Terrorism Analysis Centre which analyses intelligence to set 'terrorism threat levels'. Tom Hurd, the director general of the Office for Security and Counter-Terrorism, and reported to be a favourite to be the next head of MI6, was appointed to lead the new unit which will oversee the contact-tracing operation that I will describe in a second. Hurd is the son of former Foreign Secretary Douglas Hurd from a big-time insider family. Tom Hurd went to the elite Eton College and Oxford University with Boris Johnson. What I have been describing with this interconnecting nexus is the permanent government or Deep State that runs everything above and beyond the here today, gone tomorrow politicians. Compared with this Prime Ministers like Johnson are bit-part and seriously peripheral players as we have seen so clearly during the 'pandemic' hoax.

The 'virus nudge' – or rather smack in the back

A perfect example of systematic psychological manipulation from this network can be found in a paper prepared for government by the 'behavioural science sub-group' of the Scientific Advisory Group for Emergencies (SAGE) which is co-chaired by Sir Patrick Vallance, former executive of the massively Gates-connected GlaxoSmithKline, and Gates-funded Chief Medical Officer Christopher Whitty who have driven 'virus' policy while Prime Minister Johnson does whatever he is told. The paper, released for 'discussion' on March 23rd, 2020, is a classic agenda for behaviour control during the lockdowns. It includes under the heading 'Persuasion':

The perceived level of personal threat needs to be increased among those who are complacent, using hard-hitting Evaluation of options for increasing social distancing emotional messaging. To be effective this must also empower people by making clear the actions they can take to reduce the threat.

Such psychological games surrounding the primary themes of fear and threat have been used constantly and mercilessly since the 'pandemic' began. As I write fear of the fake 'virus', or one not at all dangerous to the overwhelming majority even if you still believe it exists, is being exploited to create a mass real-time surveillance system under the guise of 'contact tracing' that mirrors one level of the surveillance system – *of course* – in China. This is founded on the perception-manipulation that the 'virus' is 'deadly' and the tracking is needed via your phone for your protection (behaviour manipulation). Phone apps are being rolled out to track who you come into contact with to see if one of them has tested positive for 'Covid-19' with a test not testing for 'Covid-19'. Then a government operative from an army of 'contact tracers' will be knocking on your door to test you with a test not testing for 'Covid-19' and if you are positive for a genetic material that large numbers of people have in their body as a matter of course you will be told to isolate or forced into quarantine. This system is planned to take children from families as it becomes ever-more extreme which fulfils another goal of the Cult. Targeting anyone becomes easy just by claiming you have been in contact with people who have tested positive for something not being tested for. I bet pawpaws and goats in Tanzania are trembling as I speak. It's all long-planned with a European Commission proposal perfectly timed in late 2019 to introduce a 'common vaccination card/passport' for all EU citizens. Cult-owned Google, Apple and other Big Tech companies are making contact-tracing possible because they care so much about human health and one of America's contact-tracing organisations. Partners in Health, lists the Bill and Melinda Gates Foundation and the George Soros Open Society Foundations as official partners with Clinton daughter Chelsea on the Board of Trustees. A Rockefeller Foundation Paper published in April, 2020, detailing its 'National Covid-19 Testing Action Plan', called for the creation of a nationwide DNA database and mass testing and tracing for all Americans. My goodness and many people still can't see what is going on – not least the clueless, gutless pawns in the mainstream media. It's breathtaking how people can be so blind to the obvious.

The 'virus' hoax is another 'here kitty, kitty' with the story constantly changing to justify still more extreme deletions of freedom. First they said that lockdowns were necessary to 'flatten the curve', but when that happened through figure manipulation we were told that 'normality' could not return until there was a 'cure or vaccine'. No other alleged disease in human history has involved isolating the healthy and now that can only stop when there is a 'cure or vaccine'. What they mean is a vaccine to connect the population to the Smart Grid among much else. The kitty, kitty, is behaviour manipulation and we see this with social distancing and all the fine-detail rules that people think they have to conform to by law when most are only government recommendations that have no force in law. Police that have been fining and arresting people for breaking lockdown laws are being forced to admit they were policing laws that didn't exist and they had no right to enforce. This is what happens when you do what you are told without question or personal research. In the lockdown phase announced by Boris Johnson a week before I am writing this you can have an estate agent, nanny or cleaner in your house, but not your parents or grandparents. You can see one parent or grandparent at a time, but not both together. You can meet them in a park, but not in a garden because the UK Health Secretary Prat Hancock says that this could mean walking through a house to get to the garden. I guess they would also have to pass the estate agent, nanny and cleaner on the way. I could continue with a long list of such ridiculous contradictory, makes-no-sense nonsense billowing from the empty space between the government's ears. But while idiot officials impose this bizarre craziness there is method in the madness at the level of the Behaviour Insight Team and similar networks around the world. We are seeing grotesque images of children being prepared from the earliest age to fear and disconnect from their friends by being forced

Figure 4: What a testament to Cult psychopathy and human acquiesce.

Figure 5: Where is the self-respect?

to stay in marked-off playground zones while their masked parents line up six feet apart to collect them from cross markers also six feet apart (Figs 4 and 5). It is child abuse imposed by unquestioning parents and teachers at the behest of the psychopaths using the fake 'pandemic' to do anything they choose. 'It's the rules' is not a bloody good enough excuse to do this to kids who are being dehumanised by this outrage. They are training children and adults to obey fine-detail orders like domestic animals. When you have laughable and clearly contradictory rules but people still obey them you know you are getting close to total unquestioning compliance. Indeed, with large swathes of humanity they are already there. Now we have the prospect of being enslaved ongoing in small isolated groups officially known as 'Bubbles' – how appropriate given what I wrote earlier in the book. The antidote to this imposition by the few on the many is this: 'Go fuck yourself – we're not doing it.'

The plan is for the Gates 'Covid-19' vaccine to use a technique never before let loose on humans – DNA manipulation using synthetic DNA and an electrical pulse to open up cells for synthetic penetration. Given what I have written earlier in the book about the synthetic human agenda this fits the story as does my contention that the vaccine will include self-replicating nanotechnology. Having the Gates vaccine and allowing children to have it should become a new definition of insanity. The British government has refused to rule out making the Gates vaccine compulsory while ultra-Zionist lawyer Alan Dershowitz, a friend (like Gates) and legal defender of Jeffrey Epstein, insisted that Americans do not have the right to refuse the vaccine should federal or state governments makes it mandatory. He quoted a Supreme Court judgement in Jacobson v Massachusetts in 1905 which upheld the right of states to enforce compulsory vaccine laws. The Supreme Court, which is owned by the Cult, decreed that individual liberty is overridden by the power of the state. The Court shockingly found it 'immaterial' that some in the medical community believed the vaccination 'worthless or even injurious'. The state had the right to choose between opposing medical theories and to refer the decision to 'a board composed of persons residing in the affected location who are qualified to make a determination' (controlled by the Cult and Big Pharma which is the same thing). Courts would not intervene if the enforcement related 'substantially to public health, morals, or safety and was not a plain, palpable invasion of rights secured by fundamental law'. Being forced to have a potentially injurious vaccine is not 'a plain, palpable invasion of rights'? *Extraordinary*. The Court also ruled that *it is immaterial whether or not the vaccine is actually effective, so long as it is the belief of state authorities that the mandatory vaccine will promote common welfare* and such enforcement is *a reasonable and proper exercise of the police power*. It was of 'paramount necessity that a community have the right to protect itself from an epidemic of disease which threatens the safety of its members'– and clearly even when it doesn't. This, ladies and gentlemen of America, is the Supreme Court precedent that still stands as psychopath Gates prepares to inflict his vaccination on everyone.

'Outsider' (ha, ha) Donald Trump announced that he was deployir g the military to distribute the vaccine when it was ready, possibly as early as December, 2020, while the British government said its trials could lead to mass vaccination even earlier in September. The speed in which this is happening is making even vaccine proponents question how this is possible when vaccines that have caused lethal harm to children and adults take years to develop. The answer is, as I have said since the 'pandemic' began, that the vaccine was ready and waiting before the excuse to use it was even perpetrated. The idea that a vaccine could be developed in months for a 'virus' that has never been proved to exist, nor be a cause of disease, with a PCR test that doesn't even test for 'Covid-19' is patently fraudulent. You have not shown it to exist, you haven't shown it to cause a disease and you can't test for it, but you've found a vaccine in months. This is nonsense and mendacity on a historic scale. They are trying to put as much delay as they can between the 'outbreak' and the vaccine to overcome the obvious credibility gap, but they are fearful of waiting too long because the longer the delay the more people will realise that the 'pandemic' has been a gigantic hoax from start to finish. Their Plan B if enough people refuse the vaccine is to not allow anyone out of lockdown rules unless they have the vaccine and that's why we hear the mantra of 'no return to normality' until everyone is vaccinated. The 'virus' is so deadly and humanity faces such a crisis, according to the Gates script, that maybe safety may have to be compromised for speed. Gates wrote in his blog:

> If we were designing the perfect vaccine, we'd want it to be completely safe and 100 percent effective. It should be a single dose that gives you lifelong protection, and it should be easy to store and transport. I hope the COVID-19 vaccine has all of those qualities, but given the timeline we're on, it may not.

You know exactly what the vaccine is and what it contains you bloody liar. They can make the vaccine appear to work by simply changing the way they diagnose and fill in death certificates to delete 'Covid-19' in the same period as the vaccine, but no doubt they will also draw this out over years with successive 'waves' of a 'virus' that 'is mutating' and requires further vaccinations as with the flu. They are even adding new 'symptoms' including loss of smell or taste to make more people think they are 'infected' when other causes are responsible. I understand that a new symptom next week will be burping twice in 30 seconds. Apparently stop watches are going to be issued. Then there was the 'research' that told us that speaking could 'spread the virus' with a 'substantial probability that normal speaking causes airborne virus transmission in confined environments'. So stay home *and* shut the fuck up.

As I close this Postscript the economic consequences of the pandemic hoax – clearly known and planned from the start – are becoming clear with destroyed companies, employment and dreams. The numbers continue to rise of people dying through delayed treatment and diagnosis, and for suicides, drug abuse, child and domestic abuse. One study said a third of Americans are showing signs of anxiety and depression while prescriptions for mood-elevating drugs have soared. Society is crumbling because that's the whole idea. Stanford University professor Michael Levitt said lockdown saved no lives and may have cost lives (absolute certainty) while Neil Ferguson had over-estimated the death toll by '10 or 12 times' – I would say by 100 percent. US states that locked down early were no differently affected on average than those that didn't lockdown at all. Marko Kolanovic, a strategist for JP Morgan, said lockdowns failed to alter the course of the 'pandemic' and instead 'destroyed millions of livelihoods'. What was not being acknowledged is that this was the plan from the start. Even the odd mainstream article has appeared calling for the (calculated) madness of lockdown to end. In the United States the fascist control has been imposed by state governor diktats which means that at that level 50 people have been dictating the lives of 330 million. Every one of them that abused that power – and so many have – must be forced out. Is it still possible in the light of all this to dismiss that the world is controlled by a ridiculously few people as long as humans acquiesce? Or that their agenda is being orchestrated by the depths of evil? Denial is no longer an option.

We are looking global fascism in the eye and we must not blink. You can recognise politicians and mainstream 'journalists' by the break-neck speed of their eyelids and they are the problem, not the answer. *We the People* have to sort this out or no one will. Come on – *let's go.*

Appendix 1

Summary of what ultra-Zionist Cult insider Dr Richard Day said was going to happen to the world when he spoke at a meeting of paediatricians in Pittsburgh, Pennsylvania, in 1969

Population control; permission to have babies; redirecting the purpose of sex – sex without reproduction and reproduction without sex; contraception universally available to all; sex education and canalizing of youth as a tool of world government; tax-funded abortion as population control; encouraging anything-goes homosexuality; technology used for reproduction without sex; families to diminish in importance; euthanasia and the 'demise pill'; limiting access to affordable medical care making eliminating the elderly easier; medicine would be tightly controlled; elimination of private doctors; new difficult-to-diagnose and untreatable diseases; suppressing cancer cures as a means of population control; inducing heart attacks as a form of assassination; education as a tool for accelerating the onset of puberty and evolution; blending all religions ... the old religions will have to go; changing the Bible through revisions of key words; restructuring education as a tool of indoctrination; more time in schools, but pupils 'wouldn't learn anything'; controlling who has access to information; schools as the hub of the community; some books would just disappear from the libraries; changing laws to promote moral and social chaos; encouragement of drug abuse to create a jungle atmosphere in cities and towns; promote alcohol abuse; restrictions on travel; the need for more jails, and using hospitals as jails; no more psychological or physical security; crime used to manage society; curtailment of US industrial pre-eminence; shifting populations and economies – tearing out the social roots; sports as a tool of social engineering and change; sex and violence inculcated through entertainment; making boys and girls the same; implanted ID cards – microchips; food control; weather control; knowing how people respond – making them do what you want; falsified scientific research [see 'global warming']; use of terrorism; surveillance, implants, and televisions that watch you; the arrival of the totalitarian global system.

Appendix 2

Noahide Laws = human control

The seven so-called Noahide Laws are claimed to have been given by 'God' to Adam and Noah and are binding on non-Jews with *decapitation* the main penalty for not complying. Other punishments for non-Jews include death by stoning if a man has intercourse with a Jewish betrothed woman or by strangulation if the Jewish woman has completed the marriage ceremonies, but had not yet consummated the marriage. They're not racist or mad or anything.

'God' had nothing to do with the 'Seven Laws of Noah' and neither did 'Adam' and 'Noah'. They were concocted by extremist Talmudic rabbis with the goal of imposing them on the entirety of human society. The Babylonian Talmud and Jerusalem Talmud are founded on the interpretations of rabbinical crazies and incredibly racist. The deceit claims that 'Noah' is the father of all post-flood humanity and so non-Jews (Gentiles) are all subject to the Noahide Laws given to him by 'God'. 'Noah' was actually an invented character based on 'flood' heroes in many cultures long before Old Testament writers brought their composite invention to global prominence with his 'ark'. The Noahide Laws are as follows:

1. Do not worship idols.
2. Do not curse God.
3. Establish courts of justice to impose the Noahide Laws.
4. Do not murder.
5. Do not commit adultery, bestiality, or sexual immorality.
6. Do not steal.
7. Do not eat flesh from a living animal.

The Devil here, as always, is in the detail. The key 'law' is the setting up of courts to impose the Noahide Laws and decree the death sentences on non-complying non-Jews or Gentiles. These courts would be controlled by Sabbatian-Frankist Death Cult 'judges' according to their interpretation of what constitutes 'worship of idols', 'cursing god', 'adultery', 'sexual immorality' and all the rest. Some of these ultra-Zionist extremists consider Christianity as 'idolatry'. This is the point – non-compliance with the 'God' decreed by the rabbinical (Sabbatian-Frankist) 'courts' would simply mean non-compliance with the 'God' that they decide is 'God'. These zealots contend that Israel is obligated to bring the entire world to worship the Sabbatian-Frankist 'God'. All other worship, or no worship, would be decreed as 'idolatry', 'worship of idols' or cursing 'God'. The fact that they would be ordering the murder of non-compliers over a list of 'laws' that include 'do not murder' matters not to them. Hypocrisy is their very lifeblood. This is not meant to make sense to anyone with an active brain cell. It is merely a calculated excuse to kill who they like when they like. There are many other 'laws' that apply only to Gentiles, too, and even not setting up the courts to pass death sentences is punishable by death.

You could write all this off as a form of insanity except that recognition of the Noahide Laws (including therefore the demand for the creation of Noahide 'courts') has been gathering in the Gentile world. President Ronald Reagan signed a proclamation in 1982 recognising 'the eternal validity of the Seven Noahide Laws, a moral code for all of us regardless of religious faith'. The US Congress gave its support to the Noahide Laws in 1991 when establishing an 'Education Day' to honour the ultra-Zionist Russian Empire-born extremist racist lunatic Rabbi Menachem Mendel Schneerson, leader of the Chabad-Lubavitch movement, who said that non-Jews exist only to serve Jews. He also said:

> This is what needs to be said about the body: the body of a Jewish person is of a totally different quality from the body of [members] of all nations of the world ... The difference in the inner quality between Jews and non-Jews is 'so great that the bodies should be considered as completely different species.' An even greater difference exists in regard to the soul. Two contrary types of soul exist, a non-Jewish soul comes from three satanic spheres, while the Jewish soul stems from holiness.

A more racist claim you could not imagine from those who accuse the rest of the world of racism when Jewishness is not even a race, but a cultural belief system. The 1991 resolution passed by both Houses of Congress (H.J.Res.104) during the presidency of Father George Bush and included the following:

Whereas Congress recognizes the historical tradition of ethical values and principles which are the basis of civilized society and upon which our great Nation was founded;

Whereas these ethical values and principles have been the bedrock of society from the dawn of civilization, when they were known as the Seven Noahide Laws;

Whereas without these ethical values and principles the edifice of civilization stands in serious peril of returning to chaos;

Whereas society is profoundly concerned with the recent weakening of these principles that has resulted in crises that beleaguer and threaten the fabric of civilized society;

Whereas the justified preoccupation with these crises must not let the citizens of this Nation lose sight of their responsibility to transmit these historical ethical values from our distinguished past to the generations of the future;

Whereas the Lubavitch movement has fostered and promoted these ethical values and principles throughout the world.

A few things: The United States was not founded on the Noahide Laws and they have not been the 'bedrock of society from the dawn of civilization'. They were scripted by Talmudic rabbis representing a small section of a tiny section (currently 0.2 percent) of the world population but decreed by these arrogant extremists as applying to the whole of humanity on pain of death. Congressional politicians claim that the deeply racist Chabad-Lubavitch movement has 'fostered and promoted these ethical values and principles throughout the world'? Don't be ridiculous. But when you are owned by the Sabbatian-Frankist Death Cult via funding and intimidation you'll parrot any old crap that your masters tell you. The plan is to introduce a universal 'Noahide Code' founded on the Noahide Laws and imposed by rabbinical courts in a world government system controlled out of Jerusalem (see Smart Grid) and this 'code' would replace national sovereignty. The United Nations is seen as a vehicle for advancing this agenda and is 'striving to fulfil' many parts of the Noahide 'universal code'. The plan is for the global Noahide Laws to be administered by the Biblical Sanhedrin as part of the Smart Grid control system and the rebuilding of 'Solomon's Temple'. Just by coincidence, of course, the Sanhedrin Council of the Jewish nation was reconstructed for the first time in 1,600 years on October 13th, 2004. The ceremony was held in the Israeli town of Tiberias on the Western shore of the Sea of Galilee where the council's last meeting took place in 425 AD.

The pieces are being moved into place at ever greater speed and the symbol of the Noahide Laws is all around us today. It's the *rainbow colours* depicting the rainbow of Noah in the Biblical story of the Great Flood. The now ubiquitous symbol of the rainbow (including as a symbol for medical staff support during the 'pandemic') is yet another 'coincidence'?

No chance.

Bibliography

Akin, William E: *Technocracy and the American Dream: The Technocrat Movement, 1900-1941* (University of California Press, 1977)

Bastardi, Joe: *The Climate Chronicles* (CreateSpace, 2018)

Brown, Floyd, and Cefaratti Todd: *Big Tech Tyrants: How Silicon Valley's Stealth Practices Addict Teens, Silence Speech, and Steal Your Privacy* (Bombardier Books, 2019)

Brzezinski, Zbigniew: *Between Two Ages: America's Role in the Technetronic Era* (Greenwood Press, New edition, 1982)

Crockford, Susan: *The Polar Bear Catastrophe That Never Happened* (The Global Warming Policy Foundation, 2019)

Evans, David, and Naughton, Tom: *Low Cholesterol Leads to an Early Death: Evidence from 101 Scientific Papers* (Grosvenor House, 2012)

Figueres, Christiana and Rivett-Carnac, Tom: *The Future We Choose: Surviving the Climate Crisis* (Manilla Press, 2020)

Friedrichs, Rebecca: *Standing Up to Goliath* (Post Hill Press, 2018)

Gerhardt, Dr Sue: *Why Love Matters* (Routledge, 2014)

Grant, Kenneth: *Aleister Crowley & The Hidden God* (Starfire, 2013)

Groves, Barry: *Trick and Treat: How healthy eating is making us ill* (Hammersmith Press, 2008)

Huxley, Aldous: *Brave New World* (Vintage Classics, 2007)

Iserbyt, Charlotte Thomson: *The Deliberate Dumbing Down of America* (Conscience Press, 2011)

Lanza, Robert, and Berman, Bob: *Biocentrism* (BenBella Books, 2010)

Lash, John Lamb: *Not In His Image* (Chelsea Green Publishing, 2006)

Lipton, Bruce: *Biology of Belief* (Hay House UK, 2015)

Lester, Dawn, and Parker, David: *What Really Makes You Ill – Why everything you thought you knew about disease is wrong* (Independently Published, 2019)

Lovelock, James: *The Revenge of Gaia* (Penguin, 2007)

MacCormack, Patricia: *The Ahuman Manifesto* (Bloomsbury Academic, 2019)

Morano, Marc: *The Politically Incorrect Guide to Climate Change* (Regnery Publishing 2018)

Orwell, George: *Nineteen Eighty-Four* (Penguin Classics, 2004)

Siegel, Seth: *Troubled Water* (Macmillan USA, 2019)

Talbot, Michael: *Holographic Universe* (HarperCollins, 1996)

Tegmark, Max: *Our Mathematical Universe* (Penguin, 2015)

Wood, Patrick: *Technocracy Rising* (Coherent Publishing, 2014)

HeartMath website – Heartmath.com

Index

Ickonic has been a dream of mine for five years growing up around alternative information. I have always had a natural interest in what is happening in the world and what I could do to make it better.

Across the range of subjects and positions of influence occupied mainly by people who don't try to improve human society it's the mainstream media that I have always found the most frustrating and fascinating. If the media did its job then so many negative events in the world would not be happening because their background and agenda would be exposed.

A free media and free Internet would mean that those in power would be held to account for their behaviour and manipulation. They would no longer be the 'Untouchables'.

At Ickonic we engage in journalism and broadcasting as it should be – the uncensored pursuit of the truth. We have hundreds of videos, reports, series, documentaries, full-length films and weekly programmes covering a vast range of subjects with more constantly added. David Icke's public presentations over 30 years are there, plus his series unique to Ickonic, and every week he goes through the news and puts it into its real context.

Take our free seven-day trial to see the amazing information that we have. We created Ickonic as a bulwark against the hysterical censorship that we knew was coming – and is now here.

Ickonic's time has come.

Jaymie Icke, Founder, Ickonic Alternative Media

SIGN UP NOW AT ICKONIC.COM

ICKONIC
THE ALTERNATIVE

AN ICKONIC ORIGINAL FILM
DIRECTED BY JAYMIE ICKE

UNNATURAL

WHAT PRICE ARE WE PAYING FOR THE TECHNOLOGY WE LOVE?

RELEASE DATE

FRIDAY 10TH JULY

FEATURING

DR ANNIE J SASCO, DR ALASDAIR PHILLIPS, LENA PU,
DR AMELIA HARDWICK, DR ROBIN KELLY, DAVID ICKE, NAOMI COOK,
DR KLAUS BUCHER, VELMA LYRAE

NARRATED BY RICHARD GRANNON

THE TRIGGER

THE LIE THAT CHANGED THE WORLD – WHO REALLY DID IT AND WHY

DAVID ICKE

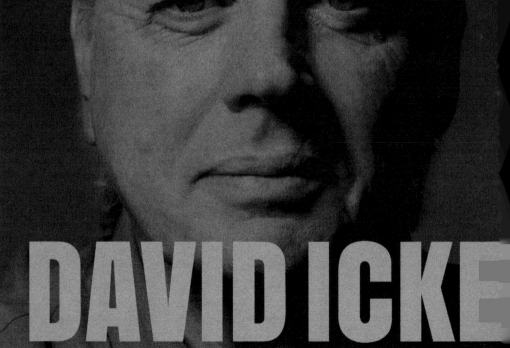

EVERYTHING YOU NEED TO KNOW
BUT HAVE NEVER BEEN TOLD

DAVID ICKE

A ground-breaking new book

ORION'S DOOR

SYMBOLS OF CONSCIOUSNESS & BLUEPRINTS OF CONTROL
- THE STORY OF ORION'S INFLUENCE *OVER* HUMANITY

NEIL HAGUE

For more details visit: *neilhague.com*

BOOKS • GRAPHIC NOVELS • ART • ILLUSTRATION • PRINTS • BLOG

Right-Brain Thinking In A Left-Brain World

Monnica Sepulveda in California has been a medium for 45 years and specialises in helping people break out of The Program – both their own and that of collective humanity.

Consultations by Skype anywhere in the world.

www.monnica.com

Contact Phone number in the USA: 1-831-688-8884
Email: monnica888@yahoo.com

Before you go ...

For more detail, background and evidence about the subjects in *The Answer* – and so much more – see my others books including *And The Truth Shall Set You Free; The Biggest Secret; Children of the Matrix; The David Icke Guide to the Global Conspiracy; Tales from the Time Loop; The Perception Deception; Remember Who You Are; Human Race Get Off Your Knees; Phantom Self; Everything You Need To Know But Have Never Been Told* and *The Trigger.*

You can subscribe to the fantastic new Ickonic media platform where there are many hundreds of hours of cutting-edge information in videos, documentaries and series across a whole range of subjects which are added to every week. This includes my 90 minute breakdown of the week's news every Friday to explain *why* events are happening and to what end.